Recent Advances in Nanocarriers for Pancreatic Cancer Therapy

Recent Advances in Nanocarriers for Pancreatic Cancer Therapy

Edited by

PRASHANT KESHARWANI

Department of Pharmaceutics, School of Pharmaceutical Education
and Research, Jamia Hamdard, New Delhi, India

NEELIMA GUPTA

Dr. Harisingh Gour Vishwavidyalaya (A Central University), Sagar,
Madhya Pradesh, India

ELSEVIER

ACADEMIC PRESS
An imprint of Elsevier

Academic Press is an imprint of Elsevier
125 London Wall, London EC2Y 5AS, United Kingdom
525 B Street, Suite 1650, San Diego, CA 92101, United States
50 Hampshire Street, 5th Floor, Cambridge, MA 02139, United States
The Boulevard, Langford Lane, Kidlington, Oxford OX5 1GB, United Kingdom

Notices
Knowledge and best practice in this field are constantly changing. As new research and experience broaden our understanding, changes in research methods, professional practices, or medical treatment may become necessary.

Practitioners and researchers must always rely on their own experience and knowledge in evaluating and using any information, methods, compounds, or experiments described herein. In using such information or methods they should be mindful of their own safety and the safety of others, including parties for whom they have a professional responsibility.

To the fullest extent of the law, neither the Publisher nor the authors, contributors, or editors, assume any liability for any injury and/or damage to persons or property as a matter of products liability, negligence or otherwise, or from any use or operation of any methods, products, instructions, or ideas contained in the material herein.

ISBN: 978-0-443-19142-8

For Information on all Academic Press publications
visit our website at https://www.elsevier.com/books-and-journals

Publisher: Stacy Masucci
Acquisitions Editor: Linda Versteeg-Buschman
Editorial Project Manager: Michaela Realiza
Production Project Manager: Paul Prasad Chandramohan
Cover Designer: Miles Hitchen

Typeset by MPS Limited, Chennai, India

Working together
to grow libraries in
developing countries

www.elsevier.com • www.bookaid.org

Dedication

I would like to dedicate this book to my parents (Mr. Hariom Kesharwani and Mrs. Anguri Kesharwani), my sister (Dr. Punam Kesharwani), and my brother (Er. Pankaj Kesharwani) for believing in me and always being there for me. Equally, the book is also dedicated to the love and sacrifices of my wife (Garima Kesharwani), my kids (Yashsavi and Vidvaan), my nephew (Adhyayan), and my niece (Prisha).

—**Prashant Kesharwani**

Contents

Part A Overview, molecular pathways and conventional therapy of pancreatic cancer

Part B Application of various nanocarriers for the management of pancreatic cancer

12. Dendrimers and carbon nanotubes-based drug delivery for pancreatic cancer 297

Mehmethan Yıldırım, Durmus Burak Demirkaya and Serap Yalcin

Part C Recent advances and future prospective for pancreatic cancer 315

13. Personalized medicine and new therapeutic approach in the treatment of pancreatic cancer 317

Hanieh Azari, Elham Nazari, Hamid Jamialahmadi, Ghazaleh Khalili-Tanha, Mina Maftooh, Seyed Mahdi Hassanian, Gordon A. Ferns, Majid Khazaei and Amir Avan

14. Clinical practice guidelines for interventional treatment of pancreatic cancer   345

Ghazaleh Pourali, Ghazaleh Donyadideh, Shima Mehrabadi, Fiuji Hamid,
Seyed Mahdi Hassanian, Gordon A. Ferns, Majid Khazaei and Amir Avan

List of contributors

Seyedeh Melika Ahmadi
Department of Pharmaceutics, Faculty of Pharmacy, Mazandaran University of Medical Sciences, Sari, Iran

Sania Ghobadi Alamdari
Department of Cell and Molecular Biology, Faculty of Basic Science, University of Maragheh, Maragheh, Iran; Immunology Research Center, Tabriz University of Medical Sciences, Tabriz, Iran

Waleed H. Almalki
Department of Pharmacology and Toxicology, Faculty of Pharmacy, Umm Al-Qura University, Makkah, Saudi Arabia

Mohammad Amini
Immunology Research Center, Tabriz University of Medical Sciences, Tabriz, Iran

Shervin Amirkhanloo
Department of Pharmaceutics, Faculty of Pharmacy, Mazandaran University of Medical Sciences, Sari, Iran

Swati Arora
School of Biosciences and Bioengineering, Lovely Professional University, Jalandhar, Punjab, India; Unite Lifescience, Hyderabad, Telangana, India

Peyman Asadi
Nano Drug Delivery Research Center, Health Technology Institute, Kermanshah University of Medical Sciences, Kermanshah, Iran

Amir Avan
Metabolic Syndrome Research Center, Mashhad University of Medical Sciences, Mashhad, Iran; College of Medicine, University of Warith Al-Anbiyaa, Karbala, Iraq; Basic Medical Sciences Institute, Mashhad University of Medical Sciences, Mashhad, Iran; School of Mechanical, Medical and Process Engineering, Science and Engineering Faculty, Queensland University of Technology, Brisbane, QLD, Australia; Faculty of Health, School of Biomedical Sciences, Queensland University of Technology, Brisbane, QLD, Australia

Hanieh Azari
Metabolic Syndrome Research Center, Mashhad University of Medical Sciences, Mashhad, Iran; Basic Sciences Research Institute, Mashhad University of Medical Sciences, Mashhad, Iran

Behzad Baradaran
Immunology Research Center, Tabriz University of Medical Sciences, Tabriz, Iran

Paula Gabriela Bercoff
Institute of Physics Enrique Gaviola (IFEG), CONICET. Faculty of Mathematics, Astronomy, Physics and Computing (FAMAF), National University of Córdoba, Ciudad Universitaria, Córdoba, Argentina

Swati Biswas
Epigenetic Research Laboratory, Department of Pharmacy, Birla Institute of Technology & Science-Pilani, Hyderabad, Telangana, India

Sanjay Ch
Epigenetic Research Laboratory, Department of Pharmacy, Birla Institute of Technology & Science-Pilani, Hyderabad, Telangana, India

Gopal Chakrabarti
Department of Biotechnology, Dr. B. C. Guha Centre for Genetic Engineering and Biotechnology, University of Calcutta, Kolkata, West Bengal, India

Mohsen Chamanara
Toxicology Research Center, AJA University of Medical Sciences, Tehran, Iran

Arindam Chatterjee
Department of Pharmaceutics, College of Pharmacy, Gupta College of Technological Sciences, Asansol, West Bengal, India

Viviana Beatriz Daboin
Physicochemical Research Institute of Córdoba (INFIQC), CONICET. Faculty of Chemical Sciences, National University of Córdoba, Ciudad Universitaria, Córdoba, Argentina

Rambabu Dandela
Department of Industrial and Engineering Chemistry, Institute of Chemical Technology, Indian Oil Odisha Campus, Samantapuri, Bhubaneswar, Odisha, India

Shwetapadma Dash
Institute of Life Sciences, Bhubaneswar, Odisha, India

Sadegh Dehghani
Pharmaceutical Research Center, Pharmaceutical Technology Institute, Mashhad University of Medical Sciences, Mashhad, Iran

Durmus Burak Demirkaya
Department of Molecular Biology and Genetics, Faculty of Science and Art, Kırsehir Ahi Evran University, Kırsehir, Turkey

Ghazaleh Donyadideh
Mashhad University of Medical Sciences, Mashhad, Iran

Gouranga Dutta
Department of Pharmaceutics, SRM College of Pharmacy, SRM Institute of Science and Technology, Kattankulathur, Tamil Nadu, India

Pedram Ebrahimnejad
Department of Pharmaceutics, Faculty of Pharmacy, Mazandaran University of Medical Sciences, Sari, Iran

Gordon A. Ferns
Division of Medical Education, Brighton & Sussex Medical School, Brighton, United Kingdom

Balaram Ghosh
Epigenetic Research Laboratory, Department of Pharmacy, Birla Institute of Technology & Science-Pilani, Hyderabad, Telangana, India

Dipanjan Ghosh
Department of Biotechnology, Dr. B. C. Guha Centre for Genetic Engineering and Biotechnology, University of Calcutta, Kolkata, West Bengal, India

Jyotirmoy Ghosh
Molecular Biology Laboratory, Divison of Physiology, National Institute of Animal Nutrition and Physiology, Bangalore, Karnataka, India

Lopamudra Giri
Department of Industrial and Engineering Chemistry, Institute of Chemical Technology, Indian Oil Odisha Campus, Samantapuri, Bhubaneswar, Odisha, India

Neelima Gupta
Dr. Harisingh Gour Vishwavidyalaya (A Central University), Sagar, Madhya Pradesh, India

Fiuji Hamid
Department of Medical Oncology, Cancer Center Amsterdam, Amsterdam U.M.C., VU. University Medical Center (VUMC), Amsterdam, The Netherlands

Seyed Mahdi Hassanian
Metabolic Syndrome Research Center, Mashhad University of Medical Sciences, Mashhad, Iran; Medical Genetics Research Center, Mashhad University of Medical Sciences, Mashhad, Iran; Basic Sciences Research Institute, Mashhad University of Medical Sciences, Mashhad, Iran

Hamid Jamialahmadi
Metabolic Syndrome Research Center, Mashhad University of Medical Sciences, Mashhad, Iran

Ananya Kar
Department of Industrial and Engineering Chemistry, Institute of Chemical Technology, Indian Oil Odisha Campus, Samantapuri, Bhubaneswar, Odisha, India

Gurleen Kaur
Department of Industrial and Engineering Chemistry, Institute of Chemical Technology, Indian Oil Odisha Campus, Samantapuri, Bhubaneswar, Odisha, India

Prashant Kesharwani
Department of Pharmaceutics, School of Pharmaceutical Education and Research, Jamia Hamdard, New Delhi, India

Ghazaleh Khalili-Tanha
Metabolic Syndrome Research Center, Mashhad University of Medical Sciences, Mashhad, Iran

Majid Khazaei
Metabolic Syndrome Research Center, Mashhad University of Medical Sciences, Mashhad, Iran; Basic Sciences Research Institute, Mashhad University of Medical Sciences, Mashhad, Iran

Mina Maftooh
Metabolic Syndrome Research Center, Mashhad University of Medical Sciences, Mashhad, Iran

Sivakumar Manickam
Petroleum and Chemical Engineering, Faculty of Engineering, Universiti Teknologi Brunei, Jalan Tungku Link Gadong, Brunei Darussalam

Atena Mansouri
Cellular and Molecular Research Center, Birjand University of Medical Sciences, Birjand, Iran

K.R. Manu
Department of Industrial and Engineering Chemistry, Institute of Chemical Technology, Indian Oil Odisha Campus, Samantapuri, Bhubaneswar, Odisha, India

Faranak Mavandadnejad
Ajmera Transplant Centre, University Health Network (UHN), Toronto, ON, Canada

Shima Mehrabadi
Metabolic Syndrome Research Center, Mashhad University of Medical Sciences, Mashhad, Iran

Ranjita Misra
Department of Biotechnology, School of Sciences, Jain University, Bangalore, Karnataka, India

Mehdi Mogharabi-Manzari
Pharmaceutical Sciences Research Center, Hemoglobinopathy Institute, Mazandaran University of Medical Sciences, Sari, Iran

Hamidreza Mohammadi
Department of Toxicology and Pharmacology, Faculty of Pharmacy, Mazandaran University of Medical Sciences, Sari, Iran; Pharmaceutical Sciences Research Center, Hemoglobinopathy Institute, Mazandaran University of Medical Sciences, Sari, Iran

Reza Mohammadzadeh
Department of Cell and Molecular Biology, Faculty of Basic Science, University of Maragheh, Maragheh, Iran

Ahad Mokhtarzadeh
Immunology Research Center, Tabriz University of Medical Sciences, Tabriz, Iran

Sara Natalia Moya Betancourt
Physicochemical Research Institute of Córdoba (INFIQC), CONICET. Faculty of Chemical Sciences, National University of Córdoba, Ciudad Universitaria, Córdoba, Argentina

Elham Nazari
Metabolic Syndrome Research Center, Mashhad University of Medical Sciences, Mashhad, Iran; Basic Sciences Research Institute, Mashhad University of Medical Sciences, Mashhad, Iran

Fatemeh Oroojalian
Natural Products and Medicinal Plants Research Center, North Khorasan University of Medical Sciences, Bojnurd, Iran

Geetha Palani
Institute of Agricultural Engineering, Saveetha School of Engineering, Saveetha Institute of Medical and Technical Sciences, Chennai, Tamil Nadu, India

Tarun Kumar Patel
Epigenetic Research Laboratory, Department of Pharmacy, Birla Institute of Technology & Science-Pilani, Hyderabad, Telangana, India

Smita C. Pawar
Department of Genetics, Osmania University, Hyderabad, Telangana, India

Venkatesan Perumal
Center for Injury Biomechanics, Materials and Medicine, Department of Biomedical Engineering, New Jersey Institute of Technology, Newark, NJ, United States

Ghazaleh Pourali
Mashhad University of Medical Sciences, Mashhad, Iran; Metabolic Syndrome Research Center, Mashhad University of Medical Sciences, Mashhad, Iran

Shalini Preethi P.
Computational Biology Special Lab, Department of Biotechnology, Bannari Amman Institute of Technology, Sathyamangalam, Tamil Nadu, India

Seyyed Mobin Rahimnia
Department of Pharmaceutics, Faculty of Pharmacy, Mazandaran University of Medical Sciences, Sari, Iran; Student Research Committee, Faculty of Pharmacy, Mazandaran University of Medical Sciences, Sari, Iran

Farzad Rahmani
Metabolic Syndrome Research Center, Mashhad University of Medical Sciences, Mashhad, Iran; Basic Medical Sciences Institute, Mashhad University of Medical Sciences, Mashhad, Iran

Arun Reddy Ravula
Center for Injury Biomechanics, Materials and Medicine, Department of Biomedical Engineering, New Jersey Institute of Technology, Newark, NJ, United States

Julieta Soledad Riva
Physicochemical Research Institute of Córdoba (INFIQC), CONICET. Faculty of Chemical Sciences, National University of Córdoba, Ciudad Universitaria, Córdoba, Argentina

Parisa Saberi-Hasanabadi
Department of Toxicology and Pharmacology, Faculty of Pharmacy, Mazandaran University of Medical Sciences, Sari, Iran

Majid Saeedi
Department of Pharmaceutics, Faculty of Pharmacy, Mazandaran University of Medical Sciences, Sari, Iran; Pharmaceutical Sciences Research Center, Hemoglobinopathy Institute, Mazandaran University of Medical Sciences, Sari, Iran

Amirhossein Sahebkar
Applied Biomedical Research Center, Mashhad University of Medical Sciences, Mashhad, Iran

Sanjeeb Kumar Sahoo
Institute of Life Sciences, Bhubaneswar, Odisha, India

Sonali Sahoo
Institute of Life Sciences, Bhubaneswar, Odisha, India; Regional Center for Biotechnology, Faridabad, Haryana, India

Zahra Salmasi
Department of Pharmaceutical Nanotechnology, School of Pharmacy, Mashhad University of Medical Sciences, Mashhad, Iran

Karthik Sambath
Department of Chemistry and Environmental Science, College of Science and Liberal Arts, New Jersey Institute of Technology, Newark, NJ, United States

Amin Shad
Department of Chemical Engineering, Ferdowsi University of Mashhad, Mashhad, Iran

Naomi Sanjana Sharath
Department of Biotechnology, School of Sciences, Jain University, Bangalore, Karnataka, India

Sumit Sheoran
School of Biosciences and Bioengineering, Lovely Professional University, Jalandhar, Punjab, India; Unite Lifescience, Hyderabad, Telangana, India

Sindhu V.
Computational Biology Special Lab, Department of Biotechnology, Bannari Amman Institute of Technology, Sathyamangalam, Tamil Nadu, India

Abimanyu Sugumaran
Department of Pharmaceutical Sciences, Assam University (A Central University), Silchar, Assam, India

Shanmuga Sundari I.
Computational Biology Special Lab, Department of Biotechnology, Bannari Amman Institute of Technology, Sathyamangalam, Tamil Nadu, India

Jorge Gustavo Uranga
Physicochemical Research Institute of Córdoba (INFIQC), CONICET. Faculty of Chemical Sciences, National University of Córdoba, Ciudad Universitaria, Córdoba, Argentina

Aayushi Velingkar
School of Biosciences and Bioengineering, Lovely Professional University, Jalandhar, Punjab, India

Sivakumar Vijayaraghavalu
Department of Life Sciences (Zoology), Manipur University, Imphal, Manipur, India

Sugunakar Vuree
Unite Lifescience, Hyderabad, Telangana, India; MNR Foundation for Research and Innovation (MNR-FRI), MNR Medical College and Hospital, Hyderabad, Telangana, India

Serap Yalcin
Department of Medical Pharmacology, Faculty of Medicine, Kırsehir Ahi Evran University, Kırsehir, Turkey

Rezvan Yazdian-Robati
Pharmaceutical Sciences Research Center, Hemoglobinopathy Institute, Mazandaran University of Medical Sciences, Sari, Iran

Mehmethan Yıldırım
Department of Molecular Biology and Genetics, Faculty of Science and Art, Kırsehir Ahi Evran University, Kırsehir, Turkey

About the editors

Dr. Prashant Kesharwani is presently working as an assistant professor at the Department of Pharmaceutics, Jamia Hamdard, New Delhi, India. He is also a recipient of the SERB Ramanujan fellowship (the most prestigious fellowship) from India. He has academic, industrial, and research experience at the international level (including the United States, Malaysia, and India). An overarching goal of his current research is the development of nano-engineered drug delivery systems for various diseases, including cancer. Dr. Kesharwani has more than 300 international publications in well-reputed journals and 22 published books (Elsevier). His h-index is 68 and i-10 index is 256 (on September 2023). He is a recipient of several internationally acclaimed awards and research funding from various funding bodies. He has presented many invited talks and oral presentations at prestigious scientific peer conferences, received international acclaim and awards for research contribution, supervised students/junior researchers, and actively participated in outreach and scientific dissemination for the service of the wider community.

Affiliation
Department of Pharmaceutics, School of Pharmaceutical Education and Research, Jamia Hamdard, New Delhi, India

Prof. Neelima Gupta, PhD, DSc, is presently working as a vice chancellor at Dr. Harisingh Gour Sagar University (A Central University), Sagar, Madhya Pradesh , India. She is a global leader having visited the five continents of the world, including countries like the the United States , the UK, Japan, Germany, France, Poland, Hong Kong, Thailand, Egypt, China, Singapore, Egypt, and Australia. She is a recipient of more than 70 awards, including the EK Janaki Ammal National Award on Animal Taxonomy, Saraswati Samman, Government of Uttar Pradesh and Vigyan Ratna, and Council of Science & Technology. She has worked extensively on parasite taxonomy, aquatic toxicology, and pollution load of the Ramganga and Ganga rivers and fish health. Research contributions include morpho-molecular-SEM taxonomy and protein profile based on 60 species of 22 genera (51 new species and 3 subspecies) and 7 Genbank submissions (GenBank: NIH genetic sequence database). She has published 216 research papers, is the author/editor of 9 books, and has adjudicated more than 150 PhD theses in India and abroad. She is represented in various national bodies (UGC, DST, CEC, UPSC, AIU, etc.). She is a pioneer in Atmanirbhar Bharat Movement launched by the Government of India.

Affiliation
Dr. Harisingh Gour Vishwavidyalaya (A Central University), Sagar, Madhya Pradesh, India

Preface

Pancreatic cancer is a devastating ailment that has a low survival rate and limited treatment options. Conventional therapy for pancreatic cancer includes surgery, chemotherapy, and radiation, but these treatments often have limited effect and can cause serious side effects. In prevailing years, owing to its distinctive attributes, a large surface area, size-tunable qualities, and surface chemistry, nanotechnology has become a viable method for cancer diagnosis, therapy, and management.

Nanotechnology has the potential to revolutionize pancreatic cancer treatment by improving drug delivery to tumor cells and reducing the after-effects of conventional therapy as nanoparticles may be engineered to focus specific tumor cells and release drugs in a controlled manner, allowing for higher drug concentrations at the tumor site while minimizing toxicity to healthy tissues.

There are numerous forms of nano-based drug delivery systems that have been studied for pancreatic cancer therapy. Hydrogels, nanoemulsions, liposomes, polymeric nanoparticles, micelle, theranostic nanoparticles, metallic nanoparticles, solid lipid nanoparticles, dendrimers, and carbon nanotube-mediated targeted drug delivery approaches are emerging options for the treatment of pancreatic cancer.

This book provides recent advances in nanocarriers explored for pancreatic cancer therapy, which help the readers to design and develop novel drug-delivery systems and devices that take advantage of recent advances in nanomedical technologies against pancreatic cancer. The book consists of an introductory chapter on an overview of the anatomy and physiology of the pancreas followed by different drug combination-based therapies pertaining to pancreatic cancer. Several chapters are devoted to the latest technologies and advances in nanotechnology and include practical solutions on how to design more effective nanocarriers for drug delivery against pancreatic cancer. Further chapters also discuss the most recent approaches such as personalized medicine, gene therapy and aptamer-mediated approaches, and photodynamic therapy. It also comprises chapters on clinical practice guidelines for interventional treatment of pancreatic cancer and future prospects of nano-based drug delivery approaches against pancreatic cancer and expected pitfalls of the technology.

This book will be a valuable resource for graduates, pharmaceutical scientists, clinical researchers, and anyone working to tackle the challenges of delivering drugs in a more targeted and efficient manner against pancreatic cancer. In totality, this book will prove to be one of the most comprehensive books available that combines both the fundamental pharmaceutical principles of nanocarriers along with the most important applications of nanotechnology in targeted drug delivery against pancreatic cancer.

Featuring contributions from field experts and researchers in industry and academia provide state-of-the-art information on nanocarriers and their use in targeted drug delivery against pancreatic cancer.

We hope that the readers of this book find it useful and stimulate further interest in the areas of drug delivery.

Prashant Kesharwani and Neelima Gupta

Acknowledgments

We sincerely thank all the contributors for offering to write comprehensive chapters within a stipulated tight schedule. This is generally an added responsibility in the hectic work schedules of the researchers. We express our earnest gratitude to the reviewers for their suggestions in framing the chapters and for providing their critical views for the improvement of the book chapters. We also thank Michaela Realiza (Editorial Project Manager, Elsevier), whose efforts during the preparation of this book proved to be very useful.

Prashant Kesharwani and Neelima Gupta

Overview, molecular pathways and conventional therapy of pancreatic cancer

PART A

Overview, molecular
pathways and conventional
therapy of pancreatic cancer

CHAPTER 1

An overview of the anatomy, physiology, and pathology of pancreatic cancer

Farzad Rahmani[1,2] and Amir Avan[1,2,3,4,5]
[1]Metabolic Syndrome Research Center, Mashhad University of Medical Sciences, Mashhad, Iran
[2]Basic Medical Sciences Institute, Mashhad University of Medical Sciences, Mashhad, Iran
[3]College of Medicine, University of Warith Al-Anbiyaa, Karbala, Iraq
[4]School of Mechanical, Medical and Process Engineering, Science and Engineering Faculty, Queensland University of Technology, Brisbane, QLD, Australia
[5]Faculty of Health, School of Biomedical Sciences, Queensland University of Technology, Brisbane, QLD, Australia

1.1 Pancreas anatomy

Pancreas is a glandular organ, which is morphologically divided into head, neck, body, and tail (Fig. 1.1). The average size of this gland is 14−18 cm long, 2−9 cm wide, 2−3 cm thick, and 80−100 g in weight [1−3]. The pancreas is a long, conical organ located behind the abdomen or behind the stomach. The widest portion on the right side of the pancreas is called the head, which is related to the duodenum. The neck of the pancreas connects the head to the body. The left side of the organ is called the body of the pancreas, which ends in the tail [4]. The tail is the narrow end of the pancreas that secretes insulin and digestive enzymes [5]. The main pancreatic duct begins in the tail portion, which transfers pancreatic secretions to the head section and often joins the bile duct in this section and forms the hepatic ampulla of the pancreas, which opens to the duodenum. The pancreas is made up of two different types of functional units including endocrine and exocrine tissues, which are introduced in the next section [6,7].

1.2 Pancreas physiology

The pancreas as an important part of the digestive system has a major role in the digestion and absorption of nutrients and regulation of body metabolism by production and release of various digestive enzymes and pancreatic hormones [8]. The pancreas consists of two separate glandular systems including exocrine and endocrine pancreas. The acinar cells that constitute most of the exocrine mass of the pancreas are involved in production and secretion of the pancreatic juice containing multiple enzymes, including peptidase, lipase, and amylase enzymes as well as alkaline fluid, which are released into the duodenum [9,10]. In contrast, the endocrine cells that make up a small part

Recent Advances in Nanocarriers for Pancreatic Cancer Therapy
DOI: https://doi.org/10.1016/B978-0-443-19142-8.00006-1

3

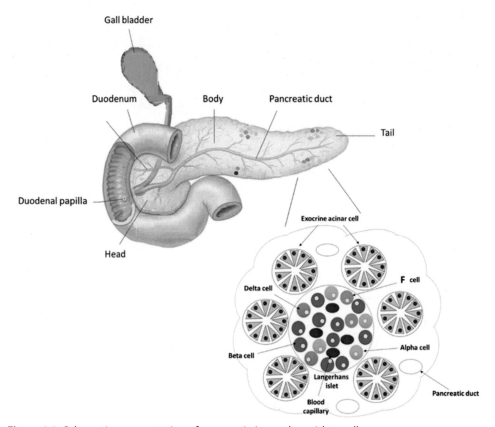

Figure 1.1 Schematic representation of pancreatic Langerhans islets cells.

(1%—2%) of the pancreas are implicated in secretion of several pancreatic hormones, which are released into the bloodstream [11]. For better understanding, the functions of pancreatic exocrine and endocrine parts are discussed separately.

1.2.1 Endocrine pancreas

The pancreatic endocrine portion consists of multiple distinct clusters of cells known as the Langerhans islet cells, which are scattered throughout the pancreas, especially in the tail area. The number of islets in the pancreas is between 1 and 2 million, but they contribute to less than 2% of the total mass of the pancreas [12]. As shown in Fig. 1.1, Langerhans islets contain various types of hormone-producing cells including alpha, beta, delta, and F cells, which can be identified by their morphological and staining characteristics. Beta cells in the center of the islets are surrounded by alpha, delta, and F cells. All cells communicate with each other through extracellular spaces and gap junctions. This type of cell arrangement makes the hormones secreted from each cell, which affects the function of other cells [13,14]. Further studies have shown that paracrine effects may play an important role in regulating hormone secretion. The way of blood supply to the islets of Langerhans also confirms the paracrine regulation of hormone secretion. In this way, the afferent blood vessels penetrate the center of the islet first, and therefore, the innermost cells of the islet receive arterial blood, while the external cells receive blood containing the secretions of internal cells [15,16]. Therefore, due to the special arrangement of cells in the islets of Langerhans, the central cells can regulate the secretion of the outer cells. In addition to the paracrine system, the autonomic nervous system is also effective in regulating the secretion of pancreatic hormones. Islet cells receive sympathetic and parasympathetic nerves and regulate hormone secretion in response to nerve input [17,18].

Beta cells, as one of the most abundant types of endocrine cells, are mainly localized in the central space of each islet and secrete insulin and amylin hormones [19]. Insulin, as the most well-known hormone produced only by beta cells, plays an important role in regulating the body's metabolism and glucose homeostasis. Release of this hormone is regulated by various factors including hormones and blood glucose. The pancreatic blood vessels originate from the splenic artery. Therefore, the islets are exposed to the systemic concentration of blood glucose and release insulin in response to hyperglycemic conditions [20].

Alpha cells as the second most abundant endocrine cells form a cortical layer at the periphery of the islets. In human pancreas, more than 90% of alpha cells are in direct contact with beta cells and their secretion is regulated by various factors including hormones, autocrine, and paracrine mechanisms [21]. Alpha cells express proglucagon gene and produce glucagon hormone, which is involved in regulating blood sugar. Proglucagon gene is also expressed in brain and intestinal L-cells and processed into various molecules including glucagon-like peptide-1 (GLP-1) and GLP-2 that implicated in glucose homeostasis [22,23].

Delta cells are generally located between the beta and alpha cells in the periphery of islets. Delta cells as well as hypothalamic cells produce somatostatin hormone, which reduces the secretion of various hormones including insulin, glucagon, gastrin, and growth hormone [24].

F cells as the least abundant hormone-producing cells constitute lower than 1% of the total islet cells. F cells produce and release pancreatic polypeptide (PP) that regulates the exocrine and endocrine secretion activities of the pancreas. The secretion of PP was shown to be negatively regulated by various factors including somatostatin and bombesin. Recent findings indicate that PP decreases secretion of gastric acid and attenuates intestinal motilities that enhanced the intestinal transit time [25,26].

1.2.2 Exocrine pancreas

Pancreas consists of two separate functional parts, exocrine and endocrine, which are involved in digestion and glucose homeostasis. The exocrine part of the pancreas, which constitutes 84% of the total pancreas mass, contains acinar and duct cells that participate

Ductal cell

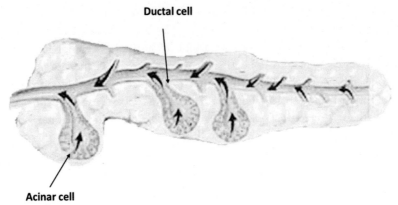

Acinar cell

Figure 1.2 Exocrine acinar and ductal cells.

in the intestinal digestion of nutrients (Fig. 1.2) [27]. Acinar cells (or acini) are the most abundant pancreatic cells that produce several types of active or inactive enzymes including amylase, lipase, trypsinogen, and chymotrypsinogen, which are released and activated in the duodenum [28]. The duct cells produce an alkaline, bicarbonate-rich fluid, which is secreted in the duodenum. In fact, the duct system, in addition to functioning as a conduit for pancreatic juice, stabilizes the exocrine proenzymes by changing the composition of pancreatic secretions by releasing bicarbonate, water, and sodium chloride [29].

1.3 Pancreas cancer pathology

Pancreatic cancers are classified based on their biological behaviors into benign and malignant tumors. According to histological differentiation, pancreatic neoplasms are classified into epithelial or nonepithelial types. Epithelial cancers can be divided into neoplasms with endocrine and exocrine differentiation [30]. Here, we present the main pathological features of exocrine tumors including pancreatic ductal adenocarcinoma (PDAC), acinar cell carcinoma (ACC), pancreatoblastoma, and endocrine tumors.

1.3.1 Pathology of the exocrine neoplasms of the pancreas

The term "exocrine pancreatic neoplasms" includes all malignancies associated with the pancreatic ductal and acinar cells [31]. More than 95% of malignant pancreatic cancers originate from the exocrine cells, which are listed in Table 1.1.

The pancreatic exocrine neoplasms are staged by the tumor, node, and metastasis (TNM) classification of the American Joint Committee on Cancer as presented in Table 1.2.

Table 1.1 Exocrine neoplasms of the pancreas.

Type	Age group	5-year survival rate (%)
Pancreatic ductal adenocarcinoma	Adults (60 years)	4
Acinar cell carcinoma	Adults (60 years)	6
Pancreatoblastoma	Children and adults	55

Table 1.2 TNM classification of pancreatic exocrine neoplasms.

TNM classification	Definition
Primary tumor (T)	
T0	No evidence of a primary tumor
T1	Tumor size <2 cm (limited to pancreas)
T2	Tumor size >2 cm (limited to the pancreas)
T3	Tumor extends to the pancreas without the involvement of the celiac axis or the superior mesenteric artery
T4	Tumor involves the celiac axis or the superior mesenteric artery
Lymph node (N)	
N0	No lymph node metastasis
N1	Lymph node metastasis
Metastasis (M)	
M0	No distant metastasis
M1	Distant metastasis
Stages	
Stage 0	Tis/ N0/M0
Stage IA	T1/ N0/M0
Stage IB	T2/ N0/M0
Stage IIA	T3/ N0/M0
Stage IIB	T1/ N1/M0
	T2/ N1/M0
	T3/ N1/M0
Stage III	T4/N/M0
Stage IV	T/N/M1

TNM, Tumor, node, and metastasis.

1.3.1.1 Pancreatic ductal adenocarcinoma

PDAC is the most aggressive tumor of the exocrine cells and contributes to about 90% of all pancreatic malignancies [32]. PDAC is often formed in the head of pancreas, but less frequently in the body or tail. Surgical resection and adjuvant chemotherapy are the only curative methods for 10%−20% of PDAC patients, while most patients are unresectable because they have either invaded nearby organs or had distant metastases [33]. PDAC metastasis can occur in any organ at various distances including liver, lung, skin, and adrenals. It has been shown that several risk factors are associated with the occurrence of PDAC including chronic disease, environmental, and genetic factors [34−36]. In addition, recent findings indicate that many cases of PDAC may originate from noninvasive epithelial precursor lesions including pancreatic intraepithelial neoplasias (PanINs). Therefore, detection of these epithelial lesions may provide an opportunity for preventing PDAC development or reducing cancer-related mortality [37,38].

The majority of PDAC patients suffer from nonspecific symptoms including abdominal pain, diarrhea, vomiting, and weight loss. Upon the tumor progression, the pancreas and bile ducts are closed resulting in alleviated bile and pancreas secretion into the duodenum. In this condition, the absorption of food and fat is reduced and weight loss occurs. The most common symptom of PDAC is jaundice, which occurs when a tumor grows in the head of the pancreas and blocks the bile duct [39]. Moreover, PDAC causes defects in the function of pancreatic beta cells, resulting in diabetes mellitus [40]. Considering that a large part of PDAC patients have impaired insulin secretion, the possibility of PDAC should also be considered in differential diagnosis with respect to type 2 diabetes [41]. The prothrombin time was also increased in PDAC due to reduced absorption of fat and vitamin K [42].

1.3.1.2 Acinar cell carcinoma
ACC is an uncommon malignant epithelial neoplasm that is mostly diagnosed in men at the age of 60 years or older. ACC can occur in any part of the pancreas but is more common in the head [43]. AAC are characterized by their morphological similarity to acinar cells and releasing pancreatic exocrine enzymes including trypsin, chymotrypsin, and lipase. Therefore, immunostaining for detection of these pancreatic digestive enzymes is very useful for confirming the diagnosis of acinar cell neoplasia [44].

1.3.1.3 Pancreatoblastoma
Pancreatoblastoma is a rare epithelial malignancy that originates from the exocrine cells of the pancreas. Pancreatoblastoma occurs in all areas of the pancreas, including the head, body, and tail with equal frequencies. Pancreatoblastoma shows acinar differentiation and therefore mimics AACs, but pancreatoblastoma occurs in children and ACC occurs in adults. In addition, the squamoid nests in pancreatoblastoma are the distinguishing feature for the correct diagnosis of pancreatoblastoma [45]. The vast majority of pancreatoblastoma has been identified in children with a mean age of 5 years. This type of tumor is slightly more common in men and two-thirds of existing tumors are reported from Asian patients. Pancreatoblastoma rarely occurs in adults and the prognosis is worse in adults than in children [46,47]. One of the clinical manifestations of

pancreatoblastoma is the increase of α-fetoprotein levels, which can be used to monitor the response to treatment [48]. Moreover, patients with pancreatoblastoma display loss of chromosome 11p, which has been reported in other infantile cancers including hepatoblastoma [49].

1.3.2 Pathology of the endocrine neoplasms of pancreas

Pancreatic endocrine neoplasms are mainly malignant neoplasms, accounting for about 5% of all pancreatic tumors. These neoplasms are epithelial tumors with endocrine differentiation, which can be located in any portion of the pancreas. Pancreatic endocrine neoplasms may arise at any age group but are most commonly diagnosed between the ages of 50 and 60 years [50,51].

Pancreatic endocrine neoplasms are classified into functional or nonfunctional categories depending on their ability to secrete specific hormones and to cause characteristic symptoms. Nonfunctional neoplasms secrete molecules, such as chromogranin, neuron-specific enolase, PP, and ghrelin, and do not cause clinical manifestations related to hormone secretion [52,53]. The classification of pancreatic endocrine neoplasms is presented in Table 1.3.

In addition, according to the type of released hormone, various functional neoplasms are diagnosed including insulinoma, gastrinoma, and glucagonoma (Table 1.4). These functional neoplasms may appear with symptoms related to excessive hormone secretion [54].

Table 1.3 Classification of pancreatic endocrine neoplasms.

Functional endocrine neoplasms	Nonfunctional endocrine neoplasms
Insulinoma Gastrinoma Glucagonoma Somatostatinoma VIPoma	PP-secreting tumor (PPoma) Poorly differentiated endocrine carcinomas: Small cell carcinoma Large cell endocrine carcinoma Mixed endocrine carcinomas

Table 1.4 Functional pancreatic endocrine tumors.

	Cell type	Clinical features
Insulinoma	Beta cells	Hypoglycemia
Gastrinoma	G cells	Peptic ulcers and diarrhea
Glucagonoma	Alpha cells	Diabetes mellitus, weight loss, and hyperglucagonemia
Somatostatinoma	Delta cells	diabetes mellitus, cholelithiasis, and steatorrhea
VIPoma	Unknown	watery diarrhea, hypokalemia, and metabolic acidosis

Insulinoma is the most frequent tumor of pancreatic endocrine cells, 90% of which are benign. However, 10% of insulinomas occur as part of multiple endocrine neoplasia type I (MEN-I) syndrome [55]. The most important symptom of insulinoma is hypoglycemia, and its related complications include headache, visual disturbances, seizures, and death in severe cases. The gold standard for the diagnosis of insulinoma is a monitored 72-hour fasting test with measurements of plasma glucose, insulin, C-peptide, and proinsulin at the onset of hypoglycemic symptoms [56,57].

Gastrinoma is one of the most common functional and malignant pancreatic endocrine tumors that release large amounts of gastrin, which leads to hyperplasia of parietal cells and increases gastric acid secretion [58]. Excessive output of stomach acid damages the mucosal defense of the stomach and causes severe peptic ulcer disease and diarrhea, which is referred to as Zollinger-Ellison syndrome. Gastrinoma is usually diagnosed between the ages of 20 and 50, which is more common in men. The diagnosis of gastrinoma is confirmed through an increase in the fasting serum gastrin concentration associated with an increase in the secretion of gastric acid or low gastric pH [59].

Glucagonoma is a rare alpha-cell tumor in the Langerhans islets, which is mainly located in the pancreatic tail. This endocrine neoplasm secretes glucagon and causes various symptoms including hyperglucagonemia, diabetes mellitus, anemia, weight loss, and diarrhea. Fasting plasma glucagon greater than 500 pg/mL can be used as a diagnostic tool for glucagonoma [60].

VIPoma is another rare pancreatic endocrine neoplasm that secretes vasoactive intestinal polypeptide (VIP). VIPoma is usually located in the body and tail of the pancreas [61]. The major clinical signs of VIPoma are watery diarrhea, hypokalemia, and metabolic acidosis [62]. VIPoma and its related symptoms are known as Verner-Morrison syndrome or pancreatic cholera. A serum level of VIP greater than 200 pg/mL may be used for the diagnosis of VIPoma [63].

Somatostatinoma, as a curious endocrine neoplasm, originates from pancreatic delta cells and produces somatostatin hormone. Increased secretion of somatostatin inhibits several gastrointestinal hormones and causes a triad of symptoms of somatostatinoma including diabetes mellitus, cholelithiasis, and steatorrhea. Increased blood levels of somatostatin can serve as a specific biomarker for tumor follow-up [64,65].

As shown in Table 1.3, a PP-secreting tumor (PPoma is a nonfunctional neoplasm that makes up approximately 50% of neuroendocrine tumors of pancreas). PPoma secretes pancreatic polypeptide and causes various nonspecific symptoms including weight loss, abdominal pain, jaundice, and diarrhea [66].

Most patients with nonfunctional endocrine neoplasms are identified with a number of nonspecific symptoms including bellyache, enlarged liver, jaundice, and obstruction of the pancreatic duct. Therefore, nonfunctional neoplasms may be diagnosed with a larger size, higher metastatic rate, and worse prognosis. Similarly, PPoma demonstrates a lower overall survival than functional neoplasms. Considering that nonfunctional neoplasms have a better prognosis than pancreatic exocrine tumors, it is very important to differentiate between a nonfunctional tumor and a functional pancreatic neoplasm [52,67].

1.4 Conclusion

Pancreatic cancer represents a challenge for identifying novel diagnostic and prognostic biomarkers. Despite recent efforts to improve the screening, diagnostic, and therapeutic methods, patients with pancreatic cancer exhibit dismal prognoses and lower survival rates. A complete understanding of the clinical symptoms related to the types of pancreatic malignancies has a central role in the correct diagnosis and treatment of patients with pancreatic cancer. In addition, the widespread use of novel methods of gene and protein analysis plays an important role in recognizing the type of neoplasm and determining the correct treatment method.

References

[1] van Erning FN, et al. Association of the location of pancreatic ductal adenocarcinoma (head, body, tail) with tumor stage, treatment, and survival: a population-based analysis. Acta oncologica 2018;57 (12):1655−62.

[2] Allen DC, Cameron RI, Loughrey MB. Pancreas, duodenum, ampulla of vater and extrahepatic bile ducts. Histopathology Specimens. Springer; 2013. p. 33−46.

[3] Kelly PJ. Ampulla of vater and head of pancreas carcinomas. Histopathology Reporting. Springer; 2020. p. 55−68.

[4] Ling Q, et al. The diversity between pancreatic head and body/tail cancers: clinical parameters and in vitro models. Hepatobiliary Pancreat Dis Int 2013;12(5):480−7.

[5] BelHadj S, et al. Inhibitory activities of Ulva lactuca polysaccharides on digestive enzymes related to diabetes and obesity. Arch Physiol Biochem 2013;119(2):81−7.

[6] Czakó L, et al. Interactions between the endocrine and exocrine pancreas and their clinical relevance. Pancreatology 2009;9(4):351−9.

[7] Das SL, et al. Relationship between the exocrine and endocrine pancreas after acute pancreatitis. World J Gastroenterol 2014;20(45):17196−205.

[8] Röder PV, et al. Pancreatic regulation of glucose homeostasis. Exp Mol Med 2016;48(3):e219.

[9] Hameed AM, Lam VW, Pleass HC. Significant elevations of serum lipase not caused by pancreatitis: a systematic review. HPB 2015;17(2):99−112.

[10] Steinberg WM, et al. Impact of liraglutide on amylase, lipase, and acute pancreatitis in participants with overweight/obesity and normoglycemia, prediabetes, or type 2 diabetes: secondary analyses of pooled data from the SCALE clinical development program. Diabetes Care 2017;40(7):839−48.

[11] D'Amour KA, et al. Production of pancreatic hormone−expressing endocrine cells from human embryonic stem cells. Nat Biotechnol 2006;24(11):1392−401.

[12] Da Silva Xavier G. The cells of the islets of Langerhans. J Clin Med 2018;7(3):54.

[13] Brereton MF, et al. Alpha-, delta-and PP-cells: are they the architectural cornerstones of islet structure and co-ordination? J Histochem Cytochem 2015;63(8):575−91.

[14] Miranda C, et al. Gap junction coupling and islet delta-cell function in health and disease. Peptides 2022;147:170704.

[15] Koh D-S, Cho J-H, Chen L. Paracrine interactions within islets of Langerhans. J Mol Neurosci 2012;48(2):429−40.

[16] Svendsen B, Holst JJ. Paracrine regulation of somatostatin secretion by insulin and glucagon in mouse pancreatic islets. Diabetologia 2021;64(1):142–51.

[17] Taborsky Jr GJ, Mundinger TO. Minireview: the role of the autonomic nervous system in mediating the glucagon response to hypoglycemia. Endocrinology 2012;153(3):1055–62.

[18] Havel PJ, Taborsky Jr GJ. The contribution of the autonomic nervous system to changes of glucagon and insulin secretion during hypoglycemic stress. Endocr Rev 1989;10(3):332–50.

[19] Kiriyama Y, Nochi H. Role and cytotoxicity of amylin and protection of pancreatic islet β-cells from amylin cytotoxicity. Cells 2018;7(8):95.

[20] Cluck MW, Chan CY, Adrian TE. The regulation of amylin and insulin gene expression and secretion. Pancreas 2005;30(1):1–14.

[21] Omar-Hmeadi M, et al. Paracrine control of α-cell glucagon exocytosis is compromised in human type-2 diabetes. Nat Commun 2020;11(1):1–11.

[22] Müller TD, et al. Glucagon-like peptide 1 (GLP-1). Mol Metab 2019;30:72–130.

[23] Hansen LB. GLP-2 and mesenteric blood flow. Dan Med J 2013;60(5):B4634.

[24] Vergari E, et al. Somatostatin secretion by Na^+-dependent Ca^{2+}-induced Ca^{2+} release in pancreatic delta cells. Nat Metab 2020;2(1):32–40.

[25] Williams JA. Pancreatic polypeptide. Pancreapedia: The Exocrine Pancreas Knowledge Base. American Pancreatic Association; 2014.

[26] Eddes EH, et al. Pancreatic polypeptide secretion in patients with chronic pancreatitis and after pancreatic surgery. Int J Pancreatol 2001;29(3):173–80.

[27] Hegyi P, Petersen OH. The exocrine pancreas: the acinar-ductal tango in physiology and pathophysiology. Rev Physiol Biochem Pharmacol 2013;165:1–30.

[28] Thrower EC, et al. Zymogen activation in a reconstituted pancreatic acinar cell system. Am J Physiol Gastrointest Liver Physiol 2006;290(5):G894–902.

[29] Hegyi P, et al. Pancreatic ductal bicarbonate secretion: challenge of the acinar acid load. Front Physiol 2011;2:36.

[30] Luchini C, et al. Malignant epithelial/exocrine tumors of the pancreas. Pathologica 2020;112 (3):210–26.

[31] Thompson ED, Wood LD. Pancreatic neoplasms with acinar differentiation: a review of pathologic and molecular features. Arch Pathol Lab Med 2020;144(7):808–15.

[32] Orth M, et al. Pancreatic ductal adenocarcinoma: biological hallmarks, current status, and future perspectives of combined modality treatment approaches. Radiat Oncol 2019;14(1):1–20.

[33] Pappalardo A, et al. Adjuvant treatment in pancreatic cancer: shaping the future of the curative setting. Front Oncol 2021;11:695627.

[34] Gu J, et al. Surgical resection of metastatic pancreatic cancer: is it worth it? - a 15-year experience at a single Chinese center. J Gastrointest Oncol 2020;11(2):319–28.

[35] Jin T, Dai C, Xu F. Surgical and local treatment of hepatic metastasis in pancreatic ductal adenocarcinoma: recent advances and future prospects. Ther Adv Med Oncol 2020;12. p. 1758835920933034.

[36] Wei M, et al. Simultaneous resection of the primary tumour and liver metastases after conversion chemotherapy versus standard therapy in pancreatic cancer with liver oligometastasis: protocol of a multicentre, prospective, randomised phase III control trial (CSPAC-1). BMJ Open 2019;9(12): e033452.

[37] Yu DY, et al. Clinical significance of pancreatic intraepithelial neoplasia in resectable pancreatic cancer on survivals. Ann Surg Treat Res 2018;94(5):247–53.

[38] Hassid BG, et al. Absence of pancreatic intraepithelial neoplasia predicts poor survival after resection of pancreatic cancer. Pancreas 2014;43(7):1073–7.

[39] Holly EA, et al. Signs and symptoms of pancreatic cancer: a population-based case-control study in the San Francisco Bay area. Clin Gastroenterol Hepatol 2004;2(6):510–17.

[40] Parajuli P, et al. Pancreatic cancer triggers diabetes through TGF-β-mediated selective depletion of islet β-cells. Life Sci Alliance 2020;3(6):e201900573.

[41] Sharma A, Chari ST. Pancreatic cancer and diabetes mellitus. Curr Treat Options Gastroenterol 2018;16(4):466–78.

[42] Matsumura K, et al. Prognostic impact of coagulation activity in patients undergoing curative resection for pancreatic ductal adenocarcinoma. In Vivo 2020;34(5):2845−50.

[43] La Rosa S, Sessa F, Capella C. Acinar cell carcinoma of the pancreas: overview of clinicopathologic features and insights into the molecular pathology. Front Med (Lausanne) 2015;2:41.

[44] Zhou W, et al. Clinical analysis of acinar cell carcinoma of the pancreas: a single-center experience of 45 consecutive cases. Cancer Control 2020;27(1) 1073274820969447.

[45] Omiyale AO. Adult pancreatoblastoma: current concepts in pathology. World J Gastroenterol 2021;27(26):4172−81.

[46] Liu T, et al. Pancreatoblastoma in children: clinical management and literature review. Transl Oncol 2022;18:101359.

[47] Huang Y, et al. Diagnosis and treatment of pancreatoblastoma in children: a retrospective study in a single pediatric center. Pediatric Surg Int 2019;35(11):1231−8.

[48] Cao G, Mendez J, Navacchia D. Pancreatoblastoma in a paediatric patient: anatomo-pathological aspects of a case with multiple hepatic metastases. Ecancermedicalscience 2018;12:861.

[49] Abraham SC, et al. Genetic and immunohistochemical analysis of pancreatic acinar cell carcinoma: frequent allelic loss on chromosome 11p and alterations in the APC/β-catenin pathway. Am J Pathol 2002;160(3):953−62.

[50] Philips S, et al. Pancreatic endocrine neoplasms: a current update on genetics and imaging. Br J Radiol 2012;85(1014):682−96.

[51] Halfdanarson TR, et al. Pancreatic endocrine neoplasms: epidemiology and prognosis of pancreatic endocrine tumors. Endocr Relat Cancer 2008;15(2):409−27.

[52] Cloyd JM, Poultsides GA. Non-functional neuroendocrine tumors of the pancreas: advances in diagnosis and management. World J Gastroenterol 2015;21(32):9512−25.

[53] Ro C, et al. Pancreatic neuroendocrine tumors: biology, diagnosis, and treatment. Chin J Cancer 2013;32(6):312−24.

[54] Ito T, Igarashi H, Jensen RT. Pancreatic neuroendocrine tumors: clinical features, diagnosis and medical treatment: advances. Best Pract Res Clin Gastroenterol 2012;26(6):737−53.

[55] Shin JJ, Gorden P, Libutti SK. Insulinoma: pathophysiology, localization and management. Future Oncol 2010;6(2):229−37.

[56] Okabayashi T, et al. Diagnosis and management of insulinoma. World J Gastroenterol 2013;19 (6):829−37.

[57] Ahn CH, et al. Clinical implications of various criteria for the biochemical diagnosis of insulinoma. Endocrinol Metab (Seoul) 2014;29(4):498−504.

[58] Dacha S, et al. Hypergastrinemia. Gastroenterol Rep (Oxf) 2015;3(3):201−8.

[59] Hung PD, Schubert ML, Mihas AA. Zollinger-Ellison syndrome. Curr Treat Options Gastroenterol 2003;6(2):163−70.

[60] Gao Y, et al. Glucagonoma syndrome with serous oligocystic adenoma: a rare case report. Med (Baltim) 2017;96(43):e8448.

[61] Bonilla Gonzalez C, et al. Pancreatic VIPoma as a differential diagnosis in chronic pediatric diarrhea: a case report and review of the literature. J Med Cases 2021;12(5):195−201.

[62] Sánchez-Salazar SM, et al. VIPoma: a rare cause of diarrhea. A case report. Rev de la Facultad de Medicina 2021;69:3.

[63] Abdullayeva L. VIPoma: mechanisms, clinical presentation, diagnosis and treatment. World Acad Sci J 2019;1(5):229−35.

[64] Mori Y, et al. Pancreatic somatostatinoma diagnosed preoperatively: report of a case. JOP J Pancreas 2014;15(1):66−71.

[65] Zhang B, et al. Pancreatic somatostatinoma with obscure inhibitory syndrome and mixed pathological pattern. J Zhejiang Univ Sci B 2010;11(1):22−6.

[66] Ligiero Braga T, Santos-Oliveira R. PPoma review: epidemiology, aetiopathogenesis, prognosis and treatment. Diseases 2018;6(1):8.

[67] Bar-Moshe Y, Mazeh H, Grozinsky-Glasberg S. Non-functioning pancreatic neuroendocrine tumors: surgery or observation? World J Gastrointest Endosc 2017;9(4):153−61.

CHAPTER 2

Different combination therapies pertaining to pancreatic cancer

Zahra Salmasi[1,*], Parisa Saberi-Hasanabadi[2,*], Hamidreza Mohammadi[2,3] and Rezvan Yazdian-Robati[3]

[1]Department of Pharmaceutical Nanotechnology, School of Pharmacy, Mashhad University of Medical Sciences, Mashhad, Iran
[2]Department of Toxicology and Pharmacology, Faculty of Pharmacy, Mazandaran University of Medical Sciences, Sari, Iran
[3]Pharmaceutical Sciences Research Center, Hemoglobinopathy Institute, Mazandaran University of Medical Sciences, Sari, Iran

2.1 Introduction

Pancreatic cancer (PC) is one of the silent cancers that progresses quietly and its symptoms appear in the final stages. This disease is one of the most fatal and aggressive cancers, which annually has more than 330,000 deaths. Men are at greater risk for PC than women [1]. Pancreas is one of the organs of the digestive system, which, along with the gallbladder, plays an important role in food digestion. Some mutations in the DNA of the pancreatic cells lead to continuous cell proliferation, which disrupts the apoptosis process and cell death that cause tumor formation. If the cancer is not treated, it spreads to the surrounding organs and blood vessels [2]. PC diagnosing can be difficult because there are no obvious symptoms at the beginning of pancreatic malignancy. But in people with pancreatic cysts or with a family background of PC, cancer screening helps in early detection [3]. To date, surgery is known as one of the earliest forms of cancer therapy. After surgery, the next standard of care is radiotherapy and chemotherapy. Most pancreatic tumors cannot be surgically removed due to metastasis and invasion of the main posterior vessels of the pancreas. Radiation combined with chemotherapy is used to slow down the progression of locally advanced cancers. Abraxane, Afinitor, everolimus, 5-FU, gemcitabine hydrochloride, gemzar, and nano–encapsulated form of bioactive compounds such as curcumin are among the most common effective chemotherapy agents for the treatment of PC [4]. Usually, there is a connective tissue called stroma around pancreatic tumors. The stroma is like a protective shield that prevents the effect of chemotherapy drugs. To solve this problem, chemotherapy drugs must be persistent so that they can pass through the stroma and reach the tumor. On the other hand, the long shelf life of the drug can poison healthy tissues and blood and be harmful to the patient. Therefore, we need to use high amounts of medicine and repeat the drug treatment many times, which

---

* These authors are equal in this work.

Recent Advances in Nanocarriers for Pancreatic Cancer Therapy
DOI: https://doi.org/10.1016/B978-0-443-19142-8.00018-8

along with the intensification of drug resistance will lead to an increase in side effects [5]. To overcome these limitations, it seems that the use of combined treatment is a suitable solution. Combination therapy, polytherapy, or multimodal treatment, all refer to the application of two or more types of treatments that are used in a different manner: simultaneously, in order, or at different times [6]. Combination drug therapy may be achieved by prescribing separate drugs in a fixed dose or in a medicinal form containing more than one active ingredient. In some cases, for detecting the best drug formulation, patients have to try several different combinations of drugs [5]. Since a pathogen or tumor is less likely to be resistant to multiple drugs simultaneously, therefore, reduction of drug resistance is considered one of the most important benefits of combination therapy [6]. In the short period of treatment, combination therapy may seem costs more than monotherapy but actually, when this treatment approach is used properly, it will save significantly during the treatment. Fewer failure rates during treatment, lower mortality, fewer side effects, less drug resistance, and, as a result, reduction in costs are among the important advantages of combination therapy usually, the main goal of developing codelivery platforms is to achieve a combination of different treatment mechanisms. Along with conventional methods, including surgery, radiation, and chemotherapy, other treatment strategies such as gene therapy, photodynamic therapy, photothermal therapy, and immunotherapy can be used in tumor treatment and seems to be more beneficial than one method alone [7,8]. In special conditions, combination therapy can not only attain a higher probability of success than monotherapy but also can do with less adverse effects on normal cells [9]. The combination of radiation and chemotherapy along with controlled drug delivery vehicles may destroy cancerous tissue without losing the organ containing the tumor [8]. The advantages of the last option compared to single drug treatment are: (1) Optimal design in line with better synergistic effects and avoiding the single use of more drugs together, (2) Optimizing patient compliance, and, (3) Accurate monitoring of individual doses and avoidance of uncertainty due to divisibility of drug doses. In this regard, coadministration of common medicinal compounds along with active ingredients of natural origin is another attractive strategy considering the general safety of phytotherapy [10−12]. For example, quercetin has received special attention in recent studies as a polyphenolic flavonoid but, unfortunately, its clinical application is limited due to inherent lipophilicity, instability in the circulation, and low bioavailability [13]. For this reason, the use of nano-carriers in combination with nanoplatforms has been considered. Some advantages of this approach are as follows: desirable biological structures, increased serum consistency, controlled medications release, high carrying capacity, long-term systemic circulation, decreased nonspecific cellular uptake, optimized selection of anticancer drug compounds to tumor tissue by increasing permeability and retention time, and ability of multidrug encapsulation for combinatorial treatment [14−16]. In this chapter, we collected the results obtained from the recent studies in developing different methods of combination therapy and their applications in PC therapy.

2.2 Carrier-free combination therapy in pancreatic cancer treatment

Drug delivery systems designed based on nano-carriers have significant potential in the field of biomedical applications due to their very suitable dispersion in water, longer duration in blood circulation, increased drug accumulation in the tumor microenvironment, and the ability to be used in combined treatments. However, most nano-carriers have some deficiencies such as low drug loading efficiency, weak therapeutic effect, possible systemic toxicity, and impermanent metabolism [17]. Carrier-free platforms that are composed of one or more drugs have received a lot of consideration in PC treatment as a result of some advantages such as improved pharmacodynamics/pharmacokinetics properties, decreased toxicity, and appropriate efficiency in drug loading [18]. Although this strategy is considered a successful approach in preclinical development, some concerns such as modulation of multiple drugs in a nano-platform and increased tumor targeting efficiency still require more attention to develop more efficient carrier-free nano-drugs. Cheng et al. [18] developed a carrier-free nanoparticle in which curcumin-erlotinib conjugate was self-assembled with size of about 105 nm. The curcumin-erlotinib conjugate nano-assembly exhibited greater lethality in tumor tissue and enhanced antimigration and anti-invasion activity especially in the case of BxPC-3 PC cell line compared to free curcumin along with erlotinib. No systemic toxicity was observed in different parts of mice treated with curcumin-erlotinib conjugate [18]. In this line, Ma et al. [19] investigated the inhibitory effect of dasatinib along with paclitaxel or gemcitabine in different human/mouse PC cell lines and compared its results with various treatments including monotherapies, paclitaxel with gemcitabine or FOLFIRINOX (combination of fluorouracil, leucovorin, irinotecan, and oxaliplatin). The data from this study showed that treating samples with dasatinib and paclitaxel or gemcitabine was a suitable technique in the case of human/mouse PC cells, which led to more reduction in the migration and the colony-forming capability of PC cells in comparison to monotherapy or administration of FOLFIRINOX [19].

In another study, Shim et al. [20] developed a preclinical process based on carrier-free pro-drug nanoparticles, which was used as an alternative plan to overcome the restrictions of conventional nano-based drug delivery systems. Increased antitumor effect with less toxicity in both technical and industrial scales was one of the advantages of this designed nano-platform. For this purpose, doxorubicin (DOX) and cathepsin B-specific cleavable peptide (Phe-Arg-Arg-Gly, FRRG) were conjugated and self-assembled using Pluronic F68 as the stabilizer. Drug loading was more than 50% and high stability of lyophilized powder was shown during long-term storage at various temperatures (-4, 37, and 60°C). Targeted cytotoxicity in cancerous cells was achieved due to the high expression of cathepsin B. In an animal study, F68-FDOX showed remarkable antitumor effects in colon, breast, and pancreatic tumor models with low toxicity in normal mice [20].

Photothermal and photodynamic therapies are the two most important phototherapy strategies. The results of numerous studies have shown that the combination of phototherapy and chemotherapy is effective and practical in cancer therapy. In this regard, Zhu et al. [21] developed a promising nano-medicine platform composed of a photodynamic agent (chlorine e6, Ce6) and peptide-gemcitabine for PC treatment. The peptide-gemcitabine conjugate consisted of a vinyl dithioether linker, which was sensitive to reactive oxygen species for the controlled release of the drug. When reached tumors, this nano-platform decomposed and gemcitabine, chlorine e6, and pro-apoptotic peptide were released under light irradiation. The significant effect of the designed drug nano-platform was observed on tumor inhibition in PC models with low systemic toxicity in animals [21].

2.3 Nanoparticle-mediated combination therapy in pancreatic cancer treatment

As mentioned, some of the major issues during PC treatments are anticancer drug resistance, narrow therapeutic window, and undesired anticancer drug side effects. Choosing suitable carriers for chemotherapy drugs and target genes is a key tool for basic research and clinical application in this field [9]. For instance, gemcitabine has been widely used as the most common chemotherapy drug in the treatment of PC in the last decade, however, its use as the first line of drug treatment suffers from obstacles such as rapid metabolism and low selectivity towards tumor cells [4]. Nanotechnology and targeted drug delivery are promising concepts in cancer treatment and have represented great results in this field. An extensive review of scientific research has shown that combined treatment along with nanomedicines generally will intensify the effects of drug synergy and inhibit or reduce drug resistance in certain cases [6].

2.3.1 Metal and metal oxide nanoparticles

2.3.1.1 Gold nanoparticles

Molecular imaging tries to discover diseases in their early stages through molecular processes in living cells/organisms and monitor the molecular impact of different treatments [22]. Gold (Au) nanoparticles are widely used in detection and treatment of various cancers because of their great features such as easy application and modification, stability, and biocompatibility. Equipping gold nanoparticle platforms with different types of functional compounds including imaging or pharmaceutical agents will lead to the improvement of the capacity of such nanosystems during multimodal imaging diagnosis and targeted therapy [23]. Qiu et al. [22] designed a theranostic nano-platform based on gold nano-cages conjugated to hyaluronic acid and anti-Glypican-1 antibody, loaded with oridonin, and attached to gadolinium and Cy7 dye. Oridonin-glypican-1-nanoparticles showed good stability in long-term storage and fluorescent/MRI features. Cellular uptake of oridonin-glypican-1-nanoparticles into PANC-1 and BXPC-3 cells was well displayed through transmission electron microscopy while these nanoparticles could not efficiently enter normal cells such as 293 T cells. In vitro studies also demonstrated that oridonin-glypican-1-nanoparticles could considerably induce apoptosis in PC cells [22]. In another study, targeted delivery of varlitinib and DOX was monitored using functionalized gold nanoparticles in human PC cell lines. Conjugated varlitinib and DOX with pegylated gold nanoparticles showed a combined effect in reducing the cancer cell (S2—013s) viability and minimizing the cytotoxicity on normal pancreatic cells (hTERT-HPNE) [24].

2.3.1.2 Silver nanoparticles
One of the possible effective nanoplatforms in PC treatment is silver nanoparticles. Silver (Ag) nanoparticles have been considered a suitable option in therapeutic strategies for all types of cancers, and they can probably be effective in the treatment of PC [25]. Barcińska et al. [26] investigated the effect of oxidative and nitro-oxidative injury when silver nanoparticles were used for inducing a cytotoxic effect in some types of PC cells. In general, they concluded that oxidative and nitro-oxidative stress and mitochondrial damage are involved in cell death and toxicity caused by silver nanoparticles in human PC cells [26].

2.3.1.3 Copper nanoparticle
Copper (Cu) oxide nanoparticles have more toxicity in human cells compared to other metal oxide nanoparticles. Pancreatic tumor growth was restricted by copper oxide nanoparticles through targeting tumor-initiating cells (TICs) in PANC-1 cells (human PC cells). These results were caused by increased levels of reactive oxygen species and enhanced mitochondrial membrane permeability in these cells. In addition, tumor growth was retarded in pancreatic tumor-bearing mice treated with CuO-NP, as well as, enhancement of apoptotic TICs was shown by flow cytometry and immunohistochemistry in this group compared to untreated mice. Overall, their results highlighted the potential of using copper oxide nanoparticles as a novel treatment for PC [27].

2.3.1.4 Selenium nanoparticles
Selenium (Se)-based drug delivery systems show excellent antioxidant activity and proper disease prevention. In addition, there is evidence supporting the biocompatibility, bioefficacy, and lower toxicity of selenium-containing nanosystems [28]. In this line, Shiri et al. [29] monitored the effect of magnesium oxide and selenium nanoparticles on the extrinsic

and intrinsic apoptosis pathways in PaTu cells treated with diazinon. The results displayed that the combination of magnesium oxide and selenium nanoparticles reduced the toxicity of diazinon more efficiently than monotherapies. In other words, this combination could modify the expression of genes in apoptosis caspase-dependent pathways [29].

2.3.1.5 Fe₃O₄ nanoparticles

Superparamagnetic iron oxide nanoparticles are inexpensive with good colloidal stability and biocompatibility and low toxicity. In recent years, use of engineered magnetic nano-particles in various fields of medical research including diagnosis through biosensing or imaging and therapeutic techniques has been widely studied [30,31]. In this line, Trabulo et al. [32] investigated multifunctionalized iron oxide nanoparticles (MNPs) for targeted delivery of therapeutic antibodies and chemotherapeutic drug (gemcitabine) to PC cells. The in vitro results revealed that anti-CD47 antibody and Gemcitabine were effectively delivered to the CD47-positive PC cells using MNPs and the cell viability was efficiently decreased through MNP-Gem-anti-CD47 in combination therapy after 6 days of treatment (Fig. 2.1) [32]. In another study, a formulation of superparamagnetic iron oxide nanoparticles loaded with curcumin was designed and its effect in combination with gemci-tabine on pancreatic tumors was investigated. The obtained results demonstrated that this system could affect cancer stem cells by inhibiting the pluripotency factors and reducing the sphere formation. In an animal study, combination therapy caused an effective reduction in tumor growth and metastasis [33].

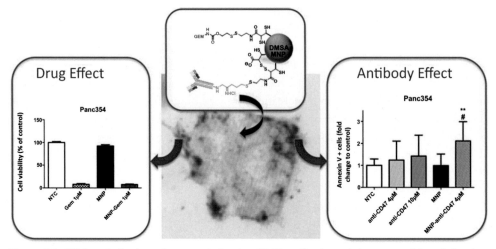

Figure 2.1 Efficient induction of apoptosis by the CD47 antibody and the cytotoxicity of the drug (gemcitabine). *Reproduced with permission from Trabulo S, Aires A, Aicher A, Heeschen C, Cortajarena AL. Multifunctionalized iron oxide nanoparticles for selective targeting of pancreatic cancer cells. Biochim Biophys Acta Gen Subj. 2017;1861(6):1597–1605.*

2.3.2 Nonmetallic nanoparticles

2.3.2.1 Carbon-based nanoparticles

Carbon nano-dots, carbon nano-tubes, carbon nano-fibers, nano-diamonds, graphene, and fullerenes are carbon-based nanomaterials that have shown significant anticancer potential. Some carbon-based nanoparticles, such as graphene oxide, have features such as great drug loading capacity, adjustable surface area, and optimal colloidal stability. Furthermore, graphene oxide is able to cause oxidative stress in a dose-dependent manner. This reaction may be considered one of the main proposed mechanisms for cytotoxicity during the use of carbon-based nanomaterials [34]. Wójcik et al. [35] investigated the impacts of some carbon-based and metallic nanomaterials on PC cell lines (AsPC-1 and BxPC-3). As a result, more intensive cytotoxic effects were shown with carbon-based nanoparticles compared to metallic nanoparticles. The lowest viability was related to nanodiamond treatment especially in BxPC-3 cell line because of reactive oxygen species (ROS) induction. Furthermore, the amount of some pro-inflammatory proteins was altered after exposure to nanodiamond and graphene oxide [35].

2.3.2.2 Silica-based nanoparticles

Porous silica nanoparticles are considered biocompatible, efficient, safe, and biodegradable drug delivery platforms due to features such as high total surface area and existence of regular porous channels [36]. Xing et al. [36] developed a nano-platform, which consists of silica and gold NPs loaded with gemcitabine, linked to IGF1 along with a temperature-sensitive gel. This system provided multimode ultrasound/computed tomography/photoacoustic imaging for precise performance of photothermal therapy against patient-derived xenograft and long-term release of gemcitabine for restricting the remaining PC cells to inhibit the recurrence [36].

Tarannum et al. [37] investigated the potential of using the sonic hedgehog inhibitor based on mesoporous silica nanoparticles containing cyclopamine and chemotherapeutic drugs combination (cisplatin/gemcitabine) to reduce the tumor stroma and, therefore, achieve more progress in pancreatic ductal adenocarcinoma therapy. The results of protein evaluation exhibited that cyclopamine-mesoporous silica NP caused significant inhibition of the sonic hedgehog pathway. Furthermore, the consecutive administration of cyclopamine-mesoporous silica NP followed by polyethylene glycol-Gemcitabine-Cisplatin-Mesoporous silica nanoparticles could efficiently modulate the stroma, increase NP accumulation in tumor environment, and enhance the therapeutic efficacy in HPAF II xenograft mice [37] (Fig. 2.2).

2.3.3 Polymeric nanoparticles

2.3.3.1 Chitosan nanoparticles

Many natural compounds have antitumor effects because of different mechanisms involved in preventing various molecular pathways in tumor cells. However, some

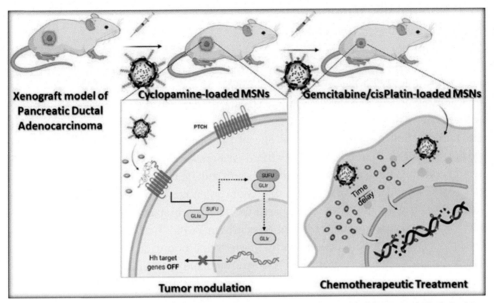

Figure 2.2 Mesoporous silica nanoparticles included SHh inhibitor cyclopamine and the combination of the chemotherapeutic drugs including cisplatin/gemcitabine for treating pancreatic ductal adenocarcinoma. *Reproduced with permission from Tarannum M, Holtzman K, Dréau D, Mukherjee P, Vivero-Escoto JL. Nanoparticle combination for precise stroma modulation and improved delivery for pancreatic cancer. J Controlled Rel. 2022;347:425–434.*

limitations, such as low bioavailability, have restricted the use of these compounds in clinical applications. To solve this problem, the use of polymeric nanoparticles (such as chitosan and polyethylene glycol as hydrophilic polymers) is encouraged as an effective carrier in drug delivery for PC treatment. The prevention of rapid absorption by phagocytic cells and final cleaning by the reticuloendothelial system are some of the advantages of using this nano-system [38]. In this context, Arya et al. [39] evaluated the effect of poly D,L-lactide-co-glycolide (PLGA) nanoparticles loaded with curcumin and modified with polyethylene glycol/chitosan against PC cells. The results displayed this platform could efficiently enter the cancer cells and increased the cytotoxicity and pro-apoptotic effects in comparison with free curcumin. Furthermore, migratory and invasive activities of PC cells were inhibited [39]. Antihuman epidermal growth factor receptor-2 (antiHER2) was grafted to gemcitabine-loaded chitosan NPs. This combination plan is reported as an efficient strategy in the treatment of PC [40]. In addition, Yu et al. [41] conducted research on chitosan gemcitabine NPs and discovered that chitosan increased gemcitabine's effect on the PC cell line SW1990 by influencing their proliferation, invasion, and migration. Additionally, they demonstrated that loading gemcitabine with cisplatin is even more effective against PC cells [41].

2.3.3.2 Dendrimers

Dendrimers are macromolecules with appropriate aspects, which make them suitable for different biomedical applications. Some of these proper features include chemical stability, monodispersity, low cytotoxicity, biocompatibility, and solubility. Dendrimers cause the effective accumulation of free drugs and simultaneous penetration and uptake into the tumor tissue [42,43]. Lin et al. [44] designed a system composed of dendrimer containing gold nanoparticles loaded with gemcitabine and miR-21 inhibitor. Cellular entrance was enhanced with a combination of gemcitabine/miR-21i with or without using ultrasound indicating significantly more cytotoxicity compared to free gemcitabine. Considerable decrease in tumor volume in the animal study proved the efficacy of this strategy for PC treatment [44]. In another study, Huang et al. [45] explored the ability of peptide dendrimers in enhancing the effect of conventional chemotherapy in a mice model PC treatment. Simultaneous coadministration of dendrimer and DOX or gemcitabine into mice with advanced pancreatic ductal adenocarcinoma tumor xenograft significantly improved drug accumulation in the tumor cells and great reduction in tumor weight in comparison with free drug [45]. Li et al. [46] used a synthesized redox-sensitive vector in their previous study, which consisted of branched poly (ethylene glycol) with dendrimers (G2) named PSPG. Then, PSPG was modified with PTP for targeted delivery of siTR3 and paclitaxel. PTP or plectin-1 targeted peptide is a new biomarker for PC, which is overexpressed on cancer cells. siTR3 is a siRNA for inhibiting TR3/Nur77 (Orphan nuclear receptor) function in cell growth and apoptosis especially in pancreatic tumors. Results indicated that this strategy could efficiently increase the cell internalization and, TR3 gene knockdown in Panc-1 cells led to decrease in tumor growth in animal models compared to monotherapy [46].

To improve the chemo-immunotherapy, Tong et al. [47] designed a novel approach for effective penetration into tumor stroma and applied the combination strategy using chemo-immunotherapy for PC treatment. For this purpose, PAMAM dendrimer was modified with the conjugation of mPEG and N,Ndipentylethylamine (DnPEA) to produce pH-sensitive NP and gemcitabine prodrug was loaded in its cavity (SPN@Pro-Gem). Interestingly, the size of this platform was changed from 120 to 8 nm when reached to the tumor site, therefore, the drug could efficiently penetrate into the tumor environment and cause more toxicity on cancerous cells. In addition, the combination of SPN@Pro-Gem and PD-1 antibody was applied in a mouse PC model and resulted in ameliorating the therapeutic outcomes [47].

2.3.3.3 Hydrogel

Tumor microenvironment has a high effect on different aspects of cancer, such as invasion, progression, and metastasis, so recently, three-dimensional (3D) culture models have had great importance in cancer research. Some hydrogels such as Matrigel, collagen, hyaluronic acid-based, and semisynthetic hydrogels have been widely used in different cancer development studies [48]. In Table 2.1, some of the 3D hydrogels

Table 2.1 Three-dimensional hydrogels used for pancreatic cancer (PC) treatment.

Materials	Cell culture	Results	References
Matrigel/soft agar–based	AsPC-1, BxPC3, COLO-357, T3M4, PK-1, PK-2, and Rlnk-2	PC cell growth was increased when TGFβ1 and epidermal growth factor were applied simultaneously The effect of gemcitabine and cisplatin was elevated by coincubation with SB431542 (TGFβ type I receptor inhibitor) and erlotinib (EGF receptor inhibitor) in pancreatic cancer cells	[49]
Poly(D,L-lactide)-poly(ethylene glycol)-poly(D,L-lactide) (PDLLAPEG-PDLLA, PLEL) triblock copolymer that could form micelles in water at room temperature and develop a micellar network for creating the hydrogel in the body	In vitro (BxPc–3 cells)/in vivo (mouse model)	– Hydrogel containing gemcitabine and cisplatin led to significant inhibition in cancer cell growth and enhancement in apoptosis	[50]
starPEG–heparin hydrogel functionalized with RGD	BxPC-3 or MIAPaCa-2 cells, cancer-associated fibroblasts (CAFs), and myeloid cells	Combination therapy composed of CD11b agonist (ADH-503) along with the checkpoint inhibitor nivolumab (αPD–1) and chemotherapy (gemcitabine and paclitaxel) remarkably reduced the cancer cell growth and metabolic activity and also modified the cytokine profile	[51]
Liposomal hydrogels encapsulated DPP–BTz (the photothermal agent) and gemcitabine	In vivo	Considerable tumor inhibition was observed via a combination of chemotherapy and photothermal therapy stimulated with the NIR–II laser	[52]

used to deal with different types of PC cells are mentioned along with a summary of the results of these studies.

2.3.4 Lipid-based nanoparticle

Lipid-based nanoparticle systems are considered one of the most encouraging nano-carriers for the delivery of different therapeutic agents to the PC microenvironment [53]. In the following, we will mention some of the most effective lipid-based nanosystems.

2.3.4.1 Liposome

One class of recent nanoparticles is lipid–polymer hybrids, which is composed of a polymeric core surrounded by a lipid shell that possesses the benefits of both polymers and liposomes. Zhao et al. [54] prepared the copolymer nanoparticles for delivery of HIF1a siRNA (hypoxia-inducible factor 1α) (si-HIF1a) and gemcitabine for the effective treatment of PC. In this platform, si-HIF1a was attached to the surface while gemcitabine was encapsulated in the core of ε-polylysine copolymer (ENPs). The results indicated this approach could efficiently prevent the expression of HIF1a and hinder tumor growth and metastasis in tumor models [54]. In another study, Xu et al. [55] developed pH-sensitive liposomes containing gemcitabine in a hydrophilic core and curcumin in a hydrophobic bilayer. Endosomal escape of liposome, cellular concentration of gemcitabine, and toxicity to MIA PaCa-2 cells were investigated in presence of curcumin as well as pharmacokinetic evaluation after IV administration in rats. They stated that cotreatment method improved cellular concentration of gemcitabine and caused more cytotoxicity in MIA PaCa-2 PC cells. Furthermore, the concentration of gemcitabine in plasma was slightly increased with the addition of curcumin possibly via the inhibition of the multidrug resistance protein 5. As a result, simultaneous delivery of curcumin with gemcitabine by pegylated pH-sensitive liposomes improved the pharmacokinetic profiles and cytotoxic effect of both medications [55].

2.3.4.2 Micelle

The high hydrophilicity of gemcitabine limits its penetration into the dense outer vessels of tumors, resulting in reduced effectiveness in cancer therapy. To achieve the desired therapeutic effect with efficient concentration, a high dosage of the drug is often required, leading to severe side effects. Utilizing a micellar platform for polymer-drug combination (prodrug) is a promising approach in drug delivery systems. This system offers dual advantages, including the benefits derived from the polymer-drug conjugate and the features obtained from the design of micellar formulations [56,57].

2.3.4.3 Solid lipid nanoparticles and nanostructured lipid carriers

Solid lipid nanoparticles (SLNs) with dimensions of $100-700$ nm can pass through capillaries and efficiently accumulate in the tumor microenvironment compared to the free form of anticancer drugs [58]. Affram et al. [58] investigated the effect of solid lipid nanoparticles loaded with gemcitabine in PC cells including PPCL-46 and MiaPaCa-2. Various solid lipid nanoparticles loaded with the drug were synthesized with cold homogenization and characterized with different evaluations. The results displayed that gemcitabine-loaded SLN had significantly more cytotoxicity in PPCL-46 cells in comparison with Mia-PaCa-2 cells as well as more toxicity was obtained through SLN platform compared to free drug [58]. In another study, Lu et al. [59] designed nanostructured lipid carriers (NLCs) loaded with a prodrug of gemcitabine-stearic acid lipid prodrug (GEM-SA) and hyaluronic acid-amino acid-baicalein (HA-AA-BCL). Baicalein (BCL) is a flavonoid extracted from a Chinese herb that has been considered an effective anticancer agent. Finally, targeted NLCs were obtained through coating with HA. This novel platform could efficiently internalize the PC cells and led to notable cytotoxicity in AsPC1 cells. In addition, tumor shrinkage was reported with in vivo administration of this formulation in mouse models of PC [59]. Thakkar et al. [60] tried to investigate the potential chemopreventive effects of a combination of ferulic acid (an antioxidant) and aspirin (anti-inflammatory drug) in a solid lipid nanoparticle coated with chitosan for treatment of PC. This study revealed that this method may increase apoptotic gene expression (p-RB, p21, and p-ERK1/2) while decreasing proliferative gene expression in MIA PaCa-2 and Panc-1 cells [60].

2.4 Combination treatment with chimeric antigen receptor T cells and oncolytic viruses

Chimeric antigen receptor (CAR) T cell is a new and developing construct that has been used to treat various types of tumors, including PC in humans. For this purpose, T cells have been genetically engineered to produce an artificial receptor, which cannot only identify the target antigen expressed on cancer cells but can also proliferate and eliminate cancer cells [61].

Watanabe et al. [62] monitored the PC therapy process with combined mesothelin-redirected CAR T cells and cytokine-armed oncolytic adenoviruses. They initially hypothesized that combined meso-CAR T cells with an oncolytic adenovirus expressing TNF-α and IL-2 genes would lead to an improvement in the treatment process. OAd-TNFa-IL2 increased the antitumor efficiency of meso-CAR T cells in human-pancreatic ductal adenocarcinoma-xenograft immunodeficient mice. The results demonstrated that combining cytokine-armed oncolytic adenovirus to augment the efficiency of CAR T-cell therapy is an encouraging strategy to dominate the immunosuppressive tumor microenvironment for pancreatic ductal adenocarcinoma therapy [62].

2.5 Compounds of natural origin and combination therapy in pancreatic cancer treatment

As mentioned above, the unfavorable consequences of cytotoxic treatment affect the patient's quality of life and may also negatively influence the treatment results and subsequently its costs. The combination of conventional chemotherapy with nontoxic structures with natural origin may lead to an appropriate therapeutic response and a better quality of life for the patient. In this way, Serii et al. [10] explored the influence of combination therapy in the treatment of PC using nanoparticles (PLGA) coated with hyaluronic acid with the loading of quercetin and gemcitabine. Hyaluronic acid was a targeting moiety for detecting CD44 receptor. The results obtained from this research showed that enhanced toxicity and cell internalization were obtained with this strategy in comparison with free drugs or nontargeted NPs. Furthermore, nanoparticles decorated with hyaluronic acid enhanced the quercetin anti-inflammatory effects, which caused a reduction in the level of interleukin in Mia-PaCa-2 and PANC-1 cells that were initially stimulated with lipopolysaccharides [10]. During the application of combination therapy, several mechanisms are used in targeting different signaling pathways, and this process will lead to the reduction of resistance to antitumor drugs. By adding a natural compound to the conventional treatment, it is more possible to overcome altered regulatory cellular pathways, which are responsible for the occurrence of drug resistance [63,64].

Furthermore, this method may be a promising strategy for reducing side effects related to conventional treatments. A number of bioactive compounds with known anticancer activity against PC include curcumin, capsaicin, genistein, ginsenosides, saikosaponin, and isoliquiritigenin. Natural ingredients can improve the chemotherapeutic effects and diminish the chemoresistance by reducing the efflux proteins belonging to the ATP-binding cassette transporters (ABC transporters), promoting cell death and reducing reverse epithelial-mesenchymal transition [65]. One of the major problems in clinical trials is the limited bioavailability of most natural active ingredients due to the high rate of metabolism and excretion of these compounds by the body. This process leads to the absence of appropriate therapeutic concentrations of these compounds in blood circulation. The application of nanotechnology creates many opportunities to improve the therapeutic effects of these plant-derived bioactive compounds. By trapping the compounds within different nano-carriers, reducing the size of the particles, and modifying their surface, we will achieve a formulated compound with suitable bioavailability [66,67]. In a review study, Thyagarajan et al. [68] highlighted the importance of some of the most considered polyphenols in the prevention of PANC. They stated that the ability of these compounds in increasing the effectiveness of chemotherapy drugs against experimental PC provides a rationale for exploring them in clinical studies [68]. It is worth mentioning that bioinformatic studies are necessary to predict the therapeutic targets of natural compounds for evaluating their pharmacological inhibitors and confirming the cellular and clinical mechanisms [68]. A brief summary of different previous studies on natural ingredients during PC treatment was presented in Table 2.2.

Table 2.2 A brief summary of different effects of natural compounds combined with chemotherapeutic agents against pancreatic cancer (PC).

Natural product	Drug	Experimental model	Results	References
Quercetin/ (5-FU)	Gemcitabine	In vitro (PANC-1cells)	Remarkable apoptosis was reported in PANC1 cells	[69]
Quercetin	Gemcitabine	In vitro (MIA PaCa-2 and BxPC-3 cells) in vivo (Orthotopic PC animal model)	No positive effect was observed with the combined gemcitabine/ quercetin treatment compared to the use of quercetin alone	[70]
Naringenin	Gemcitabine	In vitro (Aspc-1 and panc-1 cells)	naringenin inhibited the migration and invasion of PC cells resistance to gemcitabine through inhibition of TGF-β	[71]
Curcumin	Gemcitabine or Docetaxel	In vitro (PANC-1, HPAF-II, and MIAPaCa-2)	Curcumin could augment proapoptotic activity of both gemcitabine and docetaxel and reduce migration of cancer cells	[72]

(Continued)

Table 2.2 (Continued)

Natural product	Drug	Experimental model	Results	References
Thymoquinone	Gemcitabine	In vitro (BxPC-3 and HPAC) In vivo (Orthotopic PC animal model)	Reduced the proliferation of PC cells by downregulation of NF-κB, Bcl-2 family XIAP, survivin, and COX-2	[73]
cucurbitacin B	Gemcitabine	In vitro/in vivo	Reduced the proliferation of PC cells by downregulation of activated JAK2/STAT3 and Bcl-XL upregulation of caspase-3 and caspase-9	[74]
Moringa oleifera aqueous leaf extract	cisplatin	In vitro (*PANC-1, p34*, and *COLO 357*)	enhances cytotoxic effect of chemotherapy in PC by downregulation of nuclear factor-kappa B	[75]
Ginkgolide B	Gemcitabine	In vitro/in vivo	Potentiate antiproliferative effects of gemcitabine by inhibiting PAFR/NF-κB pathway	[76]

2.5.1 The role of bioactive compounds of natural origin based on nano-formulation in inhibiting the proliferation of pancreatic cancer cells

As discussed, current chemotherapy approaches are largely ineffective in the treatment of PC. Therefore, there is a need to develop alternative strategies, including the use of smart carriers in nano-dimensions and anticancer compounds of natural origin to fight this disease. In this regard, several investigations have designed and used different nano-carriers for improving some features of natural compounds such as low water solubility, poor stability, and low bioavailability to solve their limitations for use in clinical applications [77,78]. In this line, Ding et al. [79] explored the synergistic effects of triptolide and celastrol, two natural materials in Chinese medicine, which were loaded with silk fibroin nanoparticles against PC cells. A rapid release was reported at pH 4.5 and a delayed release was at neutral pH. Growth and viability of cancer cells were considerably restrained with cotreatment by these nanoparticles compared to both compounds alone [79].

2.6 Conclusions and perspectives

Five-year survival for patients with advanced PC is less than 10%, and most of these patients will die due to the drug resistance of cancer cells. Gemcitabine has been used for more than 20 years as the frontline of standard medicine in the care and improvement of PC symptoms, but it is not considered a suitable option as a single treatment. Because the only treatment option for more than 80% of PC patients who do not qualify for surgical resection is chemotherapy with or without radiation. Therefore, in the last few decades, a significant effort has been made to apply effective treatment methods for this disease. New research paradigms have emerged to use combination therapy methods for this deadly cancer. In particular, the potential use of combination therapies including immunomodulators, standard radio- and chemotherapy, and therapeutic compounds of natural origin along with the design of various nanoplatforms to optimize the delivery of medicinal compounds is discussed. This chapter addresses in vivo and in vitro efforts to identify markers that target common molecular features of pancreatic tumors and develop appropriate combination approaches based on the therapeutic mechanism.

References

[1] Siri FH, Salehiniya H. Pancreatic cancer in Iran: an epidemiological review. J Gastrointest Cancer 2020;51(2):418−24.
[2] Jia E, Ren N, Shi X, Zhang R, Yu H, Yu F, et al. Extracellular vesicle biomarkers for pancreatic cancer diagnosis: a systematic review and meta-analysis. BMC Cancer 2022;22(1):1−35.
[3] Hussain A, Weimer DS, Mani N. Diagnosing pancreatic adenocarcinoma with contrast-enhanced ultrasonography: a literature review of research in Europe and Asia. Cureus. 2022;14(2):e22080.
[4] Andersson R, Haglund C, Seppänen H, Ansari D. Pancreatic cancer − the past, the present, and the future. Scand J Gastroenterol. 2022;57(10):1169−77.
[5] Müller PC, Frey MC, Ruzza CM, Nickel F, Jost C, Gwerder C, et al. Neoadjuvant chemotherapy in pancreatic cancer: an appraisal of the current high-level evidence. Pharmacology. 2021;106(3−4):143−53.
[6] Liu L, Kshirsagar PG, Gautam SK, Gulati M, Wafa EI, Christiansen JC, et al. Nanocarriers for pancreatic cancer imaging, treatments, and immunotherapies. Theranostics. 2022;12(3):1030.
[7] Hashemi M, Abnous K, Balarastaghi S, Hedayati N, Salmasi Z, Yazdian-Robati R. Mitoxantrone-loaded PLGA nanoparticles for increased sensitivity of glioblastoma cancer cell to TRAIL-induced apoptosis. J Pharm Innov 2022;17(1):207−14.

[8] Sharkey RM, Karacay H, Govindan SV, Goldenberg DM. Combination Radioimmunotherapy and chemoimmunotherapy involving different or the same targets improves therapy of human pancreatic carcinoma Xenograft models. Mol Cancer Ther 2011;10(6):1072−81.

[9] Yazdian-Robati R, Arab A, Ramezani M, Rafatpanah H, Bahreyni A, Nabavinia MS, et al. Smart aptamer-modified calcium carbonate nanoparticles for controlled release and targeted delivery of epirubicin and melittin into cancer cells in vitro and in vivo. Drug Dev Ind Pharm 2019;45(4):603−10.

[10] Serri C, Quagliariello V, Iaffaioli RV, Fusco S, Botti G, Mayol L, et al. Combination therapy for the treatment of pancreatic cancer through hyaluronic acid-decorated nanoparticles loaded with quercetin and gemcitabine: a preliminary in vitro study. J Cell Physiol 2019;234(4):4959−69.

[11] Bayat P, Farshchi M, Yousefian M, Mahmoudi M, Yazdian-Robati R. Flavonoids, the compounds with anti-inflammatory and immunomodulatory properties, as promising tools in multiple sclerosis (MS) therapy: a systematic review of preclinical evidence. Int Immunopharmacol. 2021;95:107562.

[12] Jamshidi Z, Hashemi M, Yazdian-Robati R, Etemad L, Salmasi Z, Kesharwani P. Effects of Boswellia species on viral infections with particular attention to SARS-CoV-2. Inflammopharmacology. 2022;30 (5):1541−53.

[13] Salehi B, Machin L, Monzote L, Sharifi-Rad J, Ezzat SM, Salem MA, et al. Therapeutic potential of quercetin: new insights and perspectives for human health. ACS Omega 2020;5(20):11849−72.

[14] Hashemi M, Shamshiri A, Saeedi M, Tayebi L, Yazdian-Robati R. Aptamer-conjugated PLGA nanoparticles for delivery and imaging of cancer therapeutic drugs. Arch Biochem Biophys 2020;691:108485.

[15] Abed A, Derakhshan M, Karimi M, Shirazinia M, Mahjoubin-Tehran M, Homayonfal M, et al. Platinum nanoparticles in biomedicine: preparation, anti-cancer activity, and drug delivery vehicles. Front Pharmacol 2022;13:797804.

[16] Afsharzadeh M, Hashemi M, Mokhtarzadeh A, Abnous K, Ramezani M. Recent advances in co-delivery systems based on polymeric nanoparticle for cancer treatment. Artif Cells Nanomed Biotechnol 2018;46(6):1095−110.

[17] Huang L, Zhao S, Fang F, Xu T, Lan M, Zhang J. Advances and perspectives in carrier-free nano-drugs for cancer chemo-monotherapy and combination therapy. Biomaterials. 2021;268:120557.

[18] Cheng C, Sui B, Wang M, Hu X, Shi S, Xu P. Carrier-free nanoassembly of curcumin−erlotinib conjugate for cancer targeted therapy. Adv Healthc Mater 2020;9(19):2001128.

[19] Ma L, Wei J, Su GH, Lin J. Dasatinib can enhance paclitaxel and gemcitabine inhibitory activity in human pancreatic cancer cells. Cancer Biol Ther 2019;20(6):855−65.

[20] Shim MK, Yang S, Park J, Yoon JS, Kim J, Moon Y, et al. Preclinical development of carrier-free prodrug nanoparticles for enhanced antitumor therapeutic potential with less toxicity. J Nanobiotechnol. 2022;20(1):436.

[21] Zhu L, Lin S, Cui W, Xu Y, Wang L, Wang Z, et al. A nanomedicine enables synergistic chemo/photodynamic therapy for pancreatic cancer treatment. Biomater Sci 2022;10(13):3624−36.

[22] Qiu W, Chen R, Chen X, Zhang H, Song L, Cui W, et al. Oridonin-loaded and GPC1-targeted gold nanoparticles for multimodal imaging and therapy in pancreatic cancer. Int J Nanomed 2018;13:6809.

[23] Yazdian-Robati R, Hedayati N, Dehghani S, Ramezani M, Alibolandi M, Saeedi M, et al. Application of the catalytic activity of gold nanoparticles for development of optical aptasensors. Anal Biochem 2021;629:114307.

[24] Coelho SC, Reis DP, Pereira MC, Coelho MA. Doxorubicin and varlitinib delivery by functionalized gold nanoparticles against human pancreatic adenocarcinoma. Pharmaceutics. 2019;11(11):551.

[25] Foulkes R, Ali Asgari M, Curtis A, Hoskins C. Silver-nanoparticle-mediated therapies in the treatment of pancreatic cancer. ACS Appl Nano Mater 2019;2(4):1758−72.

[26] Barcińska E, Wierzbicka J, Zauszkiewicz-Pawlak A, Jacewicz D, Dabrowska A, Inkielewicz-Stepniak I. Role of oxidative and nitro-oxidative damage in silver nanoparticles cytotoxic effect against human pancreatic ductal adenocarcinoma cells. Oxid Med Cell Longev 2018;2018:8251961.

[27] Benguigui M, Weitz IS, Timaner M, Kan T, Shechter D, Perlman O, et al. Copper oxide nanoparticles inhibit pancreatic tumor growth primarily by targeting tumor initiating cells. Sci Rep 2019;9 (1):1−10.

[28] Ahmed HH, El-Maksoud A, Diaa M, Abdel Moneim AE, Aglan HA. Pre-clinical study for the antidiabetic potential of selenium nanoparticles. Biol Trace Elem Res 2017;177(2):267–80.

[29] Shiri M, Navaei-Nigjeh M, Baeeri M, Rahimifard M, Mahboudi H, Shahverdi AR, et al. Blockage of both the extrinsic and intrinsic pathways of diazinon-induced apoptosis in PaTu cells by magnesium oxide and selenium nanoparticles. Int J Nanomed 2016;11:6239.

[30] Mousavi S-D, Maghsoodi F, Panahandeh F, Yazdian-Robati R, Reisi-Vanani A, Tafaghodi M. Doxorubicin delivery via magnetic nanomicelles comprising from reduction-responsive poly (ethylene glycol)-b-poly (ε-caprolactone)(PEG-SS-PCL) and loaded with superparamagnetic iron oxide (SPIO) nanoparticles: preparation, characterization and simulation. Mater Sci Eng C 2018;92:631–43.

[31] Malekigorji M, Curtis AD, Hoskins C. The use of iron oxide nanoparticles for pancreatic cancer therapy. J Nanomed Res 2014;1(1):00004.

[32] Trabulo S, Aires A, Aicher A, Heeschen C, Cortajarena AL. Multifunctionalized iron oxide nanoparticles for selective targeting of pancreatic cancer cells. Biochim Biophys Acta Gen Subj 2017;1861(6):1597–605.

[33] Khan S, Setua S, Kumari S, Dan N, Massey A, Hafeez BB, et al. Superparamagnetic iron oxide nanoparticles of curcumin enhance gemcitabine therapeutic response in pancreatic cancer. Biomaterials. 2019;208:83–97.

[34] Saleem J, Wang L, Chen C. Carbon-based nanomaterials for cancer therapy via targeting tumor microenvironment. Adv Healthc Mater 2018;7(20):1800525.

[35] Wójcik B, Sawosz E, Szczepaniak J, Strojny B, Sosnowska M, Daniluk K, et al. Effects of metallic and carbon-based nanomaterials on human pancreatic cancer cell lines AsPC-1 and BxPC-3. Int J Mol Sci 2021;22(22):12100.

[36] Xing L, Li X, Xing Z, Li F, Shen M, Wang H, et al. Silica/gold nanoplatform combined with a thermosensitive gel for imaging-guided interventional therapy in PDX of pancreatic cancer. Chem Eng J 2020;382:122949.

[37] Tarannum M, Holtzman K, Dréau D, Mukherjee P, Vivero-Escoto JL. Nanoparticle combination for precise stroma modulation and improved delivery for pancreatic cancer. J Control Release 2022;347:425–34.

[38] Sadoughi F, Mansournia MA, Mirhashemi SM. The potential role of chitosan-based nanoparticles as drug delivery systems in pancreatic cancer. IUBMB Life 2020;72(5):872–83.

[39] Arya G, Das M, Sahoo SK. Evaluation of curcumin loaded chitosan/PEG blended PLGA nanoparticles for effective treatment of pancreatic cancer. Biomed Pharmacother 2018;102:555–66.

[40] Arya G, Vandana M, Acharya S, Sahoo SK. Enhanced antiproliferative activity of Herceptin (HER2)-conjugated gemcitabine-loaded chitosan nanoparticle in pancreatic cancer therapy. Nanomedicine 2011;7(6):859–70.

[41] Yu H, Song H, Xiao J, Chen H, Jin X, Lin X, et al. The effects of novel chitosan-targeted gemcitabine nanomedicine mediating cisplatin on epithelial mesenchymal transition, invasion and metastasis of pancreatic cancer cells. Biomed. Pharmacother 2017;96:650–8.

[42] Pishavar E, Oroojalian F, Salmasi Z, Hashemi E, Hashemi M. Recent advances of dendrimer in targeted delivery of drugs and genes to stem cells as cellular vehicles. Biotechnol Prog 2021;37(4):e3174.

[43] Azimifar MA, Salmasi Z, Doosti A, Babaei N, Hashemi M. Evaluation of the efficiency of modified PAMAM dendrimer with low molecular weight protamine peptide to deliver IL-12 plasmid into stem cells as cancer therapy vehicles. Biotechnol Prog 2021;37(4):e3175.

[44] Lin L, Fan Y, Gao F, Jin L, Li D, Sun W, et al. UTMD-promoted co-delivery of gemcitabine and miR-21 inhibitor by dendrimer-entrapped gold nanoparticles for pancreatic cancer therapy. Theranostics. 2018;8(7):1923.

[45] Huang S, Huang X, Yan H. Peptide dendrimers as potentiators of conventional chemotherapy in the treatment of pancreatic cancer in a mouse model. Eur J Pharm Biopharm 2022;170:121–32.

[46] Li Y, Wang H, Wang K, Hu Q, Yao Q, Shen Y, et al. Targeted co-delivery of PTX and TR3 siRNA by PTP peptide modified dendrimer for the treatment of pancreatic cancer. Small. 2017;13 (2):1602697.

[47] Tong QS, Miao WM, Huang H, Luo JQ, Liu R, Huang YC, et al. A tumor-penetrating nanomedicine improves the chemoimmunotherapy of pancreatic cancer. Small. 2021;17(29):2101208.

[48] Lin C-C, Korc M. Designer hydrogels: shedding light on the physical chemistry of the pancreatic cancer microenvironment. Cancer Lett 2018;436:22−7.

[49] Sempere LF, Gunn JR, Korc M. A novel 3-dimensional culture system uncovers growth stimulatory actions by TGFβ in pancreatic cancer cells. Cancer Biol Ther 2011;12(3):198−207.

[50] Shi K, Xue B, Jia Y, Yuan L, Han R, Yang F, et al. Sustained co-delivery of gemcitabine and cisplatinum via biodegradable thermo-sensitive hydrogel for synergistic combination therapy of pancreatic cancer. Nano Res 2019;12(6):1389−99.

[51] Kast V, Nadernezhad A, Pette D, Gabrielyan A, Fusenig M, Honselmann KC, et al. A tumor microenvironment model of pancreatic cancer to elucidate responses toward immunotherapy. Adv Healthc Mater 2022;2201907.

[52] Kong Y, Dai Y, Qi D, Du W, Ni H, Zhang F, et al. Injectable and thermosensitive liposomal hydrogels for NIR-II light-triggered photothermal-chemo therapy of pancreatic cancer. ACS Appl Bio Mater 2021;4(10):7595−604.

[53] García-Pinel B, Porras-Alcalá C, Ortega-Rodríguez A, Sarabia F, Prados J, Melguizo C, et al. Lipid-based nanoparticles: application and recent advances in cancer treatment. Nanomaterials. 2019;9(4):638.

[54] Zhao X, Li F, Li Y, Wang H, Ren H, Chen J, et al. Co-delivery of HIF1α siRNA and gemcitabine via biocompatible lipid-polymer hybrid nanoparticles for effective treatment of pancreatic cancer. Biomaterials. 2015;46:13−25.

[55] Xu H, Li Y, Paxton JW, Wu Z. Co-delivery using pH-sensitive liposomes to pancreatic cancer cells: the effects of curcumin on cellular concentration and pharmacokinetics of gemcitabine. Pharm Res 2021;38(7):1209−19.

[56] Mondal G, Almawash S, Chaudhary AK, Mahato RI. EGFR-targeted cationic polymeric mixed micelles for codelivery of gemcitabine and miR-205 for treating advanced pancreatic cancer. Mol Pharm 2017;14(9):3121−33.

[57] Khare V, Sakarchi WA, Gupta PN, Curtis AD, Hoskins C. Synthesis and characterization of TPGS−gemcitabine prodrug micelles for pancreatic cancer therapy. RSC Adv 2016;6(65):60126−37.

[58] Affram KO, Smith T, Ofori E, Krishnan S, Underwood P, Trevino JG, et al. Cytotoxic effects of gemcitabine-loaded solid lipid nanoparticles in pancreatic cancer cells. J Drug Deliv Sci Technol 2020;55:101374.

[59] Lu Z, Su J, Li Z, Zhan Y, Ye D. Hyaluronic acid-coated, prodrug-based nanostructured lipid carriers for enhanced pancreatic cancer therapy. Drug Dev Ind Pharm 2017;43(1):160−70.

[60] Thakkar A, Chenreddy S, Wang J, Prabhu S. Ferulic acid combined with aspirin demonstrates chemopreventive potential towards pancreatic cancer when delivered using chitosan-coated solid-lipid nanoparticles. Cell Biosci 2015;5(1):1−14.

[61] Rezaei R, Esmaeili Gouvarchin Ghaleh H, Farzanehpour M, Dorostkar R, Ranjbar R, Bolandian M, et al. Combination therapy with CAR T cells and oncolytic viruses: a new era in cancer immunotherapy. Cancer Gene Ther 2022;29(6):647−60.

[62] Watanabe K, Luo Y, Da T, Guedan S, Ruella M, Scholler J, et al. Pancreatic cancer therapy with combined mesothelin-redirected chimeric antigen receptor T cells and cytokine-armed oncolytic adenoviruses. JCI Insight 2018;3(7):e99573.

[63] Scaria B, Sood S, Raad C, Khanafer J, Jayachandiran R, Pupulin A, et al. Natural health products (NHP's) and natural compounds as therapeutic agents for the treatment of cancer; mechanisms of anti-cancer activity of natural compounds and overall trends. Int J Mol Sci 2020;21(22):8480.

[64] Rejhová A, Opattová A, Čumová A, Slíva D, Vodička P. Natural compounds and combination therapy in colorectal cancer treatment. Eur J Med Chem 2018;144:582−94.

[65] Marasini B, P Sahu R. Natural anti-cancer agents: implications in gemcitabine-resistant pancreatic cancer treatment. Mini Rev Med Chem 2017;17(11):920−7.

[66] Yuan R, Hou Y, Sun W, Yu J, Liu X, Niu Y, et al. Natural products to prevent drug resistance in cancer chemotherapy: a review. Ann N Y Acad Sci 2017;1401(1):19−27.

[67] Patra JK, Das G, Fraceto LF, Campos EVR, Rodriguez-Torres MdP, Acosta-Torres LS, et al. Nano based drug delivery systems: recent developments and future prospects. J Nanobiotechnol 2018;16(1):1−33.

[68] Thyagarajan A, Forino AS, Konger RL, Sahu RP. Dietary polyphenols in cancer chemoprevention: implications in pancreatic cancer. Antioxidants 2020;9(8):651.

[69] Lee JH, Lee H-B, Jung GO, Oh JT, Park DE, Chae KM. Effect of quercetin on apoptosis of PANC-1 cells. J Korean Surg Soc 2013;85(6):249−60.

[70] Angst E, Park JL, Moro A, Lu QY, Lu X, Li G, et al. The flavonoid quercetin inhibits pancreatic cancer growth in vitro and in vivo. Pancreas. 2013;42(2):223−9.

[71] Lou C, Zhang F, Yang M, Zhao J, Zeng W, Fang X, et al. Naringenin decreases invasiveness and metastasis by inhibiting TGF-β-induced epithelial to mesenchymal transition in pancreatic cancer cells. PLoS One 2012;7(12):e50956.

[72] Liu P, Ying Q, Liu H, Yu SQ, Bu LP, Shao L, et al. Curcumin enhances anti-cancer efficacy of either gemcitabine or docetaxel on pancreatic cancer cells. Oncol Rep 2020;44(4):1393−402.

[73] Banerjee S, Kaseb AO, Wang Z, Kong D, Mohammad M, Padhye S, et al. Antitumor activity of gemcitabine and oxaliplatin is augmented by thymoquinone in pancreatic cancer. Cancer Res 2009;69(13):5575−83.

[74] Thoennissen NH, Iwanski GB, Doan NB, Okamoto R, Lin P, Abbassi S, et al. Cucurbitacin B induces apoptosis by inhibition of the JAK/STAT pathway and potentiates antiproliferative effects of gemcitabine on pancreatic cancer cells. Cancer Res 2009;69(14):5876−84.

[75] Berkovich L, Earon G, Ron I, Rimmon A, Vexler A, Lev-Ari S. Moringa Oleifera aqueous leaf extract down-regulates nuclear factor-kappaB and increases cytotoxic effect of chemotherapy in pancreatic cancer cells. BMC Complementary Altern Med 2013;13(1):1−7.

[76] Lou C, Lu H, Ma Z, Liu C, Zhang Y. Ginkgolide B enhances gemcitabine sensitivity in pancreatic cancer cell lines via inhibiting PAFR/NF-κB pathway. Biomed Pharmacother 2019;109:563−72.

[77] Li Y, Zheng X, Chu Q. Bio-based nanomaterials for cancer therapy. Nano Today 2021;38:101134.

[78] Liu Y, Feng N. Nanocarriers for the delivery of active ingredients and fractions extracted from natural products used in traditional Chinese medicine (TCM). Adv Colloid Interface Sci 2015;221:60−76.

[79] Ding B, Wahid MA, Wang Z, Xie C, Thakkar A, Prabhu S, et al. Triptolide and celastrol loaded silk fibroin nanoparticles show synergistic effect against human pancreatic cancer cells. Nanoscale. 2017;9(32):11739−53.

Application of various nanocarriers for the management of pancreatic cancer

PART 3

Application of various
nanocarriers for the
management of pancreatic
cancer

CHAPTER 3

Potential application of nanotechnology in the treatment and overcoming of pancreatic cancer resistance

Shwetapadma Dash[1], Sonali Sahoo[1,2] and Sanjeeb Kumar Sahoo[1]
[1]Institute of Life Sciences, Bhubaneswar, Odisha, India
[2]Regional Center for Biotechnology, Faridabad, Haryana, India

3.1 Introduction

Cancer has afflicted the world for several thousands of years. Despite the gigantic amount of research and studies done for its therapeutic advancements, it still continues to be the leading cause of death worldwide [1]. Due to its ability to develop in almost any part of the human body, cancer can affect vital organs such as the pancreas. Cancer of the pancreas is one of the incurable ailments associated with this organ. Its differential diagnosis is connected to other pancreatic afflictions such as pancreatitis and diabetes [2]. Worldwide, pancreatic neoplasms are the seventh leading cause of cancer-related deaths [3]. With an overall survival rate of nearly 5 years, the disease incidence and mortality rate remain almost identical at $\sim 5\%$ [4,5]. Additionally, the median survival period of the pancreatic cancer is $10-12$ months and the remaining life span of a patient after its detection is measured in months [6]. The radically lowered survival rate and median survival period are mainly attributed to silent nature of the disease in its early stages [2], resulting in its systemic progression and development of multidrug resistant phenotypes [7]. Moreover, the symptoms that surface out during the advanced stages of the disease are indistinctive, which include weight loss, nausea, fatigue, shoulder pain, bloating, changes in bowel habit, lethargy, gastric pain radiating to the back, jaundice, and diabetes [8,9]. The etiology of pancreatic cancer is mainly attributed to a set of environmental/acquired risk factors as well as genetic factors. The environmental/acquired risk factors mainly include agents such as cigarette smoking, diabetes, increased body mass index (BMI), heavy liquor consumption, and chronic pancreatitis [4]. The genetic factors that play a role in augmenting the risk of pancreatic neoplasms comprise family history of the disease, genetic aberrations, and hereditary genetic syndromes. Four common signature gene alterations that have been

Recent Advances in Nanocarriers for Pancreatic Cancer Therapy
DOI: https://doi.org/10.1016/B978-0-443-19142-8.00017-6
37

found to be more frequently associated with the occurrence of pancreatic malignancies include activating mutations in KRAS (Kirsten ras) oncogene and inactivating mutations in tumor suppresser genes TP53, CDK2A, and SMAD4 [10]. Interestingly, these genetic alterations appear to occur in the form of sequential events during disease progression. For instance, the KRAS mutations are one of the earliest aberrations, while the SMAD4 and TP53 mutations are some of the late events [9,11]. Additionally, 20 other genes were found to be mutated with a frequency less than 10% from the studies conducted by the Cancer Genome Atlas (TCGA), and these alterations are called "passenger" mutations [12]. Such mutations generally play a minor role in tumor pathogenesis and are mainly responsible for tumor diversity [2]. Altogether, mutational landscape of the pancreatic tumors is associated with the deregulation of various signaling pathways in its epithelial cells and also influences the surrounding stromal cell population. This in turn highlights the major role played by the tumor-stroma crosstalk in the progression of the disease [13]. For example, mutations in SMAD4 gene found in tumor cells are involved in alteration of TGF-β pathway in tumor epithelial cells as well as stromal cell populations via paracrine signaling [9,13]. Furthermore, individuals with genetic disorders such as Lynch syndrome, hereditary pancreatitis, or Peutz—Jeghers syndrome have also been reported to be at a higher risk of developing this malignancy [4].

The global gene expression profiling studies have shown that pancreatic tumors with similar genetic profiles might differ molecularly due to differences in their transcriptome networks and, therefore can be categorized into different types [2]. However, the current classification system for pancreatic neoplasms is based on the appearance of tumor mass during its diagnosis. On this basis, the pancreatic cancers are broadly grouped into solid and cystic types. The solid pancreatic cancers constitute pancreatic ductal adenocarcinomas (PDACs), pancreatic neuroendocrine tumors, colloid tumors, medullary tumors, adenosquamous carcinoma, and pancreatoblastoma with PDACs being the most commonly observed and aggressive type. Similarly, the cystic neoplasms of the pancreas are of four types—intraductal papillary mucinous neoplasms, mucinous cystic neoplasms, solid-pseudopapillary neoplasms, and serous cystic neoplasm [4]. However, to begin with, only a few patients qualify for surgical resection after diagnosis mainly outstanding to the limitations including late detection of the disease and poor patient biology [6,14]. In addition to this, the emergence of multidrug resistance phenotype as well as a high rate of recurrence plays a major role in the failure of therapies for the treatment of pancreatic cancer.

Diagnosis of pancreatic cancer mainly relies on tumor visualization using the imaging systems such as transabdominal ultrasonography, multidetector computed tomography, magnetic resonance imaging, endoscopic ultrasound, and positron emission tomography [8,9]. Diagnosis is closely followed by the staging process, which plays a pivotal role in determining the treatment regimen. According to the staging criteria decided by American Joint Committee on Cancer (AJCC), there are four stages of pancreatic cancer: Stage I, II, III, and IV [4]. The disease treatment regimen is mainly decided by factors, such as local spread and invasiveness of the tumors, performance status of patients, associated comorbidities, and symptomatic burden [6].

3.2 Current therapeutics for pancreatic cancer

In general, there are two major types of therapeutics available for the treatment of pancreatic cancers, which comprise conventional therapeutics and targeted therapies (Fig. 3.1). Presently, vast majority of patients are endorsed for conventional treatment modalities [2,4].

3.2.1 Conventional therapies

The conventional therapies for pancreatic cancer include surgery, chemotherapy, and radiation therapy. For improving the survival period of the patient, a combination of these approaches is administered in an orderly manner.

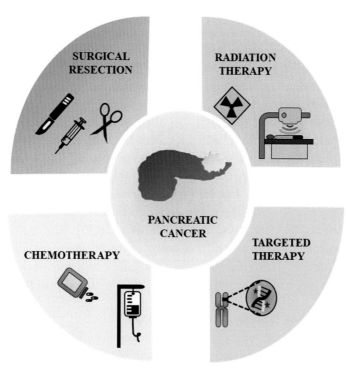

Figure 3.1 Current therapeutic approaches for pancreatic cancer treatment: treatment options for pancreatic cancer presently constitutes conventional modalities and targeted therapy. Furthermore, a combination of these approaches is also used for having a higher curative effect.

3.2.1.1 Surgery

At present, surgery is the only treatment modality, which is regarded to have a curative effect for pancreatic cancer. Based on the local spread of the tumor, patients can be categorized into four types of disease states: resectable, borderline resectable, locally advanced, and metastatic [9]. The most commonly used surgical methods include pancreaticoduodenectomy and distal, central, and total pancreatectomy. Sometimes in addition to these procedures, *en-bloc* splenectomy is also recommended. However, due to the presence of postoperational complexities in most pancreatectomies, development of minimally invasive surgical procedures such as nonoperative biliary decompression and endoscopic procedures has led to a remarkable reduction in the choice of complex operative procedures [4]. Currently, nearly 30%−40% of patients with pancreatic cancer are diagnosed as locally advanced unresectable or borderline resectable. Candidates with borderline resectable tumors are often recommended for upfront neoadjuvant therapy (NAT) or surgery. For candidates with locally advanced neoplasms, the localized therapies become questionable, and consequently treatment options are more complex outstanding to high chances of recurrence. Therefore these candidates are initially administered with systemic chemotherapy and the next procedure is decided based on the status of metastatic progression [15]. Importantly, not each of the patient that is categorized resectable maybe actually benefited from surgery. Therefore to formulate the most effective treatment plan, clinicians look for three factors, namely patient health, tumor biology, and the effect of the combinatorial treatment, which need to be considered collectively. Typically, the patient's health is mainly dictated by age, comorbidities such as cardiac diseases and dementia, and cancer-related cachexia. Similarly, tumor biology is assessed using factors such as extent of tumor tissue metastasis and infiltration with its progression. For candidates with highly aggressive tumor biology and/or poor overall health, the probability for surgery to be a potentially curative option is very less [4]. Additionally, the success rate of surgery also depends on management of postoperational complications, which commonly arise due to wound infection, metabolic disorders, cardiac ailments, cholangitis, bile leak, pancreatic fistula, etc. [16,17]. The median survival of 18 months is calculated from one of the largest series of pancreaticoduodenectomies with a survival rate of 18% [16]. Therefore treatment regimens including post and preoperative therapies are considered carefully while the diagnosis of the disease [4].

3.2.1.1.1 Neoadjuvant therapy: as a protagonist

NAT is a preoperative step that is used to test the tumor biology and expand the curative window for surgery. With respect to tumor biology, NAT helps to assess the effect of surgery on highly aggressive tumors. Consequently, this therapy provides a benefit for averting unnecessary surgical complications and at the same time provides scope for early administration of systemic treatments [9]. Because patients with poor performance status during NAT exhibit similar effects while surgery, it helps in sorting patients with better functional status [18]. NAT is also known to transform the nonoperable tumors of some locally advanced patients into surgically resectable ones by sterilizing their border, reducing their volume, and lowering their nodal positivity [4]. The above therapy also allows the administration of full-dose chemotherapy before resection, which is thought to be more effective than postoperative therapy as the resected tumor tissues are associated with poor drug uptake and reduced drug sensitivity [9].

Nevertheless, the administration of NAT is still considered controversial, the main reason for this being the lack of supporting evidence and the associated limitations [4,9]. As a consequence, there are several limitations thought to be associated with this therapy. Firstly, the eligibility criteria for this therapy require patient to have a tissue diagnosis, which can be difficult in cases where dense stroma is associated with the tumor. Secondly, it is argued that this therapy might potentially increase the risk of local progression of the disease thereby causing the patient to lose the curative surgical window [18]. Furthermore, in patients with cases of biliary obstruction, administration of NAT is thought to increase the complications and surgery-associated risks due to development of bacterobilia [19]. Therefore in such cases, the selection of surgery after preoperative therapy or surgery followed by postoperative therapy need to be addressed in a multidisciplinary manner to achieve the curative effect [4].

3.2.1.1.2 Adjuvant therapy: an afterthought

Majority of patients recommended for surgery as the only treatment option exhibit relapse and high mortality rate thereby making surgery futile. Here the function of adjuvant therapy or postoperative therapy comes into the picture. It has indicated to reduce the rate of metastatic relapse and lower the mortality rate. The administration of the therapy usually begins from 1 to 2 months after surgery thereby allowing the patient to recover from the surgical sequelae [4]. Besides, unlike NAT, the promising results of adjuvant therapy are supported by high-quality studies and trials conducted by groups such as the European Study Group for Pancreatic Cancer (ESPAC) [9]. However, clinical trials involving chemoradiotherapy have exhibited results that are inconsistent. Since more than 70% of patients display recurrence with distant metastasis, therefore systemic treatment such as chemotherapy is delivered first followed by radiotherapy if there are no concerns for metastatic relapse after completion of chemotherapy [4].

3.2.1.2 Radiation therapy

The effect of radiation therapy in the treatment of pancreatic cancer is less clear and remains controversial due to unreliable results in various trials. However, development in the delivery method of radiation is offering hope. The increased use of 3-dimensional conformal radiotherapy, which shapes the beams to exactly fit the tumor area and allows the simultaneous delivery of continuous chemoradiation has led to a substantial decrease in associated toxicities [4]. Other methods such as irreversible electroporation (IRE), stereotactic body radiation (SBRT), radiofrequency ablation (RFA), and high-intensity focused ultrasound (HIFU) can also be used for loco-regional treatment. RFA and SBRT are the most studied techniques with HIFU being the least studied form of the treatment for pancreatic cancer. RFA is generally administered during open surgery or directed by endoscopic ultrasonography, and the reported mortality is 0%–3% with 4%–28% morbidity range. SBRT has been explored in combination with various modalities and applied doses with reported morbidity of nearly 25% [20]. Additionally, IRE is believed to have the ability to kill the tumor tissues present in vicinity of important structures such as blood vessels. Moreover, IRE can also be performed percutaneously with the guidance of computed tomography (CT). It has a morbidity and mortality rate within the range of other methods such as RFA and SBRT. Research analysis of these local ablative methods has displayed tumor regression, enhanced survival, reduction in symptomatic burden, and, more importantly, converting unresectable tumors into resectable ones in numerous patients. However, due to the intrinsic biases in the patient groups and lack of meta-analytical studies, the data regarding the efficacy of such local ablative methods are regarded as inconclusive [15].

3.2.1.3 Chemotherapy

Chemotherapy is another conventional therapeutic approach, considered the backbone of pancreatic cancer treatment regimens. The current clinical practice of chemotherapy includes administration of drugs such as gemcitabine and paclitaxel, and FOLFIRINOX regimen for pancreatic cancer treatment [6]. Gemcitabine is the most commonly used drug that was first to be approved by the Food and Drug Administration (FDA) for treatment of the pancreatic neoplasms. It is a nucleoside analog with structural similarity to deoxycytidine. Following its uptake, the drug undergoes a series of metabolic reactions giving rise to multiple derivatives. These derivatives are responsible for inhibiting the enzyme thymidylate synthase, which is responsible for conversion of deoxyuridine monophosphate (dUMP) to deoxythymidine monophosphate (dTMP), thereby leading to imbalance in the dUMP-dUTP ratio. This causes obstruction of deoxyribonucleic acid (DNA) synthesis finally resulting in cellular apoptosis [21]. Another such agent is paclitaxel, commonly known as taxol. This agent is fractionated from the bark extract of Pacific yew tree, which is also used as a chemotherapeutic drug for pancreatic tumors. This drug mediates its effect mainly through induction of cell arrest at M-phase in a concentration-dependent manner inside the cell thereby leading to cytotoxicity [6,22]. However, to achieve the maximum benefit of the chemotherapeutic agents, clinicians use a specific combination of some drugs for the treatment of pancreatic cancer.

The first combination chemotherapy regimen that exhibited a substantially greater effect in terms of overall survival as compared to gemcitabine monotherapy was established in 2011 and was named FOLFIRINOX (FOL = folinic acid, F = fluorouracil, IRIN = irinotecan, and OX = oxaliplatin) [23]. 5-Fluorouracil exerts its effects on the target cells via multiple mechanisms, many of which are still not clear entirely. Similar to gemcitabine, this drug is converted into several metabolites by multiple modifying enzymes after reaching the cytoplasm. Many of these metabolites mediate cytotoxic actions by inhibiting the thymidylate synthase enzyme [6]. Additionally, 5-FU also interferes with both mRNA and tRNA maturation through different pathways, all of which cause the dysregulation of critical cell processes and decrease cell viability [24]. Many of these metabolites can also undergo incorporation into RNA, thereby affecting transcription, finally resulting in cytotoxic effects and suppression of growth, as observed in both colon and breast cancer cells [25,26]. One more agent used in FOLFIRIOX regimen is irinotecan, synthesized by modification of a natural compound camptothecin [27]. The drug was approved in 2013 for the pancreatic adenocarcinoma treatment as a part of the aforementioned regimen [28]. It undergoes extensive modification in plasma, intestinal mucosa, and liver to form a derivative called SN-38 [29]. This metabolite of irinotecan is believed to be the actual mediator of its cytotoxic effects by inhibiting topoisomerase I, introducing persistent single-stranded DNA knicks finally resulting in S-phase arrest followed by programmed cell death [30]. Oxaliplatin is a platinum-based drug used in the FOLFIRINOX regimen. The transient reactive species that are released as a result of the drug metabolism have the ability to bind to macromolecules such as the neighboring guanine moieties, finally culminating in intrastrand crosslinks. Such intrastrand crosslinks affect DNA replication and transcription and are thought to be the reason for oxaliplatin-derived cytotoxicity [31,32]. Nevertheless, this regimen displayed serious side effects, thereby making this regimen limited to patients with a good performance status [6].

Due to similar reasons, in spite of the development of several chemotherapeutic agents, which demonstrate very high efficacy, no curative treatment approach has been established for pancreatic cancer. The drugs used in conventional chemotherapy target all rapidly proliferating cells without demonstrating specificity toward tumor cells. This leads to manifestation of multiple severe side effects and dose-dependent toxicities [33]. Furthermore, over the course of therapy, cancer cells begin to develop mechanisms of protection against the cytotoxic effects induced by these drugs, culminating in reduced sensitivity of such malignant cells toward therapy. As a consequence of these drawbacks, chemotherapeutic drugs are only able to exhibit marginal effects in improvement of patient health and survival. Therefore there is an increase in the ongoing research in developing new therapies that particularly target the malignant pancreatic cells thus demonstrating enhanced efficiency [2].

3.2.2 Targeted therapies

Targeted therapies focus on the identification of the key oncogenic drivers thereby targeting the underlying signaling mechanisms, which are involved in the growth, progression, and survival of tumor cells. As a consequence of their selective targeting ability toward cancer cells, they are supposed to provide enhanced safety as compared to conventional chemotherapeutic drugs. In general, the targeted therapies include drugs that fall into two main categories of molecularly targeted therapies and tumor microenvironment (TME) targeting agents.

3.2.2.1 Molecular targeted therapies

As discussed previously, the mutational landscape of pancreatic cancer is diverse and consists of several alterations at genome as well as transcriptome level. Some of the genetic mutations can be used as a possible target for developing curative therapeutics because they are thought to be crucial for tumor pathophysiology. Based on the current information from genome and transcriptome profiles of pancreatic cancer, epidermal growth factor receptor (EGFR), vascular endothelial growth factor (VEGF), farnesyl transferase [34], DNA repair pathways, and chromatin-modifying agents can be used as a target [35]. When it comes to targeting EGFR, there are two types of inhibitors that exhibit antineoplastic effects by targeting EGFR—small molecule tyrosine kinase inhibitors (TKI) and monoclonal antibodies. Erlotinib is a FDA-approved oral TKI that selectively blocks EGFR [34,36]. Recently, Moore et al. published a phase III randomized clinical trial to compare the efficacy of erlotinib in combination with gemcitabine versus gemcitabine alone. Interestingly, this study exhibited significant survival benefits in the erlotinib arm [37]. Another TKI that targets EGFR is gefitinib. This agent blocks the EGFR phosphorylation causing the blocking of the downstream signaling cascade. Additionally, this agent also inhibits mitogen-activated protein kinase (MAPK) activity. The drug exhibited complete inhibition of EGFR-induced cell proliferation at a concentration of 2.5−10 μM [38]. In 2007, Carnerio et al. published a phase I clinical trial study regarding the maximum tolerated dose (MTD) and dose-limiting toxicities (DLTs) of gefitinib and gemcitabine combination. The overall survival was found to be 7.13 months and the time to progress was reported to be 4.57 months with the recommended dose of gemcitabine being 1200 mg/m^2 and gefitinib 250 mg daily [39].

Currently, monoclonal antibodies used for blocking EGFR in pancreatic cancer include cetuximab and matuzumab. Cetuximab is a mouse-human chimeric antibody against EGFR. It is FDA approved for head and neck squamous cell carcinoma and colorectal adenocarcinoma [34]. Its effect is being investigated in clinical and preclinical trials for pancreatic cancer studies. In this regard, the MiaPaCa-2 model of pancreatic cancer, a combination of cetuximab, gemcitabine, and radiation therapy, displayed complete inhibition of tumor regression [40]. Additionally, the same team also reported enhanced sensitivity to chemotherapy and radiotherapy after prolonged exposure to this antibody [41]. Presently, several studies evaluating the combination effect of this antibody with other biological agents and chemotherapeutic drugs, and radiotherapy on pancreatic cancer is in progress in phase I and II trials [34]. Another antibody, matuzumab is a fully-humanized monoclonal antibody binding to EGFR receptor and is currently under evaluation for its effect on pancreatic cancer. A phase I study of matuzumab in combination with gemcitabine assessing the safety and efficacy of this antibody indicated that eight out of 12 patients showed a response to this antibody and three of six patients treated with 800 mg matuzumab weekly responded partially [42]. For decades, the role of VEGF overexpression in promoting neo-angiogenesis-mediated tumor growth and progression in pancreatic cancer has been known. In regard to inhibition of VEGFR, bevacizumab is the first antibody that is humanized and binds to both VEGFR 1 and 2. This antibody is currently in clinical trials and its effect on pancreatic cancer is being evaluated in combination with other agents [34]. Additionally, vatalanib is a small molecule TKI selectively inhibiting VEGFR 1, 2, and 3. This agent displayed inhibition of tumor volume growth alone or in combination with gemcitabine in a preclinical mouse model study. Furthermore, the combinatorial arm resulted in a reduction of lymph nodes and liver metastasis [43].

KRAS is the most common and well-studied oncogene associated with pancreatic cancer with its mutation observed in more than 90% of pancreatic cancer cases. Salirasib is a salicyclic-derived RAS inhibitor. It induces membrane dislodging of all RAS isoforms and facilitates RAS degradation as reported by Weisz et al. [44]. Moreover, in combination with gemcitabine, salirasib demonstrated a median overall survival of 6.2 months and 1-year survival in advanced pancreatic ductal adenocarcinoma [45]. Moreover, since membrane transport of KRAS is essential for its activity, therefore targeting this process might aid in KRAS inhibition. In this regard, farnesylation, a crucial step mediated by farnesyl transferase enzyme for the transport of RAS proteins to the cell membrane, can be targeted. Agents such as tipifarnib and lonafarnib farnesyl transferase inhibitors (FTI) cause RAS inhibition. Tipifarnib is a competitive FTI, which is nonpeptidomimetic in nature. A phase III trial conducted in Belgium where this agent was coadministered with gemcitabine showed enhanced survival and improved outcomes as compared to gemcitabine alone [46].

In addition to mutations, the transcriptional profile of cells in humans is also dictated by epigenetic modifications. Such modifications govern the accessibility of DNA chromatin to the transcription factors. Therefore changes in both genetic and epigenetic profiles govern the transformation of a cell to attain pancreatic cancer phenotype, thereby making epigenetic therapy a possible strategy to target the pancreatic neoplastic cells. Agents such as suberoylanilide hydroxamic acid (SAHA) and trichostatin A (TSA) target the proteins responsible for such epigenetic modifications.

TSA is a histone deacetylase (HDAC) inhibitor, which induced arrest in cell growth and apoptosis in nine pancreatic cancer cell lines in vitro [47]. Additionally, a combination of TSA with irinotecan induced 80% growth suppression in cancer cell lines [48]. Similarly, SAHA, also known as vorinostat, is another HDAC inhibitor that was reported to exhibit inhibition of cell growth in pancreatic cancer cell lines COLO-357 and BxPC-3 upon coadministration with gemcitabine in vitro [49].

One of the major reasons responsible for accumulation of oncogenic mutations is DNA damage. Cells that acquire damage in DNA either undergo cell death or develop into oncogenic precursors. Therefore multiple mechanisms have been developed to prevent assemblage of such malignant lesions. One such pathway is the homologous recombination repair mechanism [50]. Some of the genes involved in homologous recombination repair pathway that are typically found mutated in pancreatic cancer are BRCA2, BRCA1, PALB2, and ATM [51]. Identification of such mutations is clinically important as homologous recombination deficiency might help foretell enhanced sensitivity to platinum-based drugs and could be a target [50]. For example, tumors with BRCA1/2 mutations demonstrate enhanced sensitivity to platinum-based poly (ADP-ribose) polymerase (PARP) inhibitors. One such drug is Olaparib, which is an FDA-approved drug used as maintenance therapy for pancreatic cancers that carry germline BRCA1 and BRCA2 mutations [35]. Another key factor of DNA damage repair pathway is ATM, which is found to be mutated in nearly 5% of PDAC cases. However, cells can make up for the loss of ATM via upregulating another repair protein ATR. PDAC tumors that carry mutations in ATM are particularly sensitive to the combination of PARP and ATR inhibitors [52].

3.2.2.2 Cancer stem cells as target

The heterogeneous cell population of pancreatic cancer also harbors a population of cancer stem cells (CSCs). This population of cells is itself heterogeneous and has the ability to self-renew and differentiate. In recent years, a large number of studies have reported that CSCs also play a key role in metastasis of pancreatic cancer [53]. Therefore targeting and eliminating CSCs can help in achieving better therapy outcomes in pancreatic cancer patients. In this regard, a better understanding of the molecular pathways by which CSCs are formed could be valuable. Studies indicate that the formation of CSCs is induced by dysregulation of signaling pathways including Wnt, Hedgehog, and Notch pathways [54].

Hedgehog pathway has been known to play a key role in the maintenance of CSCs, and embryonic development as well as its dysregulation have been found in several cancers including pancreatic cancers [55,56]. Li et al. identified increased expression of sonic hedgehog (Shh) signaling pathway in pancreatic CSCs [57]. Therefore inhibiting this pathway could eliminate CSCs and help to develop the outcomes of the candidates with pancreatic cancer. With regard to this, cyclopamine that inhibits smoothened, thereby blocking Hedgehog pathway, has been reported to decrease pancreatic CSC markers and also exhibited synergistic effect with gemcitabine by decreasing tumor volume [58]. Additionally, Yao et al. demonstrated that cyclopamine suppressed the expression of CSC markers, such as CD44 and CD133, in gemcitabine-resistant pancreatic cancer cells [59]. Furthermore, metformin, which is used commonly to reduce the blood glucose levels in type II diabetes patients, was found to reduce pancreatospheres and enhance their disintegration in pancreatic cancer cells [53]. Metformin also reduced the expression of CSCs markers including CD44, Oct4, EpCAM, and Nanog in pancreatic cancer cells [60]. Studies performed by Xia et al. suggest that this drug prevents migration, cell growth, and invasion by hindering CSC function facilitated by modulation alterations in miRNAs such as let-7a, miR-26a, 100, and 200b [60].

Moreover, the HDAC inhibitor called SAHA discussed previously has also demonstrated anti-CSC activity by prohibiting proliferation, migration, invasion, spheroid formation, and self-renewal [53]. More specifically, it increased the levels of miR-34a and downregulating expression of Bcl-2, SIRT1, survivin, VEGF, cyclin D1, and CDK6 in human pancreatic CSCs [61]. It also reduces the expression of Snail, Zeb1, and Slug thus obstructing EMT, as well as miR-34a mediated suppression Notch pathway [61]. Therefore SAHA could be a potential agent for treating pancreatic cancer stem cells.

3.2.2.3 Targeting tumor microenvironment

An important component of pancreatic cancer that represents more than 90% of the tumor mass is the stroma, commonly referred to as TME. It is characterized by a dense fibrous desmoplastic reaction at the primary tumor site [62]. The stromal compartment also plays a key role in dictating the biology of pancreatic cancer such as tumor growth, stemness, invasiveness, metastatic spread, resistance to drug, and escaping recognition by host immunity. Therefore identification of pharmacological approaches to target the stromal compartment of tumor might help in achieving enhanced drug delivery and act as a therapeutic intervention for curing pancreatic cancer [50]. There are two major stromal components of a tumor that can be targeted: cellular component and extracellular matrix. The extracellular matrix of stroma is rich in fibronectin, collagen, and hyaluronic acid, which are responsible for its enhanced density. This highly dense characteristic of stroma instigates an increase in interstitial pressure thus inhibiting diffusion of therapeutic agents into the tumor [50]. Moreover, targeting the molecules involved in tumor-stroma crosstalk can have a dual effect by eliminating the tumor cells directly as well as augmenting the treatment effect by remodeling stroma. Agents targeting such molecules include MMPs, VEGFRs, and EGFRs, which have been discussed previously as part of molecularly targeted therapies [63].

Another method to remodel the stroma is by considering its cellular components as a target. The stromal cells include various immune-related cells such as tumor-associated macrophages (TAMs), regulatory T cells, dendritic cells (DCs), and nonimmune cells such as mesenchymal cells and endothelial cells [64]. Cancer-associated fibroblasts (CAFs) are a type of mesenchymal cells and constitute a major percentage of tumor stroma, which are heterogeneous in nature. Upon activation, CAFs secret several chemokines, responsible for recruiting the myeloid cell into the tumor [65,66]. Furthermore, activation of CAF requires factors such as TGF-β, FGF-2, Shh, and PDGF, which are secreted by the tumor cells thereby making these molecules a possible target to remodel or eliminated CAFs [67,68]. Antibodies targeting TGF-β prevent CAF activation, resulting in a reduction of intratumoral fibroblasts and myeloid cell infiltration in addition to decreased CD8 + T-cell suppression [69]. An anti-TGF- β monoclonal antibody (NIS793) is currently being evaluated in combination with PD-1 blockade and gemcitabine/nab-paclitaxel (GnP) in phase II clinical trial [70]. Besides, vitamin D can also be used to achieve fibroblast quiescence, and a derivative of vitamin D called paricalcitol is currently being studied for its effect on CAF [71,72]. In addition to CAFs, the immune cells are another key constituent of the TME. These cells play a crucial role in suppression of host's antitumor immune response and mediating evasion of host immune system by tumor. Therefore targeting these cells as well as developing immunotherapeutic strategies to enhance the host immune response against tumors would enhance body's natural ability to fight this fatal disease [35]. Even though conventional immune checkpoint blockades have revolutionized the cancer treatment in numerous solid tumors; however, in case of PDAC, they have exhibited unsatisfactory results [73,74]. In addition to checkpoint blockades, numerous vaccine-based approaches are also being evaluated [35]. Some of the vaccines that are currently under study are GVAX, KIF20A-66, and survivin-2B 80−88 (SVN-2B) vaccines; algenpantucel-L; DC vaccine; K-Ras vaccine; and GV1001 vaccine. However, the efficacy of these vaccines still remains a question due to the drawbacks such as small sample number longer recruitment period, difficulty in vaccine synthesis, higher drop-out rate due to tumor progression, and most crucially difficulty in identification of immune responses and its measurement [75]. Additionally, targeting molecules such as CCR2 and CXCR2, which are involved in regulating the trafficking of short-lived immunosuppressive myeloid cells in tumor, were hypothesized to reduce tumor burden [76]. This was achieved in mice treated with CCR2 inhibitors that targeted circulating monocytes [77−79]. Combination of small molecule inhibitor of CCR2 with FOLFIRINOX in patients with locally advanced PDAC exhibited a notable reduction in the monocytic myeloid-derived suppressor cells from tumor environment, which was accompanied by huge reduction in tumor burden as well as disease downstaging and surgery eligibility in 39% of cohort [80]. Another approach that is currently under study is the CD40 agonist therapy. This strategy facilitates the reprogramming of antigen-presenting cells (APCs) such as DCs and TAMs. The above therapy is based on the interaction of CD40 on APCs with CD40 ligands on normal CD4 T-cells. This interaction activates the APCs to enhance antigen presentation and effective priming of CD8 T-cells [35,50]. The combination of CD40 agonist therapy with gemcitabine exhibited a 19% response in a cohort of 21 patients with PDAC with 52% of patients attaining stable disease at their 2-month assessment [81]. Another key immune signaling protein overexpressed by TAMs is CSF1R. This molecule was found to be involved in macrophage differentiation and production. The inhibitors of this molecule have successfully demonstrated regression of tumor, as well as increased survival in mouse models via TAM reprogramming, to improve antigen presentation and enhance anticancer T-cell response [50]. Additionally, TAMs also constitutively release IL-1β, which acts as a support for inflammatory CAFs. Blocking IL-1β have exhibited additive effects with PD-1 blockade in KPC-tumor-bearing mice models [82]. Canakinumab is an anti-IL-1β antibody in combination with PD-1 blocking antibody spartalizumab, which is currently under evaluation with GnP in phase 1 trials [83].

Adoptive cell transfer (ACT) is another modality, which is currently being studied for targeting this malignant disease. In ACT, patient's tumor antigen-specific T-cells are harvested and cultured ex vivo following which they are re-injected into the patient. The main objective of this method is to enhance the tumor-specific immune response of the patient. Presently, chimeric antigen receptor T-cell therapy is the most developed type of ACT. In CAR T-cell therapy, T-cells collected from the patient are engineered genetically to express CARs. These CARs are specific to tumor antigens such as CEA, thereby activating the T-cells upon antigen recognition [75].

3.3 Drug resistance as a pitfall

As mentioned previously, resistance to cancer therapy is one of the main reasons for the failure of conventional chemotherapeutic agents. Therefore a deep understanding of the pathology behind drug resistance is crucial for developing successful strategies to not only overcome this phenomenon but also to design novel chemotherapeutic agents with better efficacy. Based on early studies, a wide range of molecules and probable mechanisms have been suggested to contribute to drug resistance in pancreatic cancer. Typically, there are two types of resistance: firstly, the ones that impair anticancer drug delivery to tumor cells and secondly, the ones that are genetically or epigenetically acquired by the cancer cells affecting the drug sensitivity. Furthermore, the cells that selectively exhibit resistance to one drug have increased chances of displaying cross-resistance to other mechanistically and structurally unrelated drugs. This phenomenon is known as multidrug resistance and is the reason behind the decreased efficacy of treatment regimens with a combination of multiple drugs. Another phenomenon called multifactorial multidrug resistance arises due to the inherent ability of cancer cells to undergo clonal expansion and clonal selection leading to development of more than one mechanism of multidrug resistance [84].

3.3.1 Role of drug uptake and drug metabolism pathways

The phenomenon of multidrug resistance is often attributed to the increased expression of certain drug efflux pumps. These transporters reduce the intracellular accumulation of drugs by pumping drugs out of the cell. The key mediators of this process are the members of the superfamily of the ATP binding cassette (ABC). Specifically, the ABC-B, C, and G subfamilies have been studied to provide a substantial contribution to multidrug resistance by drug efflux in the pancreatic cancer cells. One of the well-studied ABC transporters is the P-glycoprotein (PGP). PGP is a broad-spectrum efflux pump constituting 12 membrane-bound regions and two ATP-binding sites. Other ABC transporters such as MRP1, MRP3, MRP4, and MRP5 all belonging to ABC-C family have been implicated in pancreatic cancer resistance toward chemotherapeutic drugs [84,85]. Changes in the activity of the key enzymes attributing to the metabolism of the drugs can also contribute to the reduced sensitivity of tumor cells toward the drug. For instance, deoxycytidine kinase (DCK), which is the rate-limiting enzyme for gemcitabine phosphorylation inside the cell, has been thought to play a key role in tumor cell responsivity toward gemcitabine [86]. Pancreatic adenocarcinoma patients with higher DCK expression have demonstrated improved overall survival upon gemcitabine treatment [85]. Moreover, HuR protein, which stabilizes DCK protein, is also associated with gemcitabine sensitivity in tumor cells. Better survival rate was seen in gemcitabine administered patients with higher HuR levels as compared with patients having lowered HuR levels [87]. Another enzyme known as ribonucleoside reductase (RNR), which induces DCK inhibition by feedback mechanisms, is blocked by a gemcitabine metabolite called gemcitabine diphosphate [88]. This enzyme is considered to be a preindicative marker for gemcitabine resistance in gemcitabine-treated patients. A differential expression analysis between five different pancreatic cancer cell lines and their gemcitabine-resistant counterparts, by Nakahira et al., revealed *rrm1* subunit of RNR to be the most upregulated enzyme [89]. In the same direction, Duxbury et al. overexpressed *rrm2* subunit of RNR in pancreatic cancer cell lines, which led to reduced sensitivity of those cell lines toward gemcitabine [90,91].

3.3.2 Role of key signaling networks

Deregulation in the levels of several transcription factors and key signaling molecules has been demonstrated to be responsible for the development of drug resistance in pancreatic cancer cells. One of them is the constitutive activation of NF-κB, which is largely associated with drug resistance in pancreatic cancer. NF-κB is a nuclear transcription factor, crucial for the regulation of several biological processes such as apoptosis, tumorigenesis, inflammation, and different autoimmune diseases [85]. Experiments revealed that gemcitabine resistant cells showed higher activity of NF-κB and its inactivation increased the sensitivity of cells toward conventional chemotherapeutics [87]. The silencing of one of the most common dimers of NF-κB known as p65/RelA has been reported to induce apoptosis and increased cytotoxicity in all gemcitabine-sensitive pancreatic cancer cells. Moreover, NF-κB pathway inversely regulates the expression of human concentrative nucleoside transporter 1 (hCNT1), which is involved in gemcitabine uptake [92]. In addition to this, one of the direct transcriptional targets of NF-κB is Shh, which also contributes to drug resistance in pancreatic cancer cells [93]. The members of Hedgehog including Shh have also been found to be overexpressed in gemcitabine resistant cancer cells. Upon induction, this pathway causes fibrosis and reduces the vascular density of the tumor stroma, thereby decreasing gemcitabine delivery to the tumor tissue [59]. Another pathway whose alteration has been associated with chemoresistance in pancreatic cancer is the phosphatidylinositol 3-kinase (PI3K)/Akt signaling pathway. This pathway facilitates drug resistance by impairment of apoptotic pathways [94]. For example, phosphorylated Akt is reported to inactivate BAD protein, which is proapoptotic in nature, thus promoting an antiapoptotic effect on the cells [87]. Effective intracellular gemcitabine concentration in PK1 and PK8 pancreatic cancer cell lines have been reported to activate PI3K/Akt/NF-κB pathway, resulting in resistance to this drug in these cells [94]. FKBP5, which is a scaffolding protein that mediates Akt dephosphorylation, is thought to be a marker of chemoresistance in pancreatic cancer. Reduced levels of FKBP5 in tumor cells are associated with resistance to chemotherapeutic agents such as gemcitabine [95]. Moreover, studies have displayed that AKT activity induces the activation of a set of survival-promoting factors such as NF-κB. Inhibition of AKT2 showed increased sensitivity to gemcitabine-mediated apoptosis and inhibition of growth by both p53-upregulated modulator of apoptosis (PUMA) upregulation and inhibition of NF-κB [96]. Additionally, increased expression of different components of Notch signaling pathway is thought to be considered a determinant of drug resistance [97]. The ERK signaling, which is one out of three MAPK, is also associated to promote chemoresistance. For instance, in the most gemcitabine sensitive pancreatic cancer cell lines, for example, MIA PaCa-2, the ERK expression levels were shown to be low, while the gemcitabine-resistant pancreatic cancer cell line PANC-1 displayed increased basal expression of ERK [87]. Moreover, neuropilin-1 (NRP-1) a VEGFR cofactor expressed only in pancreatic cancer cells but not in nonmalignant pancreatic cells. NRP-1 overexpression is associated with increased levels of MAPK and its downregulation in PANC-1 cells significantly enhanced the sensitivity of this cell line toward chemotherapy. The induction of MAPK signaling by NRP-1 is thought to induce antiapoptotic regulators, such as MCL-1, and thereby promote survival and lead to acquired chemoresistance in pancreatic cancer cells [98].

3.3.3 Tumor microenvironment

As discussed previously, the tumor stroma plays an indispensable role in progression of tumor biology including the manifestation of therapy resistance. The different components of stroma exert unique roles in attribution to therapy resistance in pancreatic cancer. The presence of an excessive volume of extracellular matrix confers to the high density of the tumor stroma. This leads to enhancement of the interstitial pressure leading to vascular constriction, which not only affects the flow of an adequate amount of oxygen and nutrients into the stroma but also impedes the penetration of chemotherapeutic drugs thereby reducing their delivery into tumor core [99]. Additionally, the hypoxia caused as a result of vascular constriction also promotes chemoresistance by activation of multiple signaling pathways including the stabilization of hypoxia inducible factor 1 alpha (HIF1α) [100]. HIF1α plays a pivotal role in activation of signaling pathways, which induce invasiveness, alter the metabolic pathways as well as stimulate drug resistance, and lead to poor disease prognosis in patients [101]. Besides, HIF1α has also been reported to support radiotherapy resistance, which acts via inducing free radical production to damage DNA. However, the lack of oxygen obstructs free radical formation thus reducing the cytotoxic effects induced by radiotherapy [100]. Besides, the chemotherapy-induced cell death is also mediated via the reactive oxygen species production, which is suppressed in hypoxic tumor cells by HIF1α, thereby leading to drug resistance in cancer cells [100]. Furthermore, to compensate for the reduced oxygen levels due to hypoxic stress, HIF1α induces uptake of glucose by the cells. This is followed by an enhancement in glycolysis, which switches the cellular metabolism toward aerobic glycolysis, a phenomenon called Warburg effect. The enhanced production of lactate from aerobic glycolysis results in extracellular acidification, which causes a pH shift. This change in the pH is further heightened by the expression of carbonic anhydrases induced by HIF1α. The swing in the pH ratio is another factor, which hinders drug absorption by the cells [102–104].

Another integral parts of tumor environment are pancreatic stellate cells. These cells have been observed to induce resistance phenotype in tumor cells by repressing H_2O_2 coupled apoptosis and enhanced pancreatic cancer cell survival in addition to reduced pancreatic tumor cell response to gemcitabine and radiotherapy [105]. Invitro experiments confirmed the PSC-induced Hes1 expression via Notch signaling to mediate gemcitabine chemoresistance [106]. Secondly, it is thought that the stellate cell-induced overexpression of periostin in the pancreatic tumor stroma also confers resistance to gemcitabine therapy in pancreatic cancer cells [107]. Besides all these mechanisms, the pancreatic stellate cells also mediate gemcitabine resistance by SDF-1α/CXCR4 signaling coupled induction of ERK1/2 and FAK-AKT pathways and a subsequent IL-6 autocrine loop in the tumor cells [108]. Recent studies have also shown that the stellate cell induces radioresistance by β-integrin-FAK pathway in tumor cells [109]. Correspondingly, the tumor macrophages that predominate the immune cell niche of pancreatic cancer stroma also confer drug resistance in an environment-mediated process. TAMs upregulate cytidine deaminase expression, which is responsible for gemcitabine inactivation in cancer cells [110]. Moreover, the TME also mediated enrichment of cancer stem cells (CSCs) via upregulation of self-renewing genes in an HIF1α dependent manner [111].

3.3.4 Cancer stem cells and epithelial to mesenchymal transition as regulators

An increasing amount of research evidence indicates that the pancreatic CSCs induce therapy resistance in pancreatic cancer and have mechanisms, which help them acquire the same phenotype. There are multiple stem cell markers that are thought to be dysregulated in therapy-resistant pancreatic tumors [85]. Recently, CD133, which was initially identified as a stem cell marker, was also suggested as a marker of therapy-insensitive CSCs [112]. Even though recent studies exhibit that Notch, Wnt/β-catenin, and DNA damage repair signaling mechanisms are involved in development of radioresistance and chemoresistance, the exact pathway inducing this phenotype in pancreatic cancer still remains to be elucidated [113]. In addition to CSCs, pancreatic cancer cells with epithelial to mesenchymal transition (EMT) phenotype have also been thought to play a pivotal role in development of resistance. Multiple pathways including the Notch, Hedgehog, Wnt, NF-κB, and TGF-β are essential for the induction of this process [114]. Furthermore, studies indicate the presence of a biological link between CSCs and EMT phenotype of cells. It was suggested that Twist was the master regulator of both CSC and EMT features. However, further studies on cells exhibiting both these features are required for deciphering this link [115].

3.3.5 Other miscellaneous pathways and factors

Dysregulation of several other genes has also been reported to be associated with therapy resistance in pancreatic cancer. Increased levels of phosphorylated FAK and Akt lead to upregulation of survivin and pBad, thereby reducing apoptosis and cytotoxicity thus, instigating potential role of this pathway in conferring resistance [116]. Substantial upregulation of antiapoptotic genes such as Bcl-2, survivin, Bcl-xL, and cIAP-1 was also reported in pancreatic cancer cells that acquired resistance to gemcitabine upon prolonged exposure to the drug [117]. Enhanced levels of phosphorylated Src (heat shock protein 27), which is a chaperone that is involved in unfolded protein response, were also observed in gemcitabine-resistant cancer cell lines [118,119].

MicroRNAs are a major landmark in the field of posttranscriptional protein expression regulation. They are hypothesized to play a critical role in cancer development. Recent studies of pancreatic cancer also suggest their involvement in development of resistant phenotype. MicroRNAs such as miR–10b, 21, 17, 34, 148, 155, 200, 204, 211, 214, 222, 320, and 365 have been validated to appear in gemcitabine-resistant pancreatic cancer cells, thereby instigating the possibility of their association with therapy resistance phenotype [87].

3.4 Nanotechnology as a therapeutic window

Considering drug resistance as a complex mechanism, more effective anticancer therapies have been designed to combat drug resistance and increase the therapeutic outcome. Among these, one rapidly emerging field in biomedicine is the development of nanotherapeutics-based approaches. Nanoparticles (NPs) have certain distinctive physicochemical properties that allow them to surmount some of the drawbacks associated with traditional medicines, such as short half-life, poor oral bioavailability, poor water solubility, and nonspecific biodistribution [120]. Nanoparticle-based drug carriers confer greater bioavailability, increased pharmacokinetics, improved targeted drug delivery, and deep tumor penetration of drugs [121,122]. At present, more than 40 therapeutic nanocarriers are approved for clinical use worldwide and at least 200 nanomaterials are undergoing clinical trials [123,124]. For this attribute, several nanoparticulate systems are now being investigated as promising drug delivery carriers for solving several forms of drug resistance [125]. For instance, several nanocarriers such as lipid- and micelle-based NPs, polymer micelles, polymeric/nonpolymeric NPs, nanoconjugates, dendrimers, carbon nanotubes, nanocapsules, nanogels, and quantum dots are successfully equipped for the enhancement of cancer therapy by imparting vast cargo without toxicity [126]. Further, the surface chemistry and plasticity of nanoparticle composition aid a wide range of design preferences. As a result, besides delivering drugs, nanocarriers also provide specific targetability to cancer cells and early diagnostics options. A nano-based drug delivery system not only carries targeted drug to overcome drug resistance but also provide specific targetability to tumor cells and diagnostics. NPs provide marvelous specificity in terms of targeted delivery through both active and passive targeting mechanisms [127,128]. In passive targeting, due to enhanced permeability and retention (EPR) effect across the abnormal leaky vasculature and lack of lymphatic drainage in TME, therapeutic nanocarriers tend to accumulate at the tumor site. However, in active targeting, the nanocarriers are conjugated with tumor-specific ligands that aid their direct interaction with the overexpressed surface receptors on target cells and induce receptor-mediated endocytosis, which allows internalization of NPs into the tumor site by reducing toxicity to normal cells [129,130]. In active targeting, several biocompatible specific ligands including antibodies, peptides, aptamers, peculiar receptors, or antigens specific to the tumor site are reengineered with the NPs [129]. In addition, active targeting may actuate combination therapy by employing the synergistic effects of different pharmaceutics

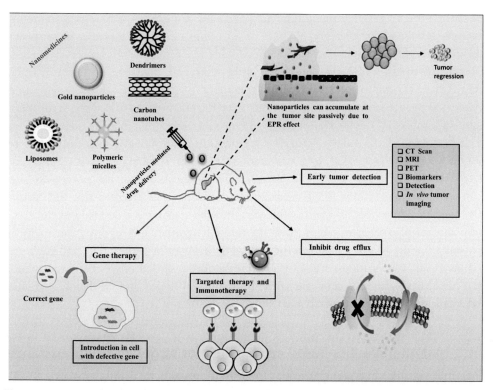

Figure 3.2 Nanotechnology-based drug delivery platform for overcoming pancreatic cancer multi-drug resistance. NPs can be made from different materials, including liposomes, polymeric micelles, metal NPs, dendrimers, and carbon nanotubes, and can deliver vast payload at the tumor site due to enhanced permeability and retention (EPR) effect. Further, cell-specific targeting of nanoparticles can be achieved via the modification of nanoparticles with ligands that bind to specific receptors present in the cancer cells, thus assisting in molecular targeted therapy and immunotherapy. Besides, delivering drug nanoparticles can transport several multidrug resistance protein specific inhibitors and siRNA to downregulate the expression of several efflux transporters thereby inhibiting drug resistance. *NPs*, Nanoparticles; *siRNA*, short-interfering RNAs.

drugs or therapeutic agents for better curative outcomes. Nanotechnology also allows for exceptional imaging opportunities by utilizing multiple forms of NPs, nanotubes, nanowires, and nanocantilevers loaded with biosensors; to increase biodistribution, it provides greater contrast in imaging and improves sensitivity [131] (Fig. 3.2). Here we have discussed some of the mechanisms through which NPs help to combat multidrug resistance for more effective pancreatic cancer therapies.

3.4.1 Nanotherapeutic strategies using chemotherapeutic drugs

At present, most of the drugs used in chemotherapy of pancreatic cancer exhibit reduced efficacy owing to their poor pharmacokinetics and development of multidrug resistance protein (MDR) phenotype in pancreatic cancer. In this regard, targeting strategies involving the delivery of these drugs using nanoparticle system have shown promising results by improving the pharmacokinetics, reducing side effects by precise targeting of tumor cells, and combating drug resistance. The first such nanoparticle system that was approved by FDA for treatment of pancreatic cancer is albumin-conjugated paclitaxel (nab-paclitaxel). This new formulation decreased the hydrophobicity and improved the bioavailability of the drug thereby lowering the adverse effects of native drugs [132–134]. Similarly, nanoliposomal irinotecan was approved by the FDA on October 2022 as a treatment strategy in combination with 5-FU and leucovorin for metastatic pancreatic cancer patients whose disease has progressed after treatment with gemcitabine [135]. Additionally, Vandana et al. reported that PEGylation of gemcitabine improves its pharmacokinetics, thereby making it a desirable platform for the treatment of pancreatic cancer [136]. In fact, Meng et al. also reported the ability of lipid-silica hybrid NPs as a platform for synergistic delivery of gemcitabine and paclitaxel in a pancreatic cancer mouse model [137]. Furthermore, several other chemotherapeutic drug-nanoparticle-based systems are currently being developed and are being examined under preclinical trials for the treatment of pancreatic cancer.

3.4.2 Nanotherapeutics-based approaches for targeting drug resistance

The mechanisms instigating tumor multidrug resistance mainly involve ATP-dependent drug efflux, inhibition of the apoptosis pathway, changes in TME cellular components, tumor heterogeneity, and changes in genetic factors, etc. [138]. Among different mechanisms allied with MDR, the drug efflux mechanism is the most crucial and has achieved more attention and intensive research. Upon prolonged stimulation with the chemotherapeutic drugs, cancer cells upregulate drug efflux–related transporters, specifically including PGP, MDR1, multidrug resistance–associated protein 1 (MRP1), and breast cancer resistance protein (BCRP) [139]. The transporters belong to the ABC transporter family. After assimilating chemotherapeutic drugs with a low molecular weight (<2000 Da), ABC proteins will pump these drugs out promptly [140]. As an upshot, the intracellular drug concentration will be lowered significantly, which leads to loss of chemotherapeutic efficiency. Therefore targeting the ABC transporter and architecting some novel nanoparticulate systems for regulating the MDR pathway have open up new possibilities for addressing these therapeutic limitations [141]. In this context, myriad of studies has reported that some chemotherapeutic-loaded NPs can circumvent the exposure of antitumor drugs to efflux transporters by entering the cell directly through receptor-mediated endocytosis and releasing the drug at a perinuclear site within the cell, away from cell membranes and efflux pumps [142]. Further, in addition to evading efflux transporters, impeding their expression and function would be another way to target efflux transporter-mediated drug resistance. Thus several PGP inhibitors have been investigated (e.g., verapamil, laniquidar, tariquidar, natural alkaloids, or herbal natural products) and many more are under clinical trial [143]. However, most of them exhibited significant limitations due to insolubility, short half-life, rapid metabolism, and systemic toxicity [144]. These drawbacks can be subdued by designing NPs that incorporate both efflux pump inhibitors and chemotherapeutics [145], or by inhibiting the ATP supply into the efflux pump [146]. Furthermore, several studies have revealed that codelivery of PGP-targeted short-interfering RNAs (siRNA) and anticancer drugs through NPs helps to surpass cancer drug-resistant by reducing the expression of ABC transporters [147]. Moreover, some nanoformulation alone (i.e., without PGP inhibitors) can inhibit the PGP-manifested MDR. For instance, specifically targeting a DOX-loaded liposomal formulation of a pancreatic cancer cell line PANC-1, which overexpresses PGP, showed similar drug accumulation both in presence and absence of verapamil and increased cytotoxicity of DOX (IC50 10-fold lower) [148,149]. In addition, another multidrug resistance protein ABCG2 is found to be highly expressed in 72% of pancreatic cancer cells [150]. In this regard, a nanoliposomal formulation loaded irinotecan together with benzoporphyrin derivative for photodynamic therapy (PDT) was able to overcome ABCG2-mediated drug resistance, reducing tumor volume from 70% to 25% in mice bearing pancreatic tumors [151]. Further, due to versatility of nanodrug delivery systems (NDDSs), it can carry a variety of active substances to the tumor site simultaneously to execute a synergistic effect. Therefore through rational design, both the inhibitors of MDR-related proteins and chemotherapeutic drugs can transport to the tumor site at the same time to mitigate MDR [152].

3.4.3 Nanotherapeutics-based approaches for targeting tumor microenvironment

TME portrays a pivotal role in instigating tumor heterogeneity and cancer progression. The heterogeneity of TME and its components, such as cells, ECM, blood vessels, and interstitial fluid, act as physical barriers and impede drugs to pervade the tumor tissue thus retard tumor sensitivity toward chemotherapeutic drugs [153]. Both the cellular and noncellular parts of TME mitigate drug resistance through different mechanisms, involving cell—cell and cell—ECM interactions, crosstalk between distinct cells, phenotypic changes, mechanosensing variation. The cellular component includes stromal cells such as cancer-associated fibroblasts, cancer-associated immune cells, cancer-associated vascular endothelial cells, cancer-associated pericytes, lymphatic endothelial cells (LECs), and CSCs and the noncellular components such as the extracellular matrix, several cytokines, growth factors, and vascular networks. An acidic environment and hypoxia drive drug resistance through several mechanisms [154]. However, TME exhibits certain characteristics and features including an acidic environment, changed pH dynamics, leaky vasculature, inadequate vascular perfusion, altered enzyme expression, altered metabolism, and hypoxic circumstances. Nanoparticle-based drug delivery systems take advantage of these attributes of TME and can target the neoplastic cells either through active or passive targeting [155]. In active targeting, NPs are specifically designed to target only the tumor cells based on molecular recognition where the surface of the NPs conjugated with either tumor-specific ligand-receptor or antibody, which makes them able to interact only with the cancerous cells. Upon binding with the receptor present on the surface of cancer cells, NPs quickly undergo receptor-mediated endocytosis or phagocytosis by cells, owing to cell-specific delivery of the encapsulated drug [156]. In the passive mechanism, tumor targeting is executed through diffusion process, and due to EPR effect, accretion of nanocarriers around the abnormal leaky vasculature occurs. Besides several nanocarriers, platform exploit the unique tumor environmental stimuli features to construct various impulse-responsive drug delivery systems to enhance drug release. For example, the specific pH difference between the TME and normal tissue is utilized by the nanovehicles to construct several pH-sensitive NPs for early dissociation and burst drug release near the vicinity of tumor tissues [157]. Based on that, several pH-responsive nanoparticulate systems were developed and such systems triggered drug release in the acidic microenvironment. Few examples of certain pH-sensitive NPs were reported as self-assembled PEG-detachable polymeric micelles DOX-PMs, zwitterionic charge-switchable polymers S-NP/DOX, pH and redox dual responsive nanoparticle RPDSG/DOX, dual-pH responsive BCP-DOX micelles [158−161]. Besides, the change in redox gradient of tumor cells can be used as another specific stimulus to escalate drug release. Glutathione (GSH) is the most commonly used redox stimulant because the concentration of GSH in the tumor cytoplasm (~ 10 mm) is about seven times elevated than that in a normal cell. Studies have reported that GSH can particularly hydrolyze the disulfide bond and enhance burst drug release by dissociating the nanocarriers. Over the last few years, the disulfide bond is broadly employed in the development of new environmentally responsive nanoparticulate drug carriers [162]. When this type of nanostructure is exposed to the tumor cytoplasm, it can rapidly unveil the therapeutic payload through self-decomposition, hence potentiate its anticancer efficacy and reduce the effect of drug resistance.

Similarly, hypoxia is another factor playing a crucial role in multidrug resistance. The increased oxygen needs of rapidly proliferating cancer cells and the irregular blood vessel supply often develop a hypoxic condition. Similarly, hypoxia-inducible factor 1α (HIF-1α) is the key modulator inducing hypoxia and silencing the HIF-1α gene, which can impede hypoxic environment [163]. Several studies have indicated the use of nanocarriers containing HIF-1α siRNA successfully combated drug resistance in different cancers [164]. Presently several nanoparticulate systems focus on targeting hypoxic-TME, pH status, or neovascularization to enhance the drug action and avoid resistance. For example, in pancreatic cancer, iRGD-functionalized pegylated polymersomes combined with azobenzene increased the accumulation of GEM in hypoxic conditions, in both in vitro and in vivo models, due to reduction in the hypoxic tumor environment, leading to burst drug release [165].

3.4.4 Pro- and antiapoptotic genes: evasion and overexpression

Cancer cells acquire strategies to decrease the expression of proapoptotic proteins or increase the expression of antiapoptotic proteins, avoiding apoptosis and increasing survival, thereby confer resistance to anticancer drugs. In this regard, several NPs have been used, which can modulate the expression of Bcl-2 protein family, including both antiapoptotic (e.g., Bcl-2, Bcl-XL, and Mcl-1) and proapoptotic members (e.g., BAX and Bak) [166]. For example, treatment of silver NPs (AgNPs) in PANC-1 cells has caused downregulation of antiapoptotic genes Bcl-2 while increasing the expression of Bax; p53 including several necroptosis- and autophagy-related proteins (RP-1, RIP-3, MLKL, and LC3-II) thus increase chemosensitivity by inducing mixed type of programmed cell death [167]. Similarly, certain toxic anticancer agents that regulate the expression of antiapoptotic or proapoptotic proteins were assembled into NPs to address this drug resistance. For example, treatment of PANC-1 cells with an ethylene glycol/poly D, L lactide copolymer loaded arsenic trioxide decreased Bcl-2 and increased caspase three expressions thus induce apoptosis [168]. In another study, Yallapu et al. evaluated the therapeutic efficacy of curcumin-loaded magnetic NPs formulation in two pancreatic cell lines, HPAF-II and PANC-1 cells, which inhibit cell proliferation and colony formation ability in vitro. Also, these NPs curtailed the tumor growth and downregulated expression of PCNA, Bcl-XL, Mcl-1, MUC1, and collagen I in in vivo model [169].

3.4.5 Nanotherapeutic strategies for targeting cancer stem cells

CSCs are a small group of cancerous cells accounting for tumor heterogeneity and retain self-renewal ability, promoting high tumorigenicity and invasiveness. These are the primary determining factors associated with tumor initiation, progression, relapse, and poor therapeutic outcome [170]. CSCs have ability to confront conventional treatment regimens such as chemotherapy and radiotherapy due to their inherent attributes including phenotypic plasticity, overexpression of antiapoptotic proteins, maintenance of a slow dividing state, highly efficient DNA repair system, drug efflux transporters, EMT, and sustained stemness features [171]. Additionally, CSCs are stable and persist in a hypoxic TME providing added resistance to anticancer therapy. Altogether, CSCs constitute a vital component responsible for resistance to conventional chemo and radiotherapy [172]. The main strategies employed for specifically targeting CSCs utilize the overexpressed pluripotency CSC markers present or molecules related to cell cycle alterations and cell survival in order to eliminate resistance to treatment. In pancreatic cancer, a large number of recent studies employed several metal-based nanoplatforms such as titanium, gold, iron, and copper to target pancreatic CSCs. In this context, Wang, et al. designed a black TiO2-based nanoprobe based on PTT loaded with Gd-DOTA and CD133 monoclonal antibodies, which specifically target and cause selective death of CD133 overexpressed PANC-1 stem cells [173]. Another study revealed that pretreatment of AuNPs with pancreatic cancer cells increased their sensitivity to the gemcitabine (GEM) by exponentially decreasing the IC_{50} and decreasing GEM-induced EMT, stemness, and MAPK activation [174]. Additionally, curcumin loaded with superparamagnetic iron oxide nanoparticle (SP-CUR) reduced resistance to GEM and enhances its cellular uptake and efficacy. Cotreatment of SP-CUR and GEM selectively reduce viability of CSCs by 50% due to downregulation of Oct-4, Nanog, Sox2, and c-Myc hence restricting tumor sphere formation [175]. Also, copper-based nanoformulations have been shown to specifically cause toxicity in CSCs by inducing high oxidative stress (ROS) [176]. Therefore the development of potent anticancer strategies, which would specifically target the tumor cells and CSCs, has gained immense research attention. In order to attempt this, nanotherapeutic-based strategies using NPs were developed to target specifically CSCs to reduce the chances of cancer recurrence and equip better curative measures.

3.4.6 Nanoparticles as delivery vehicles for RNA interference inhibitors

RNA interference (RNAi) based therapeutics are rising as progressive and promising substitutes over conventional treatment regimens in terms of specificity, toxicity, and overcoming multiple drug resistance. RNA-based therapeutics can be employed either as inhibitors of target protein expression by using siRNA and miRNA or as up regulators using mRNA [177]. The miRNA-based cancer therapeutics have significant implications in several pathophysiological processes involved in cancer progression by modulating the expression of tumor suppressor genes and oncogenes. Hence, miRNA-based transcriptional regulation emerging as a highly efficacious individualized therapeutic option for curative cancer therapy [178]. In the past few years, several miRNAs-based delivery systems were investigated; however, the short half-life, degradation by nucleases, very low endosomal and/or lysosomal degradation, broad functionality, and off-target effects restrict their clinical translation. To mitigate these limitations, nanotechnology-based miRNA delivery systems were developed for the specific targeted delivery of miRNAs/anti-miRNAs using many miRNA mimics. For instance, in the past few decades, different nanocarriers, such as lipid-based nanostructures, polymer-based nanomaterials, polymeric micelles, inorganic nanomaterials, dendrimers, and bioinspired nanovehicles, were employed for miRNA-targeted cell-specific delivery [179]. Among them, MRX34 is the first miRNA-based cancer nanotherapeutics liposomal formulation of tumor suppressor miRNA (miR-34) entered into clinical trials. MRX34 manifested highly promising results in phase 1 and phase 2 clinical trials in patients with hepatocellular carcinoma, acral melanoma, and renal cell carcinoma [179]. Presently, five more miRNA-based cancer nanotherapeutics are in clinical trials and entered either phase I or phase II stage [180]. Over the last few years, a combination approach combining the codelivery of miRNA, along with small molecule anticancer drugs, has witnessed a tremendous therapeutic outcome in cancer nanotherapeutics. In addition, the (siRNA)-mediated gene silencing has acquired much attention due to their potential to silence target gene expression both in vitro and in vivo [181]. In MDR cancer therapy, siRNA-based gene silencing has been used to downregulate MDR-related proteins such as MDR-1, MDP1 and BCL2 [182,183]. However, transport of siRNA to a target cell is challenging. The prime constraint of in vivo siRNA delivery is its inadequacy to readily enter a cell due to its high anionic (negative) charge, instability, and vulnerability to degradation in serum. NPs can overcome these limitations by fabricating with siRNA thus protecting it from serum degradation and elimination from the body. Indeed several nanoformulations, such as liposomes, lipid polymers, and dendrimers, have been developed over the last decade to act as highly effective siRNA delivery vehicles [184].

Bringing together, several studies employing combinational therapy by codelivering antitumor miRNAs/siRNAs with chemo drugs synergistically improved the disease outcome with the reduction of cancer drug resistance. These studies manifest that this approach would provide a future research direction and various hopeful avenues for cancer therapies.

3.4.7 Nanomaterials for early detection and advancing pancreatic cancer imaging for pancreatic cancer

At present, the initial screening paradigm for the early detection of pancreatic cancer includes ultrasonography (EUS) and/or magnetic resonance imaging (MRI) cholangio-pancretography (MRCP) [185,186]. However certain difficulty associated with current imaging-based screening is that it can only detect cystic tumors of a large size at preinvasive stage with standard radiological methods due to their high contrast compared to the normal pancreas and excluding the smaller (<1 cm) metastatic tumor deposits in the liver and peritoneal cavity [187]. Further, after recognition of benign lesions, subsequent invasive assessment of tissue biopsies is still required to confirm diagnosis [188]. For the refinement of detection limit of CT and MRI imaging, a large number of small organic contrast agents have been delivered to the patient to enhance the imaging signal; however, they have some constraints such as nonspecific targeting and rapid renal clearance. To alleviate this, the use of NPs can assist easy incorporation of contrast agents, subsequently increasing their sensitivity and improving biodistribution. For instance, several inorganic nanocarriers such as gold NPs and superparamagnetic iron oxide NPs have been explored as potential contrast agents for improving cancer imaging [189,190].

Nano-diagnostic platforms have renovated the cancer diagnostics discipline by developing faster, more accurate, cost-effective, and reliable biomarker detection systems [191–193]. Additionally, nanocarriers such as gold NPs, magnetic particles, quantum dots, and carbon nanotubes can incorporate several electrochemical immunosensors, thereby improving sensitivity of electrochemical tumor biomarkers detection [192,193]. For example, microfluidic biochips with highly luminescent quantum dots have shown potential as a flexible multicolor and multiplexed bioassay [194]. In summary, nanodiagnostics platforms have already been established as a powerful tool for cancer detection, prevention, and diagnosis by providing additional sensitivity, specificity early cancer biomarkers detection.

3.5 Conclusion

So far nanotechnology-based drug delivery systems have revamped pancreatic cancer therapy in several aspects and revolutionized the treatment standard. NPs accomplish a huge impact on selective recognition of cancer cells, targeted drug delivery, and overcoming restrictions associated with conventional chemotherapies. However, MDR still persists as a major summon for treating pancreatic cancers. Despite the fact that nanotechnology has made promising improvements in overcoming MDR, the following complications need to be further investigated and addressed, including the exact mechanisms underlying active delivery of functionalized nanocarriers, comprehensive knowledge of the selective pressure in the TME, and understanding the leaky vasculature; the exact pH limits in endosomes and lysosomes as well as in the extracellular environment; the harmful effects of PEGylation and ways to surmount them; and the transport kinetics of nanocarriers and aspects that can improve their transport within the tumor stroma. In addition, deep understanding of the fate of NPs in drug resistant-tumor cells, their pharmacokinetics and assessment of ideal dosage regimen of different anticancer drugs, or/and siRNA need to be optimized. Thus, employment of nanotechnology for triumphing MDR becomes more complicated and not attained the desired progress. To address this, researchers need to consider the complexity of synthesizing the NPs and their competency to combat MDR drug delivery system. In addition, over the past decades, phytochemical-based treatment regimens incorporated with nanocarrier delivery systems have gained striking research attention because of their higher safety threshold. Besides, several naturally occurring bioactive material, well known to combat multi drug resistance, are not yet explored in nanoparticulate system, which need to be investigated. In addition, late-stage detection of pancreatic cancer restricts treatment options and accounts for a dismal 5-year survival rate. Thus research using nanotechnology for the early diagnosis and progression of pancreatic cancer are urgently required. Future work must focus on using NPs for biomarkers harvesting to discover early detection biomarkers in pancreatic cancer for its early detection strategies and to decrease the death rate.

References

[1] WHO 2020. Available from: https://www.who.int/news-room/fact-sheets/detail/cancer.

[2] Grant TJ, Hua K, Singh A. Molecular pathogenesis of pancreatic cancer. Prog Mol Biol Transl Sci 2016;144:241−75.

[3] Sung H, Ferlay J, Siegel RL, Laversanne M, Soerjomataram I, Jemal A, et al. Global cancer statistics 2020: GLOBOCAN estimates of incidence and mortality worldwide for 36 cancers in 185 countries. CA Cancer J Clin 2021;71:209−49.

[4] Wolfgang CL, Herman JM, Laheru DA, Klein AP, Erdek MA, Fishman EK, et al. Recent progress in pancreatic cancer. CA Cancer J Clin 2013;63:318−48.

[5] Hausmann S, Kong B, Michalski C, Erkan M, Friess H. The role of inflammation in pancreatic cancer. Adv Exp Med Biol 2014;816:129−51.

[6] Principe DR, Underwood PW, Korc M, Trevino JG, Munshi HG, Rana A. The current treatment paradigm for pancreatic ductal adenocarcinoma and barriers to therapeutic efficacy. Front Oncol 2021;11:688377.

[7] Li D, Xie K, Wolff R, Abbruzzese JL. Pancreatic cancer. Lancet 2004;363:1049−57.

[8] Zhang L, Sanagapalli S, Stoita A. Challenges in diagnosis of pancreatic cancer. World J Gastroenterol 2018;24:2047−60.

[9] Kamisawa T, Wood LD, Itoi T, Takaori K. Pancreatic cancer. Lancet 2016;388:73−85.

[10] Hezel AF, Kimmelman AC, Stanger BZ, Bardeesy N, Depinho RA. Genetics and biology of pancreatic ductal adenocarcinoma. Genes Dev 2006;20:1218−49.

[11] Bardeesy N, Depinho RA. Pancreatic cancer biology and genetics. Nat Rev Cancer 2002;2:897−909.

[12] Cancer Genome Atlas Research Network. Integrated genomic characterization of pancreatic ductal adenocarcinoma. Cancer Cell 2017;32:185−203.e13.

[13] Mccleary-Wheeler AL, Mcwilliams R, Fernandez-Zapico ME. Aberrant signaling pathways in pancreatic cancer: a two compartment view. Mol Carcinog 2012;51:25−39.

[14] Jain A, Bhardwaj V. Therapeutic resistance in pancreatic ductal adenocarcinoma: current challenges and future opportunities. World J Gastroenterol 2021;27:6527−50.

[15] Neoptolemos JP, Kleeff J, Michl P, Costello E, Greenhalf W, Palmer DH. Therapeutic developments in pancreatic cancer: current and future perspectives. Nat Rev Gastroenterol Hepatol 2018;15:333−48.

[16] Roth MT, Cardin DB, Berlin JD. Recent advances in the treatment of pancreatic cancer. F1000Res 2020;9:F1000.

[17] Hartwig W, Werner J, Jäger D, Debus J, Büchler MW. Improvement of surgical results for pancreatic cancer. Lancet Oncol 2013;14:e476−85.

[18] Patel SH, Katz MHG, Ahmad SA. The landmark series: preoperative therapy for pancreatic cancer. Ann Surg Oncol 2021;28:4104−29.

[19] Heckler M, Mihaljevic AL, Winter D, Zhou Z, Liu B, Tanaka M, et al. *Escherichia coli* bacterobilia is associated with severe postoperative pancreatic fistula after pancreaticoduodenectomy. J Gastrointest Surg 2020;24:1802−8.

[20] Rombouts SJ, Vogel JA, Van Santvoort HC, Van Lienden KP, Van Hillegersberg R, Busch OR, et al. Systematic review of innovative ablative therapies for the treatment of locally advanced pancreatic cancer. Br J Surg 2015;102:182−93.

[21] Honeywell RJ, Ruiz Van Haperen VW, Veerman G, Smid K, Peters GJ. Inhibition of thymidylate synthase by 2',2'-difluoro-2'-deoxycytidine (Gemcitabine) and its metabolite 2',2'-difluoro-2'-deoxyuridine. Int J Biochem Cell Biol 2015;60:73−81.

[22] Cullis J, Siolas D, Avanzi A, Barui S, Maitra A, Bar-Sagi D. Macropinocytosis of Nab-paclitaxel drives macrophage activation in pancreatic cancer. Cancer Immunol Res 2017;5:182−90.

[23] Conroy T, Hammel P, Hebbar M, Ben Abdelghani M, Wei AC, Raoul JL, et al. FOLFIRINOX or gemcitabine as adjuvant therapy for pancreatic cancer. N Engl J Med 2018;379:2395−406.

[24] Longley DB, Harkin DP, Johnston PG. 5-fluorouracil: mechanisms of action and clinical strategies. Nat Rev Cancer 2003;3:330−8.

[25] Glazer RI, Lloyd LS. Association of cell lethality with incorporation of 5-fluorouracil and 5-fluorouridine into nuclear RNA in human colon carcinoma cells in culture. Mol Pharmacol 1982;21:468—73.

[26] Kufe DW, Major PP. 5-Fluorouracil incorporation into human breast carcinoma RNA correlates with cytotoxicity. J Biol Chem 1981;256:9802—5.

[27] Efferth T, Fu YJ, Zu YG, Schwarz G, Konkimalla VS, Wink M. Molecular target-guided tumor therapy with natural products derived from traditional Chinese medicine. Curr Med Chem 2007;14:2024—32.

[28] Thota R, Pauff JM, Berlin JD. Treatment of metastatic pancreatic adenocarcinoma: a review. Oncol (Williston Park) 2014;28:70—4.

[29] De Bruijn P, Verweij J, Loos WJ, Nooter K, Stoter G, Sparreboom A. Determination of irinotecan (CPT-11) and its active metabolite SN-38 in human plasma by reversed-phase high-performance liquid chromatography with fluorescence detection. J Chromatogr B Biomed Sci Appl 1997;698:277—85.

[30] Gerrits CJ, De Jonge MJ, Schellens JH, Stoter G, Verweij J. Topoisomerase I inhibitors: the relevance of prolonged exposure for present clinical development. Br J Cancer 1997;76:952—62.

[31] Woynarowski JM, Chapman WG, Napier C, Herzig MC, Juniewicz P. Sequence- and region-specificity of oxaliplatin adducts in naked and cellular DNA. Mol Pharmacol 1998;54:770—7.

[32] Di Francesco AM, Ruggiero A, Riccardi R. Cellular and molecular aspects of drugs of the future: oxaliplatin. Cell Mol Life Sci 2002;59:1914—27.

[33] Garrido-Laguna I, Hidalgo M. Pancreatic cancer: from state-of-the-art treatments to promising novel therapies. Nat Rev Clin Oncol 2015;12:319—34.

[34] Strimpakos A, Saif MW, Syrigos KN. Pancreatic cancer: from molecular pathogenesis to targeted therapy. Cancer Metastasis Rev 2008;27:495—522.

[35] Hosein AN, Dougan SK, Aguirre AJ, Maitra A. Translational advances in pancreatic ductal adenocarcinoma therapy. Nat Cancer 2022;3:272—86.

[36] FDA 2016. Available from:https://www.fda.gov/drugs/resources-information-approved-drugs/erlotinib-tarceva.

[37] Moore MJ, Goldstein D, Hamm J, Figer A, Hecht JR, Gallinger S, et al. Erlotinib plus gemcitabine compared with gemcitabine alone in patients with advanced pancreatic cancer: a phase III trial of the National Cancer Institute of Canada Clinical Trials Group. J Clin Oncol 2007;25:1960—6.

[38] Li J, Kleeff J, Giese N, Büchler MW, Korc M, Friess H. Gefitinib ('Iressa', ZD1839), a selective epidermal growth factor receptor tyrosine kinase inhibitor, inhibits pancreatic cancer cell growth, invasion, and colony formation. Int J Oncol 2004;25:203—10.

[39] Carneiro BA, Brand RE, Fine E, Knop RH, Khandekar JD, Uhlig W, et al. Phase I trial of fixed dose rate infusion gemcitabine with gefitinib in patients with pancreatic carcinoma. Cancer Invest 2007;25:366—71.

[40] Buchsbaum DJ, Bonner JA, Grizzle WE, Stackhouse MA, Carpenter M, Hicklin DJ, et al. Treatment of pancreatic cancer xenografts with Erbitux (IMC-C225) anti-EGFR antibody, gemcitabine, and radiation. Int J Radiat Oncol Biol Phys 2002;54:1180—93.

[41] Huang ZQ, Buchsbaum DJ, Raisch KP, Bonner JA, Bland KI, Vickers SM. Differential responses by pancreatic carcinoma cell lines to prolonged exposure to Erbitux (IMC-C225) anti-EGFR antibody. J Surg Res 2003;111:274—83.

[42] Graeven U, Kremer B, Südhoff T, Killing B, Rojo F, Weber D, et al. Phase I study of the humanised anti-EGFR monoclonal antibody matuzumab (EMD 72000) combined with gemcitabine in advanced pancreatic cancer. Br J Cancer 2006;94:1293—9.

[43] Solorzano CC, Baker CH, Bruns CJ, Killion JJ, Ellis LM, Wood J, et al. Inhibition of growth and metastasis of human pancreatic cancer growing in nude mice by PTK 787/ZK222584, an inhibitor of the vascular endothelial growth factor receptor tyrosine kinases. Cancer Biother Radiopharm 2001;16:359—70.

[44] Weisz B, Giehl K, Gana-Weisz M, Egozi Y, Ben-Baruch G, Marciano D, et al. A new functional Ras antagonist inhibits human pancreatic tumor growth in nude mice. Oncogene 1999;18:2579—88.

[45] Laheru D, Shah P, Rajeshkumar NV, Mcallister F, Taylor G, Goldsweig H, et al. Integrated preclinical and clinical development of S-trans, trans-Farnesylthiosalicylic Acid (FTS, Salirasib) in pancreatic cancer. Invest N Drugs 2012;30:2391–9.

[46] Van Cutsem E, Van De Velde H, Karasek P, Oettle H, Vervenne WL, Szawlowski A, et al. Phase III trial of gemcitabine plus tipifarnib compared with gemcitabine plus placebo in advanced pancreatic cancer. J Clin Oncol 2004;22:1430–8.

[47] Donadelli M, Costanzo C, Faggioli L, Scupoli MT, Moore PS, Bassi C, et al. Trichostatin A, an inhibitor of histone deacetylases, strongly suppresses growth of pancreatic adenocarcinoma cells. Mol Carcinog 2003;38:59–69.

[48] Piacentini P, Donadelli M, Costanzo C, Moore PS, Palmieri M, Scarpa A. Trichostatin A enhances the response of chemotherapeutic agents in inhibiting pancreatic cancer cell proliferation. Virchows Arch 2006;448:797–804.

[49] Arnold NB, Arkus N, Gunn J, Korc M. The histone deacetylase inhibitor suberoylanilide hydroxamic acid induces growth inhibition and enhances gemcitabine-induced cell death in pancreatic cancer. Clin Cancer Res 2007;13:18–26.

[50] Christenson ES, Jaffee E, Azad NS. Current and emerging therapies for patients with advanced pancreatic ductal adenocarcinoma: a bright future. Lancet Oncol 2020;21:e135–45.

[51] Shindo K, Yu J, Suenaga M, Fesharakizadeh S, Cho C, Macgregor-Das A, et al. Deleterious germline mutations in patients with apparently sporadic pancreatic adenocarcinoma. J Clin Oncol 2017;35:3382–90.

[52] Gout J, Perkhofer L, Morawe M, Arnold F, Ihle M, Biber S, et al. Synergistic targeting and resistance to PARP inhibition in DNA damage repair-deficient pancreatic cancer. Gut 2021;70:743–60.

[53] Xia J, Chen C, Chen Z, Miele L, Sarkar FH, Wang Z. Targeting pancreatic cancer stem cells for cancer therapy. Biochim Biophys Acta 2012;1826:385–99.

[54] Takebe N, Harris PJ, Warren RQ, Ivy SP. Targeting cancer stem cells by inhibiting Wnt, Notch, and Hedgehog pathways. Nat Rev Clin Oncol 2011;8:97–106.

[55] Ng JM, Curran T. The Hedgehog's tale: developing strategies for targeting cancer. Nat Rev Cancer 2011;11:493–501.

[56] Ruiz I Altaba A, Sánchez P, Dahmane N. Gli and hedgehog in cancer: tumours, embryos and stem cells. Nat Rev Cancer 2002;2:361–72.

[57] Li C, Heidt DG, Dalerba P, Burant CF, Zhang L, Adsay V, et al. Identification of pancreatic cancer stem cells. Cancer Res 2007;67:1030–7.

[58] Jimeno A, Feldmann G, Suárez-Gauthier A, Rasheed Z, Solomon A, Zou GM, et al. A direct pancreatic cancer xenograft model as a platform for cancer stem cell therapeutic development. Mol Cancer Ther 2009;8:310–14.

[59] Yao J, An Y, Wie JS, Ji ZL, Lu ZP, Wu JL, et al. Cyclopamine reverts acquired chemoresistance and down-regulates cancer stem cell markers in pancreatic cancer cell lines. Swiss Med Wkly 2011;141:w13208.

[60] Malanchi I, Peinado H, Kassen D, Hussenet T, Metzger D, Chambon P, et al. Cutaneous cancer stem cell maintenance is dependent on beta-catenin signalling. Nature 2008;452:650–3.

[61] Nalls D, Tang SN, Rodova M, Srivastava RK, Shankar S. Targeting epigenetic regulation of miR-34a for treatment of pancreatic cancer by inhibition of pancreatic cancer stem cells. PLoS One 2011;6:e24099.

[62] Dufort CC, Delgiorno KE, Hingorani SR. Mounting pressure in the microenvironment: fluids, solids, and cells in pancreatic ductal adenocarcinoma. Gastroenterology 2016;150:1545–57 e2.

[63] Laheru D, Jaffee EM. Immunotherapy for pancreatic cancer - science driving clinical progress. Nat Rev Cancer 2005;5:459–67.

[64] Ye J, Wu D, Wu P, Chen Z, Huang J. The cancer stem cell niche: cross talk between cancer stem cells and their microenvironment. Tumour Biol 2014;35:3945–51.

[65] Vonderheide RH, Bear AS. Tumor-derived myeloid cell chemoattractants and T cell exclusion in pancreatic cancer. Front Immunol 2020;11:605619.

[66] Hosein AN, Brekken RA, Maitra A. Pancreatic cancer stroma: an update on therapeutic targeting strategies. Nat Rev Gastroenterol Hepatol 2020;17:487–505.

[67] Aoyagi Y, Oda T, Kinoshita T, Nakahashi C, Hasebe T, Ohkohchi N, et al. Overexpression of TGF-beta by infiltrated granulocytes correlates with the expression of collagen mRNA in pancreatic cancer. Br J Cancer 2004;91:1316−26.

[68] Löhr M, Schmidt C, Ringel J, Kluth M, Müller P, Nizze H, et al. Transforming growth factor-beta1 induces desmoplasia in an experimental model of human pancreatic carcinoma. Cancer Res 2001;61:550−5.

[69] Grauel AL, Nguyen B, Ruddy D, Laszewski T, Schwartz S, Chang J, et al. TGFβ-blockade uncovers stromal plasticity in tumors by revealing the existence of a subset of interferon-licensed fibroblasts. Nat Commun 2020;11:6315.

[70] NIH 2020a. Available from: https://clinicaltrials.gov/ct2/show/NCT04390763.

[71] NIH 2018. Available from: https://clinicaltrials.gov/ct2/show/NCT03520790.

[72] Twyman-Saint Victor C, Rech AJ, Maity A, Rengan R, Pauken KE, Stelekati E, et al. Radiation and dual checkpoint blockade activate non-redundant immune mechanisms in cancer. Nature 2015;520:373−7.

[73] Royal RE, Levy C, Turner K, Mathur A, Hughes M, Kammula US, et al. Phase 2 trial of single agent Ipilimumab (anti-CTLA-4) for locally advanced or metastatic pancreatic adenocarcinoma. J Immunother 2010;33:828−33.

[74] Wainberg ZA, Hochster HS, Kim EJ, George B, Kaylan A, Chiorean EG, et al. Open-label, phase I study of nivolumab combined with nab-paclitaxel plus gemcitabine in advanced pancreatic cancer. Clin Cancer Res 2020;26:4814−22.

[75] Schizas D, Charalampakis N, Kole C, Economopoulou P, Koustas E, Gkotsis E, et al. Immunotherapy for pancreatic cancer: a 2020 update. Cancer Treat Rev 2020;86:102016.

[76] Nywening TM, Belt BA, Cullinan DR, Panni RZ, Han BJ, Sanford DE, et al. Targeting both tumour-associated CXCR2(+) neutrophils and CCR2(+) macrophages disrupts myeloid recruitment and improves chemotherapeutic responses in pancreatic ductal adenocarcinoma. Gut 2018;67:1112−23.

[77] Steele CW, Karim SA, Leach JDG, Bailey P, Upstill-Goddard R, Rishi L, et al. CXCR2 inhibition profoundly suppresses metastases and augments immunotherapy in pancreatic ductal adenocarcinoma. Cancer Cell 2016;29:832−45.

[78] Stromnes IM, Brockenbrough JS, Izeradjene K, Carlson MA, Cuevas C, Simmons RM, et al. Targeted depletion of an MDSC subset unmasks pancreatic ductal adenocarcinoma to adaptive immunity. Gut 2014;63:1769−81.

[79] Chao T, Furth EE, Vonderheide RH. CXCR2-dependent accumulation of tumor-associated neutrophils regulates T-cell immunity in pancreatic ductal adenocarcinoma. Cancer Immunol Res 2016;4:968−82.

[80] Nywening TM, Wang-Gillam A, Sanford DE, Belt BA, Panni RZ, Cusworth BM, et al. Targeting tumour-associated macrophages with CCR2 inhibition in combination with FOLFIRINOX in patients with borderline resectable and locally advanced pancreatic cancer: a single-centre, open-label, dose-finding, non-randomised, phase 1b trial. Lancet Oncol 2016;17:651−62.

[81] Beatty GL, Chiorean EG, Fishman MP, Saboury B, Teitelbaum UR, Sun W, et al. CD40 agonists alter tumor stroma and show efficacy against pancreatic carcinoma in mice and humans. Science 2011;331:1612−16.

[82] Das S, Shapiro B, Vucic EA, Vogt S, Bar-Sagi D. Tumor cell-derived IL1β promotes desmoplasia and immune suppression in pancreatic cancer. Cancer Res 2020;80:1088−101.

[83] NIH 2020b. Available from: https://clinicaltrials.gov/ct2/show/NCT04581343.

[84] Gottesman MM, Fojo T, Bates SE. Multidrug resistance in cancer: role of ATP-dependent transporters. Nat Rev Cancer 2002;2:48−58.

[85] Long J, Zhang Y, Yu X, Yang J, Lebrun DG, Chen C, et al. Overcoming drug resistance in pancreatic cancer. Expert Opin Ther Targets 2011;15:817−28.

[86] Ohhashi S, Ohuchida K, Mizumoto K, Fujita H, Egami T, Yu J, et al. Down-regulation of deoxycytidine kinase enhances acquired resistance to gemcitabine in pancreatic cancer. Anticancer Res 2008;28:2205−12.

[87] Rajabpour A, Rajaei F, Teimoori-Toolabi L. Molecular alterations contributing to pancreatic cancer chemoresistance. Pancreatology 2017;17:310−20.

[88] Sheikh R, Walsh N, Clynes M, O'connor R, Mcdermott R. Challenges of drug resistance in the management of pancreatic cancer. Expert Rev Anticancer Ther 2010;10:1647—61.

[89] Nakahira S, Nakamori S, Tsujie M, Takahashi Y, Okami J, Yoshioka S, et al. Involvement of ribonucleotide reductase M1 subunit overexpression in gemcitabine resistance of human pancreatic cancer. Int J Cancer 2007;120:1355—63.

[90] Bergman AM, Eijk PP, Ruiz Van Haperen VW, Smid K, Veerman G, Hubeek I, et al. In vivo induction of resistance to gemcitabine results in increased expression of ribonucleotide reductase subunit M1 as the major determinant. Cancer Res 2005;65:9510—16.

[91] Voutsadakis IA. Molecular predictors of gemcitabine response in pancreatic cancer. World J Gastrointest Oncol 2011;3:153—64.

[92] Skrypek N, Duchêne B, Hebbar M, Leteurtre E, Van Seuningen I, Jonckheere N. The MUC4 mucin mediates gemcitabine resistance of human pancreatic cancer cells via the Concentrative Nucleoside Transporter family. Oncogene 2013;32:1714—23.

[93] Onishi H, Katano M. Hedgehog signaling pathway as a new therapeutic target in pancreatic cancer. World J Gastroenterol 2014;20:2335—42.

[94] Ng SSW, Tsao MS, Chow S, Hedley DW. Inhibition of phosphatidylinositide 3-kinase enhances gemcitabine-induced apoptosis in human pancreatic cancer cells. Cancer Res 2000;60:5451—5.

[95] Hou J, Wang L. FKBP5 as a selection biomarker for gemcitabine and Akt inhibitors in treatment of pancreatic cancer. PLoS One 2012;7:e36252.

[96] Chen D, Niu M, Jiao X, Zhang K, Liang J, Zhang D. Inhibition of AKT2 enhances sensitivity to gemcitabine via regulating PUMA and NF-κB signaling pathway in human pancreatic ductal adenocarcinoma. Int J Mol Sci 2012;13:1186—208.

[97] Yao J, Qian C. Inhibition of Notch3 enhances sensitivity to gemcitabine in pancreatic cancer through an inactivation of PI3K/Akt-dependent pathway. Med Oncol 2010;27:1017—22.

[98] Wey JS, Gray MJ, Fan F, Belcheva A, Mccarty MF, Stoeltzing O, et al. Overexpression of neuropilin-1 promotes constitutive MAPK signalling and chemoresistance in pancreatic cancer cells. Br J Cancer 2005;93:233—41.

[99] Wang S, Li Y, Xing C, Ding C, Zhang H, Chen L, et al. Tumor microenvironment in chemoresistance, metastasis and immunotherapy of pancreatic cancer. Am J Cancer Res 2020;10:1937—53.

[100] Bristow RG, Hill RP. Hypoxia and metabolism. Hypoxia, DNA repair and genetic instability. Nat Rev Cancer 2008;8:180—92.

[101] Sermeus A, Genin M, Maincent A, Fransolet M, Notte A, Leclere L, et al. Hypoxia-induced modulation of apoptosis and BCL-2 family proteins in different cancer cell types. PLoS One 2012;7: e47519.

[102] Wykoff CC, Beasley NJ, Watson PH, Turner KJ, Pastorek J, Sibtain A, et al. Hypoxia-inducible expression of tumor-associated carbonic anhydrases. Cancer Res 2000;60:7075—83.

[103] Kondoh H. Cellular life span and the Warburg effect. Exp Cell Res 2008;314:1923—8.

[104] Maftouh M, Avan A, Sciarrillo R, Granchi C, Leon LG, Rani R, et al. Synergistic interaction of novel lactate dehydrogenase inhibitors with gemcitabine against pancreatic cancer cells in hypoxia. Br J Cancer 2014;110:172—82.

[105] Vonlaufen A, Phillips PA, Xu Z, Goldstein D, Pirola RC, Wilson JS, et al. Pancreatic stellate cells and pancreatic cancer cells: an unholy alliance. Cancer Res 2008;68:7707—10.

[106] Cao F, Li J, Sun H, Liu S, Cui Y, Li F. HES 1 is essential for chemoresistance induced by stellate cells and is associated with poor prognosis in pancreatic cancer. Oncol Rep 2015;33:1883—9.

[107] Liu Y, Li F, Gao F, Xing L, Qin P, Liang X, et al. Periostin promotes the chemotherapy resistance to gemcitabine in pancreatic cancer. Tumour Biol 2016;37:15283—91.

[108] Zhang H, Wu H, Guan J, Wang L, Ren X, Shi X, et al. Paracrine SDF-1α signaling mediates the effects of PSCs on GEM chemoresistance through an IL-6 autocrine loop in pancreatic cancer cells. Oncotarget 2015;6:3085—97.

[109] Mantoni TS, Lunardi S, Al-Assar O, Masamune A, Brunner TB. Pancreatic stellate cells radioprotect pancreatic cancer cells through β1–integrin signaling. Cancer Res 2011;71:3453—8.

[110] Amit M, Gil Z. Macrophages increase the resistance of pancreatic adenocarcinoma cells to gemcitabine by upregulating cytidine deaminase. Oncoimmunology 2013;2:e27231.

[111] Dauer P, Nomura A, Saluja A, Banerjee S. Microenvironment in determining chemo-resistance in pancreatic cancer: neighborhood matters. Pancreatology 2017;17:7–12.

[112] Hermann PC, Huber SL, Herrler T, Aicher A, Ellwart JW, Guba M, et al. Distinct populations of cancer stem cells determine tumor growth and metastatic activity in human pancreatic cancer. Cell Stem Cell 2007;1:313–23.

[113] Lee CJ, Dosch J, Simeone DM. Pancreatic cancer stem cells. J Clin Oncol 2008;26:2806–12.

[114] Gonzalez DM, Medici D. Signaling mechanisms of the epithelial-mesenchymal transition. Sci Signal 2014;7:re8.

[115] Zhou P, Li B, Liu F, Zhang M, Wang Q, Liu Y, et al. The epithelial to mesenchymal transition (EMT) and cancer stem cells: implication for treatment resistance in pancreatic cancer. Mol Cancer 2017;16:52.

[116] Huanwen W, Zhiyong L, Xiaohua S, Xinyu R, Kai W, Tonghua L. Intrinsic chemoresistance to gemcitabine is associated with constitutive and laminin-induced phosphorylation of FAK in pancreatic cancer cell lines. Mol Cancer 2009;8:125.

[117] Shi X, Liu S, Kleeff J, Friess H, Büchler MW. Acquired resistance of pancreatic cancer cells towards 5-Fluorouracil and gemcitabine is associated with altered expression of apoptosis-regulating genes. Oncology 2002;62:354–62.

[118] Mori-Iwamoto S, Kuramitsu Y, Ryozawa S, Taba K, Fujimoto M, Okita K, et al. A proteomic profiling of gemcitabine resistance in pancreatic cancer cell lines. Mol Med Rep 2008;1:429–34.

[119] Duxbury MS, Ito H, Zinner MJ, Ashley SW, Whang EE. Inhibition of SRC tyrosine kinase impairs inherent and acquired gemcitabine resistance in human pancreatic adenocarcinoma cells. Clin Cancer Res 2004;10:2307–18.

[120] Mohapatra P, Singh P, Sahoo SK. Phytonanomedicine: a novel avenue to treat recurrent cancer by targeting cancer stem cells. Drug Discov Today 2020;25:1307–21.

[121] Muntimadugu E, Kommineni N, Khan W. Exploring the potential of nanotherapeutics in targeting tumor microenvironment for cancer therapy. Pharmacol Res 2017;126:109–22.

[122] Acharya S, Sahoo SK. PLGA nanoparticles containing various anticancer agents and tumour delivery by EPR effect. Adv Drug Deliv Rev 2011;63:170–83.

[123] Bobo D, Robinson KJ, Islam J, Thurecht KJ, Corrie SR. Nanoparticle-based medicines: a review of FDA-approved materials and clinical trials to date. Pharm Res 2016;33:2373–87.

[124] Dilnawaz F, Acharya S, Sahoo SK. Recent trends of nanomedicinal approaches in clinics. Int J Pharm 2018;538:263–78.

[125] Da Silva CG, Peters GJ, Ossendorp F, Cruz LJ. The potential of multi-compound nanoparticles to bypass drug resistance in cancer. Cancer Chemother Pharmacol 2017;80:881–94.

[126] Su Z, Dong S, Zhao SC, Liu K, Tan Y, Jiang X, et al. Novel nanomedicines to overcome cancer multidrug resistance. Drug Resist Updat 2021;58:100777.

[127] Mohanty C, Das M, Sahoo SK. Emerging role of nanocarriers to increase the solubility and bioavailability of curcumin. Expert Opin Drug Deliv 2012;9:1347–64.

[128] Attia MF, Anton N, Wallyn J, Omran Z, Vandamme TF. An overview of active and passive targeting strategies to improve the nanocarriers efficiency to tumour sites. J Pharm Pharmacol 2019;71:1185–98.

[129] Bazak R, Houri M, El Achy S, Kamel S, Refaat T. Cancer active targeting by nanoparticles: a comprehensive review of literature. J Cancer Res Clin Oncol 2015;141:769–84.

[130] Sahoo SK, Parveen S, Panda JJ. The present and future of nanotechnology in human health care. Nanomedicine 2007;3:20–31.

[131] Sielaff CM, Mousa SA. Status and future directions in the management of pancreatic cancer: potential impact of nanotechnology. J Cancer Res Clin Oncol 2018;144:1205–17.

[132] Blair HA, Deeks ED. Albumin-bound paclitaxel: a review in non-small cell lung cancer. Drugs 2015;75:2017–24.

[133] Viúdez A, Ramírez N, Hernández-García I, Carvalho FL, Vera R, Hidalgo M. Nab-paclitaxel: a flattering facelift. Crit Rev Oncol Hematol 2014;92:166–80.

[134] Zong Y, Wu J, Shen K. Nanoparticle albumin-bound paclitaxel as neoadjuvant chemotherapy of breast cancer: a systematic review and meta-analysis. Oncotarget 2017;8:17360–72.

[135] NIH 2015. Available from: https://www.cancer.gov/news-events/cancer-currents-blog/2015/iri-notecan-liposome-pancreatic.

[136] Vandana M, Sahoo SK. Long circulation and cytotoxicity of PEGylated gemcitabine and its potential for the treatment of pancreatic cancer. Biomaterials 2010;31:9340−56.

[137] Yao Y, Zhou Y, Liu L, Xu Y, Chen Q, Wang Y, et al. Nanoparticle-based drug delivery in cancer therapy and its role in overcoming drug resistance. Front Mol Biosci 2020;7:193.

[138] Zhang C, Zhou X, Zhang H, Han X, Li B, Yang R, et al. Recent progress of novel nanotechnology challenging the multidrug resistance of cancer. Front Pharmacol 2022;13:776895.

[139] Bukowski K, Kciuk M, Kontek R. Mechanisms of multidrug resistance in cancer chemotherapy. Int J Mol Sci 2020;21:3233.

[140] Choi CH. ABC transporters as multidrug resistance mechanisms and the development of chemosensitizers for their reversal. Cancer Cell Int 2005;5:30.

[141] Mello FVC, De Moraes GN, Maia RC, Kyeremateng J, Iram SH, Santos-Oliveira R. The effect of nanosystems on ATP-binding cassette transporters: understanding the influence of nanosystems on multidrug resistance protein-1 and P-glycoprotein. Int J Mol Sci 2020;21.

[142] Murakami M, Cabral H, Matsumoto Y, Wu S, Kano MR, Yamori T, et al. Improving drug potency and efficacy by nanocarrier-mediated subcellular targeting. Sci Transl Med 2011;3:64ra2.

[143] Crowley E, Mcdevitt CA, Callaghan R. Generating inhibitors of P-glycoprotein: where to, now? Methods Mol Biol 2010;596:405−32.

[144] Abdallah HM, Al-Abd AM, El-Dine RS, El-Halawany AM. P-glycoprotein inhibitors of natural origin as potential tumor chemo-sensitizers: a review. J Adv Res 2015;6:45−62.

[145] Soma CE, Dubernet C, Bentolila D, Benita S, Couvreur P. Reversion of multidrug resistance by co-encapsulation of doxorubicin and cyclosporin A in polyalkylcyanoacrylate nanoparticles. Biomaterials 2000;21:1−7.

[146] Wang H, Gao Z, Liu X, Agarwal P, Zhao S, Conroy DW, et al. Targeted production of reactive oxygen species in mitochondria to overcome cancer drug resistance. Nat Commun 2018;9:562.

[147] Patil YB, Swaminathan SK, Sadhukha T, Ma L, Panyam J. The use of nanoparticle-mediated targeted gene silencing and drug delivery to overcome tumor drug resistance. Biomaterials 2010;31:358−65.

[148] Bedi D, Gillespie JW, Petrenko VA. Selection of pancreatic cancer cell-binding landscape phages and their use in development of anticancer nanomedicines. Protein Eng Des Sel 2014;27:235−43.

[149] Bernier M, Catazaro J, Singh NS, Wnorowski A, Boguszewska-Czubara A, Jozwiak K, et al. GPR55 receptor antagonist decreases glycolytic activity in PANC-1 pancreatic cancer cell line and tumor xenografts. Int J Cancer 2017;141:2131−42.

[150] Washio I, Nakanishi T, Ishiguro N, Yamamura N, Tamai I. Impact of breast cancer resistance protein expression on the in vitro efficacy of anticancer drugs in pancreatic cancer cell lines. Drug Metab Dispos 2018;46:214−22.

[151] Huang HC, Mallidi S, Liu J, Chiang CT, Mai Z, Goldschmidt R, et al. Photodynamic therapy synergizes with irinotecan to overcome compensatory mechanisms and improve treatment outcomes in pancreatic cancer. Cancer Res 2016;76:1066−77.

[152] Wang YF, Liu L, Xue X, Liang XJ. Nanoparticle-based drug delivery systems: what can they really do in vivo? F1000Res 2017;6:681.

[153] Hinshaw DC, Shevde LA. The tumor microenvironment innately modulates cancer progression. Cancer Res 2019;79:4557−66.

[154] Sükei T, Palma E, Urbani L. Interplay between cellular and non-cellular components of the tumour microenvironment in hepatocellular carcinoma. Cancers (Basel) 2021;13:5586.

[155] Roy A, Li SD. Modifying the tumor microenvironment using nanoparticle therapeutics. Wiley Interdiscip Rev Nanomed Nanobiotechnol 2016;8:891−908.

[156] Peer D, Karp JM, Hong S, Farokhzad OC, Margalit R, Langer R. Nanocarriers as an emerging platform for cancer therapy. Nat Nanotechnol 2007;2:751−60.

[157] Gao W, Chan JM, Farokhzad OC. pH-Responsive nanoparticles for drug delivery. Mol Pharm 2010;7:1913−20.

[158] Mao J, Li Y, Wu T, Yuan C, Zeng B, Xu Y, et al. A simple dual-pH responsive prodrug-based polymeric micelles for drug delivery. ACS Appl Mater Interfaces 2016;8:17109−17.

[159] Xu M, Zhang CY, Wu J, Zhou H, Bai R, Shen Z, et al. PEG-detachable polymeric micelles self-assembled from amphiphilic copolymers for tumor-acidity-triggered drug delivery and controlled release. ACS Appl Mater Interfaces 2019;11:5701–13.

[160] Yuan YY, Mao CQ, Du XJ, Du JZ, Wang F, Wang J. Surface charge switchable nanoparticles based on zwitterionic polymer for enhanced drug delivery to tumor. Adv Mater 2012;24:5476–80.

[161] Huo Q, Zhu J, Niu Y, Shi H, Gong Y, Li Y, et al. pH-triggered surface charge-switchable polymer micelles for the co-delivery of paclitaxel/disulfiram and overcoming multidrug resistance in cancer. Int J Nanomed 2017;12:8631–47.

[162] Roh YJ, Kim JH, Kim IW, Na K, Park JM, Choi MG. Photodynamic therapy using photosensitizer-encapsulated polymeric nanoparticle to overcome ATP-binding cassette transporter subfamily G2 function in pancreatic cancer. Mol Cancer Ther 2017;16:1487–96.

[163] Rey S, Schito L, Wouters BG, Eliasof S, Kerbel RS. Targeting hypoxia-inducible factors for anti-angiogenic cancer therapy. Trends Cancer 2017;3:529–41.

[164] Chen WH, Lecaros RL, Tseng YC, Huang L, Hsu YC. Nanoparticle delivery of HIF1α siRNA combined with photodynamic therapy as a potential treatment strategy for head-and-neck cancer. Cancer Lett 2015;359:65–74.

[165] Kulkarni P, Haldar MK, Karandish F, Confeld M, Hossain R, Borowicz P, et al. Tissue-penetrating, hypoxia-responsive echogenic polymersomes for drug delivery to solid tumors. Chemistry 2018;24:12490–4.

[166] Ma DD, Yang WX. Engineered nanoparticles induce cell apoptosis: potential for cancer therapy. Oncotarget 2016;7:40882–903.

[167] Zielinska E, Zauszkiewicz-Pawlak A, Wojcik M, Inkielewicz-Stepniak I. Silver nanoparticles of different sizes induce a mixed type of programmed cell death in human pancreatic ductal adenocarcinoma. Oncotarget 2018;9:4675–97.

[168] Qian C, Wang Y, Chen Y, Zeng L, Zhang Q, Shuai X, et al. Suppression of pancreatic tumor growth by targeted arsenic delivery with anti-CD44v6 single chain antibody conjugated nanoparticles. Biomaterials 2013;34:6175–84.

[169] Yallapu MM, Ebeling MC, Khan S, Sundram V, Chauhan N, Gupta BK, et al. Novel curcumin-loaded magnetic nanoparticles for pancreatic cancer treatment. Mol Cancer Ther 2013;12:1471–80.

[170] Batlle E, Clevers H. Cancer stem cells revisited. Nat Med 2017;23:1124–34.

[171] Najafi M, Farhood B, Mortezaee K. Cancer stem cells (CSCs) in cancer progression and therapy. J Cell Physiol 2019;234:8381–95.

[172] Tang L, Mei Y, Shen Y, He S, Xiao Q, Yin Y, et al. Nanoparticle-mediated targeted drug delivery to remodel tumor microenvironment for cancer therapy. Int J Nanomed 2021;16:5811–29.

[173] Wang S, Ren W, Wang J, Jiang Z, Saeed M, Zhang L, et al. Black TiO$_2$-based nanoprobes for T$_1$-weighted MRI-guided photothermal therapy in CD133 high expressed pancreatic cancer stem-like cells. Biomater Sci 2018;6:2209–18.

[174] Huai Y, Zhang Y, Xiong X, Das S, Bhattacharya R, Mukherjee P. Gold Nanoparticles sensitize pancreatic cancer cells to gemcitabine. Cell Stress 2019;3:267–79.

[175] Khan S, Setua S, Kumari S, Dan N, Massey A, Hafeez BB, et al. Superparamagnetic iron oxide nanoparticles of curcumin enhance gemcitabine therapeutic response in pancreatic cancer. Biomaterials 2019;208:83–97.

[176] Marengo A, Forciniti S, Dando I, Dalla Pozza E, Stella B, Tsapis N, et al. Pancreatic cancer stem cell proliferation is strongly inhibited by diethyldithiocarbamate-copper complex loaded into hyaluronic acid decorated liposomes. Biochim Biophys Acta Gen Subj 2019;1863:61–72.

[177] Lin YX, Wang Y, Blake S, Yu M, Mei L, Wang H, et al. RNA nanotechnology-mediated cancer immunotherapy. Theranostics 2020;10:281–99.

[178] Shenouda SK, Alahari SK. MicroRNA function in cancer: oncogene or a tumor suppressor? Cancer Metastasis Rev 2009;28:369–78.

[179] Bukhari SNA. Emerging nanotherapeutic approaches to overcome drug resistance in cancers with update on clinical trials. Pharmaceutics 2022;14:866.

[180] He B, Zhao Z, Cai Q, Zhang Y, Zhang P, Shi S, et al. miRNA-based biomarkers, therapies, and resistance in Cancer. Int J Biol Sci 2020;16:2628—47.

[181] Rana TM. Illuminating the silence: understanding the structure and function of small RNAs. Nat Rev Mol Cell Biol 2007;8:23—36.

[182] Saad M, Garbuzenko OB, Minko T. Co-delivery of siRNA and an anticancer drug for treatment of multidrug-resistant cancer. Nanomedicine (Lond) 2008;3:761—76.

[183] Liu C, Zhao G, Liu J, Ma N, Chivukula P, Perelman L, et al. Novel biodegradable lipid nano complex for siRNA delivery significantly improving the chemosensitivity of human colon cancer stem cells to paclitaxel. J Control Release 2009;140:277—83.

[184] Mainini F, Eccles MR. Lipid and polymer-based nanoparticle siRNA delivery systems for cancer therapy. Molecules 2020;25:2692.

[185] Roberts TP. Physiologic measurements by contrast-enhanced MR imaging: expectations and limitations. J Magn Reson Imaging 1997;7:82—90.

[186] Kim BH, Lee N, Kim H, An K, Park YI, Choi Y, et al. Large-scale synthesis of uniform and extremely small-sized iron oxide nanoparticles for high-resolution T1 magnetic resonance imaging contrast agents. J Am Chem Soc 2011;133:12624—31.

[187] Erkan M, Hausmann S, Michalski CW, Fingerle AA, Dobritz M, Kleeff J, et al. The role of stroma in pancreatic cancer: diagnostic and therapeutic implications. Nat Rev Gastroenterol Hepatol 2012;9:454—67.

[188] Brand R. The diagnosis of pancreatic cancer. Cancer J 2001;7:287—97.

[189] Godin B, Tasciotti E, Liu X, Serda RE, Ferrari M. Multistage nanovectors: from concept to novel imaging contrast agents and therapeutics. Acc Chem Res 2011;44:979—89.

[190] Huang HC, Barua S, Sharma G, Dey SK, Rege K. Inorganic nanoparticles for cancer imaging and therapy. J Control Release 2011;155:344—57.

[191] Cao YC. Nanomaterials for biomedical applications. Nanomedicine (Lond) 2008;3:467—9.

[192] Chikkaveeraiah BV, Bhirde AA, Morgan NY, Eden HS, Chen X. Electrochemical immunosensors for detection of cancer protein biomarkers. ACS Nano 2012;6:6546—61.

[193] Malhotra R, Patel V, Chikkaveeraiah BV, Munge BS, Cheong SC, Zain RB, et al. Ultrasensitive detection of cancer biomarkers in the clinic by use of a nanostructured microfluidic array. Anal Chem 2012;84:6249—55.

[194] Hu M, Yan J, He Y, Lu H, Weng L, Song S, et al. Ultrasensitive, multiplexed detection of cancer biomarkers directly in serum by using a quantum dot-based microfluidic protein chip. ACS Nano 2010;4:488—94.

CHAPTER 4

Application of hydrogel-based drug delivery system for pancreatic cancer

Naomi Sanjana Sharath[1], Ranjita Misra[1] and Jyotirmoy Ghosh[2]
[1]Department of Biotechnology, School of Sciences, Jain University, Bangalore, Karnataka, India
[2]Molecular Biology Laboratory, Divison of Physiology, National Institute of Animal Nutrition and Physiology, Bangalore, Karnataka, India

4.1 Introduction

Cancer is one of the deadliest and the most life threatening disease in the world. Finding a potential cure for cancer is extremely challenging because of its aggressivity and its complex nature. This in turn leads to the accountancy of exceptionally high mortality. Cancer cells can transform themselves in such a way that they can adapt themselves to an extreme tumor environment and undergo various metabolic transformations [1]. According to the mortality data collected by the National Center for Health Statistics (the latest data as of 2020), it was estimated that more than 18.1 million cancer cases were detected globally and nearly 10 million cancer deaths occurred in 2020, which is one death in every 6 months.

Pancreatic cancer (PC) is ranked 12th in place globally [2]. India, being no exception to this type of cancer, had 11,655 cases in 2020, with Mizoram showing the highest number of cases. Genetic predisposition and modifiable risk factors contribute to the cause of pancreatic cancer. Some of the factors responsible for PC are smoking, alcohol consumption, obesity, diabetes mellitus (DM), and age, whereas hereditary factors include familial PC (FPC), Peutz-Jeghers syndrome, familial adenomatous polyposis (FAP), and familial atypical multiple mole melanoma (FAMMM) [3]. It is estimated globally that 20% of PC deaths are attributable to smoking, 9% to diabetes, and 6% to obesity [4]. PC will soon be the second most malignant cancer by 2030 [2]. Thus diagnosis of PC at an early stage is necessary. In this context, presently different diagnostic strategies are available, however, each one has its own drawbacks such as various difficult detection problems, localization of the primary tumors, obscure tumor margins, and so on. Typical current cancer diagnostic methods are computed tomography (CT), magnetic resonance imaging (MRI) and ultrasound analysis (US), and biomarkers such as carbohydrate antigen CA19−9 [5]. These approaches can generate good results. However, they have their own set of drawbacks. For instance, CT scans provide a good spatial resolution and attenuation between the tumor and the background with a detail

Recent Advances in Nanocarriers for Pancreatic Cancer Therapy
DOI: https://doi.org/10.1016/B978-0-443-19142-8.00011-5

of the anatomic coverage [6]. The PC tumor appears as an unclear mass compared to a normal pancreatic tissue image. Therefore an MRI scan has to be taken in order to obtain a clearer image that is the second scan required [7]. The biomarker CA19−9, on the other hand, is not an ideal biomarker because of its low specificity [8]. Therefore there is an urgent need to develop an advanced method of detection for PC.

On the other hand, current treatments that are used for cancer are Surgery, Radiotherapy (RT), Chemotherapy, and Immunotherapy [9]. Surgical resection can be a potential source of cancer treatment but, only a certain number of patients are eligible for surgery [7]. Radiotherapy or radiation therapy enables radiation to destroy the cancer cells, hence making them nonproliferative [10]. It is usually given along with chemotherapy (neoadjuvant treatment) in order to shrink or eliminate the tumor completely [10]. However, the drawbacks of RT can cause several side effects, which include nausea, diarrhoea, and loss of appetite, which in turn leads to weight loss and lower blood count, which can cause infections and fatigue. It is used mainly for patients with locally advanced PC (LAPC), which is a nonmetastasized PC [3]. Chemotherapy utilizes cytotoxic drugs to destroy cancer cells, it has many benefits such as relieving symptoms, reduction in tumor size, increasing survival time, and improving the patient's quality of life. However, chemotherapeutics is incapable of limiting the cytotoxicity of the tumor. Some of the chemotherapeutics cannot cross the in vivo biological barrier. And some of these drugs are poorly absorbed by the tumors, leading to poor bioavailability and sometimes generate a low response. Chemotherapy can also destroy some of the healthy cells, which can in turn cause a lot of side effects such as nausea, hair loss, infections, fatigue, sore mouth, anemia, anorexia, and induced risk of sepsis (the body's extreme response to an infection) [11]. Nausea and vomiting are the most feared side effects as they can lead to dehydration and loss of appetite, which can be potentially fatal for patients.

Various other drug delivery systems have been under investigation for years for controlled drug delivery and enhancing in vivo imaging potential of the diagnostic agents. For example, the nanoparticle drug delivery systems still remain a potential strategy for cancer treatment [12]. It is faster and more efficient in delivering the drugs to the target site than the traditional drug delivery systems. Despite the current progress in the nanoparticle drug delivery systems, there are many failures that occur in this process, as well owing to its limitations such as poor circulation, low specificity in targeting tumors, poor maintenance of the drug at the target site, and toxicity issues. Therefore the requirement for an efficient drug delivery system with controlled and sustained delivery can be made with hydrogels. Hydrogels are 3D networks of cross-linked polymer chains, which are insoluble in water. They have the capacity to absorb large amounts of water and swell up due to the hydrophilic groups present in them [13]. Hydrogels have various physical and chemical properties that have the advantage to open the doors to many biomedical application fields such as wound healing, tumor study, tissue engineering, and the food industry. They have good biocompatibility, biodegradability, and negligible cytotoxicity and release the specific drug in a controlled manner and have thus been used as an excellent source for cancer treatment [14]. There are many characteristics of an ideal hydrogel such as having the highest durability and proper stability in the environment where they swell up, highest biodegradability without formation of toxic species followed by proper degradation should have neutral pH after swelling up in water, colorless, odorless, and completely nontoxic. It is obviously impossible to achieve an ideal hydrogel, but if the production reaction variables are optimized in such a way that there is a proper balance between the properties is achieved, it can therefore give rise to efficient hydrogels. Hydrogels when provided with high mechanical strength can be used for different types of research. Hydrogels can be prepared in two main ways that are physical crosslinking and chemical crosslinking [15]. Physical crosslinking methods include temperature or pH-dependent methods of hydrogel preparation. pH-dependent hydrogels have the capacity to dynamically swell or contract depending upon the pH of the surroundings, whereas temperature-sensitive hydrogels become liquid at low temperatures and start gelling at body temperature. Chemical crosslinking methods include optical polymerization, bulk polymerization, and solution polymerization. Different hydrogels consisting of different materials that can be synthetic or natural and biodegradable can be used. Hydrogels can be used in various forms, such as injectable hydrogels which can be inserted using a catheter or a syringe, local hydrogel delivery modes, where the hydrogels transport some immune cells, and immune-related proteins, without altering their biological functions. Oral drug delivery of microgels is also another method that is used. In this chapter, we will discuss the PC in detail, also various types of polymers used for hydrogel preparation and its method of formulation. Moreover, the application of the hydrogels for PC will be discussed by citing different investigations.

4.2 Pancreatic cancer

Pancreatic cancer PC, is one of the deadliest cancers in the world. Briefly, the physiology, diagnosis, and current treatments that are available for PC are described below.

4.3 Physiology

PC typically arises in the ducts of the pancreas. The small, cellular changes in the DNA, which give rise to the uncontrolled growth of cell clusters, finally result in the formation of tumors that are mostly exocrine because they develop from the epithelial cells that form a lining in the pancreatic ducts [16]. These tumors can be of different types, such as adenocarcinoma, colloid carcinoma, acinar cell carcinoma, signet ring cell carcinoma, Pancreatic Ductal Adenocarcinoma (PDAC), and Pancreatoblastoma.

PDAC is the most malignant tumor, which evolves through noninvasive precursor lesions, and it tends to have an invasive growth pattern, which can invade regional blood vessels such as the portal vein [8]. Pancreatic neoplasia/PC consists of three distinct types of neoplasias, which are intraductal papillary mucinous neoplasms, mucinous cystic neoplasms, and pancreatic intraepithelial neoplasia [8,16]. The origin of adenocarcinomas commonly occurs on the head of the pancreas, where 90% of them are adenocarcinomas. These carcinomas rarely originate from the body or the tail of the organ. This results in delayed diagnosis, leading to a worse prognosis and abdominal pain that extrudes toward the patient's back [17]. The symptoms presented by the patients include jaundice (caused by the blocking of the bile duct), itchy skin, dark-colored urine, depression, nausea, vomiting, and light-colored stools. PC begins its progression by involving the activation and deactivation of tumor suppression genes and oncogenes followed by deregulation of the cell cycle.

4.3.1 Treatment

The treatment required for PC depends upon its stage. Typical treatments include surgery, chemotherapy, RT, and palliative care. Surgical resection being the most potential method amongst all the others, is used to treat PC. If the adenocarcinoma is located at the head of the pancreas, pancreaticoduodenectomy (Whipple's Procedure) is performed. Distal resection is performed if the carcinomas are located at the tail of the organ [18]. Chemotherapy is also a prevalent approach to destroy cancer cells with the use of cytotoxic drugs (Table 4.1). Recent techniques such as hormonal therapy

Table 4.1 Standard drugs used for pancreatic cancer (PC) treatment and the new upcoming drugs, which can be used to treat PC in the future based upon previous research work.

Sl. no.	Standard drugs used for pancreatic cancer treatment	Upcoming drugs to treat pancreatic cancer	Targeted areas using these drugs to treat PC
1.	Gemcitabine (Most used)	Tretinoin	Inhibited growth of Pancreatic cell line (PANC 1)
2.	Everolimus	Vincristine	Pancreatic adenocarcinoma
3.	5-Fluorouracil (5FU)	Demecolcine	Arrests the early mitosis in both pancreatic cell lines PANC-1 and BxPC-3 cell lines
4.	Paclitaxel	Finasteride	Shows high inhibition toward pancreatic cancer cell line BxPC-3
5.	Irinotican	Progesterone	Shows high inhibition towards pancreatic cancer cell line PANC 1

and immunotherapy are used as well. Gemcitabine (GEM), also known as the gold standard drug for chemotherapy, is the cornerstone treatment for PC [19]. It is the first-line drug used for LAPC and metastatic PC [18]. Some of the other drugs are paclitaxel and 5-fluorouracil (5FU). Sometimes, a combination of drugs is also used to increase efficacy in treatment. The combination of GEM plus nanoparticle-bound paclitaxel (nab-paclitaxel) has higher activity and stronger cytotoxicity than GEM alone [4]. The survival rate at 12 months was 18% for GEM patients and 2% for 5-FU patients and it showed better antitumor activity and enhanced activity in combination with GEM in murine models of PC [20]. According to a previous work done by Curvello et al., development of a 3D collagen nanocellulose hydrogel model mimics the extracellular matrix (ECM) of PDAC and promoted formation of tumor spheroids, which increased metabolic activity and enhanced matrix stiffness [21]. Chemotherapeutic drugs such as GEM and paclitaxel were tested on them, resulting in different cell responses, which also provided a specific platform for anticancer treatments [19]. Nanoparticles, on the other hand, have received a great amount of interest because of their high efficacy in drug delivery for cancer treatment, and they have been shown to increase the intracellular concentration of the drug in cancer cells [21]. Although they have been of great significance as a promising carrier for drug delivery, they have their own set of drawbacks such as poor oral bioavailability, improper circulation and stability, and inaccurate way of distribution of the drugs in tissues. According to work done by Wilhelm et al. (2016), a literature survey consisting of nanoparticle-based drug carrier systems from the past 10 years was collected and its efficiency in drug delivery administration was statistically analyzed. It showed that only 0.7% (median) of the nanoparticle dose that was administered was delivered to tumors [12].

4.4 Limitations

There are limitations to the current PC treatment strategies available. For example, unfortunately, only less than 20% of cancer patients eligible for it surgery, whose main goal is to resect the tumor [22]. If cancer has spread throughout the pancreas, it requires pancreatectomy, which can lead to side effects such as diabetes and indigestion [23]. The drugs available, such as Gemcitabine (GEM), being widely used for PDAC. However, it has some limitations such as poor solubility, poor membrane permeability, and unstable metabolism [24]. It can also cause serious side effects such as extreme fatigue, nausea, vomiting, and muscle ache and has a low survival rate. There is also drug resistance when GEM is used due to poor vascular perfusion in PC [25]. Other alternatives such as cancer cell–based vaccines can also be used to elicit a strong tumor-specific immune response. But so far, they have failed to provide long-term benefits for Pancreatic Ductal Adenocarcinoma (PDAC) patients [22,26]. Adjuvant chemotherapy, on the other hand, cannot be used for patients with poor health. These limitations have led to the requirement of new therapeutic approaches, clinical studies, and promising future gene editing techniques. Some mechanisms of PDAC still remain unknown, leading to the prevention of the development of therapies.

4.5 Hydrogels

There are several types of research conducted over the years to develop efficient ways of drug delivery. One of the most suitable and advantageous cargos for drug delivery, which was under investigation over the years, was found to be hydrogels. Hydrogels are 3D crosslinked networks consisting of polymeric chains that have the capacity to absorb water up to a thousand times their dry weight and begin to swell up, and it has the ability to absorb body fluids in a biological environment [13]. The term Hydrogel was first coined by Van n Bemmelen in 1984 [27]. The most important properties are their mesh size and molecular weight, which leads to infinity because of their 3D network structure [28]. Their hydrophilic structure renders them to have a large water-holding capacity and gel strength [13,28]. They have a porous structure that can be modulated depending on the degree of crosslinking in the gel matrix [29]. These pores have the ability to provide efficient incorporation of the drugs and have great self-healing capacity, hence considered an effective drug delivery strategy. They act as an outstanding drug loading carrier because of their protective and convenient efficiency. And also because of their soft structure, flexibility and stimuli sensitive nature, hydrogels have attracted great attention for various types of applications in the biomedical field. Hydrogels are eco-friendly, have good biocompatibility and biodegradability, and are cost-effective. Hydrogels loaded with drugs have the unique ability to regulate the drug levels in the blood, and hence are a great boon to the drug delivery system. Hydrogels are classified as anionic, cationic, or neutral in terms of charge. Depending upon the charge of the polymer that becomes the charge of the overall network in the hydrogel [13].

Hydrogels are formed from polymers. They can be natural, synthetic polymers, polymerizable synthetic monomers, and a combination of natural and synthetic polymers. These polymers can form copolymer hydrogels, terpolymers, and so on [15]. They are prepared by cross-linking methods, which can mainly be physical, chemical, or both (Fig. 4.1) [13]. They can be of various types: (1) Polysaccharides, (2) Biological polymers like DNA/nucleic acids, (3) Polyamides, (4) Inorganic and Organic Polyesters, and (5) Polyamides.

4.6 Types of polymers used in hydrogels
4.6.1 Natural polymers

Hydrogels consisting of natural polymers are called natural hydrogels. Natural polymers can be polysaccharides. Polysaccharides are used because of their unique biological properties. For example, Chitosan, a polysaccharide obtained from a substance

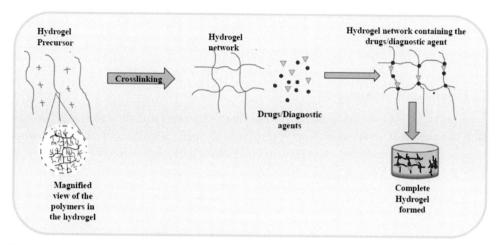

Figure 4.1 Preparation of a hydrogel.

called Chitin, which is obtained from the outer skeletons of crabs, shellfishes, and shrimps [14]. Chitosan has been used in hydrogels because of its excellent wound healing capacity, is biocompatible, biodegradable, and has remarkable antibacterial activity. Chitosan hydrogels have been synthesized through Schiff bases with other polysaccharides that are prefunctionalized, such as oxidized dextran and aldehyde Hyaluronic acid (HA) [30]. Other kinds of natural components include alginate (obtained from seaweed), aloe vera, dextran, pectin, cellulose, starch, gums, and carrageenan [31]. These polymers are easily accessible, abundant, cheap, biodegradable, and nontoxic. Alginate on the other hand, after a heart attack, has been used to return left ventricular activity to its normal state [32]. Natural polymers have large structures formed together by monomeric units held together by glycosidic bonds and are studied in great detail to be used for tissue engineering, pharmaceutical, and medical applications. Pectin is obtained from terrestrial plants consisting of α-galacturonic acid residues linked by 1, 4-glycosidic linkages. It is prepared from physically crossed hydrogels. Pectin hydrogels are prepared in such a way as to enhance their mechanical stability. They are usually prepared in two steps via a UV method using (ab N, N0 -methylene-bisacrylamide) as a crosslinking agent [14]. Another work by Delitto et al. (2021) demonstrated the development of a neoantigen-targeted hydrogel vaccine. It briefly talks about the issue of tumor involvement in major vascular structures, which causes a lot of limitations for surgical options for cancer patients, hence decreasing the chances of finding a cure and incomplete resection. This lead to further evaluation, which involved in creation of a margin tumor, which was created by performing incomplete surgical resection, bearing syngeneic flank tumors called Panc02 tumors, which is a type III adenocarcinoma pancreatic tumor, this was implanted into a set of mice. Then a previously approved gelatinized neoantigen-targeted vaccine called Panvax. This vaccine was then embedded in HA containing hydrogels and applied to the created tumors in the mice. This led to the expansion of neoantigen-specific T cells in the mice, which caused prevention of further recurrence, and it proved to be effective [33].

4.6.2 Synthetic polymers

These polymers can be produced with long chain structures and they are hydrophobic. They are preferred over natural polymers because their physical and chemical structures are highly controllable [34]. But they have low biological activity. They are generally prepared by cross-linking of polymers using chemical methods. Some of the synthetic polymers are polyethylene glycol (PEG), polyvinyl alcohol (PVA), polyacrylic acid (PAA), poly ethylene oxide (PEO), poly 2-hydroxyethyl methacrylate (PHEMA), etc. Previous research done by Swilem et al. (2014) synthesized PAA hydrogels by using an electron beam of 75 kGy to irradiate acrylic acid solution. A lot of investigation of physical properties such as swelling ratio, gel contents, adhesion, etc. was done in order to obtain the PAA hydrogel [35]. PEG is one of the most popular hydrogels used because it can resist protein absorption, does not stimulate the immune system, and is used for synthetic hydrogenation in various biomedical applications such as tissue engineering and bone prostheses [36]. According to a work done by Yu et al. (2018), it demonstrated the use of polylactic-co-glycolic acid (PLGA) core-lipid shell nanoparticles, which was developed in order to enhance diffusivity through certain complex biological barriers such as mucus or the tumor interstitial matrix whereupon the use of a general nanoparticle containing a drug provides insufficient delivery of the drug to the target site. They used a comparative study to evaluate the efficacy of these PLGA core lipid shell nanoparticles and some synthetic mucus penetration particles (MPPs). These PLGA core lipid shell nanoparticles efficiently overcame multiple intestinal barriers and resulted in increased bioavailability of the drug when administered orally [36].

4.7 Preparation of hydrogels

4.7.1 Bulk polymerization

Bulk hydrogels exhibit nanoporous meshes that inhibit entry of blood vessels and cells into their structure so that it is devoid of any biological activity. A minute amount of crosslinking agent is added for any hydrogel formulation [37]. Many materials have been processed into bulk hydrogels that have the ability to mimic any native tissue feature such as cell adhesion [13]. Bulk hydrogels can be prepared by one or more types of monomers. The polymerization reaction usually involves chemical catalysts or radiation. Polymerized hydrogel can be produced in various forms such as rods, particles, emulsions, and membranes. The process of bulk polymerization is that it utilizes monomers to make a homogeneous hydrogel to produce a transparent, glassy, and hard type of polymer matrix. Once it is immersed in water, the glassy matrix enables it to become soft and flexible. The drawback of bulk hydrogels is having homogeneous properties, thereby making it next to impossible for incorporating any diverse signaling cues to enhance the cell population, which limits the endogenous tissue repair strategies [37]. Granular hydrogels can be used as an alternative in order to overcome these limitations. They consist of inherent porosity that permits cell invasion and are composed of microgels [38]. This microporous structure enables the surrounding cells to enable numerous paths such as proliferation, migration, spreading, and infiltration. Work done by Hsu et al. (2017) demonstrated the use of granular hydrogels used to create an adaptable microporous hydrogel (AMH) composed of interconnecting pores, served as an injectable matrix and promoted gradient nerve growth factors, which were constructed by the building blocks present in the nerve conduit [39]. It proved to promote cell migration and induced the gaps present in peripheral nerve defects. Granular hydrogels can also exhibit degradation behavior. This application has been applied in the work of Griffin et al. (2020), where these hydrogels were tested in microporous annealed particle (MAP) scaffolds. This hydrogel in in vivo conditions hastened the process of material degradation and this regeneration that was imparted showed a lot of enhancement in wound healing [37].

4.7.2 Solution polymerization

This process is also known as solution cross-linking reactions. The ionic monomers are mixed with multifunctional cross-linking agents. Various typical solvents include water, ethanol, water-ethanol mixtures, and benzyl alcohol. A UV irradiation system initiates polymerization thermally. Once the hydrogels are prepared, they need to be washed thoroughly in order to eliminate monomers, cross-linking agents, oligomers, extractable polymers, and other impurities [13]. When the amount of water during the polymerization process is more than the water content corresponding to the equilibrium swelling value, phase separation occurs, leading to the formation of the heterogeneous hydrogel.

4.7.3 Optical polymerization

This method offers the advantage of controlling the rate of gelation(gel strength), and it does not require a solvent to perform the reaction [34]. The polymers used in this process are hydrophilic in nature and their molecules are light-sensitive and contain groups of acrylates and methacrylates, which are polymerized by light. Polymerization is formed when a polymer solution is taken and when exposed to UV-sensitive light, optical decomposition is initiated and free radicals are formed

[40]. Cells begin to fade during this process and the polymerization provides strength to the hydrogel also, creating a porous lattice structure. The process is performed at normal body temperatures.

4.7.4 Enzymatic polymerization

These reactions take place in a biological environment and hence have been used widely for cellular applications [41]. It has a special enzyme substrate that prevents the entry of toxic substances. A common enzyme catalyst horseradish peroxidase (HPR) is used because of its mechanical stability, and it is easily purifiable [42]. Therefore it can be used for various biomedical applications such as tissue engineering and tumor study. Another commonly used enzyme catalyst is tyrosinase [42,43]. Research work done by Liu et al. (2017) prepared cell-laden hydrogels, which were dynamically stiffened through the enzymatic reaction using tyrosinase [41]. It catalyzes the oxidation of tyrosine into dihydroxyphenylalanine (DOPA), which turns it finally into DOPA dimer. This dimer resulted in additional crosslinks thus adding stiffness to the hydrogel. This was done to study the influence of matrix stiffness on pancreatic stromal cells (PSC), which remained unexplored. These PSC-laden hydrogels were placed in a media containing tyrosinase for 6 hours. It, therefore, produced a hydrogel with great stability.

4.8 Types of some common hydrogels

Hydrogels are the main focus of research because they are applicable in many fields such as biomedical, biological, mechanical, and pharmaceutical. Hydrogels are classified into specific types. Some of them are discussed below.

4.8.1 Injectable hydrogels

These hydrogels have attracted a great amount of attention because of their controlled and sustained way of drug delivery [38]. They have been widely used in many fields such as in biomedical applications, tissue engineering, and other therapeutic purposes. It can also minimize any systemic effects of the drug such as cardiotoxic effects (affecting the heart) and nephrotoxic (affecting the kidney). These effects usually occur in the tissues that occur in tissues distant from the site of contact between the biomaterial or medical device used. They are further subdivided into temperature and pH-sensitive hydrogels. In one study, Giang Phan et al. formulated a controlled-release formulation of GEM called injectable nanobiohybrid hydrogel and used it for PC treatment. Their study described that the nanobiohybrid hydrogel is a desirable carrier for the controlled release of GEM in the treatment of PC [44].

4.8.2 Temperature-sensitive hydrogels

They are aqueous monomer polymer solutions; when undergoing a change in temperature, they change their transition from a solution into a gel. They have methyl, ethyl, or propyl groups present in them due to these groups. They are hydrophobic in nature and when they interact with the water molecules and thehydrogen bonds. This causes them to swell up. As the temperature increases, the water solubility of the polymers increases [40]. However, in some cases, the water solubility decreases. Mao et al. have formulated a thermosensitive hydrogel where they have enhanced the efficacy and toxicity of Paclitaxel (PTX) by using it as a local chemotherapy system for PC in a tumor-bearing mice model [43].

4.8.3 pH-sensitive hydrogels

The rate of glycolysis in cancer cells is very high, causing acidification in the environment near the tumor tissues and this results in a drop in the pH value in the ECM when compared to the normal tissues. This is the reason why pH-sensitive hydrogels are designed, so that they can undergo pH-dependent changes based upon the environmental pH conditions or their polymeric systems, which allows cleavage of the acidic bonds and, in turn, allows the release of the molecules that are anchored [45]. These hydrogels consist of polymers that have a hanging acidic (sulfonic acid) or basic (ammonium salts) group. With a loss or gain of a proton, they respond to the pH changes in the environment. Polyelectrolytes, such as PAA, which are anionic in nature, have a large number of such ionizable groups. In normal environmental conditions, they are deprotonated and the electrostatic changes increase, causing the water molecules to penetrate causing the hydrogel to swell up drastically. If an anionic media is used, the acidic polymer starts protonating (addition of protons), thereby resulting decrease in charge density result in a collapse in the volume of the polymer. Whereas, the cationic polyelectrolytes become acidic and swell up when the pH level becomes acidic. According to a study by Shi et al. (2014), the chemotherapy drug doxorubicin (DOX) was conjugated to succinate chitosan (S-chi) via a Schiff's base. This resulted in giving rise to a pH-sensitive polymer that could easily release DOX in an acidic tumor microenvironment, which showed a huge inhibition to the growth of MCF-7 cells in vitro and MDA-MB-231 cancer cell lines that were used to develop human xenograft breast tumors in mice [46].

4.8.4 Photosensitive hydrogels

The types of hydrogels are of great interest because of their unique ability to be administered in an aqueous solution to form hydrogels in situ, followed by the process of photopolymerization, which is a light-induced reaction, that converts a polymer into a liquid or a gel state into a solid polymer. When one adds the photosensitive molecular material to the temperature-sensitive gel and light energy is converted into heat energy, where it then reaches the phase transition temperature. The hydrogel then begins to produce photosensitivity hence becoming an efficient photosensitive hydrogel. Work done by Jafari et al. (2019) studied the evaluation of a riboflavin-mediated collagen photo crosslinking as an experimental tool to modulate the mechanical properties of ECM in a 3D in vitro tumor models, which were pancreatic tumor spheroids in this case [47]. This crosslinking process was used to manipulate the extension of invasive progression achieved by cells, which infiltrated the surrounding ECM from primary transplanted spheroids. The assay was used to study these differential therapeutic responses in primary nodule and ECM-invading populations, this response was compared to verteporfin-based photodynamic therapy (PDT) and oxaliplatin chemotherapy. The treatment response data, which were obtained, showed invading cell population, which showed that they were highly chemoresistant and have shown an increase in sensitivity in PDT. This methodology that was designed can be used for a variety of applications to target any invasive disease in the future.

4.8.5 Electrosensitive hydrogels

These type of hydrogels are polyelectrolytes, that when upon application of an electric field into them, they undergo swelling or shrinking. Under the presence of an electric field, there is a force produced on counterions and immobile charged groups, which attracts mobile ions to the electrodes. This results in shrinkage or swelling of the hydrogels at the anode or cathode. This causes an ion difference inside the hydrogel network and culture medium that is used causing them to bend. The extent of bending further depends upon electrical field characteristics, which include direction, strength, and the duration of the electric field [48]. Electrosensitive hydrogels have the ability to transform electrical energy into mechanical energy. They have a wide range of applications such as in biosensing, biomechanics, sound dampening, and tissue engineering. Hydrogels consisting of PAA have also been applied in developing electrosensitive smart muscle-based devices for training, workout purposes, etc. Luca et al. adopted a free radical-based method to fabricate some electrosensitive hydrogels using graphene oxide. They have successfully shown the biomedical applications of these developed hydrogels with greater efficacy [49].

4.9 Applications of hydrogels against pancreatic cancer

Hydrogels can be used for the PC in different ways as explained below (Fig. 4.2).

4.10 Diagnosis

Diagnosis of PC is one of the most crucial steps required before formulation of the treatment plan. Some of the diagnostic methods are MRI, Computerised

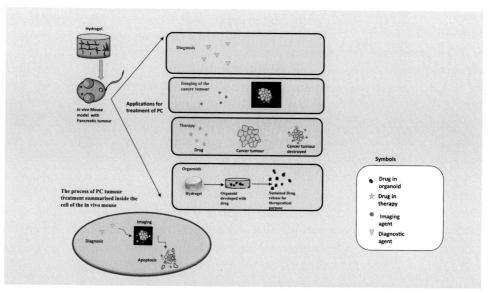

Figure 4.2 Applications of hydrogels for drug delivery for the treatment of Pancreatic Cancer (PC).

Tomography (CT,) Positron Emission Tomography (PET), and Endoscopic Ultrasound (EUS). Multidetector CT (MDCT) is one of the most widely used and best imaging tool for pancreatic adenocarcinoma detection in patients because it is inexpensive, safe, and noninvasive [50]. Histopathology analysis/Cytology is one of the most significant methods that include Endoscopic Ultrasonography (EUS) or CT guided biopsy, exploratory biopsy under laparoscopy, or an open surgery diagnosis [6]. PET CT scans can diagnose tumors early. The molecular changes of PDAC have developed significantly and require detection through immunohistochemical markers [51]. This requires development of the biomarkers related to the stage of the disease. Various techniques used to assess biomarkers include in situ hybridization, immunohistochemistry, microarray, and mutation analysis using serum, pancreatic juice, and urine [52]. Currently, there are six common tumor biomarkers (CA19−9, CA242, carcinoembryonic antigen (CEA), CA125, microRNAs, and K-RAS gene mutations) [53]. Carbohydrate antigen (CA19−9) is a Lewis antigen isolated from a tumor-associated protein, MUC1. High levels of CA19−9 indicate a poor prognosis, but low levels can be detected in early stages of PC [54]. Thus markers that focus on early diagnosis could help clinicians to select specific therapeutic agents suitable for the required cancer stage. However, future research into potent markers is required for improved diagnosis and management of PC. Rao et al. (2020) showed that the main challenge for patients with borderline resectable (BR) and LAPC is the delivery of dose-escalated RT, which includes the proximity of the duodenum adjacent to the head of pancreas (HOP), and imaging systems like CT do not give proper visualization of this boundary during this treatment. They assessed safety and feasibility of using radiopaque hydrogels between the HOP and duodenum to function as a marker and spacer in human cadaveric, porcine, and patient simulation studies. The data obtained demonstrated feasibility and safety of injecting a hydrogel marker in the pancreaticoduodenal groove in patients with BR/LAPC [55].

Hyaluronic Acid (HA), is a major glycosaminoglycan (GAG) expressed in PDAC stroma. Hyaluronidase (HAse) is an enzyme that can catalyze a reaction with utmost efficiency and its overexpression has been found to be a great way of detecting many types of cancers, PC being one of them and is a great biomarker [55]. Therefore it can be used as an important component to help in the detection of PC. Work done by Li et al. demonstrated the use of a proposed biosensor-like hydrogel where the hydrogel was made up of carboxyl-rich HA and amine-rich polyethylenimine (PEI), it also contained platinum on silica nanoparticles (Pt@SiO2). These nanoparticles can catalyze the decomposition process of H_2O_2 into O_2 [56]. HAse catalyzes the degradation of HA which, in turn, disrupts the hydrogel. The nanoparticles are released, which are mixed with the H_2O_2 in a draining device. Some of the H_2O overflowed from the device due to a pressure imbalance. This H_2O was collected and measured. This proposed biosensor system can be used to detect the activity of HAse in urine samples and can be of great help in detecting cancer [57].

The prognosis for PC is poor to date, having only a 5-year survival rate. Only a minority of cases have long-term survival. Surgical resection is one of the most potential cures, but only 20% of the PC patients are eligible for it, and there is a limited number of therapeutic options available. There are various other methods to detect PC such as CT and RT. The role of in treating Locally advanced pancreatic cancer (LAPC) is still under debate. RT has some considerations to be followed. First, insertion should be easy. Second, the complications should be a bare minimum. Third, it should be stable. Fourth, it should be visible upon imaging. And lastly, it should be degradable [50]. Natural biomaterials such as blood patches, HA, and collagen are used but have poor degradation rates and short durability.

Various investigations have recently shown a natural injectable hydrogel with PEG used as a biomaterial has attracted great attention because PEG hydrogels have high mobility in solution, lack of immunogenicity and toxicity, etc. [58]. It has also been shown to be stable in vivo for 3 months, adsorbed at 7 months, and passes out through renal filtration. Various reports have shown that PEG hydrogels used in PC are very efficient using endoscopic ultrasound (EUS).

Previous work by Kim et al. demonstrated an endoscopic ultrasound (EUS) guided PEG hydrogel delivery technique. It was shown to increase the space between HOP and the duodenum, in order for RT to be performed. The technical feasibility of EUS guided hydrogel for creation of space in a cadaveric model. It was found that the PEG hydrogel was clearly visible and showed great stability [59].

For people who are diagnosed with PC in late stages, the therapeutic options available are very limited. An ultrasound-guided high-intensity focused ultrasound (US-HIFU) can reduce the severity of the pain and improve local control in late-stage cancers and is noninvasive [60]. Sebeke et al. used pancreas of five healthy German swine, which were sonicated using a US-HIFU system. Access to the pancreas was supported using a specialized hydrogel compression device and a special diet was given to each pig. The motion artifacts and organ displacement were suspended by sleep apnea periods [61]. The size of the thermal lesions obtained was assessed using gross examination, thermal threshold, and dose profiles. MRI imaging was used to assess the effect of the compression device. Eight or ten treatments showed clear, visible damage in the target tissues of the pancreas. There was a good correlation found between the delivered energy dose and the resulting lesion sizes, which also indicated that this device had bared great significance for developing the MR-guided HIFU interventions onto the pancreas and can be used for clinical applications in the future.

4.10.1 Therapy

Despite the various treatments used for cancer treatment, they all have their set of limitations. Chemotherapy, for example, uses cytotoxic drugs to inhibit tumor recurrence, but some of the chemotherapeutics available are unable to differentiate between normal cells and cancerous cells (i.e., it is poorly specific). It causes the drug levels to rise and then decline sharply, thereby producing side effects. Comparatively, the standard drug delivery methods have a better advantage by providing a sustained release of the chemotherapeutics and hence enhancing its efficiency [62]. There are various drug delivery systems used such as hydrogels, liposomes, nanoparticles, and micelles [63]. Hydrogels are 3D networks of crosslinked hydrophilic polymer chains. They can be used in various forms for drug delivery. Chemotherapeutic drugs are wrapped in a hydrogel and implanted around a tumor to maintain a high drug concentration for a long period of time [40]. One such method is injectable hydrogels, where the materials used for the hydrogel are biodegradable and can be used for various applications such as tissue engineering, drug delivery, regeneration, and wound healing. It provides a sustained and controlled way of delivering the drug to the targeted tumor site because they are premixed with the drugs outside before getting in situ (by chemical or physical crosslinking methods) within the patient's body [64]. For example, Maspes et al. demonstrated that these in situ hydrogels based on Schiff's base cross-linked hydrogels formulated with metformin (ME) and 5FU showed a potential therapeutic application against colon cancer [65]. Some chemotherapeutics have low solubility, so injectable hydrogels help in overcoming this obstacle. There are different kinds of injectable hydrogels such as thermosensitive hydrogels, photosensitive, and pH sensitive. Thermosensitive hydrogels undergo a transition from a solution to a gel state at a particular temperature, which is called the low critical solution temperature

(LCST). When injected into the patient's body, it is in a liquid state followed by a gelation process leading to the formation of a crosslinked hydrogel. Previous work from Shabana et al. showed a comparative study of a hydrogel nanoparticle system consisting of two drugs, GEM and PTX loaded into functionalized liposomes fibronectin-mimetic peptide (PR_b), which showed sustained release of both the drugs compared to the functionalized liposomes PR_b free in drugs in the hydrogel (hydrogels encapsulating nontargeted liposomes with GEM/PTX or free drugs) [66]. The hydrogels used were thermosensitive and biodegradable (Hydrogels were made out of PEG-PLVA). The hydrogel nanoparticle system showed a better response in a reduction in the pancreatic tumor spheroids (PANC-1) also maximizing therapeutic efficiency. Bilalis et al. have fabricated another smart hydrogel composed of pentablock terpolypeptide of the type PLys-b-(PHIS-co-PBLG)-PLys-b-(PHIS-coPBLG)-bPLys and encapsulated them with GEM [42]. These pH and enzyme hydrogels worked as a convenient method of transporting the GEM drugs to the tumor cells in a controlled and sustained manner. Many proof of principle demonstrations of these injectable hydrogels in in vivo mouse tumor models have also shown encouraging results. The unique properties of hydrogels, including the ability to change from solution to solid form, make them good platforms for drug delivery applications [58].

4.10.2 Organoid development for cancer treatment

Organoids are small, self-organized 3D tissue structures that have the ability to self-organize into similar structures and behaviors to their corresponding in vivo tissue [67]. It mimics the structural and functional complexity of an organ. They enable stem cells to generate in a 3D microenvironment during differentiation into target-specific tissues. Organoids, when compared to 2D standard cultures or models, can exhibit better specificity for the patient while involving repetition in vivo, which include histological and genetic characteristics in tissue-like structures and functions in vitro [68]. They are much more convenient and accessible for biological studies and also form tissues with self-renewing capacity. It has been used for stem cell and tissue engineering research over a century. Recent advancements in hydrogels play a vital role in improving organoid systems through the close integration of the mechanical and chemical properties with various biomaterials and stem cell biology [68]. Amongst the natural hydrogels, Matrigel is the most common type of hydrogel used. Other hydrogels include collagen, alginate, cellulose, gelatin, fibrin, decellularized ECM (dECM), and HA. Gelatin methacrylate (GelMA), polyacrylamide (PAAm), and derivatives of PEG are commonly used synthetic hydrogels for organoids [69].

With the advanced engineering technology, various strategies such as the input and output flow conditions, nutrient supplies, and physicochemical stimulation can be used to construct hydrogels based on the different tissue types. Pancreatic organoid systems have shown great significance as it has been applied intensively to study pancreatic development and even for PC treatment [70]. These organoids can be generated from healthy pancreas or tumors, hence bridging the gap between in vitro and in vivo models. PDAC being one of the most malignant cancers urges the need to study the pancreatic tumors, which also allows further therapies to be investigated. Human pancreatic ductal cell lines have been used to study PDAC with the use of CRISPR Cas 9 to introduce mutations in normal pancreatic organoids to study PDAC progression. Lee et al. expressed engineered pancreatic organoids from CD133$^+$ cells to express the mutant KRASG12V (K), and the mutants CDKN2A (C), TP53 (T), and SMAD4 (S) were deleted, this gave rise to a mutant organoid and the KCTS organoid [71]. These mutant organoids, in turn, gave rise to pancreatic lesions (PanIN) but failed to give rise to PDAC [72]. The work demonstrated by Seino et al. [73] where pancreatic ductal cells from normal-like regions were used, which were adjacent to the tumor tissue, successfully established a transformation of lesions from PanIN to PDAC. This work could be used to study PDAC tumors in the future. Georgakopoulos and colleagues demonstrated the use of pancreatic organoid systems derived from human pancreatic ductal cells (hPO), using a chemically defined medium, but this failed to give rise to PDAC [74]. Another work by Seino et al. used a culture medium that could support the growth and development of hPO in a fresh or cryopreserved primary tissue [73]. This was cultured for months as it showed a high rate of expansion and efficiency. It also showed no change in chromosomal integrity and biomarker expression. Xenografts of these hPOs were grafted into immunodeficient mice and showed no signs of any origin of benign or malignant tumors. This can lead to a pathway of understanding the exocrine biology of the pancreas and its diseases, such as DM and PC, and maintain its tissue of origin.

4.11 Conclusion and future outlook

Pancreatic Cancer (PC), is one of the most malignant cancers ranking 12th worldwide. The prognosis rate still remains poor and treatments that are available for it are still limited. There are a number of standard treatments available such as chemotherapy and RT. However, they all have their own set of limitations such as poor target rate towards the tumor and poor rate of circulation. Typical current cancer diagnostic methods which are CT, MRI, etc. These approaches can generate good results but have their own set of drawbacks such as poor resolution, delayed detection of the tumor, and so on.

For the treatment of PC, standard drugs such as Gemcitabine (GEM) and Paclitaxel (PTX) can be used. However, the survival rate of patients are very low when used individually, or even in a combined state, and even if they are used along with nanoparticles. It fails to show much of therapeutic efficiency. Over the years of investigation, hydrogels have been found to be a boon for PC treatment. Hydrogels can be used for a wide variety of biomedical applications such as tissue engineering and tumor study. Hydrogels can serve as an excellent source for drug delivery. Various types of hydrogels such as natural or synthetic ones can be used. Hydrogels offer several advantages as they can deliver the drug to the target site more specifically, blend more easily with other components, and most importantly they are eco-friendly. Hydrogels used for treatment of PC combined with diagnostic instruments such as Rectal Endoscopic Ultrasound (RUS), have provided a clearer visualization between the gaps of the head of the pancreas and duodenum for better detection. They have been used for PC treatment in terms of drug delivery, and sometimes have been combined with nanoparticles for better efficacy. Many different types of researches are being conducted with hydrogels and combining them with different kinds of components, in order to improve the efficiency of PC treatment. Hydrogels combined with different other drug delivery methods such as liposomal and nanoparticle drug delivery methods, have shown a drastic increase the improvement of treating PC. Various other strategies are still being investigated for hydrogels in order to improve and enhance the progress of better PC treatment for the future.

References

[1] Siegel RL, et al. Cancer statistics, 2022. CA Cancer J Clin 2022;72(1):7−33.
[2] Rawla P, Sunkara T, Gaduputi V. Epidemiology of pancreatic cancer: global trends, etiology and risk factors. World J Oncol 2019;10(1):10−27.
[3] Vincent A, et al. Pancreatic cancer. Lancet 2011;378(9791):607−20.
[4] Zeng S, et al. Chemoresistance in pancreatic cancer. Int J Mol Sci 2019;20(18):4504.
[5] Thiel DD, et al. Comparison of patient-reported quality of life outcome questionnaire response rates between patients treated surgically for renal cell carcinoma and prostate carcinoma. BMC Urol 2015;15:58.
[6] Zhao Z, Liu W. Pancreatic cancer: a review of risk factors, diagnosis, and treatment. Technol Cancer Res Treat 2020;19. p. 1533033820962117.
[7] Zhang L, Sanagapalli S, Stoita A. Challenges in diagnosis of pancreatic cancer. World J Gastroenterol 2018;24(19):2047−60.
[8] Chang J, Schomer D, Dragovich T. Anatomical, physiological, and molecular imaging for pancreatic cancer: current clinical use and future implications. Biomed Res Int 2015;2015:269641.
[9] Semina IE, Iankina ZK. Use of an immunoblotting method for identifying the individual proteins in the antigenic complexes of *Bordetella pertussis*. Zh Mikrobiol Epidemiol Immunobiol 1989; 3:78−81.
[10] Chu LC, Goggins MG, Fishman EK. Diagnosis and detection of pancreatic cancer. Cancer J 2017;23(6):333−42.
[11] Nurgali K, Jagoe RT, Abalo R. Editorial: adverse effects of cancer chemotherapy: anything new to improve tolerance and reduce sequelae? Front Pharmacol 2018;9:245.
[12] Xin Y, et al. Recent progress on nanoparticle-based drug delivery systems for cancer therapy. Cancer Biol Med 2017;14(3):228−41.
[13] Ahmed EM. Hydrogel: preparation, characterization, and applications: a review. J Adv Res 2015;6 (2):105−21.
[14] Bashir S, et al. Fundamental concepts of hydrogels: synthesis, properties, and their applications. Polymers (Basel) 2020;12(11):2702.

[15] Misra R, Acharya S. Smart nanotheranostic hydrogels for on-demand cancer management. Drug Discov Today 2021;26(2):344—59.

[16] Kleeff J, et al. Pancreatic cancer. Nat Rev Dis Prim 2016;2:16022.

[17] Torphy RJ, Fujiwara Y, Schulick RD. Pancreatic cancer treatment: better, but a long way to go. Surg Today 2020;50(10):1117—25.

[18] Li HY, et al. Pancreatic cancer: diagnosis and treatments. Tumour Biol 2015;36(3):1375—84.

[19] Li Y, Rodrigues J, Tomas H. Injectable and biodegradable hydrogels: gelation, biodegradation and biomedical applications. Chem Soc Rev 2012;41(6):2193—221.

[20] Ertz-Archambault N, Keim P, Von D. Hoff, microbiome and pancreatic cancer: a comprehensive topic review of literature. World J Gastroenterol 2017;23(10):1899—908.

[21] Curvello R, et al. 3D collagen-nanocellulose matrices model the tumour microenvironment of pancreatic cancer. Front Digit Health 2021;3:704584.

[22] Robatel S, Schenk M. Current limitations and novel perspectives in pancreatic cancer treatment. Cancers (Basel) 2022;14(4):985.

[23] Neesse A, et al. Stromal biology and therapy in pancreatic cancer: a changing paradigm. Gut 2015;64(9):1476—84.

[24] Infante JR, et al. Peritumoral fibroblast SPARC expression and patient outcome with resectable pancreatic adenocarcinoma. J Clin Oncol 2007;25(3):319—25.

[25] Erkan M, et al. The role of stroma in pancreatic cancer: diagnostic and therapeutic implications. Nat Rev Gastroenterol Hepatol 2012;9(8):454—67.

[26] Ersek RA, Beisang 3rd AA. Physiologic tissue gel equivalent. Plast Reconstr Surg 1990;86(3):611.

[27] Aswathy SH, Narendrakumar U, Manjubala I. Commercial hydrogels for biomedical applications. Heliyon 2020;6(4):e03719.

[28] Bhattarai N, Gunn J, Zhang M. Chitosan-based hydrogels for controlled, localized drug delivery. Adv Drug Deliv Rev 2010;62(1):83—99.

[29] Sun Z, et al. Hydrogel-based controlled drug delivery for cancer treatment: a review. Mol Pharm 2020;17(2):373—91.

[30] Weng L, Chen X, Chen W. Rheological characterization of in situ crosslinkable hydrogels formulated from oxidized dextran and N-carboxyethyl chitosan. Biomacromolecules 2007;8(4):1109—15.

[31] Basu A, et al. Poly(lactic acid) based hydrogels. Adv Drug Deliv Rev 2016;107:192—205.

[32] Pena B, et al. Injectable hydrogels for cardiac tissue engineering. Macromol Biosci 2018;18(6):e1800079.

[33] Delitto D, et al. Implantation of a neoantigen-targeted hydrogel vaccine prevents recurrence of pancreatic adenocarcinoma after incomplete resection. Oncoimmunology 2021;10(1):2001159.

[34] Chamkouri H, Chamkouri M. A review of hydrogels. Their Prop Appl Med Am J Biomed Sci & Res 2021;11(6).

[35] Swilem AE, et al. Nanoscale poly(acrylic acid)-based hydrogels prepared via a green single-step approach for application as low-viscosity biomimetic fluid tears. Mater Sci Eng C Mater Biol Appl 2020;110:110726.

[36] Ho TC, et al. Hydrogels: properties and applications in biomedicine. Molecules 2022;27(9):2902.

[37] Qazi TH, Burdick JA. Granular hydrogels for endogenous tissue repair. Biomater Biosyst 2021;1:100008.

[38] Fan DY, Tian Y, Liu ZJ. Injectable hydrogels for localized cancer therapy. Front Chem 2019;7:675.

[39] Hsu RS, et al. Adaptable microporous hydrogels of propagating NGF-gradient by injectable building blocks for accelerated axonal outgrowth. Adv Sci (Weinh) 2019;6(16):1900520.

[40] Norouzi M, Nazari B, Miller DW. Injectable hydrogel-based drug delivery systems for local cancer therapy. Drug Discov Today 2016;21(11):1835—49.

[41] Liu HY, Korc M, Lin CC. Biomimetic and enzyme-responsive dynamic hydrogels for studying cell-matrix interactions in pancreatic ductal adenocarcinoma. Biomaterials 2018;160:24—36.

[42] Bilalis P, et al. Self-healing pH- and enzyme stimuli-responsive hydrogels for targeted delivery of gemcitabine to treat pancreatic cancer. Biomacromolecules 2018;19(9):3840—52.

[43] Mao Y, et al. Thermosensitive hydrogel system with paclitaxel liposomes used in localized drug delivery system for in situ treatment of tumor: better antitumor efficacy and lower toxicity. J Pharm Sci 2016;105(1):194—204.

[44] Giang Phan VH, Lee E, Maeng JH, Thambia T, Kima BS, Lee D, et al. Pancreatic cancer therapy using an injectable nanobiohybrid hydrogel. RSC Adv 2016;6:41644—55.

[45] Zeng N, et al. Synthesis of magnetic/pH dual responsive dextran hydrogels as stimuli-sensitive drug carriers. Carbohydr Res 2022;520:108632.

[46] Shi J, Guobao W, Chen H, Zhong W, Qiu X, Xing MMQ. Schiff based injectable hydrogel for in situ pH-triggered delivery of doxorubicin for breast tumor treatment. Polym Chem 2014;5:6180—9.

[47] Jafari R, Cramer GM, Celli JP. Modulation of extracellular matrix rigidity via riboflavin-mediated photocrosslinking regulates invasive motility and treatment response in a 3D pancreatic tumor model. Photochem Photobiol 2020;96(2):365—72.

[48] Murdan S. Electro-responsive drug delivery from hydrogels. J Control Rel 2003;92(1—2):1—17.

[49] di Luca M, et al. Electro-responsive graphene oxide hydrogels for skin bandages: the outcome of gelatin and trypsin immobilization. Int J Pharm 2018;546(1—2):50—60.

[50] Raman SP, Horton KM, Fishman EK. Multimodality imaging of pancreatic cancer-computed tomography, magnetic resonance imaging, and positron emission tomography. Cancer J 2012;18 (6):511—22.

[51] Hingorani SR, et al. Preinvasive and invasive ductal pancreatic cancer and its early detection in the mouse. Cancer Cell 2003;4(6):437—50.

[52] Lin MH, et al. Association between non-steroidal anti-inflammatory drugs use and the risk of type 2 diabetes mellitus: a nationwide retrospective cohort study. J Clin Med 2022;11(11):3186.

[53] Ge L, et al. Comparing the diagnostic accuracy of five common tumour biomarkers and CA19-9 for pancreatic cancer: a protocol for a network meta-analysis of diagnostic test accuracy. BMJ Open 2017;7(12):e018175.

[54] Ghaneh P, Costello E, Neoptolemos JP. Biology and management of pancreatic cancer. Gut 2007;56(8):1134—52.

[55] Lin CC, Korc M. Designer hydrogels: shedding light on the physical chemistry of the pancreatic cancer microenvironment. Cancer Lett 2018;436:22—7.

[56] Li Z, et al. Sensitive hyaluronidase biosensor based on target-responsive hydrogel using electronic balance as readout. Anal Chem 2019;91(18):11821—6.

[57] Raza A, Ki CS, Lin CC. The influence of matrix properties on growth and morphogenesis of human pancreatic ductal epithelial cells in 3D. Biomaterials 2013;34(21):5117—27.

[58] McGuigan A, et al. Pancreatic cancer: a review of clinical diagnosis, epidemiology, treatment and outcomes. World J Gastroenterol 2018;24(43):4846—61.

[59] Kim SH, et al. EUS-guided hydrogel microparticle injection in a cadaveric model. J Appl Clin Med Phys 2021;22(6):83—91.

[60] Chung AH, Jolesz FA, Hynynen K. Thermal dosimetry of a focused ultrasound beam in vivo by magnetic resonance imaging. Med Phys 1999;26(9):2017—26.

[61] Sebeke LC, et al. Feasibility study of MR-guided pancreas ablation using high-intensity focused ultrasound in a healthy swine model. Int J Hyperth 2020;37(1):786—98.

[62] Rosiak JM, Ulański P, Rzeźnicki A. Hydrogels for biomedical purposes. Nucl Instrum Methods Phys Res Sect B: Beam Interact Mater At 1995;105(1—4):335—9.

[63] Cirillo G, et al. Injectable hydrogels for cancer therapy over the last decade. Pharmaceutics 2019;11 (9):486.

[64] Ullah F, et al. Classification, processing and application of hydrogels: a review. Mater Sci Eng C Mater Biol Appl 2015;57:414—33.

[65] Maspes A, et al. Advances in bio-based polymers for colorectal cancertreatment: hydrogels and nanoplatforms. Gels 2021;7(1):6.

[66] Shabana AM, et al. Thermosensitive and biodegradable hydrogel encapsulating targeted nanoparticles for the sustained co-delivery of gemcitabine and paclitaxel to pancreatic cancer cells. Int J Pharm 2021;593:120139.

[67] Li Z, et al. Advances of engineered hydrogel organoids within the stem cell field: a systematic review. Gels 2022;8(6):379.

[68] Zhao Z, Chen X, Dowbaj AM, Sljukic A, Bratlie K, Lin K, et al. Organoids. . Nat Rev Methods Prim 2022;2::94.

[69] Clevers H. Modeling development and disease with organoids. Cell 2016;165(7):1586—97.

[70] Casamitjana J, Espinet E, Rovira M. Pancreatic organoids for regenerative medicine and cancer research. Front Cell Dev Biol 2022;10:886153.

[71] Lee J, et al. Expansion and conversion of human pancreatic ductal cells into insulin-secreting endocrine cells. Elife 2013;2:e00940.

[72] Joshi VR, Sainani GS. Rifampicin and drug interactions. J Assoc Physicians India 1988;36(6):361.

[73] Seino T, et al. Human pancreatic tumor organoids reveal loss of stem cell niche factor dependence during disease progression. Cell Stem Cell 2018;22(3):454—67 e6.

[74] Georgakopoulos N, et al. Long-term expansion, genomic stability and in vivo safety of adult human pancreas organoids. BMC Dev Biol 2020;20(1):4.

CHAPTER 5

Liposome- and niosome-based drug delivery for pancreatic cancer

Rezvan Yazdian-Robati[1], Seyedeh Melika Ahmadi[2], Faranak Mavandadnejad[3], Pedram Ebrahimnejad[2], Shervin Amirkhanloo[2] and Amin Shad[4]

[1]Pharmaceutical Sciences Research Center, Hemoglobinopathy Institute, Mazandaran University of Medical Sciences, Sari, Iran
[2]Department of Pharmaceutics, Faculty of Pharmacy, Mazandaran University of Medical Sciences, Sari, Iran
[3]Ajmera Transplant Centre, University Health Network (UHN), Toronto, ON, Canada
[4]Department of Chemical Engineering, Ferdowsi University of Mashhad, Mashhad, Iran

5.1 Introduction

Pancreatic cancer (PC), as a digestive system malignant tumor, is projected to be the second leading reason of tumor-related death in the United States by 2030 [1]. The median survival rate of PC is about 27 months if it grows from endocrine cells. However, if it grows from exocrine cells leading to pancreatic ductal adenocarcinoma (PDAC), the survival rate will be very low from a few months to one year along with a poor quality of life [2]. Unfortunately, PC is asymptomatic and considered a silent killer, so it is diagnosed after spread. Early recurrence, resistance to chemotherapy and radiotherapy, and distant metastasis are the main features of PC [3]. It is a heterogeneous disease with a complex tumor microenvironment (TME). It has been shown that the wide stroma nearby the PC cells is responsible for the metastases, tumor growth, and sequestering of chemotherapeutic agents in the tumor cells [4]. PC treatment modalities include surgery, chemotherapy, and radiation therapy [5]. The main chemotherapeutic agents used for PC treatment are paclitaxel (PTX), 5-fluorouracil (5-FU), irinotecan, oxaliplatin, gemcitabine (GEM), doxorubicin (DOX), cisplatin, and capecitabine (Cap). The failure of multiple combination routines of chemotherapeutics, for example, cisplatin or PTX, GEM with 5-FU, or FOLFIRINOX (leucovorin, fluorouracil, and irinotecan, oxaliplatin alone or with targeted therapy [such as bevacizumab and cetuximab]) in clinical settings have been demonstrated [6]. One of the major challenges in PC treatment is recurrence after surgery or chemotherapy. This is most likely due to different reasons including cancer stem cells (CSCs), which are involved in tumor regeneration and progression, epithelial—mesenchymal transition (EMT), which gives CSCs the capability to have superior resistance to treatments, and the third reason is the hypoxic nature of the pancreatic tumor, in this scenario, hypoxia-inducible factors (HIFs) control the PDAC's TME [7]. Recently, nanotechnology, as a sophisticated and new technology, has represented the nanoscale size range of materials with significantly better physiochemical features, collaborating impressively with today's medicines. Engineered nanoparticles (NPs) have unique structural features, including the ability to interact with biological molecules, a large surface-to-mass ratio, and the capability at carrying various cargo such as proteins, drugs, and nucleotides. An extensive range of metabolic and physiological properties of the targeted tissues can be targeted by NPs [8,9]. Unlike traditional drug-delivery systems, nanocarrier systems can be modified in composition, shape, size, and surface features (functional groups, charge, attachment of an array of targeting ligands, and coating). Thus, the bioavailability and biodistribution of drugs, their plasma half-life, as well as the EPR (enhanced permeability and retention) effect, would be enhanced. Indeed, their stability and solubility would be amended, leading to site-specific delivery, therapeutic agents-controlled release, and reduced toxicity [9]. As a result, the concept of nanotechnology would have vast utilization in cancer research, especially in PC [10,11]. In fact, delivery of chemotherapeutic drugs through NPs could hamper multidrug-resistant (MDR) efflux pumps existing on the surface of most tumor cells. Hence, the features of PC provide an excellent opportunity for researchers to conduct studies to manufacture novel drug delivery systems. In recent years, studies in PC have been involved with the design of vesicular carriers such as liposomes and niosomes for delivering active substances [5,12]. These lipid-based nanoparticles are a group of nano-scale particulates with the minimum toxic effect for in vivo usage. The formulations of lipid nanoparticles absolutely have an impact on drug absorption, enhancing drug solubility and membrane permeability, as well as, preventing efflux transporters. Liposome and niosome platforms are bilayer lipid vesicles prepared from phospholipids and nonionic surfactants, respectively, to act as delivery systems for both hydrophilic and hydrophobic drugs. These carriers both pose advantages and special features, which distinguish them from other drug delivery systems. Therefore, drug design in these two forms opens the gate to significant progress in the treatment of PC [13]. Our chapter offered the most current advances of the liposome and niosome platforms for PC (Fig. 5.1).

5.2 Liposome-based drug delivery

5.2.1 Components and structure of liposome

Liposomes are bi or multilayer sphere-shaped lipid vesicles that were presented in the field of drug delivery in the early 1990s by Bangham A. These lipid-based nanostructures resemble the plasma cell membrane and are able to overwhelm biological barriers [14]. Hydrophilic, amphiphilic, and hydrophobic compounds including drugs, nucleotides, imaging agents, and proteins can be incorporated within their aqueous core and/or lipid bilayers [15,16].

Liposomes are mainly composed of phospholipids, which can be neutral, positively charged (N-[1-(2,3-dioleyloxy)propyl]-N,N,N-trimethylammonium) (DOTMA) and

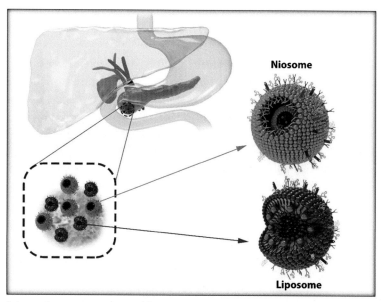

Figure 5.1 Schematic representation of liposomal and niosomal drug delivery systems for pancreatic cancer treatment.

1,2-dioleoyl-3-trimethylammonium-propane (DOTAP) and negatively charged such as 1,2-dipalmitoyl-sn-glycero-3-[phospho-rac-(1-glycerol)] (DPPG), dipalmitoylphosphatidylcholine (DPPC), and 1,2-palmitoyl-phosphatidic acid (DPPA). Phospholipids are amphiphilic and have a strong tendency to make specific structures in an aqueous environment spontaneously. Aqueous core of liposome encapsulates hydrophilic drugs, while lipophilic drugs can be merged into the membrane. However, liposomes composed only of phospholipids have a low shelf life and imperfect ability to keep loaded drugs because of high drug leakage [17,18]. To overcome this, sterols such as cholesterol are incorporated into liposomal formulation to modulate fluidity and penetrability, as well as stability of bilayer membrane [19]. Moreover, vitamin E, TPGS (D-alpha-tocopheryl polyethylene glycol 1000 succinate), and some polymers such as chitosan and polyethylene glycol (PEG) are recommended to be integrated into liposomal membranes to enhance some features such as biodistribution, stability, and even shelf-life. Considering all these characteristics, liposomes offer several distinct advantages as a drug delivery platform including high drug encapsulation efficiency, targeting ability, protecting of encapsulated drugs from degradation, reduced renal clearance, long systemic circulation, and accumulation in tumor site through EPR effects. In addition, high biocompatibility and low immunogenicity are other main advantages of liposomes [20]. Liposome or lipid-based nanoparticles are the most prevalent groups of nanomedicines (33%) existing in the market or in various phases of clinical trials [21].

5.3 Liposomal drug delivery platforms for pancreatic cancer

5.3.1 Liposome-drugs to treat pancreatic cancer

The application of liposomes for chemotherapeutic drug delivery plays an important role in PC therapy. Loading chemotherapy drugs into liposomes offers many distinct advantages over current conventional treatments. Potential benefits of exploiting this nanocarrier in the clinic include distribution of drugs constantly over an extended duration, at a steady rate, prevention of side effects of drugs, and enhanced patient compliance because of lessened dosage [22]. Very recently, in a nonclinical study, it was reported that liposomal irinotecan improved the therapeutic index fourfold in comparison to irinotecan in mice bearing IM-PAN-001 PDX pancreatic tumors [22].

One strategy to eradicate the PC is blocking the signaling pathway that promotes invasion. S100P/RAGE (receptor for advanced glycation end products) signaling pathway stimulates the growth of PC cells, invasion, and low survival rate. Overexpression of S100P has been detected in PC and is completely correlated with malignancy. Hence, Kim et al. (2011) studied pegylated liposomes of cromolyn (an anti-inflammatory drug) in mice bearing syngeneic PDAC to block RAGE/S100P signaling pathways. Results depicted disruption of S100P-RAGE interaction, decreased NF-ĸB activity, reduction in both tumor growth, and metastasis as well as improved efficacy of GEM in PDAC [23]. Considering the fact that cationic liposomes generate high levels of reactive oxygen species (ROS), therefore they are very toxic. Ichihara et al. (2019) developed a formulation of cationic liposomes aiming to prevent migration of BxPC-3 cells through the inhibition of matrix metallopeptidase 2 (MMP2), MMP9, and MMP14 [24] (Fig. 5.2).

Although PTX is a very insoluble anticancer drug with poor pharmacokinetics properties, its combination with Bovine Serum Albumin (BSA) in the pharmaceutical form of nab-paclitaxel is very effective in pancreatic cancer treatment. In this regard, Okamoto and coworkers developed PTX-loaded albumin-encapsulated liposomes with the objective of improving the cancer treatment effects. The in vitro results confirmed that this liposomal formulation consists of HEPC, cholesterol, and DSPE-PEG2000, and PTX-saturated and BSA greatly inhibited growth of AsPC-1 cells in a concentration-dependent manner. Further, the in vivo study in a mouse model inoculated with AsPC-1 cells exhibited a reduction in tumor growth after the treatment with PTX—BSA-liposomes, indicating a higher concentration drug at the tumor site via EPR mechanism compared with nab-PTX [25]. The combination of two or more drugs in a nano-liposome had greater tumor growth suppression in PDAC. A dual intervention-oriented (DIODE) tumor-targeted liposomes were fabricated to boost the therapeutic efficacy by exploiting the cocktail drug and minimization of chemotherapy-related side effects in both in vivo and in vitro settings in terms of tumor growth suppression. Liposomes are loaded with PTX, GEM, XL-184 (c-Met inhibitor, X), and erlotinib, and their combinations. Median survival was upgraded by

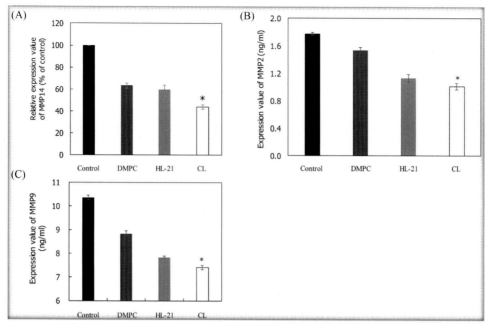

Figure 5.2 Relative expression values of (A) MMP14 and (B) expression values of MMP2 and (C) MMP9 in BxPC-3 cells treated with cationic liposomes (CL) significantly decreased. *Adapted with permission from the published work of Ichihara H, Motomura M, Matsumoto Y. Therapeutic effects and anti-metastasis effects of cationic liposomes against pancreatic cancer metastasis in vitro and in vivo. Biochem Biophys Res Commun 2019;511(3):504–9.*

novel DIODE liposomal formulations compared to GEM-loaded vehicles or liposomes [26]. The combination of autophagy inhibitors and chemotherapy has proven improvements in the treatment of PC. In this way, the synergistic cytotoxicity and coautophagy inhibition effects of TR-peptide functionalized liposomes (DSPE-PEG2000-TR) loaded with PTX and hydroxychloroquine (TR-PTX/HCQ-Lip) were examined in vitro and in vivo in the PC. In this study, hydroxychloroquine (HCQ) was used as an autophagy inhibitor and tandem peptide TH–RGD (TR) was exploited to target integrin $\alpha v\beta 3$ in pancreatic cancer cells and the surrounding stroma fibrosis. Further, TR-peptide in acidic tumor environment protonated and so help internalization via electrostatic attraction between the plasma membrane of cells with negative charge and TR-peptide. Meanwhile, TR-PTX/HCQ-Lip has suppressed the expression of SMA and collagen-1, which are correlated to the activation of cancer-associated fibroblasts (Fig. 5.3) [27].

Myeloid cell leukemia 1 (Mcl-1), as an antiapoptotic Bcl-2 family member, has emerged as a new target for PC treatment. Overexpression of Mcl-1 has been reported in human pancreatic cancer. With this concept, Wang et al. designed a cationic

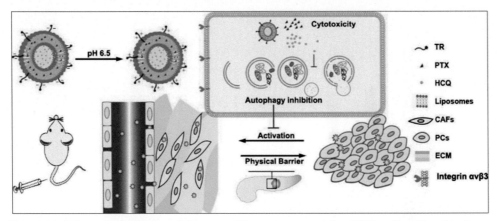

Figure 5.3 Schematic illustration of TR-targeted liposomes containing PTX (paclitaxel) and hydroxy-chloroquine TR-PTX/HCQ-Lip. *Adapted with permission from the published work of Chen X, Yu Q, Liu Y, Sheng Q, Shi K, Wang Y, et al. Synergistic cytotoxicity and co-autophagy inhibition in pancreatic tumor cells and cancer-associated fibroblasts by dual functional peptide-modified liposomes. Acta Biomat 2019;99:339–49.*

liposome loaded with GEM and Mcl-1 siRNA (Small interfering RNA) to target pancreatic cancer. Augmented cellular uptake, higher Mcl-1 down-regulation efficacy, and substantial cytotoxicity as well as tumor inhibition were observed in PANC-1 and BxPC-3 cell lines and xenograft tumor model [28].

5.3.2 Liposome—naturally derived bioactive compounds to treat pancreatic cancer

In the context of PC treatment with liposomes, natural herbal extracts, such as curcumin, berberine, and caffeic acid have been explored by scientists. For instance, application of curcumin-loaded liposome in MIAPaCa-2 PDAC cell lines and nude mice resulted in high tumor angiogenesis suppression [29]. Caffeic acid derivatives encapsulated liposomes composed of soybean phosphatidylcholine and DSPE-PEG2000 were prepared by the dry lipid film and extrusion technique and analyzed in terms of basic physical parameters. This liposomal formulation was stable and nonhemolytic, as well as had activity against PC [30]. The naturally derived flavonoid baicalein (BAI) encapsulated into a liposom with suitable size, homogeneity, and high efficiency developed for intravenous administration. The designed formulation exhibited high cytotoxicity against AsPC-1 and BxPC-3 PDAC cell lines [31]. Codelivery of irinotecan (IRI) and berberine in liposome results in enhanced drug circulation time, reduced intestinal toxicity, and excellent anticancer effects in vivo in comparison to Onivyde [29]. Hence, nanoformulations carrying natural products have a bright future in improving the PC therapy as well as can directly decline the toxicity of chemotherapy drugs and increase the safety of clinical medication.

5.3.3 Liposomal delivery of CRISPR/Cas9 to treat PC

CRISPR (clustered regularly interspaced short palindromic repeats)/Cas9 technology considered a promising therapeutic option for different cancers including PC. In the CRISPR/Cas9 platforms, transcription activator-like effector nucleases (TALENs), CRISPR, and zinc-finger nucleases (ZFNs) are fit for clinical and preclinical purposes. One recent preclinical study has exploited the CRISPR/Cas9 approach to target hypoxia-inducible factor-1 alpha with a focus on liposome as a suitable carrier for suppressing the metastasis of PC. The designed liposome was loaded with the PTX, Cas9 protein, and sgRNA protamine complex (sgRNA-encoding HIF-1α-targeting plasmid) and further modified with R8-dGR peptide on the surface. Using the liposome-CRISPR modality, the expression level of the HIF-1α, vascular endothelial growth factor (VEGF), and MMP-9 were reduced, which is associated with metastasis of PC. The tumor volumes were greatly lesser after mice were inoculated with the R8-dGR targeted CRISPR/cas9 system after 23 days compared to the HEPES control [32] (Fig. 5.4).

The outcomes of this research confirm that liposome delivery platforms could be an effective alternative to viral vectors. However, a further inclusive study is in demand before this gene editing approach is exploited in clinics.

5.4 Targeted nanoliposomes for pancreatic cancer treatment

Despite the many benefits of liposomes as drug carriers, some limitations including instability in vivo conditions, lack of target selectivity, quick clearance, and nonspecific uptake have hindered their use in the clinic. It has been proposed to use functionalized liposomes with surface-bounded ligands including antibodies and related fragments and some other moieties, for example, hyaluronic acid (HA), aptamer, transferrin, folate, and peptides, with the capability of identifying and binding to an overexpressed receptor or transporters on the tumor cell-specific cells, enhance the accumulation of liposomal in the targeted sites [19].

5.4.1 Transporter-targeted liposome for pancreatic cancer therapy

ATB° (amino acid transporter B0, + (SLC6A14, Solute carrier family 6 member 14)) is an example of the transporter whose high expression in pancreatic cancer cells consider prognostic.

So, ATB° can be considered a perfect target for drug delivery to PC cells. ATB° delivers all amino acids with exception of the acidic ones such as aspartate and glutamate [33]. Kou et al. (2020) prepared lysine-conjugated liposomes carrying GEM (Gem-loaded LYS-LPs) to target AsPC-1, BxPC-3, MIAPaca-2, and Capan-2 pancreatic cancer cells (ATB° positive). The result showed that higher cellular entry of

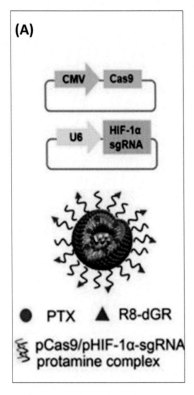
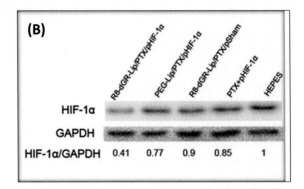
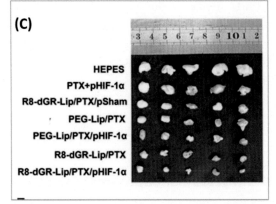

Figure 5.4 (A) Schematic illustration of targeted liposome loaded with PTX (paclitaxel) and Cas9 protein and HIF-1α-sgRNA protamine complex (R8-Dgr-Lip/PTX/p HIF-1α). (B) In R8-Dgr-Lip/PTX/p HIF-1α treated group, downregulation of HIF-1α was confirmed by Western Blot technique and (C) the tumor volume significantly decreased. *Reproduced with permission from Li M, Xie H, Liu Y, Xia C, Cun X, Long Y, et al. Knockdown of hypoxia-inducible factor-1 alpha by tumor targeted delivery of CRISPR/ Cas9 system suppressed the metastasis of pancreatic cancer. J Control Release 2019;304:204−15.*

Gem-loaded LYS-LPs in comparison to bare liposomes, a process facilitated by ATB° via endocytosis, leading to more cytotoxicity in PC cells. This novel strategy provides a way for PC therapy by targeting overexpressed transporter [34].

5.4.2 Antibody-decorated liposomes for pancreatic cancer

Tumor-specific antibodies can be fused into liposomes to target upregulated receptors, such as VEGF, MUC1 (mucin1), epidermal growth factor receptor (EGFR), and different carbohydrate antigens, on PC cells and induce strongly site-specific accumulation. Immunoliposomes (antibody-directed liposomes) are regarded as the next generation of molecular targeting drug-delivery systems, providing the potential for targeted drug delivery to cancer cells [35]. As an example, CA19−9 antibody, which is highly specific to PC cells, was conjugated to adriamycin–encapsulated liposomes for achieving targeting chemotherapy. Stronger cell damage, antitumor effect, and intratumor drug concentration were observed in the targeted liposome compared to free adriamycin and unmodified liposomal adriamycin against PC [36]. In another study, greater cell uptake was observed by administering maleimide-thiol antibody fragment conjugated with liposomes carrying PTX and GEM in comparison with nontarget liposomes, and the therapy therapeutic efficacy was improved in pancreatic cancers by applying antibody fragmented nano-systems [37]. Blockade of VEGF-A (vascular endothelial growth factor A) signaling pathway not only inhibits angiogenesis in tumor cells but may also alter or destroy tumor vessels. Within this context, Kuesters and Campbell (2010) formulated a PEGylated cationic liposome and then functionalized it by biotinylated bevacizumab (a recombinant humanized mAb against VEGF-A) to target preferentially the pancreatic tumor vasculature. Improved uptake by Capan-1, HPAF-II, and PANC-1 cells and tumor targeting received by bevacizumab-modified liposome support their future progress in the treatment of cancer [38].

5.4.3 Peptide-decorated liposome

In addition to antibodies, the targeting agents may also be proteins or peptides that have been effectively bounded to liposomes to target overexpression of appropriate receptors on the surface of the tumor cells [39]. The main issue in PC treatment is fibrotic stroma, which is a physical barrier for drug penetration and is a scaffold containing growth factor providing PC cell growth and distant metastasis. In this way, in a preclinical study, β-cyclodextrin (β-CD)-modified metalloproteinase-2 (MMP-2) responsive liposomes were developed in order to target pancreatic stellate cells (PSCs), the main source of fibrosis in the stroma. These synthesized liposomes broke down into two functional parts at the tumor site by MMP-2 enzyme. The first part contained pirfenidone (the antifibrosis drug) in the hydrophobic chamber of β-CD, which was kept in the stroma, leading to inhibition of the fibrosis by downregulation of TGF-β and collagen I in PSCs. On the contrary, the other part is composed of RGD (alanyl glycyl aspartic acid) peptide-modified-liposome carrying GEM that binds to the αVβ3 integrin overexpressing on the pancreatic tumor cells and killing them. Hence, this formulated liposomal system with joint properties improved drug perfusion with no side effects and offers an imminent strategy for PC treatment development [40]. Ferino et al. developed a functional palmityl-oleyl-phosphatidylcholine (POPC) system to target the KRAS (Kirsten rat sarcoma virus) oncogene in PDAC cells. The designed liposomes were prepared and functionalized with miR-216b and cell-penetrating peptide (TAT, transactivator of transcription) preventing KRAS expression. The authors demonstrated the functionalized liposome that could suppress the expression level of the KRAS oncoprotein (70%) in PDAC cells [41].

5.4.4 Carbohydrate-decorated liposomes

One of the main characteristics of PDAC TME is high levels of hyaluronic acid (HA) that increases significantly interstitial fluid pressure and impairs perfusion in tumors [42]. HA recognizes and binds with high affinity to the cell surface receptors, particularly glycoprotein CD44, which provides GEM resistance in PDAC through different routes, including upregulation of multidrug resistance protein 1 (MDR1), increasing GEM efflux as well as via the Wnt signaling pathway [43]. Hence, targeting the HA-CD44 signaling pathway may be a hopeful approach for GEM sensitization. In this way, HA-liposomes composed of HA-DPPE, phospholipids, and cholesterol were fabricated with two low molecular weight HA (12 and 4.8 kDa) to deliver GEM prodrug into CD44 + MiaPaCa2. Results confirmed that HA liposomes containing GEM (HA, 12 kDa) had robust efficiency, whereas nonconjugated liposomes and the 4.8 kDa HA liposomes were equally active [44]. In another example, Marengo et al. designed novel HA-decorated liposomes loaded with diethyldithiocarbamate-copper complex [Cu (DDC)2] that targeted CD44 on the PDAC CSC. Strongly improved antitumoractivity was observed on pancreatic CSCs derived from PDAC cell lines and patients [45] (Fig. 5.5).

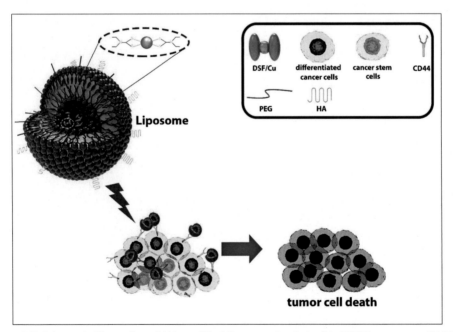

Figure 5.5 Schematic illustration of HA-modified liposome loaded with DSF/Cu to target CD44 on surface of cancer stem cells and differentiated cancer cells. *Reproduced with permission from Marengo A, Forciniti S, Dando I, Dalla Pozza E, Stella B, Tsapis N, et al. Pancreatic cancer stem cell proliferation is strongly inhibited by diethyldithiocarbamate-copper complex loaded into hyaluronic acid decorated liposomes. Biochim Biophys Acta Gen Subj 2019;1863(1):61−72.*

In another study, HA-modified pH-sensitive liposomes (HA-pSL) with a particle size of 152.3 nm and a zeta potential of -46.8 were prepared to deliver GEM into drug resistant-PC cells. The HA prompts the cellular uptake of liposomes-GEM without interfering with endosomal escape pathways as proved by confocal images. The cellular uptake of GEM improved 3.6 and 4.6 times in MIA PaCa-2 cells and Gr2000 cells, respectively, compared to the unmodified conventional liposomes. Moreover, in vivo study demonstrated a condensed tumor weight in HA-pSL treated group [46]. These studies pave the way for the development of HA-conjugated liposomes to treat PDAC (Fig. 5.6).

Glypican-1 (GPC1) is a heparan sulfate proteoglycan attached to the surface of cell membranes, which is overexpressed in a variety of cancer cells such as PC to modulate tumor growth and metastasis through influence on the TME [47]. One recent study revealed that GPC1- liposomes containing GEM could enhance the rate of apoptotic cells by up to 50% when compared to nontargeted liposomes. Overall, this targeted liposomal formulation has emerged as an attractive candidate for PDAC treatment [48].

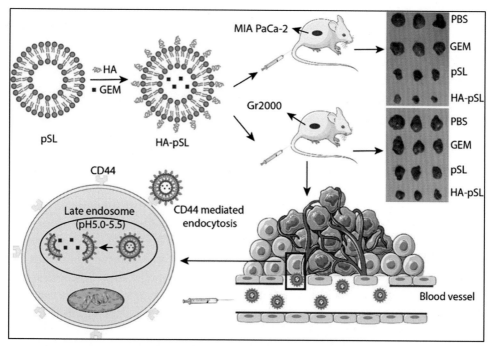

Figure 5.6 Schematic illustration of HA targeted pH-sensitive liposomes. The prepared liposome was injected into MIA PaCa-2 and resistant Gr2000 (GEM-resistance) xenograft models. Reduction in tumor weight in HA-pSL treated group was observed. *Adapted with permission from the published work of Tang M, Svirskis D, Leung E, Kanamala M, Wang H, Wu Z. Can intracellular drug delivery using hyaluronic acid functionalised pH-sensitive liposomes overcome gemcitabine resistance in pancreatic cancer? J control Release 2019;305:89–100.*

5.5 Stimuli-responsive liposomal nano-formulations for pancreatic cancer

By the continuous advancements in engineering of liposomes, with the capacity to respond to external stimuli (light, pH, temperature, enzyme, redox, ultrasound, and magnetic), and their functionalization with different ligands such as mAbs, aptamer, and peptide, the toxicity of the loaded cargo by regulating drug release at specific site decreased, resulting in clinically favorable outcomes.

5.5.1 pH-sensitive liposomes

pH-sensitive liposomes are considered favorable nanocarriers in comparison to conventional liposomes because they have endo/lysosome-escape capacities and can effectively deliver different cargoes to the cytoplasm through the endocytic pathway. Cellular internalization and controlling drug delivery are two main factors for designing pH-sensitive liposomes for specific cancer cell targeting. pH-sensitive liposomes can be employed to release drugs at an acidic pH medium such as the tumor extracellular environment of cancer cells.

CDDP, a platinum-based drug, is identified with antitumor effects against several tumors such as PC. Carlesoo et al. (2016) fabricated a cisplatin-loaded liposome (SpHL-CDDP) with two key features, including long-circulating and pH-sensitive. Therefore, when cisplatin is specifically delivered to the tumor site, its therapeutic efficacy increases while toxicity reduces. Based on antitumor efficacy evaluation, they reported the tumor volume after the regimen was followed by SpHL alone (control group) boosted rapidly over time while tumor volume exhibited a mild trend reduction compared to administrating the free-CDDP or SpHL-CDDP. Moreover, by administrating CDDP and SpHL-CDDP, necrosis was observed in tumor groups without any necrotic symptoms in the control group. In terms of toxicity, weight loss was higher in free-CDDP mice group in comparison to SpHL-CDDP treated mice [49]. Since GEM resistance is a serious issue in effectively treating PC, many investigators have highlighted overcoming this problem by introducing pH-sensitive liposomal combination therapy. Dual delivery of curcumin and GEM using PEGylated pH-sensitive liposomes in MIAPaCa-2 cells and Sprague Dawley (SD) rats lead to higher GEM concentration at the pancreatic tumor site and more cytotoxicity. It was revealed that curcumin could improve the GEM efficacy by inhibiting the multidrug resistance protein 5 (MRP5) efflux transporter, which facilitated GEM resistance in PC cells [34]. Intracellular PEG detachment is another efficient tactic for triggered release. In this regard, Kanamala et al. [50] utilized DPPE instead of DSPE and hydrazine (Hz) as a crosslinker. The mPEG-Hz-DPPE polymers revealed high stability at pH 7.4, while under mild acidic environments, protonation of acid-labile hydrazide$-$hydrazone ($-CO-NH-N=CH-$) bond occurred, and the fast release of PEG, liposome degradation, and enhanced accumulation of chemotherapeutic drug into MIA PaCa-2 pancreatic cancer cells were observed [50].

5.5.2 Magnetic sensitive and ultrasound liposomes

Ultrasound waves can activate drug release from the liposomes based on several mechanisms including thermally induced release and mechanical disruption of liposomes owing to the cavitation effects [18]. A good example including the combination of ultrasound and thermo-sensitive liposomes (TSL) was introduced by Farr et al. In a preclinical study, Farr et al. showed that temperature-sensitive liposomes carrying DOX (TSL-DOX) triggered via the mild hyperthermia (mHT), generated by controlled magnetic resonance-guided high-intensity focused ultrasound (HIFU), and improved DOX uptake by KPC mice pancreatic tumor tissue (23-fold), in comparison to TSL-DOX alone [51]. Camus et al. performed a study to assess the therapeutic efficacy of combined treatment with liposomal-DOX and ultrasound on an orthotopic model of PC. After 9 weeks, US + L-DOX treated group displayed meaningfully lower tumor volumes compared to the control group [52]. In ultrasound-targeted drug delivery, another famous approach involves the usage of microbubbles (contain a gas core encapsulated by a lipid, protein, or polymer shell) as ultrasound contrast agents to facilitate drug delivery within the body [53]. As evidence, Dwivedi et al. fabricated a DOX-loaded magneto-liposome-ligated microbubble complex. First, DOX was loaded into the iron oxide NPs and next encapsulated within oligolamellar vesicles, which were then coupled covalently to lipid-based microbubbles DSPC/cholesterol/DSPE-PEG2000-maleimide with a perfluorooctane (PFP) gas core. Improved pancreatic tumor targeting, higher apoptosis, and tumoricidal activity in both Panc-2 and BXPC-3 cell lines were observed; moreover, a significant reduction (around 80% reduction) in the tumor volume was detected after administration of DOX-loaded magneto-liposomes compare to control group in a pancreatic cancer xenograft Balb/c nude mouse. Additionally, using ultrasound stimulation deeply penetrated iron oxide nanoparticles and enhanced drug distribution and increased DOX uptake in PDAC tumors clearly detected [54]. Similarly, the ultrasound-triggered liposomes composed of DOPE-DMA, DPPC, DSPE-PEG, and CP4126 (a fatty acid ester derivative of GEM) were designed to incorporate with PFP, which can yield microscopic gas bubbles. Under ultrasound irradiation, these microbubbles create intramembrane cavities in the lipid bilayer leading to the bursting and deforming of the bilayer structure and the release of therapeutic agents from the liposomes [55].

5.5.3 Thermo-sensitive liposomes

The first class of TSLs was presented by Yatvin and coworkers (1978), which is currently known as traditional thermosensitive liposomes (TTLs) [56]. The poor penetration and limited drug release of formulated liposomes in the tumor area can be improved using an external heat source. With an increase in temperature, compositional changes occur and encapsulated drugs are released [13]. To cite an example, Affram et al. 2015 aimed to amplify the residence time and transfer a high payload of GEM to PC cells by formulating GEM-loaded PEGylated TSL nanoparticles

(GEM-TSLnps) and using mHT. With increasing temperature, the release of drug increased in vitro. In terms of in vitro cell viability, GEM-TSLnps + mHT treated cell lines demonstrated more significant cell growth inhibition than GEM-TSLnps treated cells. Moreover, the clonogenic survival assay showed a greater reduction in number of colonies in GEM-TSLnps + mHT treated group compared with free GEM. It was suggested that GEM-TSLnps + mHT is a prominent candidate for delivering a high amount of GEM [57]. In another study, Emamzadeh et al. [58], designed a thermos–responsive polymer-coated liposome nanocarrier that can carry GEM and cisplatin to enhance the drug synergism via a thermally triggered mechanism. In this study, they basically coated TSL with a synthetic polymer produced by a reversible addition – fragmentation chain transfer (RAFT) approach. This polymer-modified liposomes (PMTLs) are able to deliver both GEM and cisplatin in a thermally controlled manner. The prepared carrier accelerates drug release and can interact with the cell membrane. The result showed that the cancer cell growth was suppressed and systemic toxicity alleviates by encapsulation of the GEM and cisplatin in the liposome and incubation at 40°C [58]. The low loading efficiency is a main problem related to liposomal-GEM, so to overcome this and improve the loading and stability of the loaded drug, Tucci et al. (2019) designed a TSL consisting of lipid components that permit high GEM loading (GEM-TSLs), copper (II) gluconate, and triethanolamine (TEOA), a strong base, to improve GEM solubility and stability. The results showed that the copper complexation with GEM is pH-sensitive. Based on solubility, a combination of copper (II) gluconate, TEOA, and heat enhance solubility of GEM up to 150 mg/mL. The designed temperature-sensitive copper-GEM liposomes reduced pancreatic tumor cell viability with minimal systemic toxicity. To sum up, using elevated temperature, copper(II) and TEOA effectively increased GEM solubility and significantly affect the pancreatic tumor cell viability [59]. Oxaliplatin was loaded in a long-circulating PEGylated TSL composed of DPPC and PEG2000-DSPE as a thermosensitive and long-circulating material, respectively. Improving the retention time up to 24 h, selective release at tumor sites, remarkable tumor growth suppression, and surge survival time for the tumor-bearing mice are the main results according to the report by Li et al. [60].

5.6 Clinical studies of liposomal formulation for pancreatic cancer treatment

In this context, despite many preclinical types of research, few clinical studies are available for PC treatment (Table 5.1). Onivyde (nanoliposomal irinotecan) is the liposomal-based formulation approved in 2015 that encapsulates irinotecan (a topoisomerase I inhibitor) for metastatic pancreatic cancer therapy. Longer half-life and enhanced anticancer efficiency in comparison to nanoliposomal irinotecan are the main clinical outcomes [12]. The open clinical trial on 18 patients with a nonresectable or metastatic PDAC was conducted to assess the concentration of DOX in tumor site after

Table 5.1 Liposomal-based nanomedicine for PDAC therapy (FDA-approved or clinical-stage).

Nanomedicine	drug	Status	Reference
(CAELYX)	DOX	FDA/Phase I/II	[64]
Onivyde	Irinotecan	FDA approved	NCT03468335
Atu027-I-02	Atu027 + GEM	Completed NCT01808638	NCT01808638
SGT-53	SGT 53 + GEM + Nab-Paclitaxel	Phase II	NCT02340117
ThermoDox	DOX + focused ultrasound	Phase I	NCT04852367

administrated by ThermoDox (an encapsulated TSL form of DOX) in combination with mild hyperthermia induced by focused ultrasound in comparison to the free drug [61]. SGT-53 is a cationic liposome carrying p53 DNA sequence (NCT02340117). With the concept of silencing, protein kinase N3 (PKN3) expression could inhibit tumor metastasis and angiogenesis; a clinical trial study on 29 participants with advanced PC was performed using Atu027 combined with GEM (NCT01808638) [62]. Atu027 is a liposomal loaded with siRNA to target PKN3 and finally inhibit pancreatic cancer progression [63].

5.7 Niosome-based drug delivery

5.7.1 Structure and components of niosomes

Niosomes are the primary vesicular organic nanocarriers containing cholesterol or L-α-soya phosphatidylcholine and nonionic surfactant with a high potential for the controlled and targeted delivery of hydrophilic and hydrophobic drugs in the future. The most critical element in the development of niosomes is nonionic surfactants. Niosome are similar to liposomes in terms of structural composition and physical characteristics. They improve the solubility, stability, bioavailability, and therapeutic efficiency of poorly soluble drugs, improve photo and chemical stability of the drug utilized, and protect and prolong the blood circulation of the drug. Moreover, niosome can be modified using active materials such as peptides, aptamers, and antibodies in a controlled and targeted manner to treat different cancer [65,66]. It seems that niosomes are a viable choice for drug delivery than liposomes since they are easier and cheaper to synthesize. However, in niosomal formulation, the problem of drug leakage and aggregate formation should be addressed. Basically, niosomes are classified frequently in terms of the size and number of vesicular lipid layers including multilamellar (100−1000 nm), oligolamellar, and unilamellar. The unilamellar vesicles are further categorized into large unilamellar vesicles (LUV) and small unilamellar vesicles (SUV). Recently, several studies have been conducted on potential of niosomes to serve as a carrier for the delivery of drugs, hormones, antigens, and other bioactive agents.

Niosomes are prepared by different techniques mainly the thin-Film hydration method, ether injection method, reverse phase evaporation, supercritical reverse phase evaporation, microfluidization method, lipid injection, emulsion method, heating method, ball milling method, and the bubble method [67,68]. Components of niosomes: As a bilayer spherical structure, a niosome mainly contains the following components: nonionic surfactants: the main nonionic surfactants in the development of niosomes are the spans, tweens, and Brij. Nonionic surfactants as amphiphilic molecules contain two different regions: a hydrophilic end and a lipophilic tail. They are biocompatible and biodegradable so the niosomes consisting of them can be exploited as a suitable drug delivery system. Cholesterol: Steroids are key elements of the cell membrane, which affect the bilayer permeability and fluidity in membrane. Cholesterol as a steroid derivative is used mainly for a rigid structure and an appropriate shape of niosome. Generally, integration of cholesterol influences some features of niosome such as membrane permeability, encapsulation efficiency, and release of payload, as well as time circulation of drug [69].

Charge inducer agents: By adding some charged molecules to niosomes, the stability of niosome is increased and avoids the aggregation of the niosome particles. In addition, they facilitate drug delivery to a definite area of the body through the zeta potential parameter. Phosphatidic acid and diacetyl phosphate (DCP) are two main negative charge agents that are used for formation of niosome, while stearyl amine (SA) and stearyl pyridinium chloride are positively charged molecules utilized in niosomal preparations.

5.7.2 Niosome drug delivery for pancreatic cancer treatment

Maniam and coworkers synthesized a niosomal formulation through coloading GEM and tocotrienols, a form of vitamin E, for synergistic chemo-tocotrienol therapy of PC. The in vitro results demonstrated that such niosome not only caused PC cell death efficiently but also improved the cellular uptake activity of GEM [70]. Morusin is an isoprene flavonoid with anti-inflammatory, anticancer, antioxidant, and antibacterial properties. However, the therapeutic use of morusin was limited due to poor solubility in water. Niosome formulation can improve its therapeutic efficacy. In a study reported by Agarwal et al., morusin-loaded niosome (479 nm in diameter) prepared by a modified thin layer evaporation method using span60, and cholesterol in the ratio of 5:1w/w in 20 mL of chloroform. The morphology of the morusin- niosome demonstrated spherical shapes with a concentric bilayer. In vitro cell viability study against PANC-1 revealed that therapeutic efficacy of morusin-niosome was more effective than the free morusin [71]. While these studies showed promising results for improved PC treatment using niosome, further comprehensive assessments are essential before this nanocarrier enters clinical applications.

5.8 Conclusion

Although liposomes have come a long way and now different liposomal pharmaceutical products exist in the market, niosomes are still on the way. Liposomes are the first nano drugs approved for use in clinic as a result of extensive work over five decades. With properties such as biocompatibility, high drug loading capacity, and capability to target, liposomes have brought novel views in treating PDAC. However, drug leakage, high production cost, and special conditions for storage are some challenges in the usage of liposome-based drugs and should be addressed. On the other hand, niosomes with distinct features over liposomes, including biocompatibility, nonimmunogenicity, long shelf-life, and low production cost, are another important choice for drug delivery into PC cells. However, extensive studies on the application of niosome in PC therapy are missing and safety data in humans are not available.

Declaration of competing interest

There is no conflict of interest.

References

[1] Rahib L, Smith BD, Aizenberg R, Rosenzweig AB, Fleshman JM, Matrisian LM. Projecting cancer incidence and deaths to 2030: the unexpected burden of thyroid, liver, and pancreas cancers in the United States. Cancer Res 2014;74(11):2913−21.

[2] Perko N, Mousa SA. Management of pancreatic cancer and its microenvironment: potential impact of nano-targeting. Cancers 2022;14(12):2879.

[3] Kamisawa T, Wood LD, Itoi T, Takaori K. Pancreatic cancer. Lancet 2016;388(10039):73−85.

[4] Shinkawa T, Ohuchida K, Nakamura M. Heterogeneity of cancer-associated fibroblasts and the tumor immune microenvironment in pancreatic Cancer. Cancers. 2022;14(16):3994.

[5] Raza F, Evans L, Motallebi M, Zafar H, Pereira-Silva M, Saleem K, et al. Liposome-based diagnostic and therapeutic applications for pancreatic cancer. Acta Biomater 2023;157:1−23.

[6] Matsumoto T, Yamamura S, Nagai H, Satake H, Yasui H. Is modified FOLFIRINOX a standard regimen for 2nd line chemotherapy for pancreatic cancer after gemcitabine plus nab-paclitaxel failure?—insights from the MPACA-3 trial. Dig Med Res 2022;5:40.

[7] Shah VM, Sheppard BC, Sears RC, Alani AW. Hypoxia: friend or Foe for drug delivery in pancreatic cancer. Cancer Lett 2020;492:63−70.

[8] Charbgoo F, Taghdisi SM, Yazdian-Robati R, Abnous K, Ramezani M, Alibolandi M. Aptamer-incorporated nanoparticle systems for drug delivery. Nanobiotechnology in diagnosis, drug delivery, and treatment. Wiley; 2020. p. 95−112.

[9] Hashemi M, Shamshiri A, Saeedi M, Tayebi L, Yazdian-Robati R. Aptamer-conjugated PLGA nanoparticles for delivery and imaging of cancer therapeutic drugs. Arch Biochem Biophys 2020;691:108485.

[10] Ebrahimian M, Shahgordi S, Yazdian-Robati R, Etemad L, Hashemi M, Salmasi Z. Targeted delivery of galbanic acid to colon cancer cells by PLGA nanoparticles incorporated into human mesenchymal stem cells. Avicenna J Phytomed 2022;12(3):295−308.

[11] Moghaddam FA, Ebrahimian M, Oroojalian F, Yazdian-Robati R, Kalalinia F, Tayebi L, et al. Effect of thymoquinone-loaded lipid−polymer nanoparticles as an oral delivery system on anticancer efficiency of doxorubicin. J Nanostructure Chem 2022;12:33−44.

[12] Milano G, Innocenti F, Minami H. Liposomal irinotecan (Onivyde): exemplifying the benefits of nanotherapeutic drugs. Cancer Sci 2022;113(7):2224–31.

[13] Agarwal K. Liposome assisted drug delivery-an updated review. Indian J Pharm Sci 2022;84 (4):797–811.

[14] Maja L, Željko K, Mateja P. Sustainable technologies for liposome preparation. J Supercrit Fluids 2020;165:104984.

[15] Sheikhpour M, Sadeghizadeh M, Yazdian F, Mansoori A, Asadi H, Movafagh A, et al. Co-administration of curcumin and bromocriptine nano-liposomes for induction of apoptosis in lung cancer cells. Iran Biomed J 2020;24(1):24.

[16] Elkhoury K, Sanchez-Gonzalez L, Lavrador P, Almeida R, Gaspar V, Kahn C, et al. Gelatin methacryloyl (GelMA) nanocomposite hydrogels embedding bioactive naringin liposomes. Polymers. 2020;12(12):2944.

[17] Zhang X, Shao X, Cai Z, Yan X, Zong W. The fabrication of phospholipid vesicle-based artificial cells and their functions. N J Chem 2021;45(7):3364–76.

[18] Sang R, Stratton B, Engel A, Deng W. Liposome technologies towards colorectal cancer therapeutics. Acta Biomater 2021;127:24–40.

[19] Nsairat H, Khater D, Sayed U, Odeh F, Al Bawab A, Alshaer W. Liposomes: structure, composition, types, and clinical applications. Heliyon. 2022;8(5):e09394.

[20] Ahmed KS, Hussein SA, Ali AH, Korma SA, Lipeng Q, Jinghua C. Liposome: composition, characterisation, preparation, and recent innovation in clinical applications. J Drug Target 2019;27(7):742–61.

[21] Shan X, Gong X, Li J, Wen J, Li Y, Zhang Z. Current approaches of nanomedicines in the market and various stage of clinical translation. Acta Pharm Sin B 2022;12(7):3028–48.

[22] Salunkhe VR, Patil PS, Wadkar GH, Bhinge SD. Herbal liposomes: natural network for targeted drug delivery system. J Pharm Res Int 2021;33(29B):31–41.

[23] Kim C-E, Lim S-K, Kim J-S. In vivo antitumor effect of cromolyn in PEGylated liposomes for pancreatic cancer. J Control Release 2012;157(2):190–5.

[24] Ichihara H, Motomura M, Matsumoto Y. Therapeutic effects and anti-metastasis effects of cationic liposomes against pancreatic cancer metastasis in vitro and in vivo. Biochem Biophys Res Commun 2019;511(3):504–9.

[25] Okamoto Y, Taguchi K, Sakuragi M, Imoto S, Yamasaki K, Otagiri M. Preparation, characterization, and in vitro/in vivo evaluation of paclitaxel-bound albumin-encapsulated liposomes for the treatment of pancreatic cancer. ACS Omega 2019;4(5):8693–700.

[26] Madamsetty VS, Pal K, Dutta SK, Wang E, Mukhopadhyay D. Targeted dual intervention-oriented drug-encapsulated (DIODE) nanoformulations for improved treatment of pancreatic cancer. Cancers. 2020;12(5):1189.

[27] Chen X, Yu Q, Liu Y, Sheng Q, Shi K, Wang Y, et al. Synergistic cytotoxicity and co-autophagy inhibition in pancreatic tumor cells and cancer-associated fibroblasts by dual functional peptide-modified liposomes. Acta Biomater 2019;99:339–49.

[28] Wang Y, Gao F, Jiang X, Zhao X, Wang Y, Kuai Q, et al. Co-delivery of gemcitabine and Mcl-1 SiRNA via cationic liposome-based system enhances the efficacy of chemotherapy in pancreatic cancer. J Biomed Nanotechnol 2019;15(5):966–78.

[29] Ranjan AP, Mukerjee A, Helson L, Gupta R, Vishwanatha JK. Efficacy of liposomal curcumin in a human pancreatic tumor xenograft model: inhibition of tumor growth and angiogenesis. Anticancer Res 2013;33(9):3603–9.

[30] Zaremba-Czogalla M, Jaromin A, Sidoryk K, Zagórska A, Cybulski M, Gubernator J. Evaluation of the in vitro cytotoxic activity of caffeic acid derivatives and liposomal formulation against pancreatic cancer cell lines. Materials. 2020;13(24):5813.

[31] Markowski A, Zaremba-Czogalla M, Jaromin A, Olczak E, Zygmunt A, Etezadi H, et al. Novel liposomal formulation of baicalein for the treatment of pancreatic ductal adenocarcinoma: design, characterization, and evaluation. Pharmaceutics. 2023;15(1):179.

[32] Li M, Xie H, Liu Y, Xia C, Cun X, Long Y, et al. Knockdown of hypoxia-inducible factor-1 alpha by tumor targeted delivery of CRISPR/Cas9 system suppressed the metastasis of pancreatic cancer. J Control Release 2019;304:204–15.

[33] Bhutia YD, Babu E, Prasad PD, Ganapathy V. The amino acid transporter SLC6A14 in cancer and its potential use in chemotherapy. Asian J Pharm Sci 2014;9(6):293−303.

[34] Kou L, Huang H, Lin X, Jiang X, Wang Y, Luo Q, et al. Endocytosis of ATB0, + (SLC6A14)-targeted liposomes for drug delivery and its therapeutic application for pancreatic cancer. Expert Opin Drug Deliv 2020;17(3):395−405.

[35] Wong BCK, Zhang H, Qin L, Chen H, Fang C, Lu A, et al. Carbonic anhydrase IX-directed immunoliposomes for targeted drug delivery to human lung cancer cells in vitro. Drug Des Devel Ther 2014;993−1001.

[36] Akaishi S, Kobari M, Takeda K, Matsuno S. Targeting chemotherapy using antibody-combined liposome against human pancreatic cancer cell-line. Tohoku J Exp Med 1995;175(1):29−42.

[37] Yang W, Hu Q, Xu Y, Liu H, Zhong L. Antibody fragment-conjugated gemcitabine and paclitaxel-based liposome for effective therapeutic efficacy in pancreatic cancer. Mater Sci Eng C 2018;89:328−35.

[38] Kuesters GM, Campbell RB. Conjugation of bevacizumab to cationic liposomes enhances their tumor-targeting potential. Nanomedicine. 2010;5(2):181−92.

[39] Laufer S, Restle T. Peptide-mediated cellular delivery of oligonucleotide-based therapeutics in vitro: quantitative evaluation of overall efficacy employing easy to handle reporter systems. Curr Pharm Des 2008;14(34):3637−55.

[40] Ji T, Li S, Zhang Y, Lang J, Ding Y, Zhao X, et al. An MMP-2 responsive liposome integrating antifibrosis and chemotherapeutic drugs for enhanced drug perfusion and efficacy in pancreatic cancer. ACS Appl Mater Interfaces 2016;8(5):3438−45.

[41] Ferino A, Miglietta G, Picco R, Vogel S, Wengel J, Xodo LE. MicroRNA therapeutics: design of single-stranded miR-216b mimics to target KRAS in pancreatic cancer cells. RNA Biol 2018;15(10):1273−85.

[42] Zhao S, Chen C, Chang K, Karnad A, Jagirdar J, Kumar AP, et al. CD44 expression level and iso-form contributes to pancreatic cancer cell plasticity, invasiveness, and response to therapy CD44 and gemcitabine resistance. Clin Cancer Res 2016;22(22):5592−604.

[43] Zhao X, Li Z, Gu Z. A new era: tumor microenvironment in chemoresistance of pancreatic cancer. J Cancer Sci Clin Ther 2022;6(1):61.

[44] Dalla Pozza E, Lerda C, Costanzo C, Donadelli M, Dando I, Zoratti E, et al. Targeting gemcitabine containing liposomes to CD44 expressing pancreatic adenocarcinoma cells causes an increase in the antitumoral activity. Biochim Biophys Acta - Biomembr 2013;1828(5):1396−404.

[45] Marengo A, Forciniti S, Dando I, Dalla Pozza E, Stella B, Tsapis N, et al. Pancreatic cancer stem cell proliferation is strongly inhibited by diethyldithiocarbamate-copper complex loaded into hyaluronic acid decorated liposomes. Biochim Biophys Acta - Gen Subj 2019;1863(1):61−72.

[46] Tang M, Svirskis D, Leung E, Kanamala M, Wang H, Wu Z. Can intracellular drug delivery using hyaluronic acid functionalised pH-sensitive liposomes overcome gemcitabine resistance in pancreatic cancer? J Control Release 2019;305:89−100.

[47] Wang S, Qiu Y, Bai B. The expression, regulation, and biomarker potential of glypican-1 in cancer. Front Oncol 2019;9:614.

[48] Mu Y, Wang D, Bie L, Luo S, Mu X, Zhao Y. Glypican-1-targeted and gemcitabine-loaded liposomes enhance tumor-suppressing effect on pancreatic cancer. Aging (Albany NY) 2020;12(19):19585.

[49] Carlesso FN, Araújo RS, Fuscaldi LL, Mendes Miranda SE, Rubello D, Teixeira CS, et al. Preliminary data of the antipancreatic tumor efficacy and toxicity of long-circulating and pH-sensitive liposomes containing cisplatin. Nucl Med Commun 2016;37(7):727−34.

[50] Kanamala M, Palmer BD, Jamieson SM, Wilson WR, Wu Z. Dual pH-sensitive liposomes with low pH-triggered sheddable PEG for enhanced tumor-targeted drug delivery. Nanomedicine. 2019;14(15):1971−89.

[51] Farr N, Wang Y-N, D'Andrea S, Starr F, Partanen A, Gravelle KM, et al. Hyperthermia-enhanced targeted drug delivery using magnetic resonance-guided focussed ultrasound: a pre-clinical study in a genetic model of pancreatic cancer. Int J Hyperth 2018;34(3):284−91.

[52] Camus M, Vienne A, Mestas J-L, Pratico C, Nicco C, Chereau C, et al. Cavitation-induced release of liposomal chemotherapy in orthotopic murine pancreatic cancer models: a feasibility study. Clin Res Hepatol Gastroenterol 2019;43(6):669−81.

[53] Delaney LJ, Isguven S, Eisenbrey JR, Hickok NJ, Forsberg F. Making waves: how ultrasound-targeted drug delivery is changing pharmaceutical approaches. Mater Adv 2022;3(7):3023−40.
[54] Dwivedi P, Kiran S, Han S, Dwivedi M, Khatik R, Fan R, et al. Magnetic targeting and ultrasound activation of liposome−microbubble conjugate for enhanced delivery of anticancer therapies. ACS Appl Mater Interfaces 2020;12(21):23737−51.
[55] Wang G, Zhang C, Jiang Y, Song Y, Chen J, Sun Y, et al. Ultrasonic cavitation-assisted and acid-activated transcytosis of liposomes for universal active tumor penetration. Adv Funct Mater 2021;31 (34):2102786.
[56] Yatvin MB, Weinstein JN, Dennis WH, Blumenthal R. Design of liposomes for enhanced local release of drugs by hyperthermia. Science. 1978;202(4374):1290−3.
[57] Affram K, Udofot O, Agyare E. Cytotoxicity of gemcitabine-loaded thermosensitive liposomes in pancreatic cancer cell lines. Integr Cancer Sci Ther 2015;2(2):133.
[58] Emamzadeh M, Emamzadeh M, Pasparakis G. Dual controlled delivery of gemcitabine and cisplatin using polymer-modified thermosensitive liposomes for pancreatic cancer. ACS Appl Bio Mater 2019;2(3):1298−309.
[59] Tucci ST, Kheirolomoom A, Ingham ES, Mahakian LM, Tam SM, Foiret J, et al. Tumor-specific delivery of gemcitabine with activatable liposomes. J Control Release 2019;309:277−88.
[60] Li Y, Xu P, He D, Xu B, Tu J, Shen Y. Long-circulating thermosensitive liposomes for the targeted drug delivery of oxaliplatin. Int J Nanomed 2020;15:6721−34.
[61] Regenold M, Bannigan P, Evans JC, Waspe A, Temple MJ, Allen C. Turning down the heat: the case for mild hyperthermia and thermosensitive liposomes. Nanomed Nanotechnol Biol Med 2022;40:102484.
[62] Schultheis B, Strumberg D, Kuhlmann J, Wolf M, Link K, Seufferlein T, et al. A phase Ib/IIa study of combination therapy with gemcitabine and Atu027 in patients with locally advanced or metastatic pancreatic adenocarcinoma. J Clin Oncol 2016;34(4_suppl):385.
[63] Russo S, Saif MW. Gastrointestinal cancers symposium: update on pancreatic cancer. Ann Gastroenterol 2016;29(2):238.
[64] Halford S, Yip D, Karapetis CS, Strickland AH, Steger A, Khawaja HT, et al. A phase II study evaluating the tolerability and efficacy of CAELYX (liposomal doxorubicin, Doxil) in the treatment of unresectable pancreatic carcinoma. Ann Oncol 2001;12(10):1399−402.
[65] Aparajay P, Dev A. Functionalized niosomes as a smart delivery device in cancer and fungal infection. Eur J Pharm Sci 2022;168:106052.
[66] Shinu P, Nair AB, Kumari B, Jacob S, Kumar M, Tiwari A, et al. Recent advances and appropriate use of niosomes for the treatment of skin cancer. Indian J Pharm Educ Res 2022;56(4):1−14.
[67] Yasamineh S, Yasamineh P, Kalajahi HG, Gholizadeh O, Yekanipour Z, Afkhami H, et al. A state-of-the-art review on the recent advances of niosomes as a targeted drug delivery system. Int J Pharm 2022;121878.
[68] Mawazi SM, Ann TJ, Widodo RT. Application of niosomes in cosmetics: a systematic review. Cosmetics 2022;9(6):127.
[69] Gharbavi M, Amani J, Kheiri-Manjili H, Danafar H, Sharafi A. Niosome: a promising nanocarrier for natural drug delivery through blood-brain barrier. Adv Pharmacol Sci 2018;2018:6847971.
[70] Maniam G, Mai C-W, Zulkefeli M, Fu J-Y. Co-encapsulation of gemcitabine and tocotrienols in nanovesicles enhanced efficacy in pancreatic cancer. Nanomedicine. 2021;16(5):373−89.
[71] Agarwal S, Mohamed MS, Raveendran S, Rochani AK, Maekawa T, Kumar DS. Formulation, characterization and evaluation of morusin loaded niosomes for potentiation of anticancer therapy. RSC Adv 2018;8(57):32621−36.

CHAPTER 6

Micelles-based drug delivery for pancreatic cancer

Sanjay Ch, Tarun Kumar Patel, Swati Biswas and Balaram Ghosh
Epigenetic Research Laboratory, Department of Pharmacy, Birla Institute of Technology & Science-Pilani, Hyderabad, Telangana, India

6.1 Introduction

According to the latest epidemiological data, pancreatic cancer (PC) has become one of the world's most fatal cancers. PC ranks twelfth in cancer incidence but is the seventh leading cause of cancer mortality, with a 5-year survival rate of less than 10% [1]. However, significant progress has been made in cancer biology, genomics, proteomics, and clinical oncology in the past decades to treat cancer. Despite enormous efforts, PC remains a treatment-refractory malignancy [2]. In the PC, most cases are diagnosed at an advanced stage, and the treatment strategy includes chemotherapy, immunotherapy, surgical resection, and a combination with chemoradiotherapy (preoperative and postoperative). Typically, effective delivery of chemotherapeutic agents for PC treatment with optimum stability is still far from satisfactory. Most of the chemotherapeutic belong to biopharmaceutical classification system class-III or IV drugs; some such drugs include 5-fluorouracil, paclitaxel (PTX), docetaxel, gemcitabine (GEM), oxaliplatin, and cisplatin (Cis). These potent drugs have drawbacks such as poor solubility, bioavailability, unfavorable pharmacokinetics, lack of targetability, drug resistance, nonselective biodistribution, and adverse effects [3]. The micellar drug delivery has emerged as a novel treatment therapy in targeting drugs against PC due to their ability to deliver poorly water-soluble drugs. Polymeric micelles (PMs), below 200 nm in size, carry the small molecules through various endocytosis mechanisms to the targeted sites, unlike the conventional diffusion mechanism. After reaching the targeted sites, the drug is liberated from the micellar vesicles, internalized in the cellular compartments, and activates different cell-killing mechanisms. The PMs are amphiphilic polymers requiring hydrophilic and hydrophobic block polymers to self-assemble in an aqueous environment. The self-assembly of the micelle is entirely dependent on the hydrophilic—lipophilic balance. Depending upon the requirements, size, capability of drug loading, and micellization ability, the polymeric chain blocks can be tailored. Micelles have the advantage of targeting them into the tumor sites by surface modifications with tumor-targeting ligands. The core shell of the PMs is formed by amphiphilic polymers in which the hydrophobic

Recent Advances in Nanocarriers for Pancreatic Cancer Therapy
DOI: https://doi.org/10.1016/B978-0-443-19142-8.00001-2

part carries the hydrophobic drugs, and the hydrophilic corona imparts the hydrophilicity. The micelles' stability impacts cellular internalization, circulation, renal clearance, and strength of the interface between the external aqueous environment and the hydrophobic core [4,5]. The PMs' properties, which influence the drug release and in vivo therapeutic efficacy are shown in Fig. 6.1 [6].

6.2 Micellar uptake mechanism

Tumor uptake mechanisms can be broadly divided into active and passive. Diffusion-mediated transport is responsible for passive targeting, and the uptake mainly occurs due to the enhanced permeability and retention (EPR) effect of micelles, where micelles are accumulated within the neoplastic tissue due to the permeability of

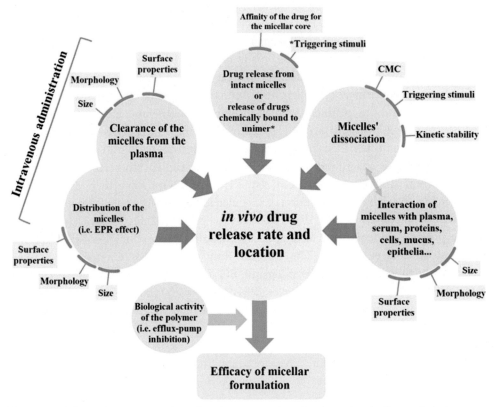

Figure 6.1 Schematic representation of various properties of polymeric micelles and their properties influencing the release and in vivo efficacy. Source: *Adapted with permission from Ghezzi M, et al. Polymeric micelles in drug delivery: an insight of the techniques for their characterization and assessment in biorelevant conditions. J Control Release 2021; 332:312—36. https://doi.org/10.1016/j.jconrel.2021.02.031. Copyright (2021), Elsevier.*

vasculature and long retention time, which significantly increases the concentration of micelles in the tumor tissue [7,8]. In Active targeting, the accumulation of micelles carrying therapeutic agents in the tumor was achieved by receptor-mediated transport. Mechanisms such as endocytosis are mainly responsible for the cellular uptake of micelles where some receptors are overexpressed to specific cancer cells, allowing the uptake of micelles carrying therapeutic agents to accumulate in the tumor environment. The various mechanisms of endocytosis are briefly discussed below and are represented in Fig. 6.2.

6.2.1 Endocytosis

Micelles placed in the external environment of a cell interact with the external plasma membrane, which leads to the uptake of micelles through a process called endocytosis. Endocytosis occurs through a series of stages where the micelles get engulfed in membranes and are deformed into a vesicle through the invagination process. Those membrane-bound vesicles are released into the cytoplasm. These membrane-bound vesicles are also called endosomes. In the next stage, these endosomes carry the micelles to different vesicular structures. In the final stage, the micelles are delivered to various intracellular compartments and all over the cells through a process called transcytosis. Endocytosis can be categorized as phagocytosis and pinocytosis.

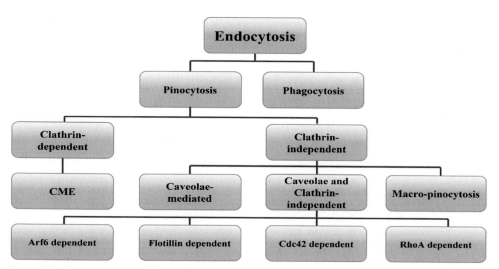

Figure 6.2 Representation of the cellular uptake mechanism of polymeric micelles through endocytosis and influence of endocytosis proteins in the cellular entry [9]. Source: *Reprinted with permission from Sahay G, Alakhova DY, Kabanov AV. Endocytosis of nanomedicines. J Control Release, 2010;145(3):182–95. https://doi.org/10.1016/j.jconrel.2010.01.036. Copyright (2010), Elsevier.*

6.2.2 Phagocytosis

Phagocytosis is expressed by very few categories of cells such as macrophages, monocytes, neutrophils, and dendritic cells. Other types of cells, such as fibroblasts and endothelial and epithelial cells, have been known to show phagocytosis but to a lower extent [10]. In phagocytosis, the cellular uptake mechanism occurs through a series of steps. In the first step, the particles in the bloodstream are recognized by a process called opsonization (opsonization is a process in which foreign particles are tagged for elimination by phagocytes). The second step involves in adhesion of opsonized particles on to the cell membrane. Ingestion of particles by the cells occurs in the third step. Opsonization happens upon coating the particles with immunoglobulins, complement proteins (C3, C4, and C5), and other proteins, such as laminin and fibronectin, which belong to blood serum. The opsonized particle attaches to the surface of the macrophage through specific receptors such as the Fc receptor or complement receptors. Mannose/fructose receptors also have a role in the phagocytosis of micelles [8,11,12].

6.2.3 Pinocytosis

Unlike phagocytosis, pinocytosis is exhibited in all cell types. It depends on the cell origin and function, and it can be classified as clathrin-mediated endocytosis (CE), clathrin-independent endocytosis, and micropinocytosis. CE is the most common route of cellular entry; it is naturally present in all mammalian cells, including pancreatic cells. CE is the most essential in uptake mechanisms of essential nutrients like cholesterol transported via low density lipoprotein receptor, transferrin receptor that carries iron. These proteins upon tagging to the micelles can be easily uptaken into the cells using CE. CE is also involved in the downregulation of cell signaling to maintain cellular homeostasis [13,14]. In CE, the receptors are engulfed in association with ligands bound on the plasma membrane. Cytosolic proteins are responsible for formation of coated pits on the cytosolic side of the membrane and produce clathrin-1, a key element for coating pits. The formed coating pits are then knocked off the membrane, by a protein known as dynamin and thereby forming clathrin-coated vesicles [15]. The micelles using this pathway are mainly targeted to degradative lysosomes where nanocarriers enter the cell through CE and carry the cargo to the endosomes at pH 6, and these endosomes are considered early endosomes. Later on, these endosomes are matured at pH 5 into late endosomes. The late endosomes will then fuse with vesicles to form lysosomes that have an acidic environment and are rich in enzymes for degradation. Only micelles carrying drugs that can sustain these harsh conditions after biodegradative release are favorable for this pathway [16]. Clathrin-independent endocytosis can be subcategorized as caveolae-mediated endocytosis (CVE) and clathrin and caveolae-independent endocytosis (CIE). CVEs are lipid rafts augmented with cholesterol and sphingolipids. These are flask-like shaped plasma membrane-bound invaginations ranging between 50−100 nm. CVE involves many functions such as cholesterol homeostasis, transduction, and in the transport of macromolecules. The internalization of extracellular molecules, ligands, and receptors takes place due to the raft-dependent endocytosis of primary structural protein called caveolae. The other types of caveolae proteins include CAV1, CAV2, and CAV3; among these, CAV1 is essential for the formation of flask-shaped vesicles and as in CE. The dynamin protein is also responsible for detecting these vesicles and fuses with the caveolae for bypassing the lysosomes, whereas CAV 2 is not and CAV 3 is muscle site-specific [17]. In case of CIE, cellular entry occurs even with the absence of CE and caveolin-1. CIE has shown carrying the micelles independently with average 90 nm vesicles along with glycosylphosphatidylinositol-linked proteins, interlukin-2, growth hormones, etc. This uptake mechanism has multiple pathways and multiple effectors (Arf6, flotillin, Cdc42, and RhoA-dependent) to regulate. All these pathways require specific lipid composition and are dependent on cholesterol [14].

6.2.4 Macropinocytosis
Compared to clathrin, caveolae-independent cytosis, the receptor activation mediates through the activation of tyrosine kinases receptors by growth factors. It acts as a signaling cascade that leads to the formation of membrane ruffles due to the changes in the actin cytoskeleton. These membrane ruffles engulf the nutrients and fluid materials present in the extracellular environment by which several nanoparticles/micelles are uptaken by the cells [18]. This pathway acts as a nonspecific entry point for several nanoparticles and can internalize large particles having a submicron size in the cells.

6.3 Polymeric micelles and their types
PMs can be broadly classified based on intermolecular forces that thrive on core segregation from the aqueous environment, such as hydrophobic interactions and electrostatic interactions (poly-ionic micelles), which can be grouped into conventional PMs and PMs based on functionalities [19].

6.3.1 Conventional polymeric micelles
The conventional PMs are formed from the self-assembly of amphiphilic polymers based on the hydrophobic interactions between the core, and shell present in the aqueous environment. The amphiphilic copolymers involved in cancer drug delivery mostly contain hydrophobic groups such as polyester or poly amino acid (PAA) derivatives. Polymers such as polylactic acid (PLA), polycaprolactone (PCL), and poly D, L-lactic-co-glycolic acid (PLGA) are extensively studied using them as a hydrophobic

core due to their biocompatibility and biodegradability. PAA derivatives such as poly (aspartic acid), poly(glutamic acid), poly (lysine), and poly (histidine) were also explored as a hydrophobic segment to carry out various drugs in treating PC [20]. Apart from these, polyethylene glycol (PEG) has emerged as a gold standard in utilizing it as a hydrophilic segment due to its versatile nature. PEG provides the stealth required for the micelles by preventing them from the reticuloendothelial system. PEG can be easily modified and conjugated with several chemical moieties [21]. In a study, salinomycin was loaded into a polymer carrier PEG-b-PLA (PEG-b-PLA) and delivered to GEM resistant PC. Significant cell mortality and apoptosis were observed, and micellar formulation successfully eradicated tumors from treated in Balb/c AsPC-1 xenograft mice [22].

6.3.1.1 Polymeric micelles based on electrostatic interactions

PMs based on electrostatic interactions (PIMs) are formed from the electrostatic interactions between the amphiphilic micelles and polyelectrolyte complexes leading through the segregation of oppositely charged polyanions/cations and precipitate in aqueous media. PIMs differ from polyelectrolyte complexes; they contain a hydrophilic segment that solubilizes the concentrates present in aqueous media. Polymers with positively charged units such as poly(ethyleneimine), poly (lysine), polyamidoamine, poly (methyl methacrylate) and negatively charged polymers such as poly (aspartic acid) and poly (methacrylic acid) are required to form PIM [23]. For example, A recent study has demonstrated that a transcriptive DNA was captured within a polyplex micellar system by utilizing PEG-b-poly(lysine) complexation. The study has shown that the formed micellar complex was rod-shaped and easily penetrated the stromal barrier after the systemic administration and has demonstrated significant antitumor efficacy in a PC mouse model through suicide gene therapy [24].

6.3.2 Polymeric micelles based on functionalities

PMs with functionalities provide various advantages compared to conventional types. They have received a lot of attention in cancer therapy due to their ability to provide specific targeting to the cancerous tissues and controlled drug release. These micelles can be functionalized based on external or internal stimuli such as pH, temperature, redox potential, photo-responsive, magnetic field, and ultrasound [25]. These stimuli-responsive micelles disassemble their structure and release the drug upon reacting to various stimuli. Stimuli-responsive micelles can be named smart micelles as they reduce the off-target drug release and precisely delivers the drug at the site of action. Fig. 6.3 represents the formation of micelles through external stimuli-responsive (temperature and pH), cellular uptake mechanism, and tumor-triggered drug release, and a few examples of stimuli-responsive PMs and their application in PC are tabulated in Table 6.1.

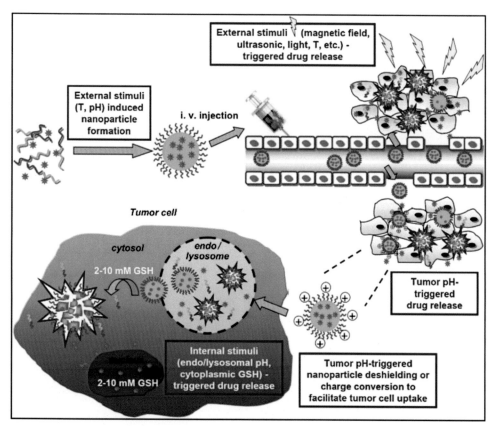

Figure 6.3 Schematic representation of micellar formation through stimuli-responsive drug delivery system via external stimulus applications (pH and temperature), tumor-triggered drug release, cellular uptake mechanism, and release under acidic effect influence and cellular uptake [26]. Source: *Reprinted with permission from Cheng R, Meng F, Deng C, Klok H-A, Zhong Z. Dual and multi-stimuli responsive polymeric nanoparticles for programmed site-specific drug delivery. Biomaterials 2013;34 (14):3647—57. https://doi.org/10.1016/j.biomaterials.2013.01.084. Copyright (2013) Elsevier.*

6.3.2.1 pH-sensitive micelles

The tumor's pH is acidic and around 6.5 compared to the normal tissue, which is about 7.4; this low pH causes a high glycolysis rate in the tumor. Due to the high glycolysis rate, lactic acid is produced under aerobic and anaerobic conditions. Tumor cells benefit from low pH and grow invasively. Upon tuning of micelles, drugs can be released from the micelles at the specific tumor site in response to low extra- or intra–cellular pH environments [40]. The underlying mechanism of drug release from the pH-sensitive micelles involves the presence of ionizable groups on the pH-sensitive polymers, which can accept or donate the protons in response to pH change. At relevant pKa, a swift change in ionization occurs with the change in pH values; thereby, weakly ionizable groups in the

Table 6.1 Represents the types of stimuli-responsive block copolymers used as micellar drug delivery systems in the treatment of pancreatic cancer.

Type of stimuli	Block copolymers	Mechanism	Therapeutic cargos	Outcome	References
pH	Poly(N, N-dimethyl aminoethyl methacrylate)	Protonation of tertiary amine group to form a cationic group	anticancer oligonucleotide, ISIS 5132	Drugs released at the basic environment and micelles were able to penetrate the AsPC-1 tumor spheroids and destroy them	[27]
	Poly-(ethylene glycol)–block–poly(dipropyl aminoethyl methacrylate)	Sulfonamide groups depending on the substitution group, pH of the polymer changes and controls the release behavior of the polymer	Triptolide-conjugated naphthalene sulfonamide	Micelles targeted to KRAS mutant pancreatic cancer-induced cell apoptosis, and have shown significant antitumor efficacy	[28]
	Vitamin E conjugated mPEG with hydrazone linkage	Polymers with linkages undergo hydrolysis under acidic pH conditions. These polymers can break the acid-sensitive groups and deliver the therapeutic agents in acidic pH	γ-tocotrienol	Cytotoxic studies on pancreatic cancer cell lines, BxPC-3, and PANC1 resulted in no toxicity, and pH-based controlled release was achieved	[29]
Temperature	Poly(2-ethylhexyl methacrylate)–b–poly[di (ethylene glycol)methyl ether methacrylate–co–oligo (ethylene glycol)methyl ether methacrylate]	Temperature-responsive micellar deformation	Gemcitabine and paclitaxel	Drug release triggered above LCST, and synergetic effect was observed in in vitro pancreatic tumor cell line studies	[30]
	Tetraethoxymethacrylate terminated with choline phosphate and dimethyl aminoethyl methacrylate	Temperature-responsive micellar deformation	Fluorescently labeled compound	Significant uptake of micelles was observed with the human pancreatic cell line (Hs766T)	[31]

Stimulus	Material	Agent	Mechanism	Observation	Ref.
Redox	Poly(L-lysine) containing thiol groups and PEG as block polymers	vascular endothelial growth factor receptor (sFlt-1) used as gene therapy	Disulfide Bond cleavage by GSH	Triggered drug release was observed with significant antitumor efficacy of micelles on BXPC3 pancreatic adenocarcinoma tumor-bearing mice	[32]
	Methoxy-polyethylene glycol-block-poly (aspartame)-graft-dodecylamine-graft-S-S by disulfide linkage	Gemcitabine and miR-519c	Disulfide bond cleavage by GSH	GSH readily breached the micelles and released the drug and synergetic effect of GEM and miR-519c on tumor growth inhibition	[33]
	PEG-poly[aspartamidoethyl(p-boronobenzyl) diethylammoniumbromide]	Tumor suppressor protein miR-34a and PLK1 inhibitor volasertib	Bond cleavage through GSH and ROS-sensitive	There was a significant reduction in the tumor volume after the micellar treatment with No systemic toxicity	[34]
Light	Poly(ethylene oxide)-block-poly(methacrylate) altered with SP chains	A fluorescently labeled dye	UV light–triggered release	Light-triggered release was observed upon UV irradiation at 365 nm	[35]
	PEG-methacrylate, 7-(2-methylacryloylethoxy)-4-methylcoumarin (CMA) and 2-(2-hydroxyethyl disulfanyl)ethyl acrylate conjugated Gemcitabine (GEM).	GEM	UV-triggered drug release	Stable micelles were formed after irradiating with UV at 365 nm. In BxPC-3 pancreatic tumor cells, micelles are effectively internalized and also inhibited the cell proliferation	[36]
Magnetic	Vitamin E succinate amphiphilic copolymer	CKAAKN	Magnetically guided tumor targeting	The CKAAKN peptide, is precisely accumulated in pancreatic cancer cells due to the specific binding to cancer cell membrane platform. It was a potential carrier for MRI contrast enhancement	[37]

(Continued)

Table 6.1 (Continued)

Type of stimuli	Block copolymers	Therapeutic cargos	Mechanism	Outcome	References
Ultrasound	PEG-PLA and PEG-polycaprolactone (PCL) as block polymer	Gemcitabine and PTX	Ultrasound-triggered structural transitions, breaking, and microbubble cavitation	Polymeric micelles with ultrasound-mediated therapy allowed controlling the invasive cancer cells by suppressing metastases and ascites	[38]
	PEG polyaspartate block copolymer	Epirubicin	Ultrasound-triggered structural transitions, breaking, and microbubble cavitation	The effectiveness and feasibility of DDS-based SDT, combined with a small dose of NC–6300 and low energy of HIFU were evaluated in mouse models of colon cancer and pancreatic cancer	[39]

polymer get ionized, which directly affects the polymer chain in which hydrodynamic diameter and molecular state of the polymeric chain get altered. The pH-sensitive polymers can be broadly divided into cationic/ anionic polymers and acid-sensitive polymers.

6.3.2.1.1 Cationic/anionic polymers

Under acidic conditions, polymers with a tertiary amine group as a side chain can bind to the protons to form a cationic group and subsequently release protons in a basic environment. For instance, poly(N, N-dimethyl aminoethyl methacrylate) (PDMAEMA) is a cationic pH-sensitive polymer with tertiary amine groups. It was used as a PM to load an anticancer oligonucleotide, ISIS 5132. In this study, albumin was conjugated to PDMAEMA. After successful loading, the therapeutic efficacy was tested on AsPC-1, PC cell line, and the prepared micellar formulation could penetrate the tumor spheroids and destroy them [27]. Recently, extensive research is going on another group of cationic polymers containing pyridine. At pH 5, pyridine groups get deprotonated and undergo a phase transition. In a study conducted, researchers used polystyrene-block-poly(4-vinylpyridine) (PS-b-P4VP) amphiphilic block copolymer that has pyridine groups and evaluated payload release and pH-responsive membrane penetration and concluded that the developed pH-sensitive micelles could be made operational under basic pH so that, the therapeutic agent can be targeted to pancreatic duct and releases the drug sustainably [41].

Most commonly used pH-sensitive polymers contain carboxylic acid and sulfonamide groups as anionic segments. At low pH, the carboxylic acid groups of such polymers are protonated and yield relatively hydrophobic neutral molecules. These molecules are converted to hydrophilic by releasing proton molecules at high pH. Poly(methyl acrylic acid) is a type of polymer that shows rapid phase transition and promotes self-aggregation. Polymers containing sulfonamide groups are anionic polymers whose pKa varies from pH 3—11 depending on the pendant substitution of sulfonamide groups. These polymers show higher sensitivity in controlling the polymer behavior over a narrow pH range because the sulfonamide groups get readily ionized with the increase in pH. This unique behavior of sulfonamide groups allows researchers to target the tumor site precisely compared to the polymers containing carboxylic acid groups [42]. In a study, ultrasensitive pH-triggered micelles were prepared by conjugating a prodrug conjugated naphthalene sulfonamide to poly-(ethylene glycol)-block-poly(dipropyl aminoethyl methacrylate) and targeted to KRAS mutant PC. The micelles went through an apparent phase transition at their apparent pKa and induced cell apoptosis. The micelles have also shown significant antitumor efficacy in KRAS mutant PC models when treated with ultra pH-sensitive micelles [28].

6.3.2.1.2 Acid-sensitive polymers

Polymers containing acid-sensitive bonds such as hydrazone, acetal, benzoic imine, and orthoester as linkages undergo hydrolysis under acidic pH conditions. These polymers can break the acid-sensitive groups and deliver the therapeutic agents in acidic pH with controlled release ability. In a study, derivatives of vitamin E, mPEG conjugates with hydrazone linkages were synthesized and evaluated on PC cell lines (BxPC-3 and PANC-1). The derivative with hydrazone linkage had the highest release at acidic pH 5.5, which suggested the pH-dependent release [29].

6.3.2.2 Temperature/thermoresponsive micelles

In response to heat stimulation, cancer cells induce apoptosis due to the deactivation and deformation of proteins at temperatures above 42°C, compared to normal cells. In particular, PC cells are susceptible to heat ablation, thus minimizing heat's negative influence on normal cells. Even though heat therapy is considered a promising therapy in treating cancers, upon repetitive treatments, tumor cells can adapt to heat and develop tolerance. In this scenario, stimuli-sensitive micelles have a greater advantage as temperature-responsive micellar preparations can effectively carry the drug load to the tumor site and the micellar systems can be prepared easily. Temperature-responsive polymers (TRPs) are abundantly available, can respond to the tumor temperature, and release the therapeutic agent [43]. TRP is extensively used in biomedical fields because it can alter their physicochemical and conformation properties throughout their phase transition temperature. Lower critical solution temperature (LCST) type polymers are widely used among several phase transition temperature types. In the aqueous phase, below LCST, these polymers have an extended coil structure and are highly hydrated. Hydrophobic globules are formed by the temperature-sensitive polymers above LCST due to the dehydration of polymers. In the aqueous phase, these chemical and structural changes occur reversibly in TRP across the LCST. TRP including poly(N-isopropyl acrylamide) (PIPAM), poly(methacrylate), poly(N-vinyl butyramide), poly(N-vinyl isobutyrate), and poly(2-isopropyl-2-oxazoline) has LCST closely to body temperature. In particular, because of the sharp TRP behavior of PIPAM, having low LCST (32°C), these polymers, upon introduction to the drug carrier surface, are highly hydrated, increasing blood circulation time and allows drug carriers to accumulate in the tumor tissues through EPR effect [44]. LCST-type TRP systems can be used as a core or corona-forming segments of the block polymer and can be integrated into the PMs. Because of the hydrophobic interaction between the dehydrated TRP chains, a core–shell micellar structure forms above the LCST when a TR polymer is used as the hydrophobic core-forming segment, whereas integrating TRP into the PMs as hydrophilic segments of block polymers, below LCST, the polymeric chains are highly hydrated and surrounded by hydrophobic core [45]. In PC, extensive research has been done on the polymers containing methacrylate groups to prepare the thermoresponsive micelles.

In a study to achieve dual controlled drug delivery for treating PC, GEM, and PTX, both drugs were loaded onto thermoresponsive PMs comprised of poly(2-ethylhexyl methacrylate)-*b*-poly[di(ethylene glycol)methyl ether methacrylate-*co*-oligo(ethylene glycol)methyl ether methacrylate] as a copolymer. The LCST value of the polymers was determined by the optical turbidity method, and drug-loaded micelles were subjected to an in vitro drug release study above LCST values, 37°C and 40°C. It was noticed that above the LCST of the polymer, both drugs could be released in a controlled manner from the micellar compartment. A synergistic effect was observed after the in vitro cytotoxicity study performed on a PC cell line [30]. In a study, a group of researchers prepared a thermoresponsive PM with an LCST below 37°C. They used tetraethoxymethacrylate terminated with choline phosphate and dimethyl aminoethyl methacrylate to prepare the micelles. Significant uptake of micelles was observed with the human pancreatic cell line (Hs766T) after treating with micellar formulation incubated at above LCST for 60 min when analyzed with laser confocal fluorescence microscopy [31].

6.3.2.3 Enzyme-sensitive micelles

Enzymes are the critical regulator of the body's biological and metabolic processes. The dysregulation of enzymes is observed in different pathological conditions associated with various diseases. The overexpression of several enzymes such as proteases, proteases, peptidases, and lipases has been seen in solid tumors and plays a vital role in the propagation of tumors. Enzyme-triggered systems enhance chemotherapeutic payloads' selective delivery, as enzymes catalyze most biological reactions under mild conditions. Various enzyme-responsive nano micelles have been developed to prepare enzyme-triggered delivery systems for chemotherapeutic payloads. The incorporation of enzyme responsiveness to the PMs for anticancer drug delivery by adding specific moieties in their main chain or side groups can be selectively recognized and degraded by overexpressed enzymes in tumor microenvironments, enabling tumor-targeted and on-demand drug release with the least untoward side effects in normal tissues. Matrix metalloproteinases, proteolytic enzymes, and extracellular matrix (ECM)-remodeling proteases are overexpressed in various tumors, including PC [2].

6.3.2.4 Redox-sensitive micelles

The fundamental design of the redox-sensitive micelles (RMs) is to deliver and release the drug and other therapeutic agents at the tumor site in response to the elevated levels of glutathione (GSH) and reactive oxygen species (ROS). Tumor microenvironment characteristics include elevated ROS levels, acidic pH environment, hypoxia, and leaky vasculature. The ROS levels in the tumor cells are significantly influenced by increased genetic mutation and metabolism. Due to the high concentrations of ROS present in the tumor cells, significant damage to the cellular proteins occurs, including lipo-oxidation and DNA/RNA damage, which finally leads to malignant tumors. Increased levels of ROS also promote apoptosis and have an essential role in various cell signaling paths such as proliferation, metastasis, apoptosis, and cell survival. The cell's balance between ROS and antioxidants can be redox hemostasis. The oxidative stress in the cells is affected by the imbalance of redox hemostasis [46].

GSH is an antioxidant that protects the cells from oxidative damage and has a primary role in scavenging ROS and regulating the redox balance. GSH is a bioproduct from synthesizing glycine and γ-glutamyl cysteine. GSH has the capability of forming a disulfide bond upon reduction and controls the tumor cells by reacting with ROS. In recent years, the reducing property of GSH came to the limelight, which made the researchers utilize this property in designing RMs for delivering therapeutic agents in cancer. In tumor cells, a ten folds increase in the levels of ROS (100 μM) and GSH (10 mM) can be observed when compared to normal cells [47] showing the potential to design RM.

To achieve ROS and GSH sensitivity, several functional moieties can be architected into the micelles to target the tumor microenvironment. Thus, RMs can disassemble in the redox and release the therapeutic agents. Strategies to impart functional moieties in the micelles and their role as RMs are briefly discussed below.

6.3.2.4.1 Disulfide bond

Both oxidizing and reducing agents sunders the disulfide bonds; GSH is a reducing agent that reduces to moieties of thiol(sulfhydryl) and is further oxidized by H_2O_2 to sulfonic, sulfenic, and sulfinic acid. Due to the less stability of the disulfide bonds at various oxidative and reductive conditions, these functional moieties are mainly considered a linker to design RMs. Chemotherapy in cancer is limited to developing resistance to multiple drugs, and efflux generated by relevant proteins causes this. To overcome this, amphiphilic polymers such as chitosan, hyaluronic acid, and PEG can be used to construct RM. In a study, disulfide bond cross-linked polyplex micelles conjugated with RGD peptides were synthesized using poly(L-lysine) containing thiol groups and PEG as block polymers and plasmid DNA from the vascular endothelial growth factor receptor (sFlt-1) used as gene therapy. Compared to the RGD conjugation, the cross-linked disulfide micelles had a prolonged circulation time, and RGD conjugation resulted in a significantly low circulation time. Micelles were tested for antitumor efficacy in BXPC3 pancreatic adenocarcinoma tumor-bearing mice. The results indicated that micelles increased the tumor accumulation, and about 15% of a significant therapeutic effect was observed with cross-linked micelle upon intravenous administration to the mice. This study concludes that disulfide cross-linking increases the tumor accumulation of micelles as a significant inhibitory effect and can be opted for antiangiogenic therapy [32]. Epidermal growth factor receptor (EGFR) overexpresses in 40%—80% of PCs, and functionalized particles are accumulated in the overexpressed EGFR, resulting in more cytotoxicity. Since micellar drug delivery poses significant advantages in the accumulation of therapeutic agents in the tumor, an attempt was made to prepare a redox-sensitive micellar system, conjugating GEM and miR-519c prepared micelles to methoxy-PEG (mPEG)-block-poly(aspartame)-graft-dodecylamine-graft-S-S by disulfide linkage and GE11 peptide mixed micelles to target EGFR was also designed for targeted release at pancreatic tumor sites with the help of disulfide bond linkage. GSH can readily break the disulfide bond present in the micelles. In 10 mM GSH, disulfide conjugated micelles released a significant amount of GEM within 60 min. It also suggests that the disulfide conjugates rapidly released GEM in the physiological environment and were stable. A desmoplastic orthotopic mouse model bearing PC was used to determine the therapeutic effect of micelles. Results showed the synergetic effect of GEM and miR-519c on tumor growth inhibition when administrated intravenously [33].

In a recent study, polyketals are used as hydrophobic segments to prepare the micelles due to their acid-responsive nature. When contacting the acidic environment, polyketals will disintegrate into water-soluble molecules, releasing the drug rapidly. To stimulate the polyketals, a redox system was chosen due to the ability of GSH to cleave the disulfide bond-containing micelles at higher concentrations. Therefore, using this advantage in this study, acid and reduction-sensitive copolymer delivered doxorubicin (DOX) at the pancreatic tumor site. mPEG was functionalized with disulfide linkage and then reacted with a polymeric precursor synthesized of resorcin and 1,4-cyclohexanedimethanol divinyl ether. The obtained redox-sensitive polymer was further analyzed for therapeutic efficacy. In this approach, the drug-entrapped micelles are influenced by the pH and GSH, rapidly releasing the drug and killing the tumor cells. The presence of mPEG as an amphiphilic polymer in these micelles improves blood circulation time and stability. This experiment's outcome significantly increased micellar internalization in an in vitro cellular uptake test conducted on the Panc-1 pancreatic cell line. The tumor growth volume was reduced considerably with Dox-loaded micelles in the Panc-1 tumor-bearing nude mice after the treatment compared to free Dox [48]. This shows that disulfide bond linkage is prominent in designing redox-sensitive micellar drug delivery systems to treat pancreatic and other cancer types efficiently.

6.3.2.4.2 Diselenide bond

Selenium belongs to the same family as sulfur, with a large diameter and weakly negative charge. Unlike the disulfide bonds, the diselenide bonds (Se-Se) show a response even at low concentrations of GSH. The diselenide bond is susceptible and breaks down quickly compared to the disulfide bond (S-S). In contrast, the diselenide bond has a bond energy of 172 KJ/mol, whereas the disulfide bond has 240 KJ/mol. This weaker bond energy makes the diselenide conjugated micellar systems release the drug rapidly upon contact with GSH or other reducing agents. Apart from these advantages, the Se-Se bond has a significant limitation of being very toxic to the cells as it undergoes selenosis. To overcome this, organic counterparts such as tellurium can be used [49].

6.3.2.4.3 Thioether, aryl boronic ester, and thioketal functional moieties

In the presence of H_2O_2, the thioether bond (C-S-C) undergoes a phase transition rapidly from the hydrophobic sulfide group to more hydrophilic groups such as sulfoxide or sulfone. Aryl boronic esters can be easily oxidized compared to aryl boronic acids by H_2O_2. Aryl boronic esters belong to the ROS-responsive linkers in which they oxidize to form a phenolic intermediate and rearrange to quinone methide and release the drug upon complete degradation of micellar nanoparticles. Peroxalate ester is another type of linker belonging to the ROS-responsive group, forming an immediate intermediate called dioxetandione upon oxidation. Thioketals are H_2O_2 responsive, where they are oxidized into thiols and ketones. In a study, both GSH and ROS-sensitive PMs were prepared using PEG-poly[aspartamidoethyl(p-boronobenzyl) diethylammoniumbromide] as block polymers. These micelles are loaded with a tumor suppressor protein miR-34a and PLK1 inhibitor volasertib. The approach of this study is to utilize the excess production of ROS in the cancer cell to target the therapeutic moiety using redox-sensitive PMs. The prepared micelles are stable due to the electrostatic interaction and nitrogen-boron coordination of nucleic acid, quaternary ammonium, and tertiary amines, boronic acid, respectively. Upon oxidation with ROS, boronic acid gets detached, forms tertiary amines and p-quinone methide, and rapidly releases the therapeutic agents at the target site. In orthotopic pancreatic tumor-bearing NSG mice, there was a significant reduction in the tumor volume after the micellar treatment. No systemic toxicity was observed from the histopathology of vital organs [34]. The role of ROS-responsive micelles and their applications in cancer therapy is gaining interest and has tremendous protential in treating PC compared to other dosage forms.

6.3.2.5 Photo-responsive polymeric micelles

Photo-responsive PMs (PRPM) differ from other stimuli as light has to be triggered from outside and can be controlled easily. The properties of the polymers can be smartly controlled by tuning the wavelength and intensity of the light. These unique properties of light-sensitive polymers gained much interest in researchers to design photo-responsive polymers in various biomedical fields, including cancer. The photo-responsive micelles can be grouped into multiple categories depending on the effect of light on the photo-responsive group and different photoreaction mechanisms: photoisomerization PMs, PMs rearrangement by photo-induction, photocleavable micelles, photo-induced cross-linkable micelles, and micelles based on photo-induced energy conversion. The self-assembly of PRPM consists of an amphiphilic block copolymer with a functional photochromic chromophore. The photochromic molecules absorb the optical signal; then the photo-irradiation is converted to a chemical signal by photoreceptor present in the chromophores through a photoreaction such as a rearrangement, isomerization, cleavage, energy conversion, and dimerization. The chemical signal converted by the photoreceptor is diverted to the functional segments of the micelles. Molecular structures and variable light sources strongly influence chromophores upon photo-irradiation [50].

6.3.2.5.1 Photoisomerization polymeric micelles

Upon photoexcitation, the structural changes between the isomers occur in photoisomerization, which is repeatable and reversible. Photoisomerization groups are potential candidates and can utilize these functionalized polymers in various applications. Some photoisomerization molecules include azobenzene (Azo), dithienylethene (DTE), and spiropyran (SP). In the Azo group containing PMs upon light irradiation (340−380 nm), conformational changes occur from the *trans* form to the *cis* form, in which both the conformations are polar. Under subsequent irradiation at 420−490 nm, this process reforms back. The self-assembly and disruption of Azo-PMs are due to the hydrophobicity of the *trans*-AZO form, and the *cis*-Azo group is more polar and less hydrophobic than the *trans* form. In a study to explain this phenomenon, a group of researchers architected a photoisomerization polymeric micellar system containing Azo groups. This amphiphilic diblock copolymer comprises an Azo conjugated poly(methacrylate) and a hydrophilic poly(t-butyl acrylate-co-acrylic acid). The side chain containing the Azo group undergoes irradiation upon UV light irradiation and transformed to *cis* from *trans* form, resulting in the bursting of micellar aggregates. When irradiated with visible light, the Azo groups changed to the *trans* form reproducing PMs [51]. The SP group containing micelles is more sensitive to light than the Azo group. SP group containing PMs, upon irradiation with visible light at 620 nm, also undergoes reversible isomerization from hydrophilic zwitterionic merocyanine state, which is considered open form to a hydrophobic SP state, which is hydrophobic and called a closed form. This process can be reversed when triggered with UV light at 365 nm. Unlike the Azo groups, the polarity is greater between the hydrophilic zwitterionic merocyanine and hydrophobic SP units. Due to this, the SP-grouped PMs are also considered a good delivery system and can be used in various biomedical fields. DTE groups containing micelles are regarded as versatile compared to other groups. In the absence of light, these contain a high thermal barrier to isomerize, and the conformational changes in shape and rigidity can be predicted between ring-open and closed photo isomers [52]. In a study, photo isomeric micelles containing poly (ethylene oxide)-block-poly(methacrylate) in which the Poly(methacrylate) group was altered with SP side chains. Upon UV irradiation, these micelles observed micellar disruption due to the conversion of SP to merocyanine-charged particles. The encapsulation and release profile of the micelles were also evaluated by loading a hydrophobic dye, coumarin 102, and its release got triggered upon excitation at 365 nm [35]. In another study to utilize DTE containing photoisomerization micelles, a thermoresponsive polymer poly(*N*-isopropylacrylamide) was used as a hydrophilic polymer, and photochromic DTE components were utilized as hydrophobic segments. Upon exposing these copolymers to light and temperature, they self-assembled to form micelles [50].

6.3.2.5.2 Polymeric micelles rearrangement by photo-induction

In photo-induced PMs, the disassembly of PMs occurs upon light induction. Hydrophobic segments of an amphiphilic polymer are converted to a hydrophilic segment, thereby disrupting micelles and releasing the payload entrapped in them. For example, we can consider a molecule containing a photo-reactive group, 2–diazo-1,2-naphthoquinone (DNQ) molecule, which is hydrophobic and converts to a hydrophilic 3-indene-carboxylic acid (3-IC) molecule of pKa of 4.5 upon Wolff rearrangement reaction induced through UV light.

6.3.2.5.3 Photocleavable polymeric micelles

Photocleavable PMs undergo photocleavage reactions in the PMs due to the presence of photocleavage groups. These photocleavage groups can randomly exist in the side, middle, and main block junctions of block polymers, and depending on various locations of photocleavage groups, photo-responsive characteristics vary. To brief their characteristics, upon irradiation, the photochromic group located on the side chain of a block polymer gets converted from hydrophobic to hydrophilic, leading to partial or complete micelles disruption and then release of payload. The photochromic groups present on the main chain of block polymers, upon irradiation, disrupt into oligomers, which leads to the rapid release of payload. Copolymers incorporated with photochromic groups at the middle, hydrophobic groups reorganize upon irradiation and split into two distinct polymeric aggregates followed by the release of payload. Some photocleavable PMs containing photochromic groups include *O*-nitrobenzyl and copolymers associated with coumarin. *O*-Nitrobenzyl and derivatives-bearing polymers are easy to synthesize, and these polymers are vulnerable to the photolysis process upon triggering through UV/NIR light containing one or two photons [53]. Coumarin and its derivative's application in polymer science, drug delivery, biology, and biomaterials have widely explored cancer applications. Coumarin moieties, upon exposure to UV/NIR irradiation, photochromic polypeptide blocks are converted to a poly (glutamic acid) hydrophilic moiety, which significantly releases the drug upon disruption. Photocleavable coumaric molecules containing PMs, on irradiating with NIR light for 220 min, tend to release the drug over a prolonged time with a significant amount of drug release.

6.3.2.5.4 Polymeric micelles induced by photo-crosslinking

Photo-cross-linkable PMs can be broadly categorized into two types: Cinnamic ester-containing crosslinkers and coumarin-containing crosslinkers. This particular method is very applicable to utilizing photo-crosslinking as a tool to stabilize the micelles. Destabilization of micelles is a major disadvantage of having less stability at higher temperatures, and these are very prone to disassembly to any solvent changes. Since light-induced cross-linking is an easy tool to apply to cross-link, there was a growing interest in developing photo-induced cross-linkable PMs in PC therapy [54]. In a study, photocrosslinkable copolymer poly(PEG-co-CMA-co-GEM) was developed from one-step radical copolymerization of PEG-methacrylate, 7-(2-Methylacryloylethoxy)-4-methylcoumarin (CMA) and 2-(2-hydroxyethyl disulfanyl)ethyl acrylate conjugated GEM. The GEM micelles cross-linked to coumarin groups by [$2\pi s + 2\pi s$] after UV irradiation at 365 nm, in which, upon irradiation, dimers are formed by coumarin leading to the formation of cyclobutene rings. The formed micelles were found to be stable. The prepared micelles do not deform below critical micellar concentration. They are even stable to the solvent changes/nonselective solvents such as DMSO/H_2O (1:1). In BxPC-3 pancreatic tumor cells, micelles are effectively internalized when analyzed using a confocal laser microscope and flow cytometer. The poly(PEG-co-CMA) micellar formulation has shown biocompatibility while analyzed through MTT assay and also exhibited high cytotoxicity of GEM-conjugated micelles against BxPC-3 cells [36].

6.3.2.6 Magnetic field-responsive polymeric micelles

Magnetic field-responsive PMs (MPM) typically consist of active magnetic components and payloads. They can be used for tumor targeting and rapid drug release, and these particles can penetrate deep inside the tumor upon exposure to an external magnetic field. This novel approach has great potential in targeting cancer and gained many researchers' attention to explore its advantages in cancer treatment. The most commonly used sensitive magnetic particles include magnetite (Fe_3O_4) and maghemite (Fe_2O_3), which are also referred to as superparamagnetic iron oxide nanoparticles. Due to their property of superparamagnetism, they form particles with 10 nm in size. After applying the magnetic field, they are attracted to the field, and after removing it, they cannot retain their magnetic properties. Other than magnetic targeting of the tumors, MPMs can also be used in biomedical applications such as magnetic resonance imaging (MRI) to detect cancers, magnetic transfection, and hypothermia. In magnetic hypothermia, the increased local temperature generated by altering the magnetic field could be used as a potential tool to kill the tumors. If chemotherapy is combined with the magnetic hypothermia approach, it destroys the tumors more effectively. This MPM has excellent potential in diagnosing, treating, and targeting the tumor with minimized side effects [2]. In a study, MRI contrast agents were targeted using an MRI micellar platform, and the delivery system was functionalized with a PC-targeting peptide, CKAAKN. This newly developed delivery system consists of hyaluronic acid-vitamin E succinate amphiphilic copolymeric micelles. Ultra-small superparamagnetic iron oxide was delivered using the developed nanocarrier. The nano micelles could be able to internalize into the BxPC-3 cells. The micelles were more specifically accumulated into the PC cells than healthy ones. This micellar system has shown 80% cell viability over HPDE6-C7 cells. This nanoplatform, by utilizing the CKAAKN peptide, can precisely accumulate in PC cells due to the specific binding of the peptide to the cancer cell membrane. These developed nano micelles are considered a better platform to diagnose cancer and potential carrier for MRI contrast enhancement [37].

6.3.2.7 Ultrasound-responsive polymeric micelles

Ultrasound-responsive PMs (URP) disintegrate/disassemble to ultrasound and release the payload at the site of action. Upon cavitation, these ultrasound waves either generate thermal effects by absorbing the energy or mechanical effects followed by micellar deformation and release the payload. Ultrasound has great potential to increase the permeability of biological barriers such as cell membranes. It could enhance the cellular uptake of drugs due to the generation of heat and the formation of cavitation bubbles. URPs have also been explored as a triggering agent to achieve spatiotemporally controlled release of many active agents encapsulated in nano micelles. Upon combination with thermoresponsive polymers, they have great potential to alter the release mechanism, and can effectively target tumors. Due to enhanced membrane permeability, low cost, and effortless administration, the URPs emerged as attractive drug delivery agents, and these can also be explored in diagnostic applications. The mostly studied polymer used for URPs includes pluronic polymers with ternary copolymers such as poly(ethylene oxide) (PEO) and poly(polypropylene oxide) [2]. In a study, a combination drug formulation of GEM-loaded PMs encapsulated with PTX-nanodroplet formulations mediated with ultrasound therapy with tumor sonication at 1 MHz ultrasound. The formulation of micelles consists of PEG-PLA and PEG-PCL as block polymers and loaded with GEM. Then PTX powder was dissolved in micellar solution. Then nanoemulsion was prepared to utilize perfluoropentacene (PFP). PFP has great potential to convert the nanoemulsions to microbubbles upon ultrasound exposure and also imparts thermal stability due to the Laplace pressure generated inside the nanodroplets. In systemic circulation, the PFP restricts the conversion of microbubbles through thermal stability and helps the nanoformulation to accumulate in the tumor through extravasation of leaky microvasculature. Pancreatic ductal adenocarcinoma xenografts were orthotopically grown in the nude mice transfected with MiaPaCa-2 cell animal model and tested for the combination therapy mediated by ultrasound results, which had shown that tumor sonication with 1 MHz ultrasound had reduced the tumor volume dramatically. PMs with ultrasound-mediated therapy allowed controlling the invasive cancer cells by suppressing metastases and ascites [38].

6.4 Pancreatic cancer—targeting sites for micelles

Conventional therapy for cancer treatment possesses many limitations, such as low concentration of drugs reaching the tumor site, multiple drug resistance, agonizing cytotoxicity, need for high doses, and poor distribution in the body. Therefore, it is important to identify the specific ligands and receptors to target chemo/therapeutic agents to the PC cells; targeting the therapeutic agents reduces the toxicity to the healthy cells, the necessity for high doses can be eliminated, and therapeutic efficacy can be significantly improved. Different ligands can be used as a targeting agents for site-specific drug sites whose receptors are specifically grown on the tumor cells. These include EGF, transferrin, urokinase plasminogen activator receptor (uPAR), fucosylated antigen, and Integrins. Potential targets in cancer therapy are illustrated in Fig. 6.4.

6.4.1 Epidermal growth factor

EGF receptor belongs to the family of human EGFRs, tyrosine kinases. EGFR over-expressed 10- to 10,000-fold in pancreatic tumor cells compared to the normal cells, and many immunohistochemistry studies revealed that it overexpresses in PC between 30% and 90%. Many intracellular signaling pathways, such as RAS/MAPK and P13K-AKT, are initiated upon EGF binding to the EGFR receptor through a series of events such as dimerization and self-phosphorylation. An increase in tumor volume, proliferation, angiogenesis, metastasis, and annexation occurs upon the upregulation of EGFR. By inhibiting the EGFR, the signaling cascade is affected, followed by the

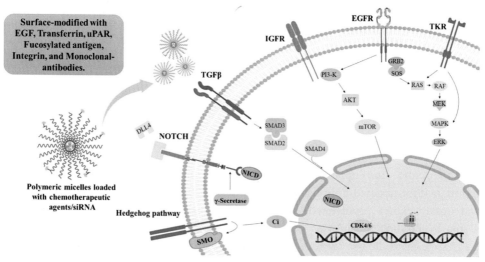

Figure 6.4 Schematic representation of potential targets in pancreatic cancer therapy [55]. *Source: Adapted permission from Lai E, et al. New therapeutic targets in pancreatic cancer. Cancer Treat Rev 2019;81:101926. https://doi.org/10.1016/j.ctrv.2019.101926. Copyright (2019), Elsevier.*

downregulation of the receptor, thereby restricting the proliferation in PC. In PC, small molecules inhibiting monoclonal antibodies that neutralize tyrosine kinase inhibitors are explored as pharmacological strategies that could effectively obstruct the EGFR. Vascular endothelial growth factor (VEGF) is an angiogenic polypeptide that plays an important role in endothelial cell growth. VEGF emerged as a new potential target site for delivering therapeutic agents, specifically in many cancers, including PC. The initial hypothesis of VEGF was that its expression is very limited to endothelial cells. However, VEGF in the tumor is overexpressed by more than 90% and stimulates the downstream signaling pathways that persuade the proliferation and endothelial cells relocation. The formation of desmoplastic stroma triggered by fibrin matrix deposition is influenced due to increased vascular permeability occurring by increased VEGF. This overexpressed VEGF has emerged as a promising target for the site-specific delivery of chemo/therapeutic agents to PC [56,57]. In a study, GEM and miR-205 conjugated EGFR-targeting monoclonal antibody cetuximab (C225). Cetuximab was conjugated to malemido-PEG-block-poly(2 methyl-2-carboxyl-propylene carbonate-graft-dodecanol) (C225-PEG-PCD). C225-PEG-PCD was used to prepare mixed micelles using PEG-b-block-poly(2-methyl-2-carboxyl-propylene carbonate-g-dodecanol-g-tetraethylenepentamine) (PEG-b-PCC-g-GEM-g-DC-g-TEPA) and targeted for codelivery of GEM and miR-205. The antibody, C225, is an FDA-approved drug and can be utilized to target EGFR in the advanced stages of PC, and tumor growth inhibition can be achieved. In MIA PaCa-2R cells, C225 conjugated mixed micelles have shown better cytotoxicity than nontargeted micelles. C225 micelles complexed with GEM-conjugated miR-225 micelles when treated in MIA PaCa-2R cells derived bearing orthotopic PC -bearing mice had shown significant tumor inhibition along with increased apoptosis. They reduced epithelial-mesenchymal transition due to the EGFR targeting via C225, thereby releasing the payload site-specifically at the pancreatic tumor site [58].

6.4.2 Transferrin

In most normal human tissues, transferrin is essential in transporting iron into the cells, and transferrin receptors are omnipresent and expressed at low levels. Transferrin receptor-bound iron uptake through the endocytosis mechanism gained a lot of importance for targeted drug delivery. Iron is abundantly consumed in highly proliferated cancer. These proliferated cells consume iron from a specific mechanism from plasma by binding the iron to the transferrin receptor, followed by endocytosis. To design a targeted delivery system, receptor-mediated endocytosis could allow the drug to release the site and accumulate in the cancer cells. Transferrin receptors are expressed more than 90% in the malignant PC cells, which could be a potential strategy to develop a targeted delivery in treating PC [59]. In a study to develop a targeting delivery for PC, a transferrin-mediated micellar system was developed using PCL-b-PEO as copolymers and doxorubicin as a drug. Here, the block copolymer chain was modified using aptamer, XQ-2d SSDNA, which has high specificity in binding toward highly expressed transferrin receptor (CD71) in PC. This XQ-2d aptamer was used in this study as a targeting moiety to enhance the deep penetration of micelles into the tumor cells. The prepared micelles were about 100−200 nm in size, and the developed micelles could bind to the Panc-1 cells due to the aptamer-specifically modified micelles. They significantly reduced the tumor cell proliferation when analyzed by CCK-8 assay, flow cytometry, and confocal laser scanning microscopy. This inhibition was due to the ability of micelles to penetrate deeply through the 3D spheroids of Panc-1 cells. This Aptamer mediated through transferrin receptor binding could be a potential strategy to deliver various therapeutic agents to treat PCs [60].

6.4.3 Urokinase plasminogen activator receptor

uPAR, along with the other receptors, is also overexpressed in PC and can be used as a potential target for receptor-targeted therapy in PC. Upon targeting uPAR, the chemo/therapeutic agents could selectively target and kill the tumor cells that express uPAR. Upon modifying with fluorescently labeled dye, these receptors can be utilized as MRI and optical tools to evaluate the severity of pancreatic lesions as they bind to the uPAR and accumulate in the cells. This allows researchers to explore its versatile advantages as a molecular imaging agent and site-specific drug delivery to treat initial and metastasis stages of PC [61].

6.4.4 Fucosylated antigen

Carbohydrate antigens (CA 19−9) belong to the fucosylated antigen, also referred to as a tumor marker, and are overexpressed in cancers related to the pancreato-biliary system. Fucosylated antigens are widely used as tumor markers to diagnose cancer and evaluate tumor efficacy, where the CA 19−9 levels are increased up to 80% in the deceased PC cells. Upon adding L-fucose linkage to the sialylated precursors, the CA 19−9 is synthesized, followed by overexpression of fucosyltransferase. Fucosylation has a significant role in cancer progression in pancreatic adenocarcinoma cells, where the increased fucosyltransferase coupling with metastasis could increase the progression. This targeting strategy is in a very early stage, has great potential in targeting drug delivery, and has a prominent role in the early diagnosis of PC. In a recent study, CA 19−9 was used as a biomarker to target pancreatic ductal carcinoma. This approach prepared three block copolymers, mPEG-PLGA-PLL modified with CA 19−9, encapsulated with PTX, and nano micelles.

Along with the active targeting of CA19−9, ultrasound-mediated microbubble destruction was used as passive targeting to deliver the drug into the pancreatic cells. The results showed low IC50, significant cell cycle arrest, and apoptosis in in vitro Capan-1 cells. In Balb/C mice bearing pancreatic tumors, the combined application of PTX and CA19−9 nano formulation had shown significant tumor growth inhibition. Due to the prolonged circulation of the formulation, an increase in AUC, t1/2, and mean residence time and a decrease in renal clearance were observed. This study is a promising strategy for the treatment of PC [62].

6.4.5 Integrins

Integrins have a role as signal transducers in migration, regulating differentiation and proliferation along with cell death. These integrins belong to the family of heterodimeric cell surface receptors and specifically bind to the ECM components. In human tumors with PC, the integrins v3 overexpresses about 58%. Integrins can bind RGD tripeptide ligands (arginine-glycine-aspartic acid). These RGD peptides have similar structures to v3. This advantage can be utilized to develop a delivery system to target pancreatic tumor cells. In a study to utilize integrins as a target to treat PC, a polyplex micellar system was developed and modified with an RGD ligand peptide. The polyplex micellar system comprises PEG-polycation block polymer. This modification was expected to increase the cellular micellar uptake, thereby increasing the accumulation of micelles in the pancreatic cells using the integrins as RGD receptors on the cell surface. The results showed that BxPC3 tumor cells internalized and increased cellular uptake. These polyplex micelles had significantly suppressed tumor growth and exhibited an antiangiogenic effect in the mice model bearing BxPC3 pancreatic tumor. This strategy of conjugating RGD to polyplex micelles successfully targeted the integrin receptors in PC [63].

6.5 Small interfering RNA-loaded micelles for pancreatic cancer therapy

Epigenetic and genetic alteration appears to be one of the major causes of the development of PC. The involvement of critical genes in PC progression promotes small interfering RNA (siRNA) as a powerful genetic tool for PC management to reduce the expression level of a targeted gene. siRNA has empowered the efficacy of current chemotherapy and radiotherapy via suppression of various oncogenes impacting the progression of PC [64]. However, their ability to facilitate gene silencing cannot completely kill cancer cells. siRNA suffers from different off-target, and their degradation by enzymes present in serum can limit their potential in gene silencing. The effective delivery of siRNA to the cytosol of target cells remains a challenge for researchers for successful RNA interference-guided gene therapy [65]. Exploring the advantages of PMs, especially poly(ethylene glycol) (PEG)-based block copolymers, which can spontaneously self-assemble with siRNA into micelles in an aqueous medium, offers a promising delivery strategy for effective systemic siRNA delivery. PMs enhance the systemic stability of siRNA, and the core can be additionally stabilized by chemical cross-linking and hydrophobic interaction due to hydrophobic chain, that is, alkyl chains and cholesteryl groups. PMs equipped with disulfide cross-linkers stabilize the micellar core and enable the release of siRNA into the cytoplasm of target cells through enzymatic reductive reaction via GSH [66]. Surface-modified PMs with targeting ligand molecules that can bind to a specific receptor overexpressed on a targeted cellular surface have significantly improved cellular uptake [67]. Recently in a study, a polyion complex micellar system equipped with 1, 2, and 3 antihuman tissue factor (TF) Fab's for the siRNA delivery via copper-free click conjugation was developed and demonstrated that the antihuman TF 3(Fab')-micelles provide a potential modality to induce apoptosis of PC cells in stroma-rich tumors [68].

6.6 Polymeric micelles in clinical studies for pancreatic cancer

Polymeric micellar delivery continues to evolve rapidly, driven by newly developed nanomaterials, with novel strategies, technologies, new treatment modalities, and challenges to current drug clinical failures for treating different cancers. The micellar delivery system offers many advantages over free drug counterparts delivered for treating PC. Currently, a polymeric micellar formulation named Genexol-PM was approved in Bulgaria, Hungary, and South Korea for treating PC, and phase-II clinical trials are under evaluation in the USA. Genexol-PM is a polymeric micellar formulation, comprises of amphiphilic diblock copolymer, monomethoxy poly(ethylene glycol)-block-poly(D, L-lactide) (mPEG-PDLLA) was synthesized by ring-opening polymerization reaction, and PTX a chemotherapeutic agent was encapsulated inside the core. Genexol-PM has encouraging results from clinical trials from various cancers, which opened up a way for combination therapy of Genexol-PM with GEM (NCT02739633) for advanced pancreatic adenocarcinoma, and phase-II trial of NCT02739633 is going on. Similarly, another PMs, NC-6004, which comprises PEG and polyaminoacid with Cis derivative, had shown linear sustained and delayed release of Cis, analyzed from a pharmacokinetic model, and exhibited longer systemic circulation time. NC-6004 has shown negligible toxicity along with significant antitumor efficacy. All the results have encouraged NC-6004 in phase-I/II clinical trials that are being conducted in Taiwan and Singapore for the treatment of advanced pancreatic adenocarcinoma. Micellar formulations that are currently in clinical trials for PC therapy are tabulated in Table 6.2.

Table 6.2 Representations of the micellar formulations in clinical trials for targeting pancreatic cancer.

Name	Block co-polymer	Therapeutic cargos	Indication	Clinical status	Reference
Genexol-PM	PEG-PLA	Paclitaxel	Pancreatic cancer	I/II	NCT00111904
NC-6004	PEG-PGlu	Cisplatin with gemcitabine conjugation	Advance pancreatic cancer	III	NCT02043288
BIND-014	PEG-PLA	Docetaxel	Advance metastatic cancer	I	NCT01300533
NK-911	PEG−P(Asp)	Doxorubicin	Pancreatic cancer	I	[21]
NK105	PEG−P(Asp)	Paclitaxel	Advance pancreatic cancer	I	[21]
NK012	PEG−P(Glu)	SN-38	Pancreatic cancer	−	[21]

6.7 Conclusion

PMs are one of the nanotechnology-based delivery systems that can deliver therapeutic agents to the specific tumor site by escaping renal clearance through the EPR effect. PMs have prolonged circulation time and can efficiently accumulate in the tumor. This gives PMs an advantage over conventional delivery as many chemotherapeutic agents suffer from poor solubility, and PM can easily solubilize the drug. PMs can also be decorated with various functional ligands targeting the tumors and increasing cellular uptake and drug internalization. Currently, drug-loaded PMs are investigated in clinical trials and have shown promising results in reducing tumor inhibition, and the applications of PM are extended to combination drug delivery, bioimaging, gene therapy, and diagnosis of cancers. To ensure the success of PMs, surface modifications of micelles can be further explored regarding drug loading, controlled release, and cellular uptake. All the research on PC suggests that PMs have become salient and give very promising hope in cancer therapy.

References

[1] Sung H, et al. Global cancer statistics 2020: GLOBOCAN estimates of incidence and mortality worldwide for 36 cancers in 185 countries. CA Cancer J Clin 2021;71(3):209−49. Available from: https://doi.org/10.3322/caac.21660.
[2] Zhou Q, Zhang L, Yang TH, Wu H. Stimuli-responsive polymeric micelles for drug delivery and cancer therapy. Int J Nanomed, 13. 2018. p. 2921−42. Available from: http://doi.org/10.2147/IJN. S158696.

[3] Springfeld C, et al. Chemotherapy for pancreatic cancer. Presse Med 2019;48(3):e159–74. Available from: https://doi.org/10.1016/j.lpm.2019.02.025 Part 2.

[4] Sawant RR, Torchilin VP. Multifunctionality of lipid-core micelles for drug delivery and tumour targeting. Mol Membr Biol 2010;27(7):232–46. Available from: https://doi.org/10.3109/09687688.2010.516276.

[5] Ghosh B, Biswas S. Polymeric micelles in cancer therapy: state of the art. J Control Release 2021;332:127–47. Available from: https://doi.org/10.1016/j.jconrel.2021.02.016.

[6] Ghezzi M, et al. Polymeric micelles in drug delivery: an insight of the techniques for their characterization and assessment in biorelevant conditions. J Control Release 2021;332:312–36. Available from: https://doi.org/10.1016/j.jconrel.2021.02.031.

[7] Bazak R, Houri M, el Achy S, Hussein W, Refaat T. Passive targeting of nanoparticles to cancer: a comprehensive review of the literature. Mol Clin Oncol 2014;2(6):904–8. Available from: https://doi.org/10.3892/mco.2014.356.

[8] Danhier F, Feron O, Préat V. To exploit the tumor microenvironment: passive and active tumor targeting of nanocarriers for anti-cancer drug delivery. J Control Release 2010;148(2):135–46. Available from: https://doi.org/10.1016/j.jconrel.2010.08.027.

[9] Sahay G, Alakhova DY, Kabanov AV. Endocytosis of nanomedicines. J Control Release 2010;145(3):182–95. Available from: https://doi.org/10.1016/j.jconrel.2010.01.036.

[10] Hillaireau H, Couvreur P. Nanocarriers' entry into the cell: relevance to drug delivery. Cell Mol Life Sci 2009;66(17):2873–96. Available from: https://doi.org/10.1007/s00018-009-0053-z.

[11] Aderem A, Underhill DM. Mechanisms of phagocytosis in macrophages. Annu Rev Immunol 1999;17(1):593–623. Available from: https://doi.org/10.1146/annurev.immunol.17.1.593.

[12] Rabinovitch M. Professional and non-professional phagocytes: an introduction. Trends Cell Biol 1995;5(3):85–7. Available from: https://doi.org/10.1016/S0962-8924(00)88955-2.

[13] Conner SD, Schmid SL. Regulated portals of entry into the cell. Nature 2003;422(6927):37–44. Available from: https://doi.org/10.1038/nature01451.

[14] Doherty GJ, McMahon HT. Mechanisms of endocytosis. Annu Rev Biochem 2009;78(1):857–902. Available from: https://doi.org/10.1146/annurev.biochem.78.081307.110540.

[15] Pucadyil TJ, Schmid SL. Conserved functions of membrane active GTPases in coated vesicle formation. Science 2009;325(5945):1217–20. Available from: https://doi.org/10.1126/science.1171004.

[16] Champion JA, Katare YK, Mitragotri S. Making polymeric micro- and nanoparticles of complex shapes. Proc Natl Acad Sci 2007;104(29):11901–4. Available from: https://doi.org/10.1073/pnas.0705326104.

[17] Chatterjee M, et al. Caveolae-mediated endocytosis is critical for albumin cellular uptake and response to albumin-bound chemotherapy. Cancer Res 2017;77(21):5925–37. Available from: https://doi.org/10.1158/0008-5472.CAN-17-0604.

[18] Mercer J, Helenius A. Virus entry by macropinocytosis. Nat Cell Biol 2009;11(5):510–20. Available from: https://doi.org/10.1038/ncb0509-510.

[19] Pham DT, Chokamonsirikun A, Phattaravorakarn V, Tiyaboonchai W. Polymeric micelles for pulmonary drug delivery: a comprehensive review. J Mater Sci 2021;56(3):2016–36. Available from: https://doi.org/10.1007/s10853-020-05361-4.

[20] Lavasanifar A, Samuel J, Kwon GS. Poly(ethylene oxide)-block-poly(l-amino acid) micelles for drug delivery. Adv Drug Deliv Rev 2002;54(2):169–90. Available from: https://doi.org/10.1016/S0169-409X(02)00015-7.

[21] Gong J, Chen M, Zheng Y, Wang S, Wang Y. Polymeric micelles drug delivery system in oncology. J Control Release 2012;159(3):312–23. Available from: https://doi.org/10.1016/j.jconrel.2011.12.012.

[22] Daman Z, et al. Polymeric micelles of PEG-PLA copolymer as a carrier for salinomycin against gemcitabine-resistant pancreatic cancer. Pharm Res 2015;32(11):3756–67. Available from: https://doi.org/10.1007/s11095-015-1737-8.

[23] Gaucher G, Dufresne M-H, Sant VP, Kang N, Maysinger D, Leroux J-C. Block copolymer micelles: preparation, characterization and application in drug delivery. J Control Release 2005;109(1):169–88. Available from: https://doi.org/10.1016/j.jconrel.2005.09.034.

[24] Tockary TA, et al. Single-stranded DNA-packaged polyplex micelle as adeno-associated-virus-inspired compact vector to systemically target stroma-rich pancreatic cancer. ACS Nano 2019; 13(11):12732−42. Available from: https://doi.org/10.1021/acsnano.9b04676.

[25] Jhaveri AM, Torchilin VP. Multifunctional polymeric micelles for delivery of drugs and siRNA Front Pharmacol 2014;25(5):77[Online]. Available:. Available from: https://www.frontiersin.org/articles/10.3389/fphar.2014.00077.

[26] Cheng R, Meng F, Deng C, Klok H-A, Zhong Z. Dual and multi-stimuli responsive polymeric nanoparticles for programmed site-specific drug delivery. Biomaterials 2013;34(14):3647−57. Available from: https://doi.org/10.1016/j.biomaterials.2013.01.084.

[27] Jiang Y, Lu H, Khine YY, Dag A, Stenzel MH. Polyion complex micelle based on albumin−polymer conjugates: multifunctional oligonucleotide transfection vectors for anticancer chemotherapeutics. Biomacromolecules 2014;15(11):4195−205. Available from: https://doi.org/10.1021/bm501205x.

[28] Kong C, et al. Targeting the oncogene KRAS mutant pancreatic cancer by synergistic blocking of lysosomal acidification and rapid drug release. ACS Nano 2019;13(4):4049−63. Available from: https://doi.org/10.1021/acsnano.8b08246.

[29] Abu-Fayyad A, Nazzal S. Synthesis, physiochemical characterization, and in vitro antitumor activity of the amide and pH cleavable hydrazone conjugates of γ-tocotrienol isomer of vitamin E with methoxy-poly(ethylene) glycol. Int J Pharm 2017;529(1):75−86. Available from: https://doi.org/10.1016/j.ijpharm.2017.06.033.

[30] Emamzadeh M, Desmaële D, Couvreur P, Pasparakis G. Dual controlled delivery of squalenoyl-gemcitabine and paclitaxel using thermo-responsive polymeric micelles for pancreatic cancer. J Mater Chem B 2018;6(15):2230−9. Available from: https://doi.org/10.1039/C7TB02899G.

[31] Yu X, Yang X, Horte S, Kizhakkedathu JN, Brooks DE. A pH and thermosensitive choline phosphate-based delivery platform targeted to the acidic tumor microenvironment. Biomaterials 2014;35(1):278−86. Available from: https://doi.org/10.1016/j.biomaterials.2013.09.052.

[32] Vachutinsky Y, et al. Antiangiogenic gene therapy of experimental pancreatic tumor by sFlt-1 plasmid DNA carried by RGD-modified crosslinked polyplex micelles. J Control Release 2011; 149(1):51−7. Available from: https://doi.org/10.1016/j.jconrel.2010.02.002.

[33] Xin X, et al. Redox-responsive nanoplatform for codelivery of miR-519c and gemcitabine for pancreatic cancer therapy. Sci Adv 2022;6(46):eabd6764. Available from: https://doi.org/10.1126/sciadv.abd6764.

[34] Xin X, Lin F, Wang Q, Yin L, Mahato RI. ROS-responsive polymeric micelles for triggered simultaneous delivery of PLK1 inhibitor/miR-34a and effective synergistic therapy in pancreatic cancer. ACS Appl Mater Interfaces 2019;11(16):14647−59. Available from: https://doi.org/10.1021/acsami.9b02756.

[35] Lee H, et al. Light-induced reversible formation of polymeric micelles. Angew Chem Int Ed 2007;46(14):2453−7. Available from: https://doi.org/10.1002/anie.200604278.

[36] Chen X, Teng W, Jin Q, Ji J. One-step preparation of reduction-responsive cross-linked gemcitabine prodrug micelles for intracellular drug delivery. Colloids Surf B Biointerfaces 2019;181:94−101. Available from: https://doi.org/10.1016/j.colsurfb.2019.05.038.

[37] Zhu X, et al. Targeting pancreatic cancer cells with peptide-functionalized polymeric magnetic nanoparticles. Int J Mol Sci 2019;20(12):2988. Available from: https://doi.org/10.3390/ijms20122988.

[38] Rapoport N, Kennedy AM, Shea JE, Scaife CL, Nam K-H. Ultrasonic nanotherapy of pancreatic cancer: lessons from ultrasound imaging. Mol Pharm 2010;7(1):22−31. Available from: https://doi.org/10.1021/mp900128x.

[39] Maeda M, et al. Sonodynamic therapy based on combined use of low dose administration of epirubicin-incorporating drug delivery system and focused ultrasound. Ultrasound Med Biol 2017;43(10):2295−301. Available from: https://doi.org/10.1016/j.ultrasmedbio.2017.06.003.

[40] Neri D, Supuran CT. Interfering with pH regulation in tumours as a therapeutic strategy. Nat Rev Drug Discov 2011;10(10):767−77. Available from: https://doi.org/10.1038/nrd3554.

[41] Moosa BA, Mashat A, Li W, Fhayli K, Khashab NM. pH responsive self-assembly of cucurbit[7]urils and polystyrene-block-polyvinylpyridine micelles for hydrophobic drug delivery. J Nanomater 2013;2013:719168. Available from: https://doi.org/10.1155/2013/719168.

[42] Gao GH, Li Y, Lee DS. Environmental pH-sensitive polymeric micelles for cancer diagnosis and targeted therapy. J Control Release 2013;169(3):180–4. Available from: https://doi.org/10.1016/j.jconrel.2012.11.012.

[43] Akimoto J, Nakayama M, Okano T. Temperature-responsive polymeric micelles for optimizing drug targeting to solid tumors. J Control Release 2014;193:2–8. Available from: https://doi.org/10.1016/j.jconrel.2014.06.062.

[44] Schild HG. Poly(N-isopropylacrylamide): experiment, theory and application. Prog Polym Sci 1992;17(2):163–249. Available from: https://doi.org/10.1016/0079-6700(92)90023-R.

[45] Cammas S, Suzuki K, Sone C, Sakurai Y, Kataoka K, Okano T. Thermo-responsive polymer nanoparticles with a core-shell micelle structure as site-specific drug carriers. J Control Release 1997;48(2):157–64. Available from: https://doi.org/10.1016/S0168-3659(97)00040-0.

[46] Mirhadi E, et al. Redox-sensitive nanoscale drug delivery systems for cancer treatment. Int J Pharm 2020;589:119882. Available from: https://doi.org/10.1016/j.ijpharm.2020.119882.

[47] Sikder A, et al. Advancements in redox-sensitive micelles as nanotheranostics: a new horizon in cancer management. J Control Release 2022;349:1009–30. Available from: https://doi.org/10.1016/j.jconrel.2022.08.008.

[48] Wang P, et al. Acid- and reduction-sensitive micelles for improving the drug delivery efficacy for pancreatic cancer therapy. Biomater Sci 2018;6(5):1262–70. Available from: https://doi.org/10.1039/C7BM01051F.

[49] Shi Z, et al. Insights into stimuli-responsive diselenide bonds utilized in drug delivery systems for cancer therapy. Biomed Pharmacother 2022;155:113707. Available from: https://doi.org/10.1016/j.biopha.2022.113707.

[50] Huang Y, Dong R, Zhu X, Yan D. Photo-responsive polymeric micelles. Soft Matter 2014;10(33):6121–38. Available from: https://doi.org/10.1039/C4SM00871E.

[51] Wang G, Tong X, Zhao Y. Preparation of azobenzene-containing amphiphilic diblock copolymers for light-responsive micellar aggregates. Macromolecules 2004;37(24):8911–17. Available from: https://doi.org/10.1021/ma048416a.

[52] Kobatake S, Takami S, Muto H, Ishikawa T, Irie M. Rapid and reversible shape changes of molecular crystals on photoirradiation. Nature 2007;446(7137):778–81. Available from: https://doi.org/10.1038/nature05669.

[53] Bochet CG. Photolabile protecting groups and linkers. J Chem Soc Perkin 1 2002;2:125–42. Available from: https://doi.org/10.1039/B009522M.

[54] O'Reilly RK, Hawker CJ, Wooley KL. Cross-linked block copolymer micelles: functional nanostructures of great potential and versatility. Chem Soc Rev 2006;35(11):1068–83. Available from: https://doi.org/10.1039/B514858H.

[55] Lai E, et al. New therapeutic targets in pancreatic cancer. Cancer Treat Rev 2019;81:101926. Available from: https://doi.org/10.1016/j.ctrv.2019.101926.

[56] Yu X, Zhang Y, Chen C, Yao Q, Li M. Targeted drug delivery in pancreatic cancer. Biochim Biophys Acta - Rev Cancer 2010;1805(1):97–104. Available from: https://doi.org/10.1016/j.bbcan.2009.10.001.

[57] Khare V, Alam N, Saneja A, Dubey RD, Gupta PN. Targeted drug delivery systems for pancreatic cancer. J Biomed Nanotechnol 2014;10(12):3462–82. Available from: https://doi.org/10.1166/jbn.2014.2036.

[58] Mondal G, Almawash S, Chaudhary AK, Mahato RI. EGFR-targeted cationic polymeric mixed micelles for codelivery of gemcitabine and miR-205 for treating advanced pancreatic cancer. Mol Pharm 2017;14(9):3121–33. Available from: https://doi.org/10.1021/acs.molpharmaceut.7b00355.

[59] Daniels TR, et al. The transferrin receptor and the targeted delivery of therapeutic agents against cancer. Biochim Biophys Acta - Gen Subj 2012;1820(3):291–317. Available from: https://doi.org/10.1016/j.bbagen.2011.07.016.

[60] Tian L, Pei R, Zhong L, Ji Y, Zhou D, Zhou S. Enhanced targeting of 3D pancreatic cancer spheroids by aptamer-conjugated polymeric micelles with deep tumor penetration. Eur J Pharmacol 2021;894:173814. Available from: https://doi.org/10.1016/j.ejphar.2020.173814.

[61] Liu S, Bugge TH, Leppla SH. Targeting of tumor cells by cell surface urokinase plasminogen activator-dependent anthrax toxin. J Biol Chem 2001;276(21):17976−84. Available from: https://doi.org/10.1074/jbc.M011085200.

[62] Xing L, et al. Ultrasound-mediated microbubble destruction (UMMD) Facilitates the delivery of CA19-9 targeted and paclitaxel loaded mPEG-PLGA-PLL nanoparticles in pancreatic cancer. Theranostics 2016;6(10):1573−87. Available from: https://doi.org/10.7150/thno.15164.

[63] Ge Z, et al. Targeted gene delivery by polyplex micelles with crowded PEG palisade and cRGD moiety for systemic treatment of pancreatic tumors. Biomaterials 2014;35(10):3416−26. Available from: https://doi.org/10.1016/j.biomaterials.2013.12.086.

[64] Kamerkar S, et al. Exosomes facilitate therapeutic targeting of oncogenic KRAS in pancreatic cancer. Nature 2017;546(7659):498−503. Available from: https://doi.org/10.1038/nature22341.

[65] Mendt M, et al. Generation and testing of clinical-grade exosomes for pancreatic cancer. JCI Insight 2018;3:8. Available from: https://doi.org/10.1172/JCI.INSIGHT.99263.

[66] Mirzaei S, et al. Pre-clinical and clinical applications of small interfering RNAs (siRNA) and co-delivery systems for pancreatic cancer therapy. Cell 2021;10(12):3348. Available from: https://doi.org/10.3390/CELLS10123348.

[67] Bertrand N, Wu J, Xu X, Kamaly N, Farokhzad OC. Cancer nanotechnology: the impact of passive and active targeting in the era of modern cancer biology ☆ HHS Public Access. Adv Drug Deliv Rev 2014;66:2−25. Available from: https://doi.org/10.1016/j.addr.2013.11.009.

[68] Min HS, et al. Tuned density of anti-tissue factor antibody fragment onto siRNA-loaded polyion complex micelles for optimizing targetability into pancreatic cancer cells. Biomacromolecules 2018;19(6):2320−9. Available from: https://doi.org/10.1021/ACS.BIOMAC.8B00507/ASSET/IMAGES/LARGE/BM-2018-00507D_0005.JPEG.

CHAPTER 7

Theranostic nanoparticles in pancreatic cancer

Sania Ghobadi Alamdari[1,2], Reza Mohammadzadeh[1], Behzad Baradaran[2], Mohammad Amini[2], Ahad Mokhtarzadeh[2] and Fatemeh Oroojalian[3]

[1]Department of Cell and Molecular Biology, Faculty of Basic Science, University of Maragheh, Maragheh, Iran
[2]Immunology Research Center, Tabriz University of Medical Sciences, Tabriz, Iran
[3]Natural Products and Medicinal Plants Research Center, North Khorasan University of Medical Sciences, Bojnurd, Iran

7.1 Introduction

Pancreatic cancer (PC) is one of the deadliest malignancies in men and women worldwide, which is attributed to its late diagnosis. This systemic disease is usually asymptomatic in the early stages, and only about 10% of patients are diagnosed in these stages [1]. In addition, the early metastasis of PC tumor may be detected even when the primary tumor is not present in the pancreas, a phenomenon that is attributed to focal inflammation and epithelial-to-mesenchymal transition. Therefore, a multidisciplinary approach to this disease is of great importance [2]. The current first-line cancer treatments, such as surgery, chemotherapy, and radiotherapy, face various challenges (e.g., low tumor specificity, high systemic toxicity, limited penetration through the dense extracellular matrix (ECM), multidrug resistance, and insufficient tumor clearance). Especially, the risk of treatment failure or metastasis and tumor recurrence continues to increase if the disease is not diagnosed in time. Therefore, strategies that integrate cancer diagnosis and treatment (i.e., theranostic) can offer great promise in this area [3].

Rapidly developing theranostic approaches combine noninvasive imaging with the specific delivery of therapeutic agents, enabling simultaneous monitoring of target detection, drug distribution, and therapeutic response [4]. Several theranostic systems have been developed for PC, combining different imaging methods (such as computed tomography (CT), positron emission tomography (PET), endoscopic ultrasonography (EUS), and magnetic resonance imaging (MRI)) with treatment modalities (e.g., chemotherapy, immunotherapy, gene therapy, photothermal therapy (PTT), and photodynamic therapy (PDT)) [5,6]. Two main strategies are used in this new biomedical technology: 1- chemical synthesis and 2- nanoparticle (NP) encapsulation. In the first method, imaging agents, anticancer drugs, and tumor-targeting molecules are conjugated together with covalent bonds, forming a macromolecular complex capable of

Recent Advances in Nanocarriers for Pancreatic Cancer Therapy
DOI: https://doi.org/10.1016/B978-0-443-19142-8.00002-4

targeting, imaging, and eradicating the tumor. In the second method, by encapsulating imaging agents and anticancer molecules in amphiphilic coatings, nanoparticles (NPs) are formed and delivered to solid tumors through the effect of enhanced permeability and retention (EPR) or specific targeting [7].

NP-based cancer diagnostic methods are being developed as promising tools for real-time, cost-effective, and convenient cancer diagnosis. A fundamental advantage of using NPs is their high surface-to-volume ratio, which can be densely covered with antibodies, aptamers, and other molecules [8]. NPs that are used for cancer detection either themselves have optical, radioactive, magnetic, and acoustic properties, or they carry other NPs or molecules that portray such features. Changing the physical properties of NPs (e.g., shape, size, shell thickness, etc.) can increase their performance by tuning these properties. Furthermore, hybrid NPs consisting of two or more types of materials can confer a variety of such properties to a single system [9]. Regarding therapeutic applications, NPs can be used as carriers for delivering drugs and other molecules (e.g., DNA, RNA, and proteins). Drugs encapsulated in NPs have numerous benefits over free chemotherapeutics administered directly, such as a lower rate of drug degradation in the bloodstream, higher targeting efficiency, lower systemic toxicity, improved drug solubility, and superior pharmacokinetic and pharmacodynamic properties [10]. In addition to their role as carriers of drugs, NPs' optical properties also increase the efficiency of these drugs during phototherapy (such as PTT and PDT) [11].

Nowadays, the use of NPs for developing targeted multimodal theranostic platforms for cancer monitoring and treatment is acquiring the utmost attention. In this chapter, we will review the NPS currently used in PC theranostic.

7.2 Metal nanoparticles

7.2.1 Gold nanoparticles

Gold NPs (AuNPs) have been studied for a long time as an ideal tool of molecular nanoprobes and drug carriers for cancer diagnosis and treatment. Due to the different sizes and shapes of AuNPs and their easy surface modification, they are widely used for cancer-targeted theranostics [12]. The exclusive optical properties of these NPs make them good noninvasive imaging agents, and their high surface-to-volume ratio enables the loading of a multitude of molecules such as targeting, imaging, and therapeutic agents. Also, targeted molecular imaging and delivery of the therapeutic component and their longer retention in target areas can reduce the circulatory concentration of NPs and, as a result, systemic toxicity [13]. The surface plasmon resonance (SPR) effect of AuNPs due to the coherent oscillation of free electrons enables them to be used as efficient biosensors, as well as imaging and photothermal agents. Moreover, amphiphilic AuNPs can be modified to become more stable in physiological environments, and the inert nature of metallic gold delivers it as a biocompatible agent [14]. AuNPs have the potential to deliver drugs and nucleic acids to cancer cells and tissues. As an efficient and safe agent, they can also be used to track drugs, opening new opportunities for cancer treatment by accurately detecting tumor boundaries. Also, AuNPs can be used in cancer phototherapy (PTT and PDT) due to their light absorption properties. Overall, AuNPs offer safe and effective nanomaterials that can be employed to diagnose and treat PC [15].

Gemcitabine (GEM), a chemotherapy drug commonly used for PC treatment, lacks satisfactory therapeutic effects due to its short half-life, poor bioavailability, and adverse cytotoxic effects against normal tissues. The fabrication of GEM-loaded and glypican-1 (GPC1)-targeted AuNCs, as a theranostic nanoplatforms for PC, was shown to overcome these limitations. The GPC1-targeted GEM-loaded NPs (GPC1-GEM@HAuNCs-Cy7/ Gd NPs) showed improved diagnostic and antitumor efficiency during near-infrared (NIR) fluorescence/MRI multimodal imaging and targeted chemotherapy against PC. By targeting the GPC1 biomarker that is selectively expressed in human PC tissues, these NPs showed great potential for early diagnosis and effective treatment of this disease. In a recent study, the results of biochemical and histological analyses revealed that the NPs prepared had negligible toxicity in vivo, offering a promising candidate for PC multipurpose treatment [16].

In another study, a photothermal theranostic nanoenvelope (PTTNe) was synthesized based on MnO_2-modified AuNPs (MnO_2@AuNPs) and then investigated for real-time monitoring of PTT by surface-enhanced Raman spectroscopy (SERS) guidance in PC cells. Considering that G protein-coupled receptors are overexpressed in PC cells, a specific peptide sequence belonging to cholecystokinin (CCK) was synthesized and conjugated with MnO_2@AuNPs to specifically target these cancerous cells. The high concentration of intracellular H_2O_2 and CCK receptors in PC cells allowed for the selective targeting of the synthesized NPs, and the destruction of the MnO_2 coating provided free AuNPs for monitoring the therapeutic response through SERS during 808-nm laser-based PTT and analyzing cell via SERS spectral analysis. Overall, the nanoprobes designed were shown to be effective not only for the targeted treatment of PC but also for monitoring the treatment in a timely manner (Fig. 7.1) [17].

Conventional chemotherapy of PC faces problems such as acquired or intrinsic drug resistance and low drug permeability. A novel transfer system based on dendrimer gold NPs (Au DENPs) was constructed for the codelivery of GEM and a miR-21 inhibitor (mir-21i) during ultrasound-targeted microbubble destruction, providing a promising strategy for PC treatment. After systematic investigation of the nanocomplexes synthesized and the confirmation of simultaneous drug and gene delivery, anticancer effects were evaluated in vivo using contrast-EUS imaging, TUNEL staining, and hematoxylin and eosin (H&E) staining. The results showed that GEM-Au DENPs/miR-21i were effectively absorbed by PC cells, which significantly reduced tumor volume and increased blood perfusion to xenograft tumors [18].

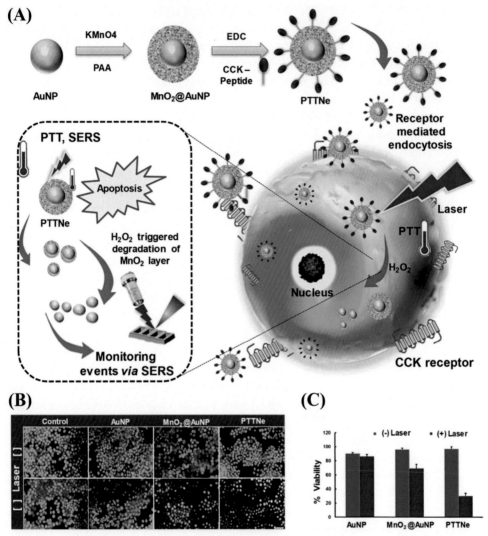

Figure 7.1 (A) Schematic representation of PTTNe for guiding a photothermal agent by SERS for detecting and treating PC. (B) Determining alive (green)-dead (orange to red) cells using different constructs with/without laser. Laser radiation (808 nm, 0.25 W) for four minutes. (C) Cell viability examined by the MTT assay with/without laser in PANC-1. *MTT*, Methyl thiazolyl tetrazolium; *PC*, pancreatic cancer; *PTTNe*, photothermal theranostic nanoenvelope; *SERS*, surface-enhanced Raman spectroscopy. *Reproduced with permission from Sujai PT, et al., Elucidating gold—MnO$_2$ core—shell nanoenvelope for real time SERS-guided photothermal therapy on pancreatic cancer cells. ACS Appl Bio Mater, 2021; 4(6): 4962—4972.*

7.2.2 Iron oxide nanoparticles

The physical and chemical properties of Iron oxide NPs (IONPs) have made them one of the most attractive candidates for many biomedical and bioengineering applications. Among various types of IONPs, one can mention maghemite (γ-Fe$_2$O$_3$), magnetite (Fe$_3$O$_4$), and mixed ferrites (MFe$_2$O$_4$ where M = Mn, Co, Ni, or Zn) [19]. The beneficial characteristics of IONPs (such as biocompatibility, good biodegradability, being minimally invasive for spatial imaging, and potential for local delivery and treatment) increase their theranostic efficiency for cancer diagnosis and treatment. Also, due to their advantageous surface chemistry, IONPs can be integrated with various imaging probes and therapeutic agents [20]. Due to the magnetic core and small size of superparamagnetic iron oxide NPs (SPIONs), these NPs deliver more localized heterogeneity in the presence of a magnetic field, delivering them suitable negative contrast agents for MRI, producing hypointense signals in T2-weighted MR images. Therefore, these particles act similarly to classical gadolinium (Gd)-based contrast agents, boosting the T1 relaxation rate and leading to positive (bright) contrast imaging [21]. Also, IONPs can be used in magnetic particle imaging (MPI) as the only signal source and the only visualized element [22]. Also, in therapeutic approaches, IONPs have been used as carriers of genes or chemotherapy drugs. So far, various hydrophilic or hydrophobic drugs and interfering RNAs or DNAs have been delivered through covalent or noncovalent bonds for cancer treatment [23]. In addition, when IONPs are exposed to strong magnetic fields, they release the received energy as heat, causing hyperthermic stress in cancer cells. In general, IONPs have shown high efficacy in cancer theranostics, including in PC [24].

Local and systemic toxicities, rapid absorption of drugs in the bloodstream, insufficient drug diffusion into large tumors, and drug resistance are among the main obstacles in intraperitoneal (IP) chemotherapy. In an orthotopic mouse model of PC, the IP transfer of urokinase plasminogen activator receptor (uPAR)-targeted IONPs increased the intratumoral accumulation of NPs. It has been observed that these targeted theranostic NPs carrying doxorubicin (Dox) or cisplatin (Cis) significantly inhibited the growth of pancreatic tumors without causing obvious systemic toxicity. In addition, uPAR-targeted theranostic IONPs were used in MRI, allowing for noninvasive monitoring of intratumor drug delivery [25].

IONPs modified with single-chain antibodies (scAbs) seem to have lower toxicity and higher efficiency in vivo than those modified with monoclonal antibodies. In a study, corresponding scAbs for MUC4, CD44V6, and CEACAM6, as potential biomarkers for pancreatic ductal adenocarcinoma (PDAC), were synthesized (scAbMUC4, scFvCD44v6, and scAbCEACAM6). Then these scAbs were conjugated to the surface of polyethylene glycol (PEG)-modified IONPs and used for the MR detection and targeted eradication of PDAC tumors. According to the results, in addition to a reduction in MRI T2-weighted signals, the synthesized nanocomposites also showed favorable anticancer effects [26].

The extreme nature of tumors and stromal barriers in the tumor microenvironment are among the reasons for poor drug delivery and resistance to chemotherapy in PC. To

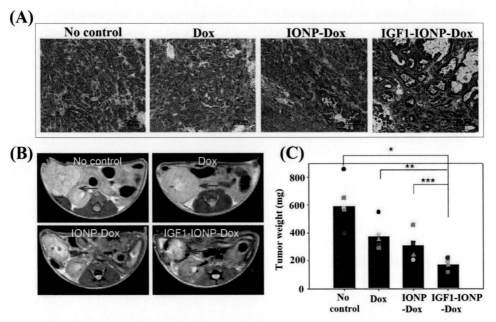

Figure 7.2 (A) Cellular density determination by the H&E staining of carcinoma tumor tissues in different treatment groups. (B) T2-weighted MRI in different treatment groups in mice (pink arrows show the location of pancreatic tumor lesions, and values in red indicate the mean relative MRI signal intensity in the entire tumor). (C) Mean tumor weight and its distribution in different treatment groups (* indicates $P < .0001$; ** indicates $P < .0006$; *** indicates $P < .005$). *Reproduced with permission from Zhou H, et al., IGF1 receptor targeted theranostic nanoparticles for targeted and image-guided therapy of pancreatic cancer. ACS Nano, 2015; 9(8): 7976—7991.*

solve these challenges, IGF1-IONP-Dox theranostic NPs were prepared by conjugating recombinant human IGF1 to IONPs to deliver the chemotherapeutic agent to stromal and cancer cells overexpressing the IGF1 receptor. The systemic delivery of the NPs prepared significantly inhibited tumor growth by suppressing cell proliferation and inducing apoptosis in an orthotopic model of PC. In a recent study, MRI-guided chemotherapy was used to evaluate the efficacy of targeted delivery of IGF1-IONP-Dox and the response to the treatment. The results suggested that these NPs can provide a promising theranostic system for the diagnosis and treatment of stroma-rich PC (Fig. 7.2) [27].

7.2.3 Silica nanoparticles

Mesoporous silica NPs (MSNPs) have been highlighted in the field of biomedicine due to their favorable properties such as high mechanical, chemical, and thermal strength, excellent biocompatibility, and easy functionalization with various components. These NPs have a structure mimicking a honeycomb pore network, where there is no connection between their pore channels, offering extraordinary drug release control [28]. There are various methods for producing MSNs with diverse characteristics, which allow for the loading of various therapeutic agents from small drugs to oligonucleotide strands or large proteins. Different modes of surface modification using the organic chains and aminopropyl groups of these NPs facilitate gradual drug release and maximum drug loading [29]. The unique properties of MSNs have led to the expansion of targeted bioimaging contrast agents. These NPs provide the possibility of imaging with different methods such as optical imaging, MRI, PET, CT, ultrasound, and multimodal imaging [30]. In general, MSNs allow for the simultaneous diagnosis and treatment of cancer, such as PC, and are suitable for loading therapeutic agents and controlling their release in the target site [31].

For the targeted delivery of GEM to PC cells, a multifunctional delivery system containing cyclic RGD peptides [cyclic (Arg-Gly-Asp-D-Phe-Glu)] (C(RGDfE)), a mesoporous silica shell, and a magnetic core was developed. Magnetic MSN (MMSN) conjugated with C(RGDfE) showed sufficient relaxation properties for MRI applications. Also, the drug nanocarriers prepared were able to increase the cellular uptake of the drug by PC cell lines overexpressing integrin $\alpha_v\beta_3$. Therefore, these multifunctional NPs fulfilled cancer-targeted therapy requirements by delivering GEM to PC cells as evidenced by MRI [32].

To develop a smart drug delivery system with a dual-active MRI contrast, Ren et al. used manganese oxide (MnO_x)-coated SPIONs as the gatekeepers of MSNs to control the release of camptothecin (CPT) from the channels of these NPs. In this platform, the thin layer of MnO_x acted as a susceptible bridge between SPION and MSN to open the cap in response to endogenous stimuli. On the other hand, manganese ions increased the T1 MRI contrast. The results showed that the MnO_x-SPION-@MSN@CPT nanosystem induced partial or even complete tumor regression in PC cells and tumor-bearing mice, suggesting the system is a useful tool for cancer diagnosis and tracking response to treatment [33].

The potential theranostic efficiency of MSNs for PC is augmented by targeting UPAR and in response to the acidic pH of the tumor microenvironment. In addition, mesoporous silica nanoparticle-urokinase plasminogen activator (MSN-UPA) NPs loaded with GEM and indocyanine green (ICG) (a multispectral optoacoustic tomography contrast material) allowed for the real-time monitoring of the intratumor accumulation of NPs and their biodistribution in an orthotopic pancreatic tumor. Also, the drug release assay revealed the pH-responsive release of GEM. In general, this system allowed for the simultaneous diagnosis and eradication of PC tumors, which could extend the survival of PC patients by shortening the time from diagnosis to treatment (Fig. 7.3) [34].

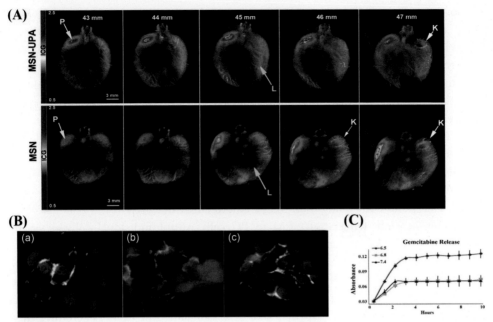

Figure 7.3 (A) S2VP10-implanted mice were injected with MSN-UPA or nontargeted MSN (*yellow arrow* = pancreatic tumor, *green arrow* = liver, red arrow = spleen, *white arrow* = kidney). (B) Fluorescence microscope images. (a) S2VP10 cells treated with unlabeled MSNs loaded with rhodamine. (b) S2VP10 cells treated with UPA ligand-targeted MSNs. (c) S2VP10 cells treated with UPAR blocking antibody. (C) Gemcitabine release kinetics. *Reproduced with permission from Gurka MK, et al., Identification of pancreatic tumors in vivo with ligand-targeted, pH responsive mesoporous silica nanoparticles by multispectral optoacoustic tomography. J Control Release, 2016; 231: 60−67.*

7.2.4 Other metal nanoparticles

TiO_2 NPs (TiO_2 NPs) have been used in an inclusive range of biomedical applications. There are various fabrication strategies for these NPs, which can be tailored according to their morphology and properties. The high surface-to-volume ratio of porous TiO_2 nanocarriers enhances drug delivery efficiency and increases loading capacity. In addition to their intrinsic properties, surface modifications can be used to produce TiO_2 NPs with special features, for example, the thermal hydrogenation of these NPs produces black TiO_2 NPs [35]. By reducing $Ti4^+$ to $Ti3^+$ in black TiO_2, a large number of oxygen vacancies are doped, and this changed surface structure makes these NPs exhibit full-spectrum absorption properties. Because of their optical properties, black TiO_2 NPs can convert absorbed NIR light into heat or produce electrons and holes upon excitation by NIR. Therefore, they can be used in thermal cancer therapies such as PTT and PDT [36]. Secondary to their imaging visibility, TiO_2 NPs can also role as a contrast agent in MRI, especially T2-weighted MRI. Therefore, by modifying the surface chemical groups of TiO_2 NPs, these NPs can be used as theranostic agents for cancer diagnosis and radiation therapy. However, their clinical application requires attentive toxicity evaluation and development of efficient surface engineering strategies [37].

Black TiO_2 NPs ($bTiO_2$ NPs) conjugated with Gd, IGF1 polypeptide, and GEM were reported to penetrate into the matrix barrier of pancreatic ductal adenocarcinoma, overcoming drug resistance. Considering that the IGF1 receptor is expressed on MIA Paca-2 cells and the respective tumor model, the nanoprobes prepared could strongly target these cancer cells. Further, $bTiO_2$-Gd-IGF1-GEM nanocomposites increased drug permeability by removing the matrix barrier and creating reverse drug resistance under the photothermal effect caused by NIR. In vivo findings demonstrated that these NPs could significantly inhibit tumor growth and cause complete tumor eradication after 12 days of treatment. Therefore, these $bTiO_2$-based nanoprobes, which enhanced the MRI signal of pancreatic tumors, can be promising agents for the dual photothermal-chemotherapy treatment of PC [38].

PC stem cells (PCSCs), which overexpress CD133, have high tumorigenic potential and resistance to chemotherapy and are considered the main targets for the diagnosis and treatment of this disease. In one study, for MRI-guided PTT of PCSCs, TiO_2 NPs were conjugated with CD133 monoclonal antibodies and DOTA-Gd. The bTiO2-Gd-CD133 mAb nanoprobes had the ability to target PCSCs, delivering a high relaxation rate and excellent thermal efficiency, offering a new strategy for the effective imaging and treatment of PC by targeting PCSCs [39].

MoS_2 nanomaterials, because of their unique semiconducting and other features and two-dimensional structure, are particularly attractive materials in the field of cancer theranostics. The controllable synthesis and flexibility of these nanomaterials, as well as easy surface modification, make them suitable nanomaterials to be used in combination with other anticancer drugs and molecules [40]. Surface modification can be utilized to boost the biochemical stability and targeting efficacy of MoS_2 nanomaterials, for example, to induce controlled and localized hyperthermia by NIR [41]. Also, MoS_2 can act as a photoacoustic tomography imaging contrast agent, where its photothermal conversion ability under NIR light enables deeper penetration into tumor tissues. Overall, MoS_2 nanostructures show great potential for simultaneous imaging-guided cancer diagnosis and treatment [42].

A versatile theranostic nanocomposite was prepared by adding Fe_3O_4 NPs on the surface of MoS_2 nanoflakes using a two-step hydrothermal technique. The biocompatibility of the MSIOs nanocomposites prepared for Mr/PAT imaging was shown to increase after being conjugated with PEG. Fe_3O_4-based magnetic targeting and MoS_2-induced photothermal conversion under NIR laser irradiation facilitated targeted magnetic photothermal ablation of PC tumors. Therefore, smart MSIOs can

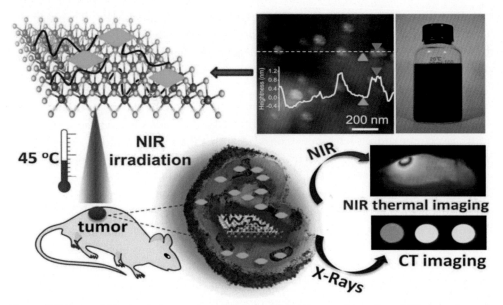

Figure 7.4 Doxorubicin loaded onto the surface of MoS_2-CS nanosheets in a NIR photothermal-triggered drug delivery system. *NIR*, Near-infrared. *Reproduced with permission from Yin W, et al., High-throughput synthesis of single-layer MoS_2 nanosheets as a near-infrared photothermal-triggered drug delivery for effective cancer therapy. ACS Nano, 2014; 8(7): 6922–6933.*

open a new horizon for monitoring the response to cancer treatments and prevent the destruction of surrounding normal tissues [42].

To improve the physiological stability and biocompatibility of MoS_2 nanosheets, polysaccharide chitosan (CS) has been suggested to be utilized during the exfoliation process of these NPs. The nanosheets constructed were used as a NIR stimuli-responsive system for concurrent chemotherapy-PTT of PC, releasing loaded Dox in response to the NIR laser. In addition, MoS_2–CS nanosheets could role as a contrast agent for CT imaging due to their ability to absorb X-rays. Therefore, 2D MoS_2 nanosheets seem to be suitable for imaging–guided diagnostic and therapeutic applications (Fig. 7.4) [43].

Some examples of metal NP-based theranostics in PC are presented in Table 7.1.

7.3 Polymeric nanoparticles

Polymers have been interesting in the field of theranostics due to their properties such as biocompatibility, tunable degradation, availability of versatile functional groups, stimulus responsiveness, and high loading capacity for biologically active molecules. Polymeric NPs can be loaded with various chromophores or fluorophores with therapeutic and diagnostic potential [50]. Drug-loaded polymeric NPs, in addition to

Table 7.1 Some examples of metal nanoparticle (NP)-based theranostics in pancreatic cancer.

Types of nanoparticles	Nanoconjugate	Size	Therapeutic agent	Imaging	Therapy	Pancreatic cancer cell lines	In vivo/ in vitro	References
Gold NPs	GPC1-Gem@HAuNCs-Cy7/Gd NPs	89 nm in hydrodynamic diameter	Gemcitabine	Near-infrared fluorescence/ MRI	chemotherapy	BxPC-3 and PANC-1	In vitro and in vivo	[16]
	MnO₂@AuNPs	150 nm	–	SERS	PTT	PANC-1	In vitro	[17]
	Gem–Au DENPs/miR–21i	In a range of 154–276 nm in hydrodynamic size	Gemcitabine and miR–21i	CEUS	Chemotherapy and gene therapy	SW1990	In vitro and in vivo	[18]
	DOX IN-Gd-AuNRs	40 nm in diameter	Doxorubicin	MRI	Chemotherapy and PTT	MIA PaCa-2	In vitro	[44]
	Au@DTDTPA NPs	2.4 nm for AuNPs core	–	Fluorescence–lifetime imaging microscopy (FLIM)	Radiotherapy	BxPC-3	In vitro	[45]
	GPC1-Gd-ORI@HAuNCs-Cy7 NPs	88 nm in hydrodynamic diameter	Oridonin and gemcitabine	Near-infrared fluorescence/ MRI	Chemotherapy	PANC-1, BxPC-3, and SW1990	In vitro and in vivo	[46]
	Antineutrophil gelatinase-associated lipocalin-gold nanoshells	>150 nm in diameter	Antineutrophil gelatinase-associated lipocalin	MRI and fluorescence optical imaging	PTT	AsPC-1	In vitro and in vivo	[47]

(*Continued*)

Table 7.1 (Continued)

Types of nanoparticles	Nanoconjugate	Size	Therapeutic agent	Imaging	Therapy	Pancreatic cancer cell lines	In vivo/ in vitro	References
Iron oxide NPs	PEG-IONP-Cis	Around 22 nm in hydrodynamic particle size	Cisplatin or doxorubicin	Near-infrared optical imaging and MRI	Chemotherapy	PANC02	In vitro and in vivo	[25]
	IONPs-PEG-MCC triple scAbs	23.6 ± 0.7 in hydrodynamic particle size	scAbMUC4, scFvCD44v6 and scAbCEACAM6	MRI	targeted therapy	BxPC-3, SW 1990, PANC-1	In vitro and in vivo	[26]
	IGF1-IONP-Dox	20.4 nm in hydrodynamic particle size	Doxorubicin	Near-infrared optical imaging and MRI	Chemotherapy	MIA PaCa-2	In vitro and in vivo	[27]
	casein-coated magnetic iron oxide-Cis	~ 30 nm in hydrodynamic particle size	Cisplatin	MRI	Chemotherapy	MIA Paca-2	In vitro and in vivo	[48]
	ATF-IONP-Gem	66 nm in hydrodynamic particle size	Gemcitabine	MRI	Chemotherapy	MIA PaCa-2	In vitro and in vivo	[49]
Silica NPs	c(RGDfE)-pMMSNs	Roughly 50 nm in diameter	Gemcitabine	MRI	Chemotherapy	BxPC-3, Panc-1, CFPAC-1	In vitro	[32]
	MnOx-SPION@MSN@CPT	100 nm for surfaced nanoparticles and 2 nm for mesoporous channels	Camptothecin	MRI	Chemotherapy	PANC-1	In vitro and in vivo	[33]
	MSN-UPA NPs	115 ± 10 nm in diameter	Gemcitabine	Multispectral optoacoustic tomography	Chemotherapy	S2VP10, S2CP9, PANC-1, MIA PaCa-2, and ASPC	In vitro and in vivo	[34]

Other metal NPs	bTiO$_2$-Gd-IGF1-GEM	159.9 nm in hydrated size	Gemcitabine	MRI	PTT and chemotherapy	MIA PaCa-2, PANC-2, and BxPC-3	In vitro and in vivo	[38]
	bTiO$_2$-Gd-CD133mAb	199.3 nm	–	MRI	PTT	SW1990 and PANC-1	In vitro	[39]
	MoS$_2$/Fe$_3$O$_4$	190.1 nm in hydrodynamic size	–	Mr/PAT imaging	PTT	PANC-1	In vitro and in vivo	[42]
	MoS$_2$-CS nanosheets	~80 nm (n $\approx$ 120 sheets)	Doxorubicin	CT imaging	PTT and chemotherapy	PANC-1	In vitro and in vivo	[43]

improving drug pharmacokinetics, increase the accumulation of drugs at the tumor site by enhancing EPR [51]. The loading of imaging or therapeutic agents in the core of polymeric NPs increases the stability of the cargo and improves its controlled release. The polymers derived from natural sources have received great attention for developing biocompatible polymeric NPs. Meanwhile, a wide range of synthetic polymers with outstanding biodegradability and biocompatibility are also available to produce polymeric NPs [52]. In general, polymer-based NPs have attracted much attention for cancer theranostic development.

7.3.1 Natural polymer nanoparticles

Natural polymers produced by plants, animals, and microorganisms are divided into three main categories: polypeptides, polysaccharides, and polyesters. The most important features of these polymers that make them suitable for manufacturing theranostic nanomedicines are the lack of immunogenicity, in most cases, biodegradability, biocompatibility, ECM mimicking features, good interaction with tissues, controllable solubility, and 3D geometry. However, some characteristics of these NPs have limited their biomedical applications, so most of these polymers must be modified to expand their scope of utilization [53]. Some natural nanopolymers undergo hydrolysis in living organisms and are excreted after being converted to biocompatible compounds in the citric acid cycle [54]. Natural polymers can act as carriers of medicinal proteins and play an important role in pharmaceutical development as they possess reactive sites that facilitate ligand conjugation, cross-linking, and other modifications [55].

CS is a natural carbohydrate capable of interacting with DNA fragments. CS NPs have been used to generate gene delivery systems for nanomedicines, such as in PC therapy [56]. The messenger RNAs (mRNA) related to CCDC88A, LAMTOR2, ARHGEF4, mTOR, WASF, and NUP85 can be effectively targeted in PDACs, suppressing the signaling pathways of these mediators and inhibiting the invasion and metastasis of PDACs. It has been shown that small interfering RNAs (SiRNAs) against these genes and PEG-CS oligosaccharide lactate (COL) modified with folic acid (FA) can be useful for imaging and targeting PDACs. The insertion of SiRNA-FA-PEG-COL NPs into PC cells in an orthotopic mouse model of PDACs was shown to target relevant mRNAs, inhibiting the metastasis and invasion of PDACs and improving the prognosis [57].

Protein-based nanocarriers with excellent biocompatibility have been used to construct multifunctional theranostic platforms. Albumin has been promising in manufacturing nano-agents for cancer imaging and treatment [58]. In a study, a GEM nanocarrier was synthesized as a theranostic agent for treating PC tumors, in which GEM and human serum albumin (HSA) were simply combined via cathepsin B cleavable peptide GFLG. Then the HSA-GEM-IR780 complex was prepared through complexation with a NIR

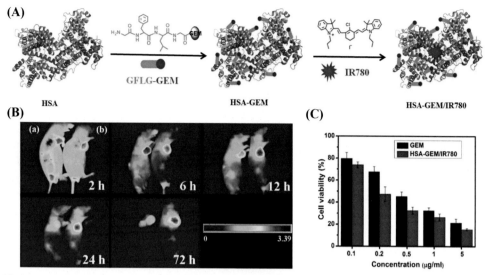

Figure 7.5 (A) Step-by-step construction of the HSA-GEM-IR780 complex. (B) In vivo NIR imaging of tumor-bearing nude mice after the injection of (a) free IR780 (left) and (b) HSA-GEM/IR780 (right) at a dosage of 1 mg/kg equivalent to IR780. (C) The viability of BxPC-3 cells treated with GEM and HSA-GEM/IR780 after 72 hours. *Reproduced with permission from Han H, et al., Enzyme-sensitive gemcitabine conjugated albumin nanoparticles as a versatile theranostic nanoplatform for pancreatic cancer treatment. J Colloid Interface Sci, 2017; 507: 217–224.*

dye, IR780. The in vivo imaging of the complex in mice carrying BXPC-3 pancreatic tumors showed long-term retention and accumulation of this nanocarrier, which effectively prevented cell proliferation. Also, compared to free GEM, the combination of HSA-GEM was able to suppress the deamination of GEM and significantly increase the concentration of the active form of GEM in the tumor tissue, hindering tumor growth with minimal side effects. Therefore, this drug nanocarrier can pave the way for the expansion of albumin-based nano-theranostics for PC (Fig. 7.5) [59].

Hyaluronic acid (HA) is a natural polysaccharide and a main component of ECM that can selectively target some receptors, such as CD44, which is overexpressed on the surface of tumor cells [60]. HA NPs are ideal carriers for imaging agents, drugs, and other biomedical substances that can accumulate in tumors via EPR and have been investigated in different formulations to assemble theranostics [61]. Nigam et al. investigated the potential of HA-functionalized HSA NPs and graphene quantum dots (GQDs) for bioimaging and targeted delivery of GEM to PC cells. The presence of HA as a targeting moiety on these NPs improved the efficacy of GEM against resistant cancer cells, and CQDs with tunable fluorescence properties developed bioimaging performance. Therefore, HSA NPs modified with HA have theranostic potential for treating PC, which should be confirmed by more in vivo and clinical experiments [62].

7.3.2 Synthetic polymer nanoparticles

To overcome some limitations related to natural polymers, many synthetic chemistry and simulation studies have been conducted to develop NPs consisting of synthetic and biodegradable polymers [63]. Among the advantages of synthetic polymer-based NPs are ease of transport and synthesis, low variability between batches, and low risk of microbial contamination. Also, synthetic polymers possessing large surfaces and numerous functional groups can be used in combination with either contrast agents for imaging purposes or bioactive agents for targeting goals. Some types of synthetic polymers used for producing nano-based formulations include polylactic acid (PLA), polyethylene imine (PEI), and PEG [64]. These polymers can be used to prepare polymeric micellar NPs that consist of a hydrophobic core and a hydrophilic corona. PEG is one of the most widely used water-soluble synthetic polymers, and hydrophobic molecules such as drugs or contrast agents are easily trapped inside its core through either covalent bonds or hydrophobic interactions [65].

A study showed that a porous ultrasound contrast nanomaterial composed of monomethoxy PEG-modified PLGA conjugated with a dual-targeted antibody loaded with an antitumor drug, paclitaxel (PTX), offering promising theranostic features in PC. In addition to intensifying imaging contrast, PTX-mPEG-PLGA NPs brought the drug onto the surface of tumor cells, facilitating the achievement of the accumulation effect. The evaluation of the contrast of the ultrasound images in vitro and in vivo displayed that these NPs increased the imaging time, leading to more potent antitumor effects. The features of these NPs should be further investigated, and their imaging efficiency is to be improved by reducing their particle sizes. In addition, boosting the loading capacity can result in more prominent tumor growth inhibitory effects [66].

One of the affordable natural products with acceptable safety, emodin (EMO), has presented great antitumor efficacy by suppressing cancer cells' proliferation through different mechanisms. Ren et al. developed a multifunctional Fe_3O_4-PEG-Cy7-EMO nanoplatform as a theranostic for PC. In this structure, the addition of PEG to Fe_3O_4 NPs improved their biocompatibility and biodistribution and prolonged their blood circulation. In addition, the incorporation of Cy7 enabled fluorescence imaging (FI). The results of transmission electron microscopy showed that the NPs prepared could be endocytosed into BXPC-3 cells, exposing these cells to growth inhibitory effects. In addition to dual FI/MRI imaging properties, Fe_3O_4-PEG-Cy7-EMO NPs were able to actively target pancreatic tumor xenografts in mice (i.e., conferring a theranostic nanoplatform) [67].

Another efficient theranostic platform for PC was constructed as reduction-sensitive polymeric micelles containing polycarbonate triblock copolymer loaded with GEM and IR820. The GEM released from these synthetic polymeric micelles (mediated via the cleavage of disulfide bonds) was shown to inhibit the proliferation of BxPC-3 cells as evidenced by the MTT cytotoxicity assay. Also, according to imaging findings in a xenograft PC tumor model, these prodrug micelles via the EPR effect could accumulate into the tumor tissue, warranting a longer blood circulation time. Overall, reduction-sensitive GEM-loaded micelles can promise an encouraging tool for NIR imaging-guided treatment of PC [68]. Table 7.2 Some examples of polymeric NP-based theranostics for PC.

7.4 Carbon nanoparticles

Recent advances have shown that carbon NPs have many applications in a wide range of biomedical fields such as theranostics. Many of these NPs, such as carbon nanotubes (CNTs), graphene derivatives, and carbon dots, have been suggested as optical imaging contrast agents due to their interesting intrinsic optical properties. Some carbon-based nanomaterials provide a very high surface area exposing numerous carbon atoms allowing for the efficient loading of biological compounds and drugs [71]. Carbon nanomaterials have unique advantages for PTT. When they accumulate in the pancreatic tumor, the thermal energy raised by the absorption of NIR promotes the death of tumor cells while showing minimal side effects against normal cells and tissues [72]. The high surface areas of carbon nanomaterials facilitate the attachment of various theranostic components such as imaging labels, targeting ligands, and therapeutic agents. Therefore, the unique physical, chemical, and mechanical properties of carbon NPs increase their theranostic efficiency [73].

Studies on invasive PC cells have shown that the overexpression of insulin-like growth factor receptor (IGFR) in these cells provides an attractive target for the treatment of this disease. In this regard, CNTs coupled with anti-IGF-1R antibodies, in addition to being able to reach the tumor through EPR, can specifically accumulate in the tumor tissue. The inhibition of IGFR-1R-mediated signaling pathways in PC cells predisposes them to antitumor agents. The pairing of SWNT (single-walled CNTs)-IGF-1Ra nanoprobes with CY7 boosts the effectiveness of NIR-based PTT and improves the photothermal conversion efficiency of NPs. Overall, SWNT-CY7-IGF-1Ra shows auspicious features for imaging-guided PTT while showing minimal side effects, contributing an important role in PC-targeted therapy [72].

The potential of graphene oxide (GO)-IONPs nanocomposites, resulting from the placement of IONPs onto the surface of GO, as a theranostic tool has been investigated in cancer. PEG-modified GO-IONPs were successfully fabricated for dual MRI and thermal ablation of PC tumors in regional lymph nodes (RLNs). In vivo and in vitro studies have revealed that PEG-GO-IONPs present low systemic toxicity and excellent efficiency in cancer PTT, as well as substantial dual lymphatic tracking capabilities. By directly injecting PEG-GO-IONPs into the tumor, these NPs migrated to

Table 7.2 Some examples of polymeric nanoparticle (NP)-based theranostics for pancreatic cancer.

Types of nanoparticles	Nanoconjugate	Size	Therapeutic agent	Imaging	Therapy	Pancreatic cancer cell lines	In vivo/in vitro	References
Natural polymer NPs	SiRNA-FA-PEG-COL NPs	80 nm	SiRNA	Confocal immunofluorescence microscopic imaging	Gene therapy	S2–013 and PANC-1	In vitro and in vivo	[57]
	HSA–GEM/IR780	–	Gemcitabine	NIR imaging	Chemotherapy	BxPC-3	In vitro and in vivo	[59]
	Cetuximab-GEM/Fe$_3$O$_4$–albumin nanospheres	200 nm in hydrodynamic diameter	Cetuximab and gemcitabine	MRI	Thermochemotherapy	AsPC-1 and MIA PaCa-2	In vitro	[69]
	Pheophorbide@Gem-HSA-NPs	165 ± 15 nm	Gemcitabine	Fluorescence imaging	PDT and chemotherapy	BxPC-3	In vitro and in vivo	[70]
Synthetic polymer NPs	HSA–HA–GQDs	56–250 nm	Gemcitabine	Fluorescence imaging	Chemotherapy	Panc-1	In vitro	[62]
	PTX-mPEG-PLGA NPs	88.6 ± 3.5 nm	Paclitaxel	Ultrasonic imaging	Antitumor therapy	CFAPC-1	In vitro and in vivo	[66]
	Fe$_3$O$_4$-PEG-Cy7-EMO NPs	9.9 ± 1.2 nm	–	Fluorescence imaging and MRI	Targeted therapy	BxPC-3	In vitro and in vivo	[67]
	PEG-b-[PLA-co-PMAC-graft-(IR820-co-GEM)]	160 nm in diameter	Gemcitabine	NIR imaging	Chemotherapy	BxPC-3	In vitro and in vivo	[68]

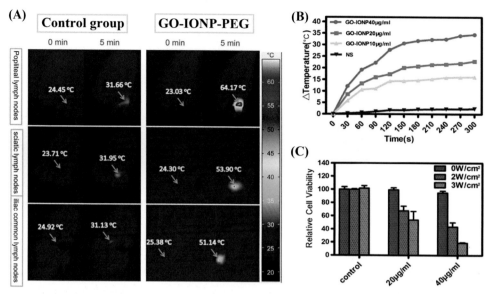

Figure 7.6 (A) Infrared thermal images of RLNs treated with normal saline and GO-IONP-PEG under 808 nm NIR laser irradiation at 2 w/cm^2 for five minutes. (B) Temperature changes in cancer cells treated with GO-IONP-PEG at the concentrations of 10, 20, and 40 mg/mL of GO along with NIR laser radiation (808 nm, 3 w/cm^2) for five minutes. (C) The relative viability of BxPC-3 cells treated with GO-IONP-PEG at the concentrations of 20 and 40 mg/mL of GO without or with NIR laser irradiation (2 and 3 w/cm^2 for 5 minutes). *RLNs*, Regional lymph nodes. *Reproduced with permission from Wang S, et al., Magnetic graphene-based nanotheranostic agent for dual-modality mapping guided photothermal therapy in regional lymph nodal metastasis of pancreatic cancer. Biomaterials, 2014; 35(35): 9473—9483.*

RLNs through lymphatic vessels as evidenced by simple mapping. Accordingly, the nano-based composite constructed can offer a useful theranostic agent to replace invasive lymph node surgery in invasive metastatic PC, as well as other cancers involving RLNs (Fig. 7.6) [74].

The combination of gold nanostars (AuNs) and reduced graphene oxide (rGO) coated with a lipid bilayer was shown to be an effective carrier for delivering anti-K-Ras antibodies (K-Ras gene is mutated in most cases of PC) to PC cells guided via dual photoacoustic/photothermal imaging. The cross-linking of FA on the surface of NPs can direct them toward cancer cells overexpressing FA receptors on their surface and improving diagnostic imaging capabilities. In addition, synergism between drugs internalized via receptor-mediated endocytosis, PTT, and gene therapy has delivered excellent anticancer activities in PC tumor-bearing mice. Therefore, rGO@AuNs-lipid-FA NPs guided via dual photoacoustic and photothermal imaging await further studies to open their path to the clinic for treating PC and other cancers [75]. Table 7.3 Some examples of carbon NP-based theranostics for PC.

Table 7.3 Some examples of carbon nanoparticle-based theranostics for pancreatic cancer.

Nanoconjugate	Size	Therapeutic agent	Imaging	Therapy	Pancreatic cancer cell lines	In vivo/ in vitro	References
SWNT–CY7–IGF-1Ra	–	–	Optical imaging	PTT	BxPC-3 and PANC-1	In vitro and in vivo	[72]
GO-IONP-PEG	165.5 nm in hydrodynamic diameter	–	MRI	PTT	BxPC-3	In vitro and in vivo	[74]
GO@AuNS	51.3 nm in hydrodynamic diameter	Anti-K-Ras gene	Photoacoustic/ photothermal imaging	PTT and gene therapy	Capan-1	In vitro and in vivo	[75]

7.5 Conclusion

Extensive research has been conducted to find new ways to fight cancer and achieve the best therapeutic outcomes while keeping drug side effects at the minimum level. The field of theranostics, concerning the simultaneous combination of diagnostic and therapeutic modalities, has promised noteworthy progress in various areas such as controlled drug release, combined treatment strategies (e.g., chemotherapy plus gene therapy), and overcoming the physical barriers hindering access to tumors (e.g., the blood-brain barrier). Many studies have shown the potential of various NPs to be used as theranostics in cancer, including PC. In this review, different NPs (metallic, polymeric, and carbon-based) used as theranostics to early diagnose and treat PC were discussed. These nanosystems provide a unique opportunity for customizing personalized medicine strategies and combining cancer imaging, diagnostic, monitoring, and therapeutic approaches. The unique optical or magnetic properties of these NPs allow for optimizing their drug-loading capacity. The intratumor accumulation of NPs via the EPR phenomenon helps determine the exact amount of the drug to be delivered to individual tumors. Besides, state-of-the-art imaging devices can provide an accurate picture of loaded drugs' recirculation in the body. Nevertheless, most of these NPs are still in the in vivo and in vitro stages and are yet to come to clinical application, requiring many challenges to be obviated, such as developing optimized nanoplatforms with low costs and plausible ligand binding efficiency, contrast probes with good degradability and sensitivity, and drugs with low toxicity and high efficacy, demanding extensive research in the field of theranostics in the future.

References

[1] Zhu H, et al. Pancreatic cancer: challenges and opportunities. BMC Med 2018;16(1):1−3.
[2] Brunner M, et al. Current clinical strategies of pancreatic cancer treatment and open molecular questions. Int J Mol Sci 2019;20(18):4543.
[3] Xue Y, et al. Recent progress of nanotechnology-based theranostic systems in cancer treatments. Cancer Biol Med 2021;18(2):336.
[4] Hapuarachchige S, Artemov D. Theranostic pretargeting drug delivery and imaging platforms in cancer precision medicine. Front Oncol 2020;10:1131.
[5] Zhao Z, Liu W. Pancreatic cancer: a review of risk factors, diagnosis, and treatment. Technol Cancer Res Treat 2020;19. p. 1533033820962117.
[6] Neoptolemos JP, et al. Therapeutic developments in pancreatic cancer: current and future perspectives. Nat Rev Gastroenterol Hepatol 2018;15(6):333−48.
[7] Zhang J, et al. Activatable molecular agents for cancer theranostics. Chem Sci 2020;11(3):618−30.
[8] Zhang Y, et al. Nanotechnology in cancer diagnosis: progress, challenges and opportunities. J Hematol Oncol 2019;12(1):1−13.
[9] Yasun E. Theranostic cancer applications utilized by nanoparticles offering multimodal systems and future insights. SN Appl Sci 2020;2(9):1−5.
[10] Kaushik N, et al. Nanocarrier cancer therapeutics with functional stimuli-responsive mechanisms. J Nanobiotechnol 2022;20(1):1−23.

[11] Pivetta TP, et al. Nanoparticle systems for cancer phototherapy: an overview. Nanomaterials 2021;11(11):3132.

[12] Zhao N, et al. Gold nanoparticles for cancer theranostics—A brief update. J Innov Opt Health Sci 2016;9(04):1630004.

[13] Vinhas R, et al. Gold nanoparticle-based theranostics: disease diagnostics and treatment using a single nanomaterial. Nanobiosens Dis Diagn 2015;4:11.

[14] Yang Y, et al. Multifunctional gold nanoparticles in cancer diagnosis and treatment. Int J Nanomed 2022;17:2041.

[15] Yang Z, et al. The applications of gold nanoparticles in the diagnosis and treatment of gastrointestinal cancer. Front Oncol 2021;11.

[16] Qiu W, et al. A GPC1-targeted and gemcitabine-loaded biocompatible nanoplatform for pancreatic cancer multimodal imaging and therapy. Nanomedicine 2019;14(17):2339—53.

[17] Sujai PT, et al. Elucidating Gold—MnO_2 core—shell nanoenvelope for real time SERS-guided photothermal therapy on pancreatic cancer cells. ACS Appl Bio Mater 2021;4(6):4962—72.

[18] Lin L, et al. UTMD-promoted co-delivery of gemcitabine and miR-21 inhibitor by dendrimer-entrapped gold nanoparticles for pancreatic cancer therapy. Theranostics 2018;8(7):1923.

[19] Dadfar SM, et al. Iron oxide nanoparticles: diagnostic, therapeutic and theranostic applications. Adv Drug Deliv Rev 2019;138:302—25.

[20] Ren X, et al. Iron oxide nanoparticle-based theranostics for cancer imaging and therapy. Front Chem Sci Eng 2014;8(3):253—64.

[21] Geppert M, Himly M. Iron oxide nanoparticles in bioimaging—an immune perspective. Front Immunol 2021;12:688927.

[22] Dulińska-Litewka J, et al. Superparamagnetic iron oxide nanoparticles—Current and prospective medical applications. Materials 2019;12(4):617.

[23] Saeed M, Ren W, Wu A. Therapeutic applications of iron oxide based nanoparticles in cancer: basic concepts and recent advances. Biomater Sci 2018;6(4):708—25.

[24] Malekigorji M, Curtis AD, Hoskins C. The use of iron oxide nanoparticles for pancreatic cancer therapy. J Nanomed Res 2014;1(1):00004.

[25] Gao N, et al. Tumor penetrating theranostic nanoparticles for enhancement of targeted and image-guided drug delivery into peritoneal tumors following intraperitoneal delivery. Theranostics 2017;7(6):1689.

[26] Zou J, et al. Nanoparticles modified by triple single chain antibodies for MRI examination and targeted therapy in pancreatic cancer. Nanoscale 2020;12(7):4473—90.

[27] Zhou H, et al. IGF1 receptor targeted theranostic nanoparticles for targeted and image-guided therapy of pancreatic cancer. ACS Nano 2015;9(8):7976—91.

[28] Baeza A, Vallet-Regí M. Mesoporous silica nanoparticles as theranostic antitumoral nanomedicines. Pharmaceutics 2020;12(10):957.

[29] Natarajan SK, Selvaraj S. Mesoporous silica nanoparticles: importance of surface modifications and its role in drug delivery. RSC Adv 2014;4(28):14328—34.

[30] Cha BG, Kim J. Functional mesoporous silica nanoparticles for bio-imaging applications. Wiley Interdiscip Rev Nanomed Nanobiotechnol 2019;11(1):e1515.

[31] Pote A, Ahirrao V, Pande V. Mesoporous silica based cancer theranostic: a modern approach in upcoming medicine. Advanced drug delivery systems. IntechOpen; 2022.

[32] Sun J, et al. A c (RGDfE) conjugated multi-functional nanomedicine delivery system for targeted pancreatic cancer therapy. J Mater Chem B 2015;3(6):1049—58.

[33] Ren S, et al. Ternary-responsive drug delivery with activatable dual mode contrast-enhanced in vivo imaging. ACS Appl Mater Interfaces 2018;10(38):31947—58.

[34] Gurka MK, et al. Identification of pancreatic tumors in vivo with ligand-targeted, pH responsive mesoporous silica nanoparticles by multispectral optoacoustic tomography. J Control Release 2016;231:60—7.

[35] Hasanzadeh Kafshgari M, Goldmann WH. Insights into theranostic properties of titanium dioxide for nanomedicine. Nano-Micro Lett 2020;12(1):1—35.

[36] Dai T, Ren W, Wu A. Cancer theranostics of black TiO_2 nanoparticles. TiO_2 nanoparticles: applications in nanobiotechnology and nanomedicine. Wiley; 2020. p. 185—215.

[37] Akasaka H, et al. Investigation of the potential of using TiO_2 nanoparticles as a contrast agent in computed tomography and magnetic resonance imaging. Appl Nanosci 2020;10(8):3143—8.

[38] Xu K, et al. IGF1 receptor-targeted black TiO_2 nanoprobes for MRI-guided synergetic photothermal-chemotherapy in drug resistant pancreatic tumor. J Nanobiotechnol 2022; 20(1):1—17.

[39] Wang S, et al. Black TiO_2-based nanoprobes for T1-weighted MRI-guided photothermal therapy in CD133 high expressed pancreatic cancer stem-like cells. Biomater Sci 2018;6(8):2209—18.

[40] Wang J, et al. MoS_2-based nanocomposites for cancer diagnosis and therapy. Bioact Mater 2021; 6(11):4209—42.

[41] Malagrino TR, et al. Multifunctional hybrid MoS_2-PEGylated/Au nanostructures with potential theranostic applications in biomedicine. Nanomaterials 2022;12(12):2053.

[42] Yu J, et al. Smart MoS_2/Fe_3O_4 nanotheranostic for magnetically targeted photothermal therapy guided by magnetic resonance/photoacoustic imaging. Theranostics 2015;5(9):931.

[43] Yin W, et al. High-throughput synthesis of single-layer MoS_2 nanosheets as a near-infrared photothermal-triggered drug delivery for effective cancer therapy. ACS Nano 2014;8(7):6922—33.

[44] Khan M, et al. Doxorubicin (DOX) gadolinium—gold-complex: a new way to tune hybrid nanorods as theranostic agent. Int J Nanomed 2021;16:2219.

[45] Ivošev V, et al. Uptake and excretion dynamics of gold nanoparticles in cancer cells and fibroblasts. Nanotechnology 2020;31(13):135102.

[46] Qiu W, et al. Oridonin-loaded and GPC1-targeted gold nanoparticles for multimodal imaging and therapy in pancreatic cancer. Int J Nanomed 2018;13:6809.

[47] Chen W, et al. Targeting pancreatic cancer with magneto-fluorescent theranostic gold nanoshells. Nanomedicine 2014;9(8):1209—22.

[48] Huang J, et al. Functionalized milk-protein-coated magnetic nanoparticles for MRI-monitored targeted therapy of pancreatic cancer. Int J Nanomed 2016;11:3087.

[49] Lee GY, et al. Theranostic nanoparticles with controlled release of gemcitabine for targeted therapy and MRI of pancreatic cancer. ACS Nano 2013;7(3):2078—89.

[50] Vijayan VM, Vasudevan PN, Thomas V. Polymeric nanogels for theranostic applications: a mini-review. Curr Nanosci 2020;16(3):392—8.

[51] Li B, et al. Drug-loaded polymeric nanoparticles for cancer stem cell targeting. Front Pharmacol 2017;8:51.

[52] Luk BT, Fang RH, Zhang L. Lipid-and polymer-based nanostructures for cancer theranostics. Theranostics 2012;2(12):1117.

[53] Jaymand M. Chemically modified natural polymer-based theranostic nanomedicines: are they the golden gate toward a de novo clinical approach against cancer? ACS Biomater Sci Eng 2019; 6(1):134—66.

[54] Ilaria Parisi O, et al. Engineered polymer-based nanomaterials for diagnostic, therapeutic and theranostic applications. Mini Rev Med Chem 2016;16(9):754—61.

[55] Hamid Akash MS, Rehman K, Chen S. Natural and synthetic polymers as drug carriers for delivery of therapeutic proteins. Polym Rev 2015;55(3):371—406.

[56] Bonferoni MC, et al. Chitosan nanoparticles for therapy and theranostics of hepatocellular carcinoma (HCC) and liver-targeting. Nanomaterials 2020;10(5):870.

[57] Taniuchi K, et al. Efficient delivery of small interfering RNAs targeting particular mRNAs into pancreatic cancer cells inhibits invasiveness and metastasis of pancreatic tumors. Oncotarget 2019; 10(30):2869.

[58] Chen Q, Liu Z. Albumin carriers for cancer theranostics: a conventional platform with new promise. Adv Mater 2016;28(47):10557—66.

[59] Han H, et al. Enzyme-sensitive gemcitabine conjugated albumin nanoparticles as a versatile theranostic nanoplatform for pancreatic cancer treatment. J Colloid Interface Sci 2017;507:217—24.

[60] Lee SY, et al. Hyaluronic acid-based theranostic nanomedicines for targeted cancer therapy. Cancers 2020;12(4):940.

[61] Zhang L, et al. Activatable hyaluronic acid nanoparticle as a theranostic agent for optical/photoacoustic image-guided photothermal therapy. ACS Nano 2014;8(12):12250—8.

[62] Nigam P, et al. Graphene quantum dots conjugated albumin nanoparticles for targeted drug delivery and imaging of pancreatic cancer. J Mater Chem B 2014;2(21):3190—5.

[63] Ali I, et al. Progress in polymeric nano-medicines for theranostic cancer treatment. Polymers 2020;12(3):598.

[64] Yhee JY, et al. Theranostic applications of organic nanoparticles for cancer treatment. MRS Bull 2014;39(3):239—49.

[65] Indoria S, Singh V, Hsieh M-F. Recent advances in theranostic polymeric nanoparticles for cancer treatment: a review. Int J pharmaceutics 2020;582:119314.

[66] Ma J, et al. Biodegradable double-targeted PTX-mPEG-PLGA nanoparticles for ultrasound contrast enhanced imaging and antitumor therapy in vitro. Oncotarget 2016;7(48):80008.

[67] Ren S, et al. Emodin-conjugated PEGylation of Fe3O4 nanoparticles for FI/MRI dual-modal imaging and therapy in pancreatic cancer. Int J Nanomed 2021;16:7463.

[68] Han H, et al. Theranostic reduction-sensitive gemcitabine prodrug micelles for near-infrared imaging and pancreatic cancer therapy. Nanoscale 2016;8(1):283—91.

[69] Wang L, et al. GEM-loaded magnetic albumin nanospheres modified with cetuximab for simultaneous targeting, magnetic resonance imaging, and double-targeted thermochemotherapy of pancreatic cancer cells. Int J Nanomed 2015;10:2507.

[70] Yu X, et al. Triple-functional albumin-based nanoparticles for combined chemotherapy and photo-dynamic therapy of pancreatic cancer with lymphatic metastases. Int J Nanomed 2017;12:6771.

[71] Liu Z, Liang X-J. Nano-carbons as theranostics. Theranostics 2012;2(3):235.

[72] Lu G-H, et al. Targeting carbon nanotubes based on IGF-1R for photothermal therapy of orthotopic pancreatic cancer guided by optical imaging. Biomaterials 2019;195:13—22.

[73] Nayak TR, Zhang Y, Cai W. Cancer theranostics with carbon-based nanoplatforms, in cancer theranostics. Elsevier; 2014. p. 347—61.

[74] Wang S, et al. Magnetic graphene-based nanotheranostic agent for dual-modality mapping guided photothermal therapy in regional lymph nodal metastasis of pancreatic cancer. Biomaterials 2014; 35(35):9473—83.

[75] Jia X, et al. Functionalized graphene@ gold nanostar/lipid for pancreatic cancer gene and photothermal synergistic therapy under photoacoustic/photothermal imaging dual-modal guidance. Small 2020;16(39):2003707.

CHAPTER 8

Recent advances in nanocarriers for pancreatic cancer therapy

Shalini Preethi P.[1], Sindhu V.[1], Karthik Sambath[2], Arun Reddy Ravula[3], Geetha Palani[4], Sivakumar Vijayaraghavalu[5], Shanmuga Sundari I.[1] and Venkatesan Perumal[3]

[1]Computational Biology Special Lab, Department of Biotechnology, Bannari Amman Institute of Technology, Sathyamangalam, Tamil Nadu, India
[2]Department of Chemistry and Environmental Science, College of Science and Liberal Arts, New Jersey Institute of Technology, Newark, NJ, United States
[3]Center for Injury Biomechanics, Materials and Medicine, Department of Biomedical Engineering, New Jersey Institute of Technology, Newark, NJ, United States
[4]Institute of Agricultural Engineering, Saveetha School of Engineering, Saveetha Institute of Medical and Technical Sciences, Chennai, Tamil Nadu, India
[5]Department of Life Sciences (Zoology), Manipur University, Imphal, Manipur, India

8.1 Introduction

8.1.1 Cancer

Cancer is an ever-increasing life-threatening disease that has to be suppressed before it reaches the advanced stages. Despite decades of advanced clinical research and trials of promising therapies, cancer continues to be playing a major part in the mortality crisis. Lifestyle, environmental destruction, and carcinogenic factors influenced human beings from having a healthy body to comorbid persons. Cancer/neoplasm is a general phrase for a wide class of dysfunction affecting any segment of the human body. The dominant aspect of cancer is the configuration of irregular cells that can grow beyond the habitual edges. This abnormality is influenced by three factors: physical carcinogen, chemical carcinogen, and biological carcinogen. Checkpoints in the cell cycle act as surveillance for DNA mechanisms to prevent genetic errors during all phases of cell division. The treatment and diagnosis of cancer seem difficult as the cancer cells become insensitive to the drugs due to molecular changes. Through factors such as age, sex, and diseases, it is estimated that one in five persons across the world is susceptible to cancer in their lifetime and the death rate is calculated to be 10 million (i.e., One in 10 dies of cancer) [1]. The methods available globally for treating cancers includes radiation therapy, chemotherapy, immunotherapy, and surgery (for solid tumors) [2]. On the other hand, early cancer prediction has effectively increased patient survival. Though several biomarkers are investigated, present invasive techniques are less specific, less sensitive, and are used for detecting tumors in later stages. So

Recent Advances in Nanocarriers for Pancreatic Cancer Therapy
DOI: https://doi.org/10.1016/B978-0-443-19142-8.00004-8

169

it is highly necessary to have an advanced, sensitive diagnostic method to bring a breakthrough in the field of cancer [3].

8.1.2 Pancreatic cancer

Long years back, food served as medicine, but now it is a barrier to human health. The food consumed is digested in a small hockey stick-shaped gland called the pancreas. It also regulates insulin and glucagon production, which involves maintaining blood sugar levels. Mutations in the cells of the pancreas are named pancreatic cancer (PC), and the risk is high for individuals whose first relatives/genetic syndromes have had PC. They are highly malignant. The occurrence of this type of cancer is high among people who smoke compared to people who have never smoked. It is said to be the second or third leading death in cancer patients. It comprises assorted distinct elements together with PC stem cells, the stroma, and the PC cell, which makes a unique tumor microenvironment for the cancer cells that play a crucial role in therapeutic resistance.

About 80% of pancreatic tissue comprises the desmoplastic stroma. Desmoplasia is referred to as a desmoplastic reaction that acts as a fundamental characteristic of pancreatic cancer, which results in a fibrous dense connective tissue thus consisting of cellular (stellate cell-derived myofibroblast-like cells and diversified immune cell types) along with noncellular components (extracellular matrix proteins; collagen types I, III, and IV; laminin; glycoprotein osteonectin; hyaluronan; and fibronectin). It is clinically differentiated into two distinct ways: (1) extensive proliferation of myofibroblast-like cells and (2) over secretion of extracellular matrix. Both cellular and noncellular components of desmoplasia are associated with the pathogenesis of PC. It also induces chemoresistance in PC. To conquer the old methods of therapeutic drugs, a new advancement in the drug delivery system (DDS) with the help of nanoparticles (NPs) is studied. For the last stages of PC, either mono or a combination of chemotherapy with radiation therapy is given. FOLFIRINOX is an effective drug used, which is a combination of four therapeutics (fluorouracil, oxaliplatin, irinotecan HCL, and leucovorin calcium), but due to its severe side effects, it is limited to patients. Broadening the field of producing new drugs with high performance, which has multidrug resistance, would be a preferable solution for PC patients [4].

8.1.3 Types of pancreatic cancer

PC is assorted into two: exocrine and neuroendocrine. 95% of PC is exocrine, they develop from exocrine cells that secrets exocrine gland and ducts of the pancreas. Additionally, it helps in breaking down fats, proteins, acids, and carbohydrates. In-depth, PC is segmented into four groups based on its metabolism, that is, glycolytic, quiescent, cholesterogenic, and mixed metabolic profiles formed on expression levels of cholesterogenic and glycolytic genes. It has been identified that patients with glycolytic tumors have the least outcome when treated with PC, while those with cholesterogenic tumors tend to have better outcomes, possibly because their energy expenditure is higher. Various types of exocrine PC are adenocarcinoma, adenosquamous carcinoma, colloid carcinoma, and squamous cell carcinoma.

Adenocarcinoma, the most periodic type among pancreatic neoplasm is pancreatic ductal adenocarcinoma (PDAC), which constitutes around 85%−90%, but the survival rate tends to be 8%−11% [5]. The ataxia telangiectasia mutated (ATM) gene plays an indispensable role in DNA damage response and repair (DDR), which is situated in chromosome 11q 22−23 and consists of 66 exons. It plays a chief role in DNA repair signaling, any defects in the ATM gene may end up in genomic mutations. It has a predominant role in the function of cell (1 mitotic spindle) during mitosis [6] and (2) telomere length [7]. MRE11-RAD50-NBS1 complex creates a physical bridge during DNA strand break (DSB), and ATM directly binds to the C terminus of NBS1. Multiple studies proved the significance of mutated KRAS, SMAD4, TP53, and CDKN24 in PDAC.

Particularly, KRAS mutations appear to be common in about 90% of PC; this cuts down the GTPase activity by preventing the GTPase activating protein to convert the active GTP bound form to the inactive GTPA bound form. It is reported that KRAS variant genes are interconnected with poor outcomes in patients with PC [8]. Mutations in TP53 make its inability to recognize DNA damage and obstruct the cell cycle arrest. Germline mutations in BRCA1/BRCA2 and CDKN2A have high risks of PDAC. The total prevalence of ATM mutations in the PDAC range is evaluated to be 6.4% [9]. Checkpoints hold a chief role in healthy cell division, mutated CDKN2A heads to loss of cyclin-dependent kinase CDK4 and CDK6 regulation. The p21 cyclin-dependent kinase inhibitor 1A (CDKN1A)-induced cell proliferation and TGF-β induced EMT can be inhibited with 4SC202, an HDAC inhibitor specifically targeted at class I [10]. At present, there are no FDA-approved targeted therapies for PC. However, studies revealed targeted therapy through inhibiting DDR response, and depending upon the specific mutation in DDR, therapies are possible.

PDAC that has mutated BRCA1/2 and PALB 2 has a promising treatment with PARP inhibitors. But the frequent mutation in PDAC is ATM mutation, though it is crucial to understand and explore the resistance mechanism of ATM/ATR/CHK1, it will be a breakthrough in targeted therapies [9]. Squamous cell carcinoma, also called "epidermoid carcinomas," is a set of cancer types with a squamous cell as a base lying above the epidermis. These cover the face area of the skin and hollow organs. The usual organs that are affected are the skin, lungs, thyroid, vaginal, and esophageal. These types of cancer are diagnosed by their appearance under the microscope. Adenoid squamous cell carcinoma is diagnosed by keratinocyte acantholysis (loss of intercellular connections) and tubular microscopic pattern. Clear cell squamous cell carcinoma is characterized by clear keratinocytes, which occurs due to intracellular edema. At present, only a few national database studies have explored pancreatic neuroendocrine tumors. Squamous cell carcinoma of the pancreas is a rare condition. It accounts for about 0.5%—5% of all exocrine cancer types and is studied as a vigorous subtype with poor diagnosis [11]. In general, pancreatic cancer is classified into three subgroups, which are as follows: (1) acinar cell carcinoma or simple cell carcinoma, which arises from parenchyma, (2) columnar cell adenocarcinoma, which arises from ducts, and (3) tumors that arise from Islets of Langerhans. Primary squamous cell carcinoma of the pancreas is very aggressive and due to the rarity of occurrence, it is been demanding to find remedial options that are hard to endure. Colloid carcinoma is an infiltrating pancreatic adenocarcinoma in which 80% of neoplasm is comprised of the colloid component. It constitutes 1%—3% of malignant cancers in the exocrine pancreas. CC often occurs in the head of the pancreas where it originates from the intraductal papillary mucinous neoplasm (IPMN), and CC in the tail is developed from mucinous cystic neoplasms (MCN). The diameter of CC changes from 1.2 to 16.0 cm. CC is usually well separated, gelatinous, and soft as on reports gained from cross-section [12].

8.2 Polymeric nanoparticles

Polymeric nanoparticles (PNPs) is currently the leading targeted therapy as its contribution is worthwhile to drug delivery, the structure or morphology of PNPs can be changed according to the need, which makes them easier and a wiser therapy to eliminate the disease. The foremost problem in cancer is multidrug resistance; all types of cancer work under this rule. Whenever a drug is administered, they tend to resist the drug for interactions and make them less reactive. Likewise, chemotherapeutic agents damage healthy tissue leading to adverse reactions inside the body, limiting the dosage intake, and resulting in toxicity that damages other organs unfortunately ending up with supplementary disease. This makes it burdensome to increase the survival rate. Hence targeting the tumor cells with a high enhanced permeability and retention (EPR), effect would be a supreme step toward making better potency of the drug. A dramatic headway in modern pharmacology begins with polymers that are made up of monomers.

Nanocarriers can overcome all the barriers and can have a secured DDS for cancer patients. They have a size range of 1—1000 nm through which therapeutic agents can be encapsulated (nanospheres) or coated on their surface (nanocapsules). It is also called as drug transporter and is made up of natural, semisynthetic, and synthetic polymers; for instance, cellulose, Polyethylene glycol (PEG), and micelles poly (N-vinyl pyrrolidone). The shape, dimensions, and ratio greatly influence the intake of the drug and have a huge effect on pharmacodynamics and pharmacokinetics. To reach the target cells, the nanocarrier must have certain parameters such as solubility, diffusion coefficients, partition, immunosurveillance, penetration, and absorption. It should also pass the natural barriers such as the stratum corneum to have a good result. Some resources for developing the PNPs from natural sources are alginate, heparin, collagen, chitosan, albumin, polyhydroxy alkanoates, and gelatin. Synthetic sources includes PEG, Poly (caprolactone), cyclodextrins, poly(lactic-co-glycolic acid), and poly-n (cyanoacrylate) which helps in transporting the drug capsules to the proteins [13].

Human serum albumin (HSA) is the most abundant serum protein and is a catabolic source of glutamine for a tumor that naturally occurs in our circulatory system, and its proved to be a safe drug carrier [14]. At the same time, polylactic-co-glycolic acid (PLGA) is meant to be utilized in tissue engineering as they possess a slow degradation rate having one month of retention time [15]. Though only limited sources are available in natural resources and extraction of these products is complicated yet, it has good biodegradability and bioavailability. It is simple to make synthetic polymers but it has poor biodegradability. They are designed in a way that makes prolonged drug action at the required site. From the perspective of drug delivery, PNPs are classified into three types: (1) solvent-activated (swelling or osmotically controlled device), (2) diffusion-controlled system (monolithic devices), and (3) chemically (biodegradable) or externally controlled devices (temperature/pH).

In the last few decades, there have been several advancements in nano theranostics to possess a controlled release and rate of drug released at the target site to kill the diseased cell. There are two ways by which targeting the cancer cell using NPs can be achieved, *viz* passive targeting and active targeting. Passive targeting aims at localizing in the specific site, and active targeting focuses on the active uptake of therapeutic drugs by the tumor cells. Both methods run behind the principle of the EPR effect, which is the dominant reason for the success of targeted therapy in cancer [16].

8.2.1 Passive targeting

In simple words, it is referred to having a superior accumulation of polymeric NPs (drug) in specific tissue. Passive targeting is directly linked with size, shape, flexibility, charge, dimension, etc. As the dimensions of the particle are extremely small, it can escape kidney filtration as well as leakage from vasculature in the tumor. When the tumor size reaches 2 mm^3, due to a lack of nutrients and oxygen, the cells form new blood vessels for their survival, this mechanism is termed as angiogenesis, which plays a critical role in the tumor environment. The size of the NP can influence the penetration rate in solid tumors and enhance the biodistribution and tumor accumulation in vivo and protect the drugs from entering the blood circulation and delivering the drug to the site of action at a necessary rate shown in Fig. 8.1 Additionally, the

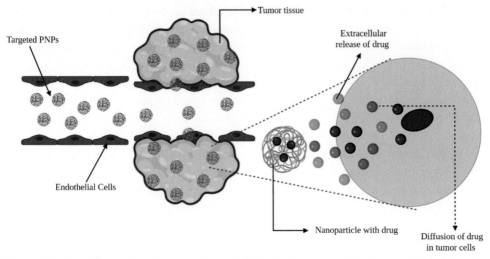

Figure 8.1 Illustration of passive targeting of PNPs that targets the tissues. *PNPs*, Polymeric nanoparticles.

nanomaterial is designed in different shapes such as cubic and star-like spherical, which affects the properties of the material that can have a high impact on cellular uptake and efficacy of loading drugs. The fusion of both leaky vasculature and poor lymphatic flow brings about an enriched EPR effect. As the designed NPs are smaller in size than the blood vessels, it stays in the tumor tissue having an increased ability of drug retention in cancer cells compared to normal tissue. They are widely used in drug delivery depending on their capacity to trap tiny hydrophobic drugs and increase the bioavailability of the therapeutics.

8.2.2 Active targeting

NP feasible with active targeting ligands have been broadly used in tumor-specific diagnosis and therapy in pancreatic cancer [17]. The ligands targeted include peptides, antibodies, nucleic acid, and proteins. Though these ligands show high specificity to tumor cells in vitro, only a few have systemically enhanced the accumulation. Research has been done to convert passive targeting to active targeting as it targets specific cells ligand which is achieved by conjugating therapeutic drugs using various moieties [18,19]. The drugs attach to the receptor of each cell present in the tumor tissue and deliver the drug as shown in Fig. 8.2. Some specific antibody for active targeting for pancreatic management are Anti -CD47 antibody, Herceptin, and Flt-1 (VEGF) antibodies. The compounds that PNP acts on for PC (Pancreatic Cancer) management are Folic acid [20], Retinoic acid, and hyaluronic acid [21,22].

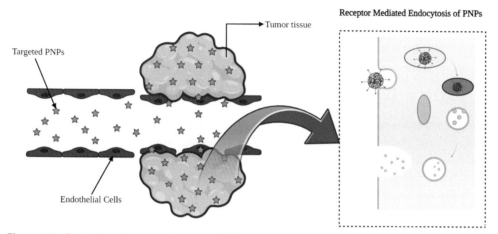

Figure 8.2 Illustration of active targeting of PNPs targeting the cells. *PNPS,* polymeric nanoparticles.

8.2.3 Responsive polymeric nanoparticles

Environmentally responsive polymers or smart polymers are incorporated with a diverse range of linear and branched or crosslinked polymer networks. The foremost property of a responsive polymer is that it can encounter different physical and chemical changes in response to exterior stimuli. These behavior changes can be triggered by physical stimuli like light, ultrasound, temperature, and electric and magnetic fields which directly change the energy level of the solvent/polymer system and stimulate their activity at some crucial levels; Chemical stimuli (i.e., chemical agents, pH, ionic strength, redox potential) induce response through modifying the subatomic interactions within the polymer and the solvent (hydrophilic/hydrophobic balance) or between hydrophobic chains. Some responsive polymers utilized for delivery of drug are broadly classified as micelles, polymer-drug conjugates, hydrogels, and polyplexes. Hydrogels have a hydrophilic co-polymeric nature which attracts water (i.e., consuming a large number of biological fluids or water), and showed a significant utility in pharmaceutical and medical areas. Currently, the headway of stimuli-responsive NPs has drastically increased in cancer treatment [23].

Liposomes are the first formulated NP in 1970. Two scientists Birrenbach and Speiser who are pioneers in the field introduced the first ever NP made up of polymers for pharmaceutical application in the 1970s [24], only one among them, which is formulated using albumin was approved by FDA for pancreatic cancer, breast cancer, and non–small cell lung cancer, that is, Abraxane (protein-bound paclitaxel) showed improved overall survival in 861 patients with metastatic PC. For patients with unresectable locally metastatic or advanced PC, gemcitabine (GEM) therapy has been the standard first-line treatment since 1997 [25]. On the whole, GEM is utilized as medication for PC with a survival rate of 5.7 months, coadministration of albumin-paclitaxel with GEM showed enhancement, and it is said to express stromal remodeling effect to alter collagen structure and get rid of cancer-associated fibroblast [26].

8.2.4 pH-responsive polymeric nanoparticles

As a consequence of rapid abnormal metabolism and augmentation, a large amount of lactic acid and end products are produced by cancer cells, which triggers toxic effects on neighboring tissue, and an acidic pH range of 5.7−6.9 is shown, as it has less capacity to oxidizes the glucose completely to produce energy for multiplying tumor cells. The PNPs that are sensitive to pH liberate therapeutic drugs having lower toxicity to the system in contrast to the free drug. It is designed in a way that the encapsulated or coated drug should be released rapidly from the PNP under acidic pH in the tumor. In comparison, normal cancer cells/tissues had an acidic microenvironment [27].

8.2.5 Synthesis of polymeric nanoparticles

NP with the potential to be included into medical applications have been blend using different strategies. The physical and chemical properties of the NP are influenced by the synthesis methods [28]. Most of the PNPs are administrated via parenteral administration. By introducing a copolymer in the process of synthesis, stable polymeric materials can be produced and can be altered as per the need. Some methods used in the synthesis are solvent diffusion, salting out, dialysis, solvent evaporation, precipitation, and supercritical fluid technology. They involve either direct synthesis or polymerization of monomers. Polymerization is achieved through microemulsion, interfacial polymerization, mini-emulsion, and controlled/living radical polymerization [29].

8.2.5.1 Solvent evaporation method

The most used, and the most convenient method to prepare PNPs for the delivery of drug molecules is the solvent extraction method. They can synthesize high-quality biodegradable polymers, which is the main purpose of using PNPs. This method dissolves the polymer and drug in an organic solvent and forms emulsions using surfactants dissolved in water. For dissolving hydrophobic drugs, solvents like chloroform or dichloromethane are used. Due to their toxicity effect, it is been replaced by ethyl acetate. The principle behind the method is a single emulsion (oil-in-water o/w), and a double emulsion (water-in-oil-in-water w/o/w). The emulsion is obtained through ultrasonication or homogenization. The size of the emulsions is shown in Fig. 8.3. In the end, solvents are been evaporated and particles are collected using ultracentrifugation. NP produced are lyophilized after the removal of surfactants. The fabrication of PLGA NPs through

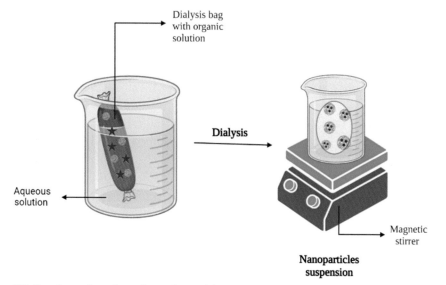

Figure 8.3 Droplet radius of emulsions formed from oil, water, and surfactant.

the solvent extraction method has been deliberated. An inspection of the duration and intensity during the sonication process with varying NP sizes and distribution has been processed. Biodegradable PNP extraction using the solvent method had a high yield. Doxorubicin (Dox)-loaded PLGA is also done using the solvent extraction method. The energy requirement, time consumption, and agglomeration of nano drops during evaporation of this process have a huge impact on the morphology and size of the particle, which acts as a barrier [28].

8.2.5.2 Salting out

Salting out is a two-step process along with emulsifying technique. This method is based on separating water-miscible solvents such as acetone, tetrahydrofuran, and ethanol. The organic phase is composed of disintegrating the polymer with the solvent. This organic phase is mixed up with an aqueous phase consisting of a stabilizer, water, and salt as an agent (electrolytes—magnesium chloride and calcium chloride; nonelectrolytes—sucrose) to enhance the diffusion of solvents and to induce the nanospheres formation [30]. Sucrose helps in encapsulating the drug. The process is carried out by constant stirring. The remaining volume is filled with water to raise the solvent diffusion into an aqueous solution and NPs are collected through the cross-filtration method. The stress exhibited on the proteins that are encapsulants can be drastically reduced using this method. This method can be implied to temperature-sensitive substances. On the other side, the main disadvantage here is the excessive washing of PNPs.

8.2.5.3 Dialysis

The dialysis method has been employed for the formation of small PNPs with a very small size distribution. The tubes of dialysis used as a physical barrier for the polymer are semipermeable membranes with an appropriate molecular weight cut-off (MWCO). The polymer is mixed with an organic solvent, which is laid down in a dialysis membrane and dialyzed. The preparation of NP suspension using dialysis method is shown in Fig. 8.4. The solvent displacement within the membrane heads to polymer aggregation, as a result, is the genesis of the homogeneous suspension of the NPs. The solvent used influences the size and morphology of the NPS. DOX is prepared using this method excluding the surfactant. The size of PNPs obtained from DMSO, DMF, and DMAc has been estimated as 100–200 nm, and it was observed that it increased with an increase in molecular weight. Acetone as a solvent yields about a mean size of 642 nm.

8.2.5.4 Supercritical fluid technology

This is a whole new world of matter, where liquids behave like gas pipes. It also has the standard densities of liquids and their solution properties. Supercritical fluids (SCFs) are emerging as an attractive alternative through environmentally friendly use, clean and reproducible scale-up, proper manipulation of structural homogeneity, and manufacturing of overly pure nanomedicine. SCF is a fluid that has been flattened and heated above its low temperature (Tc) and base stress (Pc). Supercritical carbon dioxide (scCO2) is a wide-range maximum SCF that has moderate prerequisites and is plentiful, cheap, nonflammable, nontoxic, and environmentally friendly. The SCF era generated a great deal of interest in pharmaceutical study. Many recent excellent reviews published the formation, formulation, and manipulation of pharmaceutical particles SCF. Mishima et al. outlined the formation of biodegradable debris for drug and gene delivery SCF-era use [31]. The most habitual treatment strategy for supercritical liquids is rapid-growing supercritical fluids (RESS), fuel line anti-solvent process (GAS), supercritical anti-solvent process (SAS), and debris from its various modifications and fuel saturated solutions (PGSS) method. There is extensive literature on the preparation of drug-loaded

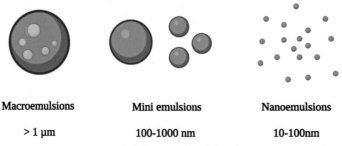

Macroemulsions	Mini emulsions	Nanoemulsions
> 1 μm	100–1000 nm	10–100nm

Figure 8.4 Schematic representation of dialysis method for the preparation of PNP. *PNPs,* polymeric nanoparticles.

microparticles for use during the SCF era. Conversely, the usefulness of SCFs has been less intensively studied. Also regardless of the supply of some fluids, the largest polymer exhibits negative solubility, or perhaps no solubility, in SCFs.

8.2.5.5 Nanoprecipitation method

A simplified way of synthesizing PNPs is nanoprecipitation method, the so-called solvent displacement method [32]. The basic principle of this technique is based on the surface deposition of a polymer after the displacement of an organic solvent from a lipophilic solution to the aqueous phase. The polymer is diffused in a water-soluble solvent of intermediate polarity, and the solution is added to the stirred aqueous solution one at a time, in stages, dropwise, or at a controlled rate of addition. Due to the rapid spontaneous diffusion of the polymer solution into the aqueous phase, the NPs form instantaneously to avoid water molecules. This process seems to be dominated by the Marangoni effect [33], where the decrease in surface tension between the two phases increases the surface area due to rapid diffusion and leads to the formation of small organic solvent droplets. As the solvent diffuses out of the NPs, the polymer will precipitate as nanocapsules or NPs. There are three ways to produce NP for drug delivery: (1) Traditional method, (2) flash method, and (3) microfluid based precipitation. In traditional method, the antisolvents are added to solvents containing hydrophobic molecules using a magnetic stirrer. Flah precipitation method was first introduced by Johnson and Prud'homme in 2003 [34]. This method aims to lower the mixing time compared to nucleation and the growth of PNPs. Various NPs of hydrophobic compounds are prepared using this method [35]. The mixing devices for Flah precipitation method are of two types, confined impinging jet (CIJ) mixer and multi-inlet vortex mixer [36]. The principle behind microfuidic-based nanoprecipitation is, in laminar flow conditions, it reduces the diffusion distance [37]. Production of PNPs using this method, especially by hydrodynamic flow focusing device, has high flexibility [38].

8.2.6 Characterization of polymeric nanoparticles

Characterization acts as an important prerequisite for preclinical development. Visualizing an accurate picture of PNPs is essential for understanding and predicting the performance of the system. The use of PNPs for pharmaceutical and biomedical packages has opened a brand new technology for the prognosis and remedy of diseases. Characterization of nanomaterials is crucial for their preclinical development, ensuring a comprehensive understanding of their properties and enabling evaluation of their safety and efficacy in various applications. Currently, there are fewer standardized methodologies or FDA regulatory protocols for the characterization of NPs. However, it is far famous that physiological interactions depend upon particle physicochemical properties. Developing a reasonably correct photograph of the PNPs is vital for information and predicting the inclusive performance of the device inside the body. A tiered technique for preclinical characterization of nanomedicines consists of physicochemical characterization, sterility and pyrogenicity assessment, biodistribution, and toxicity characterization. NPs are generally characterized inside the literature through length distribution, morphology, floor properties, balance, and drug-polymer interactions.

8.2.6.1 Determination of size and size distribution

As NP is best known for their size, it holds an important attribute in making a move through medical applications. As the therapeutics synthesized using PNP needs to creep into the cells, sinusoids, and tissues they have to be designed in small size to lucidly flow across the body. The resolution of conventional light microscopy is bounded to 1 μm as these tiny PNPs are below the diffraction limit of visible light. They can be characterized through transmission electron microscopy (TEM), dynamic light scattering (DLS), AFM, scanning electron microscopy (SEM), STM, and NSOM.

8.2.6.1.1 Scanning electron microscopy

It is a technique used for imaging the surface of the particle with the help of an electron beam making it interact with the sample and giving different signals, surface morphology, and atomic composition. It also calculates the purity of PNPs. The electron interacts with the atoms in the sample in a faster scan pattern and the intensity of the detected signal is combined with the position of the beam to produce an image. Secondary electrons emitted from the sample are used to build a three-dimensional image. Everhart Thornley scintillator-photomultiplier detector detects if any electrons are escaping from the sample surface. As PNPs are very small in size they can easily escape, for the same reason the sample is coated with a thin layer of metal (200−300 Å). This can reduce thermal damage and surface charging. Characterizing the size distribution and size morphology of PNPs requires high resolution. The electric field in field emission gun (FEG)-SEM generates high-energy electrons from a tungsten filament emitter with a tip (10 nm), which gives an increased signal-to-noise ratio.

8.2.6.1.2 Transmission electron microscopy

The TEM technique forms images using electrons transmitted through the sample and gives a two-dimensional image. It is highly efficient for measuring the polymeric wall of nanocapsules. Guinebretière et al. prepared PCL nanocapsules by the emulsion-diffusion method and measured a membrane thickness of 1−2 nm by TEM [39]. Increased computing performance, advanced detector, hardware, and software were implemented in TEM to process a good quality result. Versatile software named SerialEM has emerged for collecting the data for TEM. The principle applied here is, it connects camera hardware with the microscope across distinct manufacturers. Users can control and modify its functionality resulting in highly individualized procedures [40].

8.2.6.1.3 Dynamic light scattering

It is also known as photon correlation spectroscopy, which is widely used in the determination of the size, shape, and, diffusion behavior of the PNP. The fundamental of this technique is Brownian movement, which is characterized by light scattering from colloidal suspension and related its motion to the size of the particles [41]. DLS is applicable for monodisperse and polydisperse materials but not suitable for high-dimensional samples. Based on the strokes- Einstein's i + equation, hydrodynamic diameter can be observed. It can give whole information about the samples within a limited time. The size determination is based on the intensity (Z average), that is, the value obtained from the correlation function.

8.3 Diagnosis

More than 90% of pancreatic tumors are PDAC. Only 15%−20% of PDAC patients are appropriate for the surgical process once the initial diagnosis as a result of PDAC has some rare symptoms and a narrow diagnostic range. Therefore, the vast majority of patients had locally advanced or distant metastases at the point of diagnosis. Therefore, it is urgently necessary to develop laboratory tests and imaging technologies that are considerably more effective to detect PDAC. The overall diagnosis techniques were showed in Fig. 8.5.

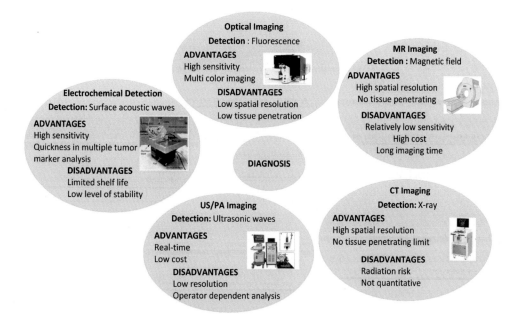

Figure 8.5 Overall schematic representation of diagnostic techniques.

8.3.1 Risk factors

In pancreatic cancer, due to its low occurrence and unfortunate endurance, the risk variables correlated to the advancement of this disease have normally been examined utilizing case-control studies. It is divided into nonmodifiable risk factors and modifiable risk factors.

8.3.1.1 Nonmodifiable risk factors
8.3.1.1.1 Age

The elderly are a common age group for PC. Under the age of 30, majority of the patients are never diagnosed and 90% of those older than 55 have the majority in their seventh and eighth decades of life [42]. The incidence rises to its maximum differs per nation based on age. For instance, the prevalence of patients in India peaks in their sixth decade of life, but in the US it peaks in its seventh decade [43].

8.3.1.1.2 Sex

Men are highly to get PC globally compared to woman (age—a standardized rate of 5.5 in males against 4.0 in females). The disparity seems to be higher pronounced in nations with higher development indices. Despite the gender disparity, a systematic assessment of data found no link between reproductive variables and PC in women. These results indicate the alternate reasons for the male preponderance may involve different exposures to environmental or genetic factors [44].

8.3.1.1.3 Ethnicity

The PC incidents are lowest among pacific islanders and Asian-American within the United States, also African-Americans have reported 50%—90% higher risk than Caucasians [44]. There is evidence for underlying genetic or gene-environment interactions to explain at least some of the observed differences in incidence between the ethnic communities. The higher incidence rates within the African-American population are proposed to be linked to greater exposure to certain risk factors for PC, such as smoking cigarettes, alcohol drinking, elevated body weight index, and higher incidence of diabetes [45], but there is also evidence for those explanations [46].

8.3.1.1.4 Blood group

Numerous sizable epidemiological types of research have demonstrated a connection between various ABO blood types and the likelihood of acquiring PC. blood group O patients had a considerably lower level risk for developing PC compared to those with blood group A (HR: 1.32, 95%Cl: 1.02—1.72), AB (HR: 1.51, 95%Cl: 1.02—2.33), or B (HR: 1.72, 95%Cl: 1.25—2.38) [47].

8.3.1.1.5 Gut microbiota

Investigation carried out in the part of gut bacteria in PC revelas, increased risk with lower levels of *Streptococcus mitis* and *Neisseria elongate* and higher levels of *Granulicatella adiacens* and *Porphyromonas gingivalis* [48].

8.3.1.1.6 Genetic susceptibility and family history

Genetic susceptibility and family history for pancreatic cancer is classified as familial when two or many first-degree relatives must already have been diagnosed with the disease, which accounts for 5%—10% of new cases [49]. Patients with PC patients have been at a ninefold increased risk compared to those without familial risk factors. This risk rises to a thirty-two-fold increased risk if three or many first-degree relatives have already been diagnosed. A PC person who is affected through family history, even if only one first-degree relative has been diagnosed, nevertheless has an 80% higher chance of getting pancreatic adenocarcinoma than someone without a history [50].

The chance of developing inherited PC increases exponentially with the number of first-degree relatives who are affected; BRCA2 and PALB mutations are most frequently identified in this group. In comparison to the general population, several disorders are also linked to a higher risk of PC [51].

8.3.1.1.7 Diabetes

Diabetes was identified as a risk variable for PC [52]. According to the findings of meta-analysis, patients who have type I diabetes had a twofold increased risk of PC development compared to those without the disease. A similar degree of raised risk of PC was seen in a person with type-2 diabetes in a different meta-analysis [53]. It should be noted that while diabetes is also considered one of the risk factors for PC, it should be highlighted that PC can potentially present as a new start to diabetes. This has increased interest in HbA1c as a prognostic biomarker for the early diagnosis of PC [52].

8.3.1.2 Modifiable risk factors
8.3.1.2.1 Smoking

Cigarette smoking is the greatest significant modifiable risk factor in PC. According to a meta-analysis, current smokers have a 74% higher possibility of PC development than non-smokers and former smokers have a 20% higher risk. The risk persists after quitting smoking for at least 10 years, according to the investigations, but early-stage research has recommended that it could take up to 20 years for the risk to return to normal [54]. E-cigarettes have generally been marked as safer (but not necessarily safe) substitutes for conventional cigarettes because they provide heated nicotine while using fewer chemicals than tobacco smoking to assess the risk/benefit ratio of e-cigarettes as exposure with unknown carcinogenic potential or as a useful smoking cessation aid helping to avoid PC [55].

8.3.1.2.2 Alcohol

Studies involving 2187 cases of the disease found that patients who consumed >30 g of alcohol per day had an elevated risk of developing PC [56]. The most recent meta-analysis discovered that low and medium levels of alcohol intake cannot raise the risk of PC, but excessive alcohol intake was related to a 15% increased risk of the disease.

The danger was higher for men who consumed large amounts of alcohol. Due to the fact that excessive alcohol use is the main cause of chronic pancreatitis, which is a known risk factor for the disease, alcohol was taken into account in this case as a risk factor for PC [56].

8.3.1.2.3 Obesity

A study on PC examined if a high body mass index (BMI) was associated with this disease, obese patients have a higher chance of PC development, and a meta-analysis of these studies found no difference in results between men and women. Every five BMI units elevated risk of PC by 10%. Given the level of information connecting obesity and PC, it seems likely that an important contributing factor to the rising pancreatic cases in the industrialized world is the rising prevalence of obesity [51].

8.3.1.2.4 Dietary factors

Taking red and processed meat is linked to the incidence of PC. Given that excessive consumption of processed and red meat was correlated to carcinogen development such as N-nitroso compounds and the potential for DNA damage, this is biologically feasible. This is a reflection of the challenges that nutritional epidemiology and suitable study techniques for predicting the risk of PC provide [51].

8.3.1.2.5 Infection

Hepatitis C or Helicobacter pylori (H-pylori) reassociated with an increased chance of developing PC, according to research investigating the relationship between numerous illnesses and this disease (H-pylori). The probable link to H-pylori prompts fascinating speculation about H-pylori eradication may have unfavorable effects on rising PC incidence [51].

8.3.2 Detection of protein-based biomarkers in blood

For PDAC diagnosis, CA19−9, a tumor-associated glycoprotein, is now the most commonly utilized biomarker. The average adult CA19−9 level is less than 37U/mL, and PDAC incidence and development are directly interconnected with the CA19−9 minor's blood rise. As an outcome, the CA19−9 blood test is advised only for tracking progress and treatment effectiveness, not for PDAC screening or diagnosis [57]. Therefore, improving the sensitivity of the CA19−9 test or looking into other PDAC biomarkers is the main focus. Promoting the sensitivity of CA19—9, probes for the early clinical diagnosis of PDAC have received a lot of attention recently [58].

In addition to CA19—9, optical nanoprobes based on gold (Au)NPs and quantum dots (QDs) are developed for PDAC diagnosis for various cancer biomarkers, such as carcinoembryonic antigen (CEA) and mucin protein MUC4 [16]. These probes range from immunoassays to live cell/tissue imaging [59]. For the detection limit of 12 ng/L for CEA in human blood samples, the enzyme-labeled Au nanoprobes outperformed the traditional enzyme-linked immunosorbent test by nearly 140 times (ELISA) [60].

8.3.3 Detection of nucleic-based biomarkers in blood

Nucleic acid-based cancer biomarkers found in patient body fluids are crucial in addition to the earlier stage cancer diagnosis by traditional cancer biomarkers without symptoms. The nucleic acid-based biomarkers for cancer diagnosis include miRNAs, which are frequently involved in cell proliferation, invasion, and metastasis in numerous malignancies (including PDAC) [61].

According to research, miR-10b, miR-21, miR30c, miR-132, miR-155, and miR-212 are significantly overexpressed in PDAC cells when compared to nonmalignant cells. This makes it possible to differentiate between PDAC-affected patients and those who do not have pancreatic pathology based on their levels. With a solid-state localized surface plasmon resonance (LSPR) sensor, PDAC patients may monitor the subfemtomolar levels of miR-21 and miR-10b in human plasma. In this plasmonic biosensor, complementary single-stranded DNA-functionalized Au nano prisms (HS-C6ssDNA) were mounted to a glass substrate, and variations in the Au nano prisms' LSPR reflected the concentration of various miRs [62]. They also used the biosensor to discriminate between miR10b and miR-10a without the need for RNA extraction and to easily discern the levels of miR-10b in PDAC patients and chronic pancreatitis [63]. A single-hemolysin (HL) nanochannel was created by the self-assembly of HL and a phospholipid bilayer at a transmembrane potential of $+180$ mV. The miR-21 signal was successfully detected by the HL signal nanochannel, and the signals from the complex molecules miR-21 probe 21, miR-155 probe 155, and miR-196a; probe 196a was properly distinguished [60].

8.3.4 Imaging techniques

8.3.4.1 Near-infrared fluorescence probes based on optical imaging

Probe indocyanine green (ICG) and green-emitting fluorescent dye, respectively, provide for the observation of cerebral vertebral arteries and the measurement of retinal blood flow [64]. But despite being widely utilized in research, molecular probes suffer from low balance and poor sensitivity. While performing cancer diagnosis by optical imaging, the photostability and sensitivity factors are prerequisites for molecular probes [65,66]. Many probe values are limited *in vivo* due to the low level of fluorescence signal amplification and stability under physiological settings following parenteral injection [67]. Brightness, higher stokes shifts, fluorescence quantum renders in the NIR region, photostability, and resistance to biological system degradation are desirable characteristics for molecular fluorescent probes [66]. The key benefits of fluorescent molecular probes are high sensitivity, spatial image resolution, simultaneous multicolor imaging, specificity, and low cost [68]. Differentiating from the spectrum range (UV exciting probes), NIR fluorescent dyes are physiologically safe for diagnostic purposes because relatively little energy is needed for activity and emission [69].

Regarding the probe's NIR wavelength emission region, it should possess high molar absorption coefficient, a high fluorescence quantum yield, sufficient photostability, and low toxicity [70]. When compared to traditional imaging, Near-infrared Fluorescence (NIRF)-based optical imaging has more advantages, such as high sensitivity, low cost, strong, reduced harmfulness, real-time visualization capabilities, noninvasive nature, and requirement for very low concentrations (nanomoles) of fluorophores for contrast amplification [71,72].

A variety of NIRF dyes have so far been created and applied in preclinical settings for the diagnosis of cancer. The compounds of cyanine, squaraine, phthalocyanine, and porphyrin can be used as NIRF dyes or probes [73]. ICG is a tri-carbone cyanine NIRF dye that was the first to be approved for use on humans by the US FDA [74]. A wide range of studies investigated the production of ICG derivatives for use in the initial stage diagnosis of cancer.

The lack of tumor specificity with the majority of NIRFs, however, is a significant problem. More specifically, in a human body with fluorescence quenching, ICG has rapid elimination, a deficient blood circulation half-life (2–4 min), and a higher level of plasma clearance (18.5% per min). While performing photodynamic treatment (PDT) diagnosis and treatment, the tumor-targeted administration of ICG and successive accumulation and retention in the tumor are important to achieve. Additionally, formulations with the desired qualities, such as fine storage and shelf life, are important elements in therapeutic applications [73].

Although different NIRF probes are employed with the use of NIRF probes, which include organic dyes, fluorescent proteins, and quantum inorganic dots, QDs in NIR fluorescence imaging are primarily constrained by their low photobleaching thresholds, enhanced cytotoxicity, and molar absorptivity. Molecular probes, in particular NIR probes that must be included within polymeric NPs to audit the surgical edges and afterward the surgical residual of cancer, are necessary to avert the tumor recurrence. For imaging-guided treatment and diagnosis, these polymeric NIR probes could be utilized successfully [75]. NPs with NIRF probe tags are recently investigated for noninvasive molecular imaging due to its adaptability, stability, and functionalization. A collection of polymeric materials, including dextran, polystyrene, PLGA, and chitosan, is used via the formation of NIR probe-based NPs [70].

There are variety of methods that are available for loading NIR probes into PNPs. Various mechanisms, including covalent bond formation, electrostatic interaction (positively charged fluorescent dye, tris(2,2-bipyridyl) dichlororuthenium (II) hexahydrate, and negative charge silica matrix), and hydrophobic-hydrophobic interactions(polystyrene) may have allowed the NIR dye to bind to the polymer matrix [73]. Polymeric NP-incorporated probes have a wide range of applications while delivering many dye molecules (up to several hundred), protecting the dyes from toxic environments, providing proper functional groups to functionalize with cancer-targeting ligands such as antibodies, peptides, and, folate, and reducing probe aggregation and subsequent self-quenching thus reducing the toxicity related with off-targeting. The most common imaging technique uses fluorescent probes, which are activated by incident radiation in the infrared or near-infrared range and emits energy at a lesser level [70].

8.3.4.2 Magnetic resonance imaging

Magnetic resonance (MR) imaging is frequently used in clinical diagnosis due to its superiority in giving extra information on tissue function and structure. Despite having adequate sensitivity for imaging tiny cystic lesions, imaging sensitivity was low while detecting solid PDAC tumors. Additionally, gadolinium (Gd)-based MR contrast agents have also been utilized to improve the sensitivity in the detection of PDAC in early stage, but their specificity in the Gd-enhanced MR imaging technique is still only 63% [76].

The usage of MR contrast chemicals for the initial observation of malignancies has received extensive research in recent times. Contrast agents typically come in two varieties: while T2-weighted contrast agents, such as superparamagnetic iron oxide NPs (SPIONPs), produce intrinsic dark signals [76], T1-weighted contrast agents, such as Gd, MnO NPs, and exceptionally tiny iron oxide NPs (ESIONPs) (4 nm) [77], can reveal a bright signal amplification and fine anatomic features. To mark and visualize the pancreas using a T1- weighted MR image, functionalized spherical Au NPs (17.2 nm) with small molecule Gd(III) contrast agents along with liposome (lip-Gd@AuNPs) were used.

After injection, a significant contrast increase was seen for distinct identification of the pancreas with contrast-to-noise ratios exceeding 35:1. Gd-based contrast agents carry a risk of toxicity, particularly in individuals with advanced renal insufficiency who run the possibility of developing nephrogenic systemic fibrosis (NSF).

Recent years have seen the emergence of biocompatible iron (Fe) oxide NPs as viable MR contrast agents that can eliminate the toxicological danger of NSF. enolase 1 (ENO1, also known as pyruvate dehydrogenase 1), which is upregulated on the cell membrane of PDAC, has been exploited for ENO1-targeted imaging of PDAC. Wang et al. reported ENO1 targeted SPIONPs for precise in vivo and in vitro MR molecular imaging of PDAC [78]. Additionally, He et al. highlighted the crucial part that CXCR4 plays in the growth and metastasis of PDAC and presented Fe oxide NPs that came to be CXCR4 mAb-modified for MR imaging of PDAC cell lines [79].

However, air, bleeding, blood clots, calcification, and other hypointense regions may be mistaken for the dark signals of lesions on T2-weighted MR images. For an accurate diagnosis, T1 contrast agents with strong signals are preferred. Due to its simple large-scale production, high r1 values, and low toxicity, ESIONPs are currently the subject of extensive research for T1-weighted MR imaging. Additionally, responsive polymers, cross-linking, and i-motif DNA can be brought into feasibly build ESIONPs-based TME responsive nano assemblies, which have the possibility to be utilized for diagnosing PDAC. The tumor-specific T1-weighted MR imaging amplification can be produced by these nano assemblies. When the low pH of the TME causes the disintegration into monodisperse ESIONPs, for instance, the ESIONPs nano assembly created by pH-sensitive i-motif DNAs could expose the T2-weighted dark MR signals in normal tissues. It can make tumor tissue the only bright tissue among the normal dark tissue. This T2-T1 inversion approach gives the possibility for the prediction of PDAC at an early stage and metastatic lesions detection by providing a clear sight for the diagnosis of small-sized tumors [60].

8.3.4.3 CT imaging

For assumed PDAC lesions, contrast-enhanced multidetector row Computed Tomography (CT) is a common diagnosis. The clinically employed iodine-based CT contrast agents, however, have a very short blood circulation half-time, and as an outcome, the imaging detection findings heavily depend on the pace of injection and the precise interval following the injection [80]. Additionally, iodine has a lesser x-ray attenuation coefficient, so patients must get substantial doses of iodine-based medications, which increases the likelihood of side effects. For PDAC imaging, a higher x-ray attenuation coefficient and greater biocompatibility in CT contrast agents are, therefore, strongly desired [81].

Au, bismuth (Bi), platinum (Pt), and other inorganic nanomaterials with exceptional x-ray attenuation effects have been suggested as feasible options as CT contrast agents. One of these, 20 nm diameter Au NPs, has a high rate of uptake in PDAC cells and it is a better option for CT imaging [82]. Bi subcarbonate nanotubes (BNTs) that are responsive to the tumor's acidic microenvironment have been detected early for use in tumor-targeted CT imaging. Additionally, in tumor sites, the large-sized BNTs would fragment into smaller bismuth subcarbonate clusters that could be safely removed by the kidney. Currently, CT is a frequently used imaging technology and a standard PDAC diagnostic method.

The improvement of specificity and sensitivity through the development of nano-materials is an appealing strategy for the early diagnosis of PDAC [60].

8.3.4.4 Ultrasound/photoacoustic imaging

Among the several imaging modalities, the US (ultrasound) method is affordable and offers real-time data, making it a popular choice for making the first diagnosis of PDAC. But the US's accuracy mostly depends on the operator's skill and the health of the patients. Additionally, contrast drugs are required to increase the US imaging sensitivity [83] for tumors with disorganized vasculature or tiny lesions.

Furthermore, laser-induced PA (photoacoustic) imaging achieves considerable penetration depths (4–6 cm) and good resolution by combining the best aspects of optical and US imaging. Tumor visualization has made extensive use of PA imaging contrast agents, such as NIR dyes (ICG, CNTs, AuNPs, transition-metal chalcogenides/Mxene-based NPs, etc.) [84]. Ag nanoplates with edges of 128 nm in length and 18 nm in thickness also demonstrated the potential for PA imaging in orthotopic pancreatic tumor models [85].

Higher local contrast and deeper penetration can be achieved using PA contrast agents made possible by nanotechnology by reason of their superior optical characteristics [60].

8.3.5 Electrochemical detection

In this method, the one-pot approach is used to create copper, cadmium, lead, and zinc-doped chitosan and poly(acrylic acid) nanospheres. These nanospheres can immobilize various tagged antibodies by reacting with glutaraldehyde (GA), as well as producing independent electrochemical signals. A sandwich-type immunosensor was created using the altered nanosphere as immunoprobes to simultaneously detect four pancreatic tumor markers (CEA, CA19–9, CA125, and CA242). The electrochemical analysis has unique benefits compared to other methods, including great sensitivity, simplicity, cheap cost, and speed in the identification of several tumor markers [86]. At the same time, identification of two or multiple tumor markers and multiple types of tags is developed, but it is still difficult to do so far with four or more markers. This is primarily due to the complications in differentiating electrochemical signals, from one another, caused by the truth that many typically used electrochemical redox probes, such as thionine, toluidine blue, and methylene blue, have a peak potential that is much like that of ferrocene, its derivatives, and hexacyanoferrate. The self-reliant peak potentials of steel ions such as Cu^{2+}, Pb^{2+}, Cd^{2+}, and Zn^{2+} allow for the parallel identification of multiple tumor markers [87,88]. Some metals ions interact with poly(acrylic acid) via way of electrostatic interactions and it might be chelated through the carboxylic acid association of poly(acrylic acid). It is reasonable to expect that a sequence of probes incorporates chitosan's excellent biocompatibility and the distinct peak potentials of metallic ions may be assembled by combining chitosan, poly(acrylic acid), and metallic ions. If this is the case, a significant problem with the parallel detection of four or multiple tumor markers may be solved.

A one-pot method is done to create metal ions (Cu2p, Pb2p, Cd2p, and Zn2p) doped chitosan poly(acrylic acid) nanospheres. The hydrophilic nanospheres were created by spontaneously polymerizing acrylic acid in a chitosan-hydrated solution that holds metallic ions (Cu2, Pb2, Cd2, or Zn2). The clear distinctive peaks are produced by those divalent metal ions in the nanosphere, which were used for the identification of four biomarkers.

In addition to providing adherence spots for immobilization of antibodies, the chitosan coating on the outside of chitosan of the nanospheres also certified the biocompatibility of the set of probes. For the detection of four tumor biomarkers, a sensitive, precise, and straightforward electrochemical immunosensor was prepared, using the analytes CEA, CA19–9, CA125, and CA242 to identify pancreatic related biomarkers.

In this electrochemical detection, the parallel detection of PC tumor markers was done by the synthesized Cu-CP, Pb-CP, Cd-CP, and Zn-CP nanospheres by one-pot method and those nanospheres were utilized as an electrochemical probe to develop quick and accurate immunosensor. These probe's benefits, including their easily synthesized nature, great biocompatibility, and ease of modification, allowed the suggested immunosensor to be auspiciously used for the parallel identification of CEA, CA19–9, CA125, and CA242. The experimental outputs appeared that the immunosensor built from chitosan poly(acrylic acid) nanospheres interfered with metallic ions has enough sensitivity to recognize the biomarkers with reasonable efficiency. Additionally, the developed electrochemical immunosensor became used to analyze clinical blood samples, and the outcomes were quite identical to those of the ELISA approach. The key benefits of the suggested immunosensor were the concurrent detection of four biomarkers with a lower detection limit and good sensitivity [89].

8.4 Surgical management

Depending on the anatomical position of the tumors, surgical options for the resection of PC include pancreaticoduodenectomy distal or total pancreatectomy. As surgeons' expertise grows, reorganizing healthcare services and limiting certain surgeries to high-volume centers has improved outcomes. Technology and surgical procedure advancements were made in an effort to further reduce unfavorable outcomes and increase survival. The goal of surgical resection is to obtain an R0 resection, which is correlated with importantly enhanced survival compared to R1 resections [90]. In an effort to accelerate microscopic clearance, neoadjuvant therapy and vascular resections have been used [91].

8.4.1 Preoperative biliary drainage

Jaundice is a familiar symptom among individuals with PC. Regarding coagulopathy and a rise in perioperative infectious problems, this may have consequences [92].

Patients with obstructive jaundice would normally have this alleviated prior to resection. Although the feature of the data was examined to be low, studies looking into preoperative biliary drainage (some using percutaneous transhepatic cholangiography and another using endoscopic retrograde cholangiopancreatography (ERCP)) revealed no evidence for or against drainage [93]. A new multicenter randomized research comparing urgent surgery to ERCP plus drainage showed a greater incidence of perioperative complications in the drainage group. This demonstrates that some people would benefit more from a quicker procedure than biliary decompression and resection [94].

8.4.2 Anastomotic technique

A pancreatic fistula and leak from pancreatic anastomosis are the main causes of morbidity after Whipple surgery [95]. Through anastomosing the pancreatic remnant to the stomach or jejunum, the Whipples could be treated while rebuilding the digestive system if these two approaches are correlated to one another, recent research observed no difference in the results. Although other anastomotic techniques have been recorded, a recent meta-analysis was unable to reveal that the "duct-to-mucosa" anastomosis was expected to cause pancreatic fistulas than the "invagination" procedure [51].

8.4.3 Minimally invasive surgery

Similar to other fields, interest has increased in pancreatic surgery's use of less invasive methods. The laparoscopic distal pancreatectomy was described as the first minimally invasive pancreatic surgery. In one meta-analysis, laparoscopic and open distal pancreatectomy had equivalent morbidity and mortality, although the minimally invasive group had lesser blood loss and a shorter hospital stay. There are no changes in the positive resection margins [96]. Laparoscopic distal pancreatectomy was at least not inferior to open pancreatectomy, according to a subsequent meta-analysis, but it could not be judged superior owing to a lack of level-one evidence. Additionally, efforts were used to enhance Whipple's process using robotic approaches. A meta-analysis of laparoscopic research studies showed that the robotic group had a reduced complication rate and less margin involvement as compared to open pancreatectomy. These studies are vulnerable to selection bias because they lack randomization. Additionally expensive in terms of capital outlay, robotic surgery lacks cost-effectiveness analyses [97].

8.4.4 Vascular resection

Any pancreatic tumor's link to the surrounding vasculature is a crucial factor in determining its ability to be removed. Although it is frequently technically possible, the advantages of resecting mesenteric and portal veins affected by malignancies are still up for debate [98]. According to a meta-analysis of research involving patients who live through Whipple's surgery with or without substantial arterial resection, those who underwent arterial reconstruction had worse results at years one and three and higher peri-operative mortality rates [99]. This is why it is generally agreed that invasion of the superior mesenteric artery or celiac trunk prevents resection. However, the outcomes of venous resection might be better. When compared to patients without vascular intervention, meta-analysis studies indicated no variation in perioperative morbidity or 1- or 3-year survival in those undergoing resection of the portal or superior mesenteric vein. Consequently, the venous resection group's operation took longer and resulted in more blood loss. As previously mentioned, the lack of randomization in these studies raises the possibility of selection bias. However, a small group of patients may benefit from incorporation of pancreatectomy and venous resection [100].

8.5 Medical management

The commonly used PNPs and their advantages, applied therapies, combined drug molecules, and outcomes are included in Table 8.1.

8.5.1 Chemotherapy

The exceptional desmoplasia of the stroma, which makes up around 80% of the tumor mass, is the primary histological hallmark for PDAC, among the most aggressive malignancies. GEM is the most frequently used drug in PDAC and has a median survival rate of approximately 5.7 months [110]. The poor prognosis of PDAC patients is largely due to their outcome of a particular microenvironment, whose defining histological characteristic is the exceptional desmoplasia of the stroma, which takes around 80% of the tumor mass. Massive stroma surrounding the local tumor alters the pancreatic tissues' typical architecture, causing poor vascularization, elevated intratumoral pressure, and decreased drug diffusion. Desmoplastic stroma also put a strain on tumor blood vessels and hinders an excessive metabolic demand that results in an environment that is anemic, hypoxic, and acidic. PC cells may eventually adjust to the hypoxic environment, go through more genetic alteration, and then develop stem-cell-like characteristics that may lessen their sensitivity to chemotherapy or radiation therapy [111,112]. Hence, designing a microenvironment pH-sensitive delivery system that can concurrently carry and release paclitaxel and GEM to the tumor's core simultaneously [113] is required for better therapy.

Using a polyethylene glycol-polyarginine-polylysine (PEG-pArg-pLys) platform, monophosphorylated GEM (p-GEM, the intermediate active product of GEM) and paclitaxel codelivery micelles were created [114]. The lysine residue of PEGpArg-pLys was connected to paclitaxel via a pH-sensitive molecule (2-propionic-3-methyl maleic anhydride, CDM). Most of the cancer cells were resistant to GEM, and p-GEM was more cytotoxic [115]. In this design, electrostatic interactions allow the guanidine

Table 8.1 Polymeric nanoparticles (NP)-enabled drug delivery [60].

Nanoparticle type	Materials used	Advantages of the materials	Applied therapies	Drug molecules	Results	References
Polymeric NPs	Dendrigraft poly-lysine–EGPLGVRGK-poly (ethylene glycol)-poly (caprolactone) (DGL–EGPLGVRGK-PEG–PCL)	Used for deep penetration into the tumor microenvironment and it inhibits proliferation and metastasis through the pathway	Chemo therapy	GEM	Enhances prolonged antitumor efficacy	[101]
Polymeric NPs	Cell-penetrating peptide (CPP)–based amphiphilic peptide (C2KG2R9)–cholesterol monomers	For effective membrane translocation and it has the ability to effectively transfer the drug across the cell membrane	Antitumor therapy	DOX	Improves the effectiveness of antitumor treatment by increasing cellular absorption of different therapeutics and tumor-targeted penetration	[102]
Polymeric NPs	Chaperonin GroEL	Used for targeted drug delivery	Gene therapy and radiation therapy	DOX	Drug administration that is efficient and highly selective has no adverse effects on vital organs	[103]
Polymeric NPs	Bovine serum albumin (BSA)	It has high water solubility and biocompatibility	Optical imaging-guided therapy	GEM	Increasing GEM stability, cellular absorption, and apoptotic effects	[104]
Polymeric NPs	Aptamers/cell-penetrating peptide-camptothecin prodrug	It has higher stability, Biocompatibility, Higher binding affinity, and low immunogenicity	Medical Imaging and anticancer therapy	Camptothecin	Increase antitumor effectiveness while minimizing cytotoxicity	[105]
Polymeric NPs	Poly(ethylene glycol)-poly(D,L-lactic acid) (PEG-PLA)	It has shown immense safety and efficacy in a variety of experimental and nontoxic formulations	Chemotherapy, immunotherapy, and synergistic therapy	Salinomycin (SAL)	Increases cell death and apoptosis, inhibition of invasion, use of EMT, eradication of the tumor, and enhances the survival rate	[106]

(Continued)

Table 8.1 (Continued)

Nanoparticle type	Materials used	Advantages of the materials	Applied therapies	Drug molecules	Results	References
Polymeric NPs	Fourth generation poly (amidoamine) (PAMAM) dendrimer–HA	Deep tumor penetration, high bioavailability, and improved drug entrapment	Targeted therapy	CDF	Improves the IC50 value and increases the safety, therapeutic range, and cellular absorption	[60]
Polymeric NPs	PCL–CDM-PAMAM/ Pt(G3,G5,G7),PEG–PCL,PCL	It exhibits balanced tumor penetration, cell internalization, and tumor retention	Anticancer therapies	Pt prodrug c, c, t-[Pt $(NH_3)_2$ $C_{12}(OH)$ $(O_2CCH_2CH_2CO_2H)$]	Optimize tumor internalization, tumor retention, and tumor penetration	[107]
Polymeric NPs	PEG_{2000}–S–S–PLA_{6000}, N_3–PEG_{2000}–PLA_{6000}	They are more stable, have longer blood circulation time, more tumor accumulation, and better intratumoral delivery ability	Targeted therapy	DOX and curcumin	Encourages cellular absorption and subsequent nuclear transport, with a preference for cancer cells	[108]
Polymeric NPs	Human serum albumin (HSA)	It has excellent biodegradability and safety	Optical imaging-guided therapy	Paclitaxel, tumor necrosis factor (TNF)–related apoptosis-inducing ligand (TRAIL)	Enhance antitumor effectiveness and apoptotic activity	[109]

groups in the side chains of pArg to transport p-GEM. Due to the higher pH, the micelle can survive in the tumor's outer layer. The therapeutic impact of coadministering GEM and albumin paclitaxel is greatly improved by contrast to that of GEM alone. HAS-PTX (albumin paclitaxel) is stated to have a stromal remodeling effect that noticeably changes collagen architecture and gets rid of fibroblasts linked to cancer. Additionally, HAS-PTX promotes intratumoral accumulation and GEM in penetration space [112]. The paclitaxel and phosphorylated GEM were coloaded into NPs using tumor central stroma targeting and microenvironment responsive method. During the raise of the antitumor efficiency of chemotherapeutics, the developed NP damaged the internal stroma while maintaining the exterior stroma. The AE105 peptide may be employed in the majority of urokinase-type plasminogen activator receptor (uPAR)-targeted imaging and therapeutic investigations because that has been proven to preferentially attach to uPAR, a receptor that is extensively expressed on the outer of tumor and stroma cells. The AE105 peptide was attached to the micelle surface to enhance the targeting effect [116]. By altering AE105, it was discovered that the T-RKP micelles could target the uPAR expressed in pancreatic tumors. Due to the increased pH in the microenvironment, the micelles stayed stable in the stroma that was external to the tumor. The entire micelle is disrupted at the tumor's core and when it enters into the tumor core was provoked by the tumor micro environment's low pH. The released PTX damaged the tumor's "internal" stroma while leaving the stroma that is "external," preventing the cancer cells from metastasis stage. Transport of the p-GEM into the cancer cells through PEG-pArg-pLys was performed. Additionally, the p-GEM- induced tumor cell death resulted in more tumor cells being killed when T cells are activated.

Improvement of a paclitaxel and p-GEM codelivery NP delivery system was prompted by the tumor microenvironment's varying pH levels. Paclitaxel and p-GEM codelivery NP delivery system is used in response to pH alterations in the tumor microenvironment. The new formulation (T-RKP) demonstrated strong biocompatibility with its PEG covering and effective tumor targeting in the systemic circulation. Based on the unique releasing characteristic of the CDM modification that occurs at the tumor core, the formulation was employed to change the drug release kinetics responsive pH stimulation in the tumor microenvironment. The core tumor stroma could be particularly disrupted while the exterior stromal layer is preserved when CDM and the AE105 peptide are used together. This technique kills tumor cells while preventing metastasis stage [26].

In another study, erlotinib and GEM -loaded macrophage-like NPs were utilized for PC surgical care. The best therapeutic choice for PC at the moment is surgical resection, and even though perioperative mortality and postoperative problems declining, everlasting adequacy is still undesirable. Active chemotherapy could extend patient survival, increase their standard of living, and enhance their prognosis, according to recent studies. Despite its great harmfulness and chemoresistance, GEM has been shown to be the only chemotherapeutic treatment to be resistant to PC. The FOLFIRINOX (folinic acid, irinotecan, fluorouracil, and oxaliplatin) regimen's effectiveness against metastatic stage PC was enhanced by the addition of GEM, although the common side effects and hazardous consequences have been markedly raised. To reduce toxicity, chemotherapeutic medicines are, therefore, increasingly being coupled with specific inhibitors.

Chemotherapeutic drugs are enclosed in NPs to decrease their level of toxicity by targeted delivery and controlled release. Drug carriers made of PLGA NPs were used. PLGA has benefits like surface modification, sustained release, biodegradability, and biocompatibility. For active targeting of cancer cells, the antiepidermal growth factor receptor (EGFR) monoclonal antibody (mAb) was coated on synthetic PEG NPs. By utilizing biomimetic NPs wrapped in natural cell membranes, drug delivery to the target cells can be improved. Additionally, hiding NPs along macrophage membranes, in specific, extends in vivo circulation, reduces their clearance through the reticuloendothelial system, avoids immunological surveillance, and also improves tumor homing.

The disguised NPs were injected into the tumor cells after which they gradually released the drugs. They prepared GEM -loaded PLGA NPs with a macrophage membrane coating (MPGNPs) to reduce the drug's toxicity and increase tumor targeting. By preventing DNA synthesis, MPGNPs and erlotinib can work together to inhibit the proliferation of PC cells.

The MPGNPS avoided phagocytosis and used the pancreatic tumors as its passive targets. Combining MOGNPS with erlotinib inhibits tumor cell growth and angiogenesis via phosphoinositide 30-kinase (PI3K)/AKT/mTOR [117].

8.5.2 Immunotherapy

Treating cancer is being revolutionized by new immunotherapeutic drugs that target the proteins cytotoxic T-lymphocyte-associated protein 4 (CTLA-4) and programmed cell death 1 and programmed cell death 1 ligand(PD-1/PD-L1). The bulk of PDAC, which eliminates mismatch repair defects, is thought to be immune-quiescent or resistant [118]. Mesothelin-specific CAR-T cells (CARTmeso cells) are used against chemotherapy-refractory metastatic PDAC in phase I trial [119] and in a Phase II study, the sole drug ipilimumab (anti-CTLA-4) was used against locally progressed or metastatic cancer.

Researchers are still working harder to overcome the severely immunosuppressive PDAC microenvironment and improve the effectiveness of immunotherapy in PDAC. For instance, Huang and his colleagues developed CXCL12 and PD-L1 targeting liposome-protamine-DNAs with plasmids encoding tiny trapping proteins (referred to as pCombo trapped NPs). The CXCL12 confine works to encourage T cell infiltration into tumor areas, while the PD-L1 trap speeds up T cell infiltration to kill PDAC cells even more. From the outcome, the double-step application of p combo trap NPs enhanced their potential for considerably decreased tumor volume, increased survival, and decreased PDAC metastasis [60].

Additionally, they added the trap genes (IL-10 and CXCL 12 traps) to LPD NPs, which significantly lessen immunosuppressive cells and stimulated immunosuppressive tolerogenic dendritic cells. The LPD NPs successfully reduced the tumor development by 20% following treatments, which were revealed by the preclinical allograft PDAC models [120]. In addition, for combining starvation theory with immunotherapy, loaded glucose oxidase (Gox) utilizing CCM-coated MSNs. The CMSNs-Gox keeps the capacity to increase the effects of immune checkpoint inhibition of PD1 while producing harmful Gox-catalyzed glucose breakdown by H_2O_2 [121].

When the metabolic enzyme indoleamine 2,3-dioxygenase (IDO) depletes the I-tryptophan (Trp) found in both tumor cells and innate immune cells, the immunosuppressive tumor microenvironment was produced. Nevertheless, IDO small molecule inhibitors such as indoximod could reverse these immunosuppressive effects (IND). In order to simultaneously load IND as an IDO inhibitor, 1-methyl-Trp as an immunological adjuvant and celastrol for PDAC chemoimmunotherapy, hyaluronidase-coated cationic albumin NPs(HNPs) was developed. Hyaluronidase-activated size-reduction and CD44 receptor—mediated endocytosis supported deep penetration into the tumor facilitating the accumulation. The immunosuppressive tumor microenvironment was most effectively reversed by the chosen IDO inhibition and chemotherapy combination. The in vivo investigations using both orthotopic and xenograft pancreatic tumor models showed an improvement in antitumor activity. Oxaliplatin and the lipid-conjugated IND prodrug are administered together in order to interfere with the immune system's IDO pathway and cause immunogenic cell death (ICD). Delicately crafted OX/IND-MSNs significantly reduced tumor size and improved survival by increasing the recruitment of CD8_T cells and downregulating Foxp3 + T cells [122].

Tumor-associated macrophages (TAMs), immune cells, are abundant highly in the immunosuppressive PDAC microenvironment. In actuality, M2 TAMs alter the tumor microenvironments and stimulate the growth of cancer using cytokines and growth factors. Reprogramming them toward predominately antitumor M1 phenotype in such situations may provide considerable possibilities for efficient cancer therapy.

In order to deliver the miR-155/miR-125b-2 expressing plasmid DNA and prepare miR-155/miR-125b-2 modified tumor-derived exosomes done through HA-PEI/HAPEG self-assembled NPs. As an outcome of these exosomes, M2 phenotype macrophages were reprogrammed to become M1 phenotype macrophages [123]. M2 TAMS that targets micelles to deliver CSF-1R—small interfering RNA (siRNA) and NVPBEZ 235, a PI3K inhibitor were developed. The simultaneous suppression of PI3K and CSF-1R may change the tumor immune microenvironment and it stimulates the antitumor immune responses for efficient PDAC treatment [124].

It is obvious that PDAC is particularly defined by several redundant hurdles to immunotherapy, despite the enormous promise and the extraordinarily fast advancement in nanotechnology for achieving effective immunotherapy on tumors. Most of the combined methods with chemotherapy as the main therapeutic component are currently undertaking clinical trials and are successful. In addition, it has recently been discovered that autophagy encourages immune evasion by destroying MHC-I [125]. Consequently, a promising treatment approach to treat PDAC may involve combining immunotherapy and autophagy suppression. The success of prospective immunotherapy that is enabled by nanotechnology will undoubtedly depend on the researcher's ongoing efforts, and we predict that immunotherapy will play an important role in future PDAC treatments.

8.5.3 Radiotherapy

Ionizing radiation is used in radiotherapy, a successful method for treating cancer in humans, to especially increase the reactive oxygen species (ROS) levels in tumor tissues. Increased ROS levels directly harm proteins, lipids, and DNA, leading to cell death [126]. PDAC is occasionally treated with radiotherapy and chemoradiotherapy in adjuvant and resectable conditions. The main objectives of radiation in these situations are to improve local control, raise the possibility of a margin-negative resection, and stop disease progression. Additionally, radiation is frequently utilized to treat PDAC patients who have localized or advanced discomfort, bleeding, or obstructive symptoms [127].

Although the incidence of tumor control increases with ionizing radiation dose in radiotherapy, the ionizing radiation excessive doses can cause serious harm to the healthy tissue in the immediate vicinity. As a result, radiosensitizers that absorb radiation have been extensively used to increase the efficacy of therapy while minimizing the negative effects on adjacent tissues. PDAC cells may turn more sensitive to radiotherapy while treated with metformin, tolfenamic acid, CPA, nimotuzumab, MK8776, and WEE1 inhibitor AZD1775 [128]. For instance, TA can enhance apoptosis and reduce cell growth by downregulating the antiapoptotic protein survival, which is linked to radiation therapy resistance [129].

Additionally, CPA is an effective SMO (sonidegib and vismodegib) inhibitor that can disrupt stroma, deplete CSCs, and improve PDAC cells' reactivity to ionizing radiation as well as depleting CSCs. Block copolymers based on hydrophobic oligo(caprolactone), poly[oligo(ethylene glycol) monomethyl ether methacrylate], poly (2-hydroxyethyl methacrylate), and poly[oligo(ethylene glycol) monomethyl ether methacrylate] to encapsulate CPA were created. The radiation response was improved by the cross-linked polymeric micelles (M-CPA), which boosted it by the respective fold changes in pancreatic cells and human pancreatic stellate cells (hPSCs). The outcomes showed that the integrated M-CPA and radiation therapy were successful in treating PDAC cells and also stellate cells [130]. Because of their excellent biocompatibility and practicable chemical manipulation, Au NPs attracted a lot of attention. To prepare molecularly imprinted microgels (AuMIP microgels) using Au NPs (24 nm), N-isopropyl acrylamide (NIPAm), and N, N′ methylene bis(acrylamide) (MBAA) as the respective seeds, primary monomers, and cross-linking agents were done through one-pot seeded precipitation polymerization method [131]. The growth of the tumor was obviously concealed by the AuMIP microgels therapy upon x-ray radiation. Additionally, superoxide dismutase (SOD)-like activity (scavenge superoxide radicals) and catalase-like activity (scavenge H_2O_2) are both present in cerium oxide NPs (CONPs) with distinct valence states (Ce3 + vs Ce4 +) and oxygen defects to modify auto-regenerative redox status. It was discovered that radiation does not have any effect on the SOD-like and catalase-like activities of CONPs at neutral pH but enhanced the SOD-like activity and lowered the catalase-like activity of CONPs in an acidic environment.

The oxidation states of Ce4 + and Ce3 + , CONPs were altered and it helped to build up radicals for tumor-specific apoptosis while preventing normal tissue from the radiation's toxicity. When considered as a whole, these outcomes showed that CONPs can function as prospective radiosensitizers for tumors, also protective agents for normal tissues to enhance PDAC treatment [132].

There can be numerous chances to lessen the indiscriminate toxicity to normal cells as a consequence of the current revolution in focused radiosensitizers. Additionally, because of the lower doses of radiation and therapeutic chemicals, radiotherapy in correlation with other therapeutic modalities may result in important activity and reduced toxicity [60].

8.5.4 Targeted therapy

On the analysis of systemic harmfulness of the chemotherapeutic agents, new focused drug delivery methods must be created immediately. GEM and DOX, two anticancer drugs, were simultaneously delivered to the PC cells' nucleus using a novel nuclear-focused, redox-sensitive, drug delivery vehicle. Sensitizing the formulation to the reducing agents' concentration requires the incorporation of a redox-sensitive polymer (PEG-S-S-PLA).

Acridine orange (AO), which has nuclear-localizing properties, was conjugated to the exterior of the polymersome. In reaction to 50 mM glutathione, the redox-sensitive, nuclear-targeted polymersomes released more than 60% of their encapsulated contents.

The drug-encapsulated vesicles are very toxic; however, the NPs are nontoxic. By directly delivering the medications to the cells' crucial organelles, the nucleus, the produced formulation can rise the drug's therapeutic index. Polymersomes are hollow vesicles made of amphiphilic polymers with a bilayer membrane that can integrate hydrophobic pharmaceuticals and an aqueous interior that can encapsulate hydrophilic chemicals. These vesicles are more reliable than liposomes because they include long-chain polymers. The outer layer's hydrophilic polymer gives the vesicles long-circulating qualities. Accumulation of the polymeric vesicles in the nuclei of pancreatic tumor cells was facilitated by the AO. The drug-encapsulated polymersomes both decreased the mass of the pancreatic tumor cell spheroids and greatly affected the vitality of pancreatic cells in monolayer and three-dimensional spheroid cultures [133].

The first-line and the most efficient drug for PC is GEM. However, due to its instability and poor cellular absorption, anticancer activity is severely constrained. The developed unique nano DDS is based on amphiphilic dendrimers and aliphatic GEM prodrugs to enhance the therapeutic efficacy of GEM. On behalf of its favorable biocompatibility, monodisperse, highly branching structure, tuneable size existence of internal cavities, and ease of functionalization, dendrimers are a prospective basis for the release of anticancer medicines and therapeutic oligonucleotides. Particularly, the spontaneous self-assembly of small amphiphilic dendrimers harnesses the benefits of a couple of lipids' capability for self-assembly and the dendrimer's distinctive structure and stability for huge drug-filling capacity, while keeping a small size and stable formulation. The nanoformulation of GEM based on dendrimers has a huge drug-filling capacity. The discovered GEM nanoformulation could efficiently accumulate at the tumor area and quickly be absorbed in cells due to its tiny size, stable formulation, and pH-responsive drug release. AmDD/Gem nano micelles' stability in a neutral environment made it possible to deliver the drugs to tumor sites effectively while minimizing systemic toxicity brought on by drug leakage into the bloodstream during transport. This GEM nanosystem, which combines amphiphilic dendrimers with drug delivery based on nanotechnology, represents a viable therapeutic possibility for treating PC.

In vivo and in vitro tests represented that the GEM nanoformulation had an effective anticancer effect than free GEM. Additionally, the nano-drug showed good biocompatibility and considerably diminished side effects. The potential application of self-assembling amphiphilic dendrimer-based nanotechnology is used for toxicity reduction and also enhancing drug efficacy [134].

8.5.5 Antibody-mediated therapy

Antibody—drug conjugates (ADCs) are gaining attention in the domain of cancer therapy because they transport anticancer medications to cancer cells highly efficacious than traditional chemotherapies. To be beneficial to exert sufficient efficacy, the drugs conjugated to the antibody must be extremely cytotoxic, such as auristatin, maytansines, and calicheamicins, which are 100−1000 times highly potent than typical anticancer medications [134]. However, there are developing concerns regarding adverse effects from the breakdown of ADC under physiological circumstances [135].

Antibodies can be added to drug-loaded nanocarriers, which have a far better delivery capacity than ADCs, to circumvent these ADC limitations. The antibody fragments (1,2-diaminocyclohexane)Pt(II)(DACHPt)(DACHPt/m) polymeric micelles with oxaliplatin as an active compound demonstrated strong therapeutic potential against many cancer models and are being assessed in phase I clinical research [136].

The efficacy of loaded Pt medicines may be increased by conjugating antibody fragments to DACHPt/m due to improved tumor cell transport and efficient intracellular drug release [137].

8.5.6 Synergistic therapy

The present research technology has changed from mono-chemotherapy to synergistic therapy improving the therapeutic benefit for cancer. The K-ras gene mutation, which affects about 90% of PC patients, is closely related to the high death rate. The downstream signal molecules that are regulated by the activated K-ras to yield the pleiotropic cellular effects that regulate cell growth, differentiation, and survival include Raf kinase, RalGEFs, and PI3K. A point mutation in the K-ras gene at codon 12 maintains the protein in the GTP-bound "on" state and maintains constitutive GTPase activity.

The K-ras gene mutation will cause the cells to take on a tumor phenotype, which will ultimately cause cancer to spread. According to studies, downregulating mutant K-ras expression increases cell death, prevents cell metastasis, and lowers treatment resistance. From those studies, the mutant K-ras gene is believed as a capable therapeutic target for preventing the spread of PC. To specifically target and cleave K-ras messenger RNA in pancreatic tumor cells, siRNA molecules and RNA interference (RNAi) was used as an effective method which limited the mutated K-ras expression [60]. SiRNA needs a carrier because, on its own, it cannot pass the hydrophobic cell membrane on its own. A new nanocarrier for treating PC was created using made of GQDs and biodegradable charged polyester vectors (BCPVs). This nanocarrier was coloaded with DOX and (siRNA), resulting in the creation of GQD/DOX/BCPV/siRNA nanocomplexes. So, to collaborate chemo and gene therapy for treating PC, initially, the cationic polymer-coated-GQDs (graphene quantum dots) were used as K-ras siRNA and DOX as a codelivery carrier. GDQs were chosen as a nanocarrier in this investigation because of their great characteristics, such as their simple production, outstanding biocompatibility, huge exterior area, and ease of conjugation with biomolecules. The option of an appropriate moderation polymer on GQD is essential to achieving the cofilling DOX function and siRNA [138]. Numerous adaptable NPs have been altered with polyethyleneimine (PEI) to create carriers that can simultaneously carry genes and drugs [139]. However, PEI exhibited some significant disadvantages, such ss a prolonged period of toxicity and the inability to degrade under physiological circumstances. The PEGylation of PEI becomes a popular solution to these issues [140]. The complexity of choosing the appropriate PEG is substantially increased by the fact that PEGylation requires extensive research on choosing the best chain number, coupling chemistry, and structural characteristics [141].

The well-developed biodegradable cationic polylactides with pendant tertiary amine groups were made after overcoming the problems and were given the designation of BCPV. BCPV incorporates siRNAs to create a particle-like shape that successfully protects siRNA from enzyme digestion. BCPV, meantime improves the cellular consumption of the filled siRNA, and it aids the siRNA's escape from the loaded endosome and entry into the cytosol, which is a vital process in RNAi- mediated clinical intervention [142,143]. BCPV was, therefore, considered to be the next prime candidate for changing GQDs because of its positively charged characteristics and excellent biodegradability.

The BCPV functionalized GQDs were utilized as a coload siRNA and DOX during the evaluation of gene/chemo combination therapy for synergistic anticancer activity. It was evident that the GQD uptake amount was increased later in the modifications in BCPV. As an outcome of the fact that negatively charged cell membranes would allow positively charged nanocomplexes to easily flow through them [144], GQD/BCPV nanocomplexes saw a change in their outer layer from negative to positive. The BCPV coating is helpful for improving the siRNA and DOX's capacity for cellular uptake.

Composed, GQD/DOX/BCPV/siRNA nanocomplexes have demonstrated their capacity for delivering the gene therapy siRNA and the anticancer medication DOX into pancreatic cells simultaneously. In pancreatic cells the K-ras gene expression was successfully diminished by the usage of nanocomplexes as the therapeutic preparation, resulting in a clear decrease in the bioactivities of cells such as cell augmentation, cell exodus, and invasion. Further crucially, through exposing the nanocomplexes to the appropriate laser beam to deliver the siRNA and DOX, the nanocomplexes' anticancer activities were markedly enhanced. The GQD/DOX/BCPV/siRNA nanocomplexes are viewed as the perfect future drug/gene delivery technologies for different cancer treatment therapies to their elevated biocompatibility, low toxicity, excellent transport efficiency, and regulated release capability [138].

8.5.7 Radiodynamic therapy

A well-tolerated dosage of high-energy x-rays is used in place of visible/near-infrared light irradiation in radio dynamic treatment (RDT), more recent development of photodynamic therapy. Greater tissue penetration is made possible, allowing for the noninvasive treatment of large, deeply seated cancers. Here, we discuss the design and evaluation of an RDT DDS that aims to enhance the photosensitizer's (PS) intra- or perinuclear localization, causing DNA damage and clonogenic cell death. This consists of cell-penetrating HIV trans-activator of transcription (TAT) peptides that are surface-functionalized with a PS (verteporfin, VP) and then integrated with PLGA NPs.

The nononcological uses of PDT includes treating many solid tumors and precancerous lesions. In order to produce single oxygen (O_2), a highly harmful ROS is used in a PS that is activated by visible or near-infrared light. However, due to the shallow tissue penetration of light, which necessitates technically hard endoscopic or interstitial fiber-optic light delivery, PDT has only found limited therapeutic utility for treating deep-seated, big, or widespread cancers. Complete tumor ablation is especially challenging due to the optical absorption and scattering's considerable tissue- and wavelength dependence [145,146]. Additionally, many molecular PSs lead to aggregate in biological media because of their hydrophobic nature, necessitating formulations such as liposomes for effective distribution to tumors in vivo and maximizing therapeutic efficacy. The external activating light source is replaced by high-energy x-rays, such as those produced by a linear accelerator (LINAC) used in radiotherapy or by appropriate radioisotopes, in RDT, often also known as X-PDT.

A PS formulation based on polymer NPs with a TAT peptide as a nuclear localizing signal was created for tumor delivery. It is based on PLGA, a biocompatible and biodegradable elastomeric copolymer with FDA approval, which is especially utilized for drug delivery. VP [147] was enclosed in PLGA for this approach, and it is anticipated that these PLGA NPs may facilitate drug accumulation in the tumor in vivo through the well-known retention (EPR) effect and enhanced permeability. To further boost their effectiveness and selectivity, they could also be coupled into tumor cell-targeting moieties.

Then, O_2 production and in vitro RDT responses in human PC (PANC-1) cells were assessed, together with the cellular uptake and intracellular localization of the PLGA-VP-TAT NPs.

The TAT peptide was incorporated into the NP surface, producing a stable PLGA-VP-TAT NP formulation, which was supported by measurements of the absorption and zeta potential over time. The PLGA-VP-TAT NP formulation was shown in Fig. 8.6.

In comparison to the nontargeted VP nanoformulation, the uptake of the NPs in human PANC-1 pancreatic cancerous cells was substantially higher with TAT targeting, including within the cell nuclei, and this resulted in significantly greater RDT cytotoxicity as evidenced by both higher DNA and cell membrane damage. Due to increased radiation-induced ROS formation, specifically single-oxygen generation from the VP molecules, RDT was significantly more harmful with targeting than the same dose of x-rays without NPs. A nuclear-targeted RDT has the potential to serve as a unique

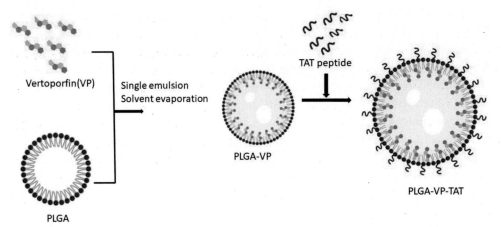

Figure 8.6 PLGA-VP-TAT NP formulation. *PLGA-VP-TAT NP*, polylactic-co-glycolic acid-verteporfin-trans-activator of transcription nanoparticles.

therapeutic option, either as a stand-alone therapy or to boost the effectiveness of fractionated radiation, along with treating deep-seated cancers like those in the pancreas.

The tumor selectivity of nuclear-targeted radio dynamic therapy will be a crucial challenge for clinical translation, as it is the major hurdle of anticancer treatments. If there is significant NP accumulation in healthy organs, even with precise spatial localization of current radiation therapy delivery, there will be activation and potential cytotoxicity in healthy tissue lying along the radiation beam paths in addition to that caused by the radiation itself. In addition, to obtain differential uptake beyond that caused by the EPR effect, it is anticipated that tumor-cell targeting will be necessary in addition to nuclear localization by the TAT or other nuclear-localizing techniques. Additionally, the danger of increased skin phototoxicity brought on by nuclear uptake needs to be taken into consideration [146].

8.6 Conclusion

PNPs have strongly registered their importance in various fields. One of the best uses of it is nanomedicine. Due to limitations in traditional therapeutics, advanced therapies using NPs have been studied as they can easily reach into a tumor. The designed NP has no harm to health, degradation time must be ensured, chemical and physical properties must be retained for a longer period, and should have no or very minimal side effects. Gene mutation is the basic cause to become cancer. It is found that about 10% of PC patients have a hereditary background caused by a single gene mutation in germline cells (BRCA2, CDKN$_2$A, p16). Early detection of any cancer has the highest rate of survivorship. Only a few changes occurred in the genes in early stages of PC, that is, pancreatic intraepithelial neoplasia, and the duct cells also do not undergo many changes during this stage. But in later phases, there are numerous mutations and abnormal cell growth. Through these conditions detection of changes in genes in pre-cancerous cells can be predicted. Biomarker is a recent trend in detecting cancer in its early stage. Cancer cells eject extracellular vesicles, which carries a huge number of cancers associated proteins called macrophage inhibitory factor. By detecting the amount of these proteins, 95.5% of an early bid of PC has been found. Other than this oral administration, near infrared based optical imaging techniques, assistance in chemotherapy, and combined polymers for effective treatment are developed. The progression of nano-based therapeutics is uplifting and we await new innovations for intractable diseases such as PC.

References

[1] Ferlay J. Cancer statistics for the year 2020: an overview. Int J Cancer 2021;149(4):778−89.
[2] Luque-Michel E, et al. Clinical advances of nanocarrier-based cancer therapy and diagnostics. Expert Opin Drug Deliv 2017;14(1):75−92.
[3] Siminska E, Koba M. Amino acid profiling as a method of discovering biomarkers for early diagnosis of cancer. Amino Acids 2016;48(6):1339−45.
[4] Madamsetty VS, et al. Tumor selective uptake of drug-nanodiamond complexes improves therapeutic outcome in pancreatic cancer. Nanomedicine 2019;18:112−21.
[5] Lambert A, et al. An update treat options pancreatic adenocarcinoma. Ther Adv Med Oncol 2019;11:1758835919875568.
[6] Palazzo L, et al. ATM controls proper mitotic spindle structure. Cell Cycle 2014;13(7):1091−100.
[7] Lee SS, et al. ATM kinase is required for telomere elongation in mouse and human cells. Cell Rep 2015;13(8):1623−32.
[8] Buscail L, Bournet B, Cordelier P. Role of oncogenic KRAS in the diagnosis, prognosis and treatment of pancreatic cancer. Nat Rev Gastroenterol Hepatol 2020;17(3):153−68.
[9] Armstrong SA, et al. ATM dysfunction in pancreatic adenocarcinoma and associated therapeutic implications. Mol Cancer Ther 2019;18(11):1899−908.
[10] Wang S, et al. The molecular biology of pancreatic adenocarcinoma: translational challenges and clinical perspectives. Signal Transduct Target Ther 2021;6(1):249.
[11] Makarova-Rusher OV, et al. Pancreatic squamous cell carcinoma: a population-based study of epidemiology, clinicopathologic characteristics and outcomes. Pancreas 2016;45(10):1432−7.
[12] Liszka L, et al. Colloid carcinoma of the pancreas: review of selected pathological and clinical aspects. Pathology 2008;40(7):655−63.
[13] Pandey P, Dureja H. Recent patents on polymeric nanoparticles for cancer therapy. Recent Pat Nanotechnol 2018;12(2):155−69.
[14] Sleep D. Albumin and its application in drug delivery. Expert Opin Drug Deliv 2015;12(2):793−812.
[15] Vazquez N, et al. Influence of the PLGA/gelatin ratio on the physical, chemical and biological properties of electrospun scaffolds for wound dressings. Biomed Mater 2019;14(4):045006.
[16] Maeda H. The 35th anniversary of the discovery of EPR effect: a new wave of nanomedicines for tumor-targeted drug delivery-personal remarks and future prospects. J Pers Med 2021;11(3):229.
[17] Etman SM, et al. Lactoferrin/Hyaluronic acid double-coated lignosulfonate nanoparticles of quinacrine as a controlled release biodegradable nanomedicine targeting pancreatic cancer. Int J Pharm 2020;578:119097.

[18] Muthu MS, Singh S. Targeted nanomedicines effective treatment modalities for cancer, AIDS and brain disorders. Nanomed (Lond) 2010;4(1):105−18.

[19] Lin MM, et al. Surface activation and targeting strategies of superparamagnetic iron oxide nanoparticles in cancer-oriented diagnosis and therapy. Nanomed (Lond) 2010;5(1):109−33.

[20] Zhou J, et al. Folate-chitosan-gemcitabine core-shell nanoparticles targeted to pancreatic cancer. Chin J Cancer Res 2013;25(5):527−35.

[21] Amanam I, Chung V. Targeted therapies for pancreatic cancer. Cancers (Basel) 2018;10(2):36.

[22] Pancreatic cancer: recent advances in nanoformulation-based therapies . Crit Rev Ther Drug Carrier Syst. 2019;36(1):59−91.

[23] Xie A, et al. Stimuli-responsive prodrug-based cancer nanomedicine. EBioMedicine 2020;56:102821.

[24] Birrenbach G, Speiser PP. Polymerized micelles and their use as adjuvants in immunology. J Pharm Sci 1976;65(12):1763−6.

[25] Burris HA, Moore MJ, Andersen J, Green MR, Rothenberg ML, Modiano MR, et al. Improvements in survival and clinical benefit with gemcitabine as first-line therapy for patients with advanced pancreas cancer: a randomized trial. J Clin Oncol 1997;15(6):2403−13.

[26] Chen X, et al. Codelivery nanosystem targeting the deep microenvironment of pancreatic cancer. Nano Lett 2019;19(6):3527−34.

[27] Dai Y, et al. Nanoparticle design strategies for enhanced anticancer therapy by exploiting the tumour microenvironment. Chem Soc Rev 2017;46(12):3830−52.

[28] Nasir A, Kausar A, Younus A. A review on preparation, properties and applications of polymeric nanoparticle-based materials. Polym Technol Eng 2014;54(4):325−41.

[29] Kumari RM, et al. Synthesis and evolution of polymeric nanoparticles. Design and development of new nanocarriers. William Andrew; 2018. p. 401−38.

[30] Reis CP, et al. Nanoencapsulation I. Methods for preparation of drug-loaded polymeric nanoparticles. Nanomedicine 2006;2(1):8−21.

[31] Mishima K, Matsuyama K, Tanabe D, Yamauchi S, Young TJ, Johnston KP. Microencapsulation of proteins by rapid expansion of supercritical solution with a nonsolvent. AIChE J 2000;46(4):857−65.

[32] Ammoury N, Fessi H, Devissaguet JP, Puisieux F, Benita S. In vitro release kinetic pattern of indomethacin from poly(D,L-lactide) nanocapsules. J Pharm Sci 1990;79(9):763−7.

[33] Sternling CA, Scriven LE. Interfacial turbulence: hydrodynamic instability and the Marangoni effect. AIChE J 1959;5(4):514−23.

[34] Johnson BK, Prud'homme RK. Chemical processing and micromixing in confined impinging jets. AIChE J 2003;49(9):2264−82.

[35] Nishikawa J, et al. Clinical importance of Epstein−Barr virus-associated gastric cancer. Cancers (Basel) 2018;10(6):167.

[36] Liu Y, Yang G, Zou D, Hui Y, Nigam K, Middelberg AP, et al. Formulation of nanoparticles using mixing-induced nanoprecipitation for drug delivery. Ind Eng Chem Res 2019;59(9):4134−49.

[37] Ding S, et al. Microfluidic nanoprecipitation systems for preparing pure drug or polymeric drug loaded nanoparticles: an overview. Expert Opin Drug Deliv 2016;13(10):1447−60.

[38] Wang J, et al. A microfluidic tubing method and its application for controlled synthesis of polymeric nanoparticles. Lab Chip 2014;14(10):1673−7.

[39] Guinebretière S, Briançon S, Fessi H, Teodorescu VS, Blanchin MG. Nanocapsules of biodegradable polymers: preparation and characterization by direct high resolution electron microscopy. Mater Sci Eng C 2002;21(1−2):137−42.

[40] Schorb M, et al. Software tools for automated transmission electron microscopy. Nat Methods 2019;16(6):471−7.

[41] Stetefeld J, McKenna SA, Patel TR. Dynamic light scattering: a practical guide and applications in biomedical sciences. Biophys Rev 2016;8(4):409−27.

[42] Wood HE, et al. Pancreatic cancer in England and Wales 1975−2000: patterns and trends in incidence, survival and mortality. Aliment Pharmacol Ther 2006;23(8):1205−14.

[43] Midha S, Chawla S, Garg PK. Modifiable and non-modifiable risk factors for pancreatic cancer: a review. Cancer Lett 2016;381(1):269−77.

[44] Zhao Z, Liu W. Pancreatic cancer: a review of risk factors, diagnosis, and treatment. Technol Cancer Res Treat 2020;19:1533033820962117.

[45] Silverman DT, Hoover RN, Brown LM, Swanson GM, Schiffman M, Greenberg RS, et al. Why do black Americans have a higher risk of pancreatic cancer than white Americans? Epidemiology 2003;14(1):45−54.

[46] Arnold LD, et al. Are racial disparities in pancreatic cancer explained by smoking and overweight/obesity? Cancer Epidemiol Biomarkers Prev 2009;18(9):2397−405.

[47] Wolpin BM, et al. ABO blood group and the risk of pancreatic cancer. J Natl Cancer Inst 2009;101(6):424−31.

[48] Memba R, et al. The potential role of gut microbiota in pancreatic disease: a systematic review. Pancreatology 2017;17(6):867−74.

[49] Hruban RH, et al. Update on familial pancreatic cancer. Adv Surg 2010;44:293−311.

[50] Permuth-Wey J, Egan KM. Family history is a significant risk factor for pancreatic cancer: results from a systematic review and meta-analysis. Fam Cancer 2009;8(2):109−17.

[51] McGuigan A, et al. Pancreatic cancer: a review of clinical diagnosis, epidemiology, treatment and outcomes. World J Gastroenterol 2018;24(43):4846−61.

[52] Huxley R, et al. Type-II diabetes and pancreatic cancer: a meta-analysis of 36 studies. Br J Cancer 2005;92(11):2076−83.

[53] Grote VA, et al. Diabetes mellitus, glycated haemoglobin and C-peptide levels in relation to pancreatic cancer risk: a study within the European Prospective Investigation into Cancer and Nutrition (EPIC) cohort. Diabetologia 2011;54(12):3037−46.

[54] Lynch SM, et al. Cigarette smoking and pancreatic cancer: a pooled analysis from the pancreatic cancer cohort consortium. Am J Epidemiol 2009;170(4):403−13.

[55] Cummings KM, Dresler CM, Field JK, Fox J, Gritz ER, Hanna NH, et al. E-cigarettes and cancer patients. J Thorac Oncol 2014;9(4):438−41.

[56] Genkinger JM, et al. Alcohol intake and pancreatic cancer risk: a pooled analysis of fourteen cohort studies. Cancer Epidemiol Biomarkers Prev 2009;18(3):765−76.

[57] Liu M, et al. Highly sensitive protein detection using enzyme-labeled gold nanoparticle probes. Analyst 2010;135(2):327−31.

[58] Wu L, Qu X. Cancer biomarker detection: recent achievements and challenges. Chem Soc Rev 2015;44(10):2963−97.

[59] Song Y, Wei W, Qu X. Colorimetric biosensing using smart materials. Adv Mater 2011;23(37):4215−36.

[60] Hu X, et al. Tailor-made nanomaterials for diagnosis and therapy of pancreatic ductal adenocarcinoma. Adv Sci (Weinh) 2021;8(7):2002545.

[61] Jayanthi V, Das AB, Saxena U. Recent advances in biosensor development for the detection of cancer biomarkers. Biosens Bioelectron 2017;91:15−23.

[62] Joshi GK, et al. Highly specific plasmonic biosensors for ultrasensitive microRNA detection in plasma from pancreatic cancer patients. Nano Lett 2014;14(12):6955−63.

[63] Joshi Gayatri K, Samantha DM, Thakshila L, Katie L, Sonali M, Rajesh S, et al. Label-free nano-plasmonic-based short noncoding RNA sensing at attomolar concentrations allows for quantitative and highly specific assay of microRNA-10b in biological fluids and circulating exosomes. ACS Nano 2015;9(11):11075−89.

[64] Santra S, Malhotra A. Fluorescent nanoparticle probes for imaging of cancer. Wiley Interdiscip Rev Nanomed Nanobiotechnol 2011;3(5):501−10.

[65] Lee J, et al. Optical imaging and gene therapy with neuroblastoma-targeting polymeric nanoparticles for potential theranostic applications. Small 2016;12(9):1201−11.

[66] Hahn MA, et al. Nanoparticles as contrast agents for in-vivo bioimaging: current status and future perspectives. Anal Bioanal Chem 2011;399(1):3−27.

[67] Yoon SM, et al. Application of near-infrared fluorescence imaging using a polymeric nanoparticle-based probe for the diagnosis and therapeutic monitoring of colon cancer. Dig Dis Sci 2011;56(10):3005−13.

[68] Peng H, et al. Polymeric multifunctional nanomaterials for theranostics. J Mater Chem B 2015;3 (34):6856−70.

[69] Larush L, Magdassi S. Formation of near-infrared fluorescent nanoparticles for medical imaging. Nanomedicine (Lond) 2011;6(2):233−40.

[70] Yang Z, et al. Pharmacokinetics and biodistribution of near-infrared fluorescence polymeric nanoparticles. Nanotechnology 2009;20(16):165101.

[71] Zhang R, et al. Peptide-conjugated polymeric micellar nanoparticles for Dual SPECT and optical imaging of EphB4 receptors in prostate cancer xenografts. Biomaterials 2011;32(25):5872−9.

[72] Gupta A, et al. Multifunctional nanoplatforms for fluorescence imaging and photodynamic therapy developed by post-loading photosensitizer and fluorophore to polyacrylamide nanoparticles. Nanomedicine 2012;8(6):941−50.

[73] Srikar R, Upendran A, Kannan R. Polymeric nanoparticles for molecular imaging. Wiley Interdiscip Rev Nanomed Nanobiotechnol 2014;6(3):245−67.

[74] Kim TH, et al. Evaluation of temperature-sensitive, indocyanine green-encapsulating micelles for noninvasive near-infrared tumor imaging. Pharm Res 2010;27(9):1900−13.

[75] Cho H, et al. In vivo cancer imaging by poly(ethylene glycol)-b-poly(varepsilon-caprolactone) micelles containing a near-infrared probe. Nanomedicine 2012;8(2):228−36.

[76] Tummala P, Junaidi O, Agarwal B. Imaging of pancreatic cancer: an overview. J Gastrointest Oncol 2011;2(3):168−74.

[77] Lee N, Hyeon T. Designed synthesis of uniformly sized iron oxide nanoparticles for efficient magnetic resonance imaging contrast agents. Chem Soc Rev 2012;41(7):2575−89.

[78] Wang L, et al. ENO1-targeted superparamagnetic iron oxide nanoparticles for detecting pancreatic cancer by magnetic resonance imaging. J Cell Mol Med 2020;24(10):5751−7.

[79] He Q, et al. Development of individualized anti-metastasis strategies by engineering nanomedicines. Chem Soc Rev 2015;44(17):6258−86.

[80] Singhi AD, et al. Early detection of pancreatic cancer: opportunities and challenges. Gastroenterology 2019;156(7):2024−40.

[81] Liu Y, Ai K, Lu L. Nanoparticulate X-ray computed tomography contrast agents: from design validation to in vivo applications. Acc Chem Res 2012;45(10):1817−27.

[82] Uesaka M, et al. Development and application of compact and on-chip electron linear accelerators for dynamic tracking cancer therapy and DNA damage/repair analysis. IOP Conf Ser Mater Sci Eng 2015;79:012015.

[83] Paefgen V, Doleschel D, Kiessling F. Evolution of contrast agents for ultrasound imaging and ultrasound-mediated drug delivery. Front Pharmacol 2015;6:197.

[84] Fu Q, et al. Photoacoustic imaging: contrast agents and their biomedical applications. Adv Mater 2019;31(6):e1805875.

[85] Homan KA, Souza M, Truby R, Luke GP, Green C, Vreeland E, et al. Silver nanoplate contrast agents for in vivo molecular photoacoustic imaging. ACS Nano 2012;6(1):641−50.

[86] Malhotra R, Patel V, Vaqué JP, Gutkind JS, Rusling JF. Ultrasensitive electrochemical immunosensor for oral cancer biomarker IL-6 using carbon nanotube forest electrodes and multilabel amplification. Anal Chem 2010;82(8):3118−23.

[87] Palecek E, et al. Electrochemistry of nonconjugated proteins and glycoproteins. Sens biomedicine Glycom Chem Rev 2015;115(5):2045−108.

[88] Feng LN, et al. Ultrasensitive multianalyte electrochemical immunoassay based on metal ion functionalized titanium phosphate nanospheres. Anal Chem 2012;84(18):7810−15.

[89] Rong Q, Feng F, Ma Z. Metal ions doped chitosan-poly(acrylic acid) nanospheres: synthesis and their application in simultaneously electrochemical detection of four markers of pancreatic cancer. Biosens Bioelectron 2016;75:148−54.

[90] Demir IE, et al. R0 versus R1 resection matters after pancreaticoduodenectomy, and less after distal or total pancreatectomy for pancreatic cancer. Ann Surg 2018;268(6):1058−68.

[91] Kim KS, et al. Impact of resection margin distance on survival of pancreatic cancer: a systematic review and meta-analysis. Cancer Res Treat 2017;49(3):824−33.

[92] Blamey SL, Fearon KC, Gilmour WH, Osborne DH, Carter DC. Prediction of risk in biliary surgery. Br J Surg 1983;70(9):535−8.

[93] Wang Q, Gurusamy KS, Lin H, Xie X, Wang C. Preoperative biliary drainage for obstructive jaundice. Cochrane Database Syst Rev 2008;16;(3):CD005444.

[94] Fang Y, et al. Pre-operative biliary drainage for obstructive jaundice. Cochrane Database Syst Rev 2012;9(9):CD005444.

[95] Hua J, et al. Duct-to-mucosa versus invagination pancreaticojejunostomy following pancreaticoduodenectomy: a systematic review and meta-analysis. J Gastrointest Surg 2015;19(10):1900−9.

[96] Venkat R, et al. Laparoscopic distal pancreatectomy is associated with significantly less overall morbidity compared to the open technique: a systematic review and meta-analysis. Ann Surg 2012;255(6):1048−59.

[97] Zhang J, et al. Robotic versus open pancreatectomy: a systematic review and meta-analysis. Ann Surg Oncol 2013;20(6):1774−80.

[98] Mollberg N, et al. Arterial resection during pancreatectomy for pancreatic cancer: a systematic review and meta-analysis. Ann Surg 2011;254(6):882−93.

[99] Yu XZ, et al. Benefit from synchronous portal-superior mesenteric vein resection during pancreaticoduodenectomy for cancer: a meta-analysis. Eur J Surg Oncol 2014;40(4):371−8.

[100] Oettle H, et al. Adjuvant chemotherapy with gemcitabine and long-term outcomes among patients with resected pancreatic cancer: the CONKO-001 randomized trial. JAMA 2013;310(14):1473−81.

[101] Chen X, et al. Co-delivery of autophagy inhibitor and gemcitabine using a pH-activatable core-shell nanobomb inhibits pancreatic cancer progression and metastasis. Theranostics 2021;11(18):8692−705.

[102] Ji T, et al. Peptide assembly integration of fibroblast-targeting and cell-penetration features for enhanced antitumor drug delivery. Adv Mater 2015;27(11):1865−73.

[103] Ji T, Kohane DS. Nanoscale systems for local drug delivery. Nano Today 2019;28:100765.

[104] Manzanares D, Cena V. Endocytosis: the nanoparticle and submicron nanocompounds gateway into the cell. Pharmaceutics 2020;12(4):376.

[105] Li Y, et al. Photodynamic therapy-triggered on-demand drug release from ROS-responsive core-cross-linked micelles toward synergistic anti-cancer treatment. Nano Res 2019;12(5):999−1008.

[106] Daman Z, et al. Polymeric micelles of PEG-PLA copolymer as a carrier for salinomycin against gemcitabine-resistant pancreatic cancer. Pharm Res 2015;32(11):3756−67.

[107] Li HJ, et al. Intratumor performance and therapeutic efficacy of PAMAM dendrimers carried by clustered nanoparticles. Nano Lett 2019;19(12):8947−55.

[108] Moquin A, et al. Encapsulation and delivery of neutrophic proteins and hydrophobic agents using PMOXA-PDMS-PMOXA triblock polymersomes. ACS Omega 2018;3(10):13882−93.

[109] Min SY, et al. Facile one-pot formulation of TRAIL-embedded paclitaxel-bound albumin nanoparticles for the treatment of pancreatic cancer. Int J Pharm 2015;494(1):506−15.

[110] Von Hoff DD, et al. Gemcitabine plus nab-paclitaxel is an active regimen in patients with advanced pancreatic cancer: a phase I/II trial. J Clin Oncol 2011;29(34):4548−54.

[111] Feig C, et al. The pancreas cancer microenvironment. Clin Cancer Res 2012;18(16):4266−76.

[112] Alvarez R, et al. Stromal disrupting effects of nab-paclitaxel in pancreatic cancer. Br J Cancer 2013;109(4):926−33.

[113] Li H, Fan X, Houghton J. Tumor microenvironment: the role of the tumor stroma in cancer. J Cell Biochem 2007;101(4):805−15.

[114] Lansakara PD, Rodriguez BL, Cui Z. Synthesis and in vitro evaluation of novel lipophilic monophosphorylated gemcitabine derivatives and their nanoparticles. Int J Pharm 2012;429(1−2):123−34.

[115] Thomas D, Radhakrishnan P. Tumor-stromal crosstalk in pancreatic cancer and tissue fibrosis. Mol Cancer 2019;18(1):14.

[116] Li D, et al. Urokinase plasminogen activator receptor (uPAR) targeted nuclear imaging and radionuclide therapy. Theranostics 2013;3(7):507−15.

[117] Cai H, et al. Combining gemcitabine-loaded macrophage-like nanoparticles and erlotinib for pancreatic cancer therapy. Mol Pharm 2021;18(7):2495−506.

[118] Pu N, Lou W, Yu J. PD-1 immunotherapy in pancreatic cancer: current status. J Pancreatology 2019;2(1):6—10.

[119] Beatty GL, et al. Activity of mesothelin-specific chimeric antigen receptor T cells against pancreatic carcinoma metastases in a phase 1 trial. Gastroenterology 2018;155(1):29—32.

[120] Bu LL, et al. Gelatinase-sensitive nanoparticles loaded with photosensitizer and STAT3 inhibitor for cancer photothermal therapy and immunotherapy. J Nanobiotechnol. 2021;19(1):379.

[121] Shen L, et al. Local blockade of interleukin 10 and C-X-C motif chemokine ligand 12 with nano-delivery promotes antitumor response in murine cancers. ACS Nano 2018;12(10):9830—41.

[122] Lu J, et al. Nano-enabled pancreas cancer immunotherapy using immunogenic cell death and reversing immunosuppression. Nat Commun 2017;8(1):1811.

[123] Su MJ, Aldawsari H, Amiji M. Pancreatic cancer cell exosome-mediated macrophage reprogramming and the role of microRNAs 155 and 125b2 transfection using nanoparticle delivery systems. Sci Rep 2016;6:30110.

[124] Li M, et al. Remodeling tumor immune microenvironment via targeted blockade of PI3K-gamma and CSF-1/CSF-1R pathways in tumor associated macrophages for pancreatic cancer therapy. J Control Release 2020;321:23—35.

[125] Yamamoto K, et al. Autophagy promotes immune evasion of pancreatic cancer by degrading MHC-I. Nature 2020;581(7806):100—5.

[126] Chang C, Li X, Cao D. Combination of gemcitabine, nab-paclitaxel, and S-1(GAS) as the first-line treatment for patients with locally advanced or advanced pancreatic ductal adenocarcinoma: study protocol for an open-label, single-arm phase I study. BMC Cancer 2021;21(1):545.

[127] Terrill JR, et al. Oxidative stress and pathology in muscular dystrophies: focus on protein thiol oxidation and dysferlinopathies. FEBS J 2013;280(17):4149—64.

[128] Tsou YA, et al. The effect of metformin use on hypopharyngeal squamous cell carcinoma in diabetes mellitus patients. BMC Cancer 2019;19(1):862.

[129] Konduri S, et al. Tolfenamic acid enhances pancreatic cancer cell and tumor response to radiation therapy by inhibiting survivin protein expression. Mol Cancer Ther 2009;8(3):533—42.

[130] Zhao J, et al. Cyclopamine-loaded core-cross-linked polymeric micelles enhance radiation response in pancreatic cancer and pancreatic stellate cells. Mol Pharm 2015;12(6):2093—100.

[131] Yoshida A, et al. Gold nanoparticle-incorporated molecularly imprinted microgels as radiation sensitizers in pancreatic cancer. ACS Appl Bio Mater 2019;2(3):1177—83.

[132] Wason MS, et al. Cerium oxide nanoparticles sensitize pancreatic cancer to radiation therapy through oxidative activation of the JNK apoptotic pathway. Cancers (Basel) 2018;10(9):303.

[133] Anajafi T, et al. Acridine orange conjugated polymersomes for simultaneous nuclear delivery of gemcitabine and doxorubicin to pancreatic cancer cells. Bioconjug Chem 2016;27(3):762—71.

[134] Laurent D, Bernhard S. Antibody — drug conjugates: linking cytotoxic payloads to monoclonal antibodies. Chemistry 2010;21(1):5—13.

[135] Wu AM, Senter PD. Arming antibodies: prospects and challenges for immunoconjugates. Nat Biotechnol 2005;23(9):1137—46.

[136] Cabral H, Kataoka K. Progress of drug-loaded polymeric micelles into clinical studies. J Control Release 2014;190:465—76.

[137] Ahn J, et al. Antibody fragment-conjugated polymeric micelles incorporating platinum drugs for targeted therapy of pancreatic cancer. Biomaterials 2015;39:23—30.

[138] Yang C, et al. Biodegradable polymer-coated multifunctional graphene quantum dots for light-triggered synergetic therapy of pancreatic cancer. ACS Appl Mater Interfaces 2019;11(3):2768—81.

[139] Du X, et al. Developing functionalized dendrimer-like silica nanoparticles with hierarchical pores as advanced delivery nanocarriers. Adv Mater 2013;25(41):5981—5.

[140] Jones CH, et al. Synthesis of cationic polylactides with tunable charge densities as nanocarriers for effective gene delivery. Mol Pharm 2013;10(3):1138—45.

[141] Pozzi D, et al. Effect of polyethyleneglycol (PEG) chain length on the bio-nano-interactions between PEGylated lipid nanoparticles and biological fluids: from nanostructure to uptake in cancer cells. Nanoscale 2014;6(5):2782—92.

[142] Yang C, et al. Biodegradable nanocarriers for small interfering ribonucleic acid (siRNA) co-delivery strategy increase the chemosensitivity of pancreatic cancer cells to gemcitabine. Nano Res 2017;10(9):3049−67.

[143] Lin G, et al. Interleukin-8 gene silencing on pancreatic cancer cells using biodegradable polymer nanoplexes. Biomater Sci 2014;2(7):1007−15.

[144] Amjad MW, et al. Recent advances in the design, development, and targeting mechanisms of polymeric micelles for delivery of siRNA in cancer therapy. Prog Polym Sci 2017;64:154−81.

[145] Benov L. Photodynamic therapy: current status and future directions. Med Princ Pract 2015;24 (Suppl 1):14−28.

[146] Clement S, et al. Radiodynamic therapy using TAT peptide-targeted verteporfin-encapsulated PLGA nanoparticles. Int J Mol Sci 2021;22(12):6425.

[147] Makadia HK, Siegel SJ. Poly lactic-co-glycolic acid (PLGA) as biodegradable controlled drug delivery carrier. Polymers (Basel) 2011;3(3):1377−97.

CHAPTER 9

Metallic nanoparticles-based drug delivery for pancreatic cancer

Sara Natalia Moya Betancourt[1], Jorge Gustavo Uranga[1], Viviana Beatriz Daboin[1], Paula Gabriela Bercoff[2] and Julieta Soledad Riva[1]

[1]Physicochemical Research Institute of Córdoba (INFIQC), CONICET. Faculty of Chemical Sciences, National University of Córdoba, Ciudad Universitaria, Córdoba, Argentina

[2]Institute of Physics Enrique Gaviola (IFEG), CONICET. Faculty of Mathematics, Astronomy, Physics and Computing (FAMAF), National University of Córdoba, Ciudad Universitaria, Córdoba, Argentina

9.1 Introduction

Pancreatic cancer is a highly deadly form of cancer with a poor prognosis due to the incidence almost equal to the mortality rate, with 5-year survival less than 9% for patients, depending on the diagnosis period of the disease 1,2 and remains one of the most fatal malignant neoplasms worldwide today [3]. Pancreatic ductal adenocarcinoma (PDAC) is one of the most lethal solid tumors with a dense desmoplastic and specifically aligned stroma, which plays an integral role in the progression of the tumor-inhibiting drug penetrations to prevent treatment [4]. The number of pancreatic cancer cases worldwide in 2020 is 495,773, while the number of deaths is 466,003 [5]. Surgical removal of the tumor is very difficult due to the location and structure of the pancreas in the body, so only about 10% of patients are suitable for potentially curative surgery [6]. Also, pancreatic cancer has a high tendency to metastasize and gain resistance to chemotherapeutic drugs over time. Surgery, chemotherapy, and/or radiotherapy constitute the basic treatment options according to the stage of pancreatic cancer. Because of this, the effectiveness of chemotherapy and radiotherapy is important in the treatment of the disease [7]. The conventional chemotherapy drugs used in this type of cancer are gemcitabine (GEM), fluorouracil (5-FU), and platinum agents such as oxaliplatin, cisplatin, and carboplatin. Given the low solubility of most anticancer drugs in aqueous media, it is difficult to administer them through an optimal route. In order to achieve the ideal efficiency of chemotherapy or adjuvant therapies, effective delivery is a key issue in pancreatic cancer treatment [8].

Using a highly efficient, nontoxic, control-released delivery system to carry anticancer drugs to cancer cells through specific receptors expressed on cancer cell surfaces has been proved to be a novel and effective approach in pancreatic cancer therapy and diagnosis [8,9].

Recent Advances in Nanocarriers for Pancreatic Cancer Therapy
DOI: https://doi.org/10.1016/B978-0-443-19142-8.00015-2

Encapsulation of drugs within nanoparticles (NPs) provides advantages when using hydrophobic, water-insoluble anticancer drugs by incorporating them into the matrix of NPs. Metallic NPs have been used as carriers for drug delivery in pancreatic cancer treatment since they can effectively deliver drugs to the target organs. The advantages of the encapsulation of drug into a carrier include increased drug solubility, prolonged drug exposure time, selective drug delivery to the target, improved therapeutic outcome, decreased toxic effects, and low drug resistance. The advantages of using NPs in drug delivery systems are summarized in Fig. 9.1.

Drug carriers are expected to remain in the bloodstream for a long time, accumulate at pathological sites with affected vasculature such as tumors through the effect of enhanced permeability and retention (EPR), and facilitate targeted drug delivery. Among several approaches to target drug-loaded NPs to specific pathological sites are passive targeting, based on EPR-mediated accumulation at pathological sites, and active targeting, based on the binding of specific ligands to the NP's surface to recognize and bind pathological cells. In active drug targeting, moieties such as antibodies, antibody fragments, and peptides are coupled to the drug-loaded NPs to act as homing devices for strapping to receptor structures expressed at the target site. This approach provides the widest opportunities and alternatives. Drug targeting by an external magnetic field is also considered active targeting. The schematic representation of drug delivery systems is shown in Fig. 9.2 [9].

Although the use of NPs in drug delivery is a topic under continuous investigation, today there are still many challenges to overcome in order to use them in an efficient

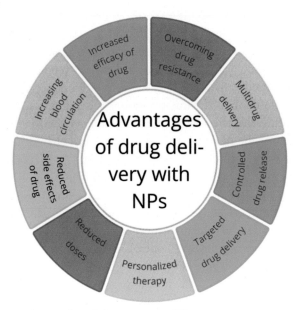

Figure 9.1 Advantages of nano-drug delivery systems [7].

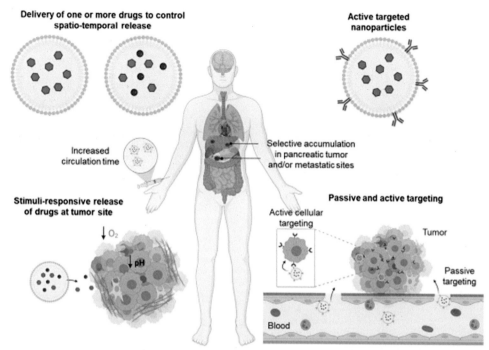

Figure 9.2 Schematic overview highlighting the use of NPs for drug delivery. NPs increase the blood circulation time and selective accumulation of drugs in tumors via passive or active targeting mechanisms. Multiple drugs can be loaded in a single NP to control their spatiotemporal release. In addition, drug release can be modulated by incorporating stimuli-responsive features via advanced nanoengineered approaches. *NPs,* nanoparticles. *Reprinted with permission from Tarannum M, Vivero-Escoto JL. Nanoparticle-based therapeutic strategies targeting major clinical challenges in pancreatic cancer treatment. Adv Drug Deliv Rev 2022;187:114357, https://doi.org/10.1016/j.addr.2022.114357. Copyright© Elsevier.*

therapy. It is necessary to find synthetic routes that can be used on a large scale so that pharmaceutical industries can carry out the production, as well as a complete characterization. In turn, these therapeutic nanoagents must be evaluated in terms of toxicity and relevant regulations, as summarized in Fig. 9.3.

This chapter summarizes the current progress on targeted drug delivery in pancreatic cancer using metallic NPs as vehicles and provides important information on new strategies for pancreatic cancer treatment.

9.2 Gold nanoparticles

Gold NPs (AuNPs) are maybe the most used NPs in biomedicine because they are easy to synthesize by simple, cheap, safe, and reliable methods. Also, they can be synthesized in a wide range of sizes, from 2–500 nm by changing the reaction parameters; they can also

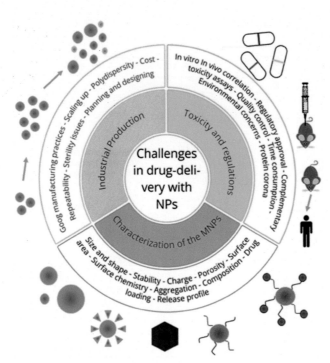

Figure 9.3 Challenges of using NPs in medical therapies. *NPs*, nanoparticles.

be easily synthesized with different shapes (spheres, rods, tubes, wires, ribbons, plate, cubic, hexagonal, and triangular) using templates and changing reaction conditions. Another characteristic is that they present a negative charge on the surface and they are highly reactive, which helps in modifying the AuNPs surface using several biomolecules. Because of the strong interaction between the gold surface and thiols or amine groups, which are present in several biomolecules such as DNA, protein, antibodies, and enzymes, the surface of AuNPs can be easily modified. In addition, it is well established that AuNPs are nontoxic and biocompatible. And finally, several research groups showed that AuNPs possess an enormous potential to improve the efficacy of cancer treatment [10]. The synthesis methods and surface modification of AuNPs are summarized in Fig. 9.4. AuNPs are being studied for theragnostic, photothermal therapies [11,12] and also for drug delivery. Conjugating AuNPs with chemotherapeutics represents a major point of interest in numerous studies (Table 9.1).

In 2008, Patra et al. conjugated gold NPs encapsulated with GEM and with cetuximab (C225) monoclonal antibody as a targeting agent for pancreatic cancer. The authors selected epidermal growth factor receptor the anti-EGFR antibody C225 as a targeting agent because pancreatic cancer cells overexpress EGFR. The targeting efficacy of antibody-targeted gold NPs (Au-C225) and control (Au-IgG) was evaluated

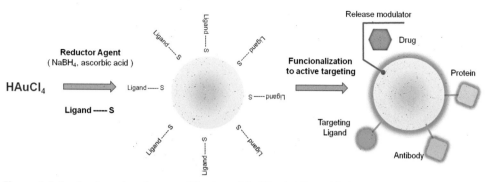

Figure 9.4 Synthesis and surface modification of AuNPs. *AuNPs*, gold nanoparticles.

against different pancreatic cancer cell lines (Mia PaCa-2, Panc-1, and AsPC-1). C225 targeted NPs showed better specificity against AsPC-1 and Panc-1 as compared to Mia Paca-2 because both PANC-1 and Mia Paca-2 are primary cell lines while AsPC-1 is a type of metastatic cell line. Therefore, efficacy of the targeted delivery system in a metastatic model (AsPC-1) was used for in vivo studies as it generates the most aggressive form of tumor. The results suggested that C225 could efficiently deliver GEM-loaded AuNPs-C225 to the tumor, as evidenced by the gold content detected among the various treatment groups through inductively coupled plasma mass spectroscopy. As can be seen in Fig. 9.5, a minimal uptake in vital organs such as the liver and kidney occurred, whereas a significant accumulation of gold was achieved in the tumor [10]. Fig. 9.5B and C represent the luciferase imaging of the control group (C225 + Gem) and experimental group (Au−C225−Gem), respectively, at the end of the study. Significant tumor growth inhibition was observed when mice were treated with Au−C225−Gem compared with its nontargeted counterpart.

Elechalawar et al. developed polyethylene glycol (PEG)-coated targeted AuNPs. They also used the anti-EGFR antibody cetuximab as a targeting agent and loaded GEM as the active ingredient. Because of the PEG coating, a stealth molecule was formed. Studies on pancreatic cell lines (PANC-1 and AsPC-1) and cancer-associated fibroblast (CAF-19) cells demonstrated that growth inhibition was better in cells treated with targeted nano-conjugates than in nontargeted systems containing IgG. Another interesting result was that the toxicity from targeted nano-conjugates in applied healthy human pancreatic cells was remarkably lower than in pancreatic cancer cells [13].

Also, hybrid nano-carriers were proven against pancreatic cancer. In 2020, Ding and coworkers fabricated gold NPs with metal−organic framework (MOF) encapsulating camptothecin (CPT) and found that the hybrid material Au/FeMOF@CPT NPs greatly improves the stability of the nanomedicine in a physiological environment. As a consequence of the high phosphate concentration inside the cancer cells, Au/FeMOF@CPT NPs effectively collapse after internalization, resulting in complete

Table 9.1 Therapies based on AuNPs as drug delivery systems in PDAC.

Design of AuNPs	Experimental model	Drug/organic dye/therapy	Treatment main outcome	References
Silica NPs with AuNPs	PANC-1	Phototherapy with methylene blue	Cellular uptake and photodynamic cytotoxicity are also dependent on the size of silica NPs and AuNPs attachment	[11]
Honeycomb-like gold NPs (HAuNPs)	SW1990 PANC-1 Mouse	Photothermal and brachytherapy	↑Tumor inhibition rate	[12]
Surface: cetuximab (C225) antibody	Mia PaCa-2, Panc-1 AsPC-1 Mouse	Gemcitabine	↓Tumor volume Uptake of AuNPs	[10]
Surface: PEG coated and C225 antibody	PANC-1 AsPC-1 CAF-19 Mouse	GEM	Growth inhibition in PDAC compared to white blood cells	[13]
AuNPs with FeMOF 20 and 60 nm AuNPs coated with N6L	Mouse PANC-1	Camptomicin GEM	↓Tumor volume ↑Cytotoxicity compared to unmodified NPs Uptake of AuNPs	[14] [15]
Surface: plectin-1-targeting peptide	PANC-1 AsPC-1	GEM	↑Cytotoxicity compared to unmodified NPs	[16]
2 nm AuNPs coated with dithiolated diethylene triamine-penta acetic acid (DTDTPA)	BxPC-3 U87-MG UM-Chor1 HeLa PC3 Dermal fibroblasts	Cy5	Uptake and excretion depending on the cell line—Better results with BxPC-3, PC3 and U87-MG cell lines	[17]

Nanoparticle	Drug	Cell lines	Results	Reference
20 nm AuNPs	GEM	PANC-1 AsPC-1 MIA PaCa-2 HPAFII	AuNPs sensitized pancreatic cancer cells to GEM	[18]
Polyethylene glycol–coated GNPs	DOXvarlitinib	MIA PaCa-2 S2-013 Healthy pancreatic cells: hTERT-HPNE	PEG-GNPs 0–1.0 nM are not toxic DOXPEG-GNPs are toxic for MIA PaCa-2, but not toxic for other cell lines Varlitinib PEG-GNPs are toxic for both MIA PaCa-2 and S2-013, but not toxic for hTERT-HPNE	[19]
AuNPs stabilized with reduced—glutathione	DOX GEM and cytarabine	Healthy pancreatic cells (hTERT-HPNE) PANC-1	AuNPs present a cytotoxic effect dependent on their concentration. Low impact on the healthy cells	[20]
GNPs linked using polydopamine to paclitaxel loaded PLGA microspheres	Paclitaxel	PANC-1	Enhanced ROS generation when using NIR Downregulation of CATALASE and SOD2	[21]

AuNPs, gold nanoparticles; *GEM*, gemcitabine; *PLGA*, poly(D,L-lactide-co-glycolide); *PEG*, polyethylene glycol; *ROS*, reactive oxygen species; *NIR*, near infrared radiation; *PDAC*, Pancreatic ductal adenocarcinoma; *NPs*, nanoparticles.

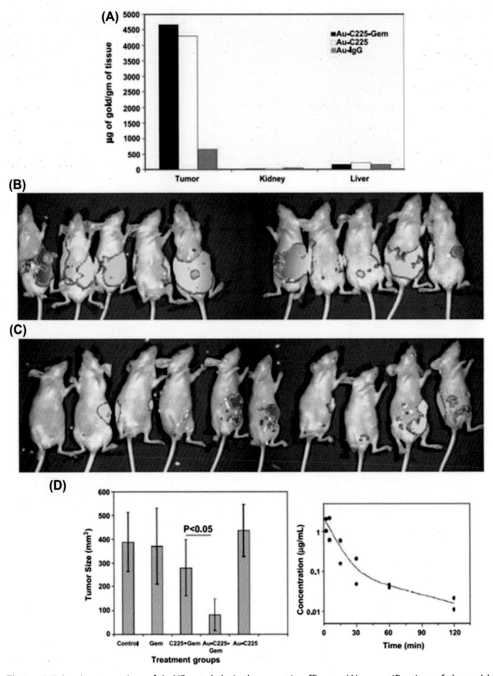

Figure 9.5 In vivo targeting of AuNPs and their therapeutic efficacy. (A) quantification of the gold amount taken up by the tumor, kidney, and liver under different treatment groups ($n = 3$). Comparative bioluminescence image from the mice treated with a mixture of C225 and GEM

(*Continued*)

drug release. Intracellular glucose can be oxidized by Au NPs to produce hydrogen dioxide, which is then used as chemical fuel for the Fenton reaction, thus achieving the synergistic anticancer efficacy. In vivo results demonstrate that the proposed therapy effectively suppresses tumor growth, and the systemic toxicity of this nanomedicine is greatly avoided [14].

In another study using AuNPs, Belbekhouche et al. used a bioactive molecule seudopeptide N6L to target nucleolin over-expressed in tumor cells [15]. Using the layer-by-layer method, the surface of the gold NPs is coated by electrolytic interactions. The coating was verified by measuring the zeta potential at each stage. In this method, direct coating was done and no purification was required. The antitumor activity of the AuNPs was evaluated using the PANC-1 cell line. AuNPs of sizes 20 and 60 nm were applied in three different forms as coated AuNPs, N6L-free AuNPs, and gold template-free NPs. N6L-coated AuNPs with 60 nm gold core decreased the viability in a dose-dependent manner. 20 nm AuNPs are approximately twice more cytotoxic because they can be coated with more N6L as a result of their smaller surface area. In addition, when the cellular deposition of 60 nm AuNPs was examined, it was observed that N6L-coated AuNPs increased the deposition proportionally over time, as compared to uncoated ones [15].

In another study, GEM conjugated with AuNPs bearing plectin-1-targeting peptide showed to be more cytotoxic in vitro in PDAC cell lines (AsPC-1 and PANC-1) and had more antitumor effect in vivo in PDAC xenograft than free GEM. The synthesis of AuNPs was via an in situ reduction of gold (III) chloride in a one-pot, green synthesis, and the modified peptide acted as a template generating highly monodispersed, spherical AuNPs with improved stability [16].

Coelho et al. evaluated the synergistic effect of conjugated PEG-coated AuNPs with DOX (DOX-PEG-GNPs) or with varlitinib (VAL-PEG-GNPs) as in vitro targeted delivery against the proliferation of cancer cells. The authors analyzed the healthy pancreatic cell line (hTERT-HPNE) and two PC cell lines (S2-013 and MIA PaCa-2). In the study, PEG-GNPs up to 1.0 nM were not toxic after an incubation period of 72 h to either cell line. Also, it was revealed that DOX-PEG-GNPs were toxic for MIA PaCa-2 cells but

(C225 + Gem); (B) or Au−C225−Gem (C) i.p. (*n* = 10). (D) Effect of different treatment groups on tumor growth inhibition in vivo (left). Tumor volume was measured after sacrificing the mice at the end of the experiment. Right, the plasma concentration of gold over time is determined by ICP analysis. Blood samples were collected from the mice under isoflurane anesthesia at different time points in heparinized tubes containing tetrahydrouridine to prevent GEM degradation by cytidine-deaminase after i.v. drug administration. *GEM*, gemcitabine. *Reprinted with permission from Patra CR, Bhattacharya R, Mukhopadhyay D, Mukherjee P. Fabrication of gold nanoparticles for targeted therapy in pancreatic cancer. Adv Drug Deliv Rev 2010; 62: 346–61, https://doi.org/10.1016/j.addr.2009.11.007. Copyright© Elsevier.*

not toxic for other cell lines. In addition, VAL-PEG-GNPs were not toxic for hTERT-HPNE, but they were toxic for both MIA PaCa-2 and S2-013 (derived from metastatic pancreatic tumors). Furthermore, the toxicity of drugs conjugated with PEG-GNPs in the normal pancreatic cell line was smaller compared to the toxicity induced by unconjugated free drugs [19]. In another study, Steckiewicz et al. evaluated the antitumor potential of AuNPs stabilized with reduced glutathione and conjugated with cytarabine, DOX, and GEM. The cytotoxic effect was corroborated by MTT assay in vitro in different cell lines. The results showed that AuNPs present cytotoxic effect that is dependent on their concentration, with a lower impact on the healthy cell lines compared to the cancer cell lines [20]. Banstola et al. developed paclitaxel-loaded poly(D,L-lactide-co-glycolide) (PLGA) microspheres linked to AuNPs using polydopamine, which they further assessed with and without NIR treatment in PANC-1 cells. It was revealed that using near infrared radiation (NIR) resulted in a larger production of reactive oxygen species (ROS) and also in the downregulation of the expression levels of two important antioxidant enzymes, CATALASE and SOD2. The effect of chemo–photothermal therapy was demonstrated to be synergistic in inducing the apoptosis of cancer cells [21].

AuNPs have been shown to be suitable for treating pancreatic cancer, inducing apoptosis of these cancer cells and even making PDAC cells more sensitive to the drugs used in chemotherapy. Currently, the literature has limited but promising data on this topic. More studies are required to find the most efficient design of NPs that can be used safely *in vivo* in patients carrying this disease with the intention of curing it. The studies presented in this chapter can be an ideal starting point for new studies to emerge that can provide more information on this field.

9.3 Silver nanoparticles

Silver nanoparticles (AgNPs) are commonly used as a bactericide, antifungal, and antimicrobial substance; bare AgNPs were also proposed as a potent anticancer agent since the administration of bare AgNPs into pancreatic tumors results in tumor reduction or retardation. In this sense, Zielinska and coworkers have observed a higher cytotoxic effect of 2.6 and 18 nm AgNPs on human pancreas ductal adenocarcinoma cells compared with nontumor cells of the same tissue [22]. The treatment with AgNPs resulted in important and concentration- and size-dependent inhibition of pancreatic cancer cell proliferation as well as induction of apoptosis, necroptosis/necrosis, and autophagic and mitotic catastrophe. Furthermore, they observed cellular uptake of AgNPs and the PANC-1 cells death was associated with morphological changes and biological events. These alterations were associated with a significant increase in the level of autophagy (LC3-II), necroptosis (RIP1, RIP3, and MLKL) and apoptosis (Bax) proteins as well as a decreased level of antiapoptotic marker (Bcl-2). Additionally, the authors determined an elevated level of the tumor suppressor p53 protein, characteristic for apoptosis, autophagy, and necroptosis [22].

In addition, He and coworkers used green-synthesized AgNPs to analyze their inhibitory effects in cancer cells, such as prostate cancer VCaP, pancreas cancer BxPC-3, and lung cancer H129 [23]. In this study, AgNPs were obtained by longan peel powder as a reducing and stabilizing agent. Firstly, ten grams of peels were immersed in 250 mL of distilled water for 1 hour at 50°C. Cooled filtrates were centrifuged at 3000 rpm for 5 minutes and then kept at 4°C. Finally, 50 mL of the extract solutions reacted drop-wise with 50 mL of AgNO$_3$ 2.0 mM solution by stirring at 80°C for 5 hours, obtaining AgNPs of diameters between 8 and 22 nm. The IC50 values of AgNPs for H1299, VCaP, and BxPC-3 cells were 5.33 ± 0.37, 87.33 ± 4.80, and 38.9 ± 2.10 µg/mL, respectively, indicating that the major effect was obtained with lung cancer cells. Guo et. al also employed a green-synthesis using *Berberis thunbergii* leaf, which is a plant bulked principally in China and Japan, and it has significant anticancer, anti-inflammatory, immunomodulatory, analgesic, antibacterial, antioxidant, antifungal, antiviral, and antiparasitic activities [24]. These authors determined the pancreatic cancer activities of AgNO$_3$, *B. thunbergii* leaf aqueous extract, and AgNPs against pancreatic (PANC-1, AsPC-1, and MIA PaCa-2) cancer cell lines. AgNPs had very low cell viability and antihuman pancreatic cancer effects dose-dependently against PANC-1, AsPC-1, and MIA PaCa-2. The IC50 values of the AgNPs were 259, 268, and 14 µg/mL against PANC-1, AsPC-1, and MIA PaCa-2 cell lines, respectively. These NPs had effective antipancreatic cancer activities dose-dependently without any cytotoxicity on the normal cell line (HUVEC); in addition, the Ag NPs revealed excellent antioxidant properties against common free radicals.

Regarding the use of AgNPs in drug transport systems against pancreatic cancer, Karuppaiah et al. in 2020 studied the delivery of anticancer drug GEM using AgNPs [25]. GEM is a pharmaceutical drug employed to cure different types of cancer, namely pancreas, lung, and breast cancers and can cause side effects such as low blood cell counts, fever and liver problems [26]. To synthesize the AgNPs, the authors were based on a procedure involving a silver nitrate solution being added drop-wise to a cold sodium borohydride solution, which is a very strong reducing agent, with magnetic stirring until a bright yellow color was obtained. Polyvinylpyrrolodone (PVP) was used as a capping agent in order to prevent aggregation, and the as-prepared AgNPs presented an average particle size of 9.16 nm. Finally, GEM was added to the AgNPs suspension stirring during 24 hours, forming GEM-AgNPs through electrostatic interactions since the drug is positively charged and the NPs were negatively charged because of the PVP capping. The adsorption efficiency was calculated as 75.6%. The authors evaluated the system GEM-AgNPs in MDA-MB-453 human triple-negative metastatic breast cancer cells, and the results demonstrated a synergistic cytotoxic effect of GEM conjugated with noncytotoxic dose of AgNP, obtaining a IC50 = 37.64 µM, indicating better cytotoxic activity when compared to individual treatments of GEM (IC50 = 56.54 μM) or AgNP (IC50 = 71.45 μg/mL) [25]. However, this promising system has not been evaluated in PDAC cells, yet. Another study considered the folic acid conjugated AgNPs anticancer drug DOX, electrostatically attached onto the NPs surface as a drug delivery system [27]. The study showed that drug release occurred in the cytoplasm after 4 hours, with significant cell death observed after 8 hours. It is anticipated that the data reported to date in these kinds of cancers will spark the interest of pancreatic cancer researchers and that further studies will be initiated in this area.

The analyzed articles showed that AgNPs can have a synergistic effect with anticancer drugs, which could allow the use of smaller amounts or AgNPs or smaller doses. Therefore, these nanoagents also provide less toxicity in healthy cells, potentially reducing the side effects caused by anticancer agents. However, silver is not extensively used in drug delivery nanosystems because there are some concerns regarding the toxicity and stability. It is expected, in the coming years, that this research area will be expanded, with a greater diversity of anticancer drugs to be used and greater knowledge of the in vivo behavior of the nanosystems, in terms of absorption, distribution, metabolism, excretion, and toxicity.

9.4 Iron oxide nanoparticles

Another interesting type of NPs are the magnetic nanoparticles (MNPs), which have been explored during the last decades in several scientific fields, based on their excellent physical and chemical properties, such as superparamagnetism, good colloidal stability, low toxicity, and good biocompatibility [28,29]. Among several types of iron oxides, magnetite Fe_3O_4 is the most used in biomedical applications and has been widely investigated for using in biomedical applications, including diagnosis via magnetic biosensing or magnetic resonance imaging (MRI), magnetic separation techniques, and as drug-delivery agent [29].

Among the different methods to obtain magnetite, thermal decomposition, coprecipitation, and electrochemical synthesis stand out. Thermal decomposition is an innovative synthesis route, which is based on the decomposition of metal precursors (e.g., acetylacetonates, carbonyls, or oleates) at high temperatures (150°C−300°C) in the presence of organic solvents characterized with high boiling point (250°C−300°C) such as octadecene or benzyl ether [30]. The presence of dispersants and hydrophobic ligands, including oleic acid, lauric acid, oleylamine, and hexadecyl amine, is required to control the size and shape of the desired NPs and prevents their aggregation. To carry out the synthesis, a mixture of solvent with organometallic precursors, surfactants, and stabilizing agents is heated at a constant rate to reach the nucleation or decomposition temperature of the precursor. Next, the solution is heated to the boiling point of the solvent, which leads to the formation of small nanocrystals, and the final step consists of phase growth in which the solution is refluxed for some time and cooled to room temperature. The schematic representation of this type of synthesis is presented in Fig. 9.6A. The main advantage of this method is that the obtained Fe_3O_4 NPs have a very narrow size distribution, as well as defined shapes, sizes, and crystallinity, and also well-defined magnetic properties. However, the synthesis procedure is more complex, time-consuming, and more difficult to scale than others. Also, the MNPs prepared in this way are dispersible only in nonpolar solvents, being immiscible in water, which can be a major limitation in biomedical applications.

On the other hand, the coprecipitation reaction is the most popular method to obtain magnetite Fe_3O_4 NPs. This route is widely used for the preparation of magnetite for biomedical applications due to the nontoxic reagents. In this method, solutions of iron (II) and (III) salts are basically mixed in an alkaline medium, at temperatures around 90°C. During this procedure, it is necessary to keep anaerobic reaction conditions to prevent the conversion of magnetite to iron (III) oxide. The scheme of magnetite NPs synthesis from alkaline solutions of iron (II) and (III) salts is presented in Fig. 9.6B.

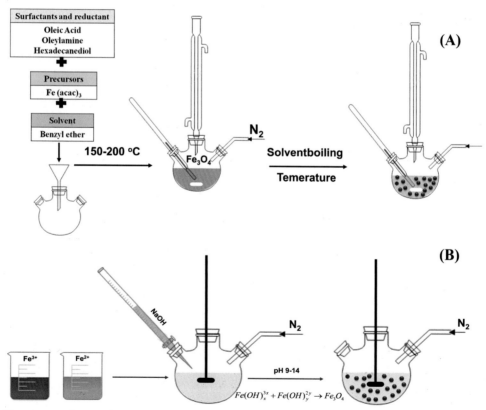

Figure 9.6 Scheme of Fe_3O_4 NPs synthesis route by (A) thermal decomposition and (B) coprecipitation. *NPs*, nanoparticles.

The typical method of electrochemical preparation of magnetic NPs is based on the electro-oxidation using iron as an electrode material: anode and cathode. In the electrolyte solution, a surfactant is added, and the reaction is carried out in a short period of time (around 30 minutes) and at relatively low temperature [30,31]. This methodology produces a clean product with a well-controlled NP size (in the order of 20−30 nm), a narrow size distribution plus excellent magnetic properties, which is convenient for biomedical uses. In addition, this method is suitable for scaling-up production by enlarging the size and number of electrodes. The current density, the applied cell potential, temperature, electrolyte composition, and the distance between the electrodes are the most typical parameters to establish [31].

The hydrothermal method is carried out at high temperature and high pressure, using autoclaves or special reactors. The general system is composed of Fe salts, organic additives, citric acid, glycolic acid, picolinic acid, nicotinic acid or pyridine, and a hydrothermal water−ethanol solution [30]. There are other less-used methods to obtain magnetite such as sonochemical and micro-emulsion syntheses. Comparison of each method's advantages and disadvantages are presented in Fig. 9.7.

Once the MNPs are obtained, the next stage is their surface modification in order to attach molecules of interest to these particles. In this sense, Moya et al. synthesized magnetite MNPs by coprecipitation and coated their surface with polysaccharides

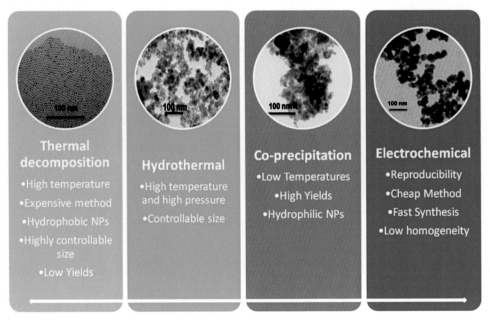

Figure 9.7 Comparison of the different chemical methods of magnetic NPs synthesis. *NPs,* nanoparticles.

commonly used in biomedicine, chitosan (CHI), and diethylaminoethyl dextran (DEX) [32,33]. Subsequently, they analyzed the interaction of different drugs with these MNPs using an electrochemical technique. These authors concluded that CHI presented greater efficiency in the anchoring of drugs to these MNPs because, although the structures of both polymers are similar, DEX displays a branched structure, which means that the amine groups are not as available as in the case of CHI to interact with pharmaceutical drugs.

On the other hand, Daboin et al. successfully designed CHI and PVP coated $Co_xFe_{3-x}O_4$ NPs [34]. The prepared coated NPs exhibited higher SAR values compared to the bare NPs due to the presence of CHI and PVP, demonstrating that the coating can drastically modify the physicochemical properties of the MNPs [34]. Theses authors also developed MNPs coated with silica oxide, observing that the structural and magnetic properties of the $CoFe_2O_4/SiO_2$ nanocomposites were significantly different depending of the type of dispersing agents used (PVP, cetyl trimethyl ammoniumbromide (CTAB) and PEG) before the surface modification with silica SiO_2 [34,35].

Regarding the use of MNPs as drug delivery carriers, Khan et al. used a superparamagnetic iron oxide formulation of Fe_3O_4 NPs loaded with curcumin (SP-CUR) and GEM. In that report, the authors showed that SP-CUR effectively delivered curcumin to pancreatic tumors enhancing both, GEM uptake and its efficacy at the same time. An orthotopic mouse model indicated an improved accumulation of SP-CUR in its pancreas to decrease tumor growth and metastasis. When the tumor tissues were analyzed, it was thought that the treatment inhibited the tumor stoma and caused changes in cell stiffness [36].

Also, the MNPs can be coated with specific biomolecules to produce an intelligent delivery. In this sense, Trabulo et al. reported the use of Fe_3O_4 NPs, which were functionalized with monoclonal antibodies CD47 or with GEM, and also with the mixture of MNP-Gem-anti-CD47 [29]. The functionalized Fe_3O_4 NPs with GEM act as a linker that allow performing the release of the GEM selectively, with a strong dependence on the reducing environment, allowing the release in an intracellular environment. Pancreatic cancer cells expressing the CD47 receptor were used, and Prussian blue staining was used to verify the presence of iron inside the cells. Nonfunctionalized Fe_3O_4 NPs were almost undetected by Prussian blue staining inside two pancreatic cancer cultures (Panc215 and Panc354), but the Fe_3O_4 NPs functionalized with anti-CD47 were detected in the cytoplasm of all the tested cell types, proving that Fe_3O_4 NPs functionalization greatly improves the cellular uptake by pancreatic cancer cells.

Arachchige et al. reported the use of superparamagnetic Fe_3O_4 NPs coated with DEX conjugated with DOX and a fluorescent tracker (isotiocianato de fluoresceína, FITC) for tracking the Fe_3O_4 NPs entry into the human pancreatic cancer MIA PaCa-2 cells [36]. They demonstrated a rapid entry (15 mintes compared to the nearly 6 h for free DOX), subcellular drug release, and accumulation in the nucleus. This rapid cellular uptake of Fe$_3$O$_4$ NPs is most likely via endocytosis, while the mechanism for the free DOX is through Fickian diffusion, which is much slower. Functionalized NPs enable tracking the rapid entry and release of DOX in human pancreatic cancer cells.

More recently, Albukhaty et al. also reported the use of superparamagnetic iron oxide NPs synthesized by coprecipitation, coated with DEX and conjugated with folic acid (FA-DEX-MNPs) for a better delivery and uptake of vinblastine (VBT) in PANC-1 pancreatic cancer cells [37]. The authors proved that the VBT formulated in the FA-DEX-MNPs are efficiently internalized inside the cancer cells, and this internalization can be due to folate-receptor-mediated endocytosis. In addition to being used by themselves for drug delivery, MNPs are also used in conjunction with another type of nano-carriers to provide the property of responding to an external magnetic field, therefore being able to carry out active targeting. In this sense, Andrada et al. produced magnetic vesicles using magnetite Fe$_3$O$_4$ NPs and 1-methylimidazolium bis-(2-ethylhexyl) phosphate (imim-DEHP) as surfactant, loaded with DOX. Some vesicles were then coated with chitosan to improve their stability and biocompatibility. After 24 hours, DOX release percentages ranging between 43%—53% were achieved. The prepared vesicles responded to an external magnetic field, making them good candidates to be used in active targeting [38].

9.5 Other metallic nanoparticles (Pd, Pt, CuO, ZnO, TiO$_2$)

There are few reports about the use of other metallic NPs; among them, there are some that refer to the use of palladium NPs (Pd-NPs) for the treatment of pancreatic cancer. In 2019, the use of Pd-NPs with Tris(dibenzylideneacetone)dipalladium (Tris DBA-Pd), a novel inhibitor of N-myristoyltransferase 1 (NMT-1), which had been proven in vivo activity against melanoma and also hyaluronic acid (Tris DBA-Pd HANP), was evaluated against in vivo xenografts of LM36R [39]. The authors also modified the Pd-NPs surface with the IGF1R antibody to give them specificity. However, Tris DBA-Pd HANP group without the antibody was the most responsive to treatment and showed the greatest effect. After 4 weeks, the tumor volume was around 10 times less than the control. Recently, PdNs were also proposed by Gulbagca and coworkers [40]. The authors used a green synthesis that enhanced the therapeutic effects of Pd-NPs. In that study, various biological activities such as antimicrobial, anticancer, antioxidant, and DNA cleavage activities of Urtica-mediated green-synthesized Pd-NPs were investigated. For the cytotoxic effects of Pd-NPs, the MDA-MB-231 breast cancer cell line, HT-29 colon cancer cell line, Mia Paca-2 human pancreatic cancer cell line, and healthy cell line L929-Murine fibroblast were used. IC$_{50}$ values of Pd-NPs against MDA-MB-231, HT-29, and MIA PaCa-2 cancer cell lines were calculated, resulting in 31.175, 20.383, and 29.335 µg/mL, respectively. No significant cytotoxic effect was observed in the healthy lines L929.

Platinum NPs, Pt-NPs, were tested by Wójcik et al. in 2021 in the BxPC-3 cell lines in which at the concentration of 5 mg/L exhibited a potential toxic effect, with a cytotoxicity of 6% [41]. In the AsPC-1 cell line, the highest toxic effect was observed after Pt administration at a concentration of 5 mg/L, which caused a cytotoxicity of 5%, a higher effect than with Au-NPs, which produced a cytotoxicity of 3%. In addition, the cytotoxic effects of Pt-NPs on human lung adenocarcinoma (A549), ovarian teratocarcinoma (PA-1), pancreatic cancer (Mia-Pa-Ca-2) cells, and normal peripheral blood mononucleocyte (PBMC) were examined [42]. The cytotoxic effect exerted on cancer cell lines was observed, whereas no cytotoxic effect was observed at highest dose on normal cells. Furthermore, it seems that the pancreatic cancer cells are less prone than lung cancer (A549) or ovarian adenocarcinoma (PA-1) to the negative effects that are caused by Pt-NPs. The results showed that Pt-NPs had potent anticancer activities against PA-1 cell line via induction of apoptosis and cell cycle arrest.

Another type of NPs, such as copper oxide NPs (CuO-NPs), were also tested against pancreatic cancer. In 2018, the cytotoxic effect of these NPs was evaluated in cancer stem cells, also called tumor initiating cells (TICs), a rare population of cells that initiate tumor growth and metastasis [43]. In pancreatic cancer, TICs significantly contribute to tumor regrowth after therapy, due to their intrinsic resistance. CuO-NPs were cytotoxic against TIC-enriched PANC1 human pancreatic cancer cell cultures. Specifically, treatment with CuO-NPs decreases cell viability and increases apoptosis in TIC-enriched PANC1 cultures to a greater extent than in standard PANC1 cultures. These effects are associated with increased ROS levels as well as reduced mitochondrial membrane potential. Furthermore, the authors demonstrated that CuO-NPs inhibit tumor growth in mice compared to untreated mice. Recently, the properties of a starch capped CuO-NPs against gastric cancer (AGS and KATO III), pancreatic cancer (AsPC-1 and MIAPaCa-2), and colon cancer (HCT 116 and HCT-8) were evaluated. The viability of malignant cancer cell lines reduced dose-dependently in the presence of CuO-NPs@Starch [44]. IC_{50} against AsPC-1 and MIA PaCa-2 was 329 and 250 µg/mL, respectively, being theses values somewhat larger than those obtained in gastric and colon cancer lines.

Besides, the effect of PEG-coated zinc oxide NPs (ZnO-NPs) was studied in pancreatic cancer cells [45]. In that report, the authors demonstrated the cytotoxic effect of ZnO-NPs in PANC1 cells. The PEG-coated ZnO-NPs were more cytotoxic than uncoated ZnO-NPs in PANC1 cancer cells. The authors demonstrated that apoptosis is the main mode of cytotoxic activity. It is worth noting that PEGylation of ZnO-NPs did not decrease the cell killing activity, whereas it further increased its anticancer effect in the pancreatic cancer cells. Overall, PEGylation of ZnO-NPs could be an effective strategy to improve the stability, while at the same time its anticancer activity could be enhanced for a better therapeutic response [45]. Also, Zao et al. prepared hexagonal ZnO-NPs with an average particle size of 33 nm, which exhibited concentration-dependent cytotoxicity against pancreatic cancer cell lines. The cell viability was studied by evaluating the activity of mitochondrial succinate dehydrogenase enzyme by MTT assay [46]. ZnO-NPs exhibited a significant growth inhibition toward Panc-1 and AsPC-1 cells in a concentration-dependent manner. Calculated IC_{50} values were $40 \pm 6 \, \mu M$ and $30 \pm 5 \, \mu M$ for Panc-1 and AsPC-1, respectively, indicating that ZnO-NPs are more effective toward AsPC-1 cells when compared to Panc-1 cells. Hence, 40 and 30 μM concentrations of ZnO-NPs were considered for their use in in vivo experiments on Panc-1 and AsPC-1cells, correspondingly. On the other hand, ZnO-NPs showed concentration-dependent inhibition toward the viability of the Hu02 cell line with IC_{50} values of $80 \pm 2 \, \mu M$. From these results, it is possible to conclude that the cytotoxicity of prepared ZnO-NPs on pancreatic cancer cells is considerably higher when compared to normal fibroblast cells [46].

Titanium dioxide (TiO_2) has been widely used in many nanotechnology areas including nanomedicine, where it has been proposed for photodynamic and sonodynamic cancer therapies. In 2018, the cellular toxicity of a DOX release system based on TiO_2 nanotubes (TiO_2-NTs) in pancreatic cancer cells (SW1990) was evaluated [47]. The DOX release from the nanotubes was found to be pH dependent. The toxicological effects were studied after coincubation of SW1990 with TiO_2-NTs-DOX, TiO_2-NTs, and DOX, respectively. The cellular effect of DOX released from the TiO_2-NTs. DOX was the same as when DOX was used alone, indicating that the synthesized TiO_2-NTs are well qualified as drug carriers in antitumor drug controlled-release system. Also in 2018, polyacrylic acid (PAA)-modified titanium oxide NPs (TiO_2-PAA NPs) were synthesized and their tissue distribution and acute toxicity were evaluated using healthy mice and mice bearing tumors derived from xenografted MIAPaCa-2 human pancreatic cancer cells. Healthy mice were injected with 25 mg/kg body weight TiO_2-PAA NPs via the tail vein, and tumor-bearing mice were injected either into the tumor locally or via the tail vein. After 1 hour, 12% of the TiO_2-PAANP dose had accumulated in the tumor, and 2.8% of the dose remained after 1 week. Such a high accumulation could be associated only with EPR effects of the tumor, as the injected NPs did not have specific molecules attached. The liver accumulated the largest proportion of the injected NPs, up to 42% in tumor-bearing mice, which indicates that TiO_2-PAA NPs should be modified to prevent accumulation in the liver.

9.6 Mesoporous silica nanoparticles

Although silicon is a metalloid and not a metal, silicon oxide has a very interesting pore structure, so mesoporous silica nanoparticles (MSNs) have been proven to be promising vehicles for drug delivery. MSNs have several attractive properties such as stability, large surface area and dual-function surfaces (exterior and interior), controllable particle size and shape, and ease of large-scale synthesis, as well as convenient pore sizes where chemotherapeutic drugs can be loaded.

Among the articles related to the use of MSNs for anticancer drug delivery, Jie Lu et al. have reported an animal tumor study using MSNs in pancreatic cancer xenografts [48]. They demonstrated that CPT-loaded MSNs conjugated with folic acid (targeting the folate receptor, F-MSNs) exhibit significant tumor-suppressive effects, as can be seen in Fig. 9.8. Different doses were also examined for dose-dependent inhibition of tumor growth, establishing 0.5 mg of CPT-loaded MSNs per mouse as a minimum dose sufficient for achieving complete tumor growth inhibition. MSNs were found to be excreted in the urine [48].

Slapak et al. functionalized MSNs with an avidin—biotin gatekeeper system containing a protease linker that is specifically cleaved by tumor cells. By a bioinformatic analysis, identified ADAM9 as a PDAC-enriched protease and PDAC cell-derived conditioned medium efficiently cleaved protease linkers containing ADAM9 substrates. They efficiently functionalized MSNs with a protease-linker and capped the NPs with avidin, and the cap was removed in the presence of PDAC cell-derived ADAM9, but not by leukocytes. Subsequently, they treated PDAC cells in vitro with paclitaxel-loaded MSNs, showing high cytotoxicity in cultured cells, while no cell death was

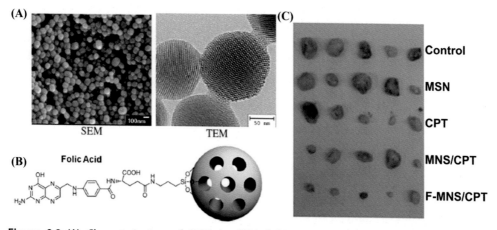

Figure 9.8 (A) Characterization of MSN by SEM (left) and TEM (right) images of F-MSN. (B) Schematic illustration of MSNs modified with folic acid targeting ligands on the surface. (C) Images of tumors collected at the end of experiment. *MSNs*, mesoporous silica nanoparticles. *Reprinted with permission from Lu J, Li Z, Zink JI, Tamanoi F. In vivo tumor suppression efficacy of mesoporous silica nanoparticles-based drug-delivery system: enhanced efficacy by folate modification, Nanomed Nanotechnol Biol Med 2012; 8: 212—20, https://doi.org/10.1016/j.nano.2011.06.002. Copyright© Elsevier.*

observed in cell lines derived from white blood cells, confirming the efficacy of the NPs-mediated drug delivery system. All in all, this research presented a novel ADAM9-responsive and protease-dependent drug delivery system for PDAC as a promising tool for reducing the cytotoxicity of systemic chemotherapy [49,50].

Kusum Saini et al. achieved superior delivery of the anticancer drug GEM with MSNs to cancer cell lines MIA Paca-2. They synthesized MSNs with particle diameters between 42−64 nm and internal pores of 2.5−5.2 nm by changing the synthesis conditions [51]. They observed that a greater drug release in extracellular cancer is reached at cellular pH (5.5), compared to the physiological pH (7.4) of healthy cells; with the optimal sample having a pore diameter of 5.2 nm, they achieved a GEM loading of 14.92% and a cumulative release of 58% at pH 5.5, compared to a low release of 22% at pH 7.4. Consequently, they obtained a 60% cell growth inhibition of the pancreatic cancer cell line (MIA Paca-2), via GEM -loaded MSNs, simultaneously demonstrating good target selectivity of MSNs as a drug carrier [51]. In a later work, in order to achieve superior drug delivery and to improve its controlled release, they functionalized the NPs surfaces with amine groups (NH_2-MSN) [52]. The authors first coated the MSNs with pH-sensitive polymers, such as either chitosan or PLGA, to prevent premature release of the drug at physiological pH 7.4 and also to achieve its controlled release at a lower pH 5.5 (extracellular cancer cell pH), and finally, they added transferrin (Tf)-conjugated, for better uptake of MSNs by the MIA PaCa-2cells, through ligand − receptor interactions. The highest drug loading of 27.2% was achieved for the functionalized MSNs with larger pore diameter of 5.2 nm. Besides, with PLGA as coating agent, a more controlled and desirable constant release rate of GEM with time was achieved at pH 5.5. Finally, for Tf-conjugated, polymer-coated MSNs, 70 − 75% of MIA PaCa-2 cells killing was achieved, as compared to 60% without Tf conjugation, due to the better uptake of NPs by cancer cells via ligand − receptor interactions [52].

The four-drug regimen, FOLFIRINOX (comprising irinotecan, 5–FU, oxaliplatin, and leucovorin) has a better survival outcome than the more frequently used GEM, but FOLFIRINOX is highly toxic especially because of the irinotecan, restricting its use in patients. For that, Liu et al. coated the MSNs with a lipid bilayer (LB) in order to decrease the toxicity of irinotecan [53]. LB-coated MSNs (LB-MSNs) permitted systemically reduced drug leak with an increased drug concentration at the tumor sites of an orthotopic Kras-derived PDAC model, compared to liposome NPs. The amount of irinotecan in the tumor increased 5 times compared to the free drug and approximately 2.5 times compared to the liposome NPs. In addition, LB-MSNs were observed to be more effective in the treatment of tumor metastases [53]. A summary of the different therapies to enhance the release of anticancer drugs using MSNs is shown in Table 9.2.

Table 9.2 Therapies based on MSNs (mesoporous silica nanoparticles) for improved drug delivery in PDAC (pancreatic ductal adenocarcinoma).

Suface MSN modification	Experimental model	Drug	Treatment main outcome	References
Folic acid	Mice	Camptothecin	↓Tumor volume compared to free drug and unmodified MSNs	[48]
ADAM9-linker biotin–avidin	PDAC and white blood cells	Paclitaxel	↑Cytotoxicity in PDAC compared to white blood cells	[49,50]
	MIA Paca-2 PDAC cells	Gemcitabine	↑Cytotoxicity compared to unmodified MSNs	[51]
Transferrin/chitosan or poly(D, L–lactide-co-glycolide)	MIA Paca-2 PDAC cells	GEM	↑Cytotoxicity compared to unmodified MSNs pH–sensitive cargo release	[52]
Lipid bilayer	PDAC cells	Irinotecan	↓Tumor weight and metastasis, improved survival compared to free drug ↓Liver, GIT, and bone marrow toxicity	[53]
Chitosan/urokinase plasminogen activator	PDAC cells	GEM	pH-specific cargo release	[54]

9.7 Conclusion

Pancreatic cancer is an aggressive disease often diagnosed at its later stages, so surgery is no longer an option. Therefore conventional chemotherapy is the main treatment alternative. However, this therapy often fails due to the inability of traditional drugs to reach the site of action, making targeted delivery an important option for future cancer treatment. The stability of metallic NPs in biological media can be carefully tailored by using surface functionalization with various organic molecules. Drug delivery systems using NPs, drugs, and specific receptors, expressed on cancer cell surfaces, provide selectivity by enhancing anticancer activity. For this reason, targeted drug delivery is a novel and potential approach in the diagnosis and therapy of pancreatic cancer. In particular, a growing number of in vitro and in vivo studies using metal-based NPs have emerged in the research community, showing promising results in the treatment of pancreatic cancers. These NPs often have intrinsic anticancer properties, in addition to being used as nano-platforms with other therapeutic options. Most of the metal-based formulations have not yet been translated to clinical settings, mainly due to toxicity concerns. For that, the use of specific metallic NPs in cancer research remains an open and promising research field, and more studies are needed to determine optimal production and characterization of NPs, as well as their effects on cancer cells. In conclusion, metal-based nanostructures hold great promise for developing more effective cancer therapies and deserve further special interdisciplinary research efforts to overcome current limitations.

Acknowledgments

Julieta S. Riva, Jorge G. Uranga, and Paula G. Bercoff are researchers of Consejo Nacional de Investigaciones Científicas y Tecnológicas (CONICET). Sara N. Moya Betancourt and Viviana Daboin acknowledge doctoral fellowships from CONICET.

Conflicts of interest

There are no conflicts to declare.

References

[1] Baker LA, Tiriac H, Clevers H, Tuveson DA. Modeling pancreatic cancer with organoids, Trends. Cancer 2016;2(4):176−90. Available from: https://doi.org/10.1016/j.trecan.2016.03.004.

[2] Cancer. Net. Pancreatic Cancer: Statistics. Available from: https://www.cancer.net/cancer-types/pancreatic-cancer/statistics; 2022 [accessed 11.07.22].

[3] Hand F, Conlon KC. Pancreatic cancer. Surgery 2019;37(6):319−26. Available from: https://doi.org/10.1016/j.mpsur.2019.03.005.

[4] Wei D, Cheng X, Du C, Wang Y, Sun J, Li C, et al. Stroma-targeted nanoparticles that remodel stromal alignment to enhance drug delivery and improve the antitumor efficacy of Nab-paclitaxel in pancreatic ductal adenocarcinoma models. Nano Today 2022;45:101533. Available from: https://doi.org/10.1016/j.nantod.2022.101533.

[5] GLOBOCAN. Available from: https://gco.iarc.fr/today/data/factsheets/cancers/13-Pancreas-fact-sheet.pdf; 2020 [accessed on 11.07.22].

[6] Yu X, Zhang Y, Chen C, Yao Q, Li M. Targeted drug delivery in pancreatic cancer. Biochim Biophys Acta 1805;2010:97−104. Available from: https://doi.org/10.1016/j.bbcan.2009.10.001.

[7] Demirtürk N, Bilensoy E. Nanocarriers targeting the diseases of the pancreas. s, Eur J Pharm Biopharm 2022;170:10−23. Available from: https://doi.org/10.1016/j.ejpb.2021.11.006.

[8] Yu X, Zhang Y, Chen C, Yao Q, Li M. Targeted drug delivery in pancreatic cancer. J Biomed Nanotech 2014;10:3462−82. Available from: https://doi.org/10.1016/j.bbcan.2009.10.001.

[9] Tarannum M, Vivero-Escoto JL. Nanoparticle-based therapeutic strategies targeting major clinical challenges in pancreatic cancer treatment. Adv Drug Deliv Rev 2022;187:114357. Available from: https://doi.org/10.1016/j.addr.2022.114357.

[10] Patra CR, Bhattacharya R, Mukhopadhyay D, Mukherjee P. Fabrication of gold nanoparticles for targeted therapy in pancreatic cancer. Adv Drug Deliv Rev 2010;62:346−61. Available from: https://doi.org/10.1016/j.addr.2009.11.007.

[11] Roy I. Gold nanoparticle-enhanced photodynamic therapyfrom photosensitiser-entrapped ormosil nanoparticles. J Nanosci Nanotechnol 2019;19:6942−8. Available from: https://doi.org/10.1166/jnn.2019.16719.

[12] Zhang F, Han X, Hu Y, Wang S, Liu S, Pan X, et al. Interventional photothermal therapy enhanced brachytherapy: a new strategyto fight deep pancreatic cancer. Adv Sci (Weinh) 2019;6:1801507. Available from: https://doi.org/10.1002/advs.201801507.

[13] Elechalawar CK, Hossen MN, Shankarappa P, Peer CJ, Figg WD, Robertson JD, et al. Targeting pancreatic cancer cells and stellate cells using designer nanotherapeutics in vitro. Int J Nanomed 2020;15:991−1003. Available from: https://doi.org/10.2147/IJN.S234112.

[14] Ding Y, Xu H, Xu C, Tong Z, Zhang S, Bai Y, et al. Fabricated from gold nanoparticles-decorated metal−organic framework for cascade chemo/chemodynamic cancer therapy. Adv Sci 7 2020;2001060. Available from: https://doi.org/10.1002/advs.202001060.

[15] Belbekhouche S, Cossutta M, Habert D, Hamadi S, Modjinou T, Cascone I, et al. N6L-functionalized nanoparticles for targeted and inhibited pancreatic cancer cells. Colloids Surf A 2020;607:125461. Available from: https://doi.org/10.1016/j.colsurfa.2020.125461.

[16] Pal K, Al-Suraih F, Gonzalez-Rodriguez R. Multifaceted peptide assisted one-pot synthesis of gold nanoparticles for plectin-1 targeted gemcitabine delivery in pancreatic cancer. Nanoscale 2017;9 (40):15622−34. Available from: https://doi.org/10.1039/C7NR03172F.

[17] Ivošev V, Jiménez Sánchez G, Stefancikova L, Haidar DA, González Vargas CR, Yang X, et al. Uptake and excretion dynamics of gold nanoparticles in cancer cells and fibroblasts. Nanotechnology 2020;31:135102. Available from: https://doi.org/10.1088/1361-6528/ab5d82.

[18] Huai Y, Zhang Y, Xiong X, Das S, Bhattacharya R, Mukherjee P. Gold nanoparticles sensitize pancreatic cancer cells to gemcitabine. Cell Stress 2019;3:267−79. Available from: https://doi.org/10.15698/cst2019.08.195.

[19] Coelho SC, Reis DP, Pereira MC, Coelho MAN. Doxorubicin and varlitinib delivery by functionalized gold nanoparticles against human pancreatic adenocarcinoma. Pharmaceutics 2019;11:551. Available from: https://doi.org/10.3390/pharmaceutics11110551.

[20] Steckiewicz KP, Barcinska E, Sobczak K, Tomczyk E, Wojcik M, Inkielewicz-Stepniak I. Assessment of anti-tumor potential and safety of application of glutathione stabilized gold nanoparticles conjugated with chemotherapeutics. Int J Med Sci 2020;17:824−33. Available from: https://doi.org/10.7150/ijms.40827.

[21] Banstola A, Pham TT, Jeong JH, Yook S. Polydopamine-tailored paclitaxel-loaded polymeric microspheres with adhered NIR-controllable gold nanoparticles for chemo-phototherapy of pancreatic cancer. Drug Deliv 2019;26:629−40. Available from: https://doi.org/10.1080/10717544.2019.1628118.

[22] Zielinska E, Zauszkiewicz-Pawlak A, Wojcik M, Inkielewicz-Stepniak I. Silver nanoparticles of different sizes induce a mixed type of programmed cell death in human pancreatic ductal adenocarcinoma. Oncotarget 2018;9:4675−97. Available from: https://doi.org/10.18632/oncotarget.22563.

[23] He Y, Du Z, Ma S, Liu Y, Li D, Huang H, et al. Effects of green-synthesized silver nanoparticles on lung cancer cells in vitro and grown as xenograft tumors in vivo. Int J Nanomed 2016;11:1879−87. Available from: https://doi.org/10.2147/IJN.S103695.

[24] Guo J, Li Y, Yu Z, Chen L, Chinnathambi A, Almoallim HS, et al. Novel green synthesis and characterization of a chemotherapeutic supplement by silver nanoparticles containing *Berberis thunbergii* leaf for the treatment of human pancreatic cancer. Biotechnol Appl Biochem 2022;69:887−97. Available from: https://doi.org/10.1002/bab.2160.

[25] Karuppaiaha A, Sirama K, Selvaraj D, Ramasamye M, Babuf D, Sankar V. Synergistic and enhanced anticancer effect of a facile surface modified noncytotoxic silver nanoparticle conjugated with gemcitabine in metastatic breast cancer cells. Mater Today Commun 2020;23:100884. Available from: https://doi.org/10.1016/j.mtcomm.2019.100884.

[26] Gomes HIO, Martins CSM, Prior JAV. Silver nanoparticles as carriers of anticancer drugs for efficient target treatment of cancer cells. Nanomaterials 2021;11:964. Available from: https://doi.org/10.3390/nano11040964.

[27] Foulkes R, Asgari MA, Curtis A, Hoskins C. Silver-nanoparticle-mediated therapies in the treatment of pancreatic cancer. ACS Appl Nano Mater 2019;2:1758−72. Available from: https://doi.org/10.1021/acsanm.9b00439.

[28] Khan S, Setua S, Kumari S, Dan N, Massey A, Hafeez BB, et al. Superparamagnetic iron oxide nanoparticles of curcumin enhance gemcitabine therapeutic response in pancreatic cancer. Biomaterials 2019;208:83−97. Available from: https://doi.org/10.1016/j.biomaterials.2019.04.005.

[29] Trabulo S, Aires A, Aicher A, Heeschen C, Cortajarena AL. Multifunctionalized iron oxide nanoparticles for selective targeting of pancreatic cancer cells. Biochim Biophys Acta - Gen Subj 2017;1861(6):1597−605. Available from: https://doi.org/10.1016/j.bbagen.2017.01.035.

[30] Mylkie K, Nowak P, Rybczynski P, Ziegler-Borowska M. Polymer-coated magnetite nanoparticles for protein immobilization. Materials 2021;14:248. Available from: https://doi.org/10.3390/ma14020248.

[31] Lozano I, Casillas N, Ponce de Leon C, Walsh FC, Herrasti P. New insights into the electrochemical formation of magnetite nanoparticles. J Electrochem Soc 2017;164(4):D184−91. Available from: https://doi.org/10.1149/2.1091704jes.

[32] Moya Betancourt SN, Cámara CI, Juarez AV, Pozo López G, Riva JS. Effect of magnetic nanoparticles coating on their electrochemical behaviour at a polarized liquid/liquid interface. J Electroanal Chem 2022;911:116253. Available from: https://doi.org/10.1016/j.jelechem.2022.116253.

[33] Moya Betancourt SN, Uranga JG, Cámara CI, Juarez AV, Pozo López G, Riva JS. Effect of bare and polymeric-modified magnetic nanoparticles on the drug ion transfer across liquid/liquid interfaces. J Electroanal Chem 2022;919:116502. Available from: https://doi.org/10.1016/j.jelechem.2022.116502.

[34] Suárez J, Daboin V, González G, Briceño S. Chitosan-polyvinylpyrrolidone $Co_xFe_{3-x}O_4$ ($0.25 \leq x \leq 1$) nanoparticles for hyperthermia applications. Int J Biol Macromol 2020;164:3403−10. Available from: https://doi.org/10.1016/j.ijbiomac.2020.08.043.

[35] Daboin V, Briceño S, Suárez J, Carrizales-Silva L, Alcalá O, Silva P, et al. Magnetic $SiO_2Mn_{x-1}Co_xFe_2O_4$ nanocomposites decorated with $Au@Fe_3O_4$ nanoparticles for hyperthermia. J Magn Magn Mater 2019;479:91−8. Available from: https://doi.org/10.1016/j.jmmm.2019.02.002.

[36] Arachchige MP, Laha SS, Naik AR, Lewis KT, Naik R, Jena B. Functionalized nanoparticles enable tracking the rapid entry and release of doxorubicin in human pancreatic cancer cells. Micron 2017;92:25−31. Available from: https://doi.org/10.1016/j.micron.2016.10.005.

[37] Albukhaty S, Al-Musawi S, Abdul Mahdi S, Sulaiman GM, Alwahibi MS, Dewir YH, et al. Investigation of dextran-coated superparamagnetic nanoparticles for targeted vinblastine controlled release, delivery, apoptosis induction, and gene expression in pancreatic cancer cells. Molecules 2020;25:4721. Available from: https://doi.org/10.3390/molecules25204721.

[38] Andrada HE, Venosta L, Jacobo SE, Silva OF, Falcone RD, Bercoff PG. Highly stable nanostructured magnetic vesicles as doxorubicin carriers for field-assisted therapies. ChemNanoMat 2022;8:e202100409. Available from: https://doi.org/10.1002/cnma.202100409 (1 of 12).

[39] Elsey J, Bubley JA, Zhu L, Rao S, Sasaki M, Pollack BP, et al. Palladium based nanoparticles for the treatment of advanced melanoma. Sci Rep 2019;9(3255):1−9. Available from: https://doi.org/10.1038/s41598-019-40258-6.

[40] Gulbagca F, Aygün A, Gülcan M, Ozdemir S, Gonca S, Sen F. Green synthesis of palladium nanoparticles: preparation, characterization, and investigation of antioxidant, antimicrobial, anticancer, and DNA cleavage activities. Appl Organomet Chem 2021;e6272:1−9. Available from: https://doi.org/10.1002/aoc.6272.

[41] Wójcik B, Sawosz E, Szczepaniak J, Strojny B, Sosnowska M, Daniluk K, et al. Effects of metallic and carbon-based nanomaterials on human pancreatic cancer cell lines AsPC-1 and BxPC-3. Int J Mol Sci 2021;22:12100. Available from: https://doi.org/10.3390/ijms222212100.

[42] Bendale Y, Bendale V, Paul S. Evaluation of cytotoxic activity of platinum nanoparticles against normal and cancer cells and its anticancer potential through induction of apoptosis. Integr Med Res 2017;6:141−8. Available from: https://doi.org/10.1016/j.imr.2017.01.006.

[43] Benguigui M, Weitz IS, Timaner M, Kan T, Shechter D, Perlman O, et al. Copper oxide nanoparticles inhibit pancreatic tumor growth primarily by targeting tumor initiating cells. Sci Rep 2019;9:12613. Available from: https://doi.org/10.1038/s41598-019-48959-8.

[44] Chen J, Karmakar B, Salem MA, Alzahrani AY, Bani-Fwaze MZ, Abdel-Daim MM, et al. CuO NPs@Starch as a novel chemotherapeutic drug for the treatment of several types of gastrointestinal system cancers including gastric, pancreatic, and colon cancers. Arab J Chem 2022;15:103681. Available from: https://doi.org/10.1016/j.arabjc.2021.103681.

[45] Du Y, Zhang J, Yan S, Tao Z, Wang C, Huang M, et al. PEGylated zinc oxide nanoparticles induceapoptosis in pancreatic cancer cells throughreactive oxygen species. IET Nanobiotechnol 2019;13:80−4. Available from: https://doi.org/10.1049/iet-nbt.2018.5327.

[46] Zhao C, Zhang Xg, Zheng Y. Biosynthesis of polyphenols functionalized ZnO nanoparticles: characterization and their effect on human pancreatic cancer cell line. J Photochem Photob B: Biol 2018;183:142−6. Available from: https://doi.org/10.1016/j.jphotobiol.2018.04.031.

[47] Wang Y, Yuan L, Yao C, Fang J, Wu M. Cytotoxicity evaluation of pH-controlled antitumor drug release system of titanium dioxide nanotubes. J Nanosci Nanotechnol 2015;15:4143−8. Available from: https://doi.org/10.1166/jnn.2015.9792.

[48] Lu J, Li Z, Zink JI, Tamanoi F. In vivo tumor suppression efficacy of mesoporous silica nanoparticles-based drug-delivery system: enhanced efficacy by folate modification. Nanomed Nanotechnol Biol Med 2012;8:212−20. Available from: https://doi.org/10.1016/j.nano.2011.06.002.

[49] Slapak EJ, Kong L, Mandili M, Nieuwland R, Kros A, Bijlsma MF, et al. ADAM9-responsive mesoporous silica nanoparticles for targeted drug delivery in pancreatic cancer. Cancers 2021;13:3321. Available from: https://doi.org/10.3390/cancers13133321.

[50] Slapak EJ, Mandili M, Bijlsma MF, Spek CA. Mesoporous, silica nanoparticle-based drug, delivery systems for the treatment of, pancreatic cancer: a systematic, literature overview. Pharmaceutics 2022;14:390. Available from: https://doi.org/10.3390/pharmaceutics14020390.

[51] Saini K, Prabhuraj RS, Bandyopadhyaya R. Development of mesoporous silica nanoparticles of tunable pore diameter for superior gemcitabine drug delivery in pancreatic cancer cells. J Nanosci Nanotechnol 2020;20:5. Available from: https://doi.org/10.1166/jnn.2020.17381.

[52] Saini K, Bandyopadhyaya R. Transferrin-conjugated polymer-coated mesoporous silica nanoparticles loaded with gemcitabine for killing pancreatic cancer cells. ACS Appl Nano Mater 2020;3:229−40. Available from: https://doi.org/10.1021/acsanm.9b01921.

[53] Liu X, Situ A, Kang Y, Villabroza KR, Liao Y, Chang CH, et al. Irinotecan delivery by lipid-coated mesoporous silica nanoparticles shows improved efficacy and safety over liposomes for pancreatic cancer. ACS Nano 2016;10(2):2702−15. Available from: https://doi.org/10.1021/acsnano.5b0778110.1021/acsnano.5b07781.s001.

[54] Gurka MK, Pender D, Chuong P, Fouts BL, Sobelov A, McNally MW, et al. Identification of pancreatic tumors in vivo with ligand-targeted, pH responsive mesoporous silica nanoparticles by multispectral optoacoustic tomography. J Control Release 2016;231:60−7. Available from: https://doi.org/10.1016/j.jconrel.2015.12.055.

CHAPTER 10

Empowering treatment strategies for pancreatic cancer by employing lipid nanoparticle-driven drug delivery

Sumit Sheoran[1,2,*], Swati Arora[1,2,*], Aayushi Velingkar[1], Smita C. Pawar[3] and Sugunakar Vuree[2,4]

[1]School of Biosciences and Bioengineering, Lovely Professional University, Jalandhar, Punjab, India
[2]Unite Lifescience, Hyderabad, Telangana, India
[3]Department of Genetics, Osmania University, Hyderabad, Telangana, India
[4]MNR Foundation for Research and Innovation (MNR-FRI), MNR Medical College and Hospital, Hyderabad, Telangana, India

10.1 Introduction

Solid lipid nanoparticles (LNPs) are being produced as spinel delivery systems for the administration of liquid soluble drugs and effective dynamic treatment adjustment [1]. According to a recent study, SLNs (solid lipid nanoparticles) constitute a flexible, diversified, and adaptable system for delivering drugs. This technology has the capability to improve medication strength as well as regulate drug release from the matrix over time. Furthermore, encapsulating pharmaceuticals in solid LNPs helps them resist enzymatic destruction before they reach their target sites [2]. An agreement has arisen among scientists that lipids are effective good adsorbents for drug administration due to their intrinsic potential to promote stomach solubilization and the immersion of poorly accessible therapeutic ingredients through the lymph system [3,4]. SLNs are one of the innovative prospective dispersion transport systems utilized in lieu of polymers as an alternative to oil-in-water (O/W) emulsifiers for enteral administration, and they are identifiable from O/W emulsions. A solid lipid nanoparticle can replace the fluid lipid in the O/W emulsion [5]. Solid LNPs are created using methodologies such as high-pressure homogenization and solvent evaporation [6,7]. Moreover, the characteristics of SLNs may be modified to increase their efficiency. This is especially beneficial for drugs that are insoluble in water. In order to understand solid LNPs and their prospective uses in the pharmaceutical sector, detailed literature research on the different varieties of SLNs and conventional matrices utilized as drug delivery techniques are required.

For many years, the pharmaceutical industry has used lipid components that really are room-temperature solids to make a range of formulations [8]. Further, Earlier research also

* First equal authorship.

Recent Advances in Nanocarriers for Pancreatic Cancer Therapy
DOI: https://doi.org/10.1016/B978-0-443-19142-8.00016-4

indicates that SLNs are nontoxic and biodegradable colloidal transporters [9]. It is vital to highlight that SLNs are nanoscale in size, and their strong capability at the intracellular membrane and in the intracellular compartment permits them to successfully infiltrate the cells [10]. Solid LNPs have gotten a lot of interest since they can carry medicines and genes efficiently and can also be utilized for specific therapies [11]. Because of their greater bioactivity, enhanced capacity for drug loading, and scalability, they may have a benefit over other nanoparticle. The lipids employed in the production of the matrix in solid LNPs are consistent with the body's natural defense and also have minimal side effects and acceptable ratings. According to Basha and colleagues, solid LNPs form vibrant, varied, and configurable pharmaceutical carrier systems with enhanced capacity for increasing drug stability and attempting to control drug release from the composite over period, and packaging drugs in solid LNPs aids in trying to resist proteolytic degradation first before drugs reach the desired sites [2]. Additionally, pharmaceutical companies may employ solid LNPs to develop medications for particular human organs depending on their biochemical makeup and kind of responses. Furthermore, the features of the SLNs may be altered to increase their efficiency. This is especially beneficial for medications that are poorly soluble in water. Fig. 10.1 depicts a diagrammatic depiction of SLNs and their targeted particularities from several perspectives.

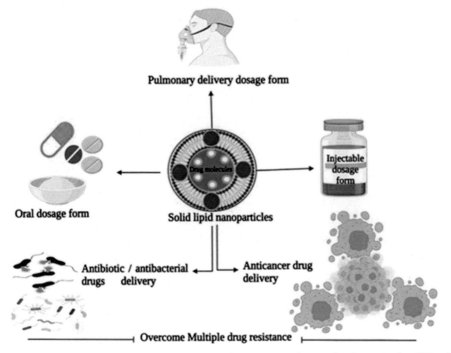

Figure 10.1 Solid LNPs and their targeted identifications are depicted schematically. *LNPs*, lipid nanoparticles.

The current research concentrates on the various kinds of SLN and conventional matrices used as drug delivery strategies in pancreatic cancer, as well as to understand SLNs and their potential applications.

10.2 Symptoms and risk factors of pancreatic cancer

As pancreatic cancer is challenging to detect, it is frequently discovered as an advanced disease. Jaundice and weight loss are symptoms of pancreatic cancer. Diabetes and exposure to certain toxins are a major risk factors. Treatment is based on the size and location of the tumor, in addition to whether or not it really has expanded to other areas of the system.

Pancreatic cancer develops when abnormalities (mutations) in pancreatic cells cause them to grow uncontrollably. A clump of tissue can form as a result. This tumor is often harmless (not cancerous). However, with pancreatic cancer, the mass is malignant (cancerous).

The majority of people do not notice early indications of pancreatic cancer (Fig. 10.2). However, as the condition advances, individuals can observe:

1. Inflammation in the upper abdomen may move to the posterior.
2. Discoloration of the skin and the whites of the eyes (jaundice).
3. Exhaustion.
4. Hunger loss.
5. Light-colored feces.
6. Pitch black poop
7. Malnutrition.
8. The presence of thrombosis in the system.
9. Dry, itching skin.
10. Diabetic, whether new or increasing.
11. Puking and discomfort.

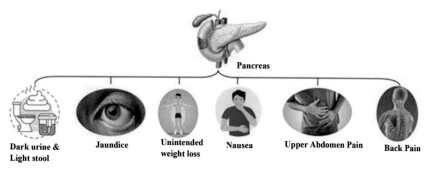

Figure 10.2 Symptoms of pancreatic cancer.

If you experience these signs and have suddenly established diabetes or pancreatitis—a painful condition caused by pancreatic irritation—your healthcare provider may consider pancreatic cancer.

The average lifetime chance of acquiring pancreatic cancer is roughly 1 in 64. A risk factor is anything that increases your chances of getting an illness. There are danger variables (shown in Fig. 10.3) that are a result of behavior and may be modified. Following are some major risk factors for pancreatic:

1. Smoking.
2. Obesity poses a risk factor as well. Having extra weight all around waistline is a danger concern even if you are not obese.
3. Diabetes, particularly type diabetes patients, that is connected to overweight. The emergence of diabetes at an advanced age and in somebody of normal body weight or BMI might be a symptom of pancreatic cancer.
4. Coming in contact with chemicals used by dry cleaners and metal workers.
5. Having chronic pancreatitis.

There are some risk factors that you cannot change, some of which are as follows:

1. Genetic recurrent pancreatitis is caused by gene alterations (mutations) that are handed down from parent to kid.
2. Being a Male.

Figure 10.3 Risk factors of pancreatic cancer.

3. Being an African American.
4. Being of Ashkenazi Jewish descent.

If you experience certain symptoms or have suddenly established diabetic or pancreatitis, your doctor may suspect pancreatic cancer.

Pancreatic neuroendocrine cancer can vary from classic pancreatic cancer signs, such as losing weight. This is due to the fact that some Pancreatic neuroendocrine tumors (PNETs) increase the production of hormones.

10.2.1 The stages of pancreatic cancer?

Pancreatic cancer is divided into five categories (Fig. 10.4). Your prognosis is influenced by the size and location of the tumor, in addition to whether or not really the disease has progressed:

1. Phase 0: Stage 0 cancer, also known as cancer in situ, is distinguished by malignant growth in the pancreatic lining. The cells might develop into cancer and migrate to neighboring tissue.
2. Phase 1: The cancer is in the pancreas.
3. Phase 2: The tumor has migrated to regional lymph nodes, organs, or lymphatic system from the pancreas.
4. Phase 3: The malignancy has progressed to massive blood arteries in the vicinity of the pancreas. It might potentially have migrated to adjacent lymph nodes.
5. Phase 4: The disease has migrated to remote parts of the body in fourth stage of pancreatic cancer. It may have spread to other tissues, organs, or lymph nodes.

10.3 Lipid nanoparticles

"Fat" appears to be a synonym for "lipid." Lipids appear to be a substance that cannot dissolve in water but may dissolve in alcohol, (C2H5)2 O, and chcl3 [12]. Individual cells required lipids to thrive. Animal and plant cells were primarily composed of lipids, Cx (H2O)y, and protein. Both triglycerides and cholesterol are lipids. Fats are quickly obtained and maintained inside the system. It is a crucial component of the cell's structure and acts as an energetic benchmark. Fats sometimes are classified as

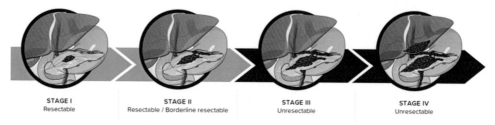

STAGE I
Resectable

STAGE II
Resectable / Borderline resectable

STAGE III
Unresectable

STAGE IV
Unresectable

Figure 10.4 Stages of pancreatic cancer.

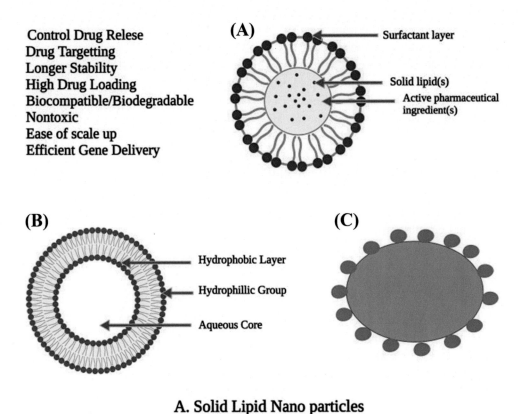

Control Drug Release
Drug Targetting
Longer Stability
High Drug Loading
Biocompatible/Biodegradable
Nontoxic
Ease of scale up
Efficient Gene Delivery

(A)

Surfactant layer

Solid lipid(s)

Active pharmaceutical
ingredient(s)

(B)

Hydrophobic Layer

Hydrophillic Group

Aqueous Core

(C)

A. Solid Lipid Nano particles
B. Liposome
C. Lipid Emulsion

Figure 10.5 The entire configuration of solid LNPs, which offer advantages over LNPs and lipids emulsions, is graphically represented [13]. A) Solid Lipid Nanoparticles (SLNs), B) Liposomes, C) Lipid Emulsion. *LNPs*, lipid nanoparticles.

aquaphobic or amphoteric low molecular weight compounds; the amphiphilic property of particular lipids allows us to produce watery forms such as vesicles, huge uniflagellar liposomes, or membranes. The biochemical constituents or "building blocks" of biological lipids are ketoacyl and isoprene groups. Fig. 10.5 depicts the structures of SLN, liposomes, and lipid emulsion.

Fats have received a nice deal of interest since the commencement of the pharmaceutical era because of their biocompatibility as a transporter. Because they are very repellent, they have low oral absorption [14]. As a result, the ambition to broaden the variety of uses for such transporters fell short, and they were not used in propulsion systems until 1900 after they were enclosed in colloidal delivery methods [15—18]. In the development of nanomaterials delivery systems, LNPs were shown to be more helpful than polymeric NPs [19]. LNPs are considered to as "Nano safe" carriers since they are constructed of physiologic and/or disposable lipids [20]. Solid LNPs are a well-known LNP synthesis that was created in the early 1990s [21]. Due to the numerous advantages of previous transporters, such as emulsifying agents, lipid membranes, and polymeric nanoparticles (NPs), delivery approach was developed [22]. The practicality of the manufacturing techniques and leveling-up process, the GRAS grade of all formulations, and absence of polar components separate SLNs from liposomes [23].

Tumor nanotechnology is presently being developed as a possible cancer therapy approach for antitumor medication delivery [24]. NPs with sizes ranging from one to 1000 nm improve therapeutic bioavailability and antitumor drug selectivity [25]. Fig. 10.6 depicts a number of NPs and nanotech cancer therapy techniques that have recently been published. Semiconducting quantum dots can really be employed as a versatile composite structure with significant potential for biomedical activities because of its peculiar optical properties, large excitation range, and extremely constrained symmetrical intensity distribution. Semiconductor quantum dots are a novel type of fluorescent element. They are used in cell imaging, biolabeling, and biosensing. Quantum dots have a stronger influence than conventional fluorophores. They are bright, possess better control over emission intensity, and are less photobleached. Different colored quantum dots with wide absorption and narrow emission spectra can be stimulated by a single light source. The previously described quantum dots appear

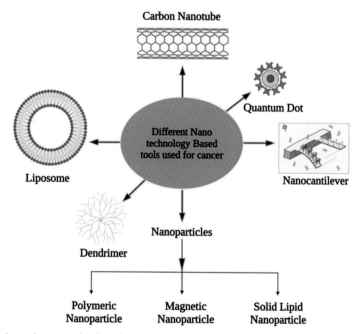

Figure 10.6 Several nanotechnology-based cancer therapy techniques are in use [13]. *Taken from S. Sheoran, S. Arora, and G. Pilli, "Lipid based nanoparticles for treatment of cancer," Heliyon, p. e09403, 2022.*

to be the most effective option for screening cell receptors. To make good fluorescence probes, the surfaces of quantum dots must be altered using diverse biological molecules [26].

Among the numerous NP formulations used in the treatment of cancer depicted in Fig. 10.6, we highlight ones relying on liquid that flows since significant advances in production and alternative compositions have been made in the last decades. Chemical modifications to lipid nanosystems can be employed to avoid detection by the immune system or to boost pharmaceutical availability. These might also be made in pH-sensitive formulations to boost the release of the drug in acidic conditions, and they could be combined with antibodies that recognize tumor cells and their receptors, such as folic acid (FoA) [27]. Nanomedicines may be used in concert with other therapy techniques to improve patient's response.

Several antitumor drugs, including cisplatin, have already been studied in nanoformulations, and others have been studied in clinical studies and/or are industrially available for medical use [28]. Doxil, a liposome formulation containing DOX, was the first commercially used anticancer medication nanosystem that presents an overview of the many types of LBNPs (Fig. 10.7) that have been developed in recent years, as well as their uses and benefits in various types of malignancies.

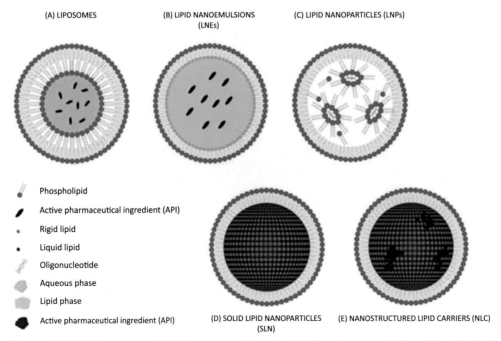

Figure 10.7 (A) Liposomes, (B) lipid nanoemulsions in lipid-based nanoparticles, (C) solid lipid nanoparticles, (D) and nanostructured lipid carriers. *Taken from S. Sheoran, S. Arora, and G. Pilli, "Lipid based nanoparticles for treatment of cancer," Heliyon, p. e09403, 2022.*

10.4 Solid lipid nanoparticles

These really are solid sizes ranging from 1−1000 nm. Nanoparticles range in size between 150 to 300 nm. Solid LNPs are solid, submicronic colloidal nanocarriers with diameters ranging from 1e1000 nm [13]. The granular size ranges from 150 to 300 nm. Nanoparticles, for example, provide a framework for controlled drug release [29]. Their solid SLN method enables them to limit medicine movement and provide greater stability, combining the benefits of polymeric NPs and liposomes and consists of high emulsifiers [30]. Furthermore, experiments reveal that SLNs were particularly beneficial in a variety of ways (Fig. 10.8),

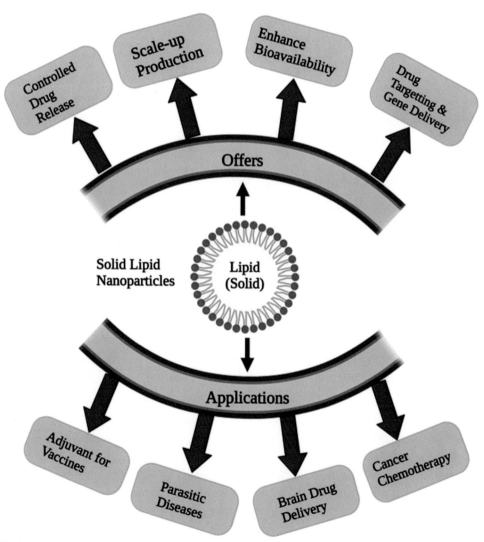

Figure 10.8 The advantages and applications of SLN are represented graphically [13]. *SLN,* solid lipid nanoparticles.

including the avoidance of using organic solvents during manufacture, the possibility of scaling [31], and the incorporation of both lipophilic and hydrophilic medications in substantial quantities [32]. SLNs are formed by substituting a solid lipid or a mixture of solid lipids for the liquid lipid (oil) in the formation of an oil and water dispersion. One distinguishing property of SLNs is that they are rigid both at room and body temperatures [33]. These drug delivery systems are composed of 0.1%– 30% (w/w) solid lipids distributed in an aqueous media. SLNs are often made up of solid-form lipids such as higher-grade triglycerides, free fatty acids, free fatty alcohols, complex glyceride blends, and even wax (all of which are well-known physiologic lipids) [34]. It is also possible to employ more complex systems [35].

10.5 Limitations of solid lipid nanoparticles and way to overcome

Though SLNs are typically composed of solid lipids, deterioration and unstable may be an issue. Excessive pressure-induced drug disintegration, the coexistence of diverse lipid alterations and colloidal species, the minimum drug-loading potential, and the kinetics of the delivery are all things to consider.

10.6 High pressure-induced drug degradation

The principal reasons for drug disintegration are molecular mass and organization, and high-pressure uniformity has been demonstrated to diminish polymer molecular mass. Regardless of the fact that multiple studies suggest that elevated homogenization-induced drug breakdown is not a problem for the vast majority of bioactive metabolites, high molecular weight composites or chain-length components are significantly more sensitive. However, big molecular weight compounds such as DNA, albumin, and dextrose are more susceptible to breaking; hence, integrating these materials into SLNs requires a unique strategy.

10.7 Lipid crystallization and drug incorporation

Another essential issue to consider is lipids crystallization. Scientists have already been examining the association between lipid changes and medicine-based treatment over the past few years. The investigation of lipid alterations is widely recognized. X-ray and differential scan calorimeter studies are used in the bulk of the approaches. Nonetheless, the majority of the evidence has come from large-scale lipid investigations. The efficiency of SLNs may vary greatly due to the evident nanosize of the carrier, and a large number of interface active participants required to sustain colloidal lipid dissemination. As a result, lipid crystallization and drug inclusion have an effect on the characteristics of lipid particles. When considering medication capture inside solid LNPs, the following important factors must be considered:

(1) the presence of supercooled melts; (2) the presence of various lipid modifications; (3) the shape of lipid nanodispersions; and (4) gelation processes.

10.8 Several colloidal species coexist

Researchers have given little consideration to the coexistence of many nanomaterials within solid LNPs, despite the fact that it is an important issue to solve. Surfactants are present on both the lipid surface and the inside of the lipid. Diverse micelles must be recognized in glycocholate/lecithin stabilized and similar systems. Because micelles, mixed micelles, and lipid membranes may dissolve drugs, they can be employed as therapeutic incorporation targets. Because dynamic models are crucial for drug stability and release, the existence of diverse heterogeneous entities alone is inadequate to define the structure of colloidal lipid phase separation. As a result, the kinematics of delivery process must be considered. Enzymatic hydrolysis drugs, for example, breakdown faster in water-soluble and interface-localized chemicals than in lipid molecules.

The rate of disintegration will be governed by two factors: (1) the chemical makeup of the medication and (2) the drug concentration in the aqueous phase or at the lipid/water border. When buoyant drugs come into contact with liquid, they swiftly hydrolyze, disrupting the drug's dispersion balance between diverse habitats. Carriers are only useful if they keep drugs from being redistributed. Increasing the matrix width naturally affects the mass transfer coefficient of the drug within the transporter, hence SLNs are expected to outperform lipid nanoemulsions.

10.9 Nanostructured carriers of lipid (solid lipid nanoparticles and nanostructured lipid carriers)

Despite their safety and efficiency, solid LNPs have a number of significant drawbacks, including increased moisture concentrations (70%—99.9%), inadequate drug content due to crystalline shape, drug ejection during preservation, and probable polymorphisms transitions and particle formation during storage. As a consequence, modifications to the Solid LNPs organization are required to meet these limits. At the turn of 2000, further research resulted in the invention of a "second generation" of LNPs: the NLCs [29]. Dr. Rimpler (Wedemark, Germany) then created the first NLC concepts: Nano Repair Q10 cream, Nano Repair Q10 serum, and Chemisches Laboratorium's Nano lipid CLR Restore (Berlin, Germany). Solid LNPs will be at the forefront of nanotechnology innovation, with several potential applications and a short time between discovery and commercialization [36]. Despite the reality that medication loaded with aquaphilic molecules is quite low, previous data shows that SLNs and NLCs were appropriate for the integration of lipophilic drugs [37]. Early research on the subject indicates that only highly potent aquaphilic medications with low effectiveness might be thoroughly integrated through the solid lipid matrix [38].

10.9.1 Solid lipid nanoparticles and nanostructured lipid carriers for drug delivery

Liposomes and different versions have indeed been utilized in lipid-based medicinal compositions since the 1960s and are regarded as the classic forms. Previous research has linked liposomes to inherent failures and poor characteristics in terms of depolymerization, an absence of massive production technology, merging and drug leaking, polymer matrix degradation and cytotoxicity, phospholipid degradation, high production costs, and sterilization issues [20,39−42]. Müller and colleagues coined the words "solid LNPs" and "nanostructured lipid carriers" (NLCs) in 2002. These developed from a natural notion that combined the beneficial properties of NPs with nontoxic and biodegradable lipid components to generate nontoxic and biodegradable parenteral emulsions that could be delivered directly [20].

The nanoparticle is categorized according to its contents, distribution method, and doctors and medical. Depending on their content, a nanoparticle is classified into two types: solid SLNs and NLCs. Since 1990 [42], SLNs have been touted as viable alternatives to liposomes, emulsions, and polymeric nanoparticle carrier systems. They have a spherical shape with an average size of 40−1000 nm and may be studied using transmitted and scanning electron microscopes.

10.9.2 Solid lipid nanoparticles as delivery carriers for anticancer agents

Cancer is distinguished by uncontrollable cell proliferation, susceptibility to apoptosis, and the ability to spread to other tissues [43]. Chemotherapeutic, which would be administered through regular medication delivery channels, is the most thorough cancer treatment. However, there are significant disadvantages to this method, including limited solubility, low sensitivity, potential toxicity, and low therapeutic efficacy [44]. Cancer medication resistance is the most challenging obstacle to overcome in cancer treatment. Resistance to chemotherapy medications is common in cancer cells, resulting in treatment failure (Fig. 10.9). Resistance to cancer drugs may be produced by genetic changes that result in parallel changes in signaling pathways. Multidrug treatment with multiple target pathways has been found in studies to be more successful than mono-drug therapy [45].

External factors and obtained resistance to antibiotics, the two leading causes of chemotherapy failure, have a major adverse effect on chemotherapeutics treatment outcomes. Recent advancements in nanotechnology have provided new treatment options for tumors that have grown resistant to traditional treatments [46]. Fig. 10.9 depicts how solid LNPs can bypass medication tolerance by successfully penetrating

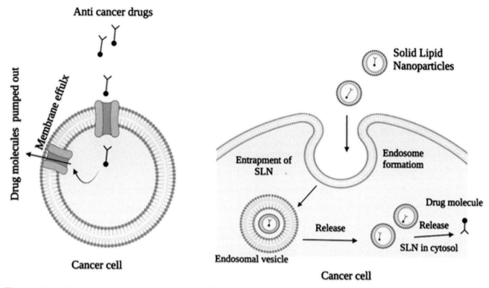

Figure 10.9 Escape mechanism of solid LNPs that contain anticancer drugs. *LNPs*, lipid nanoparticles.

cancer cells. Based on the nanoparticle composition and manufacturing process, SLNs can hold both hydrophilic and lipophilic anticancer drugs. Drug particles may be included in three ways: (1) they can be spread uniformly in the lipid matrix; (2) they can be incorporated into the nanoparticles; and (3) they can be incorporated into the shell of the nanoparticles. Docetaxel, a natural lipid-soluble molecule, exhibits favorable characteristics for incorporation into Solid Lipid Nanoparticle (SLN) formulations. The inherent properties of docetaxel make it suitable for utilization in SLN systems. Notably, a previous study demonstrated that SLN formulations enhanced the cytotoxicity of docetaxel when tested on MCF-7 breast tumor cells, surpassing the effectiveness of the medication in its conventional form during characterization [47].

In vivo and in vitro research have been conducted to explore the efficacy of SLN absorption in various systems. SLNs have indeed been demonstrated to have less side effects while enhancing the occupancy length and effectiveness of cytotoxic medications. Doxorubicin is a natural drug compound with potent anticancer properties. Its use has a number of negative side effects, including cardiac problems. Doxorubicin may be integrated into SLNs, and when paired with alpha-tocopherol succinate, which also has anticancer potential, it demonstrated excellent cytotoxicity and uptake in drug-resistant MCF-7 human cancer cells [48].

Despite the reality that cancer cells represent for further than 80% points of all malignancies in people, a treatment regimen of solid tumors continues to pose major issues due to poor responses that have been anticipated to be as low as 20% in esophageal cancer, pancreatic cancer, and ovarian cancer [49]. An earlier study indicated that miRNA-200c might be effectively trapped in SLNs to prevent development of resistance. According to one study, paclitaxel-loaded SLNs might be employed to treat drug-resistant breast cancer cells. This was corroborated by later study findings. Paclitaxel-SLNs demonstrated significant effectiveness in both drug-resistant and drug-sensitive MCF-7 cells. According to a recent survey, doxorubicin SLNs have great promise as a beneficial therapeutic method for overcoming multidrug resistance [50].

10.9.3 Routes of delivering

The SLN technique has made tremendous progress in the treatment of a variety of ailments. Hydrophilic and lipophilic medicines are encapsulated in SLNs, which decreases their degradation in the body all while allowing for sustained strategic drug release. NPs of various sorts have indeed been developed for the following purposes:

10.9.3.1 Oral delivery

SNLs can be transformed into traditional oral dosage forms. Furthermore, SLN dispersal can be utilized instead of granule fluid in a technique like wet granulation [51]. If the SLN suspensions are powdery, they can be tableted immediately after preparation by lyophilization and spray drying. To enhance expense, crisped SLN powder can be packed in gelatin capsules, generated as liquid polyethylene glycol 600 and packed in soft gel capsules, or turned into a powder form and wrapped in packets following lyophilization [2]. Numerous investigations on bioactive chemicals for SLNs for oral administration have been done. Research effectively proved that SLNs are appropriate delivery systems for oral insulin delivery [52]. Moreover, the solid structure of SLN has been demonstrated to shield insulin from degradation processes in the gastrointestinal system while boosting insulin uptake through the intestinal lining. Recent research revealed that docetaxel-loaded SLNs are potential drug transporters in the prevention and treatment of metastases of breast cancer [53]. In another study, solid LNPs (SLNs) combined with transferrin in the treatment of breast cancer showed a significant ability to transport tamoxifen citrate to tumor cells, resulting in increased therapeutic benefits [54].

10.9.3.2 Parenteral delivery

Administered is the most effective technique for administering bioactive chemotherapeutic drugs with narrow absorption indexes and limited bio-availability, especially for drugs prescribed to patients who have difficulty [55]. Parenteral drug delivery has benefitted from considerable technical advances, which have resulted in the development of complex devices that enable drug targets as well as prolonged or changed outcomes of parenteral drugs [56]. Protein and peptide medicines are more vulnerable to enzymatic breakdown, necessitating regular compensation when administered orally. SLNs with a controlled release mechanism for a route of administration have been found to be effective treatment techniques for preventing enhanced patient adherence and repeated administration [57]. Parenteral SLN delivery might take various forms, ranging from intravenous to intraarticular. Several studies have been carried out on the pharmacokinetic and distribution of doxorubicin content in SLNs in tissues [2,44]. Just the synaptic connections of rabbits were shown to contain doxorubicin in these experiments. Hidden compounds were incorporated into the SLNs to increase dispersion to the brain. Doxorubicin oral dosing, on the other hand, resulted in lower bioavailability in the heart and liver.

10.9.3.3 Pulmonary delivery

Respiratory drug delivery is a noninvasive mode of delivery that has many advantages for local treatment of airway illnesses; it immediately enters the epithelium, avoids first metabolizing in the liver, and has minimal toxicity [58]. A study on the pulmonary injection of amikacin-loaded SLNs was conducted with the purpose of increasing its intensity for the treatment of cystic fibrosis-associated lung infections in male rats [59]. Both free medicine and cholesterol-loaded drug administration strategies, such as intravenous and pulmonary delivery routes, were employed. Earlier research found that pulmonary medication release had less negative impacts on the kidneys and a larger drug dosage interval than intravenous administration, leading to higher patient compliance [56,58]. People who do have trouble adhering to SLN drugs or who suffer from renal problems may benefit from pulmonary administration of SLN medications. Other important administration routes for SLN-packaged medications, in addition to oral and parenteral administration, are ocular and rectal delivery, each of which comes with its very own set of benefits.

10.10 Applications of solid lipid nanoparticles in pancreatic cancer

Solid LNPs are one of several kinds of NPs that can be utilized to treat cancer. They are used as potential nanocarriers for the encapsulation of chemotherapeutic medications in addition to enhancing the stability and efficacy of the encapsulated anticancer therapeutics. The high drug loading capacity of solid LNPs is comparable to that of polymeric NPs. Additional benefits of solid LNPs include enhanced pharmacokinetic characteristics and lower in vivo toxicity, which make them an adaptable nanodrug carrier for anticancer medications. delivering these medicines by solid LNPs can considerably reduce the difficulties associated with anticancer drugs, including the assessment of normal tissue toxicity, lower specificity and stability, and the high prevalence of resistance-related problems [60].

Currently, specific cancer cells are killed using magnetic NPs and hyperthermia in the treatment of cancer. A more recent method for treating cancer that involves mixing chemotherapeutic drugs with magnetic NPs has been proven to be effective in treating a variety of tumors because it offers cancer cells a twofold boost from both hyperthermia and chemotherapy. Chemothermia, a treatment for several types of malignancies, including breast, colon, bladder, and pancreatic cancer, is defined as the combination of hyperthermia with chemotherapy. The results of this study showed how effectively and significantly anticancer medications had improved. The use of NPs can lessen the major adverse effects associated with chemotherapy [61,62].

The total survival time for patients with pancreatic cancer ranges from a few months to five years. Pancreatic cancer is recognized for having a low survival rate. By employing medications, such as curcumin (CUR), sulforaphane (SFN), 5-FU, and GEM, several NPs have been developed to treat pancreatic cancer and have shown encouraging outcomes in preclinical investigations when compared to traditional chemotherapy [61].

According to the study by Inkoom et al., 2022, it is crucial to check the anticancer activity of 4NSG-solid LNPs (4-(N)-stearoyl-gemcitabine) on patient-derived pancreatic cancer cells in vitro using (PPCL-46, PPCL-68) and (PPCL -192, PPCL-135) cell lines obtained from Caucasian (White) and African American (AA) patients, respectively, and to further evaluate the antitumor efficacy in pancreatic cancer PDX mice bearing tumors from both of these populations. It is crucial to note that while several gemcitabine (GEM) analogs have been shown to be successful, in a number of commercially accessible cell lines, there is little evidence available comparing the effectiveness of GEM analogs in patient-derived pancreatic cancer cells from White and AA patients. This study supports the use of patient-derived pancreatic cancer cells to assess the effectiveness of GEM analogs in White and AAs through scientific research investigations [63].

Recent research on nanodrug delivery methods demonstrates enhanced cellular absorption of the solid LNPs formulation in comparison to GEM in numerous organs and cancer types and regulated drug release [64]. To enhance the therapeutic efficacy against pancreatic cancer cells, an unusual solid lipid NP with a substantial payload of GEM was created. To avoid drug dispersion into the aqueous phase, temperature-induced drug degradation, and crystallization modification [65], 4NSG-solid LNPs were prepared using the cold homogenization technique. The selection of surfactants has a significant influence on solid LNPs particle size. Labrasol, tween 80, and lecithin surfactant compositions were kept below 2% in order to create solid LNPs with small particle sizes and to mitigate any potential toxicity concerns brought on by high surfactant amounts [66]. Using TEM for the analysis of 4NSG-solid LNPs formulation revealed spherical NPs with diameters ranging from 63−100 nm, which validated the particle size reduction in 4NSG-solid LNPs. In comparison to the comparable results for GEM-HCL, the IC50 values of 4NSG-solid LNPs were considerably lower in the PPCL-46, PPCL-68, PPCL-192, and PPCL-135 produced from White and AA individuals, respectively. The IC50 results indicate that 4NSG-solid LNPs have a strong antiproliferative effect on the PPCL-46, PPCL-68, PPCL-192, and PPCL-135 cultures. This might be explained by the unique properties of 4NSG-solid LNPs, which are most likely the result of the alteration of the polar nature of GEM-HCL to moderately lipophilic by conjugation of GEM to stearic acid. Additionally, it has been discovered that GEM heavily depends on nucleoside transporters such as hENT1 in order to move between and accumulate inside cancer cells. It has been shown that underexpression of these transporters confers pancreatic cancer resistance [67]. According to earlier published efforts that employ delivery methods for the targeted transport of GEM derivatives [68], the lipophilic nature of 4NSG-solid LNPs implies that it enters pancreatic cancer cells via passive diffusion. Using flow cytometry and confocal imaging, the cellular uptake of 4NSG-solid LNPs was assessed. In their flow cytometry and confocal tests, FITC-solid LNPs displayed a ten-fold increase in geometric fluorescence intensity compared to FITC-exposed cells. This shows that the solid LNPs might capture a larger payload of 4NSG, confirming the FITC-increased solid lipid nanoparticle's intensity above FITC alone. A crucial parameter of cell viability is used in the clonogenic test to assess a cell's capacity for growth and metastasis in colonies of at least 50 cells [69]. According to the results, 4NSG-solid LNPs were more successful than GEM-HCL at preventing cell growth. PPCL-46 and PPCL-192 cells were used in a cell migration experiment to investigate the function of 4NSG-solid LNPs in cell mobility. According to the research, 4NSG-solid LNPs dramatically decreased cell migration in both cells when compared to GEM-HCl. One method for reducing tumor development is thought to be the inhibition of cell cycle progression in cancer cells [70]. The genetic characterization of cell cycle regulators is crucial since the majority of cancer-related disorders are often mutated [71]. The results of the investigation showed that treatment of PPCL-46 and PPCL-192 cells with 4NSG-solid LNPs at a concentration of 5 M significantly stopped the advancement of the cell cycle in the G1 phase. This shows that 4NSG-solid LNPs may have antiproliferative effects that prevent the advancement of the cell cycle. At a concentration of 20, 4NSG-solid LNPs may have caused apoptosis in the PPCL-46 and PPCL-192 cells, confirming that only a small percentage of the cell population had accumulated in the S and G2/M phases. The outcomes of their cell cycle experiments further substantiate our claim that 4NSG-solid LNPs had a more powerful cytotoxic impact than GEM-HCL. The process of cell migration plays a crucial role in promoting tumor spread. In this work, PPCL-192 and PPCL-46 cells' ability to move around was reduced by 4NSG-solid LNPs. Compared to GEM-HCL, the 4NSG-solid LNPs dramatically lowers cellular migration. Very few cells were found in the wound area after administration of the 4NSG-solid LNPs formulation at a dose of 20 mM, demonstrating its superior capacity to inhibit cellular mobility when compared to GEM-HCL. It was demonstrated that the half-life and AUC parameters significantly lengthened the residence duration and increased the proportion of 4NSG-solid LNPs that remained intact in systemic circulation when the pharmacokinetic profiles of 4NSG-solid LNPs and GEM-HCL were compared.

The prognostic value of EGFR, which is overexpressed in 30%–89% of pancreatic cancer, is still debatable [72,73]. Similar to EGFR, which is overexpressed in between 4% and 50% of pancreatic cancer patients, it is unknown how HER2 affects prognosis [74]. HER2 expression predicts a poorer outcome in certain PDAC patients while showing no correlation in others [75,76]. On the other hand, VEGFR and VEGF overexpression in PDAC is an excellent indicator of advanced stage and recurrence following resection. In this work, they examined the expressions of VEGFR, HER2, and EGFR in pancreatic tumor-bearing PDX mice models treated with GEM-HCL and 4NSG-solid LNPs. Lower expressions of VEGFR, HER2, and EGFR were seen in the tumors of the $4NSG-SLN_{AAT}$ and $4NSG-SLN_{WT}$ treated groups in this particular PDX model made up of members of the White and AA populations. This finding suggests that 4NSG-solid LNPs could be used as an effective VEGFR, HER2, and EGFR-specific therapy [77,78]. In comparison to GEM-HCL treatments, 4NSG-solid LNPs significantly reduced the expression of the VEGFR, HER2, and EGFR receptors in the tumor tissues of the White and AA patients. Clinical evidence suggests that VEGFR, HER2, and EGFR receptor targeting may overcome innate tumor resistance and improve therapy results in pancreatic cancer. This might lead them to hypothesize that 4NSG-capacity solid LNPs to target VEGFR, HER2, and EGFR receptors is what most likely caused the tumor's development to be significantly reduced. In comparison to GEM-HCL, 4NSG-antitumor solid lipid nanoparticle's efficacy demonstrated considerable tumor growth suppression in both White and AA's tumors during a 25-day period. To a significant extent, tumor inhibition was shown in animals carrying White and AA tumors throughout the research period, suggesting that the solid LNPs may play a key role in encapsulating a greater payload of 4NSG that resulted in high build-up in the tumor location. The exceptional tumor effectiveness of 4NSG-solid LNPs might be explained by a number of important aspects, including (1) The 4NSG lacked a free NH2 group, which prevented the cysteine deaminase enzyme from properly metabolizing GEM. The duration of circulation, greater bioavailability, and enhanced therapeutic effectiveness of 4NSG were most likely made possible by this occurrence. (2) To preserve 4NSG from severe conditions and boost its payload for targeted transport to tumors of interest, it is enclosed in a solid LNP delivery system. (3) The conjugation of GEM to stearic acid may have given 4NSG some degree of lipophilicity, which in turn may help facilitate its delivery to tumor cells.

In this investigation, Inkoom and his team showed that 4NSG improved the permeability and plasma metabolic stability of GEM, which increased its therapeutic effectiveness. The pharmacokinetic properties of GEM were enhanced by chemically converting it to 4NSG and then forming it into 4NSG-solid LNPs, which led to the longer system circulation shown in their study. Comparing the mice with pancreatic tumors from White and AA patients to the mice treated with GEM, 4NSG-solid LNPs significantly inhibited tumor development in all of the animals [63].

Ferulic acid (FA) is one of the most abundant antioxidants in wheat bran. In cases of breast, skin, colon, and liver cancer, it exhibits anticancer potential [79]. FA has an inferior oral bioavailability due to its weak water solubility. Solid LNPs can compensate for FA's low bioavailability. Glyceryl behenate was used to make solid LNPs that were loaded with FA by Zhang et al. [80]. When compared to aqueous dispersion (10.0 mg/mL and 2.1 hours, respectively), the pharmacokinetic characteristics for solid LNPs exhibited a greater C_{max} and half-life (18.7 mg/mL and 4.6 hours, respectively), indicating a sustained release from the lipid matrix. Using the in vivo imaging technology, it was also shown that solid LNPs retained in the small intestine for a longer period of time than in the free control. For the treatment of pancreatic cancer, Thakkar et al. [81] loaded aspirin (ASP) and FA in chitosan-coated solid LNPs. The lipid core of solid LNPs coated with chitosan demonstrated good durability in an acidic environment thanks to the development of a thick coating around it. The muco-adhesion of solid LNPs was similarly enhanced by this biopolymer covering [82]. Pancreatic cancer cells MIA Panc-1 and PaCa-2 were suppressed by modest dosages of free FA (200 mm) and ASP (1 mm), respectively, by 45% and 60%. After solid LNPs entrapment, it was shown that FA (40 mM) and ASP (25 mM) showed equivalent cytotoxicity at 5- and 40-fold lower doses. Oral administration of a combination of FA (75 mg/kg) and ASP (25 mg/kg) in solid LNPs effectively decreased tumor development by 45% when compared to the reference group in the in vivo pancreatic cancer xenograft mice research.

Accordingly, the 2015 study by Thakkar et al. looked at the possible chemopreventive effects of a combination of free ASP and FA as well as encapsulated ASP and FA in c-solid LNPs. For the first time, the ASP and FA c-solid LNPs combination inhibiting cell survival in a synergistic manner and causing apoptosis in MIA PaCa-2 and Panc-1 human pancreatic cancer cells was demonstrated. Even while this was not statistically significant, additional in vivo experiments showed that the c-solid LNPs combination might decrease tumors. Studies using immunohistochemistry show that the regimen promotes apoptosis due to greatly increased protein expression. The preliminary results from these studies provide a basis for further research to confirm if this combination regimen based on nanotechnology is possibly useful as a chemopreventative therapy for pancreatic cancer [83].

Sutaria et al.'s research has mostly examined the chemopreventive effects of low doses of the ACS (ASP, CUR, and SFN e) combination solid LNPs against pancreatic cancer cells, MIA Panc-1 and PaCa-2 [84]. It was assumed that delivering two or more chemopreventative medications at low concentrations together might have an additive or synergistic effect on the cancer cells because administering a single agent at low concentrations has been demonstrated to be ineffective. This is because carcinogenesis has a multifaceted nature and cancer arises from a number of cellular modifications over a long period of time. Among the several chemopreventive medications under investigation, ASP, SFN, and CUR have been found to be effective in the chemoprevention of pancreatic cancer [85–87]. Nonsteroidal anti-inflammatory drugs (NSAIDs) such as ASP and celecoxib have been proven in several in vivo and in vitro studies to aid in the prevention of pancreatic cancer development. Researchers have looked at the chemopreventive effects of CUR and SFN, two substances that are both efficient and nontoxic in nature [88–90]. Therefore using a multidisciplinary approach, this study investigated the synergistic effects of solid LNPs combinations of chemopreventive medicines, especially ASP in combination with CUR and SFN.

However, a number of factors, such as these drugs' limited oral bioavailability after delivery, have greatly impeded their clinical translation. By designing a solid LNPs drug delivery system for these medicines, it is possible to increase their bioavailability in tissues and plasma compared to their free form, thus enhancing their therapeutic efficacy. Additionally, administering medications at lower dosages with a decreased risk of adverse side effects while preserving effectiveness is possible thanks to the drug's encapsulation inside the lipid matrix. Combining drugs with different modes of action makes it easier to achieve the required preventative effect while reducing the dose concentration and its adverse consequences [91]. Both CUR and ASP solid LNPs were discovered to have excellent encapsulation efficiency, good stability at or below room temperature in terms of formulation development, and ideal particle sizes. The use of an organic solvent during the manufacturing procedure may have enhanced the lipid's hygroscopic properties, which might account for the improved stability. The lipophilic properties of both ASP and CUR are responsible for high encapsulation. Additionally, it was discovered that the particles were in the nm range, indicating a higher likelihood of the medications being taken up by cells. The fact that the designed solid LNPs are composed of physiological lipids like stearic acid makes them nontoxic.

In order to establish an additive or synergistic effect on the cancer cells, the effectiveness of these medications was first evaluated by calculating their IC50 values, and then by combining the ineffective levels to show that they were more effective at lower concentrations. It was compared to how the two drug delivery methods—free form and solid lipid nanoparticle form—performed. When compared to the drug's free form, it was seen that the CUR and ASP solid LNPs IC50 concentrations had decreased by around 38 and 3 times, respectively. there have been studies showing that drug-loaded solid LNPs had a superior cytotoxicity profile than the free drug [92]. This has mostly been attributed to the NPs' smaller particle size, which improves drug absorption. The surfactant used in the development process determines the inhibitory effect on the cells. Poloxamer 188 was used, which has been shown in the past to target malignant cells, due to differences in the membrane of these cells compared to the noncancer cells. Poloxamer has been demonstrated to increase proto-apoptotic signalling and reduce antiapoptotic defence in multiple drug-resistant (MDR) cells in addition to inhibiting MDR proteins and other drug efflux transporters on the surface of cancer cells [93]. Three different concentrations of SFN (5 M), ASP (25 M), and CUR (2.5 M) were used in the MTS test on drug-entrapped solid LNPs. The viability of these two cell lines alone exhibited little to no decline, but when the two were mixed, a substantial drop of 60% was seen in MIA Panc1 and PaCa2 cells. Apoptosis assay, which identified the advancement of a cancer cell from four different phases following the addition of the drug—living cell, early apoptotic cell, late apoptotic cell, and necrotic cells—was used to confirm the effectiveness of the combination regimen. These outcomes appear to be in line with what we discovered in the MTS experiment. The suppression of the COX-2 enzyme, control of the P53 suppressor pathway, and manipulation of the Nrf2 pathway are potential processes that might result in a major change for the combination; however, additional research needs to be carried out to verify these findings.

Given that pancreatic cancer cannot be detected at an early stage, it is reasonable to assume that chemoprevention is an effective method of preventing the illness. This study examined the synergistic effects of combining free SFN with ASP and CUR solid LNPs using a multidisciplinary approach. It was observed that the combination of solid LNPs decreased cell viability and induced apoptosis in human pancreatic cancer cell lines for the first time. The effectiveness of this solid LNP combination has to be investigated further in vivo, though. The findings from cell-based tests and formulation studies thus amply show the potential for creating drug-encapsulated solid LNPs formulations that combine several drugs to prevent pancreatic cancer [94].

CUR has been shown to be an effective pancreatic cancer chemo-preventive agent among the many chemo-preventive drugs under investigation. However, this agent's limited oral bioavailability following administration has considerably impeded its clinical translation [84]. In contrast to the free form, it is possible to improve the bioavailability in the plasma and tissues of CUR by developing a solid lipid NP drug delivery system, which will boost therapeutic efficacy.

Given the positive outcomes of in vitro cytotoxicity tests conducted on CFPAC-1 and PANC-1 cultures, the in vivo findings may serve as a good starting point for further research into in vivo pancreatic cancer models. According to the study on c-solid LNPs, their findings support the idea of using the created solid LNPs-based delivery systems for entrapping CUR to increase both its chemical stability and water dispersibility, allowing its use in treatment.

Even though the aforementioned results may not meet the ideal standards for in vivo delivery, they offer promising insights and a plethora of possibilities for modifying the composition and surface characteristics of SLNs. These findings inspire us to explore ways to enhance the circulation time of SLNs while simultaneously reducing opsonization, thereby opening avenues for improved drug delivery strategies [93].

With a five-year survival rate of <5%, pancreatic cancer is the fourth most prevalent cancer mortality in the United States. The American Cancer Society estimated that in 2014, 46,420 people would be diagnosed with pancreatic cancer in the United States alone, and 39,590 of them would face death [95]. The poor patient survival rate suggests a greater need for cutting-edge methods of battling this fatal illness. Chemoprevention has lately drawn a lot of interest as a cutting-edge pancreatic cancer treatment method [96,97]. In addition, current research has focused on the use of chemopreventive drugs that have different modes of action and target numerous pathways [84,98]. This strategy offers a low-dose therapeutic method with more efficacy and lesser damage. Studies on combination treatment, especially for the prevention of pancreatic cancer, are still in their early stages.

Numerous epidemiological and animal studies have shown that NSAIDs, such as ASP, that are widely used can lower the incidence and death of many cancer forms [96,97]. Ibuprofen (IBU), an NSAID, has lately been demonstrated to prevent the growth and spread of malignancies in both in vitro and in vivo investigations [99−101]. IBU has a good chemopreventive potential, however, side effects such as increased gastrointestinal ulcers might make it unsuitable for long-term usage [102,103]. According to current literature, encapsulation inside NP formulations may provide the chance to lessen these medications' negative effects while preserving their high efficacy [104,105]. Formulations that may be helpful in chemoprevention include LNPs with a solid matrix, such as solid LNPs and polymeric NPs [96,97,106]. The ability of the drug to reduce renal and hepatic passage, cross mucosal barriers, lower immune recognition, increased stability, enhanced apparent half-lives of the drugs, and increased solubility are just a few of the benefits that these nanosized drug delivery systems have over standard delivery systems [107,108]. The ability of solid LNPs to boost the oral bioavailability of lipophilic drugs, however, is their most significant benefit. The necessity for more study in this field is justified by the rising importance of NPs in cancer treatment and chemoprevention.

SFN is an isothiocyanate that contains sulfur that is naturally occurring and is present in cruciferous vegetables including brussels sprouts, broccoli, cabbage, and cauliflower [109]. In animal models, SFN has been demonstrated to be beneficial in avoiding a variety of chemically generated malignancies and inhibiting the development of preexisting tumors [110−112]. The expression of NF-B-mediated genes that code for adhesion molecules, inflammatory cytokines, growth factors, and antiapoptotic factors is impacted by SFN, which has been demonstrated to decrease NF-B activity [95].

In this experiment by Thakkar et al., lipid matrices of stearic acid, compritol ATO 888, and tripalmitin were combined with either (1) Poloxamer 188 or (2) Tween-80 as the surfactant to improve IBU-loaded solid LNP formulations. The generated IBU-solid LNPs were examined for their entrapment effectiveness, particle size, in vitro drug dissolving rates, and zeta potential. Another group has not yet studied the impact of low-dose free IBU, IBU-solid LNPs, or IBU-solid LNPs coupled with free SFN on pancreatic cancer cells. In order to assess their combined chemopreventive activity in MIA PaCa-2 and Panc-1 human pancreatic cancer cells, they thus adjusted IBU-solid LNPs formulations [113].

10.11 Conclusion

Pancreatic cancer therapy is still difficult. Because pancreatic cancer is relatively resistant to traditional therapies, innovative specific target medications have garnered a lot of interest. These focused nanomaterials would have been capable of recognizing cancerous cells, visualizing their spot inside the body, releasing the drug to such cells only, thwarting drug resistance, killing cancer cells without harming normal tissue to minimize adverse effects, and supervising therapeutic efficacy in instantaneously, as well as provide responses about whether sick people react effectively to the treatment options, allowing the diagnosis to be stopped on period. NP materials have demonstrated extremely encouraging outcomes in improving the pharmacological properties of this anticancer medication while also enhancing antitumor activity against experimental solid tumors. In current history, nano-drug means of delivery technology have emerged as a prominent topic. The utilization of nanomaterials as drug-carrier systems is an appealing technique for achieving regulated drug delivery.

References

[1] Mehnert W, Mäder K. Solid lipid nanoparticles: production, characterization and applications. Adv Drug Deliv Rev 2012;64:83–101.
[2] Basha SK, Dhandayuthabani R, Muzammil MS, Kumari VS. Solid lipid nanoparticles for oral drug delivery. Mater Today Proc 2021;36:313–24.
[3] Rehman M, et al. Solid lipid nanoparticles for thermoresponsive targeting: evidence from spectrophotometry, electrochemical, and cytotoxicity studies. Int J Nanomed 2017;12:8325.
[4] Mukherjee S, Maity S, Ghosh B, Chakraborty T, Mondal A, Bishayee A. Assessment of the antidiabetic potentiality of glyburide loaded glyceryl monostearate solid lipid nanoparticles. J Drug Deliv Sci Technol 2020;55:101451.
[5] Garud A, Singh D, Garud N. Solid lipid nanoparticles (SLN): method, characterization and applications. Int Curr Pharm J 2012;1(11):384–93.
[6] Dong Z, Xie S, Zhu L, Wang Y, Wang X, Zhou W. Preparation and in vitro, in vivo evaluations of norfloxacin-loaded solid lipid nanopartices for oral delivery. Drug Deliv 2011;18(6):441–50.
[7] Li H, Zhao X, Ma Y, Zhai G, Li L, Lou H. Enhancement of gastrointestinal absorption of quercetin by solid lipid nanoparticles. J Control Release 2009;133(3):238–44.
[8] De Blaey CJ, Polderman J. Rationales in the design of rectal and vaginal delivery forms of drugs. Medicinal chemistry, vol. 9. Elsevier; 1980. p. 237–66.
[9] Duan Y, et al. A brief review on solid lipid nanoparticles: part and parcel of contemporary drug delivery systems. RSC Adv 2020;10(45):26777–91.

[10] Scioli Montoto S, Muraca G, Ruiz ME. Solid lipid nanoparticles for drug delivery: pharmacological and biopharmaceutical aspects. Front Mol Biosci 2020;7:587997.

[11] Tekade RK, Maheshwari R, Tekade M, Chougule MB. Solid lipid nanoparticles for targeting and delivery of drugs and genes. Nanotechnology-based approaches for targeting and delivery of drugs and genes. Elsevier; 2017. p. 256−86.

[12] IUPAC, Compendium of chemical terminology (Gold Book). Blackwell Scientific Publications, Oxford, 1997.

[13] Sheoran S, Arora S, Pilli G. Lipid based nanoparticles for treatment of cancer. Heliyon 2022; e09403.

[14] Tang J, Sun J, He Z-G. Self-emulsifying drug delivery systems: strategy for improving oral delivery of poorly soluble drugs. Curr Drug ther 2007;2(1):85−93.

[15] Humberstone AJ, Charman WN. Lipid-based vehicles for the oral delivery of poorly water soluble drugs. Adv Drug Deliv Rev 1997;25(1):103−28.

[16] Kuentz M. Lipid-based formulations for oral delivery of lipophilic drugs. Drug Discov Today Technol 2012;9(2):e97−e104.

[17] Patel AR, Velikov KP. Colloidal delivery systems in foods: a general comparison with oral drug delivery. LWT-Food Sci Technol 2011;44(9):1958−64.

[18] Pouton CW, Porter CJH. Formulation of lipid-based delivery systems for oral administration: materials, methods and strategies. Adv Drug Deliv Rev 2008;60(6):625−37.

[19] zur Mühlen A, Schwarz C, Mehnert W. Solid lipid nanoparticles (SLN) for controlled drug delivery−drug release and release mechanism. Eur J Pharm Biopharm 1998;45(2):149−55.

[20] Pardeike J, Hommoss A, Müller RH. Lipid nanoparticles (SLN, NLC) in cosmetic and pharmaceutical dermal products. Int J Pharm 2009;366(1):170−84. Available from: https://doi.org/10.1016/j.ijpharm.2008.10.003.

[21] Gasco M.R. Method for producing solid lipid microspheres having a narrow size distribution. Google Patents US5250236A, Oct. 05, 1993.

[22] Geszke-Moritz M, Moritz M. Solid lipid nanoparticles as attractive drug vehicles: composition, properties and therapeutic strategies. Mater Sci Eng C 2016;68:982−94. Available from: https://doi.org/10.1016/j.msec.2016.05.119.

[23] Doktorovova S, Souto EB, Silva AM. Nanotoxicology applied to solid lipid nanoparticles and nanostructured lipid carriers−a systematic review of in vitro data. Eur J Pharm Biopharm 2014;87(1):1−18.

[24] Bor G, Mat Azmi ID, Yaghmur A. Nanomedicines for cancer therapy: current status, challenges and future prospects. Ther Deliv 2019;10(2):113−32.

[25] Miele E, et al. Nanoparticle-based delivery of small interfering RNA: challenges for cancer therapy. Int J Nanomed 2012;7:3637.

[26] Fatima I, Rahdar A, Sargazi S, Barani M, Hassanisaadi M, Thakur VK. Quantum dots: synthesis, antibody conjugation, and HER2-receptor targeting for breast cancer therapy. J Funct Biomater 2021;12(4):75.

[27] Rama AR, et al. Last advances in nanocarriers-based drug delivery systems for colorectal cancer. Curr Drug Deliv 2016;13(6):830−8.

[28] Alavi M, Hamidi M. Passive and active targeting in cancer therapy by liposomes and lipid nanoparticles. Drug Metab Pers Ther 2019;34(1).

[29] Muller RH, Shegokar R, Keck CM. 20 years of lipid nanoparticles (SLN and NLC): present state of development and industrial applications. Curr Drug Discov Technol 2011;8(3):207−27.

[30] Kathe N, Henriksen B, Chauhan H. Physicochemical characterization techniques for solid lipid nanoparticles: principles and limitations. Drug Dev Ind Pharm 2014;40(12):1565−75.

[31] Teeranachaideekul V, Müller RH, Junyaprasert VB. Encapsulation of ascorbyl palmitate in nanostructured lipid carriers (NLC)—Effects of formulation parameters on physicochemical stability. Int J Pharm 2007;340(1−2):198−206.

[32] Jaiswal P, Gidwani B, Vyas A. Nanostructured lipid carriers and their current application in targeted drug delivery. Artif Cells, Nanomed, Biotechnol 2016;44(1):27−40.

[33] Lima AM, et al. Hypericin encapsulated in solid lipid nanoparticles: phototoxicity and photodynamic efficiency. J Photochem Photobiol B Biol 2013;125:146−54.

[34] Wissing SA, Kayser O, Müller RH. Solid lipid nanoparticles for parenteral drug delivery. Adv Drug Deliv Rev 2004;56(9):1257−72.

[35] Svilenov H, Tzachev C. Solid lipid nanoparticles—a promising drug delivery system. Nanomedicine 2014;2:187−237.

[36] Iqbal MA, Md S, Sahni JK, Baboota S, Dang S, Ali J. Nanostructured lipid carriers system: recent advances in drug delivery. J Drug Target 2012;20(10):813−30.

[37] Almeida AJ, Souto E. Solid lipid nanoparticles as a drug delivery system for peptides and proteins. Adv Drug Deliv Rev 2007;59(6):478−90.

[38] Almeida AJ, Runge S, Müller RH. Peptide-loaded solid lipid nanoparticles (SLN): influence of production parameters. Int J Pharm 1997;149(2):255−65.

[39] Naseri N, Valizadeh H, Zakeri-Milani P. Solid lipid nanoparticles and nanostructured lipid carriers: structure, preparation and application. Adv Pharm Bull Sep. 2015;5(3):305−13. Available from: https://doi.org/10.15171/apb.2015.043.

[40] Mishra V, et al. Solid lipid nanoparticles: emerging colloidal nano drug delivery systems. Pharmaceutics 2018;10(4):191.

[41] Thatipamula RP, Palem CR, Gannu R, Mudragada S, Yamsani MR. Formulation and in vitro characterization of domperidone loaded solid lipid nanoparticles and nanostructured lipid carriers. Daru 2011;19(1):23.

[42] Shazly GA. Ciprofloxacin controlled-solid lipid nanoparticles: characterization, in vitro release, and antibacterial activity assessment. Biomed Res Int 2017;2017:2120734.

[43] ud Din F, et al. Effective use of nanocarriers as drug delivery systems for the treatment of selected tumors. Int J Nanomed 2017;12:7291.

[44] Bayón-Cordero L, Alkorta I, Arana L. Application of solid lipid nanoparticles to improve the efficiency of anticancer drugs. Nanomaterials 2019;9(3):474.

[45] Sivakumar SM. Therapeutic potential of chitosan nanoparticles as antibiotic delivery system: challenges to treat multiple drug resistance. Asian J Pharm 2016;10(2).

[46] Liu J, Wang T, Wang D, Dong A, Li Y, Yu H. Smart nanoparticles improve therapy for drug-resistant tumors by overcoming pathophysiological barriers. Acta Pharmacol Sin 2017;38(1):1−8.

[47] Qureshi OS, et al. Sustained release docetaxel-incorporated lipid nanoparticles with improved pharmacokinetics for oral and parenteral administration. J Microencapsul 2017;34(3):250−61.

[48] Oliveira MS, Aryasomayajula B, Pattni B, Mussi SV, Ferreira LAM, Torchilin VP. Solid lipid nanoparticles co-loaded with doxorubicin and α-tocopherol succinate are effective against drug-resistant cancer cells in monolayer and 3-D spheroid cancer cell models. Int J Pharm 2016;512(1):292−300.

[49] Nami S, Aghebati-Maleki A, Aghebati-Maleki L. Current applications and prospects of nanoparticles for antifungal drug delivery. EXCLI J 2021;20:562.

[50] Kang KW, et al. Doxorubicin-loaded solid lipid nanoparticles to overcome multidrug resistance in cancer therapy. Nanomed Nanotechnol Biol Med 2010;6(2):210−13.

[51] Carvalho PM, Felício MR, Santos NC, Gonçalves S, Domingues MM. Application of light scattering techniques to nanoparticle characterization and development. Front Chem 2018;6:237.

[52] Sarmento B, Martins S, Ferreira D, Souto EB. Oral insulin delivery by means of solid lipid nanoparticles. Int J Nanomed 2007;2(4):743.

[53] Gulati N, Gupta H. Parenteral drug delivery: a review. Recent Pat Drug Deliv Formul 2011;5(2):133−45.

[54] Bhagwat GS, et al. Formulation and development of transferrin targeted solid lipid nanoparticles for breast cancer therapy. Front Pharmacol 2020;11:614290.

[55] Patel R, Patel KP. Advances in novel parentral drug delivery systems. Asian J Pharm 2010;4(3).

[56] Deshpande A, Mohamed M, Daftardar SB, Patel M, Boddu SHS, Nesamony J. Solid lipid nanoparticles in drug delivery: opportunities and challenges. Emerging nanotechnologies for diagnostics, drug delivery and medical devices. Elsevier; 2017. p. 291−330.

[57] Weber S, Zimmer A, Pardeike J. Solid lipid nanoparticles (SLN) and nanostructured lipid carriers (NLC) for pulmonary application: a review of the state of the art. Eur J Pharm Biopharm 2014;86(1):7−22.

[58] Badilli U, Gumustas M, Uslu B, Ozkan SA. Lipid-based nanoparticles for dermal drug delivery. Organic materials as smart nanocarriers for drug delivery. Elsevier; 2018. p. 369—413.

[59] Chattopadhyay N, Zastre J, Wong H-L, Wu XY, Bendayan R. Solid lipid nanoparticles enhance the delivery of the HIV protease inhibitor, atazanavir, by a human brain endothelial cell line. Pharm Res 2008;25(10):2262—71.

[60] Newton, AM J, & Kaur, S. Solid lipid nanoparticles for skin and drug delivery. Nanoarchitectonics biomedicine, Elsevier, 295—334, 2019. doi:10.1016/b978-0-12-816200-2.00015-3

[61] Lu QZ, Yu A, Xi Y, Li H, Song Z, Cui J, et al. Development and evaluation of penciclovir-loaded solid lipid nanoparticles for topical delivery. Int J Pharm 2009;372:191—8.

[62] Paliwal R, Rai S, Vaidya B, Khatri K, Goyal AK, Mishra N, et al. Effect of lipid core material on characteristics of solid lipid nanoparticles designed for oral lymphatic delivery. Nanomed Nanotechnol Biol Med 2009;5(2):184—91.

[63] Inkoom A, Ndemazie N, Smith T, Frimpong E, Bulusu R, Poku R, et al. Application of modified GEMcitabine-loaded solid lipid nanoparticle in the treatment of pancreatic cancer patient-derived xenograft model. Preprint: Research Square, 2022.

[64] Affram KO, Smith T, Ofori E, Krishnan S, Underwood P, Trevino JG, et al. Cytotoxic effects of gemcitabine-loaded solid lipid nanoparticles in pancreatic cancer cells. J Drug Deliv Sci Technol 2020;55:101374. Available from: https://doi.org/10.1016/j.jddst.2019.101374.

[65] Ganesan P, Narayanasamy D. Lipid nanoparticles: different preparation techniques, characterization, hurdles, and strategies for the production of solid lipid nanoparticles and nanostructured lipid carriers for oral drug delivery. Sustain Chem Pharm 2017;6:37—56.

[66] Kalaycioglu GD, Aydogan N. Preparation and investigation of solid lipid nanoparticles for drug delivery. Colloids Surf A: Physicochem Eng Asp 2016;510:77—86.

[67] Wonganan P, Lansakara PD, Zhu S, Holzer M, Sandoval MA, Warthaka M, et al. Just getting into cells is not enough: mechanisms underlying 4-(N)-stearoyl gemcitabine solid lipid nanoparticle's ability to overcome gemcitabine resistance caused by RRM1 overexpression. J Control Release 2013;169:17—27. Available from: https://doi.org/10.1016/j.jconrel.2013.03.033.

[68] Bildstein L, Dubernet C, Marsaud V, Chacun H, Nicolas V, Gueutin C, et al. Transmembrane diffusion of gemcitabine by a nanoparticulate squalenoyl prodrug: an original drug delivery pathway. J Control Release 2010;147:163—70. Available from: https://doi.org/10.1016/j.jconrel.2010.07.120.

[69] Kal H, Barendsen G. Radiosensitivity of surviving cells in tumours pretreated with continuous irradiation. Br J Radiol 1973;46:1083.

[70] Graña X, Reddy EP. Cell cycle control in mammalian cells: role of cyclins, cyclin dependent kinases (CDKs), growth suppressor genes and cyclin-dependent kinase inhibitors (CKIs). Oncogene 1995;11:211—20.

[71] Kastan MB, Canman CE, Leonard CJ. P53, cell cycle control and apoptosis: implications for cancer. Cancer Metastasis Rev 1995;14:3—15.

[72] Tobita K, Kijima H, Dowaki S, Kashiwagi H, Ohtani Y, Oida Y, et al. Epidermal growth factor receptor expression in human pancreatic cancer: significance for liver metastasis. Int J Mol Med 2003;11:305—9.

[73] Bloomston M, Bhardwaj A, Ellison EC, Frankel WL. Epidermal growth factor receptor expression in pancreatic carcinoma using tissue microarray technique. Dig Surg 2006;23:74—9.

[74] Safran H, Steinhoff M, Mangray S, Rathore R, King TC, Chai L, et al. Overexpression of the HER-2/neu oncogene in pancreatic adenocarcinoma. Am J Clin Oncol 2001;24:496—9.

[75] Stoecklein NH, Luebke AM, Erbersdobler A, Knoefel WT, Schraut W, Verde PE, et al. Copy number of chromosome 17 but not HER2 amplification predicts clinical outcome of patients with pancreatic ductal adenocarcinoma. J Clin Oncol 2004;22:4737—45.

[76] Komoto M, Nakata B, Amano R, Yamada N, Yashiro M, Ohira M, et al. HER2 overexpression correlates with survival after curative resection of pancreatic cancer. Cancer Sci 2009;100:1243—7.

[77] Morgan MA, Parsels LA, Kollar LE, Normolle DP, Maybaum J, Lawrence TS. The combination of epidermal growth factor receptor inhibitors with gemcitabine and radiation in pancreatic cancer. Clin Cancer Res 2008;14:5142—9. Available from: https://doi.org/10.1158/1078-0432.CCR-07-4072.

[78] Friess H, Berberat P, Schilling M, Kunz J, Korc M, Buchler MW. Pancreatic cancer: the potential clinical relevance of alterations in growth factors and their receptors. J Mol Med (Berl) 1996;74:35–42. Available from: https://doi.org/10.1007/BF00202070.

[79] Henderson AJ, Ollila CA, Kumar A, Borresen EC, Raina K, Agarwal R, et al. Chemopreventive properties of dietary rice bran: current status and future prospects. Adv Nutr 2012;3:643e53.

[80] Zhang Y, Li Z, Zhang K, Yang G, Wang Z, Zhao J, et al. Ethyl oleate-containing nanostructured lipid carriers improve oral bioavailability of trans-ferulic acid as compared with conventional solid lipid nanoparticles. Int J Pharm 2016;511:57e6.

[81] Thakkar A, Chenreddy S, Wang J, Prabhu S. Ferulic acid combined with aspirin demonstrates chemopreventive potential towards pancreatic cancer when delivered using chitosan-coated solid-lipid nanoparticles. Cell Biosci 2015;5:46.

[82] Luo Y, Teng Z, Li Y, Wang Q. Solid lipid nanoparticles for oral drug delivery: chitosan coating improves stability, controlled delivery, mucoadhesion and cellular uptake. Carbohydr Polym 2015;122:221e9.

[83] Lin C-H, Chen C-H, Lin Z-C, Fang J-Y. Recent advances in oral delivery of drugs and bioactive natural products using solid lipid nanoparticles as the carriers. J Food Drug Anal 2017;25(2):219–34. Available from: https://doi.org/10.1016/j.jfda.2017.02.001.

[84] Sutaria D, Grandhi BK, Thakkar A, Wang J, Prabhu S. Chemoprevention of Pancreatic cancer using solid-lipid nanoparticulate delivery of a novel aspirin, curcumin and sulforaphane drug combination regimen. Int J Oncol 2012;41(6):2260–8.

[85] Fendrich V. Chemoprevention of pancreatic cancer-one step closer. Langenbecks Arch Surg 2012;397:495–505. Available from: https://doi.org/10.1007/s00423-012-0916-x22350613.

[86] Logsdon CD, Abbruzzese JL. Chemoprevention of pancreatic cancer: ready for the clinic? Cancer Prev Res (Phila) 2010;3:1375–8. Available from: https://doi.org/10.1158/1940-6207.CAPR-10-021621084259.

[87] Husain SS, Szabo IL, Tamawski AS. NSAID inhibition of GI cancer growth: clinical implications and molecular mechanisms of action. Am J Gastroenterol 2002;97:542–53. Available from: https://doi.org/10.1111/j.1572-0241.2002.05528.x11922545.

[88] Kuo ML, Huang TS, Lin JK. Curcumin, an antioxidant and anti-tumor promoter, induces apoptosis in human leukemia cells. Biochim Biophys Acta 1996;1317(2):95–100. Available from: https://doi.org/10.1016/S0925-4439(96)00032-48950193.

[89] Moragoda L, Jaszewski R, Majumdar AP. Curcumin induced modulation of cell cycle and apoptosis in gastric and colon cancer cells. Anticancer Res 2001;21(2A):873–8 11396178.

[90] Lampe JW. Sulforaphane: from chemoprevention to pancreatic cancer treatment? Gut 2009;58:900–2. Available from: https://doi.org/10.1136/gut.2008.16669419520886 58900902.

[91] Chaudhary A, Sutaria D, Huang Y, Wang J, Prabhu S. Chemoprevention of colon cancer in a rat carcinogenesis model using a novel nanotechnology-based combined treatment system. Cancer Prev Res (Phila) 2011;4:1655–64. Available from: https://doi.org/10.1158/1940-6207.CAPR-11-0129.

[92] Miglietta A, Cavalli R, Bocca C, Gabriel L, Gasco MR. Cellular uptake and cytotoxicity of solid lipid nanospheres (solid lipid nanoparticles) incorporating doxorubicin or paclitaxel. Int J Pharm 2000;2:106–67. Available from: https://doi.org/10.1016/S0378-5173(00)00562-711163988.

[93] Yan F, Zhang C, Zheng Y. The effect of poloxamer 188 on nanoparticle morphology, size, cancer cell uptake, and cytotoxicity. Nanomedicine 2010;6:170–178,. Available from: https://doi.org/10.1016/j.nano.2009.05.00419447200.

[94] Chirio D, Peira E, Dianzani C, Muntoni E, Gigliotti CL, Ferrara B, et al. Development of solid lipid nanoparticles by cold dilution of microemulsions: curcumin loading, preliminary in vitro studies, and biodistribution. Nanomaterials 2019;9(2):230.

[95] Kallifatidis G, Rausch V, Baumann B, et al. Sulforaphane targets pancreatic tumour-initiating cells by NF-kappaB-induced anti-apoptotic signalling. Gut. 2009;58:949–63.

[96] Grandhi BK, Thakkar A, Wang J, Prabhu S. A novel combinatorial nanotechnology-based oral chemopreventive regimen demonstrates significant suppression of pancreatic cancer neoplastic lesions. Cancer Prev Res 2013;6:1015–25.

[97] Chaudhary A, Sutaria D, Huang Y, Wang J, Prabhu S. Chemoprevention of colon cancer in a rat carcinogenesis model using a novel nanotechnology-based combined treatment system. Cancer Prev Res 2011;4:1655−64.

[98] Thakkar A, Sutaria D, Grandhi BK, Wang J, Prabhu S. The molecular mechanism of action of aspirin, curcumin and sulforaphane combinations in the chemoprevention of pancreatic cancer. Oncol Rep 2013;29:1671−7.

[99] Palayoor ST, Bump EA, Calderwood SK, Bartol S, Coleman CN. Combined antitumor effect of radiation and ibuprofen in human prostate carcinoma cells. Clin Cancer Res 1998;4:763−71.

[100] Yao M, Zhou W, Sangha S, et al. Effects of nonselective cyclooxygenase inhibition with low-dose ibuprofen on tumor growth, angiogenesis, metastasis, and survival in a mouse model of colorectal cancer. Clin Cancer Res 2005;11:1618−28.

[101] Bonelli P, Tuccillo FM, Federico A, et al. Ibuprofen delivered by poly(lactic-co-glycolic acid) (PLGA) nanoparticles to human gastric cancer cells exerts antiproliferative activity at very low concentrations. Int J Nanomed 2012;7:5683−91.

[102] Lanas A. A review of the gastrointestinal safety data - a gastroenterologist's perspective. Rheumatology 2010;49(Suppl 2):ii3−ii10.

[103] Mallen SR, Essex MN, Zhang R. Gastrointestinal tolerability of NSAIDs in elderly patients: a pooled analysis of 21 randomized clinical trials with celecoxib and nonselective NSAIDs. Curr Med Res Opin 2011;27:1359−66.

[104] Brigger I, Dubernet C, Couvreur P. Nanoparticles in cancer therapy and diagnosis. Adv Drug Deliv Rev 2002;54:631−51.

[105] Potta SG, Minemi S, Nukala RK, et al. Preparation and characterization of ibuprofen solid lipid nanoparticles with enhanced solubility. J Microencapsul 2011;28:74−81.

[106] Kokawa A, Kondo H, Gotoda T, et al. Increased expression of cyclooxygenase-2 in human pancreatic neoplasms and potential for chemoprevention by cyclooxygenase inhibitors. Cancer 2001;91:333−8.

[107] O'Driscoll CM. Lipid-based formulations for intestinal lymphatic delivery. Eur J Pharm Sci 2002;15:405−15.

[108] Mehnert W, Mäder K. Solid lipid nanoparticles: production, characterization and applications. Adv Drug Deliv Rev 2001;47:165−96.

[109] Matusheski NV, Juvik JA, Jeffery EH. Heating decreases epithiospecifier protein activity and increases sulforaphane formation in broccoli. Phytochemistry. 2004;65:1273−81.

[110] Fahey JW, Haristoy X, Dolan PM, et al. Sulforaphane inhibits extracellular, intracellular, and antibiotic-resistant strains of Helicobacter pylori and prevents benzo[a]pyrene-induced stomach tumors. Proc Natl Acad Sci USA 2002;99:7610−15.

[111] Kuroiwa Y, Nishikawa A, Kitamura Y, et al. Protective effects of benzyl isothiocyanate and sulforaphane but not resveratrol against initiation of pancreatic carcinogenesis in hamsters. Cancer Lett 2006;241:275−80.

[112] Chung FL, Conaway CC, Rao CV, Reddy BS. Chemoprevention of colonic aberrant crypt foci in Fischer rats by sulforaphane and phenethyl isothiocyanate. Carcinogenesis. 2000;21:2287−91.

[113] Thakkar A, Chenreddy S, Wang J, Prabhu S. Evaluation of ibuprofen loaded solid lipid nanoparticles and its combination regimens for pancreatic cancer chemoprevention. Int J Oncol 2015;46:1827−34. Available from: https://doi.org/10.3892/ijo.2015.2879.

CHAPTER 11

Solid lipid nanoparticle-based drug delivery for pancreatic cancer

Dipanjan Ghosh[1], Gouranga Dutta[2], Arindam Chatterjee[3], Abimanyu Sugumaran[4], Gopal Chakrabarti[1] and Sivakumar Manickam[5]

[1]Department of Biotechnology, Dr. B. C. Guha Centre for Genetic Engineering and Biotechnology, University of Calcutta, Kolkata, West Bengal, India
[2]Department of Pharmaceutics, SRM College of Pharmacy, SRM Institute of Science and Technology, Kattankulathur, Tamil Nadu, India
[3]Department of Pharmaceutics, College of Pharmacy, Gupta College of Technological Sciences, Asansol, West Bengal, India
[4]Department of Pharmaceutical Sciences, Assam University (A Central University), Silchar, Assam, India
[5]Petroleum and Chemical Engineering, Faculty of Engineering, Universiti Teknologi Brunei, Jalan Tungku Link Gadong, Brunei Darussalam

11.1 Introduction

Cancerous pancreatic ductal adenocarcinoma, often known as pancreatic cancer, is a fatal malignancy with a low prognosis. This cancer is the fourth major contributor to cancer-related mortality globally (accounting for 2.5% of all cancer cases) and is projected to emerge as the second most common by 2040. In the previous two decades, little progress has been made in extending life expectancy and/or reducing mortality associated with various types of pancreatic cancer. 60%−70% of pancreatic cancers originate in the pancreas, head, and neck. However, tumors may also be found in the pancreas, body, and tail [1−3]. The early stages of pancreatic cancer are symptomless. Because of bile obstruction, patients may first experience mild gastrointestinal difficulties and indigestion pain but subsequently develop symptoms such as persistent constipation, jaundice, darker urine, and chronic pancreatitis [4−6]. In most situations, the diagnosis of pancreatic cancer is discovered too late for 75%−80% of patients. Patients typically only have 1−2 years to survive after diagnosis. 90% of pancreatic tumors are late-stage metastatic liver tumors that spread to adjacent organs, resulting in several additional difficulties. Early screening with CT and MRI has proven challenging as they generally cannot identify precancerous pancreatic intraductal malignant transformation ulcers tinier than 5−8 mm. This is the phase where many cancerous cells are in a progressive state of growth [1,3,7]. It is conceivable that activating pancreatic stellate cells is the first step in developing pancreatic cancer. This ultimately results in fibrosis formation, followed by chronic pancreatitis, frequently a precursor to pancreatic carcinoma. The activation of the pancreatic stellate cells may be avoided, and the cytokines might instead

Recent Advances in Nanocarriers for Pancreatic Cancer Therapy
DOI: https://doi.org/10.1016/B978-0-443-19142-8.00005-X

travel straight to the oncogenic KRAS cells, where they would aggressively stimulate cancer growth [7,8].

The current treatment methods, such as chemotherapy, radiation therapy, and surgical resection, are prevalent in other forms of cancer. The treatment success is based on the course of the disease as well as an individual's general condition at the time of diagnosis. Chemotherapy has been considered the gold-standard treatment for pancreatic cancer for many decades. However, they have substantial limitations, such as difficulty in effectively and promptly penetrating through stromal barriers in pancreatic stellate cells. In conjunction with chemotherapy medicines, radiation treatments are also employed to diagnose and treat pancreatic cancer.

Similarly, surgical excision for pancreatic cancer is another widely used and traditional first therapy strategy. In most instances, however, systemic metastases develop shortly after resection, compromising the hepatic and gastric systems and causing several additional problems [6,8,9]. Other additional challenges include pancreatic fibroblastic cells and fibrous stroma, which are significant barriers to the biodistribution of conventional chemotherapeutic drugs used to treat pancreatic cancers. Pancreatic stellate cells contribute to forming a highly thick and impenetrable barrier, hindering the ability of CT and MRI to identify tumor development and staging. In addition to dysregulating bile secretion, blood glucose levels, hormonal functions, and thrombosis, the tumor's growth in the pancreas diminishes the organ's function over time [6,9,10]. These limitations indicate the need for innovative ways that provide early diagnosis and noninvasive treatment of pancreatic cancer. Therefore nanotechnology is the most effective method for addressing this concern.

Nanotechnology may provide great possibilities for comprehending and treating the intricacies of pancreatic cancer. Several nanoscale structures/formulations (10−1000 nm particle size) are generated for the administration of different therapeutic agents, including polymeric nanoparticles, lipid-based nanoparticles, carbon-based nanoparticles, metal nanoparticles, nanomicelles, and nanoemulsions. These nanostructured materials may readily infiltrate the microtumor environment and release regulated amounts of chemotherapeutic medicines and imaging probes. In addition, several nanoparticles exhibit bioimaging features relevant to the theranostic activity of pancreatic cancer. These nanoparticles may be customized with various active targeting agents, drugs, and biological components to obtain a more effective cancer therapy.

Among the many nanoparticles, lipid-based nanoparticles, especially solid lipid-based nanoparticles (SLNs), are the most effective drug-delivery vehicles for many diseases. SLNs were initially found and developed utilizing biodegradable lipids in the early 1990s. It has been shown that SLNs possess numerous qualities, making them excellent nanocarriers for various hydrophobic and hydrophilic therapeutic agents. SLNs are a stable mixture of solid and liquid lipids in water stabilized by a surfactant [11,12]. Nanocarrier systems such as SLNs have been intensively explored for cancer therapies and be effective. This chapter demonstrates the application of SLNs in pancreatic cancer as drug delivery nanocarriers and the current clinical status. Also, a brief discussion on the methods of SLN preparation and their advantages over cancer treatment is presented.

11.2 Lipid classifications for solid–lipid nanoparticle synthesis

Lipid nanoparticles (LNPs) are lipid droplets suspended in an aqueous solution. Surfactants stabilize the LNPs in the aqueous solution. Generally, lipids or oils are immiscible in water. Surfactants act as a barrier to stabilize the lipid and prevent unwanted coalescence [13]. SLNs are synthesized using many lipids, including cationic, anionic, neutral, and ionizable lipids. In general, three categorized lipids are used for the preparation of LNPs; such as cationic lipid, anionic lipid, and neutral lipid. The integrated differences rely on their structures. Cationic lipids have a positively charged head group; similarly, anionic lipids have negatively charged polar head groups. Examples of ionizable cationic lipids are DOTMA (1,2-di-O-octadecenyl-3-trimethyl-lammonium propane), DODAP (1,2-Dioleoyl-3-trimethylammonium propane), DLin-KC2-DMA, and DLin-MC3-DMA [14–17]. Besides, they are also pH-responsive, highly functional, or potent lipids for in vivo transfection. Researchers utilize different kinds of lipids for different purposes.

For instance, cationic lipids are specially used for biomolecule (gene, DNA, RNA, and peptides) delivery. The details of the lipid category are described in Table 11.1. Generally, biomolecules, such as proteins, DNA, RNA, and genes, are negatively charged, and they can readily be packed with the cationic charged lipids, forming a protein-lipid complex. The conjugates are called lipoplex [18,19]. Similarly, neutral lipids and ionizable lipids are also used for drug delivery. All lipids must be biocompatible and biodegradable, implying they are nontoxic and do not produce toxic metabolites in the hepatic circulation. Due to their low removal rate and high tolerance, cationic lipids are positively charged at low pH but stay mostly unchanged at blood pH [20]. The ability to use LNPs in clinical settings was greatly improved by adjusting the ionizable cationic lipid structure and acid dissociation constant. Dioleoylphosphatidylcholine (DOPE) and 1,2-Dioleoyl-sn-glycero-3-phosphocholine (DOPC) [21] are two of the most often utilized neutral lipids for the fabrication of SLNs, which are employed chiefly for gene delivery using DOPE instead of DOPC as the helper lipid increases transfection efficiency. This is because DOPE at low pH induces a conformational change to an inverted hexagonal packing shape [22]. In contrast to lamellar packing, the inverted hexagonal packing structure resembles a honeycomb of tubular structures that condense DNA within the tubes by electrostatic interactions. Additional lipids are anionic lipids, which are only occasionally used to produce LNPs. This is because anionic lipids have a repellant electrostatic interaction with the phosphate backbone of DNA and the ionic head group of lipids, preventing DNA from being compressed.

Table 11.1 Some of the lipids used for the synthesis of LNPs (lipid nanoparticles) from PubChem Database (https://pubchem.ncbi.nlm.nih.gov/).

Lipid category	Lipid	Description	Molecular formula	Topological surface area ($Å^2$)	Molecular weight (gm/mol)	XLogP3-AA
Cationic lipid	D-Lin-MC3-DMA	It is an effective carrier for the transport of siRNA, an ionizable cationic lipid	$C_{43}H_{79}NO_2$	29.5	642.1	16
	ALC-0315	A lipid aids in the cellular delivery and release of mRNA from endosomes by ionizable amino acid destabilization. ALC-0315 may be employed to generate LNP delivery vehicles	$C_{48}H_{95}NO_5$	76.1	766.3	17.3
	DOTAP chloride	It does not need to use an intermediary fat such as a helper lipid; DOTAP chloride is a very efficient and beneficial transfection lipid for DNA (plasmids and bacmids) and modified nucleic acids (antisense oligonucleotides)	$C_{42}H_{80}ClNO_4$	52.6	698.5	–
	DLin-KC2-DMA	To distribute siRNA, the siRNA delivery method of choice is DLin-KC2-DMA	$C_{43}H_{79}NO_2$	21.7	642.1	15.7
	SM-102	LNPs can be formed using SM-102, an ionizable amino acid lipid. LNPs based on SM-102 might be used to deliver mRNA-based vaccinations	$C_{44}H_{87}NO_5$	76.1	710.2	15.5
	CKK-E12	LNPs utilized to deliver RNA-based therapies include the ionizable lipid CKK-E12 and other lipids. Liver parenchymal cells were a primary target of cKK-E12 in vivo	$C_{60}H_{120}N_4O_6$	146	993.6	18.7

Name	Description	Molecular formula			
Vaxfectin	It is a cationic lipid-based adjuvant compatible with plasmid DNA and protein-based vaccinations	$C_{81}H_{163}BrN_3O_{10}P$	179	1450.1	—
DLinDMA	DLinDMA, an ionizable cationic lipid, is a crucial component of stable nucleic acid-lipid particles (SNALPs). DLinDMA is used to deliver siRNA	$C_{41}H_{77}NO_2$	21.7	616.1	14.5
DODAP	The cationic lipid is DODAP. The ionotropic lipid DODAP is a lipid present in SLNs	$C_{41}H_{77}NO_4$	55.8	648.1	15.1
DOTMA	As a tetra-methylated DOTA analog, DOTMA is a cationic lipid that may be employed as a nonviral gene therapy vector. It has been used as a component of liposomes that may be used to encapsulate siRNA, microRNAs, and oligonucleotides, as well as for in vitro gene transfection. Gene transfection is efficient in in vitro and in vivo. DOTMA creates a positive charge on liposomes, facilitating their contact with the cell membrane	$C_{42}H_{84}ClNO_2$	18.5	670.6	—
L319	L319 is an ionizable cationic lipid used to synthesize liposomes and deliver short interfering RNAs (siRNAs)	$C_{41}H_{75}NO_6$	82.1	678	12.5
Fluorescent DOTAP	The cationic lipid fluorescent DOTAP may be used to study nucleic acid and protein transport	$C_{36}H_{60}ClN_5O_7$	149	710.3	—

(Continued)

Table 11.1 (Continued)

Lipid category	Lipid	Description	Molecular formula	Topological surface area ($Å^2$)	Molecular weight (gm/mol)	XLogP3-AA
	L343	L343 is an ionizable cationic lipid that may be included in synthetic liposomes for the systemic administration of RNAi-based therapies	$C_{51}H_{95}NO_6$	82.1	818.3	16.5
	C13–112-tetra-tail	C13–112-tetra-tail is a cationic lipid-like molecule with four hydrophobic carbon-13 tails and a PEG2 linker. C13–112-tetra-tail could be formed into LNPs	$C_{58}H_{120}N_2O_6$	106	941.6	19.9
	MVL5	MVL5 is a nondegradable multivalent cationic lipid. MVL5 is a very effective DNA and siRNA vector.	$C_{59}H_{116}Cl_5N_7O_4$	170	1164.9	–
	DOSPA	IUPAC name of the lipid is 2-[3-[4-(3-aminopropylamino) butylamino] propylcarbamoylamino]ethyl-[2,3-bis[[(Z)-octadec-9-enoyl] oxy]propyl]–dimethylazanium. The cationic lipid is DOSPA. DOSPA DNA formulation is an upcoming transfection technique	$C_{54}H_{107}N_6O_5 +$	144	920.5	13.9
	ZA3–Ep10	It is a zwitterionic lipid that generates LNPs for in vivo RNA administration and nonviral CRISPR/Cas gene editing	$C_{66}H_{138}N_6O_9S$	209	1191.9	13.3

Transfectam	It is a cationic lipid capable of interacting with DNA to generate complexes to facilitate the effective transfer of genes into diverse eukaryotic cells	$C_{49}H_{102}N_6O_2$	126	807.4	15.8
7-Oxotridecanedioic acid	It is a cationic lipid intermediate for synthesizing biodegradable LNPs. It is possible to insert 7-oxotridecanedioic acid into lipid particles to deliver active drugs	$C_{13}H_{22}O_5$	91.7	258.31	1.3
18:0 DAP	18:0 DAP may generate LNPs that incorporate mRNA inside their core	$C_{41}H_{81}NO_4$	55.8	652.1	16.9
503O13	503O13 is an ionizable, biodegradable lipid for siRNA delivery	$C_{73}H_{144}N_4O_8$	118	1205.9	24.5
DOBAQ	DOBAQ, a cationic lipid, is a pH-sensitive lipid. DOBAQ may be used for drug delivery of liposomes	$C_{49}H_{83}NO_6$	92.7	782.2	16.7
98N12−5	The new multitail ionizable lipid 98N12−5 efficiently transported siRNA to the liver and pancreas in vivo	$C_{81}H_{163}N_9O_5$	167	1343.2	24.1
18:0 EPC chloride (2-(((R)-2,3-Bis (stearoyloxy)propoxy) (ethoxy)phosphoryl) oxy)-N,N,N-trimethylethana-minium chloride)	Cationic phospholipid 18:0 EPC chloride is synthetic	$C_{46}H_{93}ClNO_8P$	97.4	854.7	–
14:0 DAP	14:0 Drug distribution may be made easier with DAP (1,2-dimyristoyl-3-dimethylammonium-propane)	$C_{33}H_{65}NO_4$	55.8	539.9	12.6

(Continued)

Table 11.1 (Continued)

Lipid category	Lipid	Description	Molecular formula	Topological surface area (Å^2)	Molecular weight (gm/mol)	XLogP3-AA
Neutral lipid	DOPE (D-serine 1,2-dioleoyl-3-phosphoglycero-3 (sodium salt))	As a replacement for brain PS, DOPS is a good option. It is more resistant to oxidation and has many of the same physical features as the original. For coagulation experiments, lipid mixes, including DOPS, DOPC, and DOPE, have been employed to simulate platelet membranes	$C_{41}H_{78}NO_8P$	134	744	10.6
	DOPC	1,2-Dioleoyl-sn-Glycero-3-Phosphocholine	$C_{44}H_{84}NO_8P$	111	786.1	13.8
Anionic lipid	DSPA	1,2-Distearoyl-sn-glycero-3-phosphate, sodium salt (DSPA) is a form of phosphatidic acid (PA), a major component of cell membranes	$C_{39}H_{76}NaO_8P$	122	727	–
	DMPG	1,2-dimyristoyl-sn-glycero-3-phospho-(1'-rac-glycerol)	$C_{34}H_{67}O_{10}P$	149	666.9	10

11.3 Preparations techniques of solid lipid-based nanoparticles

SLNs may be prepared using lipids, surfactants/emulsifiers, and solvents in a dispersion system. The particle size may range between 10 and 1000 nm, depending on the technique. These methods might be classified as "high energy," "low energy," or "solvent-based." The high-energy techniques include high-pressure homogenization, ultrasonication, microwaves, and supercritical fluids. Low-energy techniques include microemulsion, double emulsion, and phase inversion [12,23]. High shear forces are required to decrease the particle size in high-energy methods. In contrast, low shear forces are sufficient to reduce particle size independently in low-energy techniques.

11.3.1 High-pressure homogenization

High-pressure homogenization is the safest method for producing SLNs. SLNs are generated using melt emulsification. In high-pressure homogenization, the liquid is forced at high pressure (100−2000 bar) through a few microns of space of piston-gap homogenizer. In this approach, the fluid travels rapidly over a limited distance. Even the high lipid content is turned into nanodispersion with homogenization. The process of hot and cold homogenization may be used to generate SLNs [23].

11.3.1.1 Hot homogenization

Hot homogenization is one form of the high-pressure processes used in producing SLNs. Generally, in this technique, the process temperature must be greater than the melting point of the lipid, and it must thus be regarded as emulsion homogenization. The high-shear mixing equipment is employed to obtain the pre-emulsion (O/W type emulsion). After generating pre-emulsion, the product is cooled to develop lipid crystals and SLNs. 3−5 homogenization cycles are required to produce emulsions, and the pressure must be kept between 500 and 1000 bar. In high-pressure homogenization, the growth of particle sizes depends on the increase in temperature or the rise in the number of cycles or the pressure. The nanoemulsion is eventually cooled to ambient temperature. Following this, lipids recrystallize, resulting in the production of SLNs [11,24,25].

11.3.1.2 Cold homogenization

Cold homogenization is a high-pressure process used in producing SLNs. This method is designed to replace hot homogenization, such as accelerated degradation owing to elevated temperature and drug degradation through homogenization into the aqueous medium. The most crucial step is compared to hot homogenization; the drug-containing liquid is often frozen with liquid nitrogen or solid carbon dioxide to ensure the drug is spread out evenly in the lipid matrix. Ball mill was then primarily used for crushing materials into fine dust particles. The diameters of the collected dust particles vary from 50 to 100 μm. The small fragments were then spread with a cold aqueous surfactant. The dispersion was homogenized under high pressure to increase the production of SLNs. Despite this, cold homogenization products often have larger particle sizes and a broader size distribution than hot homogenization products. In reality, the cold homogenization procedure reduces heat exposure [11,12].

11.3.2 Ultrasonication

Ultrasonication, or high-velocity stirring, is the most practical method for producing SLNs by high share energy. The lipid-containing dispersed emulsion is subsequently subjected to ultrasonic energy directly. Most droplet sizes decrease in the emulsion due to acoustic cavitation. The more extensive particle size distribution hinders utilizing this ultrasonication approach, and the larger particle size is maintained in the micrometer range, which is the primary reason for physical instability. Numerous investigations and significant research have proved that ultrasonication and high-speed stirring in conjunction with high temperatures provide a stable formulation [12,26,27].

11.3.3 Coacervation

Recently, a novel approach for the regulated preparation of SLNs via coacervation has been established. This approach's antecedent for SLNs preparation is a soap micellar solution prepared at a temperature above the Krafft point. To manufacture the micellar solution, the salt of fatty acid and the stabilizing agent is chosen as the surface-active nonionic polymers. This method permits pharmaceutical integration without the need for highly sophisticated equipment or hazardous chemicals and is consequently affordable for industrial and laboratory use. The drug may be mixed directly in the micellar system or with a small quantity of ethanol to facilitate micellization. As with microemulsion templates, the solubilizing capabilities of micellar solutions allow them to load many pharmaceuticals into SLNs, particularly poorly soluble compounds. The ability to adjust the size of SLNs by altering the reaction conditions is critical to this approach. The correct coupling between the alkaline salt of the fatty acid and the correct coacervating solution is essential for producing a stable and homogenous nanoparticle suspension [23,28,29].

11.3.4 Solvent emulsification evaporation

Evaporation of a solvent is a popular method for producing SLNs. In this process, hydrophobic drugs and lipophilic compounds are liquefied in the organic phase and are composed of a volatile or partially water-miscible solvent. With homogenization at high speed, the mixture is emulsified into O/W or W/O/W emulsions. Immediately, the coarse emulsion is allowed to run through a microfluidizer to reduce the particle size. When the solvent is evaporated by evaporation using a rotary evaporator, nanoparticles are produced. The primary capability of this method is to withstand thermal stress. Consequently, there are possibilities to introduce the thermolabile drug. The most problematic aspect of this technique is its reliance on organic solvents, which might react with drug molecules [23,30,31].

11.3.5 Microemulsions

Microemulsions are transparent, thermodynamically controlled, isotropic liquid combinations of oil, water, and surfactant, usually accompanied by a cosurfactant. SLNs were prepared to lower the microemulsion concentration. The solid lipid is melted over its melting point to form the oil phase. SLNs may be produced by combining hot microemulsion with cold water (microemulsion dilution method) or by cooling the hot microemulsion on its own (microemulsion cooling technique). An amount of water 10−200 times more than the microemulsion volume may be used to dilute the microemulsions. Using this method, it is possible to administer weakly water-soluble drugs through SLNs [23,32].

11.4 Role of pancreatic lipase and lipid nanoparticle in pancreatic cancer therapy

One of the most characteristic features of pancreatic cancer is the fibrotic stroma, accounting for up to 80% of the tumor mass. Increased stromal material has been associated with poor survival in human pancreatic cancer patients. This desmoplastic reaction compresses and distorts tumor blood vessels by creating an extraordinarily dense network of extracellular matrix proteins around tumor components [33,34]. The abnormal vasculature in pancreatic cancer tumors also promotes chemoresistance, another benefit of hypoxia. Numerous scientific evidences established that in a healthy pancreas, pancreatic stellate cells (PSCs), which are quiescent but become active when a cross-talk mechanism enhances the aggressiveness of pancreatic cancer, are attracted to cancer cells. This severe fibrosis is the result of the activity of PSCs. Because of this, pancreatic stellate cells are becoming recognized as attractive therapeutic targets for reprogramming fibrosis and inhibiting cancer cells' bidirectional pro-tumorigenic signaling in pancreatic cancer. Consequently, future pancreatic cancer therapies must focus on the tumor and surrounding tissue as a new target [35−37]. Generally, the pancreas plays two major roles in human bodies; the exocrine function that produces substances (enzymes) assisting digestion and the endocrine function that sends out hormones to control the amount of sugar in the bloodstream. Pancreatic lipase (PNLIP) is usually secreted by the pancreas and transferred to the duodenum to participate in the hydrolysis and digestion of fat, cholesterol esters, and fat-soluble vitamins [38].

PNLIP is the super-family of the enzyme that helps to digest or metabolize the absorbing fat. Surprisingly, it has been shown that PNLIP is overexpressed in pancreatic cancer. As evidenced, Sanh et al. showed that various kinds of proteins (such as proteins identified included "transferrin, ER-60 protein, pro-apolipoprotein, tropomyosin 1, alpha 1 actin precursor, ACTB protein, gamma 2 propeptide, aldehyde dehydrogenase 1A1 (ALDH1A1), PNLIP and annexin A1)" were overexpressed in pancreatic cancer tissue samples, which were identified and evaluated by MALDI-TOF mass spectrometry [39,40]. As per genetic diversity, PNLIP is generally categorized into three different genes such as "PNLIP-related protein 1 (PNLIPRP1), PNLIP-related protein 2 (PNLIPRP2) and PNLIP-related protein 3 (PNLIPRP3)". The NCBI gene database retrieved these four genes (human) genetic sequences. A phylogenic tree was constructed by MUSCLE alignment, including with MEGA, to investigate the structural diversity of the genes. Besides, the structural diversity of the gene was investigated to identify the homologous and nonhomologous parts of the genes by BRIG (Blast ring image generator), including with the NBLAST algorithm [41,42]. Fig. 11.1A illustrates the phylogenic tree where the genetic diversity is shown. Fig. 11.1B describes the circular genome comparison of the lipolytic pancreatic genes (PNLIP, PNLIPPR1, PNLIPPR2, and PNLIPPR3). The PNLIP gene was the control or reference gene (Fig. 11.1B). The homologous region is plotted into the circular map by which the genome part could be identified precisely. Pancreatic lipase-related protein 1 (PNLIPPR1), pancreatic lipase-related protein 2 (PNLIPPR2), and pancreatic lipase-related protein 3 (PNLIPPR3) genes are referred to as different color ballots. Similarly, the label is shown in a different color in the outer layer of the circular genome map. Also, GC content and skewness of the reference gene (PNLIP) are shown on the circular map. There were 14 numbers of conserved locations identified and the similarity % was also denoted in the circular genome comparison map (Fig. 11.1B). These genes are responsible for lipoidal degradation in the pancreatic cell. Lipids in nanosized droplets (LNPs) are also broken down by these pancreatic lipase gene-encoded proteins. Multiple experimental findings confirmed the temporal pattern of PNLIPRP2 mRNA expression, suggesting that PNLIPRP2 likely plays an important role in the metabolism of milk lipids in lactating mammals [43].

The duodenum has several different lipases, including the conventional pancreatic triglyceride lipase (PTL), PLRP1 and 2, respectively, bile salt-induced lipase (BSSL), and pancreatic phospholipase A2. PLRP1 and PLRP2 have 68% and 66% amino acid sequence identity with PTL, respectively. Studies have demonstrated that the length of PNLIPRP2 mRNA in humans, rats, and mice is 1500 base pairs, and the protein produced by this mRNA has a molecular weight of 53 kilodaltons. PNLIPRP2 lipase possesses two distinct domains: an N-terminal domain spanning residues 18−353 and a C-terminal domain spanning residues 354−466. The N-terminal domain adopts an α/β hydrolase fold, while the C-terminal domain exhibits a β-sandwich structure [44,45]. The length of the peptide can be either 16 or 30 amino acids. In mice and rats, the signal peptide consists of 30 amino acids, while in humans and coypu, it is only 16 amino acids long. However, the human and coypu cDNAs have a shorter 5' sequence compared to the cDNAs obtained from mice or rats [46].

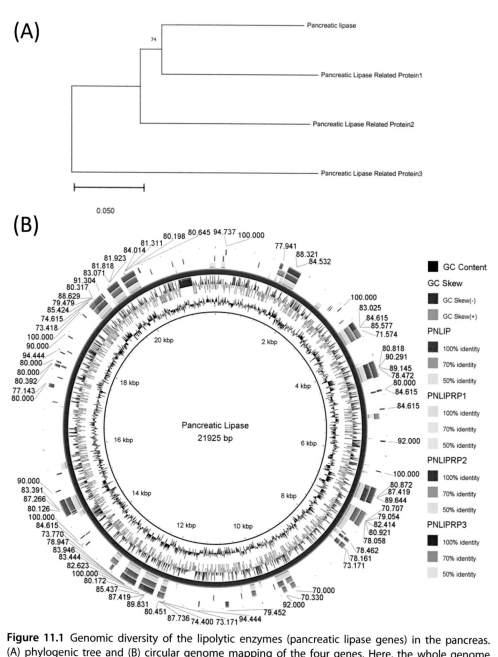

Figure 11.1 Genomic diversity of the lipolytic enzymes (pancreatic lipase genes) in the pancreas. (A) phylogenic tree and (B) circular genome mapping of the four genes. Here, the whole genome sequences of the four genes have been considered for comparison. There are seven rings, and the different genes are considered different colors. The homologous region is mapped in the circle. The first circle is considered the GC content, and the second and third circles are considered GC (+) and GC (−) skewness. Simultaneously, the fourth circle is the PNLIP gene, considered the reference gene. The fifth, sixth, and seventh circles are PNLIPPR1, PNLIPPR2, and PNLIPPR3, respectively. *PNLIP*, pancreatic lipase.

PLRP2 is expressed in lymphocytes and colonic epithelial cells, suggesting that it may have a role in the inflammatory response as well as in the regulation of the intestinal flora [45,47,48]. Some animals, including humans, may release bile salt stimulated lipase (BSSL) during lactation from the mammary gland, which can then be given to children via milk to aid with fat digestion and absorption in the early stages of life. It is possible that BSSL plays a function in inflammation, arteriosclerosis, and other conditions because it is expressed in a variety of organs, including the liver, inflammatory cells, endothelial cells, and platelets [49,50]. These key pancreatic lipases digest lipids such as triglycerides, cholesterol, and phosphatidylcholine, so dietary fats are entirely used. Therefore, LNPs have many advantages as a delivery system. The pancreatic cells avidly uptake the nanoparticle made by lipids and try to metabolize them. This could help to release the encapsulating or loading molecules (anticancer drugs and different biomolecules, such as siRNA, mRNA, peptide, and DNA) into the cytomatrix. Notably, it has been shown that the drug-loaded LNPs have more potent anticancer efficacy against pancreatic cancer. Gemcitabine-loaded LNPs were more potent and effective against pancreatic cancer. The Pancreatic cancer cell line PPCL-46 cells and Mia–PaCa-2 cells were used as in-vitro anti-cancer model. They validated the results in 2D and 3D cell cultures. As a result, for the PPCL-46 cell line, the IC50 value of gemcitabine-loaded LNPs was $27 \pm 5\,\mu M$; whereas free gemcitabine molecules exhibited $126 \pm 3\,\mu M$ in 2D cell culture. In contrast, for Mia PaCa-2 culture, the value of gemcitabine-loaded LNPs was $56 \pm 16\,\mu M$; whereas for free gemcitabine molecule, it was $188 \pm 46\,\mu M$. This data imply that LNPs have more power to destroy cancer cells than bare anticancer drug molecules [51].

11.5 Enhancing cancer therapeutic efficacy with lipid-based nanoparticles

Nanotechnology plays a key role in targeted chemotherapy. Evidence suggests that nanotechnology is beneficial for targeted drug delivery against cancer. Dose reductants and targeted phenomenon are the two essential distinct advantages of using nanotechnology; also able to overcome drug resistance. In contrast, the tumor vasculatures are leaky, irregular, abrupt, and have a rough microenvironment. Consequently, the cancer cells collect nutrients from blood circulation through this leaky vasculature. Thus, nanoparticles can readily reach the tumor site and penetrate through the leaky vasculature of the blood capillaries of the tumor site. This magical phenomenon is known as the "EPR effect" (Enhanced Permeation and Retention effect). This is a passive targeting strategy by which the evil effect of cancer can be removed.

In Addition, LNPs can be useful for high-loading hydrophobic anticancer drugs and efficiently deliver them into the cancer cells. Many lipids have been developed to deliver chemotherapeutic drug molecules into cancer cells. Generally, hydrophobic drug molecules are employed to encapsulate for delivery into the cancer cells using lipids as the matrix. The drug molecules are dispersed into the lipid matrix. Cancer cells preferentially uptake lipids for uncontrolled growth, proliferation, migration, and invasion. This phenomenon is known as "lipophagy" [52,53]. However, several drug molecules are available for pancreatic cancer. The US-FDA-approved anticancer drugs for pancreatic cancer are capecitabine, 5-Fluorouracil, gemcitabine, irinotecan, leucovorin, nab-paclitaxel, and oxaliplatin [54]. These drugs are transported through a lipid-based nanosystem as carrier to the pancreas and exhibit anticancer activity, and some related studies have been described for better understanding at the below sections.

11.5.1 Gemcitabine

Gemcitabine, an anticancer drug, is the first-line therapy for pancreatic adenocarcinoma in advanced nonresectable Stage II or III and metastatic Stage IV, and the adult dose of gemcitabine is 200 mg/single vial dose and 1 gm/single vial dose. Gemcitabine diphosphate and gemcitabine triphosphate are the essential metabolites in cancer cells [55]. Two forms of gemcitabine inhibit DNA synthesis: gemcitabine diphosphate (dFdCTP) and gemcitabine triphosphate (dFdCTP). The most likely method by which gemcitabine kills cancer cells is by integrating dFdCTP into DNA. Much research shows that gemcitabine LNPs are more effective than free gemcitabine for targeted delivery. Affram et al. developed gemcitabine encapsulated SLNs for targeted anticancer therapy against patient-derived primary pancreatic cancer cell lines (PPCL-46) and Mia PaCa-2. The authors used glyceryl monostearate as a lipid base, polysorbate 80 (Tween® 80), and poloxamer 188 (Pol 188) as surfactants. The optimized resultant lipid nanoparticles' size, polydispersity index (PDI), and zeta-potential were 603 ± 19 nm, 0.266 ± 0.07, and -24.9 ± 0.2 mV, respectively. The results indicated that gemcitabine-loaded LNPs were ~ 4.6-fold more potent than free-gemcitabine as a drug molecule. They denoted that the IC_{50} value of free gemcitabine against PPCL-46 cells was 126 ± 3 μM, whereas, for gemcitabine-loaded LNPs, it was 27 ± 5 μM. Besides, the IC_{50} value of free gemcitabine and gemcitabine-loaded LNPs against the Mia PaCa-2 cell line were 188 ± 46 and 56 ± 16 μM, respectively. The study suggests that the lipid nanocarrier-mediated gemcitabine shows more potential efficacy than only free gemcitabine [51]. Similarly, the lipid-modified prodrug is another approach to improving the bioavailability of gemcitabine. Bulanadi et al. recently developed novel amphiphilic lipid prodrug nanoparticles against human pancreatic cancer cell lines: CFPAC-1, BxPC3, and MiaPaCa-2 [56]. At first, they individually developed three separate amphiphilic lipid-prodrugs (Gem-Oleyl, Gem-linoleyl, and Gem-phytanyl) with gemcitabine. XRD study revealed that Gem-phytanyl, the lipid prodrug exhibited only an amorphous peak (lattice parameter:

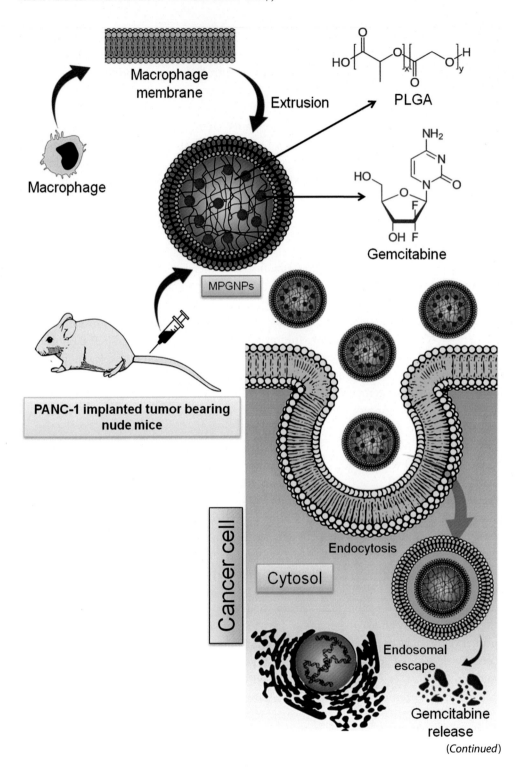

Macrophage membrane

Extrusion

PLGA

Gemcitabine

Macrophage

MPGNPs

PANC-1 implanted tumor bearing nude mice

Cancer cell

Endocytosis

Cytosol

Endosomal escape

Gemcitabine release

(Continued)

39.0 ± 0.5 Å), representing a rather disordered phase, which transformed into a cubic mesophase with an Ia3d space group at hydration with excess water. Then, they developed LNPs using 1,2-dimyristoyl-sn-glycero-3-phosphocholine (DMPC), cholesterol, and Gem-phytanyl ester prodrug.

Gemcitabine is also used in combination therapy, but gemcitabine and erlotinib in combination therapy showed unsatisfied activity with more toxicity. Cai et al. established a novel advanced delivery system. Furthermore, toxicity can be alleviated by surface decorating with the lipid membrane of macrophages and encapsulating gemcitabine into polylactic-co-glycolic acid (PLGA) nanoparticles [57]. It has been shown that it is possible to hide the nanoparticles from the immune system by covering them with macrophage membranes. The macrophage lipid membrane is used to encapsulate the PLGA-gemcitabine NPs to reduce the unwanted toxicity in the systemic circulation with increasing tumor accumulation against pancreatic cancer. The schematic of this strategy is represented in Fig. 11.2. The particle size of the drug-loaded PLGA nanoparticles was ~ 179 nm, whereas macrophage membrane-coated PLGA nanoparticles were 192 nm. Notably, the deviation of surface charge also signifies that the nanoparticles were successfully macrophage coated. Also, the antiproliferative effects on pancreatic cancer cells in vitro and in vivo were achieved using the combination of macrophage membrane-coated PLGA nanoparticles and erlotinib. Consequently, the macrophage membrane-coated gemcitabine-loaded PLGA nanoparticles might potentially target pancreatic tumors passively. However, when macrophage membrane-coated PLGA-drug nanoparticles were combined with erlotinib, they showed synergistic antitumor action.

11.5.2 Paclitaxel

Paclitaxel is another anticancer drug that can inhibit cancer growth by depolymerizing microtubules during cell division. The paclitaxel and gemcitabine combination therapy is also used against pancreatic cancer [58]. Meng et al. developed a PEGylated core-shell nanoparticle as the codelivery system of both paclitaxel and gemcitabine, targeted anticancer therapy against pancreatic cancer. The core-shell nanoparticle comprised gemcitabine encapsulated mesoporous silica nanoparticles as the core, while paclitaxel was dispersed into the outer lipid bi-layer (DPPC/cholesterol/DSPE-PEG) as the

◀ **Figure 11.2** Schematic representation of MPGNPs (Macrophage lipid membrane surface decorated gemcitabine-PLGA nanoparticle). It is a novel delivery system for the targeted delivery of gemcitabine using MPGNPs as a nanocarrier against pancreatic cancer. This study used macrophage's lipid-membrane to evade the immuno-interactions of gemcitabine-embedded PLGA nanoparticles. In addition, as a combination therapy, erlotinib, the inhibitor of EGFR, was administered with these synthesized nanoparticles. The authors used male BALB/c nude mice where the PANC-1 cell line (human pancreatic cell line) was xenografted. *PLGA*, polylactic-co-glycolic acid.

shell. The nanoparticles were 65–75 nm, with a 2.75 nm hexagonal hole remaining in the core section and a uniform coating of the surfaces with a 7 nm intact lipid bi-layer. Furthermore, they demonstrated that paclitaxel (2.5 wt.%) and gemcitabine (40 wt.%) were highly loaded in the nanoparticles. A tumor xenograft model was done with a PANC-1 cell line in the mouse model as an in vivo anticancer therapy. The novel nanoformulation showed significantly more synergistic anticancer properties than free drug molecules. It has been shown that the novel synthesized nanoformulation was able to shrink tumors ∼12 times more than free Abraxane. Based on the HPLC results, lipid bi-layer coated mesoporous silica nanoparticles increased the phosphorylated DNA-interactive gemcitabine metabolite 13-fold and decreased the inactivated and de-aminated metabolites fourfold compared to free gemcitabine [59]. Similarly, Wu et al. [60] synthesized tumor-specific MUC1 antibody conjugated poly-lactic glycolic acid-based nanoparticles where fluorescent agent and chemotherapeutic drug paclitaxel were encapsulated. Mucin-1 (MUC1) is a glycoprotein shown to be extensively O-linked glycosylated in its extracellular domain. It is a transmembrane glycoprotein in cellular or luminal epithelial cells of the glandular or luminal epithelial cells of the mammary glands. MUC1 is often found in the ducts of the esophagus and stomach, as well as in the pancreas and prostate [61,62]. A spacer moiety was also attached to the surface of the nanoparticles. The resultant nanoparticles could be used for bioimaging, and paclitaxel was used as the targeted anticancer therapy. The fluorescent molecules, such as fluorescein diacetate, indocyanine green, and Nile red, were used to encapsulate the nanoparticles. This study used a spacer moiety as a successful linker for surface passivation with the MUC1 antibody. The hydrodynamic diameters of the paclitaxel, fluorescein diacetate, Nile red, and indocyanine green loaded nano-particles were ∼142, ∼172, ∼205, and ∼180, respectively. The zeta potential of the paclitaxel, fluorescein diacetate, Nile red, and indocyanine green loaded nanoparticles were −7.6, −6.4, −6.7, and −6.8 mV, respectively. Cellular uptake studies were carried out with these resultant nanoparticles against MUC1 high-expressive BxPC3 cells and MUC1 low-expressive BxPC3 Neo cells. The authors claimed that after posttreatment of nanoparticles, the antibody (TAB004) functionalized nanoparticles were more retained in the MUC1 high-expressing cancer cells than free nanoparticles [60]. Recently, Yu et al. developed an albumin-bound paclitaxel-loaded lipid nanoformulation against pancreatic cancer [63]. The nanoformulation comprised a novel delivery strategy, as depicted in Fig. 11.3. They synthesized nanoparticles made by albumin-bound paclitaxel, which were further coated with PEGylated cationic lipid (DPPC, Dipalmitoyl phosphatidylcholine) as well as surface passivized by CAP peptide (AC-Ala-Thr-Lys(C18)-Asp-Ala-Thr-Gly-Pro-Ala-Lys(C18)-Thr-Ala-NH2) for recognizing FAP-α (Fibroblast Activating Protein–α). FAP-α is the biomarker in the tumor microenvironment [64,65]. The lipid–albumin nanoparticles are thermo-responsive. They studied in vivo anticancer efficacy in the animal model and used

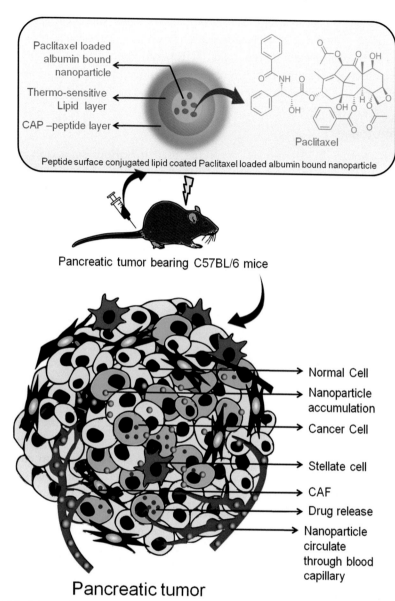

Figure 11.3 Schematic representation of the targeted delivery of paclitaxel through novel lipid nanoformulation. In this strategy, the novel nanoparticles were surface decorated by CAP-peptide, selectively recognized by cancer-associated fibroblast cells in the tumor microenvironment. The nanoformulation was administered via the i.v route. The nanoparticles are comprised of thermoresponsive lipid (DPPC) that was degraded with NIR applied externally. The nanoparticles are specifically enriched into the tumor site through a passive targeting strategy (EPR effect) and selective uptake by cancer-associated fibroblast cells. The remaining parts of the particles were degraded by applying NIR externally. *DPPC*, dipalmitoyl phosphatidylcholine; *NIR*, near infrared light; *EPR*, enhanced permeation and retention effect.

C57/BL-6 mice as tumor-bearing mice. Undoubtedly, after successful tumor implantation, the novel nanoparticles were administered via the intravenous (i.v) route and simultaneously applied near infrared light (NIR) into the tumor site for the NIR-induced thermo-responsive paclitaxel release at the tumor site. The synthesized novel nanoparticles showed higher anticancer activity than free paclitaxel [63].

11.5.3 Irinotecan

Irinotecan is another FDA-approved molecule used in various solid tumors, such as breast cancer and colorectal cancer. DNA damage and cell death occur when the drug molecules inhibit the topoisomerase I enzyme. In addition, USFDA approved irinotecan (CAMPTOSAR) as an anticancer drug molecule against pancreatic cancer in April 2000. Irinotecan belongs to the BCS II class, implying that it has low water solubility but high permeability into the cells [66–68]. Clinical pharmacokinetic profiling was depicted by Chabot et al. [69]. They described that irinotecan (CPT11) has a terminal half-life ($t_{1/2}$) of 12 h, a steady state volume of distribution of 168 lit/m^2, and a total body clearance of 15 lit/m^2/h in the clinical pharmacokinetic model. Besides, the plasma protein binding capacity of irinotecan is 65%. Despite their poor hydrophilicity, the molecules cannot spread quickly throughout the body. Hence, the nanoparticle-mediated drug delivery system is a platform that can reach a specific cell and permeate with the nanocarrier.

In contrast, Irinophore C is the lipid nanoformulation that encapsulates and stabilizes the lactone ring of the irinotecan [70–72]. Waterhouse et al. claimed that Irinophore C could completely nullify the toxicity of irinotecan in the GIT tract of rat models, which is supported by their pharmacokinetic profiling and histopathological assessment [73]. A significant number of studies focused on irinotecan encapsulated in LNs. However, Liu et al. synthesized lipid bi-layer coated mesoporous silica nanoparticles to deliver irinotecan to reduce the irinotecan-related toxicity. The drug molecules were stabilized and efficiently packed with the lipid bilayer. Furthermore, they used the trapping agent triethylammonium sucrose octasulfate (TEA8SOS) to encapsulate irinotecan into the lipid bi-layer vesicle [74].

11.5.4 Capecitabine

Capecitabine is a chemotherapeutic anticancer molecule used for pancreatic cancer. US-FDA approved this anticancer drug molecule on April 30, 1998, with the brand name Xeloda [75]. Capecitabine is a highly water-soluble drug (solubility: 26 mg/mL and logP value: 0.4) and remains in BCS class 1; it implies capecitabine has high solubility and high permeability. During oral administration of capecitabine to target tumor tissue, it is preferentially metabolized to the cytotoxic component fluorouracil (5-fluorouracil; 5-FU) by a sequence of three metabolic processes. Capecitabine is a carbamate ester that produces three active metabolites in the cells, such as "5-fluoro-2-deoxyuridine mono-phosphate, 5-fluoro-2-deoxyuridine diphosphate, and 5-fluoro-2-deoxyuridine triphos-phate." Both normal and tumor cells metabolize 5-FU to 5-fluoro-2-deoxyuridine monophosphate (FdUMP) and 5-fluorouridine triphosphate (FUTP) [75]. Reigner et al. discussed the pharmacokinetic profiles of capecitabine in detail. They described that after oral administration of a dose of 1250 mg/m^2, capecitabine is rapidly and extensively absorbed from the gastrointestinal tract (T_{max}: 2 h and C_{max}: 3−4 mg/L) and presented a short elimination half-life ($t_{1/2}$): 0.55−0.89 h. These values are based on the drug reaching its peak concentration in 2 h. The amount of drug-related material that may be recovered from urine and feces is close to 100%. The cytotoxic fluorouracil moiety is present in plasma at extremely low quantities [with a C_{max} ranging from 0.22 to 0.31 mg/L and an area under the concentration-time curve (AUC) of 0.461 to 0.698 mg h/L]. [76] Being a short half-life of elimination and less plasma-bound capac-ity, the drug molecules are readily excreted from the body and cannot reach the thresh-old concentration in the tumor microenvironment. Hence, nanoparticle-mediated delivery systems are the most promising approach. Dudhipala et al. developed capecitabine-loaded SLNs for drug delivery against colon cancer. This study used glyc-eryl trimyristin as a lipid and poloxamer-188 and Lecithin E-80 as cosurfactants in this nanoformulation. The particle size of the synthesized SLNs was 145.6 ± 3.6 nm and PDI was 0.203 ± 0.004 with a zeta-potential of −26.9 ± 2.7 mV. This data imply that the nanoparticles are monodispersed and negatively charged in nature, preventing unwanted coalescence or aggregation. The cancer cells can avidly uptake the nanoparti-cles and try to metabolize the lipid particles into the cytomatrix. The drug molecules were released into the cancer cell and showed anticancer properties significantly [77].

11.5.5 5-fluorouracil

5-fluorouracil is another anticancer drug that can directly bind with DNA molecules and damage the DNA of cancer cells. The antineoplastic drug fluorouracil (5-FU), a pyrimidine analog, is an active metabolite of capecitabine. It is used to treat a wide variety of solid tumors, including colon, rectal, breast, gastric, pancreatic, ovarian, bladder, and liver. 5-fluorouracil is a BCS-III classification drug, implying that it has good aqueous solubility but poor permeability in the cell [78,79]. Hence, fluoroura-cil encapsulated lipid nanocarrier is a better choice against pancreatic cancer. Smith et al. showed higher loading of hydrophilic anticancer molecules. They used a lipid nanocarrier for 5-FU to deliver against cancer cells. The particle size was 263 ± 3 nm, and the zeta potential was 0.1 ± 0.02 with 81% entrapment into LNPs. They used three lipids: Compritol 888 ATO (glyceryl behenate), mPEG2000-DSPE, and Precirol ATO 5 (glyceryl palmitostearate). Besides, as surfactants, they used mPEG2000-DSPE to stabilize the particle in the aqueous solution. In this study, the IC_{50} of 5-Fu and 5-Fu-loaded SLNs were 17.7 ± 0.03 and $7.4 \pm 0.02\ \mu M$, respectively, implying that the synthesized nanoformulation was 2.4-fold potent against colorectal carcinoma cells (HCT116 cell line). The in vivo study showed that the resultant nanoformulation significantly inhibited tumor growth, while the plasma concentration of the nanoformulation was 3.6-fold higher compared to free 5-fluorouracil [80].

11.5.6 RNA-based delivery system

A group of newly discovered genes associated with cancer has been identified, which have significant implications for both pancreatic and stromal cells encompassing the tumor. These genes promote tumor formation, metastasis, and resistance to therapy. Several of these genes and proteins are "undruggable" since they provide no primary pharmacological functions, such as inhibitory and antagonistic activities. The anticancer drug molecules have distinct molecular mechanisms and target the cancer cell. Those targets are also active in noncancer or normal cells. Therefore the anticancer drug molecules can show their toxicity against noncancer or normal cells.

In contrast, inhibiting small ligands is challenging because their binding sites (in the case of RNA molecules) are difficult to anticipate. In certain circumstances, the anticancer drug molecules may not perform effectively against the target as their sequence is identical to other proteins. Although nanoformulations of RNA interference (RNAi) may silence target genes, the end consequence is a considerable reduction in tumor development and an increase in overall patient survival [81–84]. However, nowadays, it is established that RNA-based molecules, such as sequence interfering RNA (siRNA) and short hairpin RNA (shRNA), have the benefit of increased selectivity over pharmaceutical inhibitors, which are often not specific to their target gene. A typical siRNA molecule consists of two strands, each 19 to 21 nucleotides in length, with 3' overhangs of two nucleotides on each strand, for a total duplex length of 21 to 23 base pairs. Besides, RNA-induced silencing complex (RISC) recognizes and breaks down the target transcript, resulting in silence and degradation of siRNA's 5'-terminal region [85,86]. After cleavage, the RISC-siRNA complex previously recycled may be employed in other cleavage processes.

For this reason, researchers harness the power of siRNA to cure many illnesses, including cancer. However, getting siRNA into cells is a significant hurdle in developing siRNA-based cancer therapies. The difficulty in delivering siRNA into cells is a significant barrier. Various barriers are present to successfully deliver the RNA molecules into the cell, such as negatively charged RNA molecules having an enormous molecular weight (about 13.5 kDa). The negatively charged RNA molecules create repulsion while interacting with the cell membrane, resulting in their inability to enter the cell. Also, the body's reticuloendothelial system can quickly pick up and get rid of naked (not changed) siRNA

[87]. Hence, lipid-based nanoformulations are suitable for delivering RNA molecules into cancer cells as they have excellent biocompatibility, biodegradability, low toxicity and immunity, structural flexibility, and ease of mass production. Generally, RNA molecules are negatively charged, and researchers employ cationic lipids to pack the RNA molecules into lipoplexes. The inverse ionic interaction assists in stabilizing lipoplex formation [88]. Several types of siRNA-encapsulated lipid-based nanoparticles are considered for targeted anticancer therapies. Patisiran (ONTATTRO), a lipid-based nanoparticle synthesized with siRNA targeting transthyretin, was authorized by the FDA in 2018 as the first siRNA medication to treat transthyretin-type amyloid polyneuropathy [89].

shRNA molecules were delivered against pancreatic desmoplastic stroma cells presenting into the tumoral micro-environment of pancreatic adenocarcinoma by Han et al. [88]. The strategy of this work is described in detail in Fig. 11.4. Primarily, gold nanoparticles were functionalized to deliver both siHSP47 (a siRNA of HSP47, a collagen-specific molecular chaperone) and gemcitabine with ATRA (All-Trans Retinoic Acid, an inducer of pancreatic desmoplastic stroma cells quiescence) surface conjugated LNPs. ATRA is a water-insoluble compound that could help coat the resultant nanoparticles and recognize PSC. Also, the synthesized gold nanoparticles were pH-responsive. The negatively charged ATRA and siRNA were surface-functionalized readily onto the PEG-grafted polyethyleneimine (PEI)-coated gold nanoparticles. The nanocomplex is "activated" in the acidic microenvironment of pancreatic tumor (pH ~ 6.5) and exhibited pH and ATRA dual-enhanced cellular uptake and HSP47 knockdown in pancreatic desmoplastic stroma cells. While activated, the nanocomplex attributed the structural phenomena, such as PEG shedding, decreased particle size, increased surface charge, and hydrophobic ligand exposure.

However, KRAS is the most abundant mutation in several types of tumors, such as colon adenocarcinoma, lung adenocarcinoma, pancreatic carcinoma, and multiple myeloma, which is the undruggable (a protein that is not pharmacologically capable of being targeted) target for anticancer therapy [90]. Pramanik et al. developed a lipid-based nanoformulation to deliver the p53 transcriptional network component miR-34a and miR-143/145 cluster. In this, miR-34a regulates cancer stem cell survival and the miR-143/145 cluster constraining the expression of KRAS2 and its downstream effector system Ras-responsive element binding protein-1 (RREB1) [91]. The authors used positively charged lipids (DOTAP and DSPE-PEG-OMe) for packing the negatively charged RNA molecules. There is no evidence of toxicity as histopathological or biochemical indication after i.v injection of the lipid nanocomplex. Increasing apoptosis and a reduction in proliferation accompanied the tumor growth suppression for administering the resultant lipid nanovector. A considerable increase in the matching miRNA and significant reduction in particular miRNA targets (SIRT1, CD44, aldehyde dehydrogenase, and KRAS2 for miR34a and KRAS2 and RREB1 for miR-143/145) were noted in the treated xenografts. It has been concluded that the nanovector is a potential delivery

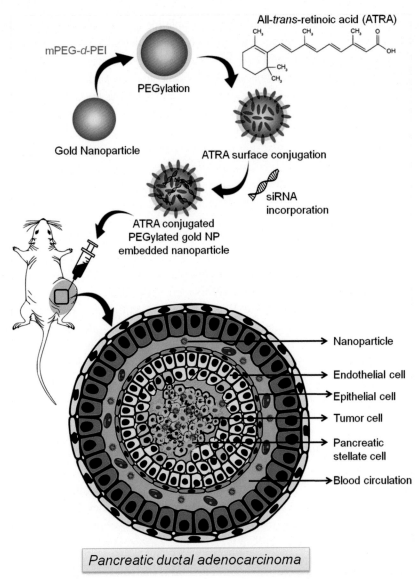

Figure 11.4 Schematic representation of All-trans-retinoic acid (ATRA; the lipophilic moiety)-PEG surface decorated gold nanoparticle to deliver gemcitabine and siRNA (siRNA of heat shock protein 47, a collagen-specific molecular chaperone) as the targeted combination therapy.

system for the distribution of miRNA to cancer cells. Moreover, few molecules have been used in recent studies as a druggable treatment for KRAS [92]. Sasayama et al. developed an LNP formulation to deliver KRAS-targeting siRNA to Mia PaCa-2 cells in vitro and tumors in vivo, resulting in food protein knockdown indicating anticancer effectiveness [93]. They used a novel lipid (LNPK15) as a base composed of cholesterol, DSPC, and 3.3% PEGylated PEG-DSPE (1,2-distearoyl-sn-glycero-3-phosphatidyletha-nolamine N-(polyethylene glycol-2000) and two novel cationic lipids (SST-01 and SST-31)). Also, PEGylated lipid increases the circulation time through blood [94,95]. The nanoparticles could encapsulate KRAS siRNA and showed excellent siRNA delivery to tumor sites and prolonged circulation time. The KRAS-targeting novel lipid nanoformu-lation played a substantial antitumor effect in tumor-bearing xenograft mice with pancre-atic cancer cell lines (Mia PaCa-2). They established that the lipid PEG-DSPE used as a mixture of their nanoformulation was hydrolyzed by phospholipase 2 (PLA2).

11.6 Future aspects

Pancreatic cancer is deadly and is often identified in its metastatic phase. Several tradi-tional methods exist for therapy and diagnostics. However, these methods have many limitations. Due to these disadvantages, nanotechnological techniques are emerging to enhance the bioavailability of chemotherapeutic medicines and decrease their toxicity. In the future, cancer patients will no longer receive chemotherapeutic drugs alone. The greatest weapon for targeted anticancer drug delivery will be lipid nanoformula-tions. LNPs will be delivered therapeutic molecules and diverse biomolecules such as mRNA, siRNA, and DNA. LNPs are biodegradable, biocompatible, and nontoxic. PEGylated LNPs are superior to nonPEGylated LNPs as they can aggregate in sys-temic circulation. As a result of being PEGylated, nanoparticles exhibit a negative sur-face charge and are hydrophilic, enhancing blood circulation. Notably, LNPs are readily taken up by cancer cells, and the delivery drug molecules exhibit anticancer efficacy. There have been relatively few studies on the domain of drug delivery by the SLNs carrier system in pancreatic cancer. Hence there is a need for more research in this area. In addition, LNPs may be the optimal delivery mechanism for targeted anti-cancer therapies.

References

[1] Sielaff CM, Mousa SA. Status and future directions in the management of pancreatic cancer: potential impact of nanotechnology. J Cancer Res Clin Oncol 2018;144(7):1205–17.
[2] Birhanu G, Javar HA, Seyedjafari E, Zandi-Karimi A. Nanotechnology for delivery of gemcitabine to treat pancreatic cancer. Biomedicine & pharmacotherapy, 88. Elsevier Masson; 2017. p. 635–43.
[3] Siegel RL, Miller KD, Jemal A. Cancer statistics, 2018. CA Cancer J Clin 2018;68(1):7–30.
[4] Ko A. Nanomedicine developments in the treatment of metastatic pancreatic cancer: focus on nanoli-posomal irinotecan. Int J Nanomed 2016;11:1225.
[5] National Cancer Institute. Pancreatic Cancer - Patient Version, NCI; 2018.
[6] Vincent A, Herman J, Schulick R, Hruban RH, Goggins M. Pancreatic cancer. Lancet. 2011;378 (9791):607–20.
[7] McCarroll J, Teo J, Boyer C, Goldstein D, Kavallaris M, Phillips PA. Potential applications of nano-technology for the diagnosis and treatment of pancreatic cancer. Front Physiol 2014;5:2.

  [8] Edderkaoui M, Eibl G. Risk factors for pancreatic cancer: underlying mechanisms and potential targets. Front Physiol Front 2014;5:415.
  [9] Hartwig W, Werner J, Jäger D, Debus J, Büchler MW. Improvement of surgical results for pancreatic cancer. Lancet Oncol 2013;14(11):e476—85.
 [10] Erkan M, Hausmann S, Michalski CW, Schlitter AM, Fingerle AA, Dobritz M, et al. How fibrosis influences imaging and surgical decisions in pancreatic cancer. Front Physiol 2012;3:389.
 [11] Garud A, Singh D, Garud N. Solid lipid nanoparticles (SLN): method, characterization and applications. Int Curr Pharm J 2012;1(11):384—93.
 [12] Gordillo-Galeano A, Mora-Huertas CE. Solid lipid nanoparticles and nanostructured lipid carriers: a review emphasizing on particle structure and drug release. Eur J Pharm Biopharm 2018;133:285—308.
 [13] Pons R. Polymeric surfactants as emulsion stabilizers. In: Alexandridis P, Lindman B, editors. Amphiphilic block copolymers. Amsterdam: Elsevier; 2000. p. 409—22.
 [14] Hou X, Zaks T, Langer R, Dong Y. Lipid nanoparticles for mRNA delivery. Nat Rev Mater 2021;6(12):1078—94.
 [15] Semple SC, Akinc A, Chen J, Sandhu AP, Mui BL, Cho CK, et al. Rational design of cationic lipids for siRNA delivery. Nat Biotechnol 2010;28(2):172—6.
 [16] Tam Y, Chen S, Cullis P. Advances in lipid nanoparticles for siRNA delivery. Pharmaceutics. 2013;5(4):498—507.
 [17] Ren T, Song YK, Zhang G, Liu D. Structural basis of DOTMA for its high intravenous transfection activity in mouse. Gene Ther 2000;7(9):764—8.
 [18] Meisel JW, Gokel GW. A simplified direct lipid mixing lipoplex preparation: comparison of liposomal-, dimethylsulfoxide-, and ethanol-based methods. Sci Rep 2016;6(1):27662.
 [19] Bansal SK, Rajpoot K, Sreeharsha N, Youngren-Ortiz SR, Anup N, Tekade RK. Endosomal escape tendency of drug delivery systems to mediate cytosolic delivery of therapeutics. In: Tekade RK, editor. The future of pharmaceutical product development and research. Elsevier; 2020. p. 227—58.
 [20] Carrasco MJ, Alishetty S, Alameh MG, Said H, Wright L, Paige M, et al. Ionization and structural properties of mRNA lipid nanoparticles influence expression in intramuscular and intravascular administration. Commun Biol 2021;4(1):956.
 [21] Hattori Y, Suzuki S, Kawakami S, Yamashita F, Hashida M. The role of dioleoylphosphatidylethanolamine (DOPE) in targeted gene delivery with mannosylated cationic liposomes via intravenous route. J Control Rel 2005;108(2—3):484—95.
 [22] Yanagisawa M, Sakaue T, Yoshikawa K. Characteristic behavior of crowding macromolecules confined in cell-sized droplets. In: Hancock R, Jeon KW, editors. International review of cell and molecular biology. Academic Press; 2014. p. 175—204.
 [23] Battaglia L, Gallarate M, Panciani PP, Ugazio E, Sapino S, Peira E, et al. Techniques for the preparation of solid lipid nano and microparticles. Application of nanotechnology in drug delivery. IntechOpen; 2014.
 [24] Siekmann BWK. Melt-homogenized solid lipid nanoparticles stabilized by the nonionic surfactant tyloxapol. I. Preparation and particle size determination. Pharm Pharmacol Lett 1994;3:194—7.
 [25] Mehnert W. Solid lipid nanoparticles production, characterization and applications. Adv Drug Deliv Rev 2001;47(2—3):165—96.
 [26] Joshi SARK. Solid lipid nanoparticle: a review. IOSR J Pharm 2012;2(6):34—44.
 [27] Leong TSH, Wooster TJ, Kentish SE, Ashokkumar M. Minimising oil droplet size using ultrasonic emulsification. Ultrason Sonochem 2009;16(6):721—7.
 [28] Battaglia L, Gallarate M, Cavalli R, Trotta M. Solid lipid nanoparticles produced through a coacervation method. J Microencapsul 2010;27(1):78—85.
 [29] Bianco MA, Gallarate M, Trotta M, Battaglia L. Amphotericin B loaded SLN prepared with the coacervation technique. J Drug Deliv Sci Technol 2010;20(3):187—91.
 [30] Fadda P, Monduzzi M, Caboi F, Piras S, Lazzari P. Solid lipid nanoparticle preparation by a warm microemulsion based process: influence of microemulsion microstructure. Int J Pharm 2013;446 (1—2):166—75.
 [31] Trotta M, Debernardi F, Caputo O. Preparation of solid lipid nanoparticles by a solvent emulsification-diffusion technique. Int J Pharm 2003;257(1—2):153—60.

[32] Hu L, Tang X, Cui F. Solid lipid nanoparticles (SLNs) to improve oral bioavailability of poorly soluble drugs. J Pharm Pharmacol 2004;56(12):1527−35.

[33] Phillips P. Pancreatic stellate cells and fibrosis [Internet]. In: Grippo PJ, Munshi HG, editors. Pancreatic cancer and tumor microenvironment. Trivandrum (India): Transworld Research Network; 2012.

[34] Elahi-Gedwillo KY, Carlson M, Zettervall J, Provenzano PP. Antifibrotic therapy disrupts stromal barriers and modulates the immune landscape in pancreatic ductal adenocarcinoma. Cancer Res 2019;79(2):372−86.

[35] Wu Y, Zhang C, Jiang K, Werner J, Bazhin AV, D'Haese JG. The role of stellate cells in pancreatic ductal adenocarcinoma: targeting perspectives. Front Oncol 2021;10:: 621937.

[36] Walsh JC, Lebedev A, Aten E, Madsen K, Marciano L, Kolb HC. The clinical importance of assessing tumor hypoxia: relationship of tumor hypoxia to prognosis and therapeutic opportunities. Antioxid Redox Signal 2014;21(10):1516−54.

[37] McCarroll JA, Naim S, Sharbeen G, Russia N, Lee J, Kavallaris M, et al. Role of pancreatic stellate cells in chemoresistance in pancreatic cancer. Front Physiol 2014;5:: 141.

[38] A-Kader HH, Ghishan FK. The pancreas. Textbook of clinical pediatrics. berlin, heidelberg. Berlin Heidelberg: Springer; 2012. p. 1925−36.

[39] Lowe AW, Olsen M, Hao Y, Lee SP, Taek Lee K, Chen X, et al. Gene expression patterns in pancreatic tumors, cells and tissues. PLoS One 2007;2(3):e323.

[40] Sanh N, Fadul H, Hussein N, Lyn-Cook BD, Hammons G, Ramos-Cardona XE, et al. Proteomics profiling of pancreatic cancer and pancreatitis for biomarkers discovery. J Cell Sci Ther 2018;9(4). Available from: https://doi.org/10.4172/2157-7013.1000287.

[41] Ruinelli M, Schneeberger PHH, Ferrante P, Bühlmann A, Scortichini M, Vanneste JL, et al. Comparative genomics-informed design of two LAMP assays for detection of the kiwifruit pathogen *Pseudomonas syringae* pv. *actinidiae* and discrimination of isolates belonging to the pandemic biovar 3. Plant Pathol 2017;66(1):140−9.

[42] Edgar RC. MUSCLE: multiple sequence alignment with high accuracy and high throughput. Nucleic Acids Res 2004;32(5):1792−7.

[43] Li X, Lindquist S, Lowe M, Noppa L, Hernell O. Bile salt−stimulated lipase and pancreatic lipase-related protein 2 are the dominating lipases in neonatal fat digestion in mice and rats. Pediatr Res 2007;62(5):537−41.

[44] Ollis DL, Cheah E, Cygler M, Dijkstra B, Frolow F, Franken SM, et al. The α/β hydrolase fold. Protein Eng Des Sel 1992;5(3):197−211.

[45] Lowe M. Properties and function of pancreatic lipase related protein 2. Biochimie. 2000;82(11):997−1004.

[46] Zhu Guoying, Fang Qing, Zhu Fengshang, Huang Dongping, Yang Changqing. Structure and function of pancreatic lipase-related protein 2 and its relationship with pathological states. Front Genet 2021;12:693538. Available from: https://doi.org/10.3389/fgene.2021.693538.

[47] Lowe ME, Kaplan MH, Jackson-Grusby L, D'Agostino D, Grusby MJ. Decreased neonatal dietary fat absorption and T cell cytotoxicity in pancreatic lipase-related protein 2-deficient mice. J Biol Chem 1998;273(47):31215−21.

[48] Hill DA, Artis D. Intestinal bacteria and the regulation of immune cell homeostasis. Annu Rev Immunol 2010;28(1):623−67.

[49] Lindquist S, Andersson EL, Lundberg L, Hernell O. Bile salt-stimulated lipase plays an unexpected role in arthritis development in rodents. PLoS One 2012;7(10):e47006.

[50] Panicot-Dubois L, Thomas GM, Furie BC, Furie B, Lombardo D, Dubois C. Bile salt−dependent lipase interacts with platelet CXCR4 and modulates thrombus formation in mice and humans. J Clin Invest 2007;117(12):3708−19.

[51] Affram KO, Smith T, Ofori E, Krishnan S, Underwood P, Trevino JG, et al. Cytotoxic effects of gemcitabine-loaded solid lipid nanoparticles in pancreatic cancer cells. J Drug Deliv Sci Technol 2020;55:101374.

[52] Maan M, Peters JM, Dutta M, Patterson AD. Lipid metabolism and lipophagy in cancer. Biochem Biophys Res Commun 2018;504(3):582−9.

[53] Kounakis K, Chaniotakis M, Markaki M, Tavernarakis N. Emerging roles of lipophagy in health and disease. Front Cell Dev Biol 2019;7:185.

[54] National Cancer Institute. Drugs approved for rhabdomyosarcoma [Internet]. National Cancer Institute; 2013. p. 2021.

[55] Plunkett W, Huang P, Xu YZ, Heinemann V, Grunewald R, Gandhi V. Gemcitabine: metabolism, mechanisms of action, and self-potentiation. Semin Oncol 1995;22(4):3–10.

[56] Bulanadi JC, Xue A, Gong X, Bean PA, Julovi SM, Campo L, et al. Biomimetic gemcitabine–lipid prodrug nanoparticles for pancreatic cancer. Chempluschem. 2020;85(6):1283–91.

[57] Cai H, Wang R, Guo X, Song M, Yan F, Ji B, et al. Combining gemcitabine-loaded macrophage-like nanoparticles and erlotinib for pancreatic cancer therapy. Mol Pharm 2021;18(7):2495–506.

[58] Corrie PG, Qian W, Basu B, Valle JW, Falk S, Lwuji C, et al. Scheduling nab-paclitaxel combined with gemcitabine as first-line treatment for metastatic pancreatic adenocarcinoma. Br J Cancer 2020;122(12):1760–8.

[59] Meng H, Wang M, Liu H, Liu X, Situ A, Wu B, et al. Use of a lipid-coated mesoporous silica nanoparticle platform for synergistic gemcitabine and paclitaxel delivery to human pancreatic cancer in mice. ACS Nano 2015;9(4):3540–57.

[60] Wu Sta, Fowler AJ, Garmon CB, Fessler AB, Ogle JD, Grover KR, et al. Treatment of pancreatic ductal adenocarcinoma with tumor antigen specific-targeted delivery of paclitaxel loaded PLGA nanoparticles. BMC Cancer 2018;18(1):457.

[61] Nath S, Mukherjee P. MUC1: a multifaceted oncoprotein with a key role in cancer progression. Trends Mol Med 2014;20(6):332–42.

[62] Chen W, Zhang Z, Zhang S, Zhu P, Ko JKS, Yung KKL. MUC1: structure, function, and clinic application in epithelial cancers. Int J Mol Sci 2021;22(12):6567.

[63] Yu Q, Qiu Y, Li J, Tang X, Wang X, Cun X, et al. Targeting cancer-associated fibroblasts by dual-responsive lipid-albumin nanoparticles to enhance drug perfusion for pancreatic tumor therapy. J Control Rel 2020;321:564–75.

[64] Xin L, Gao J, Zheng Z, Chen Y, Lv S, Zhao Z, et al. Fibroblast activation protein-α as a target in the bench-to-bedside diagnosis and treatment of tumors: a narrative review. Front Oncol 2021;11:648187.

[65] Zi F, He J, He D, Li Y, Yang L, Cai Z. Fibroblast activation protein α in tumor microenvironment: recent progression and implications. Mol Med Rep 2015;11(5):3203–11.

[66] Jandu H, Aluzaite K, Fogh L, Thrane SW, Noer JB, Proszek J, et al. Molecular characterization of irinotecan (SN-38) resistant human breast cancer cell lines. BMC Cancer 2016;16(1):34.

[67] Fujita KIchi. Irinotecan, a key chemotherapeutic drug for metastatic colorectal cancer. World J Gastroenterol 2015;21(43):12234.

[68] US-FDA. Clinical Pharmacology and Biopharmaceutics Review (NDA 20–571 SE8–021). Vol. 2022. 2000.

[69] Chabot GG, Robert J, Lokiec F, Canal P. Irinotecan pharmacokinetics. Bull Cancer 1998; Spec No:11–20.

[70] Ramsay E, Alnajim J, Anantha M, Taggar A, Thomas A, Edwards K, et al. Transition metal-mediated liposomal encapsulation of irinotecan (CPT-11) stabilizes the drug in the therapeutically active lactone conformation. Pharm Res 2006;23(12):2799–808.

[71] Ramsay E. A novel liposomal irinotecan formulation with significant anti-tumour activity: use of the divalent cation ionophore A23187 and copper-containing liposomes to improve drug retention. Eur J Pharm Biopharm 2008;68(3):607–17.

[72] Ramsay EC, Anantha M, Zastre J, Meijs M, Zonderhuis J, Strutt D, et al. Irinophore C: a liposome formulation of irinotecan with substantially improved therapeutic efficacy against a panel of human xenograft tumors. Clin Cancer Res 2008;14(4):1208–17.

[73] Waterhouse DN, Sutherland BW, Santos NDos, Masin D, Osooly M, Strutt D, et al. Irinophore C™, a lipid nanoparticle formulation of irinotecan, abrogates the gastrointestinal effects of irinotecan in a rat model of clinical toxicities. Invest N Drugs 2014;32(6):1071–82.

[74] Liu X, Situ A, Kang Y, Villabroza KR, Liao Y, Chang CH, et al. Irinotecan delivery by lipid-coated mesoporous silica nanoparticles shows improved efficacy and safety over liposomes for pancreatic cancer. ACS Nano 2016;10(2):2702–15.

[75] U.S. Food and Drug Administration. Drug approval package. ELELYSO (Taliglucerase alfa) Inject. 2012.

[76] Reigner B, Blesch K, Weidekamm E. Clinical pharmacokinetics of capecitabine. Clin Pharmacokinet 2001;40(2):85−104.

[77] Dudhipala N, Puchchakayala G. Capecitabine lipid nanoparticles for anti-colon cancer activity in 1,2-dimethylhydrazine-induced colon cancer: preparation, cytotoxic, pharmacokinetic, and pathological evaluation. Drug Dev Ind Pharm 2018;44(10):1572−82.

[78] Zhang N, Yin Y, Xu SJ, Chen WS. 5-Fluorouracil: mechanisms of resistance and reversal strategies. Molecules. 2008;13(8):1551−69.

[79] Dadwal S, Kumar R, Wadhwa S. Formulation strategies to improve the permeability of BCS class III drugs: special emphasis on 5 fluorouracil. Int J Emerg Technol Innov Res 2020;5(12):822−30.

[80] Smith T, Affram K, Nottingham EL, Han B, Amissah F, Krishnan S, et al. Application of smart solid lipid nanoparticles to enhance the efficacy of 5-fluorouracil in the treatment of colorectal cancer. Sci Rep 2020;10(1):16989.

[81] Kokkinos J, Ignacio RMC, Sharbeen G, Boyer C, Gonzales-Aloy E, Goldstein D, et al. Targeting the undruggable in pancreatic cancer using nano-based gene silencing drugs. Biomaterials. 2020;240:119742.

[82] Zuckerman JE, Davis ME. Clinical experiences with systemically administered siRNA-based therapeutics in cancer. Nat Rev Drug Discov 2015;14(12):843−56.

[83] Wu SY, Lopez-Berestein G, Calin GA, Sood AK. RNAi therapies: drugging the undruggable. Sci Transl Med 2014;6(240) 240ps7.

[84] Zhou J, Shum KT, Burnett J, Rossi J. Nanoparticle-based delivery of RNAi therapeutics: progress and challenges. Pharmaceuticals. 2013;6(1):85−107.

[85] Rana TM. Illuminating the silence: understanding the structure and function of small RNAs. Nat Rev Mol Cell Biol 2007;8(1):23−36.

[86] Tatiparti K, Sau S, Kashaw S, Iyer A. siRNA delivery strategies: a comprehensive review of recent developments. Nanomaterials. 2017;7(4):77.

[87] Xin Y, Huang M, Guo WW, Huang Q, Zhang LZ, Jiang G. Nano-based delivery of RNAi in cancer therapy. Mol Cancer 2017;16(1):134.

[88] Han X, Li Y, Xu Y, Zhao X, Zhang Y, Yang X, et al. Reversal of pancreatic desmoplasia by re-educating stellate cells with a tumour microenvironment-activated nanosystem. Nat Commun 2018;9(1):3390.

[89] Kim YK. RNA therapy: current status and future potential. Chonnam Med J 2020;56(2):87.

[90] Cook JH, Melloni GEM, Gulhan DC, Park PJ, Haigis KM. The origins and genetic interactions of KRAS mutations are allele- and tissue-specific. Nat Commun 2021;12(1):1808.

[91] Pramanik D, Campbell NR, Karikari C, Chivukula R, Kent OA, Mendell JT, et al. Restitution of tumor suppressor microRNAs using a systemic nanovector inhibits pancreatic cancer growth in mice. Mol Cancer Ther 2011;10(8):1470−80.

[92] Huang L, Guo Z, Wang F, Fu L. KRAS mutation: from undruggable to druggable in cancer. Signal Transduct Target Ther 2021;6(1):386.

[93] Sasayama Y, Hasegawa M, Taguchi E, Kubota K, Kuboyama T, Naoi T, et al. In vivo activation of PEGylated long circulating lipid nanoparticle to achieve efficient siRNA delivery and target gene knock down in solid tumors. J Control Rel 2019;311−312:245−56.

[94] Suk JS, Xu Q, Kim N, Hanes J, Ensign LM. PEGylation as a strategy for improving nanoparticle-based drug and gene delivery. Adv Drug Deliv Rev 2016;99(Pt A):28−51.

[95] Fan W, Peng H, Yu Z, Wang L, He H, Ma Y, et al. The long-circulating effect of pegylated nanoparticles revisited via simultaneous monitoring of both the drug payloads and nanocarriers. Acta Pharm Sin B 2022;12(5):2479−93.

CHAPTER 12

Dendrimers and carbon nanotubes-based drug delivery for pancreatic cancer

Mehmethan Yıldırım[1], Durmus Burak Demirkaya[1] and Serap Yalcin[2]
[1]Department of Molecular Biology and Genetics, Faculty of Science and Art, Kırsehir Ahi Evran University, Kırsehir, Turkey
[2]Department of Medical Pharmacology, Faculty of Medicine, Kırsehir Ahi Evran University, Kırsehir, Turkey

12.1 A brief overview of pancreatic cancer

Pancreatic cancer or the type of cancer we know as pancreatic cancer refers to pancreatic ductal carcinoma. Pancreatic cancer is especially leading of cancer deaths in the world. Considering the survival rates within 5 years in the United States, it is seen that the rate 12.5% (2013−2019) [1]. Again, for both gender groups, the highest incidence rates of pancreatic cancer are in North America, Europe, New Zealand and Western Europe. In contrast, lower incidences were found in South-Central Asia and Central Africa [2].

Incidence rates in both male and female individuals are directly proportional to increasing age. Generally, approximately 90% of pancreatic cancer cases are in people aged 55 and over [2].

Considering the risk factors of pancreatic cancer, the exact etiology of this type of cancer has never been fully elucidated. However, in epidemiological studies, many risk factors for pancreatic cancer have emerged in a genetic or nongenetic way. Old age, high body mass index (BMI), long-term smoking, high-fat diet, and chronic pancreatitis can be counted among the nonhereditary risk factors. Considering the hereditary risk factors, in other syndromes, such as familial malignant syndrome, Peutz-Jeghers syndrome, Lynch Syndrome, Von Hippel Lindau syndrome, multiple endocrine neoplasia type 1 syndrome called MEN1, in which mutations in CDKN2A, PALB2, and BRCA1/2 genes reveal a familial pancreatic relationship, a 10% incidence rate is observed. It can be said that pancreas is a risk factor [2,3].

Pancreatic adenocarcinoma is one of the deadliest types of cancer. Reducing the increasing incidence rate and preventing a consistently poor prognosis are the primary goals in treatment studies. Although there are incidences that can be alleviated by the patient with lifestyle changes, this is not enough. It is known that scientists investigate the pharmaceutical benefits of risk reduction in their recent studies and use biomolecules

Recent Advances in Nanocarriers for Pancreatic Cancer Therapy
DOI: https://doi.org/10.1016/B978-0-443-19142-8.00012-7

that can be combined such as beta-blockers, statins, ASA, and metformin in carcinomas. Although it is known that these pharmaceuticals have a low-risk profile and benefits, studies on the administration dose, duration of action, and disease progression of these molecules should continue [4].

More than 90% of pancreatic adenocarcinomas are duct cell adenocarcinomas. Other types are called acinar cell carcinoma and cystadenocarcinoma. Two-thirds arise in the head of the pancreas, and the remaining one-third occurs in the body or tail of the pancreas. When their toxicokinetic structures were investigated by scientists, two tumor markers that were associated with pancreatic cancer, namely CA 19—9 and carcinoembryonic antigen (CEA), were found (Fig. 12.1).

In addition, the stages of pancreatic cancer are divided as follows:

Stage 1: The tumor is only in the pancreas and has not spread to another place.
Stage 2: The tumor infiltrates the bile duct and other nearby structures, but the lymph nodes are negative.
Stage 3: At this stage, the tumor has any positive lymph nodes.
Stage 4A: Tumor: it metastasizes to nearby organs such as the liver, adrenals, stomach, and diaphragm.
Stage 4B: The tumor easily infiltrates distant parts of the body and metastasizes [2].

12.2 Drug delivery for cancer therapy

By 1960, the concept of nanotechnology by Feynman had become an exploratory attribute. With the studies carried out from those years until today, many researches

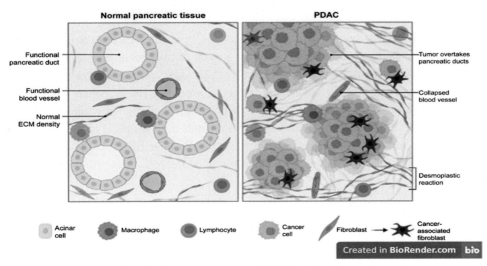

Figure 12.1 Pancreatic ductal adenocarcinoma. *Available from: http://www.Biorender.com.*

have enabled the realization of discoveries [5]. Nanotechnology has been developed and evolved today, from healthcare products to many therapeutics at the molecular level.

Nanomaterials, which have entered our lives with nanotechnology, are one of the areas with rapid integration into cancer therapeutics. All of the structures we call nano-carrier systems; they are systems that interact with target cells and tissues, facilitate a controlled response to stimuli, and can be used to induce desired physiological responses [6,7]. Nanocarriers work to release drugs directly to the site of action, but for this, they first need a specific design. The designed nanocarriers minimize the exposure of drugs to healthy tissues when they enter the correct domain. Along with this advantage, the enhanced permeability and retention (EPR) effect and enhanced permeability elicited by nanocarriers play a major role in drug delivery by nanocarriers [8−10]. While nanoparticles are generally in the range of 20−200 nm, endothelial pores range from 10 to 1000 nm. For this reason, the tumor has the opportunity to accumulate easily by extravasation into the interstitial space [9].

In addition to existing cancer treatment regimens, the development of more effective cancer treatments in direct proportion to technology has enabled us to obtain nanosized drug delivery systems such as liposomes, dendrimers, and carbon nanotubes (CNTs), which can selectively deliver the drug load to cancer cells. Although dendrimers and CNTs are frequently involved in biomedical applications, including many areas such as oncology, liposomes and nanoparticles are within the scope of research today.

Dendrimers represent a class of three-dimensional monodisperse synthetic macromolecules with a series of layered branches extending regularly from a central core molecule; CNTs CNTare potential needle-like carriers of bioactives, including drugs, proteins, and genes [9]. Detailed information about dendrimers and CNTs will be given to the readers in more detail in other chapters.

12.3 Carbon nanotubes

In the field of nanomaterials, CNTs are used in drug delivery, tissue engineering, cancer therapy, and bioimaging. CNTs can extend the lifespan of drugs as well as facilitate their delivery directly to targeted cells. Thus they are recognized as highly efficient biocompatible bioimaging and biosensor agents. CNTs were also used to detect the SARS-COVID-19 virus, which had a great impact on our lives at the end of 2019 and showed great results in the field of cancer therapy and tissue engineering, which is largely necessary considering the current conditions. General concerns with CNTs are the cytotoxicity values encountered in in vivo biomedical applications. In addition, the high production cost is among the disadvantages (Fig. 12.2).

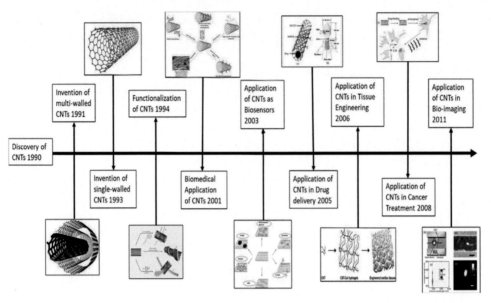

Figure 12.2 Timeline and demonstration of biomedical applications of CNTs [11]. *CNTs*, carbon nanotubes.

Carbon is one of the most versatile elements. It has many allotropes and conformations with various properties. With these properties, it provides the formation of various structures ranging from a few nanometers to hundreds of millimeters. Carbon materials have become a center of attraction in the field of nanotechnology that can be synthesized and characterized at the nano level. Carbon nanomaterials have unique properties such as high specific area, flexibility and optical transparency, higher electrical conductivity, and high carrier mobility. Therefore they are found in various fields such as drug delivery, molecular imaging, tissue engineering, and biosensing [12–14].

CNTs are divided into two types according to the number of carbon layers present: single-walled CNTs (SWCNTs) and multi-walled CNTs (MWCNTs) containing a single layer of graphene. SWCNTLs have diameters ranging from 0.4–2 nm and are usually hexagonally bundled bundles. It has a total of two regions with different chemical and physical properties. These two regions are the end wall of the pipe and the side wall of the pipe [11,15] (Fig. 12.3).

MWCNTs have a complex conformation of two or more cylinders (usually no more than 50), each composed of sheets of graphene. They have diameters in the 1–3 nm range and are also used in flexible sensors such as high-frequency semiconductor devices, microelectric devices, and electromyography [17].

(A)   (B)

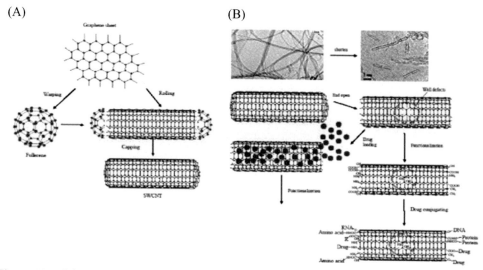

Figure 12.3 Schematic representation of the modification of CNTs with various molecules [16]. (A) A schematic representation of CNTs. (B) A schematic representation of the method for constructing CNT-based medication delivery systems. *CNTs,* carbon nanotubes.

CNTs have a hydrophobic nature and are therefore insoluble in water. They are also difficult to dissolve in other solvents. Various molecules with different chemical structures can be conjugated with CNTs, leading to potential applications in the biomedical field [11,18]. CNTs have started to be used in drug delivery because they improve the penetration of the drug used in the studies in the cells and lead to a higher drug effect. Its use in anticancer therapies includes selective targeting through surface functionalization. In the field of tissue engineering, it provides the realization of sensation in the microambiance of the cell in order to improve the mechanoelectrical aspects of the scaffold and to allow chemical reactions to take place inside the cells [19].

With the development of nanotechnology and the emergence of new treatment applications, new strategies and methodologies have begun to be developed for effective cancer treatment. Current treatment modalities include radiotherapy, chemotherapy, surgical interventions, and immunotherapy. These methods can have serious side effects. For this reason, the emergence of cancer treatments including targeted drug delivery, diagnosis, and imaging with the formation of systems based on nanomaterials is also observed as a major role in drug delivery. The CNTs being tested for these specific applications have been developed with Zhou and other colleagues using MTX, known as an analytical device, the detection model system, to detect the anticancer drug in blood. However, in practice, it is necessary to regulate the MTX concentration, create an optimized dosage for patients, and minimize the possibility of poisoning [20].

Properties of CNTs such as large surface area, encapsulation ability, conjugation, high drug capacity, target-specific action, and strong near-infrared (NIR) radiation absorbance make them suitable for use as a vehicle in chemotherapy and photothermal applications. In addition, carbon nanoparticles can cross the cell membrane and penetrate tumor cells due to their increased permeability and retention effects. CNTs can also achieve target specificity with a certain type of functionalization. Acid-treated CNTs develop a -COOH group on the surface that can be further modified by adding amines, antibodies, thiols, carbohydrates, and glycoproteins to achieve target specificity [21−23].

12.4 Dendrimers

Dendrimers are known in the literature as a specific and synthetic macromolecule class consisting of branches built around a central core with many functions. Each branch point layer creates a new generation and these branches depend on the type of terminal functions. Dendrimers, often regarded as three-dimensional soft nanoparticles, have even greater molecular size branching than a branched polymer of glucose or some branched lignin. Many expectations have been set for this conformation, leading to the emergence of many patents and publications related to medicine [24−26] (Fig. 12.4).

There is a nucleus in the center of dendrimers, and this nucleus consists of an atom or groups of atoms consisting of carbon branches and other added elements as a result of repeated chemical reactions to produce a structure called dendric structure [28−30]. Within the central core, there are branches that give rise to multiple inner layers with repeating units. The structure is surrounded by these branches [31]. It has been determined that flexible cavities that facilitate the encapsulation of the molecules of other

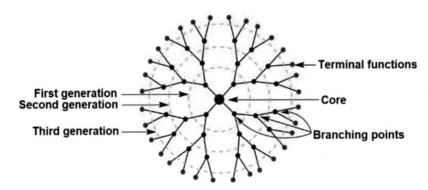

Figure 12.4 A schematic third-generation dendrimer showing the main structural features [27].

added atoms are formed in the spaces inside the dendrimer building blocks, and the number of branching points from this central core to the surface is called the generation number [32,33]. To give an example, a dendrimer with 4 branching points gets a designation called the G4 dendrimer and is called the fourth generation. For this reason, a fourth-generation polyamidoamine (PAMAM) dendrimer is referred to as G4-PAMAM.

There is an increase in each generation as dendrimers are synthesized. These increases are called G. It is one of the biggest known features of dendritic structures to cause their masses to double [34]. There are many functional groups on the outer surfaces of dendrimeric structures, and these groups have very important roles in the biological interactions or physicochemical properties of dendrimeric structures [35]. Generally, the functional groups found on these surfaces are more appropriate to be synthesized specifically to modulate cell interactions in targeted biological systems.

In addition, seedless dendrimers can also be found. These structures have taken place in the literature as dendrons. Various dendrimers can be synthesized by combining two or more dendrons [36].

12.4.1 Poly-L-lysine-based dendrimers

The first large dendrimer structures synthesized and patented were based on poly-L-lysine. Initially functionalized with 24 macrocyclic gadolinium complexes on the surface, these dendrimers provided a high relaxation agent for magnetic resonance imaging. This compound, designated SHL 643 A, was put into practice by first imaging healthy aortoiliac regions, then injecting it into patients with coronary artery disease. However, a new published result with this compound could not be detected in the literature [37,38].

12.4.2 Polyamidoamine dendrimers

PolyAMidoAMine, abbreviated PAMAM dendrimers, is the most widely used dendrimer type. In native form, they have NH2 terminal functions as poly-L-lysine dendrimers. These features allow them to be changed easily when they want. The risk of reverse Michael addition, which causes the structure to break especially in acidic conditions, has prevented the use of PAMAM dendrimers in clinical studies for a long time. However, recently, PAMAM dendrimers have been retested and the form obtained with the change of terminal functions to hydroxyl has started to be used again [27,39].

12.4.3 Polypropylene imine dendrimers

Polypropylene imine (PPI) dendrimers are some of the earliest known dendrimers with the propylamine spacer parts best specified by Vogtle. In general, it has been observed that the primary amine terminal groups are composed of poly-alkylamines and the inner parts are composed of tertiary Tris(3-hydroxypropyltriazolylmethyl) amine. These dendrimers have been studied before in biological sciences based on bio-materials and are also referred to in the literature by names such as polypropylene amine or diamino butane. Polyethylene imine dendrimers, on the other hand, consist of a subclass of PPI dendrimers and are known to consist of diamino ethane and diamino propane [31].

12.4.4 Frechet-type dendrimers

These dendrimers are the dendrimer types discovered by Hawker and Frechet as hyper-branched architecture of poly-benzyl ether [40,41]. Frechet dendrimers contain -COOH in their terminal region and therefore offer a good branching region for modulation of terminal groups. A good aspect of the presence of these polar-charged groups in these dendrimers is that they increase their solubility in aqueous environments and in environments where these polar-loaded solvents are present [28].

12.4.5 Core-shell tecto dendrimer

This type of dendrimer consists of structures that use the other as a core by covalently surrounding the dendrimer molecules with the shells of other dendrimers. Usually, the number of nuclei found is even higher than the dendrimers around them. The addition of additional shells is controlled by synthetic procedures [42].

12.4.6 Chiral dendrimers

Various branches are used while synthesizing these dendrimers structurally. However, it is known that they are chemically similar to the chiral nucleus. This chiral is located on the axis of the functional groups. Chiral only, the Chirality of dendrimers containing a core, and with it their optical activity, decrease at the right rate with the increase in the size of the dendrimers [43,44].

12.4.7 Liquid crystal dendrimers

Potential industry applications have been used in the synthesis of liquid crystals and have been studied by many researchers [31]. These dendrimers are composed of mesogenic liquid crystal monomers. It is known that the formation of liquid crystal phases is formed by rod-like or disk-like molecules [45].

12.4.8 Peptide dendrimers

These dendrimers consist of peptidyl-branched nuclei or radial or wedge-like branched macromolecular structures composed of covalently linked terminal functional groups.

Peptide dendrimers are generally synthesized using different and convergent synthesis methods [31]. It is seen that peptide dendims are used as multidrug peptides in the biomedical field known as surfactants in sweetening proteins and in applications such as drug and gene transfer [46,47].

12.4.9 Polyester dendrimers

The development of therapeutic indices of drugs and making them more effective has been an important area in ailments such as cancer, inflammatory diseases, and other infectious diseases such as HIV. Polyester dendrimers are seen as one of the most promising in this field due to their biocompatibility and degradation within the cell. It shows the lowest toxicity in drug delivery systems due to reduced exposure of these dendrimers to healthy tissues. Similar to the commonly used dendrimers, these dendrimers contain a lot of space inside and can, therefore serve to transport drugs, metals, and imaging parts [48−52] (Fig. 12.5).

12.5 Dendrimers and carbon nanotubes-based drug delivery for pancreatic cancer

Pancreatic cancer is one of the tumor types, with a high mortality rate and five-year survival time of about 5%. Pancreatic cancer has proven to be difficult to treat through traditional methods, including surgery and chemotherapy [54]. Nanomedicine researchers have unique drug delivery systems to treat especially pancreatic cancer. The drug delivery systems are the new smart drugs where the carrier is loaded with both diagnostic and therapeutic agents [55] (Fig. 12.6).

Recent studies have emerged based on CNTs and dendrimers acting as drug carriers. In particular, CNTs are used as the third allotropic form of carbon fullerene wrapped in cylindrical tubes. It is modified in a therapeutically active structure by forming supramolecular assemblies with stable covalent bonds or noncovalent bonds to ensure integration in biological systems. This enables it to be functional. Due to their biocompatibility and cell specificity along with their high carrying capacity, they have been investigated in various cancer cells in the evaluation of pharmacokinetic parameters, cytotoxicity, cell viability, and drug delivery in tumor cells. This process is also valid for the dendrimer and has been tested in drug combinations based on the specificity of its conformation and configuration [56].

A study by Huang et al. in January 2022 on pancreatic ductal adenocarcinoma designed peptide dendrimers as boosters of chemotherapy. Chemotherapy could not be used effectively due to the presence of a dense dysplastic tumor stroma that prevents drug accumulation and deep penetration in tumors. It markedly promoted the accumulation of free doxorubicin upon coincubation of the synthesized dendrimers and their deep progression into three-dimensional multicellular pancreatic ductal adenocarcinoma (PDAC) tumor

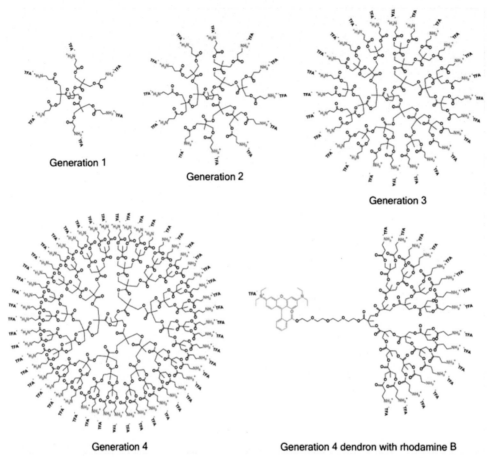

Generation 1

Generation 2

Generation 3

Generation 4

Generation 4 dendron with rhodamine B

Figure 12.5 Generation one to four amino-functional bis-MPA dendrimers included in a 2018 study by Stenstrom et al. Illustration of rhodamine B-labeled generation 4 dendron structures synthesized to study the subcellular localization of these materials as well as the BU dendrimer. TFA is short for trifluoroacetate [53].

cultures. It greatly increased the doxorubicin concentration of the designed dendrimers. Dendrimer also promoted free doxorubicin internalization into PDAC cells mimicking the tumor microenvironment [57].

A significant increase in the anticancer activity of doxorubicin and gemcitabine was observed when any of the drugs were administered to mouse models carrying PDAC tumor xenografts with a dendrimer, and this procedure was performed for each mouse separately. This result was particularly evident for the treatment of the dendrimer and gemcitabine combination, resulting in a reduction of up to 12.9% in tumor weight compared to gemcitabine treatment alone. Looking at the work can be attributed to the combination of

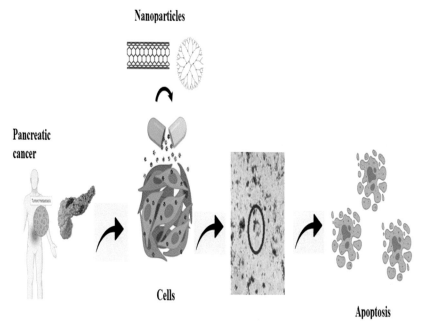

Figure 12.6 Schematic representation of targeted drug delivery in pancreatic cancer therapy. *Available from: http://www.biorender.com.*

multiple functionalities of the dendrimer. In short, it promotes free drug accumulation and deep penetration into tumors and internalization into cancer cells [58].

In another article published by Seidu et al., transfection by fluoridation of dendrimers in pancreatic adenocarcinomas enabled dendrimers to be highly efficient gene vectors and to internalize fluorine on drug molecules. The fluorinated dendrimers provide enhanced cellular uptake and increase transfection efficiency due to endosomal escape. With their proper size and zeta-potentials, these materials exhibit significant DNA condensation and screen ability and make a difference in drug delivery. In a different study, Wang et al. found that more than 90% of gene transfection occurred in HeLa and HEK293 cells as well as pancreatic cells [59–61] (Fig. 12.7).

In a study published by Bura et al., considering that epidermal growth factor (EGF) is overexpressed in pancreatic cancer, SWCNTs s were functionalized with EGF. These were applied to pancreatic cancer cells (PANC-1), providing a kinetic characterization of the nanoprobe's kinetics with the drug delivery system. Raman spectroscopy and enzyme-linked immunosorbent assay (ELISA) were used for characterization detection. The study showed that laser irradiation of PANC-1 cells containing nanoprobes induces significant apoptosis compared to untargeted probes, revealing large aggregates of tumor cells that play a major role in EGF

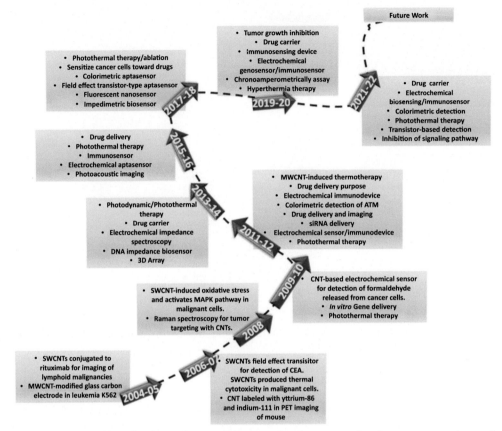

Figure 12.7 A roadmap for the evolution of the use of carbon nanotubes in cancer targeting and diagnosis is shown in the diagram [62].

conjugation. Thus this process has become available for specific targeting of pancreatic adenocarcinomas [63] (Fig. 12.8).

The use of dendrimers and CNTs in biomedical and medical fields is increasing, and especially in the field of oncology, they help drugs reach the required target areas and persist in that region despite the tumor microenvironment. In addition to the studies, new studies are still coming, and studies are continuing with great insistence to be used in new therapeutic treatments of cancer types that pose serious dangers and cause death today, especially pancreatic cancer. It is thought that the cost of dendrimers and CNTs will decrease in the future and will enable the formation of new therapeutic treatments.

Table 12.1 has shown several dendrimers and CNT-based therapeutics for pancreatic cancer therapy.

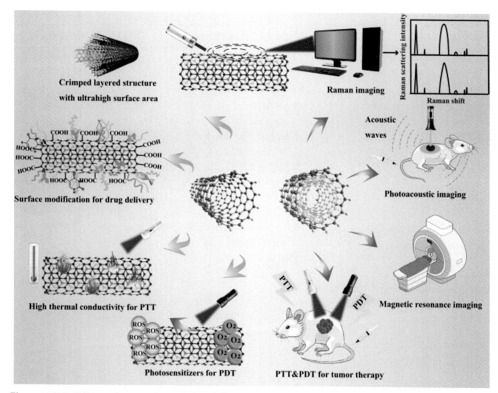

Figure 12.8 Schematic overview of the different applications of CNTs in cancer theranostics [64]. *CNTs*, carbon nanotubes.

Table 12.1 Dendrimer and carbon-based nanoparticles for pancreatic cancer therapy.

Drug/gene	Type of nanoparticle	Disease	References
Gemcitabine and retinoic acid	PAMAM dendrimer	Pancreatic cancer	[65]
Paclitaxel (PTX) and TR3 small interfering RNA (siRNA)	Peptide modified dendrimer	Pancreatic cancer	[66]
Gemcitabine (Gem) and miR-21 inhibitor (miR-21i)	Dendrimer-entrapped gold nanoparticles	Pancreatic cancer	[67]
3, 4-difluorobenzylidene curcumin (CDF)	Hyaluronic acid-conjugated polyamidoamine dendrimers	Pancreatic cancer	[68]
Flt-1 (a receptor for vascular endothelial growth factors (VEGF)) antibody	Polyethylene glycol (PEG)-cored PAMAM dendrimers	Pancreatic cancer	[69]

(*Continued*)

Table 12.1 (Continued)

Drug/gene	Type of nanoparticle	Disease	References
5-fluorouracil (5Fu)	Amino-capped polyamidoamine (PAMAM) dendrimer	Pancreatic cancer	[70]
Doxorubicin and gemcitabine	TAEA-cored peptide dendrimers	Pancreatic cancer	[58]
Gemcitabine	Amphiphilic dendritic nanomicelle	Pancreatic cancer	[71]
siRNA	Single walled carbon nanotubes (SWNTs)	Pancreatic cancer	[72]
IGF-1R	CNTs	Pancreatic Cancer	[73]
MBD1siRNA	LyP-1-functionalized multiwalled CNTs	Pancreatic cancer	[74]
—	PEG-ylated multiwalled CNTs	Pancreatic cancer	[75]
Ginseng secondary metabolites (ginsenoside Rb1 or Rg1)	CNT	Pancreatic cancer	[76]
DNA	Single-walled carbon nanotubes (SWCNT)	Pancreatic cancer	[77]

12.6 Conclusion

The use of dendrimers and CNTs in biomedical and medical fields is increasing, and especially in the field of oncology, they help drugs reach the required target areas and persist in that region despite the tumor microenvironment. In addition to the studies, new studies are still coming, and studies are continuing with great insistence to be used in new therapeutic treatments of cancer types that pose serious dangers and cause death today, especially pancreatic cancer. It is thought that the cost of dendrimers and CNTs will decrease in the future and will enable the formation of new therapeutic treatments.

References

[1] Cancer Stat Facts: Pancreatic Cancer. Available from: https://seer.cancer.gov/statfacts/html/pancreas.html.
[2] Puckett Y, Garfield K. Pancreatic cancer. StatPearls [Internet]. Treasure Island (FL): StatPearls Publishing; 2022. Jan.
[3] Health Commission Of The People's Republic Of China. National guidelines for diagnosis and treatment of pancreatic cancer 2022 in China (English version). Chin J Cancer Res 2022;34(3): 238—55.
[4] Miyaki C, Lynch LM. An update on common pharmaceuticals in the prevention of pancreatic cancer. Cureus 2022;14(5):e25496.

[5] Cho K, Wang XU, Nie S, Chen Z, Shin DM. Therapeutic nanoparticles for drug delivery in cancer. Clin Cancer Res 2008;14(5):1310−16.

[6] Bharali DJ, Khalil M, Gurbuz M, Simone TM, Mousa SA. Nanoparticles and cancer therapy: a concise review with emphasis on dendrimers. Int J Nanomed 2009;4:1−7.

[7] Tekade RK, Kumar PV, Jain NK. Dendrimers in oncology: an expanding horizon. Chem Rev 2009;109(1):49−87.

[8] Li Y, Wang J, Wientjes MG, Au JLS. Delivery of nanomedicines to extracellular and intracellular compartments of a solid tumor. Adv Drug Deliv Rev 2012;64(1):29−39.

[9] Maeda H, Bharate GY, Daruwalla J. Polymeric drugs for efficient tumor-targeted drug delivery based on EPR-effect. Eur J Pharm Biopharm 2009;71(3):409−19.

[10] Mody N, Tekade RK, Mehra NK, Chopdey P, Jain NK. Dendrimer, liposomes, carbon nanotubes and PLGA nanoparticles: one platform assessment of drug delivery potential. AAPS PharmSciTech 2014;15(2):388−99.

[11] Murjani BO, Kadu PS, Bansod M, Vaidya SS, Yadav MD. Carbon nanotubes in biomedical applications: current status, promises, and challenges. Carbon Lett 2022;32(5):1207−26.

[12] Patel KD, Singh RK, Kim HW. Carbon-based nanomaterials as an emerging platform for theranostics. Mater Horiz 2019;6(3):434−69.

[13] Rauti R, Musto M, Bosi S, Prato M, Ballerini L. Properties and behavior of carbon nanomaterials when interfacing neuronal cells: How far have we come? Carbon 2019;143:430−46.

[14] Tiwari SK, Pandey R, Wang N, Kumar V, Sunday OJ, Bystrzejewski M, et al. Progress in diamanes and diamanoids nanosystems for emerging technologies. Adv Sci 2022;9(11):2105770.

[15] Aqel A, Abou El-Nour KM, Ammar RA, Al-Warthan A. Carbon nanotubes, science and technology part (I) structure, synthesis and characterisation. Arab J Chem 2012;5(1):1−23.

[16] Zhang W, Zhang Z, Zhang Y. The application of carbon nanotubes in target drug delivery systems for cancer therapies. Nanoscale Res Lett 2011;6(1):555.

[17] Jha R, Singh A, Sharma PK, Fuloria NK. Smart carbon nanotubes for drug delivery system: a comprehensive study. J Drug Deliv Sci Technol 2020;58:101811.

[18] Simon J, Flahaut E, Golzio M. Overview of carbon nanotubes for biomedical applications. Materials 2019;12(4):624.

[19] Raphey VR, Henna TK, Nivitha KP, Mufeedha P, Sabu C, Pramod KJMS. Advanced biomedical applications of carbon nanotube. Mater Sci Eng C 2019;100:616−30.

[20] Zhou H, Ran G, Masson JF, Wang C, Zhao Y, Song Q. Novel tungsten phosphide embedded nitrogen-doped carbon nanotubes: a portable and renewable monitoring platform for anticancer drug in whole blood. Biosens Bioelectron 2018;105:226−35.

[21] Jeyamohan P, Hasumura T, Nagaoka Y, Yoshida Y, Maekawa T, Kumar DS. Accelerated killing of cancer cells using a multifunctional single-walled carbon nanotube-based system for targeted drug delivery in combination with photothermal therapy. Int J Nanomed 2013; 8:2653.

[22] Kam NWS, Dai H. Carbon nanotubes as intracellular protein transporters: generality and biological functionality. J Am Chem Soc 2005;127(16):6021−6.

[23] Madani SY, Tan A, Dwek M, Seifalian AM. Functionalization of single-walled carbon nanotubes and their binding to cancer cells. Int J Nanomed 2012;7:905−14.

[24] Majoral JP, Zablocka M, Ciepluch K, Milowska K, Bryszewska M, Shcharbin D, et al. Hybrid phosphorus−viologen dendrimers as new soft nanoparticles: design and properties. Org Chem Front 2021;8(16):4607−22.

[25] Roach PJ, Depaoli-Roach AA, Hurley TD, Tagliabracci VS. Glycogen and its metabolism: some new developments and old themes. Biochem J 2012;441(3):763−87.

[26] Xia Y, Matham MV, Su H, Padmanabhan P, Gulyas B. Nanoparticulate contrast agents for multi-modality molecular imaging. J Biomed Nanotechnol 2016;12(8):1553−84.

[27] Caminade AM. Dendrimers, an emerging opportunity in personalized medicine? J Pers Med 2022;12(8):1334.

[28] Elham FA, Sedigheh A, Abolfazl M, Morteza TN, Hamid WJ, Sang H, et al. Dendrimers: synthesis, applications, and properties. Nanoscale Res Lett 2014;9:247.

[29] Zeng FW, Zimmrman SC. Dendrimers in supramolecular chemistry:from molecular recognition to self-assembly. Chem Rev 1997;97:1681.

[30] Zimmerman SC. Dendrimers in molecular recognition and self-assembly. Curr Opin Colloid Interface Sci 1997;2(1):89−99.

[31] Sherje AP, Jadhav M, Dravyakar BR, Kadam D. Dendrimers: a versatile nanocarrier for drug delivery and targeting. Int J Pharm 2018;548(1):707−20. Available from: https://doi.org/10.1016/j.ijpharm.2018.07.030.

[32] Tomalia DA. Birth of a new macromolecular architecture: dendrimers as quantized building blocks for nanoscale synthetic polymer chemistry. Prog Polym Sci 2005;30:294−324.

[33] Noriega-Luna LA, Godínez FJ, Rodríguez A, Rodríguez GZ, Larrea CF, Sosa-Ferreyra RF, et al. Applications of dendrimers in drug delivery agents, diagnosis, therapy, and detection BustosJ Nanomater 2014;2014. Available from: https://doi.org/10.1155/2014/507273.

[34] Hao-Jui H, Jason B, Seung-ri L, Seungpyo H. Dendrimer-based nanocarriers: a versatile platform for drug delivery. Wiley Interdiscip Rev Nanomed Nanobiotechnol 2017;(9) Article e1409.

[35] Caminade AM, Turrin CO. Dendrimers for drug delivery. J Mater Chem 2014;2:4055−66.

[36] Boas U, Christensen JB, Heegaard PMH. Dendrimers: design, synthesis and chemical properties. Dendrimers in medicine and biotechnology new molecular tools. RSC Publishing; 2006.

[37] Herborn CU, Schmidt M, Bruder O, Nagel E, Shamsi K, Barkhausen J. MR coronary angiography with SH L 643 A: initial experience in patients with coronary artery disease. Radiology 2004;233 (2):567−73.

[38] Runge VM, Heverhagen JT. Advocating the development of next-generation high-relaxivity gadolinium chelates for clinical magnetic resonance. Invest Radiol 2018;53(7):381−9.

[39] McCarthy TD, Karellas P, Henderson SA, Giannis M, O'Keefe DF, Heery G, et al. Dendrimers as drugs: discovery and preclinical and clinical development of dendrimer-based microbicides for HIV and STI prevention. Mol Pharm 2005;2(4):312−18.

[40] Hawker, Frechet JMJ. A new convergent approach to monodisperse dendritic macromolecules. J Chem Soc Chem Commun 1990;15:1010−13.

[41] Hawker CJ, Wooley KL, Frechet JMJ. Unimolecular micelles and globular amphiphiles: dendritic macromolecules as novel recyclable solubilisation agents. J Chem Soc Perkin Trans 1993;1(12):1287−97.

[42] Li J, Swanson DR, Qin D, Brothers HM, Piehler LT, Tomalia D, et al. Characterizations of core-shell tecto-(dendrimer) molecules by tapping mode atomic force microscopy. Langmuir 1999;15: 7347−50.

[43] Kremers JA, Meijer EW. Synthesis and characterization of a chiral dendrimer derived from pentaerythritolore. J Org Chem 1994;59:4262−6.

[44] Seebach RP, Beat G, Greiveldinger T, Butz H, Sellner. Chiral dendrimers − dendrimers. Topics in current chemistry. Berlin, Heidelberg: Springer; 1998. p. 125−64.

[45] Frey H, Lorenz K, Mulhaupt R. Dendritic polyols based on carbosilanes-lipophilic dendrimers with hydrophilic skin. Macromol Symp 1996;102:19−26.

[46] Kinberger GA, Cai W, Goodman M. Collagen mimetic dendrimers. J Am Chem Soc 2002;124: 15162−3.

[47] Sadler K, Tam JP. Peptide dendrimers: applications and synthesis. Mol Biotechnol 2002;90:195−229.

[48] Gillies ER, Dy E, Frechet JMJ, Szoka FC. Biological evaluation of polyester dendrimer: poly (ethylene oxide) "Bow-Tie" hybrids with tunable molecular weight and architecture. Mol Pharm 2005;2:129−38.

[49] Jain K, Kesharwani P, Gupta U, Jain NK. Dendrimer toxicity: let's meet the challenge. Int J Pharm 2010;394:122−42.

[50] Jean-d'Amour Twibanire K, Bruce Grindley T. Polyester dendrimers: smart carriers for drug delivery. Polymers 2014;6:179−213.

[51] Morgan MT, Carnahan MA, Immoos CE, Ribeiro AA, Finkelstein S, Lee SJ, et al. Dendritic molecular capsules for hydrophobic compounds. J Am Chem Soc 2003;125:15485−9.

[52] Antoni P, Hed Y, Nordberg A, Nyström D, von Holst H, Hult A, et al. Bifunctional dendrimers: from robust synthesis and accelerated one-pot post-functionalization strategy to potential applications. Angew Chem Int Ed 2009;48:2126−30.

[53] Stenström P, Manzanares D, Zhang Y, Ceña V, Malkoch M. Evaluation of amino-functional poly-ester dendrimers based on bis-MPA as nonviral vectors for siRNA delivery. Molecules (Basel, Switzerland) 2018;23(8):2028.

[54] Kurtanich T, Roos N, Wang G, Yang J, Wang A, Chung EJ. Pancreatic cancer gene therapy deliv-ered by nanoparticles. SLAS Technol 2019;24(2):151−60.

[55] Jaidev LR, Chede LS, Kandikattu HK. Theranostic nanoparticles for pancreatic cancer treatment. Endocr Metab Immune Disord Drug Targets 2021;21(2):203−14.

[56] Rastogi V, Yadav P, Bhattacharya SS, Mishra AK, Verma N, Verma A, et al. Carbon nanotubes: an emerging drug carrier for targeting cancer cells. J Drug Deliv 2014;2014:670815.

[57] Huang S, Huang X, Yan H. Peptide dendrimers as potentiators of conventional chemotherapy in the treatment of pancreatic cancer in a mouse model. Eur J Pharm Biopharm 2022;170:121−32.

[58] Huang S, Huang X, Yan H. Peptide dendrimers as potentiators of conventional chemotherapy in the treatment of pancreatic cancer in a mouse model. Eur J Pharm Biopharm 2022; 170:121−32.

[59] Seidu TA, Kutoka PT, Asante DO, Farooq MA, Alolga RN, Bo W. Functionalization of nanoparti-culate drug delivery systems and its influence in cancer therapy. Pharmaceutics 2022;14(5):1113.

[60] Wang H, Wang Y, Wang Y, Hu J, Li T, Liu H, et al. Self-assembled fluorodendrimers combine the features of lipid and polymeric vectors in gene delivery. Angew Chem 2015;127(40):11813−17.

[61] Wang M, Liu H, Li L, Cheng Y. A fluorinated dendrimer achieves excellent gene transfection effi-cacy at extremely low nitrogen to phosphorus ratios. Nat Commun 2014;5:3053.

[62] Singh R, Kumar S. Cancer targeting and diagnosis: recent trends with carbon nanotubes. Nanomaterials (Basel, Switzerland) 2022;12(13):2283.

[63] Bura C, Mocan T, Grapa C, Mocan L. Carbon nanotubes-based assays for cancer detection and screening. Pharmaceutics 2022;14(4):781.

[64] Tang L, Xiao Q, Mei Y, He S, Zhang Z, Wang R, et al. Insights on functionalized carbon nano-tubes for cancer theranostics. J Nanobiotechnol 2021;19(1):423.

[65] Yalçin S, Erkan M, Ünsoy G, Parsian M, Kleeff J, Gündüz U. Effect of gemcitabine and retinoic acid loaded PAMAM dendrimer-coated magnetic nanoparticles on pancreatic cancer and stellate cell lines. Biomed Pharmacother 2014;68(6):737−43.

[66] Li Y, Wang H, Wang K, Hu Q, Yao Q, Shen Y, et al. Targeted Co-delivery of PTX and TR3 siRNA by PTP peptide modified dendrimer for the treatment of pancreatic cancer. Small 2017;13(2). Available from: https://doi.org/10.1002/smll.201602697 Epub 2016 Oct 20. PMID: 27762495.

[67] Lin L, Fan Y, Gao F, Jin L, Li D, Sun W, et al. UTMD-promoted co-delivery of gemcitabine and miR-21 inhibitor by dendrimer-entrapped gold nanoparticles for pancreatic cancer therapy. Theranostics. 2018;8(7):1923−39.

[68] Kesharwani P, Xie L, Banerjee S, Mao G, Padhye S, Sarkar FH, et al. Hyaluronic acid-conjugated polyamidoamine dendrimers for targeted delivery of 3,4-difluorobenzylidene curcumin to CD44 overexpressing pancreatic cancer cells. Colloids Surf B Biointerfaces 2015;136:413−23.

[69] Öztürk K, Esendağh G, Gürbüz MU, Tülü M, Çalış S. Effective targeting of gemcitabine to pancre-atic cancer through PEG-cored Flt-1 antibody-conjugated dendrimers. Int J Pharm 2017;517 (1−2):157−67. Available from: https://doi.org/10.1016/j.ijpharm.2016.12.009.

[70] Chen J, Qiu M, Zhang S, Li B, Li D, Huang X, et al. A calcium phosphate drug carrier loading with 5-fluorouracil achieving a synergistic effect for pancreatic cancer therapy. J Colloid Interface Sci 2022;605:263−73.

[71] Zhao W, Yang S, Li C, Li F, Pang H, Xu G, et al. Amphiphilic dendritic nanomicelle-mediated deliv-ery of gemcitabine for enhancing the specificity and effectiveness. Int J Nanomed 2022;17:3239−49.

[72] Anderson T, Hu R, Yang C, Yoon HS, Yong KT. Pancreatic cancer gene therapy using an siRNA-functionalized single walled carbon nanotubes (SWNTs) nanoplex. Biomater Sci 2014;2(9): 1244−53.

[73] Lu GH, Shang WT, Deng H, Han ZY, Hu M, Liang XY, et al. Targeting carbon nanotubes based on IGF-1R for photothermal therapy of orthotopic pancreatic cancer guided by optical imaging. Biomaterials. 2019;195:13−22.

[74] Lin QJ, Xie ZB, Gao Y, Zhang YF, Yao L, Fu DL. LyP-1-fMWNTs enhanced targeted delivery of MBD1siRNA to pancreatic cancer cells. J Cell Mol Med 2020;24(5):2891–900.

[75] Mocan T, Matea CT, Cojocaru I, Ilie I, Tabaran FA, Zaharie F, et al. Photothermal treatment of human pancreatic cancer using PEGylated multi-walled carbon nanotubes induces apoptosis by triggering mitochondrial membrane depolarization mechanism. J Cancer 2014;5(8):679–88.

[76] Lahiani MH, Eassa S, Parnell C, Nima Z, Ghosh A, Biris AS, et al. Carbon nanotubes as carriers of Panax ginseng metabolites and enhancers of ginsenosides Rb1 and Rg1 anti-cancer activity. Nanotechnology. 2017;28(1):015101.

[77] Bhattacharya S, Gong X, Wang E, Dutta SK, Caplette JR, Son M, et al. DNA-SWCNT biosensors allow real-time monitoring of therapeutic responses in pancreatic ductal adenocarcinoma. Cancer Res 2019;79(17):4515–23.

Recent advances and future prospective for pancreatic cancer

Part C

Recent advances and future
prospective for pancreatic
cancer

CHAPTER 13

Personalized medicine and new therapeutic approach in the treatment of pancreatic cancer

Hanieh Azari[1,2],*, Elham Nazari[1,2],*, Hamid Jamialahmadi[1], Ghazaleh Khalili-Tanha[1],*, Mina Maftooh[1], Seyed Mahdi Hassanian[1,2], Gordon A. Ferns[3], Majid Khazaei[1,2] and Amir Avan[1,4,5,6]

[1]Metabolic Syndrome Research Center, Mashhad University of Medical Sciences, Mashhad, Iran
[2]Basic Sciences Research Institute, Mashhad University of Medical Sciences, Mashhad, Iran
[3]Division of Medical Education, Brighton & Sussex Medical School, Brighton, United Kingdom
[4]College of Medicine, University of Warith Al-Anbiyaa, Karbala, Iraq
[5]School of Mechanical, Medical and Process Engineering, Science and Engineering Faculty, Queensland University of Technology, Brisbane, QLD, Australia
[6]Faculty of Health, School of Biomedical Sciences, Queensland University of Technology, Brisbane, QLD, Australia

13.1 Introduction

Pancreatic cancer (PC) is the seventh most common cause of death in men and women and is predicted to become the second most important cause of cancer-related death by 2030 [1]. The etiology of PC is poorly understood, and few prevention strategies are available. Despite substantial epidemiological data on this multifactorial disease, few risk factors have been identified, include: family history, smoking, obesity, diabetes mellitus, Helicobacter pylori infection, hepatitis B, human immunodeficiency virus infection, and dietary intake. Lack of symptoms can make the early diagnosis of this condition difficult and lead to cancer detection in more advanced stages [2−7].

Various treatments have been used: such as chemotherapy, radiotherapy, and surgery, and often a combination of these. Complications during surgery and poor response to chemotherapy or radiotherapy have been a concern for metastatic PC. Extensive efforts have been made to improve traditional therapy, but there has been a slight improvement in the survival of this particularly devastating cancer. The challenges with treatment are partly due to the multiple genetic alterations/mutations associated with the disease, frequent tumor microenvironment, and inefficient drug delivery [5,6].

A better understanding of cellular and molecular signaling mechanisms, tumor microenvironments, and genetic mutations offers the opportunity to introduce novel promising therapeutics [3].

---

* Equally contributed as the first author.

Recent Advances in Nanocarriers for Pancreatic Cancer Therapy
DOI: https://doi.org/10.1016/B978-0-443-19142-8.00010-3
317

Recently personalized medicine (PM) has gained much attention as an emerging field based on a biological approach that can make a real difference in offering better treatment by identifying the causing genomic makeup of each patient. In doing so, the focus will be a combination of genetic, environmental, and behavioral factors to improve the targeted therapy and reduce costs. PM has the potential for oncogenic drivers for tailoring therapy of the tumor, optimizing tumor response, and therapy-induced toxicities for each patient, and modulating the tumor immune environment. PIK3CA signaling pathway, DNA repair dysfunction, and next-generation sequencing analyses can be mentioned as PM approaches in PC therapy. Furthermore, four genes, KRAS, TP53, CDKN2A, and SMAD4, can be considered for genetic mutations in this regard. PM is an opportunity that care providers would adopt to offer better treatment options, improve the quality of care, decrease the error of medicine, and reduce cost. It is undeniable that the PM can be served to aid patients, physicians, policymakers, and health care providers in better achieving the main goals of care. Also, it would play a pivotal role in revolutionizing the future of healthcare that must be addressed [4,8,9]. Owing to the paramount importance of PM, the present chapter provides a starting point for introducing PM in PC therapy to confront with challenges of current treatment practice. Therefore, we will endeavor to deal with novel therapies highlighted by PM for PC.

13.1.1 Pancreatic cancer: common treatment

Based on the stage of disease, various treatments can be used for PC that include: chemotherapy, radiation therapy, immunotherapy, and surgery. Sometimes, combining several treatment options may be appropriate. For example, immunotherapy might be advised before surgery. For advanced-stage PC, treatment options might focus on pain relief and keeping symptoms manageable as much as possible. In addition to the advantages of each treatment method, disadvantages can also be listed, such as hair loss in chemotherapy, dose adjustment in radiotherapy, and invasiveness in surgery. The side effects are summarized in Table 13.1 [5,10–12].

To overcome the challenges of current treatments, new approaches have attracted the attention of researchers and care providers in recent years. PM is one of the recommended therapy models.

13.2 Could personalized medicine transform healthcare?

Recently, with Advances in omics technologies such as genomics, there has been a notable shift from traditional medicine to PM. PM is an emerging approach to medicine that uses an individual's genetic profile for better decision-making and could lead to new insights into the diagnosis, treatment of disease, and prevention. It fundamentally focuses on a combination of genetic, environmental, and behavioral factors to

Table 13.1 Current side effects of PC (pancreatic cancer) treatment.

Radiation therapy Using radiation to destroy cancer cells	Chemotherapy Using small molecules to destroy cancer cells	Immunotherapy Using certain parts of the immune system to fight cancer	Surgery Removal of cancer
• Damage to surrounding tissues • Skin changes in the irradiated areas, from redness to blisters and scaling • Nausea and vomiting • Diarrhea • Tiredness • Loss of appetite • Weight Loss • Lowers the number of blood platelets and increases the risk of serious infection	• Fatigue • Hair loss • Easy bruising and bleeding • Infection • Anemia • Nausea and vomiting • Appetite changes • Diarrhea • Constipation • Multidrug resistance • Systemic toxicity • Chemoresistance peculiar adverse event • Unpleasant skin changes such as spots, sagging, and wrinkles • Headache, Muscular pain, Stomach ache, or pain in the fingers and toes • Mouth and throat sores • Blood disorders • Changes in memory and concentration • Sexual and reproductive issues	• Can cause the immune system to attack the patient's kidney, heart, and other organs • Lethally treatment • It may not work • Low response rate • Immune-related adverse effects • Use of small drugs to target cancer-specific hallmarks • Support the body's immune system and fight cancer	• Reconstructive surgery may be needed • It is one of the invasive methods for the patient • Inability to kill microscopic disease around the edge of the tumor • may leave tumor cells in the PC patient • The patient must tolerate the agony and anesthesia

improve the quality-of-care services and reduce costs. Diagnosis and intervention, drug development, theranostics, radiotheranostics, respiratory proteomics, cancer genomics, and population screening are PM applications.

ICPerMed has developed a vision that includes five perspectives for "next-generation" medicine in 2030 with some promising directions for PM approaches, leading to increased effectiveness, equitable access for possible healthcare, and economic value. The perspectives are oriented as follows:

Perspective 1: Empowered, informed, engaged citizens: Health care monitoring can be controlled by the individual citizen.

Perspective 2: Empowered, informed, engaged health providers: Clinical decisions need to integrate novel health-related multidisciplinary professions. The education of health care providers should be considered in the aspect of PM.

Perspective 3: Improved service delivery: Healthcare systems can optimize health promotion at the level of disease prevention, diagnosis, and treatment. If resource allocation is aligned with social values, PM services will improve in equity and effectiveness.

Perspective 4: Available health-related information for better treatment, prevention, and research: For more efficient PM, healthcare providers and researchers can use personal data in electronic health records (EHRs).

Perspective 5: Economic value of establishing the next generation of medicine: A reasonable balance between investment and profit for the citizen is a reality for PM.

The goals of ICPerMed vision are well-being, promoting healthy lifestyles, prevention, and efficient healthcare for everyone. To successfully implement PM, data and technology, healthcare system reforms, intersectoral synergies, and education and literacy will be crucial tools. It would shed light on the latest development in the field of medicine and will crystalize the need for paradigm shifts in healthcare services (Fig. 13.1) [13,14].

PM promises to revolutionize health care, by exploring the most appropriate treatment for the right patient at the right time, and, therefore, has the potential to facilitate quality of care and help to decrease healthcare costs.

13.2.1 What is personalized medicine?

PM uses genomics and other features, such as the personality of the patient and environmental factors, to design a customized plan for treatment individually. These factors can be used for prevention, diagnosis, and predicting the response to medicines. PM based on individual genetic makeup is beginning to overcome traditional medicine's obstacles.

From another point of view, PM is a new approach to medical science in which a specially tailored medicine is administered to the patients considering various factors such as genetic, age, environment, and family [15–18].

PM uses various sciences, such as bioinformatics, biomathematics, biostatistics, and systems biology to integrate, analyze, and interpret genomics, transcriptomics,

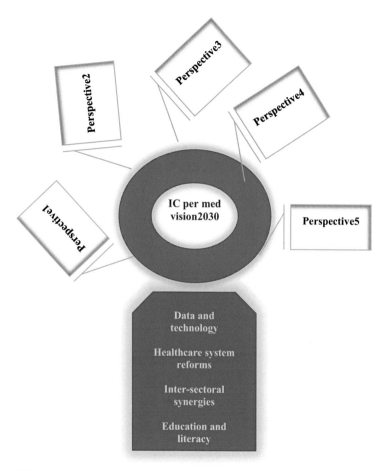

Figure 13.1 ICPerMed vision 2030 for PM. *ICPerMed*, International Consortium for Personalised Medicine; *PM*, personalized medicine.

proteomics, phenomics, nutrition, exposomics, epigenomics, microbiomics, and metabolomics data, to achieve better personalization of a population and right risk stratification of individual in population (Fig. 13.2).

13.2.2 Precision or personalized medicine: what's the difference?

PM and Precision are sometimes used interchangeably. The terms "Personalized Medicine" and "precision medicine" refer to genetic information for "individuals" treatment. However, recent technological advances in genetics play a major role in assessing this information regarding individual patients more accurately. Precision medicine is the new phrase for PM. The difference is that precision medicine is a medical strategy or model that seeks to adopt more precise new therapies by targeting disease

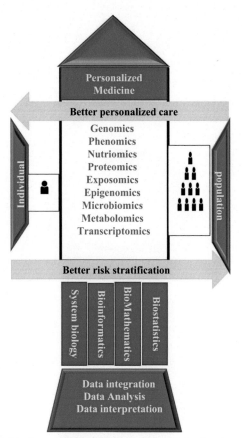

Figure 13.2 PM from individual to population health. *PM*, personalized medicine.

subgroups. It will need to rely on genomics, data science, data sharing, digital health, and other molecular technologies [19,20].

13.2.3 Advantages of personalized medicine

The idea of PM holds great promise, and many of its advantages for patients, providers, and populations are as follows:

As can be deducted from Table 13.2, the PM has many benefits for healthcare organizations, care providers, patients, and policymakers to achieve the main goals of health care consist of improving the quality of care and reducing costs. Integrative healthcare with PM has gained much attention and would lead to a remarkable revolution in service delivery.

It has facilitated health promotion, disease prevention, diagnosis and treatment, patient engagement, monitoring treatment adherence, and surveillance.

Table 13.2 Advantages of PM (personalized medicine) for patients, providers, and population [21–27].

Advantages for		
Patients	**Providers**	**Population**
• Increases patient involvement and engagement • Reduce costs for patients • Higher probability of the desired outcomes • Increases patient adherence to treatment • Enhances the ability to predict the best treatment for a specific patient • Individualized targeted medicine (finding the proper medication without error) • Reduces high-risk invasion testing procedures	• Increases the chances of a doctor using the patient's genetic and molecular information • Improves the ability to understand the underlying mechanisms of the disease • Captures more characteristics and heterogeneity of cancer • improves disease detection • Accurately predict disease • allows health care providers to offer better treatment options • predicts dosing and prescribes more effective drugs • Reveals additional or alternative uses for drug candidates • avoids prescribing drugs with predictable side effects • avoids adverse drug reactions • predicts susceptibility to disease • preempts disease progression • Reduces trial-and-error prescribing	• Focus on preventative medicine for population health • customizes disease prevention strategies • Improves the diagnosis and medical management of many diseases • helps in preventing, diagnosing, and treating a range of diseases

• Reduce the time, cost, and failure rate of clinical trials
• reduce error medicine
• The efficiency of care
• Decrease mortality

13.3 The role of personalized medicine in pancreatic cancer

Considering the heterogeneous nature of PC, lifestyle, tumor immune environment, and limits on the targeted therapy of PC, recent research has focused on early-stage detection. Advances in biomarker identification and imaging technology have contributed significantly to the early detection of disease before the incurable metastatic state. In oncology, precision medicine is a new approach to redefining cancer and its treatment. On the other hand, the PM is offering unique treatment for every patient.

Precision medicine, according to the genetics and molecular biology of cancer, has aided PC patients in discovering essential biomarkers, and more targeted approaches to therapy and immunotherapy could then improve survival outcomes.

Furthermore, the PM has the potential for oncogenic drivers for tailoring therapy of the tumor, optimizing tumor response, therapy-induced toxicities for the individualized patient, and modulating the tumor immune environment. A deep understanding of the tumor's cellular and molecular biology can help establish effective treatment strategies for cancers. Ultimately, this ensures better patient care [28,29].

13.4 Recent progress in personalized medicine for pancreatic cancer therapy

Many studies have revealed the promise of precision medicine. PIK3CA signaling pathway, Notch signaling, DNA repair dysfunction, cancer antigen 19-9, and next generation sequencing analyses can be mentioned as PM approaches in PC. Furthermore, four genes, KRAS, TP53, CDKN2A, and SMAD4, are most frequently mutated in pancreas cancer and can be considered for genetic alteration in PM. Here, we will mention the latest research on PC therapy with PM according to actionable gene mutations or molecular subtypes [30].

13.5 The molecular landscape of pancreatic cancer

Recently, the whole exome and whole genome sequencing have identified an extensive range of genetic, transcriptomic, and epigenetics variations of PC. These findings have led to valuable improvement in diagnosis, prognosis, and better treatments for PC. Most of these alterations are associated with pathways related to the proliferation, apoptosis, and repairing systems [31].

13.6 Genomic subgroups

The four most frequent mutations in PC have been detected in KRAS, CDKN2A, TP53, and SMAD4, which played a critical role in the cell cycle and apoptosis. These predominant mutations were reported in approximately 90% of PC patients. KRAS and CDKN2A variations were observed frequently in low-grade pancreatic lesions (PanIN1 and PanIN2), while mutated TP53 and SMAD4 were identified in the higher grade (PanIN3). The KRAS mutation is the first and foremost step in initiating PC or PanIN1, and the percentage of KRAS mutations ranges between 88% and 100%. The mutated gene activates RAS protein, which continuously hydrolysis DTP to GDP, resulting in increased cell proliferation. A previous study showed that KRAS mutation decreases the overall survival (OS) rate and is related to poor prognosis.

A wide range of mutations of KRAS was reported in PC; among them, mutations in codon 12 (G12D and G12R) with 48% and 31% are the most frequent in PC. Therefore, KRAS inhibitors could be a promising therapy for tumor growth inhibition. In-vivo and in-vitro studies showed that novel treatment silences the RAS pathway by targeting the RAS domains such as RBD and RA [32,33]. The CDKN2A is another well-known gene with an incidence rate of 75%—95% in PC. CDKN2A encodes two proteins, INK4 and p16, which arrest the cell cycle in the G1 phase. The inactivation of CDK2A increases tumor growth [34]. TP53 is a tumor suppressor protein that plays a pivotal role in apoptosis and cell cycle arrest. The inactivated p53 leads to proliferating damaged cells and cancer formation. The p53 mutations were found in 75% up to 85% of PC [35]. SMAD4 is a mediator of the TGF-B pathway regulating apoptosis and cell cycle. The data reported that SMAD4 inactivation in about 50% of PC patients.

DNA damage frequently occurs in cells, and repairing them is critical for cell survival. Various repairing systems maintain genome integrity, including base excision repair (BER), nucleotide excision repair (NER), mismatch repair system (MMR), homologous recombination (HR), and non-homologous end joining (NHEJ). BRCA1 and BRCA2 are members of the NHEJ system, which repair the DNA double-strand break (DSB). The studies showed BRCA1/2 mutations in about 5% of PC patients, while the mutation of BRCA2 accounts for approximately 20% of familial patients [36]. PALB2 is another member of the NHEJ system, which is necessary for the localization of BRCA2 in the nucleus. Previous investigations found that PALB2 mutation increased the risk of PC with familial history [37]. Ataxia telangiectasia mutated (ATM) is a member of the repairing system in DNA DSB. A Study reported that the risk of PC in patients with a germline ATM mutation accounts for 1.1% (age 50 years), 6.3% (age 70 years), and 9.5% (age 80 years) [38].

Approximately 20% of PC is related to chromatin alteration in remodelers. These mutations reported in the structural subunits of SWI/SNF complex included PBRM1, ARID1A, and ARID1B, which are bonded to DNA, and also in enzymatic subunits consisting of SMARCA4 and SMARCA2 catalyzed ATP for reorganizing complex [39] (Fig. 13.3).

13.7 Transcriptomic subgroup

Recently, new approaches categorized PC according to transcriptional profile. Collisson et al. predict three subgroups for PC: classical, quasi-mesenchymal (QM), and exocrine-like. The first subgroup identifies the expression level of KRAS and GATA6 genes with a higher OS. The QM group shows overexpression of mesenchyme-associated genes and poor survival rate, whereas the patients in the exocrine-like subgroup experience a moderate survival rate and high expression of tumor cell-derived digestive enzyme genes [40].

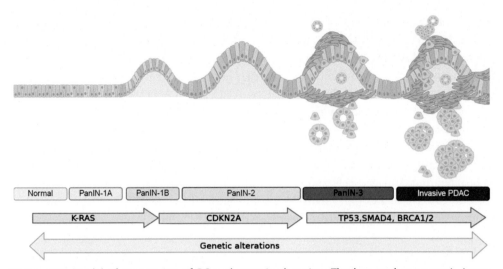

| Normal | PanIN-1A | PanIN-1B | PanIN-2 | PanIN-3 | Invasive PDAC |

K-RAS → CDKN2A → TP53,SMAD4, BRCA1/2 →

← Genetic alterations →

Figure 13.3 Model of progression of PC and genetic alteration. The low-grade pancreatic intrae-pithelial lesions (PanIN-1A and PanIN-1B) have K-RAS mutations, while the low-grade PanIN-2 shows CDKN2A mutations. Progression of low-grade PC to high-grade (PanIN-3) and the invasive tumor is associated with genetic variations in TP53, BRCA1/2, and SMAD4. *PC*, pancreatic cancer.

Moffitt et al. categorized PC into two main groups: tumor-specific and stromal-specific groups. The tumor-specific group has two subgroups, classical and basal-like, the basal-like subgroup shows overexpression of basal-like genes, such as keratin and lamin, and has a better response to chemotherapy, while this subgroup has a weak OS compared to the classical subgroup. The stromal-specific group was introduced into two subgroups, normal and activated. The normal stromal-specific groups displayed a better OS rate and prognosis than other subgroups [41].

Bailey et al. reported four subgroups for PC through RNASeq analysis, including squamous, immunogenic, pancreatic progenitor, and aberrantly differentiated endo-crine exocrine (ADEX). The squamous subgroup showed a high expression of genes in various inflammation pathways and hypoxia, such as P53, KDM6A, and transform-ing growth factor-b (TGF-B). The immunogenic subgroup displayed the dysregula-tion of the immune system. Another subgroup is pancreatic progenitor, which is known by differential apomucin expression. Lastly, the ADEX is featured by the over-expression of genes involved in endocrine and endocrine differentiation, including NR5A2, RBPJL, NEUROD1, and NKX2−2 [42].

Puleo et al. (2018), Aung et al. (2018), and Brinbaum et al. (2017) identified other transcriptomic subgroups, which overlap with the groups mentioned above. Overall, PC is separated into two main groups classical and basal-like/squamous subgroups. The classical subgroup showed a favorable survival rate and better prognosis, while the basal-like category resisted chemotherapy and had a poor prognosis [35,43,44].

13.8 Predictive markers of pancreatic cancer for personalized therapy

Researchers have recently focused on finding novel predictive markers to offer the best treatment for PC patients.

The previous studies reported the thymidylate synthase (TS) expression as a predictive marker. TS plays a pivotal role in dTMP synthesis, which is targeted by 5-fluorouracil (5-FU). The low expression of TS is a positive prognosis factor in patients with 5-fu-based chemotherapy [45]. The other studies found that the low expression of TS was associated with more prolonged disease-free survival (DFS) in PC patients who received 5-fu [46]. The result of phase III clinical trial (RTOG9704) showed that the patients with a high expression of deoxycytidine kinase (dCK), an enzyme that phosphorylated numerous deoxyribonucleosides, had longer OS and better response to 5-fu and gemcitabine [47,48].

Platinum-based drugs are a class of chemo agents such as oxaliplatin and cisplatin that bind to purine bases on DNA, resulting in DNA DSB. There is accumulating evidence that the patients with deficient DNA repairing systems, for example, a mutation in BRCA1/2, FANCG, and FANCC, showed better to radiation and platinum-based drugs [49,50]. It has been shown that a high expression of excision repair cross-complementing group 1 (ERCC1) gene, which is a key player in the NER system, is related to shorter OS in the patients who received FOLFIRINOX [51].

Gemcitabine therapy is the standard gold treatment for advanced PC. Two clinical trials (RTOG 9704 and ESPAC-3) indicated that the hENT1 gene, human equilibrative nucleoside transporter 1, is a transporter of gemcitabine into tumor cells overexpressed in patients with higher OS and DFS rates [52,53]. The result revealed that the combination of gemcitabine and erlotinib, an epidermal growth factor receptor (EGFR), had a better outcome in patients with wild-type KRAS. They had improved OS and a better prognosis [54].

The investigations showed that the patients with a BRCA1/2 mutation have a better response to Olaparib, a Poly-ADP ribose polymerase (PARP) inhibitor. The PARP inhibitors are a class of drugs that inhibit PARP. PARP plays a critical role in the BER system and actives different enzymes, resulting in repairing damage in DNA [55,56]

13.9 Examples of precision medicine in pancreatic cancer

13.9.1 Patient derived xenograft

Patient derived xenograft (PDX) provide a promising new tool for personalized cancer treatment based on the patient's genetics, tumor heterogeneity, and cancer microenvironment of the primary tumor. PDX is performed by engrafting the patients' tumor specimens, instead of cancerous cell lines, into immune-deficient animal models. Traditional cancer cell cultures and animal xenografts using cell lines are limited to the general pancreatic genetic profile and do not reflect the tumor heterogeneity and TME variations in patients. In contrast, PDX using the patient's tumor engraftments opens new opportunities to assess the pharmacogenetics and pharmacodynamics of treatments based on precision medicine [57].

Several studies have evaluated the different therapeutics, mainly the previously established drugs, by PDX in PC. Viqueira et al. tested several drugs in pancreatic ductal adenocarcinoma (PDAC) models involving PDX. They represented that the association of EGFR and phosphor-EGFR should be considered in response to some of the drugs [58]. In another study, it was shown that among 10 tested drugs in pancreatic PDX, cobimetinib and trametinib as MEK inhibitors caused tumor regression more efficiently [59]. Some of the other studies compared and correlated the pharmacological results in PDX with the clinical outcomes. For example, in a study on pancreatic PDX models, it was shown that the tumor regression in 88% of models was consistent with the response of patients to the treatments [60]. Moreover, to find the appropriate treatment regimen, in a clinical study of a gemcitabine resistance PC patient, the sensitivity of PDX generated by the patient's tumor to DNA-damaging agents such as cisplatin and mitomycin C was shown, and according to this finding, conducted chemotherapy with these drugs resulted to 3 years lack of symptoms in the patient with 3 months predicted surveillance [61].

PDX, in conclusion, mirrors the patient's tumor heterogeneity, genetic profile, and sensitivity to therapies. Despite all these merits, it has some shortcomings including the lack of standardization, the slowness of technique for clinical application, and many others that should be addressed for more implementation of pancreatic PDXs in clinical PM.

13.9.2 Patient's derived organoid

Considering the poor outcomes associated with PC due to multiple factors including late diagnosis and rapid progression and metastasis of the cancer besides the resistance to chemotherapies and high heterogenicity of individuals tumor behavior, this is an urgent need to simulate PC and its TME based on patient tumor profile for discovering effective drugs that cannot be achieved by a 2D or 3D cell culture [62,63]. The patient's derived organoid technology (PDO) is a form of 3D culture of cells that has been obtained from primary tissues, embryonic stem cells, or pluripotent stem cells on a 3D structure, with the ability to self-renewal and self-organization while maintaining the functionality as the original tissue. These organoids can be kept up through unlimited cultures and conserve their genetic stability [64].

PDO technology provides a more accurate evaluation of the cancer cell interactions both inside of tumor and between the tumor microenvironment without the need for animal models or xenograft models. In contrast to 3D cell cultures or spheroids, organoids provide conditions for cell differentiation and self-organization. Moreover, these devices do not put some parts of cells in hypoxic or nutrient stress due to the presence of a lumen that provides a nutrient gradient and oxygen flow [62].

An organoid mainly consists of cells, cell niche factors, and ECM, which is constructed in a microfluidic chip. Some of the features of the microfluidic chips that make them a robust approach for the study of tumor interaction with therapeutics are their transparency for imaging, safety, and eco-friendly material used for chips. A chip model enables us to simulate and control the physical conditions such as the mechanical stress, hypoxia, and matrix stiffness, by controlling the flow rate of the culture medium in the chamber. In addition, the ability to culture several types of cells made these chips a desirable in vitro platform for modeling more complex organs such as pancreas [62,65].

13.10 The advantages of microfluidic devices

The advantages of microfluidic devices include:
1. interaction with cancer cells with other cells and components in TME such as fibroblasts and with perivascular cells.
2. For modeling the angiogenesis in cancer and the interaction of antiangiogenetic drugs and cancer cells and other TME factors.
3. These devices can determine and control different mechanical properties, which influence the metastasis, such as confinement and stiffness, and also can mimic the in vivo cell-cell interaction and signaling involved in metastasis [65].
4. There is no attending for ethical concerns including xenograft or animal models
5. Due to using the primary tumor cells of patient, this is a robust approach for personalized therapeutic methods and evaluation of chemoresistance resulting from tumor heterogenicity or patient's specific TME 6. It needs small parts of tumor samples [65].

13.11 General scheme of producing a pancreatic organoid

The first step for formation of an organoid is preparing the primary pancreatic tumor cells by digesting the samples via enzymatic or mechanical processes. The samples can be provided by biopsy of aspiration of fine needle through endoscopy. In addition, iPSCs with KRAS/tp3 modification can be used as cell sources. Then in the next step, the cells are cultured in a 3D matrix on a microfluidic chip consisting of collagen, Matrigel (which is one of the widely used materials), or other synthetic scaffold materials such as basement membrane extracted from the Engelbreth—Holm—Swarm mouse sarcoma (BME2) and an air-liquid interface that consists of collagen gel-packed cells directly exposed to air (high oxygen). In addition, some growth factors and differentiation regulating factors are necessary for induction of the formation of organoids, including EGF, FGF, Wnt3a, nicotinamide, Rspo1 (induction of Wnt signaling), prostaglandin E2, and some other supplements. It is noteworthy to mention that although most procedures use Wnt and its stimulators, some other methods use Wnt-free medium [63,64].

13.12 Some applications of pancreatic organoids

The pancreatic organoids provide many applications in PC studies including:

1. Provides an in vitro model of human PC for studying cancer progression [63].
2. Identification of novel biomarkers according to the genetic profile of patients, especially in the initial phases of PC [63].
3. Pancreatic organoids for genomic studies, for example, for validation of genetic alterations involved in cancer progression and defining responsible genes in tumor progression, prognosis, and its response to therapeutics in different stages of cancer [63,64].
4. Biobanks of tumor organoids.

   The samples investigated in many cancer data banks including the Cancer Genome Atlas (TCGA) somehow consists of primary tumor samples due to the fact that the metastatic tumors are associated with the patient's death. In contrast, theoretically, the pancreatic organoids can expand the limit of tumor samples and provide different stages of samples. Some positive attempts for access to organoid biobanks and information have been conducted by ub4organoids (http://www.hub4organoids.eu) and the Human Cancer Models Initiative (https://ocg.cancer.gov/programs/HCMI). However, such biobanks should solve some challenges that are associated with such biobanks and should be further assessed, including the ethical issues and informed consent difficulties for samples, storing of living materials and the loss of some organoids maintained for extended times, and also the uncertain tumoral heterogeneity in these organoid cultures [63,64].

5. Finding drugs for precision medicine.

   As an auxiliary tool for PM, pancreatic organoids can be used for rapid drug assessment based on patient's tumor profile before or in accordance with treatment. This method potentially can illustrate the patient's possible response to therapeutics based on its genetic profile and helps to determine the alternative therapy when the first line of therapy is unsuccessful. Moreover, this technique can be used in combination with dynamic live imaging to functional optical metabolic assessments and help to define heterogeneity, nonresponsive subclones, and differentiation premalignant from invasive tumors. Pharmacotyping with pancreatic organoids provides the opportunity to determine a more effective drug regimen at an appropriate time [63,64].

   In conclusion, pancreatic organoids provide extended sources of tumor biomimetic cultures, which are resembled in morphology, cell polarity, and metabolic heterogeneity, to the primary tumor and are genetically stable across many passages for precision medicine according to the patient tumor profile. On the other hand, the cost and time-consuming procedures besides their uncertain growth and heterogeneity nature are challenging issues that should be defined [63].

13.12.1 RNA-based therapeutic tool for personalized PDAC treatment

Targeted therapy based on RNAs has encountered many difficulties because they are relatively large, charged molecules, and one obstacle is crossing the cell membrane and targeting inside the cells. On the other hand, the small RNAs are usually unstable and have relatively rapid renal clearance. To address these issues, some targeted therapy approaches have been developed for the delivery of antimiRNAs inside specific targets. In a study by Gilles et al., the antimiRs delivered to PDAC cells in PDX and PDO avatars via tumor-penetrating nanocomplexes (TPN). They reported that a specific nano–drug, TPN-21, can effectively diminish tumor growth and survival in gemcitabine-resistant patients [66].

13.12.2 Radiomics and deep learning in personalized medicine

These two quantitative imaging methods interpret the medical imaging data that are poorly realized by conventional imaging analysis via mining and comparing routine image information. The resulting data are promising for personalized management of PC such as the differentiative diagnosis and detection in early steps of disease, and also treatment follow-up. Radiomics extracts hand-crafted features of segmented radiography images such as tumor shape, size, texture, and intensity. Indeed, it uses the feature extracted data from row images, and the outputs involve the analysis and comparison of these metrics with other pancreatic images through algorithms. Many radiomic models, for example, which have been developed for evaluating pancreatic lesions such as cyst's malignancies, have shown that these were more accurate in comparison with conventional radiology, especially in the early small-size lesions [67].

On the other hand, deep learning as a machine learning method applies algorithms for predicting and analyzing row unsegmented data from images or image patches. It takes pancreas images as input and provides outputs that include predicting tumor malignancy, histological detection, and expected patient surveillance [67].

13.13 The quantitative imaging methods for pancreatic cancer diagnosis, prognosis, and prediction

The accumulative studies data resulting from radiomic and deep learning are helpful for diagnosis of early progressing cancer and provide drug response for PM. In a study, for instance, the endoscopic ultrasound images of intraductal papillary mucinous neoplasm (IPMN) patients were analyzed with a developed convolutional neural network (CNN) model for IPMN malignancy diagnosis with 94% accuracy compared with the 56% diagnosed cases by a human. Tang et al. reported that via radiomic modeling, high-recurrence risk patients can be predicted in early phases and can receive more aggressive treatments or alternative regimens [68]. In addition, combining radiomics and deep learning by using radiomic features as input for deep learning algorithms makes robust fusion models, which outperform both models lonely. Dmitriev et al. successfully combined a radiomics model and a CNN model for classifying and diagnosing pancreatic cyst lesion types accurately [69]. Additionally, radiogenomics, as a radiomic subtype, evaluates the association of imaging phenotype with genomic profile, which can be more helpful in prognosis and prediction of treatment. Concerning radiogenomics, in a study, the correlation of different mutation profiles in panNENs with morphological changes in images was shown. In another study, the association of patients' telomere length with pancreatic neuroendocrine tumors via CT-based radiomic features was determined [67].

All in all, the quantitative imaging methods may present new ways for noninvasive cancer detection and prognosis prediction of the disease, but some challenges should be tackled for applying these methods in the clinical workplaces such as inherent heterogeneity in image acquisition, difficulties in interpretation of deep learning results in clinic, and improper image processing steps [67].

13.14 Challenges and innovations in personalized medicine care

PM originates from the fact that the differences in the molecular, environmental, and behavioral levels and the heterogeneity of the occurrence of the disease in each person determine the need for interventions tailored to the person himself. In this way, many problems can be mentioned, including obtaining approval, conflicting with the interests of different people, and pharmaceutical and insurance companies. Due to the genetic range, various environmental factors, epigenetics, etc., the effect of each drug and treatment method can be different from one person to another, so now doctors prescribe warfarin, PQ, and imatinib based on the individual's phenotypic and genetic characteristics and adjust the appropriate dose [70,71].

PM has changed the strategies for screening and follow-up of patients so that today we are talking about personal thresholds instead of population thresholds. For example, cholesterol over 400 is considered a risk factor for cardiovascular diseases, but in new studies, the standard deviation for this case is very high, and it is better to consider a personal threshold for each person separately. The strategies used in PM include (1) patient-derived cells and organoid avatars, (2) using personal and monitored protocols to determine disease symptoms and phenotype, (3) developing personal digital therapeutic methods, and (4) treating infertile patients [70].

Personal medicine has 3 main goals: (1) Improving the level of health care. (2) Helping to identify the pathological mechanism of each patient individually. (3) Reaching the most accurate and effective treatment for each person. With scientific and technical advances, patients are divided into different groups according to their biological characteristics, lifestyle, genetic risk, and environmental influences. This division, based on patients' genotype and phenotype, can speed up patient treatment by avoiding the slow and dangerous process of trial-and-error prescription before finding the most suitable treatment. One of the latest concepts of PM is accurate public health, which is the most correct intervention in the population at the most correct time. This requires the accurate collection of detailed genetic information on a large population and its division into different groups, which is very difficult and challenging [71].

In personal medicine, because the patient is at the core of decision-making for diagnosis and treatment, it confronts us with various ethical challenges, which must be done with respect for privacy, informed consent, and awareness of the risks and benefits of the designed treatment method, with which it was encountered. Another challenge that we face in the discussion of PM is the economic and health inequality in different parts of the world because the approaches and methods in PM are expensive, and they are used only at the research level in practice in many countries. but according to the investigations conducted by WHO, the expansion and use of PM over 50 years will lead to a reduction in medical and health costs. Finally, another thing that is very important is operational errors (preparation, sample handling, study design, and reproducibility) and interpretation errors (data analysis, interpretation of false positives, validation, and prediction), which are predicted by passing the time and collection of genetic information in databases will gradually reduce these issues [13,71].

13.15 Challenges in the treatment of pancreatic cancer

Treatment challenges related to the pancreatic disease are divided into several groups:

1. *Pathobiology:* The complex molecular nature of cancer is perhaps the most basic and important challenge related to the treatment of the disease. The absence of a specific driver mutation and the wide heterogeneity of the disease and the acquisition of mutations resistant to cytotoxic treatment are among the factors that cause these challenges. Also, the microenvironment of the tumor is a suppressor of the immune system and helps the tumor to escape from this barrier. Due to the very key role of KRAS in PC, most treatments are being developed based on this target, although no success has been achieved so far.

2. *Biospecimen acquisition:* The anatomical position of the pancreas is one of the challenges. To obtain samples, methods such as percutaneously guided needle biopsy, core needle biopsy, and endoscopic ultrasound were used to obtain samples, but with the increased focus on PM and finding predictive markers, the need to obtain larger tissue samples required modification of the current methods and/or utilizing alternative methods such as the use of circulating tumor cells (CTCs) and

circulating cell-free DNA (cfDNA), which are challenging because despite the reports of cases indicating the connection of CTCs with the early stages of cancer, basically their observation is considered a poor prognosis and the role of the methods mentioned in the clinic needs further investigation [72].

3. *Molecular profiling:* Despite the wide importance of NGS in finding specific genetic changes related to PC and increasing the diagnostic power of existing methods, identifying people at risk of this cancer, or identifying treatment-resistant mutations in people that cause cancer-specific treatment options, this technique still needs more confirmations for use in the clinic because the majority of the mutations found are of low prevalence and currently the drug that targets the common mutations in PC, KRAS, CDKN2A, TP53, and SMAD4 is still not developed [73].

4. *Preclinical models:* A better understanding of pathogenesis and, as a result, finding suitable treatments is achieved by using preclinical models. About PC, preclinical models are classified into two categories: in vivo and in vitro. In in-vitro models, at first, cell lines such as MiaPaCa-2, PANC-1, AsPC-1, HPAC, and BxPC-3 were used, but the problem associated with them is that due to the two-dimensional culture pattern, the conditions and events of real tumors do not imitate, as a result, to solve this problem, models that imitate the 3D pattern of the tumor and preserve the genotypic and phenotypic characteristics of the tumor, such as organoids, were developed and used. On the other hand, in vivo models include cancer cell models that are transplanted subcutaneously or orthotopically into mice, genetically engineered mouse models (GEMMs), and PDXs. Among them, in vivo models, especially PDX, which are established by transplanting a human tumor mass into immunodeficient mice, such as athymic nude mice, are more important for testing the efficacy of new therapies due to their presumed similarity to the disease pathology in humans. Of course, in the PDX model, mice have immunodeficiency, and as a result, they are limited for use in immunotherapy experiments [72,73].

5. *Hierarchizing molecular targets:* The lack of discovery of a reliable and actionable molecular target in PC has led to little progress despite extensive research on this cancer. As a result, the need to discover a molecular target with such characteristics requires the use of the knowledge of calculation and analysis of the obtained data at the genomic, proteomic, and metabolomic levels in combination with artificial intelligence. However, the challenge in using these cases is their significance and confirmation in the clinic, which is possible with the help of clinical trial studies [72].

6. *Clinical trial design:* One of the existing challenges of clinical trial enrollment of patients is uncertainty about related risks, fear of randomization, and strict eligibility criteria in clinical trial design. There are various experimental studies related to PC, such as umbrella, basket, etc., and since conventional approaches have failed to find effective treatment, there will be a need for more comprehensive coordination and guidance of patients in new clinical trials [72].

13.16 The challenges from an oncologist's perspective

As mentioned earlier, despite decades of efforts to find the right treatment combination for this disease, there has been little progress in treatment related to the disease. Factors slowing down this progress are as follows:

Pancreatic adenocarcinoma is characterized by significant genetic heterogeneity among people, which occurs at different levels such as histology inside and outside the tumor. This genetic heterogeneity creates many challenges in finding appropriate and comprehensive treatment. Many studies related to this cancer also show a wide range of changes in the genomic structure as a result of damage to the DNA repair system and suppressive mutations of tumor suppressor genes. Heterogeneity at the phenotypic level has also been identified in this disease, and it is considered a big challenge in the field of clinical trial studies. Based on the genetic background and molecular profile, as well as considering the four major common critical mutations (KRAS, TP53, SMAD4, and CDKN2A), PC is divided into four categories: stable ($<$50 genetic events), focal (between 50 and 200 events, 50% on a single chromosome), sporadic (between 50 and 200 widespread mutations) and unstable (more than 200 widespread mutations). The microenvironment around the pancreatic tumor by creating hypoxic conditions following the desmoplastic reaction inside the tumor causes the drug to enter the tumor environment. Cancer stroma-targeted therapies have the potential to develop a therapy for PC. Another target as a therapeutic goal is cancer stem cells. These stem cells with the ability of self-renewal, radiation, and chemical resistance can be effective in the process of tumor invasion and development. Regarding PC, so far *tarextumab* and the combination of *napabucasin, gemcitabine*, and *nab-paclitaxel* targeting STAT3 have been included in clinical trials. Finally, another challenge that exists concerning PC is errors arising from the directional interpretation and strategic and method errors, which have caused failure in the results of clinical trials and caused a break in finding effective treatment, which emphasizes the need to develop a strategy [72–77].

13.17 Opportunities for personalized therapy in the near future

Part of the failure in finding the right treatment can be due to the lack of suitable predictive biomarkers and targets. Recently, several studies have suggested potential diagnostic targets:

*   *Targeting the DNA repair pathway (BRCA)*

    Considering the key role of the repair pathway and its players i.e. BRCA in maintaining the integrity of the genome and also as a checkpoint in the cycle of cell repair in response to damage, it seems to be logical to target it as a drug target. Much evidence supports this choice: carriers of BRCA1 mutations appear to be 2–3 times more likely to develop PC than the general population and 3–6 times more likely to develop BRCA2 mutations than the general population. Response to platinum-based therapies and radiation therapy is better in patients with defects in repair pathways than in others. Responding to PARP inhibitor drugs in BRCA mutation carriers is also considered another treatment strategy [78].

- *Targeting hyaluronic acid*

  Hyaluronic acid is a mucopolysaccharide made by HA synthases, the increase of which in a group of patients with PC is considered a drug resistance factor caused by the collapse of the internal vessels of the tumor delivering the drug receptor, following the increase in interstitial fluid pressure. The mentioned case, along with considering its role in increasing tumor proliferation, adhesion, migration, invasion, and immune resistance, has caused it to be considered a very attractive therapeutic target [75].

- *Targeting DNA mismatch repair*

  Targeting this pathway using poly (ADP-ribose) polymerase inhibitors in people with PC can be promising because it causes unbearable damage to tumor DNA. Currently, trials based on the drug *Olaparib* in PC have been promising [79].

- *Targeting metabolic pathways*

  Reprogrammed metabolism is a mechanism that tumor cells adopt after challenges such as hypoxia and nutrient deprivation. This mechanism is associated with a poor prognosis and causes this cancer to be resistant to existing treatments. As a result, targeting this path can be a suitable therapeutic target. A lot of single-drug and combined clinical trial studies have been conducted in this regard, targeting lipid metabolism, amino acid, redox balance, glycolysis, and mitochondrial metabolism [79].

- *Targeting mesothelin*

  Mesothelin is a surface glycoprotein produced by pancreatic tumor cells, which plays a role in tumor adhesion, metastasis, and resistance to chemotherapy by binding to MUC16 (CA125) factor. It is one of the targets of antibody-based treatments, and SS1P (CAT-5001) and MORAb-009 are among the treatments targeting mesothelin [23,78].

- *Targeting the ERBb (HER) family*

  Members of this family are membrane tyrosine kinases that are involved in processes such as cell survival, proliferation, differentiation, and migration. Combined treatments based on targeting this family, such as the combination of *Erlotinib-Lapatinib* and *Trastuzumab*, etc. with *Gemcitabine* have been associated with improvement in patient survival [77].

- Another HER2-based adjuvant therapy in PC patients is the new approach of CAR-Tcell therapy, which is also called adaptive cell therapy.

- It is also important to use natural herbal products as anticancer drugs. The combination of these products with conventional chemotherapy has been performed in

PC patients and the results are being investigated. Clinical trials are investigating the effect of several natural compounds and their results in this cancer, including the anticancer product BMS–247550, a new epothilone derivative BMS–247550, a semisynthetic analog of the natural product epothilone B that has similar activity to *paclitaxel*, and *Minnelide*, a triptolide analog, reduced tumor growth, and spread and improved survival in human PDAC xenograft models [73].

- *Irinotecan* is currently used for the treatment of metastatic PC, both in the first line (as part of the FOLFIRONOX regimen) and in the second line (in the form of nanoliposomal *irinotecan* in combination with *5FU*). Some patients who receive *irinotecan* have severe complications due to blood and gastrointestinal toxicity. These are patients who may be deficient in the enzyme UDP-glucuronosyltransferase 1A1 (UGT1A1), which catalyzes the glucuronidation of the active metabolite *irinotecan*, SN–38. Various studies have shown that the polymorphism of the UGT1A1 gene, which leads to the incomplete activity of the enzyme, causes severe poisoning in the patient [78].

- *Gemcitabine transfer molecule*: hENT1– *Gemcitabine* (2, 2-difluorodeoxycytidine) is the basic and systemic treatment for patients with PDAC, especially in the adjuvant setting. *Gemcitabine* is a polar molecule and, therefore, does not cross the cell membrane easily. Human equilibrated nucleoside transporter (hENT) 1 is the major transporter protein for the cellular uptake of *Gemcitabine* in PC cells. In a retrospective study of PC patients with increased hENT1 expression, it was seen that when treated with *Gemcitabine*, patients with low hENT1 expression had better response and survival outcomes. However, there is heterogeneity in the predictive value of increased hENT1 expression so hENT1 has not been accepted as a predictive biomarker as a standard marker [80].

- SMAD4–SMAD4/DPC4 (deleted in PC) encodes a key intracellular messenger in the TGF signaling cascade. The combination of RUNX3 and SMAD4 status has been suggested as a prognostic factor in the disease. Compared to SMAD4 alone, it is much more useful. The role of SMAD4 or SMAD4/RUNX3 as a biomarker in the care of patients with PDAC needs to be established in prospective studies before it can be widely applied in the clinic, especially in situations where radiation therapy is considered or be tested [81].

- Finally, another drug targets in PC are microRNAs or a group of noncoding RNAs, whose dysregulation has been seen in a group of diseases, including PC, and who naturally are involved in a wide range of cellular mechanisms and functions such as control growth, proliferation, differentiation, development, and apoptosis. As mentioned earlier, the use of these molecules as drug targets faces challenges such as instability and rapid renal clearance, and as a result, more studies regarding the use of this target in PC treatments are in the preclinical stages [82].

13.18 Conclusion

Recent discoveries in genetics and techniques developed to identify DNA have given rise to a new concept called personalized or precision medicine. The characteristics and differences of people in the molecular, physiological, environmental, and behavioral fields make it necessary to treat each person with interventions that match their unique characteristics. With the sequencing of human DNA and the emergence of new technologies that led us to obtain genomics, transcriptomics, metabolomics, and epigenomics data, today we can measure molecular components at all histological levels. The metabolic pathways of chemical reactions that take place in every cell of the body are affected by a wide range of DNA mutations, SNPs, gene deletions, duplications, etc. Pharmacogenetics has gradually identified the gene variants that affect the metabolism of drugs. PM tries to achieve the best treatment for each person using modern methods and genetic data [83].

Today, genetic tests are used to estimate the risk of developing diseases in a personalized way and to guide medicine, which includes: (1) Specific single gene tests. (2) Specific gene panels. (3) Genotyping panels for specific predisposing variants.

PC is the seventh leading cause of death in men and women and is predicted to become the second leading malignancy by 2030. The cause of PC is not fully understood and few prevention strategies are available. Despite the significant epidemiological study of this multifactorial disease, several risk factors including family history, smoking, obesity, diabetes, Helicobacter pylori infection, hepatitis B, human immunodeficiency virus infection, and dietary intake have been identified. Lack of symptoms can make diagnosis difficult and lead to cancer being diagnosed at a more advanced stage [84].

Defining the concept of precision medicine for PC patients has become very common in recent years. New initiatives and methods have been developed around the world to determine the biological characteristics of the tumor and provide the best treatment options for PC, and all these actions are known in the United States as the panCAN network. The preliminary results of PANCAN data show that 50% of patients with the pancreas have a functional molecular change for which targeted treatment can be available. Similar projects and plans are underway in other countries. By increasing the identification of biomarkers and gene profiles, it is hoped that with the completion of genetic databases, we can have a clear vision of precision medicine in PDAC [83].

In addition, PM has the potential of oncogenic stimuli to tailor tumor therapy, optimize tumor response, treat patient-specific toxicities, and modulate the tumor immune milieu. A deep understanding of the cellular and molecular biology of tumors can help to develop effective treatment strategies for cancer. Ultimately, this ensures better patient care. Although targeting cancer metabolism is a promising strategy, its success depends on the accurate identification of tumor subtypes or specific metabolic profiles. PDAC is classified into three subtypes (slow proliferative, glycolytic, and lipogenic) through the metabolic profile [85].

The only serum marker that is usually measured in PDAC is CA19-19, the increase of which indicates more advanced PDAC and a poorer prognosis for the patient. However, this biomarker changes only in 65% of affected cases. In some studies, other metabolites such as different amino acids, fatty acids, and nucleotide intermediates have been used. It is hoped that shortly, panels consisting of different biomarkers will be created to determine the tumor risk in each person individually and more accurately [86].

All the changes and reactions of PDAC cannot be explained by genetic changes, so many studies have investigated the effects of epigenetics in the development, occurrence, and prognosis of the disease. No evidence-based personalized treatment for pancreatic adenocarcinoma is currently available for clinical practice. While new agents or compounds are widely investigated in hopes of improving disease outcomes, new development strategies and better research methods are eagerly needed to bolster therapeutic progress in PC [84].

In conclusion, the progress and new initiatives in the field of genetics and new-generation sequencing techniques have raised hope in PM in PC patients, although more research and clinical trials studies on a larger scale are needed to increase the survival rate and better management of the patients.

Declarations of interest

The authors declare no conflicts of interest.

References

[1] Abbassi R, Schmid RM. Evolving treatment paradigms for pancreatic cancer. Visc Med 2019;35 (6):362−72.
[2] Rawla P, Sunkara T, Gaduputi V. Epidemiology of pancreatic cancer: global trends, etiology and risk factors. World J Oncol 2019;10(1):10.
[3] Chen X, Liu F, Xue Q, Weng X, Xu F. Metastatic pancreatic cancer: mechanisms and detection. Oncol Rep 2021;46(5):1−10.
[4] Mishra V, Chanda P, Tambuwala MM, Suttee A. Personalized medicine: an overview. Int J Pharm Qual Assur 2019;10(2):290−4.
[5] Ducreux M, Cuhna AS, Caramella C, Hollebecque A, Burtin P, Goéré D, et al. Cancer of the pancreas: ESMO Clinical Practice Guidelines for diagnosis, treatment, and follow-up. Ann Oncol 2015;26:v56−68.
[6] Li J, Wientjes MG, Au JL-S. Pancreatic cancer: pathobiology, treatment options, and drug delivery. AAPS J 2010;12(2):223−32.
[7] Kolodecik T, Shugrue C, Ashat M, Thrower EC. Risk factors for pancreatic cancer: underlying mechanisms and potential targets. Front Physiol 2014;4:415.

[8] Schwartz GG. Is cadmium a cause of human pancreatic cancer? Cancer Epidemiol Biomarkers Prev 2000;9(2):139−45.

[9] Kalra DJPM. The importance of real-world data to precision medicine. Future Med 2019;79−82.

[10] Alyass A, Turcotte M, Meyre D. From big data analysis to personalized medicine for all: challenges and opportunities. BMC Med Genom 2015;8(1):1−12.

[11] Prins BP, Leitsalu L, Pärna K, Fischer K, Metspalu A, Haller T, et al. Advances in genomic discovery and implications for personalized prevention and medicine: estonia as example. J Pers Med 2021;11(5):358.

[12] Mathur S, Sutton J. Personalized medicine could transform healthcare. Biomed Rep 2017;7(1):3−5.

[13] Vicente AM, Ballensiefen W, Jönsson J-I. How personalised medicine will transform healthcare by 2030: the ICPerMed vision. J Transl Med 2020;18(1):1−4.

[14] Horgan D, Lal JA. Making the most of innovation in personalised medicine: an EU strategy for a faster bench to bedside and beyond process. Public Health Genomics 2018;21(3−4):101−20.

[15] Lee I-H, Kang H-Y, Suh HS, Lee S, Oh ES, Jeong H. Awareness and attitude of the public toward personalized medicine in Korea. PLoS One 2018;13(2):e0192856.

[16] Offit K. Personalized medicine: new genomics, old lessons. Hum Genet 2011;130(1):3−14.

[17] Snyderman R. Personalized health care: from theory to practice. Biotechnol J 2012;7(8):973−9.

[18] Pokorska-Bocci A, Stewart A, Sagoo GS, Hall A, Kroese M, Burton H. 'Personalized medicine': what's in a name? Per Med 2014;11(2):197−210.

[19] Juengst E, McGowan ML, Fishman JR, Settersten Jr RA. From "personalized" to "precision" medicine: the ethical and social implications of rhetorical reform in genomic medicine. Hastings Cent Rep 2016;46(5):21−33.

[20] Ashley EA. Towards precision medicine. Nat Rev Genet 2016;17(9):507−22.

[21] Vellekoop H, Versteegh M, Huygens S, Ramos IC, Szilberhorn L, Zelei T, et al. The net benefit of personalized medicine: a systematic literature review and regression analysis. Value Health 2022;25(8):1428−38.

[22] Martorell-Marugán J, Tabik S, Benhammou Y, del Val C, Zwir I, Herrera F, et al. Deep learning in omics data analysis and precision medicine. Exon Publ 2019;37−53.

[23] Sun W, Lee J, Zhang S, Benyshek C, Dokmeci MR, Khademhosseini A. 5th Anniversary Article: Engineering Precision Medicine (Adv. Sci. 1/2019). Adv Sci 2019;6(1):1970001.

[24] Hoggatt J. Personalized medicine—trends in molecular diagnosticsy. Mol Diagn Ther 2011;15(1):53−5.

[25] Evangelatos N, Satyamoorthy K, Brand A. Personalized health in a public health perspective. Springer; 2018. p. 433−4.

[26] Verma M. Personalized medicine and cancer. J Pers Med 2012;2(1):1−14.

[27] Brammer M. The role of neuroimaging in diagnosis and personalized medicine-current position and likely future directions. Dialogues Clin Neurosci 2019;11(4):389−96.

[28] Wong K, Qian Z, Le Y. The role of precision medicine in pancreatic cancer: challenges for targeted therapy, immune modulating treatment, early detection, and less invasive operations. Cancer Transl Med 2016;2(2):41.

[29] Gambardella V, Tarazona N, Cejalvo JM, Lombardi P, Huerta M, Roselló S, et al. Personalized medicine: recent progress in cancer therapy. Cancers. 2020;12(4):1009.

[30] Hayashi H, Higashi T, Miyata T, Yamashita Y, Baba H. Recent advances in precision medicine for pancreatic ductal adenocarcinoma. Ann Gastroenterol Surg 2021;5(4):457−66.

[31] Raphael BJ, Hruban RH, Aguirre AJ, Moffitt RA, Yeh JJ, Stewart C, et al. Integrated genomic characterization of pancreatic ductal adenocarcinoma. Cancer Cell 2017;32(2):185−203 e13.

[32] Canon J, Rex K, Saiki AY, Mohr C, Cooke K, Bagal D, et al. The clinical KRAS (G12C) inhibitor AMG 510 drives anti-tumour immunity. Nature 2019;575(7781):217−23.

[33] Waters AM, Der CJ. KRAS: the critical driver and therapeutic target for pancreatic cancer. Cold Spring Harb Perspect Med 2018;8(9):a031435.

[34] Hustinx SR, Leoni LM, Yeo CJ, Brown PN, Goggins M, Kern SE, et al. Concordant loss of MTAP and p16/CDKN2A expression in pancreatic intraepithelial neoplasia: evidence of homozygous deletion in a noninvasive precursor lesion. Am J Surg Pathol 2005;18(7):959−63.

[35] Aung KL, Fischer SE, Denroche RE, Jang G-H, Dodd A, Creighton S, et al. Genomics-driven precision medicine for advanced pancreatic cancer: early results from the COMPASS Trial. Clin Cancer Res 2018;24(6):1344—54.

[36] Murphy KM, Brune KA, Griffin C, Sollenberger JE, Petersen GM, Bansal R, et al. Evaluation of candidate genes MAP2K4, MADH4, ACVR1B, and BRCA2 in familial pancreatic cancer: deleterious BRCA2 mutations in 17%. Cancer Res 2002;62(13):3789—93.

[37] Yang X, Leslie G, Doroszuk A, Schneider S, Allen J, Decker B, et al. Cancer risks associated with germline PALB2 pathogenic variants: an international study of 524 families. J Clin Oncol 2020;38 (7):674.

[38] Hsu F-C, Roberts NJ, Childs E, Porter N, Rabe KG, Borgida A, et al. Risk of pancreatic cancer among individuals with pathogenic variants in the ATM gene. JAMA Oncol 2021;7(11):1664—8.

[39] Shain AH, Giacomini CP, Matsukuma K, Karikari CA, Bashyam MD, Hidalgo M, et al. Convergent structural alterations define SWItch/Sucrose NonFermentable (SWI/SNF) chromatin remodeler as a central tumor suppressive complex in pancreatic cancer. Proc Natl Acad Sci U S A 2012;109(5):E252—9.

[40] Collisson EA, Sadanandam A, Olson P, Gibb WJ, Truitt M, Gu S, et al. Subtypes of pancreatic ductal adenocarcinoma and their differing responses to therapy. Nat Med 2011;17(4):500—3.

[41] Moffitt RA, Marayati R, Flate EL, Volmar KE, Loeza S, Hoadley KA, et al. Virtual microdissection identifies distinct tumor-and stroma-specific subtypes of pancreatic ductal adenocarcinoma. Nat Genet 2015;47(10):1168—78.

[42] Bailey P, Chang DK, Nones K, Johns AL, Patch A-M, Gingras M-C, et al. Genomic analyses identify molecular subtypes of pancreatic cancer. Nature 2016;531(7592):47—52.

[43] Puleo F, Nicolle R, Blum Y, Cros J, Marisa L, Demetter P, et al. Stratification of pancreatic ductal adenocarcinomas based on tumor and microenvironment features. Gastroenterology 2018;155 (6):1999—2013.e3.

[44] Birnbaum DJ, Finetti P, Birnbaum D, Mamessier E, Bertucci F. Validation and comparison of the molecular classifications of pancreatic carcinomas. Mol Cancer 2017;16(1):1—7.

[45] Hu YC, Komorowski RA, Graewin S, Hostetter G, Kallioniemi O-P, Pitt HA, et al. Thymidylate synthase expression predicts the response to 5-fluorouracil-based adjuvant therapy in pancreatic cancer. Clin Cancer Res 2003;9(11):4165—71.

[46] Formentini A, Sander S, Denzer S, Straeter J, Henne-Bruns D, Kornmann M. Thymidylate synthase expression in resectable and unresectable pancreatic cancer: role as predictive or prognostic marker? Int J Colorectal Dis 2007;22(1):49—55.

[47] McAllister F, Pineda DM, Jimbo M, Lal S, Burkhart RA, Moughan J, et al. dCK expression correlates with 5-fluorouracil efficacy and HuR cytoplasmic expression in pancreatic cancer: a dual-institutional follow-up with the RTOG 9704 trial. Cancer Biol Ther 2014;15(6):688—98.

[48] Costantino CL, Witkiewicz AK, Kuwano Y, Cozzitorto JA, Kennedy EP, Dasgupta A, et al. The role of HuR in gemcitabine efficacy in pancreatic cancer: HuR Up-regulates the expression of the gemcitabine metabolizing enzyme deoxycytidine kinase. Cancer Res 2009;69(11):4567—72.

[49] Van Der Heijden MS, Brody JR, Dezentje DA, Gallmeier E, Cunningham SC, Swartz MJ, et al. In vivo therapeutic responses contingent on Fanconi anemia/BRCA2 status of the tumor. Clin Cancer Res 2005;11(20):7508—15.

[50] Blair AB, Groot VP, Gemenetzis G, Wei J, Cameron JL, Weiss MJ, et al. BRCA1/BRCA2 germline mutation carriers and sporadic pancreatic ductal adenocarcinoma. J Am Coll Surg 2018;226 (4):630—7.e1.

[51] Strippoli A, Rossi S, Martini M, Basso M, D'Argento E, Schinzari G, et al. ERCC1 expression affects outcome in metastatic pancreatic carcinoma treated with FOLFIRINOX: a single institution analysis. Oncotarget 2016;7(23):35159.

[52] Farrell JJ, Elsaleh H, Garcia M, Lai R, Ammar A, Regine WF, et al. Human equilibrative nucleoside transporter 1 levels predict response to gemcitabine in patients with pancreatic cancer. Gastroenterology 2009;136(1):187—95.

[53] Poplin E, Wasan H, Rolfe L, Raponi M, Ikdahl T, Bondarenko I, et al. Randomized, multicenter, phase II study of CO-101 versus gemcitabine in patients with metastatic pancreatic ductal

adenocarcinoma: including a prospective evaluation of the role of hENT1 in gemcitabine or CO-101 sensitivity. J Clin Oncol 2013;31(35):4453−61.

[54] Boeck S, Jung A, Laubender RP, Neumann J, Egg R, Goritschan C, et al. KRAS mutation status is not predictive for objective response to anti-EGFR treatment with erlotinib in patients with advanced pancreatic cancer. J Gastroenterol 2013;48(4):544−8.

[55] Kaufman B, Shapira-Frommer R, Schmutzler RK, Audeh MW, Friedlander M, Balmaña J, et al. Olaparib monotherapy in patients with advanced cancer and a germline BRCA1/2 mutation. 2015;33(3):244.

[56] Golan T, Hammel P, Reni M, Van Cutsem E, Macarulla T, Hall MJ, et al. Maintenance olaparib for germline BRCA-mutated metastatic pancreatic cancer. N Engl J Med 2019;381(4):317−27.

[57] Sereti E, Karagianellou T, Kotsoni I, Magouliotis D, Kamposioras K, Ulukaya E, et al. Patient Derived Xenografts (PDX) for personalized treatment of pancreatic cancer: emerging allies in the war on a devastating cancer? J Proteom 2018;188:107−18.

[58] Rubio-Viqueira B, Jimeno A, Cusatis G, Zhang X, Iacobuzio-Donahue C, Karikari C, et al. An in vivo platform for translational drug development in pancreatic cancer. Clin Cancer Res 2006;12 (15):4652−61.

[59] Kawaguchi K, Igarashi K, Murakami T, Kiyuna T, Lwin TM, Hwang HK, et al. MEK inhibitors cobimetinib and trametinib, regressed a gemcitabine-resistant pancreatic-cancer patient-derived orthotopic xenograft (PDOX). Oncotarget. 2017;8(29):47490−6.

[60] Izumchenko E, Paz K, Ciznadija D, Sloma I, Katz A, Vasquez-Dunddel D, et al. Patient-derived xenografts effectively capture responses to oncology therapy in a heterogeneous cohort of patients with solid tumors. Ann Oncol 2017;28(10):2595−605.

[61] Villarroel MC, Rajeshkumar NV, Garrido-Laguna I, De Jesus-Acosta A, Jones S, Maitra A, et al. Personalizing cancer treatment in the age of global genomic analyses: PALB2 gene mutations and the response to DNA damaging agents in pancreatic cancer. Mol Cancer Ther 2011;10(1):3−8.

[62] Haque MR, Rempert TH, Al-Hilal TA, Wang C, Bhushan A, Bishehsari F. Organ-chip models: opportunities for precision medicine in pancreatic cancer. Cancers (Basel) 2021;13(17):4487.

[63] Yao J, Yang M, Atteh L, Liu P, Mao Y, Meng W, et al. A pancreas tumor derived organoid study: from drug screen to precision medicine. Cancer Cell Int 2021;21(1):398.

[64] Moreira L, Bakir B, Chatterji P, Dantes Z, Reichert M, Rustgi AK. Pancreas 3D organoids: current and future aspects as a research platform for personalized medicine in pancreatic cancer. Cell Mol Gastroenterol Hepatol 2018;5(3):289−98.

[65] Frappart PO, Hofmann TG. Pancreatic Ductal Adenocarcinoma (PDAC) organoids: the shining light at the end of the tunnel for drug response prediction and personalized medicine. Cancers (Basel) 2020;12(10):2750.

[66] Gilles ME, Hao L, Huang L, Rupaimoole R, Lopez-Casas PP, Pulver E, et al. Personalized RNA medicine for pancreatic cancer. Clin Cancer Res 2018;24(7):1734−47.

[67] Preuss K, Thach N, Liang X, Baine M, Chen J, Zhang C, et al. Using quantitative imaging for personalized medicine in pancreatic cancer: a review of radiomics and deep learning applications. Cancers (Basel) 2022;14(7):1654.

[68] Tang TY, Li X, Zhang Q, Guo CX, Zhang XZ, Lao MY, et al. Development of a novel multi-parametric MRI radiomic nomogram for preoperative evaluation of early recurrence in resectable pancreatic cancer. J Magn Reson Imaging 2020;52(1):231−45.

[69] Dmitriev K, Kaufman AE, Javed AA, Hruban RH, Fishman EK, Lennon AM, et al. Classification of pancreatic cysts in computed tomography images using a random forest and convolutional neural network ensemble. Med Image Comput Comput Assist Interv 2017;10435:150−8.

[70] Goetz LH, Schork NJ. Personalized medicine: motivation, challenges, and progress. Fertil Steril 2018;109(6):952−63.

[71] Sedda G, Gasparri R, Spaggiari L. Challenges and innovations in personalized medicine care. Future Oncol 2019;15(29):3305−8.

[72] Peretti U, Zanon S, Michele R. The personalized medicine for pancreatic ductal adenocarcinoma patients: the oncologist perspective. Endoscopic Ultrasound 2017;6(Suppl 3):S66.

[73] Tesfaye AA, Kamgar M, Azmi A, Philip PA. The evolution into personalized therapies in pancreatic ductal adenocarcinoma: challenges and opportunities. Expert Rev Anticancer Ther 2018;18 (2):131−48.

[74] Murakami T, Hiroshima Y, Matsuyama R, Homma Y, Hoffman RM, Endo I. Role of the tumor microenvironment in pancreatic cancer. Ann Gastroenterol Surg 2019;3(2):130−7.

[75] Sahin IH, Lowery MA, Stadler ZK, Salo-Mullen E, Iacobuzio-Donahue CA, Kelsen DP, et al. Genomic instability in pancreatic adenocarcinoma: a new step towards precision medicine and novel therapeutic approaches. Expert Rev Gastroenterol Hepatol 2016;10(8):893−905.

[76] Cros J, Raffenne J, Couvelard A, Poté N. Tumor heterogeneity in pancreatic adenocarcinoma. Pathobiology. 2018;85(1−2):64−71.

[77] Galvin R, Chung C, Achenbach E, Dziadkowiec O, Sen S. Barriers to clinical trial enrollment in patients with pancreatic adenocarcinoma eligible for early-phase clinical trials. Oncology 2020;34 (10):407−12.

[78] Meti N, Kelly D, Allen MJ, Lanys A, Fazelzad R, Ramjeesingh R, et al. Genomic sequencing to inform therapy in advanced pancreatic cancer: a systematic review and meta-analysis of prospective studies. Cancer Treat Rev 2021;101:102310.

[79] Perkhofer L, Gout J, Roger E, de Almeida FK, Simões CB, Wiesmüller L, et al. DNA damage repair as a target in pancreatic cancer: state-of-the-art and future perspectives. Gut. 2021;70 (3):606−17.

[80] de Sousa Cavalcante L, Monteiro G. Gemcitabine: metabolism and molecular mechanisms of action, sensitivity and chemoresistance in pancreatic cancer. Eur J Pharmacol 2014;741:8−16.

[81] Kruger S, Haas M, Ormanns S, Bächmann S, Siveke JT, Kirchner T, et al. Translational research in pancreatic ductal adenocarcinoma: current evidence and future concepts. World J Gastroenterol 2014;20(31):10769.

[82] Qadir MI, Faheem A. miRNA: A diagnostic and therapeutic tool for pancreatic cancer. Crit Rev Eukaryot Gene Expr 2017;27(3):197−204.

[83] Noori-Daloii MR, Zafari N. The personalized medicine: today and tomorrow. Med Sci 2019;29 (1).

[84] Regel I, Mayerle J, Ujjwal, Mukund M. Current strategies and future perspectives for precision medicine in pancreatic cancer. Cancers. 2020;12(4):1024.

[85] Chandana S, Babiker HM, Mahadevan D. Therapeutic trends in pancreatic ductal adenocarcinoma (PDAC). Expert Opin Investig Drugs 2019;28(2):161−77.

[86] Kiczmer P, Seńkowska AP, Szydło B, Świętochowska E, Ostrowska Z. Assessing the merits of existing pancreatic cancer biomarkers. Biuletyn Polskiego Towarzystwa Onkologicznego Nowotwory. 2017;2(3):251−5.

CHAPTER 14

Clinical practice guidelines for interventional treatment of pancreatic cancer

Ghazaleh Pourali[1,2,*], **Ghazaleh Donyadideh**[1,*], **Shima Mehrabadi**[2,*],
Fiuji Hamid[3,*], **Seyed Mahdi Hassanian**[2,4,5], **Gordon A. Ferns**[6], **Majid Khazaei**[2,4]
and Amir Avan[2,7,8]

[1]Mashhad University of Medical Sciences, Mashhad, Iran
[2]Metabolic Syndrome Research Center, Mashhad University of Medical Sciences, Mashhad, Iran
[3]Department of Medical Oncology, Cancer Center Amsterdam, Amsterdam U.M.C., VU. University Medical Center (VUMC), Amsterdam, The Netherlands
[4]Basic Sciences Research Institute, Mashhad University of Medical Sciences, Mashhad, Iran
[5]Medical Genetics Research Center, Mashhad University of Medical Sciences, Mashhad, Iran
[6]Division of Medical Education, Brighton & Sussex Medical School, Brighton, United Kingdom
[7]College of Medicine, University of Warith Al-Anbiyaa, Karbala, Iraq
[8]Faculty of Health, School of Biomedical Sciences, Queensland University of Technology, Brisbane, QLD, Australia

14.1 The definition of pancreatic cancer and its classification in clinic

Pancreatic cancer (PC) usually has a poor prognosis; it is rarely detected at an early stages, by which time it has often spread locally, or metastasized. There are several types of PCs, but the most common is pancreatic adenocarcinoma that comprises 85% of cases [1]. Adenocarcinomas develop in areas of the exocrine gland, that secrete digestive enzymes. About 1%−2% of PCs arise in the nerves and endocrine gland. In generally, the aggressiveness of the latter tumors is less than for those developing in the exocrine pancreas [2].

The initial symptoms of PCs include weight loss, back pain, loss of appetite, and dark urine; the latter due to biliary tract involvement. But the early stages are often asymptomatic. PCs are often diagnosed only when it is widely disseminated [3,4]. PCs arising from the exocrine pancreas may spread to other organs of the digestive system including the duodenum. The PC might invade locally and affect bile ducts and blood vessels. It may also affect other organs by metastatic spread via the blood or lymphatic system [4].

The stage of PC at diagnosis determines the choice of the best intervention and categorize patients in clinical studies. The stages of PC include PC stage 0 with no

---

* Authors Ghazaleh Pourali, Ghazaleh Donyadideh, Shima Mehrabadi and Hamid Fiuji equally contributed as first author.

Recent Advances in Nanocarriers for Pancreatic Cancer Therapy
DOI: https://doi.org/10.1016/B978-0-443-19142-8.00008-5

spread involving one layer of cells in the organ. PC cancer is not detectable through imaging or even direction inspection. PC stage I and local growth is at the stage that the disease is limited to the pancreas. When the diameter of cancerous mass is smaller <2 or >2 cm, these are termed stage IA and IB respectively. PC stage II or local spread are featured with spreads outside the pancreas and adjacent lymph nodes. PC stage III is featured with a wider spread and spread of the tumor to adjacent nerves or main vessels without metastasis. PC IV or distant spread is when the cancer spreads to distant organs [5,6] (Table 14.1) (Fig. 14.1).

14.2 Incidence and epidemiology and risk factors

PC is usually seen in older individuals and the risk of the disease increases with age [7]. Around 80% of the patients are >60 years [8]. Several other environmental factors (modifiable) and genetic factors (nonmodifiable) have been established [9] (Fig. 14.2).

14.2.1 Modifiable risk factors

14.2.1.1 Tobacco use and smoking, are important risk factors for pancreatic cancer

The risk of PC is twice as high in smokers compared to nonsmokers. Around 25% of PC are due to smoking and consuming other tobacco products increase the risk of PC and the risk falls after cessation [10].

Table 14.1 Staging of PC (pancreatic cancer) classification. PC progression and treatment strategy for patient determined by this classification.

Stage	Tumor description
0	• Limited to the top layer of pancreatic duct cells • Has not spread anywhere • Has not visible on imaging or even in direct vision
IA	• Limited to pancreas • 2 cm or less in longest dimension
IB	• Limited to pancreas • More than 2 cm in longest dimension
II	• Extends beyond the pancreas • Has spread to nearby lymph nodes
III	• Has spread to nearby nerves or major vessels • Has not metastasized
IV	• Pancreatic cancer has spread to distant organs • Metastatic cancer

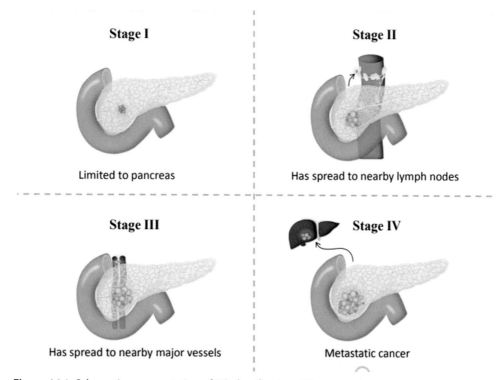

Figure 14.1 Schematic representation of PC classification. *PC*, pancreatic cancer.

14.2.1.2 Large epidemiological studies have shown the link between obesity and pancreatic cancer

Case control studies demonstrated that obesity was associated with a statistically significant 50%–60% increased risk of PC [11,12]. A recent study between 2008 and 2015 including 110 cases, indicated that there was a direct connection between precancerous lesions of the pancreas, intralobular fibrosis, pancreatic fatty infiltration, high BMI, and intravisceral fat [13].

14.2.1.3 Chemical and carcinogenic agents exposure

Specific chemicals like pesticides, cleaning agents, chemicals, and paints used for metal refining intensify the risk of PC [14].

14.2.1.4 Dietary factors

The risk of PC increases with high consumption of meat (mostly grilled), fried foods, and foods containing nitrosamines [15]. The risk of PCs increases with excessive use of sugar and sweetened soft drinks [16]. In addition, excessive use of citrus fruits and

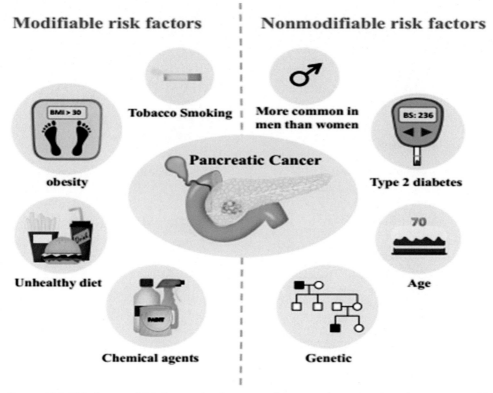

Figure 14.2 Risk factors of PC. Two major factors are known to have a major role in causing PC, namely, environmental factors (modifiable) and genetic factors (nonmodifiable). *PC*, pancreatic cancer.

flavonoids as natural antioxidants in plants is related to a modest reduction in PC risk [17]. There also appears to be an inverse association between high 25-hydroxyvitamin D with PC risk [17,18].

14.2.2 Nonmodifiable risk factors

14.2.2.1 Age
The risk of developing PC grows with aging so that the majority of patients are older than 45 years old and two-thirds of the patients are >65 years old. The average age of patients at the time of diagnosing PC is approximately 70 years [19].

14.2.2.2 Gender
The risk of PC in men is slightly higher which might be due to tobacco smoking which is more common in men [20].

14.2.2.3 Family history

The PC gene seems to be inherited by some patients. In some families the risk of PC is high because of genetic syndromes [20].

14.2.2.4 Diabetes mellitus

PC is more prevalent in individuals with diabetes and type 2 diabetes in particular. This type of diabetes is usually seen in adulthood and it is related to obesity and being over-weight. The relationship between PC and type 2 diabetes is not completely clear [21].

14.2.2.5 Chronic pancreatitis

Chronic pancreatitis is known as a long-term inflammation of the pancreas and it is related to a higher risk of PC. However, many cases of pancreatitis do not develop into PC. Chronic pancreatitis can be due to genetic mutations (see below). In this case, the risk of developing a PC is higher [22].

14.2.2.6 Other diseases

Some studies have shown that gastric Helicobacter pylori infection, cirrhosis, peri-odontal disease, hepatitis B, and gingivitis increase the risk of PC [23–25].

14.2.2.7 Genetic syndrome

Up to 10% of PC cases have a heritable component. Genetic development include hereditary pancreatitis, familial atypical multiple mole melanoma (FAMMM) syndrome, Peutz-Jeghers syndrome, familial breast cancer (BRCA-2), hereditary nonpolyposis colo-rectal cancer syndrome (HNPCC), and Li-Fraumeni syndrome [26]. In some cases, the changes result in syndromes that increase the risk of other types of cancers that can be diagnosed using genetic tests. Instances of genetic syndrome that may cause PC are hereditary ovarian and breast cancer syndromes [27]. These are due to a mutation in the BRCA2 or BRCA1 gene [28]. Hereditary breast cancer is due to a mutation in the PALB2 gene [29]. Familial pancreatitis is mostly due to mutations in the PRSS1 gene [30]. Hereditary nonpolyposis colorectal cancer (HNPCC) or Lynch syndrome is due to a defect in MSH2 or MLH1 gene [31].

Peutz-Jeghers syndrome (PJ) is an inherited disease caused by a defect in the STK11 gene. The syndrome is associated with gastrointestinal polyps and other cancers. Without proper medical monitoring, the risk of cancer in people with PJ syndrome may be higher than 93% [32]. FAMMM syndrome was described in 1975 as a syndrome associated with dysplastic nevi and melanomas and was linked to development of pancreatic cancer. FAMMM is developed by mutations in the p16/CDKN2A gene and accounts for the majority of high-density melanoma-prone families [33].

14.3 Surgical treatment of pancreatic cancer

The only potential cure for PC is surgery; however, due to late diagnosis, only 15%−20% of patients can be treated with pancreatectomy. PC has a poor prognosis and even if diagnosed early, the improvement rate after the intervention is poor despite all the advances in surgery and adjuvant therapy. PDAC is staged based on the classification of tumor metastasis so the patient is categorized into three stages: resectable, locally advanced, and metastatic disease [34]. Contrast-enhanced computed tomography (CT), using multislice scanners with arterial and portal venous phases of contrast enhancement, is the "gold standard" method for clinical staging; with 80% accuracy in terms of assessing potential resectability. MRI and endoscopic ultrasound are valuable modalities in the case of diagnostic difficulties. Vascular involvement, tumor size, comorbidity, and age need to be taken into account in the preoperative stage and making decisions about surgical resection [35]. Pancreatoduodenectomy (Whipple), total pancreatectomy, or distal pancreatectomy are usually based on staging and location of tumor [36].

Major contraindications for resection are metastases in the liver, or extra-abdominal site and also omentum. The other criteria for unresectability are encasement (> 50% of the vessel circumference) or thrombus/occlusion of the superior mesenteric artery (SMA); superior mesenteric vein (SMV)-portal confluence occlusion or unreconstructable SMV; or direct involvement of aorta, inferior vena cava, or celiac axis detected by lack of a fat plane separating low-density tumor and these structures on CT scan or EUS [37,38]. Factors that do not contraindicate resection include continuous invasion of the duodenum, stomach, or colon; lymph node metastasis within the operative field; venous impingement or minimal invasion of the superior mesenteric vein−splenic vein−hepatic portal vein trifurcation; gastroduodenal artery encasement; and the age of the patient [39].

When a PC is diagnosed early before it is spreading, surgery may be effective. There is a higher risk of cancer in organs around the pancreas, liver tissue, tissue behind the pancreas, and spleen. Before advancement and spread of the disease, the patient needs to go through an accurate examination and then the physician assesses the stage of disease, which can be highly gratifying by carrying out by taking samples and surgery [39]. The type of surgery depends on the position of the tumor and these methods include:

1. Whipple method or pancreatoduodenectomy: The standard resectional therapy for cancer of the pancreatic head is the partial pancreaticoduodenectomy, first performed by *Kausch* in 1912 and *Whipple* in 1934. The Whipple method is a complicated method to remove a part of the pancreas, intestine, and gallbladder. This method is usually used for PC treatment when the disease is limited to the head of the gland. It is recommended to treat tumors and other issues in the pancreas, bile duct, and small intestine. With this surgery, around 30% of individuals need an enzyme supplement to help with digestion. The intervention involves an invasive and long operation

while the recovery is easy compared to the whole pancreatectomy. The Whipple is a complicated approach for the patient and surgeon as well [40].

Distal pancreatectomy: In the case of distal pancreatectomy, the trunk and tail of the gland are removed along with spleen (in most cases) and part of the intestine, stomach, left adrenal gland, left diaphragm, and left kidney. Similar to the Whipple method, distal pancreatectomy is a complicated and long procedure that is recommended only by the physician. The method is implemented whether by laparoscopic or open surgery. In the latter case, a large incision is performed on the abdomen, and in the former method, many small incisions are performed on the skin to enter surgical instruments [41]. The abdomen is filled with carbon dioxide and the surgeon can have a better view of the space inside using cameras. In the case of a partial pancreatectomy, the surgeon clamps and cuts the vessels to free the gland for removal. If the cases include invasion of the vessels or arteries of the spleen, the organs and the pancreas are both removed [42]. The operation risks severe complications and is not recommended if other options are available. Pancreatectomy is indicated for pancreatic necrosis, chronic pancreatitis (chronic inflammation), chronic pancreatic disease with trauma cancer and pain shock [Adenocarcinoma (85% of cases)], cystadenoma tumor or the islets of Langerhans (neuroendocrine tumors), papillary cystic neoplasms lymphoma, scinar cell tumor, and severe hyperinsulinemia [43].

A complete pancreatectomy is performed only when it is necessary to remove the whole pancreas, part of the small intestine, part of the stomach, gallbladder, common bile ducts, adjacent lymph nodes, spleen, and the lymph nodes nearby so that even part of the immune system is removed. Surgery is very risky and can change the lives of patients. Following pancreatectomy, the patients usually develop diabetes and this requires a new lifestyle, diet, or use of insulin. The patient cannot survive without digestive enzymes and insulin. As shown by the studies, around 75% of people without cancer survive at least seven years without pancreas. In PC patients, the 7-year survival rate is between 30% to 64%, which depends on the type of cancer and its level of spread [43]. The advantage of pancreatic surgery is that it is the most efficient treatment for the disease and increases the chance of living.

14.4 Nonsurgical therapies

For individuals with nonmetastatic PC, surgical excision is the main option for cure. However, only 15%—20% of individuals have a resectable tumor at the time of diagnosis. Approximately 40% of patients develop distant metastases, while the remaining 30%—40% of patients have locally advanced, unresectable tumors [2]. Nonsurgical treatment options for locally advanced PC (LAPC) now include systemic chemotherapy, radiotherapy (RT), and minimally invasive image-guided treatments [44]. Minimally invasive image-guided techniques have evolved in recent years and include radiofrequency ablation (RFA), microwave ablation (MWA), laser ablation, cryoablation (CA), irreversible electroporation

(IRE), reversible electrochemotherapy (ECT), high intensity focused ultrasound, and trans-arterial embolization procedures [45]. In certain conditions, a response to initial therapy will be adequate to allow for a future resection attempt. Preoperative staging contrast-enhanced CT scans and, less frequently, laparotomy/laparoscopy are used to determine resectability. In some cases, additional imaging modalities such as magnetic resonance imaging, endoscopic ultrasonography, and staging laparoscopy may be required [46]. The most common cause of local unresectability is vascular invasion, particularly affecting the superior mesenteric artery (SMA). After multiagent treatment, a satisfactory down-staging response will be achieved, allowing future resection to be considered. A multiphasic CT scan of the chest, abdomen, and pelvis should be conducted prior to therapy to determine the stage of the disease. Cancer antigen 19—9 (CA19—9) serum levels should be monitored at the start of therapy and then every one to three months afterward if increased [47]. The treatment of nonmetastatic PC is evolving, however, early chemotherapy with combination regimens is becoming more popular.

14.4.1 Chemotherapy

The assessment of the patient's PS is the initial step before deciding on the best treatment approach. Patients with a low PS may be candidates for single-agent chemotherapy, palliative radiation therapy, or optimum supportive care; patients with a high PS may be candidates for a more aggressive oncological strategy, such as chemotherapy or chemoradiation [44]. Fig. 14.3 summarizes the treatment algorithm in patients with LAPC.

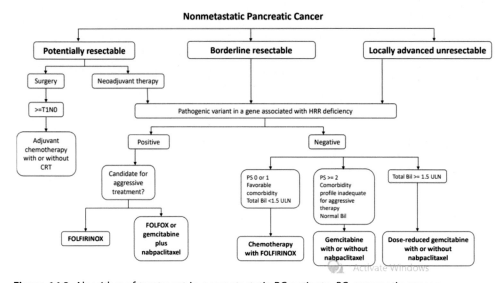

Figure 14.3 Algorithm of treatment in nonmetastatic PC patients. *PC*, pancreatic cancer.

The standard treatment was previously gemcitabine (GEM) for a duration of six months [48]. In 2016, a metanalysis of 11 studies was performed (315 patients) and found that LAPC patients treated with FOLFIRINOX (oxaliplatin plus irinotecan with leucovorin and short-term infusional fluorouracil) had a 24.2 months median overall survival (OS), which was significantly longer than that achieved by GEM therapy (6—13 months) [49]. Because surgery is the only possibly curative treatment, the discovery of a novel neoadjuvant treatment, which improves survival rate, is critical [50].

Following the development of combination chemotherapy regimens, such as FOLFIRINOX (short-term infusion of fluorouracil [FU] with leucovorin, irinotecan, and oxaliplatin) and nanoparticle albumin-bound paclitaxel (nabpaclitaxel) plus GEM, which resulted in significantly higher objective response rates (ORR) than GEM alone (23 percent [nabpaclitaxel plus GEM] and 39 percent [FOLFIRINOX] versus approximately 10 percent with GEM alone), many institutions have adopted neoadjuvant combination chemotherapy for initial therapy of LAPC patients [46,51]. The significance of RT in accomplishing a microscopically complete resection in patients treated initially with multiagent neoadjuvant chemotherapy is uncertain, and the use of RT in this context is decreasing [52].

1. Combination treatment with modified FOLFIRINOX is preferable for patients with confirmed variations who have a satisfactory PS and comorbidity profile.

Starting with FOLFOX (leucovorin plus short-term infusional FU and oxaliplatin) is one option for those with borderline PS or comorbidities. If mutations in a gene related to homologous recombination repair (HRR) deficiency are detected and the patient has tolerated FOLFOX well, irinotecan may be given for subsequent cycles.

1. GEM with nab-paclitaxel or FOLFIRINOX are alternatives for patients who do not have HRR pathway mutations in their germline or tumor.

After four to six months of neoadjuvant treatment, resectability should be carefully evaluated.

14.4.1.1 FOLFIRINOX

For patients with LAPC and a satisfactory PS, neoadjuvant FOLFIRINOX has been adopted. Although the primary tumor ORRs appear to be good, there are few data on rates of resectability, perioperative morbidity, and mortality in patients who undergo surgery after receiving FOLFIRINOX for LAPC; few data on long-term outcomes; and no adequately powered robust phase III randomized trials demonstrating benefit over less intensive chemotherapy regimens in this setting [49,53—56].

14.4.1.2 Gemcitabine alone and combinations

Conversion to resectable in the locally advanced context is unusual with GEM monotherapy (5%), hence treatment is not regarded as potentially curative. Single-agent GEM is only advised for individuals who are unable to handle multiagent chemotherapy [57].

There are little data on the relative effectiveness of GEM-containing regimens versus FOLFIRINOX in LAPC. The phase II NEOLAP study started with two cycles of neoadjuvant GEM/nab-paclitaxel and then randomly allocated patients to two further courses of GEM/nab-paclitaxel or two months of FOLFIRINOX. Sequential FOLFIRINOX was not significantly superior in terms of surgical exploration (approximately 63% in each group) or rate of complete macroscopic tumor resection (R0 or microscopically positive [R1] margins, 45 versus 31%, odds ratio 0.54, 95% CI 0.26−1.13), according to a preliminary report [58]. A retrospective study of 485 consecutive patients treated over an eight-year period yielded further data; 285 received FOLFIRINOX as the first-line treatment, whereas 200 received GEM with nab-paclitaxel. FOLFIRINOX patients were usually younger and had higher overall PS but had more locally advanced cancers. Many serologic and radiographic indicators of response were similar across the two groups; however, partial response was more likely with FOLFIRINOX (19% vs 6%), and pancreatectomy was performed more frequently in this group as well (27% vs 16%). Despite this, the OS length was comparable at a median follow-up of 33 months (median 21 vs 20 months) [59].

14.4.1.3 Adjuvant therapy

Adjuvant treatment is frequently advised for individuals undergoing resection of potentially resectable PC. Randomized studies have shown that administering six months of adjuvant chemotherapy has a considerable survival advantage [60]. Modified FOLFIRINOX is favored over GEM alone or GEM plus capecitabine for individuals with great PS who can tolerate it. GEM with capecitabine is a strategy for less fit people [61].

14.4.2 Chemoradiotherapy

In cases where surgery is not an option after induction chemotherapy, chemoradiotherapy may be used to induce tumor shrinkage and, in a small number of patients, enable secondary resection. In such cases, palliating cancer-related pain is also important. An updated 2018 meta-analysis of 41 trials indicated a substantial survival advantage for chemoradiation following induction chemotherapy in situations where treatment lasted at least 3 months [62]. Currently, based on median OS and median progression-free survival (PFS), the SCALOP phase 2 study results suggest that a capecitabine-based approach should be favored over a GEM-based strategy in the setting of chemoradiotherapy following a course of induction chemotherapy for LAPC [63]. The LAP 07 phase III research did not show any substantial improvement in OS, but it did show a significantly lower local progression rate for chemoradiotherapy without an increase in toxicity (except nausea) [64]. Novel minimally invasive techniques, including IRE, have just lately been investigated for the treatment of LAPC following induction chemotherapy. The safety and effectiveness of percutaneous CT-guided IRE monotherapy or after GEM or FOLFIRINOX initiation chemotherapy were examined in the multicenter, single-arm PANFIRE-2 research. The desired median survival was exceeded in patients with LAPC and those who had local recurrence (50 patients overall; 40 with LAPC and 10 with local recurrence). Notably, there were 14 mild and 21 serious complications, and there was one fatality that was probably associated with IRE [65]. Some data point to a possible function of IRE following FOLFIRINOX treatment since improved outcomes have been observed in some patient subgroups. IRE could be thought of as a less invasive, perhaps curative method for treating LAPC [66]. However, in order to compare the effectiveness of these three approaches, randomized clinical studies are required.

14.4.3 Radiotherapy

Nearly 80%−90% of PC patients have locally advanced disease when diagnosed, giving them an extremely poor prognosis of fewer than 5% OS at five years. To achieve adequate local control in this group of patients, systemic treatment in combination with RT is essential. The tumor must receive a greater radiation dosage during RT, with doses to healthy tissue being kept to a minimum. Conventionally, the usual RT dose has been set at 50−54 Gy given over a period of 6 weeks. This dose was first established based on the at-risk organs' tolerance to large-field radiation. These levels, however, only partially suppressed the tumor, whilst greater doses frequently cause treatment-related toxicity that might adversely influence the patient's quality of life (QOL) [67]. Modern technological advancements over the past ten years, including intensity-modulated RT (IMRT), the development of respiratory control techniques, and enhanced imaging guidance during treatment, have made dose-escalation therapy possible and made it possible to reduce treatment volumes, increase ablative doses to the tumor, and subsequently improve clinical outcomes while concurrently lowering treatment toxicity [68]. A 2015 systematic review examined the toxicity and tumor outcomes of two different RT-techniques for the therapy of LAPC by comparing 13 IMRT trials with 7 3D-CRT series. IMRT was associated with a lower risk of adverse effects even if OS and PFS results did not change [69]. Undoubtedly, the regularly administered dosage, which is insufficient to effectively manage the disease, might be used to explain why there is no OS gain [44]. In a study by Krishnan et al. [70], in comparison to patients who got a conventional dosage with an effective biological dose (BED) less than 70 Gy, those who received treatment with a BED >70 Gy showed greater OS. In this setting, where the major limitation is possible severe intestinal toxicity, stereotactic body RT (SBRT) has been extensively researched as a beneficial treatment for patients with LAPC [71−76].

SBRT can deliver large doses of radiation accurately to smaller tumor volumes. However, the advantage of SBRT persists unknown since it is unclear whether median survival is higher than would be predicted with other kinds of treatment, and toxicity has been higher in some studies [77−79]. Others who used narrower treatment fields, more conformal procedures, and hypofractionated regimens reported better results [80−82].

Recent SBRT data for LAPC therapy demonstrated substantial variation in total dose prescription and fractionations. In most cases, the total doses applied ranged from 30 to 45 Gy, resulting in BED of more than 60 Gy [71−76]. Because of the aggressiveness of cancer, which promotes fast development of metastasis, OS is not significantly reduced in SBRT series, and high rates of late toxicity have limited its usage. As a result, multifraction therapy techniques are preferred. In a study of 167 LAPC patients, the five-fraction procedure was found to have much reduced gastrointestinal toxicity than the single-fraction therapy. However, both groups had a high LC rate [73]. Several retrospective investigations reached similar findings, recognizing the benefits of multifractionated RT regimens versus single-fraction therapy in terms of toxicity, while achieving the same effectiveness [74,75,83]. Patients in these studies received systemic therapy (mostly GEM) at various stages throughout SBRT treatment (before, after, or both before and after SBRT), and therapeutic results varied according to the patients' clinical condition and disease grade. SBRT and standard fractionated RT were compared in just a few nonrandomized, retrospective trials [84]. When compared to standard fractionated RT, SBRT was linked with considerably better OS. Furthermore, in the neo-adjuvant context, SBRT was linked with considerably higher rates of pathological full response and margin-negative resection. These are encouraging findings that should be considered for further validation. However, the significant metastatic potential of cancer may influence the rationale for SBRT to strengthen local therapy.

14.4.4 Ablative techniques

Patients who have a stable or partial response to neoadjuvant therapy and are not surgical candidates should be regarded as candidates for ablative therapies [65,85−87]. There are two types of ablative treatment: first is thermal (RFA, CA, and MWA) and second is nonthermal (RE and IRE).

14.4.4.1 Thermal ablation

RFA applies high-frequency alternating current to solid tumors via needle electrodes. High temperatures are generated during this process and result in thermal coagulation, protein denaturation, and necrosis within the tumor [86]. RFA is typically used for debulking the tumor rather than complete ablation. This treatment is not recommended for small tumors that have perivascular growth. Early research into the efficacy and safety of RFA for the treatment of LAPC found high rates of morbidity and mortality. This is mainly due to thermal injury to the bile ducts, pancreatic duct, duodenum, and vital vessels. Recent research indicates that combining RFA with chemotherapy improves OS by determining the best temperature range parameters (less than 90 degrees), treatment duration, and probe positioning [86,88].

CA causes rapid freezing of target lesions using argon gas. Freeze-thaw cycles destroy cells through endothelial injury, vascular-mediated toxicity, and cellular death. A retrospective study examined CA with and without immunotherapy for the treatment of LAPC. The median OS was 13 mo in cryoimmunotherapy group and 7 mo in cryotherapy group, which was significantly higher than the chemotherapy group (3.5 mo), and the cryo-immunotherapy group had significantly higher median OS than the cryotherapy and immunotherapy groups (5 mo) [86].

MWA is another method that results in tissue necrosis by making water molecules oscillate. This technique has several advantages over RFA in terms of ease of setup and broader ablation zones in a shorter time period, but there is very little recent research on its use in PC with survival data [86].

14.4.4.2 Nonthermal ablation

IRE creates an electric field through the cell membrane by using high-voltage direct current pulses. As a result, membrane homeostasis is disturbed and causes irreversible changes in transmembrane potential, activating the apoptotic pathway and resulting in cell death. The extracellular matrix, critical vessel structures, bile ducts, and intestines are all preserved by IRE. The Food and Drug Administration (FDA) has approved the technology for the ablation of soft tissue tumors [89]. Aside from its cytoreductive abilities, through active in vivo immunization against PC cells, IRE can cause systemic immunomodulation. Following tumor cell apoptosis and necrosis, IRE triggers a systemic immune response by releasing antigens and damage-associated molecular pattern molecules (DAMPs). These DAMPs stimulate the maturation of antigen-presenting cells, resulting in a long-lasting antitumor T-cell response. This response may result in regression of distant metastases. These effects, when combined with immunotherapy, could open the way for a new treatment for tumors with low immunogenic potential, such as PDAC [87]. Because pancreatic IRE procedures have a high-risk profile, it is critical to consider contraindications and carefully assess patients for treatment. The involvement of the duodenum is regarded as a contraindication. If the patient has a biliary blockage, biliary drainage must be established prior to treatment, and biliary protection is strongly indicated if the tumor is near the common bile duct. Portal vein stenting should be performed if a patient has a partly occluded portal vein prior to having IRE to avoid acute full obstruction because of postprocedural edema. Gastrointestinal symptoms such as discomfort, diarrhea, nausea, vomiting, lack of appetite, and delayed stomach emptying are the most prevalent side effects [87]. A recent systematic review of all studies that have used IRE for LAPC shows a median OS after IRE ranging from 7 to 27 months. This difference could be attributed to the IRE approach used, the diverse LAPC tumor biology, adjuvant chemotherapy protocols, comorbidities, and other patient differences. Major complications including portal vein thrombosis, bleeding, and duodenal perforation have been reported in up to 30% of patients, with mortality rates of up to 11% [88].

Reversible ECT is another new nonthermal ablation technique that combines chemotherapeutic drugs (bleomycin) and electric pulses for cell membrane electroporation to avoid potential thermal injury to the peripancreatic vessels. Electric pulses determine the permeability of a transient cell membrane, allowing the cell to be exposed to chemotherapeutic drugs [90]. According to the lack of immediate intraoperative side effects associated with electroporation and bleomycin, ECT has been shown to be safe [90]. Nonetheless, there are few studies on ECT in the literature and more research is needed [91].

14.4.4.3 Intra-arterial therapies

Decades ago, regional intra-arterial chemotherapy (RIAC) was introduced to improve cancer treatment. Intra-arterial chemotherapy produces high drug concentrations at the target site while keeping systemic drug concentrations low. A meta-analysis of six RCTs comparing systemic chemotherapy to RIAC found that RIAC resulted in higher partial remission, clinical advantages, and response rates, as well as fewer complications such as myelosuppression [92]. Other authors considered RIAC as a neoadjuvant regional therapy with continuous GEM infusion to improve resectability rates in LAPC [93]. Novel infusion techniques, such as Trans-Arterial Micro-Perfusion (TAMP), which was recently FAD-approved, offer promising future prospects in local chemotherapy. TAMP involves isolating an arterial segment with proximal and distal balloons, increasing intra-arterial luminal pressure, and forcing the drug throughout the arterial wall to the tumoral tissue. The catheter might provide greater medication concentrations within the tumor while reducing systemic adverse effects. A phase III randomized clinical study is presently recruiting LAPC patients to compare TAMP to systemic chemotherapy. The trial's purpose is to demonstrate longer median survival and enhanced QOL by targeted treatment administration. TAMP resulted in above two-year survival in more than half of patients in Phase I/II trials. The phase III study is now ongoing (clinicaltrials.gov NCT03257033).

Hence, neoadjuvant chemotherapy may be administered to allow for curative surgical resection, radiation treatment, or ablation. SBRT may be used to achieve adequate LC while minimizing adverse effects. Increasing expertise with percutaneous thermal ablation and IRE results in better outcomes with fewer complications. Given the current poor outcomes in terms of OS improvement, various therapeutic strategies for optimizing therapy should be examined.

14.5 Treatment in metastatic patient

Improved survival, palliation, and QOL are the main targets of treatment for metastatic PC (MPC). Most chemotherapeutic medications have been explored in the treatment of MPC, but only a small number have been chosen as standards of care [94].

To date, few medicines are approved for the basic treatment of Stage IV(advanced) PC. Although numerous chemotherapy regimens have improved PFS, the OS does not increase in the majority of the cases. There has been limited innovation in this situation's first treatment [95]. As a result, we have compiled a list of the most relevant studies and the most up-to-date suggestions.

14.5.1 First-line chemotherapy

Prior to the approval of GEM in 1997, FU was the first line treatment for advanced PC [96]. In phase II randomized study, comparing with bolus FU, GEM significantly enhanced clinical benefit response, OS (between 4.4 to 5.7 months; $P = .0025$), and median PFS with adequate tolerability [96].

More than twenty randomized trials have directly compared GEM to GEM plus another cytotoxic agent or targeted therapy. There was no improvement in survival rates shown by any of them [95]. More than 20 randomized controlled trials have compared GEM alone to GEM plus another cytotoxic drug or targeted treatment. However, erlotinib showed a statistically noteworthy, even if modest, improvement in the average OS, with a 23% versus 17% one-year survival rate ($P = .023$) and 6.24 versus 5.91 months for 6-month survival ($P = .038$) (569 patients) [97]. Reni and colleagues made the first direct comparison between GEM monotherapy and polychemotherapy using cisplatin, epirubicin, 5-FU, and GEM (PEFG). There was not a significant statistical difference in the survival rate between the two different groups. (99 individuals in total), despite a 38.5% response rate in the PEFG group and an 8.5% response rate in the GEM group [98].

In the key PRODIGE 4-ACCORD11 study, combining oxaliplatin, irinotecan hydrochloride, leucovorin calcium (folinic acid), and FU is known as FOLFIRINOX, which was compared to GEM in individuals with metastatic PC younger than 75 years of age [99]. The OS was significantly improved, with a median survival of 11.1 months for FOLFIRINOX versus 6.8 months for GEM (Death hazard ratio 0.57; 95% confidence interval 0.45−0.73; P .001) [100]. In addition, in comparison to GEM, FOLFIRINOX dramatically postponed the decline in QOL [101]. In an additional, unreported phase III study, those who were given FOLFIRINOX had a significantly longer median OS time than those who were given GEM. Patients treated with FOLFIRINOX had a median survival of 11.1 months, while those treated with GEM had a median survival of 6.8 months (P .001) [102]. Ever since, FOLFIRINOX has been the choice treatment for otherwise healthy MPC patients who have a status of ECOG performance of either 0 or 1, no considerable cardiac comorbidities, and no bilirubin elevation (Table 14.2).

In 2013, Von Hoff et al. reported that for first-line treatment, the combination of GEM and nab-paclitaxel was advantageous to GEM alone in the MPACT trial for

Table 14.2 Eastern cooperative oncology group (ECOG) PS.

Performance status	Definition
0	Completely active
1	Strenuous physical activity restriction, able to perform light activities
2	Capable of self-care, unable to work
3	Capable of limited self-care, confined to bed
4	Complete disabled

patients with metastatic PC; 861 individuals with ECOG PS between 0 and 2 participated in this clinical trial. Those who received nab-paclitaxel had a median OS of 8.5 months, while those who received GEM alone had a median OS of 6.7 months (Hazard ratio 0.72; 95% confidence interval 0.62−0.80; P .001) [103].

For MPC patients with a favorable comorbidity profile and good ECOG PS either 0 or 1, as a standard treatment, FOLFIRINOX is recommended for metastatic PC by the National Comprehensive Cancer Network (NCCN), the American Society of Clinical Oncology (ASCO), and the European Society for Medical Oncology (ESMO) [47,104−106].

The elderly and the physically weak should not attempt this regimen. In a study conducted from 2008 through 2015, Baldini et al. enrolled 42 patients with an average age of 70−79 and mild comorbidities (median Charlson index of 10) [107]. In MPC patients, decreasing the FOLFIRINOX dose from the first cycle was beneficial in 57% of cases. In comparison to the landmark PRODIGE 4-ACCORD11 trial, the average OS was 12.2 months.

The average OS did not differ significantly between the two groups (11.7 vs 16.6 months, $P = .69$). One could handle toxicology with relative ease. In their study, Kang and colleagues found that mFOLFIRINOX was well tolerated and had similar efficacy to FOLFIRINOX [108]. mFOLFIRINOX typically includes either a dose reduction in irinotecan or a suppression of a FU bolus (or both).

In the face of these alternatives, prognostic variables must be taken into account. Historically, Karnofsky's index of PS (KPS) and the Eastern Cooperative Oncology Group PS Scale (ECOG PS) have proven to be the most accurate survival predictors, but a phase III MPACT study analysis found that liver metastases, age, and the number of metastatic sites were also favorable survival prognostic factors and should be taken into account when choosing treatments [109]. Sarcopenia at the time of diagnosis and reduction in skeletal muscle after chemotherapy are other predictive markers for survival [110] as well as nutritional index, which may also be taken into consideration [111]. In a retrospective chart review, a high blood level of carcinoembryonic antigen, neutrophilia, sarcopenia, and synced metastatic disease (stage IV), and a high serum level of lactate dehydrogenase were verified as independent predictive markers for OS [112].

Clearly, the most important factor is PS while selecting a FOLFIRINOX regimen. In a retrospective analysis conducted at a single institution, Sehdev and colleagues found that the presence of DNA damage response (DDR) gene mutations is associated with increased OS in MPC patients who were administered FOLFIRINOX [113]. Mutations in the BRCA tumor suppressor gene are also associated with improved survival when exposed to platinum-based chemotherapy [114].

1. The mFOLFIRINOX regimen (oxaliplatin plus irinotecan with leucovorin and short-term infusional FU) is well tolerated and preferred for patients with MPC who have a favorable comorbidity profile and good ECOG PS (0 or 1).

2. GEM plus nab-paclitaxel is preferable for MPC patients with ECOG PS 0−2 and improved median OS compared to GEM alone.

3. Patients with MPC who have mutations in the BRCA tumor suppressor gene should prefer chemotherapy based on platinum.

14.5.2 Second-line chemotherapy

About 40%−50% of patients suffering from advanced PC are eligible for second-line or additional chemotherapy when first-line chemotherapy fails to stop the progression [115]. After GEM failure, 45% and 21% of MPC patients received two or more treatment regimens, respectively [116]. The average pooled rate of second-line therapy in 24 first-line published studies (52 different modalities) from 1998 to 2012 was 43% (range, 16%−68%) [117]. This percentage rose from 35% before 2007 to 48% after 2007. All of these studies were completed before FOLFIRINOX and nab-paclitaxel−GEM and featured predominantly GEM-based first-line regimens. More anticancer treatment was given to 47% of patients in the combination chemotherapy arm of the PRODIGE 4-ACCORD 11159 [99,102].

Since upfront combination regimens tend to be more effective, more patients will be able to progress to second-line treatment, improving OS. A change in general health, in addition to the presence of a solid tumor, is considered a sufficient cause to advise against cancer-specific therapies, as recommended by guidelines [118]. Most clinical trials only enrolled individuals with an ECOG PS of either 0 or 1, despite guidelines recommending against such treatments for patients with solid tumors and compromised general health. The majority of patients in the real world do not qualify for clinical trials like these, and they have a dismal outlook (median OS with best supportive care (BSC) alone is about 2 months, comparison to 5−6 months in treated patients) [119]. When disease progresses despite initial chemotherapy, there is currently no accepted treatment protocol. A meta-analysis of second-line treatments found that compared to single-agent treatments, combinations improved PFS (2.5 vs 1.9 months; P .018) but not overall survival (5.1 vs 4.3 months; P .169). Meta-analyses of second-line studies show no significant difference in survival outcomes between GEM-platinum and fluoropyrimidine-platinum combination regimens [117,120]. Patients were randomly assigned to receive either the oxaliplatin, folinic acid, and 5-FU (OFF regimen) or BSC alone in a phase III trial conducted by the German CONKO group [121]. 182 Due to slow accrual, this trial was stopped early with only 46 patients enrolled. However, the OFF group had a significantly higher OS rate than the CON group (4.8 vs 2.3 months; $P = .008$). Hematological, gastrointestinal, and sensory neurotoxicity of grades 1—3 was more common in the OFF group, but there was no significant increase in the incidence of toxicity of grades 2—4. The median OS for the OFF regimen was 5.9 months, compared to 3.3 months for the 5-FU-folinic acid (FF regimen) in the subsequent CONKO-003 trial (HR = 0.66, $P = .01$) [122].

In contrast, the PANCREOX trial found that the modified FOLFOX6 regimen (mFOLFOX6) was not superior to 5-FU-folinic acid in terms of PFS (the primary endpoint), objective response rate, or time to deterioration; in fact, patients in the 5-FU-folinic acid arm had longer OS (median, 9.9 months vs 6.1 months; $P = .02$). This unexpected finding was attributed to a disparity in the use of post-progression therapies (7% vs 23%; $P = .015$), as well as to higher rates of grade 3—4 adverse events (63% vs 11%) and withdrawal from the study due to adverse events (20% vs 2%) [123]. The vast majority of patients are better off with FOLFIRINOX or nab-paclitaxel-GEM as their initial treatment, and the outcomes of these randomized trials, conducted when single-agent GEM was the only standard of therapy, cannot be applied to this population (both being neurotoxic). In fact, the contentious randomized trial results may only apply to a subset of patients: those who are deemed unfit for upfront combination chemotherapy and treated with single-agent GEM, but who are deemed fit for oxaliplatin-based combination chemotherapy in the second-line situation. A novel formulation of irinotecan, called nanoliposomal irinotecan (MM-398), has been developed to increase the therapeutic index of irinotecan by increasing the exposure of tumor tissue to this drug, with irinotecan nanoliposomes accumulating in tumor-associated macrophages and decreasing the exposure of normal tissues as potential sites of toxicity [124,125].

After a phase II study of 40 patients with metastatic disease who had progressed on first-line GEM-containing regimens, and where 75% of patients survived for at least 3 months, the NAPOLI-1 phase III trial randomly assigned 417 patients with MPC previously treated with GEM-containing regimens to receive 5-FU-folinic acid (every 2 weeks), irinotecan monotherapy (120 mg/m^2 every 3 weeks), due to a change in protocol, folinic acid (every 2 weeks), nanoliposomal irinotecan (80 mg/m^2), and 5-FU [126]. About one-third of the patients had previously been treated with at least two lines of chemotherapy for metastatic disease. OS was better for those who received nanoliposomal irinotecan in addition to 5-FU and folinic acid compared to those who received 5-FU and folinic acid alone (median, 6.1 months vs 4.2 months; $P = .012$; HR, 0.75). Patients in the experimental arm also fared better than those in the 5-FU and folinic acid arms on a number of secondary efficacy endpoints, including PFS, objective response rate, time to treatment failure, and CA19—9 responses. However, irinotecan nanoliposomal delivered alone had no effect on survival time when compared to 5-FU-folinic acid [127]. In spite of this, patients' QOL remained stable throughout treatment, and there were no discernible differences between their QOL and that of treated patients with 5-FU-folinic acid [128]. Combining nanoliposomal irinotecan with 5-FU and folinic acid was found to be effective due to these research results. It may be preferable to the neurotoxic oxaliplatin-based regimens following first-line nab-paclitaxel-GEM treatment (as a third-line treatment option) [129].

Additional research is needed before clinical application of nanoliposomal irinotecan to evaluate if it may have a major clinical function in irinotecan-pretreated patients (especially with upfront FOLFIRINOX). There is a lack of prospective data on second-line treatment options for patients whose metastatic PC has progressed while receiving GEM plus FOLFIRINOX or nab-paclitaxel [130—133]. In 2015, Potal et al. concluded that response to first-line FOLFIRINOX had no impact on response to nab-paclitaxel GEM; the medians for progression-free and OS with these agents after FOLFIRINOX failure were 5.1 and 8.8 months, respectively [133]. Approximately 40% of patients in the MPACT phase III post hoc analysis were given a second-line treatment. Overall median survival for 18 patients who underwent FOLFIRINOX as second-line treatment following nab-paclitaxel-GEM failure was 15.7 months [130].

Other targeted or cytotoxic agents analyzed in the second-line setting (and beyond) for patients with advanced PC (such as Jak1 and Jak2 or glufosfamide or tyrosine kinase inhibitor ruxolitinib) have not shown any benefit in randomized studies or were only examined in small, Phase II trials with a single treatment arm [134,135].

Notably, patients who had immunohistochemistry (IHC), polymerase chain reaction (PCR), or next-generation sequencing results that indicated deficient mismatch repair (dMMR) or high microsatellite instability (MSI-H) are an exception to the rule (NGS). Pembrolizumab, an anti-PD-1 immune checkpoint inhibitor, showed a complete radiographic response in 21% of cases, objective response in 53% of cases, and disease control in 77% of cases in a study of 86 patients with 12 different types of cancer who tested positive for dMMR and had received a minimum one prior therapy and evidence of progressive disease [136]. Two of the eight patients in this trial with PC had a full radiographic response, while six patients had their disease under control.

Pembrolizumab, developed in the United States, was given approval by the Food and Drug Administration in 2017 to treat tumors with dMMR/MSI-H mutations in any part of the body. Therefore, even though tumors with this characteristic are expected in only about 1% of PCs, the potential for effective treatment is high [137].

APC patients and a known BRCA mutation are being studied for a potential response to poly ADP-ribose polymerase (PARP) inhibitors, which are being studied because of their promise as a targeted therapy [138–140].

Both the American and European guidelines recommend basing the selection of second-line therapy on the patient's PS, the presence or absence of comorbidities, the state of the patient's organs, any lingering toxicities from the first-line treatment, and the availability of a support system for intensive medical treatment [103,141] (Fig. 14.4).

1. In patients with a good PS (ECOG 0–1) and a favorable comorbidity profile and a normal or subnormal serum bilirubin level (<1/5 ULN):
   a. To follow up initial treatment with GEM and nab-paclitaxel, 5-FU and nanoliposomal irinotecan (naI-IRI) is the treatment of choice. When nanoliposomal irinotecan is not readily available, when first-line therapy-related toxicities persist, or when the patient's comorbidity profile does not allow for its use, 5-FU (5-FU) plus either irinotecan or oxaliplatin (or both) can be substituted. Considerations such as the presence of limiting neuropathy following upfront nab-paclitaxel may influence a decision between 5-FU plus irinotecan and 5-FU plus oxaliplatin.

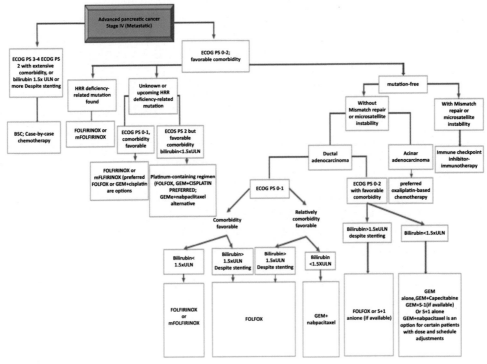

Figure 14.4 Algorithm of treatment in metastatic PC patients. *PC*, pancreatic cancer.

The few patients who are candidates for second-line therapy after first-line GEM monotherapy may benefit from these recommendations (5-FU + naI-IRI, irinotecan, or oxaliplatin).

b. Following FOLFIRINOX in first-line treatment, GEM plus nab-paclitaxel is preferential. (in the EU, off-label use); GEM alone must be offered when nab-paclitaxel is unavailable.

2. Individuals with an ECOG PS of 2 or a comorbidity profile that prevented extra aggressive treatment regimens and who would like to pursue cancer-directed treatment or bilirubin >1/5 ULN are advised to use either GEM or 5-FU.

3. When an ECOG score is >3, only the BSC should be provided to the individual.

4. Pembrolizumab (if available) is suggested as a second-line therapy for individuals with dMMR or MSI tumors, and routine testing for dMMR or MSI using IHC, PCR, or NGS is recommended for individuals who are considered to be candidates for checkpoint inhibitor therapy (when available).

14.5.3 Side effects and future perspective

Patients with PC not only face a poor prognosis but also a reduced QOL as a result of side effects of treatment methods (surgery, chemotherapy, and RT), as demonstrated by FACT-hep scores from before to after treatment. The complications caused by various types of treatment are described below.

Complications with nutrition after pancreatic surgery are common and can include nutrient deficiencies, diabetes, fatty liver, and metabolic bone disease. Each of these, beyond causing additional medical issues, can have profound effects on one's QOL and functional status [142]. Moreover, depending on the type of substance employed, anesthetics have a variety of side effects that affect various body organs [143].

Cancer-related fatigue is one of the distressing side effects that 92% of chemotherapy patients experience and negatively impacts QOL [144]. In 2018, Altun et al. conducted a study that showed the most frequent side effects of chemotherapy are nausea and vomiting, fatigue, reduced appetite, taste changes, hair loss, dry mouth, and constipation [145]. Other notable side effects of chemotherapy include diarrhea, tingling or numbness in hands and/or feet, skin changes (such as dry skin, skin irritation, and pruritus), fever, mouth mucosa damage (mucositis), flu–like clinical signs, allergic reaction, memory problems, reduced renal function, deafness and/or ringing in the ears, an increased risk of infection, weight loss, and pain caused by chemotherapy [145,146] Moreover, 43% of cancer patients experienced insomnia syndrome while receiving chemotherapy treatment, making sleep disturbances common among cancer survivors [147]. The management of adverse side effects can increase the effectiveness of cancer treatment. To improve the QOL for cancer patients, it is necessary to identify new treatments to alleviate the side effects of chemotherapy [145].

Patients who were treated with RT have been shown to experience a rise in distress, anxiety, and depression, according to studies [148,149]. Up to 80% of patients having RT experience acute fatigue, and up to 30% of individuals experience chronic fatigue for months or even years after treatment [150].

The current treatments for PC have many side effects that reduce QOL, so there is a strong demand for new, high-quality treatments with fewer side effects and personalized medicine.

Grant

This study was supported by a grant from Mashhad University of Medical Sciences.

Conflict of interest

The authors have no conflict of interest to disclose.

References

[1] Lambert A, Schwarz L, Borbath I, Henry A, Van Laethem J-L, Malka D, et al. An update on treatment options for pancreatic adenocarcinoma. Ther Adv Med Oncol 2019;11 1758835919875568.
[2] Rawla P, Sunkara T, Gaduputi V. Epidemiology of pancreatic cancer: global trends, etiology and risk factors. World J Oncol 2019;10(1):10.
[3] Mizrahi JD, Surana R, Valle JW, Shroff RT. Pancreatic cancer. Lancet 2020;395(10242):2008−20.
[4] Aguila EJT, Francisco CPD, Co JT. Pancreatic cancer masquerading as ischemic enteritis on endoscopy. JGH Open 2021;5(1):157−9.
[5] Nevala-Plagemann C, Hidalgo M, Garrido-Laguna I. From state-of-the-art treatments to novel therapies for advanced-stage pancreatic cancer. Nat Rev Clin Oncol 2020;17(2):108−23.
[6] Kamisawa T, Wood LD, Itoi T, Takaori K. Pancreatic cancer. Lancet 2016;388(10039):73−85.
[7] Nipp R, Tramontano AC, Kong CY, Pandharipande P, Dowling EC, Schrag D, et al. Disparities in cancer outcomes across age, sex, and race/ethnicity among patients with pancreatic cancer. Cancer Med 2018;7(2):525−35.
[8] Banda L., Lishimpi K., Bechtold M., Phiri G., Simuyandi M., Madsen M., et al. Pancreatic cancer. 2017.
[9] Midha S, Chawla S, Garg PK. Modifiable and non-modifiable risk factors for pancreatic cancer: a review. Cancer Lett 2016;381(1):269−77.
[10] Pandol SJ, Apte MV, Wilson JS, Gukovskaya AS, Edderkaoui M. The burning question: why is smoking a risk factor for pancreatic cancer? Pancreatology. 2012;12(4):344−9.
[11] Renehan AG, Tyson M, Egger M, Heller RF, Zwahlen M. Body-mass index and incidence of cancer: a systematic review and meta-analysis of prospective observational studies. Lancet 2008;371 (9612):569−78.
[12] Xu M, Jung X, Hines OJ, Eibl G, Chen Y. Obesity and pancreatic cancer: overview of epidemiology and potential prevention by weight loss. Pancreas. 2018;47(2):158.
[13] Catanzaro R, Cuffari B, Italia A, Marotta F. Exploring the metabolic syndrome: nonalcoholic fatty pancreas disease. World J Gastroenterol 2016;22(34):7660.
[14] Boonhat H, Lin R-T. Global burden of pancreatic cancer incidence and mortality attributable to residential exposure to the petrochemical industry in 2030. Saf Health 2022;13 S87eS310.

[15] Huang BZ, Wang S, Bogumil D, Wilkens LR, Wu L, Blot WJ, et al. Red meat consumption, cooking mutagens, NAT1/2 genotypes and pancreatic cancer risk in two ethnically diverse prospective cohorts. Int J Cancer 2021;149(4):811−19.

[16] Dewi NU, Diana R. Sugar intake and cancer: a literature review. Amerta Nutr 2021;5(4):387−94.

[17] Nam SY, Jo J, Lee WK, Cho CM. The sex discrepancy effects of fruit and vegetable intake on pancreatic cancer risk; a large Korean cancer screening cohort study. Dig Liver Dis 2022;54(3):365−70.

[18] Wei D, Wang L, Zuo X, Bresalier RS. Vitamin D: promises on the horizon and challenges ahead for fighting pancreatic cancer. Cancers. 2021;13(11):2716.

[19] Gaddam S, Abboud Y, Oh J, Samaan JS, Nissen NN, Lu SC, et al. Incidence of pancreatic cancer by age and sex in the US, 2000−2018. JAMA. 2021;326(20):2075−7.

[20] Ilic M, Ilic I. Epidemiology of pancreatic cancer. World J Gastroenterol 2016;22(44):9694.

[21] Cui Y, Andersen DK. Diabetes and pancreatic cancer. Endocr-Relat Cancer 2012;19(5):F9−26.

[22] Pinho AV, Chantrill L, Rooman I. Chronic pancreatitis: a path to pancreatic cancer. Cancer Lett 2014;345(2):203−9.

[23] Kunovsky L, Dite P, Jabandziev P, Dolina J, Vaculova J, Blaho M, et al. Helicobacter pylori infection and other bacteria in pancreatic cancer and autoimmune pancreatitis. World J Gastrointest Oncol 2021;13(8):835.

[24] Bartel MJ, Asbun H, Stauffer J, Raimondo M. Pancreatic exocrine insufficiency in pancreatic cancer: a review of the literature. Dig liver Dis 2015;47(12):1013−20.

[25] Xu J-H, Fu J-J, Wang X-L, Zhu J-Y, Ye X-H, Chen S-D. Hepatitis B or C viral infection and risk of pancreatic cancer: a meta-analysis of observational studies. World J Gastroenterol 2013;19(26):4234.

[26] Solomon S, Das S, Brand R, Whitcomb DC. Inherited pancreatic cancer syndromes. Cancer J (Sudbury, Mass) 2012;18(6):485.

[27] Kleeff J, Korc M, Apte M, La Vecchia C, Johnson CD, Biankin AV, et al. Pancreatic cancer. Nat Rev Dis Prim 2016;2(1):1−22.

[28] Iqbal J, Ragone A, Lubinski J, Lynch H, Moller P, Ghadirian P, et al. The incidence of pancreatic cancer in BRCA1 and BRCA2 mutation carriers. Br J Cancer 2012;107(12):2005−9.

[29] Principe DR. Precision medicine for BRCA/PALB2-mutated pancreatic cancer and emerging strategies to improve therapeutic responses to PARP inhibition. Cancers. 2022;14(4):897.

[30] Liu Q, Guo L, Zhang S, Wang J, Lin X, Gao F. PRSS1 mutation: a possible pathomechanism of pancreatic carcinogenesis and pancreatic cancer. Mol Med 2019;25(1):1−11.

[31] Steinke V, Engel C, Büttner R, Schackert HK, Schmiegel WH, Propping P. Hereditary nonpolyposis colorectal cancer (HNPCC)/Lynch syndrome. Dtsch Ärzteblatt Int 2013;110(3):32.

[32] Taheri D, Afshar-Moghadam N, Mahzoni P, Eftekhari A, Hashemi SM, Emami MH, et al. Cancer problem in Peutz−Jeghers syndrome. Adv Biomed Res 2013;2:35.

[33] Korsse SE, Harinck F, van Lier MG, Biermann K, Offerhaus GJA, Krak N, et al. Pancreatic cancer risk in Peutz-Jeghers syndrome patients: a large cohort study and implications for surveillance. J Med Genet 2013;50(1):59−64.

[34] Strobel O, Neoptolemos J, Jäger D, Büchler MW. Optimizing the outcomes of pancreatic cancer surgery. Nat Rev Clin Oncol 2019;16(1):11−26.

[35] Strobel O, Hank T, Hinz U, Bergmann F, Schneider L, Springfeld C, et al. Pancreatic cancer surgery. Ann Surg 2017;265(3):565−73.

[36] Hartwig W, Hackert T, Hinz U, Gluth A, Bergmann F, Strobel O, et al. Pancreatic cancer surgery in the new millennium: better prediction of outcome. Ann Surg 2011;254(2):311−19.

[37] Derogar M, Blomberg J, Sadr-Azodi O. Hospital teaching status and volume related to mortality after pancreatic cancer surgery in a national cohort. J Br Surg 2015;102(5):548−57.

[38] Tentes A-AK, Kyziridis D, Kakolyris S, Pallas N, Zorbas G, Korakianitis O, et al. Preliminary results of hyperthermic intraperitoneal intraoperative chemotherapy as an adjuvant in resectable pancreatic cancer. Gastroenterol Res Pract 2012;2012:506571.

[39] Ichikawa T, Haradome H, Hachiya J, Nitatori T, Ohtomo K, Kinoshita T, et al. Pancreatic ductal adenocarcinoma: preoperative assessment with helical CT versus dynamic MR imaging. Radiology. 1997;202(3):655−62.

[40] Bhosale P, Fleming J, Balachandran A, Charnsangavej C, Tamm EP. Complications of Whipple surgery: imaging analysis. Abdom Imaging 2013;38(2):273—84.

[41] Björnsson B, Larsson AL, Hjalmarsson C, Gasslander T, Sandström P. Comparison of the duration of hospital stay after laparoscopic or open distal pancreatectomy: randomized controlled trial. J Br Surg 2020;107(10):1281—8.

[42] Ikenaga N, Ohtsuka T, Nakata K, Watanabe Y, Mori Y, Nakamura M. Clinical significance of postoperative acute pancreatitis after pancreatoduodenectomy and distal pancreatectomy. Surgery. 2021;169(4):732—7.

[43] Nakata K, Shikata S, Ohtsuka T, Ukai T, Miyasaka Y, Mori Y, et al. Minimally invasive preservation versus splenectomy during distal pancreatectomy: a systematic review and meta-analysis. J Hepatobiliary Pancreat Sci 2018;25(11):476—88.

[44] Spiliopoulos S, Zurlo MT, Casella A, Laera L, Surico G, Surgo A, et al. Current status of non-surgical treatment of locally advanced pancreatic cancer. World J Gastrointest Oncol 2021;13(12):2064—75.

[45] Ierardi AM, Lucchina N, Bacuzzi A, Bracchi E, Cocozza E, Dionigi G, et al. Percutaneous ablation therapies of inoperable pancreatic cancer: a systematic review. Ann Gastroenterol 2015;28(4):431.

[46] Balaban EP, Mangu PB, Khorana AA, Shah MA, Mukherjee S, Crane CH, et al. Locally advanced, unresectable pancreatic cancer: American Society of Clinical Oncology clinical practice guideline. J Clin Oncol 2016;34(22):2654—68.

[47] Sohal DPS, Kennedy EB, Khorana A, Copur MS, Crane CH, Garrido-Laguna I, et al. Metastatic pancreatic cancer: ASCO clinical practice guideline update. J Clin Oncol 2018;36(24):2545.

[48] Ishii H, Furuse J, Boku N, Okusaka T, Ikeda M, Ohkawa S, et al. Phase II study of gemcitabine chemotherapy alone for locally advanced pancreatic carcinoma: JCOG0506. Japanese J Clin Oncol 2010;40(6):573—9.

[49] Suker M, Beumer BR, Sadot E, Marthey L, Faris JE, Mellon EA, et al. FOLFIRINOX for locally advanced pancreatic cancer: a systematic review and patient-level meta-analysis. Lancet Oncol 2016;17(6):801—10.

[50] Barcellini A, Peloso A, Pugliese L, Vitolo V, Cobianchi L. Locally advanced pancreatic ductal adenocarcinoma: challenges and progress. Onco Targets Ther 2020;13:12705.

[51] Su Y-Y, Ting Y-L, Wang C-J, Chao Y-J, Liao T-K, Su P-J, et al. Improved survival with induction chemotherapy and conversion surgery in locally advanced unresectable pancreatic cancer: a single institution experience. Am J Cancer Res 2022;12(5):2189.

[52] Tempero MA, Malafa MP, Chiorean EG, Czito B, Scaife C, Narang AK, et al. NCCN guidelines insights: pancreatic adenocarcinoma, version 1.2019: featured updates to the NCCN guidelines. J Natl Compr Canc Netw 2019;17(3):202—10.

[53] Boone BA, Steve J, Krasinskas AM, Zureikat AH, Lembersky BC, Gibson MK, et al. Outcomes with FOLFIRINOX for borderline resectable and locally unresectable pancreatic cancer. J Surgical Oncol 2013;108(4):236—41.

[54] Marthey L, Sa-Cunha A, Blanc JF, Gauthier M, Cueff A, Francois E, et al. FOLFIRINOX for locally advanced pancreatic adenocarcinoma: results of an AGEO multicenter prospective observational cohort. Ann Surgical Oncol 2015;22(1):295—301.

[55] Auclin E, Marthey L, Abdallah R, Mas L, Francois E, Saint A, et al. Role of FOLFIRINOX and chemoradiotherapy in locally advanced and borderline resectable pancreatic adenocarcinoma: update of the AGEO cohort. Br J Cancer 2021;124(12):1941—8.

[56] Janssen QP, van Dam JL, Doppenberg D, Prakash LR, van Eijck CHJ, Jarnagin WR, et al. FOLFIRINOX as initial treatment for localized pancreatic adenocarcinoma: a retrospective analysis by the trans-atlantic pancreatic surgery consortium. J Natl Cancer Inst 2022;114(5):695—703.

[57] Tempero MA, Malafa MP, Al-Hawary M, Behrman SW, Benson AB, Cardin DB, et al. Pancreatic adenocarcinoma, version 2.2021, NCCN clinical practice guidelines in oncology. J Natl Compr Canc Netw 2021;19(4):439—57.

[58] Kunzmann V, Algül H, Goekkurt E, Siegler GM, Martens UM, Waldschmidt D, et al. Conversion rate in locally advanced pancreatic cancer (LAPC) after nab-paclitaxel/gemcitabine-or FOLFIRINOX-based induction chemotherapy (NEOLAP): Final results of a multicenter randomised phase II AIO trial. Ann Oncol 2019;30:v253.

[59] Perri G, Prakash L, Qiao W, Varadhachary GR, Wolff R, Fogelman D, et al. Response and survival associated with first-line FOLFIRINOX vs gemcitabine and nab-paclitaxel chemotherapy for localized pancreatic ductal adenocarcinoma. JAMA Surg 2020;155(9):832–9.

[60] Khorana AA, Mangu PB, Berlin J, Engebretson A, Hong TS, Maitra A, et al. Potentially curable pancreatic cancer: American Society of Clinical Oncology clinical practice guideline. J Clin Oncol 2016;34(21):2541–56.

[61] Mas L, Schwarz L, Bachet J-B. Adjuvant chemotherapy in pancreatic cancer: state of the art and future perspectives. Curr Opin Oncol 2020;32(4):356–63.

[62] Chang JS, Chiu Y-F, Yu J-C, Chen L-T, Ch'ang H-J. The role of consolidation chemoradiotherapy in locally advanced pancreatic cancer receiving chemotherapy: an updated systematic review and meta-analysis. Cancer Res Treat 2018;50(2):562–74.

[63] Hurt CN, Falk S, Crosby T, McDonald A, Ray R, Joseph G, et al. Long-term results and recurrence patterns from SCALOP: a phase II randomised trial of gemcitabine-or capecitabine-based chemoradiation for locally advanced pancreatic cancer. Br J Cancer 2017;116(10):1264–70.

[64] Hammel P, Huguet F, van Laethem JL, Goldstein D, Glimelius B, Artru P, et al. Effect of chemoradiotherapy vs chemotherapy on survival in patients with locally advanced pancreatic cancer controlled after 4 months of gemcitabine with or without erlotinib: the LAP07 randomized clinical trial. JAMA. 2016;315(17):1844–53.

[65] Ruarus AH, Vroomen LGPH, Geboers B, et al. Percutaneous irreversible electroporation in locally advanced and recurrent pancreatic cancer (PANFIRE-2): a multicenter, prospective, single-arm, phase II study S, et al. Radiology. 2020;294(1):212–20.

[66] Melisi D, Oh D-Y, Hollebecque A, Calvo E, Varghese A, Borazanci E, et al. Safety and activity of the TGFβ receptor I kinase inhibitor galunisertib plus the anti-PD-L1 antibody durvalumab in metastatic pancreatic cancer. J Immunother Cancer 2021;9(3):e002068.

[67] Cattaneo GM, Passoni P, Longobardi B, Slim N, Reni M, Cereda S, et al. Dosimetric and clinical predictors of toxicity following combined chemotherapy and moderately hypofractionated rotational radiotherapy of locally advanced pancreatic adenocarcinoma. Radiother Oncol 2013;108(1):66–71.

[68] Garibaldi C, Jereczek-Fossa BA, Marvaso G, Dicuonzo S, Rojas DP, Cattani F, et al. Recent advances in radiation oncology. Ecancermedicalscience. 2017;11:785.

[69] Bittner M-I, Grosu A-L, Brunner TB. Comparison of toxicity after IMRT and 3D-conformal radiotherapy for patients with pancreatic cancer—a systematic review. Radiother Oncol 2015;114 (1):117–21.

[70] Krishnan S, Chadha AS, Suh Y, Chen H-C, Rao A, Das P, et al. Focal radiation therapy dose escalation improves overall survival in locally advanced pancreatic cancer patients receiving induction chemotherapy and consolidative chemoradiation. Int J Radiat Oncol Biol Phys 2016;94(4):755–65.

[71] Goyal K, Einstein D, Ibarra RA, Yao M, Kunos C, Ellis R, et al. Stereotactic body radiation therapy for nonresectable tumors of the pancreas. J Surgical Res 2012;174(2):319–25.

[72] Gurka MK, Collins SP, Slack R, Tse G, Charabaty A, Ley L, et al. Stereotactic body radiation therapy with concurrent full-dose gemcitabine for locally advanced pancreatic cancer: a pilot trial demonstrating safety. Radiat Oncol 2013;8(1):1–9.

[73] Herman JM, Chang DT, Goodman KA, Dholakia AS, Raman SP, Hacker-Prietz A, et al. Phase 2 multi-institutional trial evaluating gemcitabine and stereotactic body radiotherapy for patients with locally advanced unresectable pancreatic adenocarcinoma. Cancer. 2015;121(7):1128–37.

[74] Mellon EA, Hoffe SE, Springett GM, Frakes JM, Strom TJ, Hodul PJ, et al. Long-term outcomes of induction chemotherapy and neoadjuvant stereotactic body radiotherapy for borderline resectable and locally advanced pancreatic adenocarcinoma. Acta Oncol 2015;54(7):979–85.

[75] Comito T, Cozzi L, Clerici E, Franzese C, Tozzi A, Iftode C, et al. Can stereotactic body radiation therapy be a viable and efficient therapeutic option for unresectable locally advanced pancreatic adenocarcinoma? Results of a phase 2 study. Technol Cancer Res Treat 2017;16(3):295–301.

[76] Mazzola R, Fersino S, Aiello D, Gregucci F, Tebano U, Corradini S, et al. Linac-based stereotactic body radiation therapy for unresectable locally advanced pancreatic cancer: risk-adapted dose prescription and image-guided delivery. Strahlenther Onkol 2018;194(9):835–42.

[77] Chang DT, Schellenberg D, Shen J, Kim J, Goodman KA, Fisher GA, et al. Stereotactic radiotherapy for unresectable adenocarcinoma of the pancreas. Cancer. 2009;115(3):665−72.

[78] Mahadevan A, Jain S, Goldstein M, Miksad R, Pleskow D, Sawhney M, et al. Stereotactic body radiotherapy and gemcitabine for locally advanced pancreatic cancer. Int J Radiat Oncol Biol Phys 2010;78(3):735−42.

[79] Didolkar MS, Coleman CW, Brenner MJ, Chu KU, Olexa N, Stanwyck E, et al. Image-guided stereotactic radiosurgery for locally advanced pancreatic adenocarcinoma results of first 85 patients. J Gastrointest Surg 2010;14(10):1547−59.

[80] Chuong MD, Springett GM, Freilich JM, Park CK, Weber JM, Mellon EA, et al. Stereotactic body radiation therapy for locally advanced and borderline resectable pancreatic cancer is effective and well tolerated. Int J Radiat Oncol Biol Phys 2013;86(3):516−22.

[81] Schellenberg D, Kim J, Christman-Skieller C, Chun CL, Columbo LA, Ford JM, et al. Single-fraction stereotactic body radiation therapy and sequential gemcitabine for the treatment of locally advanced pancreatic cancer. Int J Radiat Oncol Biol Phys 2011;81(1):181−8.

[82] Polistina F, Costantin G, Casamassima F, Francescon P, Guglielmi R, Panizzoni G, et al. Unresectable locally advanced pancreatic cancer: a multimodal treatment using neoadjuvant chemoradiotherapy (gemcitabine plus stereotactic radiosurgery) and subsequent surgical exploration. Ann Surg Oncol 2010;17(8):2092−101.

[83] Lin J-C, Jen Y-M, Li M-H, Chao H-L, Tsai J-T. Comparing outcomes of stereotactic body radiotherapy with intensity-modulated radiotherapy for patients with locally advanced unresectable pancreatic cancer. Eur J Gastroenterol Hepatol 2015;27(3):259−64.

[84] Zhong J, Patel K, Switchenko J, Cassidy RJ, Hall WA, Gillespie T, et al. Outcomes for patients with locally advanced pancreatic adenocarcinoma treated with stereotactic body radiation therapy versus conventionally fractionated radiation. Cancer. 2017;123(18):3486−93.

[85] Lafranceschina S, Brunetti O, Delvecchio A, Conticchio M, Ammendola M, Currò G, et al. Systematic review of irreversible electroporation role in management of locally advanced pancreatic cancer. Cancers. 2019;11(11):1718.

[86] Narayanan G, Ucar A, Gandhi RT, Nasiri A, Inampudi P, Wilson NM, et al. Emerging ablative and transarterial therapies for pancreatic cancer. Dig Dis Interv 2020;4(04):389−94.

[87] Moris D, Machairas N, Tsilimigras DI, Prodromidou A, Ejaz A, Weiss M, et al. Systematic review of surgical and percutaneous irreversible electroporation in the treatment of locally advanced pancreatic cancer. Ann Surgical Oncol 2019;26(6):1657−68.

[88] van Veldhuisen E, van den Oord C, Brada LJ, Walma MS, Vogel JA, Wilmink JW, et al. Locally advanced pancreatic cancer: work-up, staging, and local intervention strategies. Cancers. 2019;11(7):976.

[89] Narayanan G, Hosein PJ, Beulaygue IC, Froud T, Scheffer HJ, Venkat SR, et al. Percutaneous image-guided irreversible electroporation for the treatment of unresectable, locally advanced pancreatic adenocarcinoma. J Vasc Interv Radiol 2017;28(3):342−8.

[90] Casadei R, Ricci C, Ingaldi C, Alberici L, Di Marco M, Guido A, et al. Intraoperative electrochemotherapy in locally advanced pancreatic cancer: indications, techniques and results—A single-center experience. Updates Surg 2020;72(4):1089−96.

[91] Girelli R, Prejanò S, Cataldo I, Corbo V, Martini L, Scarpa A, et al. Feasibility and safety of electrochemotherapy (ECT) in the pancreas: a pre-clinical investigation. Radiol Oncol 2015;49(2):147.

[92] Liu F, Tang Y, Sun J, Yuan Z, Li S, Sheng J, et al. Regional intra-arterial vs. systemic chemotherapy for advanced pancreatic cancer: a systematic review and meta-analysis of randomized controlled trials. PLoS One 2012;7(7):e40847.

[93] Davis JL, Pandalai P, Ripley RT, Langan RC, Steinberg SM, Walker M, et al. Regional chemotherapy in locally advanced pancreatic cancer: RECLAP trial. Trials. 2011;12(1):1−8.

[94] Ko AH. Progress in the treatment of metastatic pancreatic cancer and the search for next opportunities. J Clin Oncol 2015;33(16):1779−86.

[95] Chin V, Nagrial A, Sjoquist K, O'Connor CA, Chantrill L, Biankin AV, et al. Chemotherapy and radiotherapy for advanced pancreatic cancer. Cochrane Database Syst Rev 2018;3(3):Cd011044.

[96] Burris 3rd HA, Moore MJ, Andersen J, Green MR, Rothenberg ML, Modiano MR, et al. Improvements in survival and clinical benefit with gemcitabine as first-line therapy for patients with advanced pancreas cancer: a randomized trial. J Clin Oncol 1997;15(6):2403−13.

[97] Moore MJ, Goldstein D, Hamm J, Figer A, Hecht JR, Gallinger S, et al. Erlotinib plus gemcitabine compared with gemcitabine alone in patients with advanced pancreatic cancer: a phase III trial of the National Cancer Institute of Canada Clinical Trials Group. J Clin Oncol 2007;25(15):1960−6.

[98] Reni M, Cordio S, Milandri C, Passoni P, Bonetto E, Oliani C, et al. Gemcitabine versus cisplatin, epirubicin, fluorouracil, and gemcitabine in advanced pancreatic cancer: a randomised controlled multicentre phase III trial. Lancet Oncol 2005;6(6):369−76.

[99] Conroy T, Desseigne F, Ychou M, Bouché O, Guimbaud R, Bécouarn Y, et al. FOLFIRINOX versus gemcitabine for metastatic pancreatic cancer. N Engl J Med 2011;364(19):1817−25.

[100] Gourgou-Bourgade S, Bascoul-Mollevi C, Desseigne F, Ychou M, Bouché O, Guimbaud R, et al. Impact of FOLFIRINOX compared with gemcitabine on quality of life in patients with met-astatic pancreatic cancer: results from the PRODIGE 4/ACCORD 11 randomized trial. J Clin Oncol 2013;31(1):23−9.

[101] Cintas C, Douché T, Therville N, Arcucci S, Ramos-Delgado F, Basset C, et al. Signal-targeted therapies and resistance mechanisms in pancreatic cancer: future developments reside in proteomics. Cancers. 2018;10(6):174.

[102] Singhal MK, Kapoor A, Bagri PK, Narayan S, Singh D, Nirban RK, et al. A phase III trial comparing FOLFIRINOX versus gemcitabine for metastatic pancreatic cancer. Ann Oncol 2014;25 iv210.

[103] Von Hoff DD, Ervin T, Arena FP, Chiorean EG, Infante J, Moore M, et al. Increased survival in pancreatic cancer with nab-paclitaxel plus gemcitabine. N Engl J Med 2013;369(18):1691−703.

[104] Sohal DPS, Mangu PB, Khorana AA, Shah MA, Philip PA, O'Reilly EM, et al. Metastatic pancre-atic cancer: American Society of Clinical Oncology clinical practice guideline. J Clin Oncol 2016;34(23):2784.

[105] Sinn M, Bahra M, Liersch T, Gellert K, Messmann H, Bechstein W, et al. CONKO-005: adjuvant chemotherapy with gemcitabine plus erlotinib versus gemcitabine alone in patients after R0 resection of pancreatic cancer: a multicenter randomized phase III trial. J Clin Oncol 2017;35(29):3330−7.

[106] Tempero MA, Malafa MP, Al-Hawary M, Asbun H, Bain A, Behrman SW, et al. Pancreatic ade-nocarcinoma, version 2.2017, NCCN clinical practice guidelines in oncology. J Natl Compr Canc Netw 2017;15(8):1028−61.

[107] Baldini C, Escande A, Bouché O, El Hajbi F, Volet J, Bourgeois V, et al. Safety and efficacy of FOLFIRINOX in elderly patients with metastatic or locally advanced pancreatic adenocarcinoma: a retrospective analysis. Pancreatology. 2017;17(1):146−9.

[108] Kang H, Jo JH, Lee HS, Chung MJ, Bang S, Park SW, et al. Comparison of efficacy and safety between standard-dose and modified-dose FOLFIRINOX as a first-line treatment of pancreatic cancer. World J Gastrointest Oncol 2018;10(11):421.

[109] Tabernero J, Chiorean EG, Infante JR, Hingorani SR, Ganju V, Weekes C, et al. Prognostic factors of survival in a randomized phase III trial (MPACT) of weekly nab-paclitaxel plus gem-citabine versus gemcitabine alone in patients with metastatic pancreatic cancer. Oncologist 2015;20(2):143−50.

[110] Choi Y, Oh D-Y, Kim T-Y, Lee K-H, Han S-W, Im S-A, et al. Skeletal muscle depletion pre-dicts the prognosis of patients with advanced pancreatic cancer undergoing palliative chemother-apy, independent of body mass index. PLoS One 2015;10(10):e0139749.

[111] Geng Y, Qi Q, Sun M, Chen H, Wang P, Chen Z. Prognostic nutritional index predicts survival and correlates with systemic inflammatory response in advanced pancreatic cancer. Eur J Surgical Oncol 2015;41(11):1508−14.

[112] Park I, Choi SJ, Kim YS, Ahn HK, Hong J, Sym SJ, et al. Prognostic factors for risk stratification of patients with recurrent or metastatic pancreatic adenocarcinoma who were treated with gemcitabine-based chemotherapy. Cancer Res Treat 2016;48(4):1264−73.

[113] Sehdev A, Gbolahan O, Hancock BA, Stanley M, Shahda S, Wan J, et al. Germline and Somatic DNA damage repair gene mutations and overall survival in metastatic pancreatic adenocarcinoma patients treated with FOLFIRINOXDNA repair gene mutations and survival in pancreatic cancer. Clin Cancer Res 2018;24(24):6204−11.

[114] Fogelman D, Sugar EA, Oliver G, Shah N, Klein A, Alewine C, et al. Family history as a marker of plat-inum sensitivity in pancreatic adenocarcinoma. Cancer Chemother Pharmacol 2015;76(3):489−98.

[115] Walker EJ, Ko AH. Beyond first-line chemotherapy for advanced pancreatic cancer: an expanding array of therapeutic options? World J Gastroenterol 2014;20(9):2224.

[116] Bachet JB, Mitry E, Lièvre A, Lepere C, Vaillant JN, Declety G, et al. Second-and third-line chemotherapy in patients with metastatic pancreatic adenocarcinoma: feasibility and potential benefits in a retrospective series of 117 patients. Gastroentérol Clin Biol 2009;33(10—11):1036—44.

[117] Nagrial AM, Chin VT, Sjoquist KM, Pajic M, Horvath LG, Biankin AV, et al. Second-line treatment in inoperable pancreatic adenocarcinoma: a systematic review and synthesis of all clinical trials. Crit Rev Oncol Hematol 2015;96(3):483—97.

[118] Schnipper LE, Smith TJ, Raghavan D, Blayney DW, Ganz PA, Mulvey TM, et al. American Society of Clinical Oncology identifies five key opportunities to improve care and reduce costs: the top five list for oncology. J Clin Oncol 2012;30(14):1715—24.

[119] Ueda A, Hosokawa A, Ogawa K, Yoshita H, Ando T, Kajiura S, et al. Treatment outcome of advanced pancreatic cancer patients who are ineligible for a clinical trial. Onco Targets Ther 2013;6:491.

[120] Rahma OE, Duffy A, Liewehr DJ, Steinberg SM, Greten TF. Second-line treatment in advanced pancreatic cancer: a comprehensive analysis of published clinical trials. Ann Oncol 2013;24(8):1972—9.

[121] Pelzer U, Schwaner I, Stieler J, Adler M, Seraphin J, Dörken B, et al. Best supportive care (BSC) versus oxaliplatin, folinic acid and 5-fluorouracil (OFF) plus BSC in patients for second-line advanced pancreatic cancer: a phase III-study from the German CONKO-study group. Eur J Cancer 2011;47(11):1676—81.

[122] Oettle H, Riess H, Stieler JM, Heil G, Schwaner I, Seraphin J, et al. Second-line oxaliplatin, folinic acid, and fluorouracil versus folinic acid and fluorouracil alone for gemcitabine-refractory pancreatic cancer: outcomes from the CONKO-003 trial. J Clin Oncol 2014;32(23):2423—9.

[123] Gill S, Ko YJ, Cripps C, Beaudoin A, Dhesy-Thind S, Zulfiqar M, et al. PANCREOX: a randomized phase III study of fluorouracil/leucovorin with or without oxaliplatin for second-line advanced pancreatic cancer in patients who have received gemcitabine-based chemotherapy. J Clin Oncol 2016;34(32):3914—20.

[124] Kang MH, Wang J, Makena MR, Lee JS, Paz N, Hall CP, et al. Activity of MM-398, nanoliposomal irinotecan (nal-IRI), in Ewing's family tumor xenografts is associated with high exposure of tumor to drug and high SLFN11 expression. Clin Cancer Res 2015;21(5):1139—50.

[125] Chang TC, Shiah HS, Yang CH, Yeh KH, Cheng AL, Shen BN, et al. Phase I study of nanoliposomal irinotecan (PEP02) in advanced solid tumor patients. Cancer Chemother Pharmacol 2015;75(3):579—86.

[126] Wang-Gillam A, Li CP, Bodoky G, Dean A, Shan YS, Jameson G, et al. Nanoliposomal irinotecan with fluorouracil and folinic acid in metastatic pancreatic cancer after previous gemcitabine-based therapy (NAPOLI-1): a global, randomised, open-label, phase 3 trial. Lancet. 2016;387(10018):545—57.

[127] Chen LT, Siveke JT, Wang-Gillam A, Li CP, Bodoky G, Dean AP, et al. Survival with nal-IRI (liposomal irinotecan) plus 5-fluorouracil and leucovorin versus 5-fluorouracil and leucovorin in per-protocol and non-per-protocol populations of NAPOLI-1: Expanded analysis of a global phase 3 trial. Eur J Cancer 2018;105:71—8.

[128] Hubner RA, Cubillo A, Blanc JF, Melisi D, Von Hoff DD, Wang-Gillam A, et al. Quality of life in metastatic pancreatic cancer patients receiving liposomal irinotecan plus 5-fluorouracil and leucovorin. Eur J Cancer 2019;106:24—33.

[129] Li D, Xie K, Wolff R, Abbruzzese JL. Pancreatic cancer. Lancet. 2004;363(9414):1049—57.

[130] Chiorean EG, Von Hoff DD, Tabernero J, El-Maraghi R, Ma WW, Reni M, et al. Second-line therapy after nab-paclitaxel plus gemcitabine or after gemcitabine for patients with metastatic pancreatic cancer. Br J Cancer 2016;115(2):188—94.

[131] Lee MG, Lee SH, Lee SJ, Lee YS, Hwang JH, Ryu JK, et al. 5-Fluorouracil/leucovorin combined with irinotecan and oxaliplatin (FOLFIRINOX) as second-line chemotherapy in patients with advanced pancreatic cancer who have progressed on gemcitabine-based therapy. Chemotherapy. 2013;59(4):273—9.

[132] Assaf E, Verlinde-Carvalho M, Delbaldo C, Grenier J, Sellam Z, Pouessel D, et al. 5-fluorouracil/leucovorin combined with irinotecan and oxaliplatin (FOLFIRINOX) as second-line chemotherapy in patients with metastatic pancreatic adenocarcinoma. Oncology. 2011;80(5—6):301—6.

[133] Portal A, Pernot S, Tougeron D, Arbaud C, Bidault AT, de la Fouchardière C, et al. Nab-paclitaxel plus gemcitabine for metastatic pancreatic adenocarcinoma after Folfirinox failure: an AGEO prospective multicentre cohort. Br J Cancer 2015;113(7):989—95.

[134] Hurwitz HI, Uppal N, Wagner SA, Bendell JC, Beck JT, Wade 3rd SM, et al. Randomized, double-blind, phase II study of ruxolitinib or placebo in combination with capecitabine in patients with metastatic pancreatic cancer for whom therapy with gemcitabine has failed. J Clin Oncol 2015;33(34):4039−47.

[135] Ciuleanu TE, Pavlovsky AV, Bodoky G, Garin AM, Langmuir VK, Kroll S, et al. A randomised Phase III trial of glufosfamide compared with best supportive care in metastatic pancreatic adeno-carcinoma previously treated with gemcitabine. Eur J Cancer 2009;45(9):1589−96.

[136] Le DT, Durham JN, Smith KN, Wang H, Bartlett BR, Aulakh LK, et al. Mismatch repair defi-ciency predicts response of solid tumors to PD-1 blockade. Science. 2017;357(6349):409−13.

[137] Hu ZI, Shia J, Stadler ZK, Varghese AM, Capanu M, Salo-Mullen E, et al. Evaluating mismatch repair deficiency in pancreatic adenocarcinoma: challenges and recommendations. Clin Cancer Res 2018;24(6):1326−36.

[138] Holter S, Borgida A, Dodd A, Grant R, Semotiuk K, Hedley D, et al. Germline BRCA mutations in a large clinic-based cohort of patients with pancreatic adenocarcinoma. J Clin Oncol 2015;33 (28):3124−9.

[139] Domchek SM, Hendifar AE, McWilliams RR, Geva R, Epelbaum R, Biankin A, et al. RUCAPANC: an open-label, phase 2 trial of the PARP inhibitor rucaparib in patients (pts) with pancreatic cancer (PC) and a known deleterious germline or somatic BRCA mutation. Am Soc Clin Oncol 2016;34(15).

[140] Golan T, Oh D-Y, Reni M, Macarulla TM, Tortora G, Hall MJ, et al. POLO: a randomized phase III trial of olaparib maintenance monotherapy in patients (pts) with metastatic pancreatic cancer (mPC) who have a germline *BRCA1/2* mutation (g*BRCA*m). Am Soc Clin Oncol 2016;;34(15).

[141] Ducreux M, Cuhna AS, Caramella C, Hollebecque A, Burtin P, Goéré D, et al. Cancer of the pancreas: ESMO Clinical Practice Guidelines for diagnosis, treatment and follow-up. Ann Oncol 2015;26:v56−68.

[142] Petzel MQB, Hoffman L. Nutrition implications for long-term survivors of pancreatic cancer sur-gery. Nutr Clin Pract 2017;32(5):588−98.

[143] Aronson JK. Meyler's side effects of drugs used in anesthesia. Elsevier; 2008.

[144] Hartvig P, Aulin J, Hugerth M, Wallenberg S, Wagenius G. Fatigue in cancer patients treated with cytotoxic drugs. J Oncol Pharm Pract 2006;12(3):155−64.

[145] Altun I, Sonkaya A. The most common side effects experienced by patients were receiving first cycle of chemotherapy. Iran J Public Health 2018;47(8):1218−19.

[146] Sun V. Symptom concerns and quality of life in hepatobiliary cancers. Oncol Nurs Forum 2008;35 (3):E45−52.

[147] Palesh OG, Roscoe JA, Mustian KM, Roth T, Savard J, Ancoli-Israel S, et al. Prevalence, demographics, and psychological associations of sleep disruption in patients with cancer: University of Rochester Cancer Center−Community Clinical Oncology Program. J Clin Oncol 2010;28(2):292.

[148] Takahashi T, Hondo M, Nishimura K, Kitani A, Yamano T, Yanagita H, et al. Evaluation of qual-ity of life and psychological response in cancer patients treated with radiotherapy. Radiat Med 2008;26(7):396−401.

[149] Clark KL, Loscalzo M, Trask PC, Zabora J, Philip EJ. Psychological distress in patients with pan-creatic cancer—an understudied group. Psychooncology 2010;19(12):1313−20.

[150] Turriziani A, Mattiucci GC, Montoro C, Ferro M, Maurizi F, Smaniotto D, et al. Radiotherapy-related fatigue: incidence and predictive factors. Rays. 2005;30(2):197−203.

CHAPTER 15

Aptamer-mediated nano-therapy for pancreatic cancer

Seyyed Mobin Rahimnia[1,2], Sadegh Dehghani[3], Majid Saeedi[1,4], Amin Shad[5] and Rezvan Yazdian-Robati[4]

[1]Department of Pharmaceutics, Faculty of Pharmacy, Mazandaran University of Medical Sciences, Sari, Iran
[2]Student Research Committee, Faculty of Pharmacy, Mazandaran University of Medical Sciences, Sari, Iran
[3]Pharmaceutical Research Center, Pharmaceutical Technology Institute, Mashhad University of Medical Sciences, Mashhad, Iran
[4]Pharmaceutical Sciences Research Center, Hemoglobinopathy Institute, Mazandaran University of Medical Sciences, Sari, Iran
[5]Department of Chemical Engineering, Ferdowsi University of Mashhad, Mashhad, Iran

15.1 Introduction

Pancreatic cancer (PC) has a 5-year survival rate of less than 5%, making it one of the deadliest cancers. Clinically, PC refers to a malignant tumor developed in the epithelial cells of glandular structures in the pancreatic ductal cells, known as pancreatic ductal adenocarcinoma (PDAC), accounting for more than 90% of pancreatic malignancies. PDAC is considered a highly lethal metastatic tumor despite the use of multiple chemotherapy regimens. Several risk factors for PC have been identified, including smoking, a sugar- and fat-rich diet, family history, diabetes, chronic pancreatitis, coffee and alcohol, obesity, age, gender, and mutation of some genes, such as the Kras gene [1,2]. The GLOBOCAN estimations are the foundation for the most current international epidemiological trends. According to GLOBOCAN 2018 estimates, PC is the 14th most common neoplasm in the world, based on the number of new cases each year, and is predicted to be the second leading cause of cancer-related death in the United States by 2030 [3]. The incidence of PC varies by geography and demographic. In 2018, 458,918 new occurrences of PC were reported globally, accounting for 2.5% of all malignancies. Regarding incidence rates, there is not much difference between men and women. PC is the seventh fastest-growing cause of cancer mortality in both men and women (432,000 death per 459,000 cases) [1]. Many patients are diagnosed at a later stage (around 80% of PC patients have no symptoms) due to the absence of a successful initial diagnosis. Only 10%−20% of all identified cases are resectable and chemotherapy is still used to treat the majority of individuals who are not able to receive surgical cancer treatment [4]. For patients without medical therapeutic support, the average survival duration is just 12−14 weeks [5]. However, the conventional treatments for PC are often

Recent Advances in Nanocarriers for Pancreatic Cancer Therapy
DOI: https://doi.org/10.1016/B978-0-443-19142-8.00013-9

unsuccessful due to the dense stroma, hypovascularity, and chemoresistance of PDAC, which result in a decrease in the bioavailability of systemically administrated drugs [6]. So, the disruption of the vascularity of the pancreatic TME (tumor microenvironment) not only affects the cellular composition but also affects the response to systemic treatments [7,8]. Due to inherent physical and biological challenges followed by PCs, therapeutic drugs within the pancreatic TME are unstable and have diminished effectiveness [9,10]. As a result, innovative PC treatment options are urgently required.

15.2 Nanotechnology as a novel cancer therapeutic strategy

The term "nanotechnology" describes the study and creation of objects with at least one dimension of 1−100 nm. Nanocarriers can increase the therapeutic index of presently accessible medications by boosting drug effectiveness, decreasing drug toxicity, and reaching steady-state therapeutic concentrations of pharmaceuticals over a prolonged time [11]. Nanocarriers have the potential to provide the way for the development of multipurpose systems for targeted drug delivery [12,13], combination therapies, or systems for concurrent therapeutic and diagnostic purposes [14]. Nanoparticles (NPs) enable the delivery of specific drugs to their targeted lesions, in appropriate concentration, and reduce the drug amount in unwanted organs/tissues due to their unique cell uptake and trafficking processes [15]. NPs have been a gift in the revolutionized area of oncotherapy, overcoming biological obstacles and reducing the dosage and severity of chemotherapy-induced adverse effects. Due to the fact that EPR depends on the leaky structure of cancer cells, only 20% of the medicine may move into the cell, while the rest is destroyed by the body [16−18]. The antitumor effects of chemotherapy medicines have been enhanced using a variety of nanotechnology-based targeted drug delivery strategies, including liposomes, micelles, solid lipid NPs (LPNs), gold NPs (AuNPs), polymeric NPs (PNPs), carbon dots, carbon nanotubes, iron oxide NPs, and dendrimers [19−22]. Many efforts have been explored to increase the bioavailability and effectiveness of therapeutic medicines against PDAC by targeting the tumor matrix and the vascularity of the tumor [8,23,24]. In this context, nanotechnology has made great progress over the last two decades, introducing not only strong strategies for effective drug delivery in pancreatic tumors but also important approaches for the design of vaccination platforms for PDAC [23−26]. Despite the issues discussed above with the pancreatic TME that restrict the delivery and effectiveness of both chemo and immunotherapies for PC, developments in nanotechnology-based techniques may play an important role in resolving these difficulties. In addition to nanotechnology, several specific targeting technologies, such as vaccines, antibodies, or aptamer-drug conjugates, have been created for the treatment of PC [27]. Targeted drug delivery systems (TDDS) provide several benefits, including the ability to fight off drug-resistant cancer cells, protect normal cells from cytotoxic substances, and reduce dose-limiting side effects [28].

15.3 Aptamers as an advance targeted strategy in cancer diagnosis and treatment

Aptamers are known as synthetic short single-stranded oligonucleotides. They are synthesized using the in vitro molecular technique systematic evolution of ligands by exponential enrichment (SELEX) (Fig. 15.1) [29]. These sequences have a high selective binding and affinity for certain targets such as polypeptides, proteins, ions, small-molecule, bacteria, viruses, cells, and tissues [30,31]. Aptamers offer beneficial features compared to antibodies, including smaller size, stronger affinity, more selectivity, more biocompatibility, better stability, and lower immunogenicity, all of which led to their

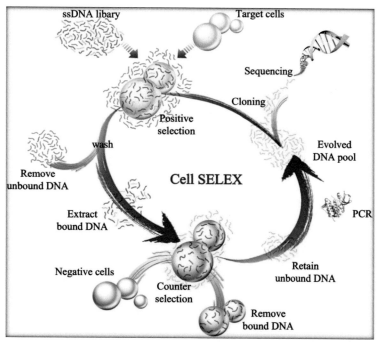

Figure 15.1 Cell SELEX showed schematically. The procedure began with the incubation of a library of single-stranded nucleic acids with the desired cells. The bound DNAs were eluted by heating at 95 C after washing. Incubation of the eluted DNAs with nontarget cells served as a counter-selection step (negative cells). The free DNAs were then amplified using PCR after being eluted. Single-stranded DNA (ssDNA) was isolated from the PCR byproducts so that the next selection cycle could begin. This procedure is repeated until a DNA pool is created that has high selectivity and affinity for the target cells. *Adapted with permission from Yazdian-Robati R., et al. Application of aptamers in treatment and diagnosis of leukemia. Int J Pharm 2017;529(1–2):44–54.*

considerable employment in the biomedical area [32–34]. Moreover, aptamers have lower manufacturing costs than antibodies, making them more economical [35]. Aptamers are appropriate ligands in biosensors (aptasensors), which may provide colorimetric [36], electrochemical [37], and fluorescent signals [38]. A large variety of aptasensors with clinically relevant sensitivities have been created for the clinical diagnosis of cancer. Aptamers may serve as players of different roles such as antagonists of protein-protein or receptor-ligand interactions, oncosuppressors, drug carriers, and detectors for PC [39]. It has been demonstrated that free aptamers and their conjugates with NPs enhance the effectiveness of destroying cancer cells [40].

15.4 Aptamer design approaches

SELEX technique was developed by Tuerk and Ellington in 1990 to find aptamers with high affinitive and selective properties [41,42]. SELEX is categorized into several classes depending on the target including cell-SELEX, protein-SELEX, secretome-SELEX, and so on. Secretome-SELEX consists of the utilization of a cell type's total secreted factors as a target. Protein-SELEX targets exogenously generated or purified proteins or peptides, which may not be in their natural conformation or environment, while cell-SELEX generates aptamers for protein targets in their natural conformation [43]. With the improvement and progression of the SELEX technique, a various range of targets, such as proteins, small molecules, bacteria, viruses, living cells, and even tissues, might be employed directly in the selection process [44]. Proteins are the most popular targets used by SELEX to identify aptamers [45]. However, it is challenging to generate sufficient quantities of recombinant human proteins with native structures, particularly for transmembrane and intracellular proteins. To address these issues, scientists have been inventing novel aptamer selection techniques. In 1998, Morris and Jensen developed an in vitro method for isolating high-affinity aptamers against a group of possible targets by using human red blood cell membranes as a platform for cell-based SELEX technology (cell-SELEX) [46]. In contrast to conventional SELEX techniques, cell-SELEX selects aptamer against a complete cell, such that molecular targets on the cell surface are in their original state and would reflect their normal folding structures [47]. In the last two decades, aptamers have been produced for a wide range of living cells and other complicated systems, particularly cancer cells [48]. Aptamers selected in this manner can target overexpressed proteins on the cell surface and even detect minor abnormal cell-surface proteins [48].

15.5 Methods for coupling aptamers to nanoparticles

Aptamers may be directly or indirectly attached to NPs via a linker (a bridge or spacer). Direct and indirect conjugation may be accomplished by covalent or noncovalent bonding. In covalent conjugation, a functional group (like a primary amino group or a thiol group) is typically linked to one end of the aptamer. This group can interact with a functional group (such as a carboxylic acid, maleimide, or aldehyde group) on the surface of the NP or at one end of the linker molecule. It can also interact with gold or another metal element or an inorganic molecule to form inorganic NPs [20,49]. Covalent conjugation refers to the interactions between different functional groups like carboxylic acid groups and amino groups, which result in the formation of amide (or carboxamide) linkages. Similarly, interactions between carboxylic acid groups and thiol groups produce thioester bonds, while those between carboxylic acid groups and alcohol groups result in ester bonds. Primary amine groups and thiol groups interact to produce thioamide bonds, and thiol groups can also interact with each other. For noncovalent conjugation, the simple strategy is through electrostatic interactions. Moreover, avidin−biotin and streptavidin−biotin interactions are exploited in many biotechnological applications. However, sometimes a linker molecule is employed, which causes an interaction between the opposite charges on the linker molecule and the aptamer [50−53]. The direct and covalent approach was used in most of the aptamer-nanoparticle conjugates that have been described so far [54]. Covalently coupled bioconjugates may result in increased stability in physiological salt and pH while eliminating the unneeded addition of biological components (e.g., streptavidin), hence limiting immunological responses and possible toxicity [54]. These different strategies of aptamer-NPs conjugation are shown in Fig. 15.2.

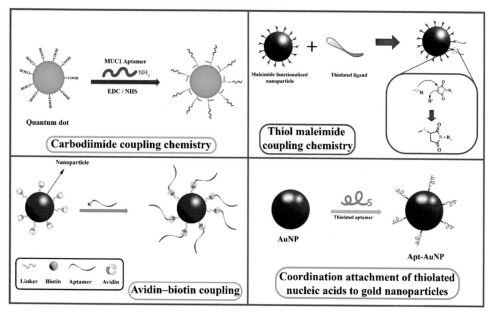

Figure 15.2 Schematic illustration of various types of aptamer-NP attachments [55]. *NP*, nanoparticles.

15.6 Tumor markers for pancreatic cancer

PDAC is a very heterogeneous disease, especially in terms of genetics and biology. Recent studies indicate that many oncogenes and signaling pathways are critically attributed to the process of PDAC tumorigenesis and may therefore be potentially valuable therapeutic targets [56]. Diagnosing PC may be accomplished by identifying tumor markers in peripheral blood, and aptamers may play a key role in this endeavor [40]. Cyclophilin B (CypB) and carbohydrate antigen 19−9 (CA 19−9) are two molecules that have been examined as promising biomarkers of PC [57]. CypB and CA 19−9 can be raised in other cancers and medical conditions. Currently, in order to predict treatment response and provide prognostic information, the CA 19−9 level in the serum of a patient with PDAC was analyzed [58,59]. In addition, tumor-associated molecules on the surface of PC cell membranes are also important diagnostic biomarkers for PC. As indicators for the identification of metastatic PC, $CD24^+CD44^+EpCAM^+$ on PC membranes and the metastasis-associated molecules vimentin and alkaline phosphatase placental-like 2 (ALPPL-2) may be employed. PC cells that exhibit $CD24^+CD44^+EpCAM^+$ are often referred to as PC stem cells (PCSCs) [60]. Tumor cells that have spread out from their original site and are able to circulate in the body's bloodstream are called circulating tumor cells (CTCs), and they may be used as biomarkers for early clinical diagnosis of PDAC [61]. Recently, it was found that some cancershave overexpression of glypican 1 (GPC1), a family of heparan sulfate proteoglycans, which is also associated with tumorigenesis. Some studies reported its level was increased in the samples from patients with PDAC, holding great promise as a biomarker in early diagnosis and potential usage in cancer development [62]. Cholecystokinin-B receptor (CCKBR) is another established biomarker that is overexpressed on the surface of human PC cells and plays a significant role in PDAC proliferation. Human PC has a high expression of a novel gene known as pancreatic adenocarcinoma up-regulated factor (PAUF), which plays a significant role in the progression of PC [63]. A PAUF-specific RNA-aptamer (P12FR2) was created by Kim and colleagues and modified with 2'-fluoropyrimidine. P12FR2 aptamers prevented PAUF-induced migration of PANC-1 cells in vitro and decreased tumor growth by 60% in a PDAC xenograft mouse model without significantly reducing weight in the treatment group [64]. MicroRNA (miRNAs) are a subclass of noncoding RNA that play a role in the expression of posttranscriptional regulatory mechanisms [65]. MiRNA dysregulation in pancreatic tissue, blood, stool, and saliva has been profiled and has grown in significance as a biomarker for PC early detection [66]. Among a variety of miRNAs, miR-21, miR-155, and miR-196 have been shown to be upregulated in PDAC and to be able to distinguish from precancerous lesions [67−69]. The autocrine regulatory molecule macrophage inhibitory cytokine 1 (MIC-1) is a distant member of the transformer growth factor beta (TGF-β) superfamily. Serum

MIC-1 levels may serve as an innovative diagnostic biomarker for PC early detection [70]. Mucin 1 (MUC1) protein is another main target in PC therapy. This highly glycosylated protein is overexpressed in many malignancies including PC and is responsible for drug resistance by over-activating Erk1/2 and P13K pathways that impede apoptosis in tumor cells [71].

15.7 Aptamers against pancreatic cancer

Since 2004, many PC-targeting aptamers have been identified (Table 15.1). These aptamers may play a pivotal role in the diagnosis and therapy of PC. Primarily, cell-SELEX, protein-SELEX, and secretome-SELEX were exploited to obtain PC-specific aptamers. Regardless of the approach used for selection, the low K_d (less than 100 nM) for all of the aptamers against PC make them potentially effective for PC screening and clinical diagnosis.

15.8 Aptamers in clinical trials for pancreatic cancer

NOX-A12, an RNA aptamer from the Spiegelmer company with the following sequence: (5′-GCGUGGUGUGAUCUAGAUGUAUUGGCUGAUCCUAGUCAGGUACGC-3′), binds and inactivates Chemokine (C-X-C motif) ligand 12 (CXCL12), an essential component for accommodating and maintenance of chronic lymphocytic leukemia (CLL) cells [89,90]. This aptamer was used to treat nonHodgkin's lymphoma and multiple myeloma. There is no report on NOX-A12 conjugation to NP systems [22]. In 2019, twenty patients suffering from metastatic microsatellite-stable (MSS) colorectal or PC were enrolled in the Opera study (NCT03168139) to investigate their response to a novel combined treatment including NOX-A12 aptamer and pembrolizumab (programmed death-1 (PD-1) receptor monoclonal antibody). According to the results, 25% of patients attained a stable stage of their disease and 35% of patients showed a longer survival time compared to the traditional therapy. The incidence rate of side effects of the mentioned combination therapy was similar to that of pembrolizumab alone in advanced cancer patients. Thus, NOX-A12 aptamer revealed safe, targeted, and efficient therapeutic potential in combination with pembrolizumab. More clinical trials are needed to develop the application of different aptamers in the treatment of PDAC [91].

15.9 Aptamer-functionalized nanocarriers against pancreatic cancer

The combination of targeted drug delivery and controlled release systems may be advantageous in the treatment of cancers. The targeted strategy aims to give cancer

Table 15.1 List of currently identified aptamers against PC (pancreatic cancer).

Aptamer name	Target	sequencing	Role of aptamer	SELEX approach	References
Aptamer 146 and Aptamer 1	CD44, CD24, ESA, and CD133	AAGGAGCAGCGTGGAGGATA ACCACTAGTCTAAAAGACAGC CGTAGAGCCGGGACCGGTGCC ACTTAGGGTGTGTCGTCGTGG TAAGGAGCAGCGTGGAGGATA TCCGTTCGTACTCGCAAGCTG ATCCGCGGCGACTTGTGACA ATTAGGGTGTGTCGTCGTGGT	Detection	Cell-SELEX (HPAC[a] cell line)	[72]
M9−5	Cyclophilin B	GGACCUAUGCAGUAGCCAGU GUGGACUGGGCUGCCCCCC	Detection	Secretome-SELEX (conditioned media of Mia PaCa-2 cell line)	[57]
P15	Vimentin	GGGAGACAAGAAUAAACGCU CAAAGUUGCGGCCCAACCGU UUAAUUCAGAAUAGUGUGAU GCCUUCGACAGGAGGCUCAC AACAGGC	Oncosuppressive; Detection	Cell-SELEX (PANC-1 cell line)	[73]
BC-15	hnRNP A1[b]	5'-GCAATGGTACGGTACTTCCTG TGGCGAGGTAGGTGGGGTGTG TGTGTATCCAAAA GTGCACGCTACTTTGCTAA-3'	Detection	Tissue-SELEX	[74,75]
XQ-2d	PL45[c]	ACTCATAGGGTTAGGGGCTGC TGGCCAGATACTCAGATGGTA GGGTTACTATGAGC	Detection	Cell-SELEX (PL45 and hTERT-HPNE cells)	[76]
APTA-12	Nucleolin	5'-GGT GGT GGT GGT TZT GGT GGT GGT GG-3'	Oncosuppressive; Targeted delivery	Designed based on the AS1411 structure	[77]
P12FR2	PAUF[d]	5'-GGGCGUGCUGGGCCUGUAAA UACACGCAUCGUAUCUGCAU UCGCAUCCCUGACUCAUAAC CCAGAGGUCGAUG-3'	Oncosuppressive	Protein-SELEX	[64]

Name	Target	Sequence	Application	Selection method	Ref.
AP1153	CCKBRᵉ	5'-CATGGTGCAGGTGTGGCTGGGATTCATTTGCCGTGCTGGTGCGTCCGCGGCCGCTAATCCTGTTC-3'	Oncosuppressive	Cell-SELEX (PANC-1 cell line)	[78]
SQ-2 (RNA aptamer)	ALPPL-2ᶠ	AUACCAGCUUAUUCAAUUGCCUGAAAAGCUAUCGCCAAUUCGCAGUGAUAUCCUUUAAGAUAGUAAGUGCAAUCU	Targeted delivery; Detection	Cell-SELEX (Panc-1 and Capan-1 cells)	[79]
GBI-10	Tenascin-C	GGCTGTTGTGAGCCTCCTCCCAGAGGGAAGACTTTAGGTTCGGTTCACGTCCCGCTTATTCTTACTCCC	Targeted delivery	Cell-SELEX (U251 cell line)	[80]
PL-8	PL45	5'-CGC TCG GAT GCC ACT ACA GCA TAT ATC CTC CCC CCA TGC GTG GTC ACC GAG TCT GAG GCT GG-3'	Targeted delivery	Cell-SELEX (PL45 cell line)	[81]
C2	Transferrin receptor	UCAAACAUCUCACAGAUCAAUCCAAGGGACCUCGGUUAAAGGACGACUCCC	Targeted delivery	Protein-SELEX	[82,83]
E07	EGFRᵍ	UGCCGCUAUAAUGCACGGAUUUAAUCGCCGUAGAAAGCAUGUCAAAGCCG	Targeted delivery	Protein-SELEX	[84,85]
Waz	Transferrin receptor	GGGUUCUACGAUAAACGGUUAAUGACCAGCUUAUGGGCUGGCAGUUCCC	Targeted delivery	Protein-SELEX and a single round of internalization selection against HeLa Cells	[86]
P1 and P19	C/EBPα protein	GGGAGACAAGAAUAAACGCUCAAUGCGGCUGAAUGCCCAGCCGUGAAAGGCGUCGAUUUCCAUCCUUCGACAGGAGGCUCACAACAGCGGGAGACAAGAAUAAAACGCUCAAUGGCGAAUGCCCUAAUAGGGCGUUAUGACUUGUUGAGUUCGACAGGAGGCUCACAACAGGC	Oncosuppressive	Live Cell-SELEX (PANC-1 cell line)	[87]

(Continued)

Table 15.1 (Continued)

Aptamer name	Target	sequencing	Role of aptamer	SELEX approach	References
CA19-9	Cancer antigen 19-9	GACTGGCCCAGGCCCCTCCT CCCGCTGCTGCCCGCCCTC GACGTGACCCGGATACAT GCCCCTCCTCTCCCCGCCCGTC GGGCGGGGCCGTGGCGATG TTACTGCGTGTGTTCGTG AGGCGGGCGGCGTGGCGA TGTTACTGCGTGTGTTCGTA GACTGGCCCAGGCCCCTCCT CCCGCTGCTGCCCGCCCT	Detection	Trypsin enhanced SELEX	[88]

[a]Human pancreatic adenocarcinoma cell line.
[b]Heterogeneous nuclear ribonucleoprotein A1.
[c]A pancreatic carcinoma cell line.
[d]Pancreatic adenocarcinoma up-regulated factor.
[e]The G-protein-coupled cholecystokinin B receptor.
[f]Alkaline phosphatase placental-like 2.
[g]Epidermal growth factor receptors.

cells a dose of the drug over a prolonged period while preventing the surrounding healthy tissue from being destroyed [92]. Advances in diagnosis and therapy have been accelerated by the creation of numerous nanomaterials. On the other hand, NPs modified with ligands can specifically recognize the cancer cells and be able to selectively deliver cargo to tumor cells, thus greatly improving the therapeutic index (improving therapeutic efficacy and reducing toxicity). To date, many moieties have been explored to functionalize NPs for specific targeting, and aptamers are one of them [93]. Consequently, several aptamers-nanomaterial complexes have been created and used in various fields, such as biosensing, cancer research, drug delivery, etc. [21,36,94−96]. In the following, we will refer to several studies conducted on surface-modified NPs with aptamers against PC. Table 15.2 briefly displays some of these efforts. A variety of nanomaterials, such as calcium phosphosilicate NPs (CPSNPs), AuNPs, LPNs, magnetic nanoparticles (MPNs), superparamagnetic iron oxide NPs (SPIONs), PNPs, and albumin NPs were utilized to be functionalized with aptamers, and their potential in the field of PC research was investigated (see Fig. 15.3) [78,97−104].

15.9.1 Aptamer-functionalized calcium phosphosilicate nanoparticles

Amorphous CPSNPs are biocompatible and biodegradable nanomaterials with pH-dependent solubility profiles, making them desirable for bioimaging and medicinal delivery applications [78]. CPSNPs stay intact in the bloodstream, but a breakdown in the low pH of endocytic vesicles, therefore, releasing their cargo intracellular [105]. High-affinity DNA aptamers against CCKBR, which is overexpressed by PDAC, were selected by dual SELEX protocol by Clawson et al. in 2017 [78]. Numerous cancer types have increased expression of the cell surface G protein-coupled receptor CCKBR (Gene 1D#887), which promotes the growth of tumor cells [40]. The selected aptamer (AP1153) had a $K_d \sim 15$ pM and internalize via a CCKBR-mediated pathway and do not initiate CCKBR signaling or promote proliferation. Additionally, bioconjugation of the aptamer to the surface of CPNSPs using the EDC/NHS coupling method led to a significant increase in uptake by orthotopic PDAC tumors in vivo (even when compared to gastrin, the natural CCKBR ligand) [78].

15.9.2 Aptamer-functionalized gold nanoparticles

Among metal NPs, AuNPs have received the greatest attention for application in targeted cancer therapy, due to their ability to be modified by ligands with terminal groups such as thiols, phosphines, and amines; biocompatibility; low cytotoxicity; stability; simplicity in synthesis; passive targeting; and special surface plasmon characteristics [106,107]. Moreover, AuNPsexploited in other cancer therapies such as photothermal therapy and radio sensitization because of their special optical properties.

Table 15.2 List of aptamer–functionalized NPs (nanoparticles) against PC (pancreatic cancer).

Type of NPs	aptamer	The sequence of the aptamer	Aim of study	Conjugation Methodology	References
CPSNPs	AP1153	5′-CATGGTGCAGGTGTGGCTGGGATTC ATTTGCCGTGCTGGTGCGTCCGCG GCCGCTAATCCTGTTC-3′	Treatment	EDC–NHS coupling agent	[78]
AuNPs	AS1411	5′-GGTGGTGGTGGTTGTGGTGGTGGT GG-3′	Treatment	Protonation of the citrate layer on AuNPs and aptamer at pH 3	[97]
LNPs	J10	5′-ACGCTCGGATGCCACTACAGGGAT GGGAGGGGAGGGGGCTCGTGGCGG CTAGGGGGTATAAACTCATGGACGT GCTGGTGAC-3′	Treatment	thiol maleimide reaction	[98]
MNPs	HIF-1α	(5′-ACAACAAGTATGTGGAGCAACTG TGTGG-3′)	Imaging and Diagnosis	DCC–NHS coupling agent	[99]
MNPs	AS1411	NH2–5′-(GGTGGTGGTGGTTGTGGT GGTGGTGG)-3′	Imaging and treatment	EDC–NHS coupling agent	[100]
SPIONs	MUC1 aptamer	5′ GCAGTTGATCCTTTGGATACCCT GG 3′	Imaging and Diagnosis	covalent cross-linking of carboxyl groups on the surface of the NPs to the amino groups of the aptamer	[101]
PNPs	AS1411	5′-GGTGGTGGTGGTTGTGGTGGTGG TGG-3′	Treatment	EDC–NHS coupling agent	[102]
PNPs	XQ-2d	5′–COOH–ACTCATAGGGTTAGGGG CTGCTGGCCAGATACTC. AGATGGTAGGGTTACTATGAGC-3′	Treatment	with coupling agent	[103]
Albumin NPs	MUC1 aptamer	5′ COOH-GGA GTT GAT CCTTTG GAT ACC CTG G 3′	Treatment	EDC–NHS coupling agent	[104]

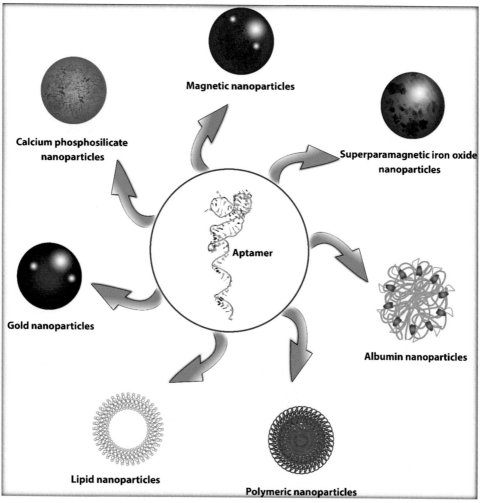

Figure 15.3 Schematic illustration of some aptamer functionalized NPs against PC. *NPs*, nanoparticles; *PC*, pancreatic cancer.

Huay et al. demonstrated that pretreatment of PC cells with AuNPs(20 nm diameter) sensitized the pancreatic cells to gemcitabine (Gem) and lessened the Gem-induced EMT, stemness, and MAPK activation [108].

Aptamer-loaded gold nanostars (AuNS) demonstrated an improvement in in-vitro effectiveness of 20% on average in a variety of cancer cells compared to free aptamer medication more than 10 times [109,110]. According to another research, a 10-fold increase of DNA on AuNPs caused a threefold increase in uptake in cancer cells [111]. There are many different kinds of aptamers that have been developed for different targets, but only a few have been used for the delivery using AuNPs [112]. AS1411, a 26-base guanine-rich aptamer with the following sequences (5′-GGTGGTGGTGGTTGTGGTGGTGGTGG-3′), has been the most studied aptamer for targeting AuNP. It binds to nucleolin, a phosphoprotein that is overexpressed in cancer cells [20,113]. In 2014, Dam et al. conjugated a ssDNA onto citrate-capped AuNS at pH = 3 [97]. Secondary-structured oligonucleotides were loaded onto AuNSusing trisodium citrate (CIT-3) at greater densities than the salt-aging approach. In the following step, using this method, they grafted an AS1411 aptamer onto AuNS at a high density. This highly loaded nanoconstruct (*Apt-AuNS) was taken up effectively by both PC and fibrosarcoma cells. interestingly, they discovered that an increase in Apt attachment on AuNS led to a more potent in vitro response [97].

15.9.3 Aptamer-functionalized lipid nanoparticles

Lipid-based nanocarriers may be actively targeted toward tumors by attaching various molecules to their surface. In 2021, Huang et al. created an LNP-based drug delivery system with an active targeting scaffold, which functions as a vehicle and is able to selectively adhere to the surface of circulating monocytes in the bloodstream (see Fig. 15.4) [98]. To build a high-affinity monocyte-targeting drug delivery carrier, this

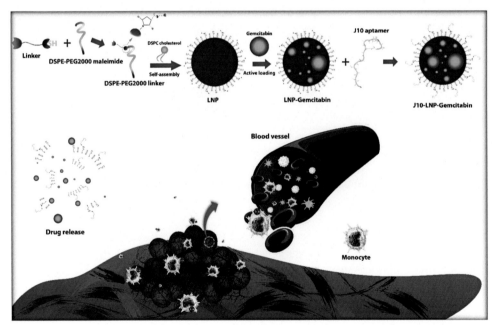

Figure 15.4 Schematic representation of the fabrication process of J10-LPN-GEM conjugates and their transfer route by monocytes in blood circulation for targeted drug delivery of PC cells. *GEM,* Gemcitabine; *PC,* pancreatic cancer. *Reproduced from Huang S.-S., et al. Immune cell shuttle for precise delivery of nanotherapeutics for heart disease and cancer. Sci Adv 2021;7(17):eabf2400.*

group employed cutting-edge technology to select a specific aptamer that targets monocytes and then fused it with LNP as an active-targeting scaffold. Aptamer J10 was selected after multiple rounds of SELEX against two monocyte/macrophage cell lines [98]. LNP were prepared using a thiolated linker DNA that can simply bind to maleimide-containing DSPE-PEG and then could be hybridized with J10 aptamer (aptamers: linker, 2.5:1) to generate the monocyte-targeted LNP. The Gem was loaded into LNP, and then the J10 aptamer was grafted on the LNP surface as a potent monocyte-targeting scaffold to infiltrate the injured pancreatic tumor site. The capacity of this targeted nanosystem was specifically examined in vitro and in vivo using different techniques. Flow cytometry examination with DiD-labeled J10-LNPs demonstrated that J10-Gem-LNPs attach to monocytes more effectively than nondecorated LNPs, with negligible binding to endothelial cells in vitro. This was validated in vivo by flow cytometry, which revealed a binding preference for monocytes over lymphocytes and granulocytes. The therapeutic efficacy of J10-Gem-loaded LNP was evaluated in the orthotopic PDAC mouse model using TUNEL assay, in vivo imaging system (IVIS), and functional magnetic resonance imaging (fMRI) monitoring. The results revealed that this targeted platform increased tumor cell apoptosis and diminished tumor cell proliferation effectively hindering the growth of the pancreatic tumor [98]. Moreover, as the liver is one of the most typical metastatic sites for PC, they evaluated the therapeutic potential of the NPs using a mouse model of PC with hepatic metastasis [114]. The development of metastatic liver tumorigenesis was equally inhibited in the targeted group. According to their research, this drug delivery vehicle not only could be effective in the treatment of PC with liver metastasis but also be exploited for other diseases with monocyte recruitment in their pathophysiology. Monocytes are attracted to the liver before the development of metastasis to assist the growth and proliferation of the invasive tumor cells that ultimately lead to metastasis [115,116].

15.9.4 Aptamer-functionalized magnetic nanoparticles for treatment of pancreatic cancer

Magnetic nanoparticles (MNPs) are an interesting subclass of NPs that are generally manufactured from pure metals (Fe, Co, Ni, and some rare earth metals) or a combination of metals and polymers [117]. MNPs have also been targeted with aptamers for PC diagnosis and therapy. For example, based on the unique hypoxic character of solid tumors, Zhu et al. [99] designed PEG- and Mn (II)-modified MNPs (Fe3O4@PMn) targeted with HIF-1α aptamer (5′-ACAACAAGTATGTGGAGCAACTGTGTGG-3′) to warrant the special accumulation of the NPs in the hypoxic area of cancer stem cells. Furthermore, the high sensitivity of iron oxide NPs in this complex provided significant contrast enhancement in T1- and T2-weighted magnetic resonance imaging (MRI) in vitro and in vivo [99].

In order to control drug retention and nuclear delivery of curcumin (Cur) and Gem, Sivakumar et al. [100] developed a targeted delivery system using AS1411 aptamer and PLGA MNPs for PC imaging and therapy both in vitro and in vivo. Using multiple in vitro cytotoxic assays, including apoptosis assay, flow cytometry analysis, and confocal laser scanning microscopy, the targeted nanocomplex (Apt-Cur-Gem-PLGA-MNPs) was found to be capable of specifically and effectively delivering both Gem and Cur to PANC-1, MIA PaCa, and PK-1cancer cells. Importantly, blocking the vascularization, proliferation and the migration of PC cells, as well as inducing apoptosis, were observed. The findings demonstrated that aptamer-targeted MNPs were highly selective to nucleolin receptors, which are overexpressed in PC cells. Furthermore, hyperthermia generated by MNPs incorporated in PLGA revealed that the PC cell viability decreased remarkably by the exposure to the AC magnetic field after Apt-Cur-Gem-PLGA-MNPs intervention. Moreover, by adjusting the direction of the applied magnetic field, the migration of cells that have taken up Apt-Cur-Gem-PLGA-MNPs may be effectively regulated [100].

15.9.4.1 Aptamer-functionalized superparamagnetic iron oxide nanoparticles

Recently, SPIONs have shown the inherent magnetism of MRI, as well as the safety of biocompatible coatings and surface functional moieties [118]. SPIONs have been used for research, diagnosis, and treatment in the field of molecular imaging using MRI [119]. MRI is an effective noninvasive technique for examining cells and human bodies in three dimensions. Conjugating SPIONs with tumor-targeting moieties enhances their localization in the region of cancer cells in comparison to nontargeted SPIONs. The modification of SPIONs by different molecular ligands boosted the selectivity and diagnostic capacity of conjugates further [120]. Surface-active SPIONs possess the ability to be used for imaging purposes, cross cell or tissue barriers, and aggregate specifically in cancerous tissues. He et al. created a CXCR4-USPIO ultrasmall superparamagnetic iron oxide molecular probe to precisely identify PCs with CXCR4-positive expression [121]. In a different work in 2014, Zuo et al. examined a novel polylysine-like peptide (iRGD), which may boost tumor cell permeability and facilitate cellular internalization to enhance imaging sensitivity for use in PC cell labeling [122]. MUC1, a member of the mucin family of glycoproteins that are often overexpressed and abnormally glycosylated in PC, controls the activity of cancer cells to invasion and metastasize [123]. As a targeted molecular probe, Zou et al. investigated the diagnostic potential of MUC1 aptamer-SPION conjugates via the development of an MRI imaging platform for the human PC [101]. In this regard, 5′ amino-modified anti-MUC1 aptamer with a sequence of 5′ GCAGTTGATCCTTTGGATACCCTGG 3′ was employed in their study. The selectivity and absorption pattern of MUC1-functionalized SPIONs, as well as MRI conspicuity, were verified in vitro (in BxPC-3 cells) and in vivo.

The synthesized molecular probe had a particle size of 63.5 $\pm$ 3.2 nm and a surface charge of 10.2 mV. Prussian blue staining, a common histopathology staining, was utilized for the detection of iron and an MTS assay was used for evaluating cytotoxicity. The T2 relaxation duration and relaxation rate (R2) were found to be considerably shortened when using the nanoprobe solution and had a linear relationship to the concentration of iron in the solution. Functionalization of SPION with MUC1 aptamer aided in higher specific targeting and accumulation of the developed nanoprobe in PC tissues but lower in normal pancreatic tissues as confirmed by western blot and immunohistochemistry analysis. In conclusion, in-vitro and in-vivo MRI investigations revealed that MUC1-SPIONs had significant tumor-targeting and contrast-enhanced MRI imaging capabilities. These findings imply that nano-sized MUC1-SPIONs are a potential MRI contrast agent for the early and precise diagnosis of PC. To properly employ SPIONs in the clinics, however, several issues must be resolved. These include the effects of SPIONs in the body and the toxicity of the surface modification of the degradation products. Scientists believe that active research will gradually find solutions to each of these upcoming issues [101].

15.9.5 Aptamer-functionalized polymeric nanoparticles

PNPs are colloidal particles with a polymer backbone in the nanometer range. One or more anticancer agents of interest are adsorbed, encapsulated, or conjugated onto the inside or shell of the PNPs. A drug-loaded PNP-based targeted delivery system is employed for the sustained release of antitumor agents to specific target sites [124]. In 2016, Wang et al. synthesized a smart targeted PEG-PDLLA (poly(ethylene glycol)-block-poly(D,L–lactide)) micelle loading herb-derived compound triptolide (TP) to prevent the proliferation of chemo-resistant PC (CPC). This biodegradable and biocompatible nano smart micelle system was developed in which a carboxyl terminated PEG-PDLLAwere self-assembled with a TP that was previously modified with AS1411 aptamer [102]. In a xenograft mouse model of Gem-resistant human PC (MIA PaCa-2), this smart nano system had greater antitumor efficacy than the nontargeted group, effectively extending the longevity of mice bearing MIA PaCa-2 cells compared to mice treated with the anticancer drug Gemzar. These targeted systems have been verified beneficial in improving TP accumulation within nuclei of CPC cells where TP is released to induce much stronger toxicity than Gemzar. Tian et al. focused their efforts in 2020 on the fabrication of aptamer-functionalized PNPs for the targeted delivery of doxorubicin [103]. A complete screening was carried out utilizing Panc-1 cells (2D and 3D cell culture model) and bladder cancer cells, as well as renal epithelial cells, to understand the particular targeting of aptamers toward PC cells. To improve the specific binding effectiveness and deep penetration of the PNP delivery system toward PC cells, the XQ-2d aptamer with the following sequences: 5′−COOH−ACTCATAGGGTTAGGGGCTGCTGGCCAGATACTC.AGATGGT AGGGTTACTATGAGC-3′ was employed as a targeting moiety. CCK-8 test findings demonstrated that the anticancer effectiveness of the aptamer-functionalized PNPs loaded with DOX (DOX@PCL-b-PEO-aptamer micelles) was double in comparison to free DOX and nonmodified drug-loaded micelles. Fig. 15.5 depicts the schematic attachment of aptamer to DOX@PCL-b-PEO NPs and the process of attaching the aptamer-NPs complex to its target (nucleolin) on the surface of the PC cell and subsequently entering the cell.

Flow cytometric test confirmed the antiproliferative impact of DOX@PCL-b-PEO-aptamer micelles against Panc-1 cells. Additionally, under the same incubation conditions, confocal laser scanning microscopy demonstrated that the micelles modified with aptamer have more affinity to penetrate and accumulate within Panc-1 tumor cells than T-24 and HEK293 cells. Based on the 3D multicellular spheroids of Panc-1 cells study, this targeted system showed greater deep tumor penetration compared to unmodified micelles, which may account for the improved therapeutic efficiency of the aptamer-functionalized drug delivery system [125,126]. The effectiveness of targeting and improved deep tumor penetration of the nanoparticulate system after aptamer conjugation are confirmed by this study. The aforementioned research establishes the rationale for enhancing the anticancer medicine DOX's bioavailability and

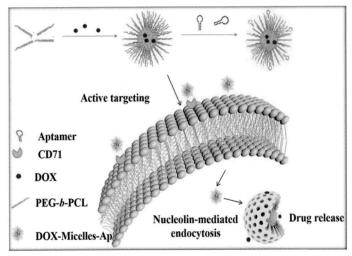

Figure 15.5 Schematic representation of XQ-2d aptamer attachment to PCL NPs containing DOX against PC cell surface nucleolin. *PC*, pancreatic cancer; *NPs*, nanoparticles. *Adapted with permission from Tian L., et al. Enhanced targeting of 3D pancreatic cancer spheroids by aptamer-conjugated polymeric micelles with deep tumor penetration. Eur J Pharmacol 2021;894:173814.*

therapeutic impact while minimizing its adverse effects. It also illustrates the clinical applicability of the aptamer-PNPs targeted drug delivery.

15.9.6 Aptamer-functionalized albumin nanoparticles

Human serum albumin (HSA) is the most prevalent protein in blood plasma with a molecular weight of 66.5 kDa, which can bind to a broad range of molecules and substances including therapeutic drugs, long-chain fatty acids, nutrients, metal ions,antibodies, and peptides. These special features make albumin an important carrier in drug delivery approaches [127]. Due to its inherent capabilities as a blood transporter, a single molecule of albumin may be loaded with and/or conjugated to various therapeutic payloads to improve its pharmacokinetics [128]. Moreover, albumin can be readily synthesized at the nanoscale sizes, showing benefits for the fabrication of safe and cost-effective nanovectors [129]. There are several amine and carboxyl functional groups on the surface of albumins that may be employed for its surface modification, resulting in enhanced targeting ability and responsibility [130]. For the first time, Nigam et al. conjugated MUC-1 aptamer (5′ COOH-GGA GTT GAT CCTTTG GAT ACC CTG G 3′) and fluorescent silver NPs to HSA NPs to target MUC1 expressing PC cells. Capsaicin (Cap), a main ingredient in chili pepper, was delivered to PC by this nanoformulation. According to the MTT test, the Apt A-HSA-Cap formulation was the most effective, which may be attributed to its focused internalization in Panc-1 cells that express MUC-1 [104].

15.10 Conclusion

Bioconjugates consisting of NPs and aptamers are a potentially strong tool for the development of innovative PC screening and treatment strategies. As drug delivery systems for cancer treatment, nanoparticle—aptamer bioconjugates may be developed to target and be taken up by pancreatic cancerous cells for the targeted delivery and controlled release of chemotherapeutic medicines over a prolonged period directly at the tumor site. A better clinical outcome may be obtained through the targeted delivery of chemotherapeutic drugs by reducing their adverse effects and increasing their cytotoxicity to PC cells. Another benefit would be the capacity to distribute two or more chemotherapeutic drugs at the same time and control their rates of release. This would enable successful combination chemotherapy, which is often used to treat various cancers. For this purpose, isolating aptamers that selectively bind to the external antigens that are overexpressed on the plasma membrane of cancer cells or in the extracellular matrix of tumor tissue is important. In addition, NPs must be created with optimum features that assist in targeting and distribution of medications to the appropriate tissues, while avoiding pickup by the body's mononuclear phagocytic system.

Conflict of interest

Declarations of interest: none.

References

[1] Bray F, Ferlay J, Soerjomataram I, Siegel RL, Torre LA, Jemal A. Global cancer statistics 2018: GLOBOCAN estimates of incidence and mortality worldwide for 36 cancers in 185 countries. CA Cancer J Clin 2018;68(6):394−424.

[2] Bryant KL, Mancias JD, Kimmelman AC, Der CJ. KRAS: feeding pancreatic cancer proliferation. Trends Biochem Sci 2014;39(2):91−100.

[3] Rahib L, Smith BD, Aizenberg R. Projecting cancer incidence and deaths to 2030: the unexpected burden of thyroid, liver, and pancreas cancers in the United States. Cancer Res. 2014;74(11): 2913−21.

[4] Mokdad AA, Minter RM, Zhu H, Augustine MM, Porembka MR, Wang SC, et al. Neoadjuvant therapy followed by resection versus upfront resection for resectable pancreatic cancer: a propensity score matched analysis. J Clin Oncol 2017;35(5):515−22.

[5] Carmichael J, Fink U, Russell RC, Spittle MF, Harris AL, Spiessi G, et al. Phase II study of gemcitabine in patients with advanced pancreatic cancer. Br J Cancer 1996;73(1):101−5.

[6] Laheru D, Jaffee EM. Immunotherapy for pancreatic cancer - science driving clinical progress. Nat Rev Cancer 2005;5(6):459−67.

[7] Ligorio M, Sil S, Malagon-Lopez J, Nieman LT, Misale S, Di Pilato M, et al. Stromal microenvironment shapes the intratumoral architecture of pancreatic cancer. Cell 2019;178(1):160−75.

[8] Vennin C, Murphy KJ, Morton JP, Cox TR, Pajic M, Timpson P. Reshaping the tumor stroma for treatment of pancreatic cancer. Gastroenterology 2018;154(4):820−38.

[9] Neesse A, Bauer CA, Öhlund D, Lauth M, Buchholz M, Michl P, et al. Stromal biology and therapy in pancreatic cancer: ready for clinical translation? Gut 2019;68(1):159−71.

[10] Nia HT, Munn LL, Jain RK. Mapping physical tumor microenvironment and drug delivery. Clin Cancer Res 2019;25(7):2024−6.

[11] Alexis F, Rhee J-W, Richie JP, Radovic-Moreno AF, Langer R, Farokhzad OC, editors. New frontiers in nanotechnology for cancer treatment. Urologic oncology: seminars and original investigations. Elsevier; 2008.

[12] Bae Y, Jang W-D, Nishiyama N, Fukushima S, Kataoka K. Multifunctional polymeric micelles with folate-mediated cancer cell targeting and pH-triggered drug releasing properties for active intracellular drug delivery. Mol Biosyst 2005;1(3):242−50.

[13] Nasongkla N, Bey E, Ren J, Ai H, Khemtong C, Guthi JS, et al. Multifunctional polymeric micelles as cancer-targeted, MRI-ultrasensitive drug delivery systems. Nano Lett 2006;6(11): 2427−30.

[14] Larina IV, Evers BM, Ashitkov TV, Bartels C, Larin KV, Esenaliev RO. Enhancement of drug delivery in tumors by using interaction of nanoparticles with ultrasound radiation. Technol Cancer Res Treat 2005;4(2):217−26.

[15] Attia MF, Anton N, Wallyn J, Omran Z, Vandamme TF. An overview of active and passive targeting strategies to improve the nanocarriers efficiency to tumour sites. J Pharm Pharma 2019;71 (8):1185−98.

[16] Sheikh A, Md S, Kesharwani P. Aptamer grafted nanoparticle as targeted therapeutic tool for the treatment of breast cancer. Biomed Pharmacother 2022;146:112530.

[17] Hillaireau H, Couvreur P. Nanocarriers' entry into the cell: relevance to drug delivery. Cell Mol life Sci 2009;66(17):2873−96.

[18] Park K. Nanotechnology: what it can do for drug delivery. J Control Release 2007;120(1−2):1.

[19] Su S, Kang M. Recent advances in nanocarrier-assisted therapeutics delivery systems. Pharmaceutics 2020;12(9):837.

[20] Bayat P, Abnous K, Balarastaghi S, Taghdisi SM, Saeedi M, Yazdian-Robati R, et al. Aptamer AS1411-functionalized gold nanoparticle-melittin complex for targeting MCF-7 breast cancer cell line. Nanomed J 2022;9(2):164–9.

[21] Hashemi M, Shamshiri A, Saeedi M, Tayebi L, Yazdian-Robati R, et al. Aptamer-conjugated PLGA nanoparticles for delivery and imaging of cancer therapeutic drugs. Arch Biochem Biophys 2020;691:108485.

[22] Charbgoo F, Taghdisi SM, Yazdian-Robati R, Abnous K, Ramezani M, Alibolandi M. Aptamer-incorporated nanoparticle systems for drug delivery. Nanobiotechnology in Diagnosis. Drug Deliv Treat 2020;95–112.

[23] He X, Chen X, Liu L, Zhang Y, Lu Y, Zhang Y, et al. Sequentially triggered nanoparticles with tumor penetration and intelligent drug release for pancreatic cancer therapy. Adv Sci 2018;5(5):1701070.

[24] Yu Q, Qiu Y, Li J, Tang X, Wang X, Cun X, et al. Targeting cancer-associated fibroblasts by dual-responsive lipid-albumin nanoparticles to enhance drug perfusion for pancreatic tumor therapy. J Control Release 2020;321:564–75.

[25] Han X, Li Y, Xu Y, Zhao X, Zhang Y, Yang X, et al. Reversal of pancreatic desmoplasia by re-educating stellate cells with a tumour microenvironment-activated nanosystem. Nat Commun 2018;9(1):3390.

[26] Ji T, Li S, Zhang Y, Lang J, Ding Y, Zhao X, et al. An MMP-2 responsive liposome integrating antifibrosis and chemotherapeutic drugs for enhanced drug perfusion and efficacy in pancreatic cancer. ACS Appl Mater Interfaces 2016;8(5):3438–45.

[27] Kim D-H, Seo J-M, Shin K-J, Yang S-G. Design and clinical developments of aptamer-drug conjugates for targeted cancer therapy. Biomater Res 2021;25(1):1–12.

[28] Kumari P, Ghosh B, Biswas S. Nanocarriers for cancer-targeted drug delivery. J Drug Target 2016;24(3):179–91.

[29] Yazdian-Robati R, Arab A, Ramezani M, Abnous K, Taghdisi SM. Application of aptamers in treatment and diagnosis of leukemia. Int J Pharm 2017;529(1–2):44–54.

[30] Di Primo C, Dausse E, Toulmé JJ. Surface plasmon resonance investigation of RNA aptamer-RNA ligand interactions. Methods Mol Biol 2011;764:279–300.

[31] Hedayati N, Taghdisi SM, Yazdian-Robati R, Mansouri A, Abnous K, Mohajeri SA. Selection of DNA aptamers for tramadol through the systematic evolution of ligands by exponential enrichment method for fabrication of a sensitive fluorescent aptasensor based on graphene oxide. Spectrochim Acta A Mol Biomol Spectrosc 2021;259:119840.

[32] He F, Wen N, Xiao D, Yan J, Xiong H, Cai S, et al. Aptamer-based targeted drug delivery systems: current potential and challenges. Curr Med Chem 2020;27(13):2189–219.

[33] He XY, Ren XH, Peng Y, Zhang JP, Ai SL, Liu BY, et al. Aptamer/peptide-functionalized genome-editing system for effective immune restoration through reversal of PD-L1-mediated cancer immunosuppression. Adv Mater 2020;32(17):e2000208.

[34] Keefe AD, Pai S, Ellington A. Aptamers as therapeutics. Nat Rev Drug Discov 2010;9(7):537–50.

[35] Dunn MR, Jimenez RM, Chaput JC. Analysis of aptamer discovery and technology. Nat Rev Chem 2017;1(10):1–16.

[36] Yazdian-Robati R, Hedayati N, Ramezani M, Abnous K, Taghdisi SM. Colorimetric gold nanoparticles-based aptasensors. Nanomed J 2018;5(1):1–5.

[37] Liu Y, Lai Y, Yang G, Tang C, Deng Y, Li S, et al. Cd-aptamer electrochemical biosensor based on AuNPs/CS modified glass carbon electrode. J Biomed Nanotechnol 2017;13(10):1253–9.

[38] Danesh NM, Yazdian-Robati R, Ramezani M, Alibolandi M, Abnous K, Taghdisi SM. A label-free aptasensor for carcinoembryonic antigen detection using three-way junction structure and ATMND as a fluorescent probe. Sens Actuators B Chem 2018;256:408–12.

[39] Morita Y, Leslie M, Kameyama H, Volk DE, Tanaka T. Aptamer therapeutics in cancer: current and future. Cancers 2018;10(3):80.

[40] Gao G, Liu C, Jain S, Li D, Wang H, Zhao Y, et al. Potential use of aptamers for diagnosis and treatment of pancreatic cancer. J Drug Target 2019;27(8):853–65.

[41] Tuerk C, Gold L. Systematic evolution of ligands by exponential enrichment: RNA ligands to bacteriophage T4 DNA polymerase. Science 1990;249(4968):505–10.

[42] Ellington AD, Szostak JW. In vitro selection of RNA molecules that bind specific ligands. Nature 1990;346(6287):818−22.

[43] Mercier M-C, Dontenwill M, Choulier L. Selection of nucleic acid aptamers targeting tumor cell-surface protein biomarkers. Cancers 2017;9(6):69.

[44] Sun H, Zhu X, Lu PY, Rosato RR, Tan W, Zu Y. Oligonucleotide aptamers: new tools for targeted cancer therapy. Mol Ther Nucleic Acids 2014;3(8):e182.

[45] Gopinath SC. Methods developed for SELEX. Anal Bioanal Chem 2007;387(1):171−82.

[46] Morris KN, Jensen KB, Julin CM, Weil M, Gold L. High affinity ligands from in vitro selection: complex targets. Proc Natl Acad Sci U S A 1998;95(6):2902−7.

[47] Sefah K, Shangguan D, Xiong X, O'Donoghue MB, Tan W. Development of DNA aptamers using Cell-SELEX. Nat Protoc 2010;5(6):1169−85.

[48] Fang X, Tan W. Aptamers generated from cell-SELEX for molecular medicine: a chemical biology approach. Acc Chem Res 2010;43(1):48−57.

[49] Yazdian-Robati R, Bayat P, Dehestani S, Hashemi M, Taghdisi SM, Abnous K. Smart delivery of epirubicin to cancer cells using aptamer-modified ferritin nanoparticles. J Drug Target 2022;30(5):567−76.

[50] Cai L, Chen Z-Z, Chen M-Y, Tang H-W, Pang D-W. MUC-1 aptamer-conjugated dye-doped silica nanoparticles for MCF-7 cells detection. Biomaterials 2013;34(2):371−81.

[51] Medley CD, Bamrungsap S, Tan W, Smith JE. Aptamer-conjugated nanoparticles for cancer cell detection. Anal Chem 2011;83(3):727−34.

[52] Bruno JG. Aptamer−biotin−streptavidin−C1q complexes can trigger the classical complement pathway to kill cancer cells. Vitro Cell Dev Biol Anim 2010;46(2):107−13.

[53] Liu J, Zeng J, Tian Y, Zhou N. An aptamer and functionalized nanoparticle-based strip biosensor for on-site detection of kanamycin in food samples. Analyst 2018;143(1):182−9.

[54] Farokhzad OC, Karp JM, Langer R. Nanoparticle-aptamer bioconjugates for cancer targeting. Expert Opin Drug Deliv 2006;3(3):311−24.

[55] Odeh F, Nsairat H, Alshaer W, Ismail MA, Esawi E, Qaqish B, et al. Aptamers chemistry: chemical modifications and conjugation strategies. Molecules 2019;25(1):3.

[56] Kang X, Lin Z, Xu M, Pan J, Wang ZW. Deciphering role of FGFR signalling pathway in pancreatic cancer. Cell Prolif 2019;52(3):e12605.

[57] Ray P, Rialon-Guevara KL, Veras E, Sullenger BA, White RR. Comparing human pancreatic cell secretomes by in vitro aptamer selection identifies cyclophilin B as a candidate pancreatic cancer biomarker. J Clin Invest 2012;122(5):1734−41.

[58] Pan L, Zhao J, Huang Y, Zhao S, Liu Y-M. Aptamer-based microchip electrophoresis assays for amplification detection of carcinoembryonic antigen. Clinica Chim Acta 2015;450:304−9.

[59] Liu J, Zuo Y, Qu G-M, Song X, Liu Z-H, Zhang T-G, et al. CypB promotes cell proliferation and metastasis in endometrial carcinoma. BMC Cancer 2021;21(1):1−8.

[60] Li C, Heidt DG, Dalerba P, Burant CF, Zhang L, Adsay V, et al. Identification of pancreatic cancer stem cells. Cancer Res 2007;67(3):1030−7.

[61] Zippelius A, Pantel K. RT-PCR-based detection of occult disseminated tumor cells in peripheral blood and bone marrow of patients with solid tumors: an overview. Ann N Y Acad Sci 2000;906 (1):110−23.

[62] Nagarajan A, Malvi P, Wajapeyee N. Heparan sulfate and heparan sulfate proteoglycans in cancer initiation and progression. Front Endocrinol 2018;9:483.

[63] Kim SA, Lee Y, Jung DE, Park KH, Park JY, Gang J, et al. Pancreatic adenocarcinoma up-regulated factor (PAUF), a novel up-regulated secretory protein in pancreatic ductal adenocarcinoma. Cancer Sci 2009;100(5):828−36.

[64] Kim YH, Sung HJ, Kim S, Kim EO, Lee JW, Moon JY, et al. An RNA aptamer that specifically binds pancreatic adenocarcinoma up-regulated factor inhibits migration and growth of pancreatic cancer cells. Cancer Lett 2011;313(1):76−83.

[65] Bünger S, Laubert T, Roblick UJ, Habermann JK. Serum biomarkers for improved diagnostic of pancreatic cancer: a current overview. J Cancer Res Clin Oncol 2011;137(3):375−89.

[66] Hernandez YG, Lucas AL. MicroRNA in pancreatic ductal adenocarcinoma and its precursor lesions. World J Gastrointest Oncol 2016;8(1):18−29.

[67] Bloomston M, Frankel WL, Petrocca F, Volinia S, Alder H, Hagan JP, et al. MicroRNA expression patterns to differentiate pancreatic adenocarcinoma from normal pancreas and chronic pancreatitis. JAMA 2007;297(17):1901–8.

[68] Caponi S, Funel N, Frampton AE, Mosca F, Santarpia L, Van der Velde AG, et al. The good, the bad and the ugly: a tale of miR-101, miR-21 and miR-155 in pancreatic intraductal papillary mucinous neoplasms. Ann Oncol 2013;24(3):734–41.

[69] Szafranska AE, Davison TS, John J, Cannon T, Sipos B, Maghnouj A, et al. MicroRNA expression alterations are linked to tumorigenesis and non-neoplastic processes in pancreatic ductal adenocarcinoma. Oncogene 2007;26(30):4442–52.

[70] Koopmann J, Rosenzweig CN, Zhang Z, Canto MI, Brown DA, Hunter M, et al. Serum markers in patients with resectable pancreatic adenocarcinoma: macrophage inhibitory cytokine 1 versus CA19-9. Clin Cancer Res 2006;12(2):442–6.

[71] Supruniuk K, Radziejewska I. MUC1 is an oncoprotein with a significant role in apoptosis. Int J Oncol 2021;59(3):1–11.

[72] Kim YJ, Lee HS, Jung DE, Kim JM, Song SY. The DNA aptamer binds stemness-enriched cancer cells in pancreatic cancer. J Mol Recognit 2017;30(4):e2591.

[73] Yoon S, Armstrong B, Habib N, Rossi JJ. Blind SELEX approach identifies RNA aptamers that regulate EMT and inhibit metastasis. Mol Cancer Res 2017;15(7):811–20.

[74] Li S, Xu H, Ding H, Huang Y, Cao X, Yang G, et al. Identification of an aptamer targeting hnRNP A1 by tissue slide-based SELEX. J Pathol 2009;218(3):327–36.

[75] Zhang J, Li S, Liu F, Zhou L, Shao N, Zhao X. SELEX aptamer used as a probe to detect circulating tumor cells in peripheral blood of pancreatic cancer patients. PLoS One 2015;10(3):e0121920.

[76] Wu X, Zhao Z, Bai H, Fu T, Yang C, Hu X, et al. DNA aptamer selected against pancreatic ductal adenocarcinoma for in vivo imaging and clinical tissue recognition. Theranostics 2015;5(9):985.

[77] Park JY, Cho YL, Chae JR, Moon SH, Cho WG, Choi YJ, et al. Gemcitabine-incorporated G-quadruplex aptamer for targeted drug delivery into pancreas cancer. Mol Ther Nucleic Acids 2018;12:543–53.

[78] Clawson GA, Abraham T, Pan W, Tang X, Linton SS, McGovern CO, et al. A cholecystokinin B receptor-specific DNA aptamer for targeting pancreatic ductal adenocarcinoma. Nucleic Acid Ther 2017;27(1):23–35.

[79] Dua P, Kang HS, Hong S-M, Tsao M-S, Kim S, Lee D-K. Alkaline phosphatase ALPPL-2 is a novel pancreatic carcinoma-associated protein. Cancer Res 2013;73(6):1934–45.

[80] Daniels DA, Chen H, Hicke BJ, Swiderek KM, Gold L. A tenascin-C aptamer identified by tumor cell SELEX: systematic evolution of ligands by exponential enrichment. Proc Natl Acad Sci 2003;100(26):15416–21.

[81] Champanhac C, Teng I, Cansiz S, Zhang L, Wu X, Zhoa Z, et al. Development of a panel of DNA aptamers with high affinity for pancreatic ductal adenocarcinoma. Sci Rep 2015;5(1):1–8.

[82] Wilner SE, Wengerter B, Maier K, Magalhães MDLB, Del Amo DS, Pai S, et al. An RNA alternative to human transferrin: a new tool for targeting human cells. Mol Ther Nucleic Acids 2012;1:e21.

[83] Porciani D, Tedeschi L, Marchetti L, Citti L, Piazza V, Beltram F, et al. Aptamer-mediated codelivery of doxorubicin and NF-κB decoy enhances chemosensitivity of pancreatic tumor cells. Mol Ther Nucleic Acids 2015;4:e235.

[84] Li N, Nguyen HH, Byrom M, Ellington AD. Inhibition of cell proliferation by an anti-EGFR aptamer. PLoS One 2011;6(6):e20299.

[85] Ray P, Cheek MA, Sharaf ML, Li N, Ellington AD, Sullenger BA, et al. Aptamer-mediated delivery of chemotherapy to pancreatic cancer cells. Nucleic Acid Ther 2012;22(5):295–305.

[86] Maier KE, Jangra RK, Shieh KR, Cureton DK, Xiao H, Snapp EL, et al. A new transferrin receptor aptamer inhibits new world hemorrhagic fever mammarenavirus entry. Mol Ther Nucleic Acids 2016;5:e321.

[87] Yoon S, Rossi JJ. Treatment of pancreatic cancer by aptamer conjugated C/EBPα-saRNA. RNA activation. Springer; 2017. p. 173–88.

[88] Gu L, Yan W, Liu S, Ren W, Lyu M, Wang S. Trypsin enhances aptamer screening: a novel method for targeting proteins. Anal Biochem 2018;561:89–95.

[89] Turner JJ, Hoos JS, Vonhoff S, Klussmann S. Methods for L-ribooligonucleotide sequence determination using LCMS. Nucleic Acids Res 2011;39(21):e147.

[90] Sayyed S, Hägele H, Kulkarni O, Endlich K, Segerer S, Eulberg D, et al. Podocytes produce homeostatic chemokine stromal cell-derived factor-1/CXCL12, which contributes to glomerulosclerosis, podocyte loss and albuminuria in a mouse model of type 2 diabetes. Diabetologia 2009; 52(11):2445−54.

[91] Halama N, Prüfer U, Frömming A, Beyer D, Eulberg D, Jungnelius JU, et al. Phase i/ii study with cxcl12 inhibitor nox-a12 and pembrolizumab in patients with microsatellite-stable, metastatic colorectal or pancreatic cancer. Ann Oncol 2019;30:v231.

[92] Langer R. Drug delivery and targeting. Nature 1998;392(6679 Suppl):5−10.

[93] Fu Z, Xiang J. Aptamer-functionalized nanoparticles in targeted delivery and cancer therapy. Int J Mol Sci 2020;21(23):9123.

[94] Yang L, Zhang X, Ye M, Jiang J, Yang R, Fu T, et al. Aptamer-conjugated nanomaterials and their applications. Adv Drug Deliv Rev 2011;63(14−15):1361−70.

[95] Wang H, Yang R, Yang L, Tan W. Nucleic acid conjugated nanomaterials for enhanced molecular recognition. ACS Nano 2009;3(9):2451−60.

[96] Liu Q, Jin C, Wang Y, Fang X, Zhang X, Chen Z, et al. Aptamer-conjugated nanomaterials for specific cancer cell recognition and targeted cancer therapy. NPG Asia Mater 2014;6(4):e95.

[97] Dam DHM, Lee RC, Odom TW. Improved in vitro efficacy of gold nanoconstructs by increased loading of G-quadruplex aptamer. Nano Lett 2014;14(5):2843−8.

[98] Huang S-S, Lee K-J, Chen H-C, Prajnamitra RP, Hsu C-H, Jian C-B, et al. Immune cell shuttle for precise delivery of nanotherapeutics for heart disease and cancer. Sci Adv 2021;7(17):eabf2400.

[99] Zhu H, Zhang L, Liu Y, Zhou Y, Wang K, Xie X, et al. Aptamer-PEG-modified Fe3O4@ Mn as a novel T1-and T2-dual-model MRI contrast agent targeting hypoxia-induced cancer stem cells. Sci Rep 2016;6(1):1−12.

[100] Sivakumar B, Aswathy RG, Nagaoka Y, Iwai S, Venugopal K, Kato K, et al. Aptamer conjugated theragnostic multifunctional magnetic nanoparticles as a nanoplatform for pancreatic cancer therapy. RSC Adv 2013;3(43):20579−98.

[101] Zou Q, Zhang CJ, Yan YZ, Min ZJ, Li CS. MUC-1 aptamer targeted superparamagnetic iron oxide nanoparticles for magnetic resonance imaging of pancreatic cancer in vivo and in vitro experiment. J Cell Biochem 2019;120(11):18650−8.

[102] Wang C, Liu B, Xu X, Zhuang B, Li H, Yin J, et al. Toward targeted therapy in chemotherapy-resistant pancreatic cancer with a smart triptolide nanomedicine. Oncotarget 2016;7(7):8360.

[103] Tian L, Pei R, Zhong L, Ji Y, Zhou D, Zhou S. Enhanced targeting of 3D pancreatic cancer spheroids by aptamer-conjugated polymeric micelles with deep tumor penetration. Eur J Pharmacol 2021;894:173814.

[104] Nigam P, Waghmode S, Yeware A, Nawale L, Dagde P, Dhudhane A, et al. Aptamer functionalized multifunctional fluorescent nanotheranostic platform for pancreatic cancer. J Nanopharm Drug Deliv 2014;2(4):280−7.

[105] Bussard KM, Gigliotti CM, Adair BM, Snyder JM, Gigliotti NT, Loc WS, et al. Preferential uptake of antibody targeted calcium phosphosilicate nanoparticles by metastatic triple negative breast cancer cells in co-cultures of human metastatic breast cancer cells plus bone osteoblasts. Nanomed Nanotechnol Biol Med 2021;34:102383.

[106] Herne TM, Tarlov MJ. Characterization of DNA probes immobilized on gold surfaces. J Am Chem Soc 1997;119(38):8916−20.

[107] Giljohann DA, Seferos DS, Daniel WL, Massich MD, Patel PC, Mirkin CA. Gold nanoparticles for biology and medicine. Spherical nucleic acids. Jenny Stanford Publishing; 2020. p. 55−90.

[108] Huai Y, Zhang Y, Xiong X, Das S, Bhattacharya R, Mukherjee P. Gold Nanoparticles sensitize pancreatic cancer cells to gemcitabine. Cell Stress 2019;3(8):267.

[109] Dam DHM, Lee JH, Sisco PN, Co DT, Zhang M, Wasielewski MR, et al. Direct observation of nanoparticle−cancer cell nucleus interactions. ACS Nano 2012;6(4):3318−26.

[110] Dam DHM, Culver KS, Odom TW. Grafting aptamers onto gold nanostars increases in vitro efficacy in a wide range of cancer cell types. Mol Pharma 2014;11(2):580−7.

[111] Giljohann DA, Seferos DS, Patel PC, Millstone JE, Rosi NL, Mirkin CA. Oligonucleotide loading determines cellular uptake of DNA-modified gold nanoparticles. Spherical nucleic acids. Jenny Stanford Publishing; 2020. p. 413—23.

[112] Yazdian-Robati R, Hedayati N, Dehghani S, Ramezani M, Alibolandi M, Saeedi M, et al. Application of the catalytic activity of gold nanoparticles for development of optical aptasensors. Anal Biochem 2021;629:114307.

[113] Yazdian-Robati R, Bayat P, Oroojalian F, Zargari M, Ramezani M, Taghdisi SM, et al. Therapeutic applications of AS1411 aptamer, an update review. Int J Biol Macromol 2020;155:1420—31.

[114] Lee JW, Stone ML, Porrett PM, Thomas SK, Komar CA, Li JH, et al. Hepatocytes direct the formation of a pro-metastatic niche in the liver. Nature 2019;567(7747):249—52.

[115] Condeelis J, Pollard JW. Macrophages: obligate partners for tumor cell migration, invasion, and metastasis. Cell 2006;124(2):263—6.

[116] Gil-Bernabé AM, Ferjančič Š, Tlalka M, Zhao L, Allen PD, Im JH, et al. Recruitment of monocytes/macrophages by tissue factor-mediated coagulation is essential for metastatic cell survival and premetastatic niche establishment in mice. Blood. J Am Soc Hematol 2012;119(13):3164—75.

[117] Farzin A, Etesami SA, Quint J, Memic A, Tamayol A. Magnetic nanoparticles in cancer therapy and diagnosis. Adv Healthc Mater 2020;9(9):1901058.

[118] Laurent S, Saei AA, Behzadi S, Panahifar A, Mahmoudi M. Superparamagnetic iron oxide nanoparticles for delivery of therapeutic agents: opportunities and challenges. Expert Opin Drug Deliv 2014;11(9):1449—70.

[119] Estelrich i Latràs J, Sánchez Martín M, Busquets i Viñas M. Nanoparticles in Magnetic Resonance Imaging: from simple to dual contrast agents. Int J Nanomed 2015;10(1):1727—41.

[120] Seneci P, Rizzi M, Ballabio L, Lecis D, Conti A, Carrara C, et al. SPION-Smac mimetic nano-conjugates: putative pro-apoptotic agents in oncology. Bioorg Med Chem Lett 2014;24(10):2374—8.

[121] He Y, Song W, Lei J, Li Z, Cao J, Huang S, et al. Anti-CXCR4 monoclonal antibody conjugated to ultrasmall superparamagnetic iron oxide nanoparticles in an application of MR molecular imaging of pancreatic cancer cell lines. Acta Radiol 2012;53(9):1049—58.

[122] Zuo HD, Yao WW, Chen TW, Zhu J, Zhang JJ, Pu Y, et al. The effect of superparamagnetic iron oxide with iRGD peptide on the labeling of pancreatic cancer cells in vitro: a preliminary study. BioMed Res Int 2014;2014:852352.

[123] Hanson RL, Brown RB, Steele MM, Grandgenett PM, Grunkemeyer JA, Hollingsworth MA. Identification of FRA-1 as a novel player in pancreatic cancer in cooperation with a MUC1: ERK signaling axis. Oncotarget 2016;7(26):39996.

[124] Masood F. Polymeric nanoparticles for targeted drug delivery system for cancer therapy. Mater Sci Eng C 2016;60:569—78.

[125] Lee GY, Kenny PA, Lee EH, Bissell MJ. Three-dimensional culture models of normal and malignant breast epithelial cells. Nat Methods 2007;4(4):359—65.

[126] Cen P, Ni X, Yang J, Graham DY, Li M. Circulating tumor cells in the diagnosis and management of pancreatic cancer. Biochim Biophys Acta 2012;1826(2):350—6.

[127] Karami E, Behdani M, Kazemi-Lomedasht F. Albumin nanoparticles as nanocarriers for drug delivery: focusing on antibody and nanobody delivery and albumin-based drugs. J Drug Deliv Sci Technol 2020;55:101471.

[128] Cho H, Jeon SI, Ahn C-H, Shim MK, Kim K. Emerging albumin-binding anticancer drugs for tumor-targeted drug delivery: current understandings and clinical translation. Pharmaceutics 2022;14(4):728.

[129] Parodi A, Miao J, Soond SM, Rudzińska M, Zamyatnin Jr AA. Albumin nanovectors in cancer therapy and imaging. Biomolecules 2019;9(6):218.

[130] Kouchakzadeh H, Shojaosadati SA, Tahmasebi F, Shokri F. Optimization of an anti-HER2 monoclonal antibody targeted delivery system using PEGylated human serum albumin nanoparticles. Int J Pharm 2013;447(1—2):62—9.

CHAPTER 16

Photodynamic therapy for pancreatic cancer

Rezvan Yazdian-Robati[1], Atena Mansouri[2], Peyman Asadi[3], Mehdi Mogharabi-Manzari[1] and Mohsen Chamanara[4]

[1]Pharmaceutical Sciences Research Center, Hemoglobinopathy Institute, Mazandaran University of Medical Sciences, Sari, Iran
[2]Cellular and Molecular Research Center, Birjand University of Medical Sciences, Birjand, Iran
[3]Nano Drug Delivery Research Center, Health Technology Institute, Kermanshah University of Medical Sciences, Kermanshah, Iran
[4]Toxicology Research Center, AJA University of Medical Sciences, Tehran, Iran

16.1 Pancreatic cancer

Pancreatic cancer (PC) remains a high aggressive and deadly malignancy with restricted choices for effective therapy. This gastrointestinal cancer is on path to become the second leading cause of cancer related death in the USA in the next 20–30 years [1,2]. The two primary kinds of PC are pancreatic adenocarcinoma (pancreatic ductal adenocarcinoma (PDAC)), which occurs in 85% of cases and mostly develops from the exocrine pancreas glands, and pancreatic neuroendocrine tumor (PanNET), which is less prevalent (less than 5%) and develops from the pancreatic endocrine tissue [3]. Only 24% of persons with PDAC survive for one year following diagnosis, and only 9% make it to 5 years [4]. There are four different forms of PC, depending on the clinical stage of the tumor: I (no spread or treatable), the cancer has developed no more than 2 cm in the pancreas (IA), or more than 2 cm but no more than 4 cm (IB); II (local spread or borderline resectable), the cancer has spread locally to the adjacent lymph nodes or is larger than 4 cm and restricted to the pancreas; Cancer cells may have spread to adjacent blood vessels or nerves in stage III (wider spread or unresectable), but it has not spread to other organs of the body; Cancer at stage IV (metastatic) has spread to distant organs [1]. PDAC, are frequently discovered at an advanced stage (stage III or IV) [5]. As the tumor grows, nonspecific symptoms including weariness, stomach pain, light-colored faces, and jaundice gradually appear [6]. This disease has an insidious beginning, and the majority of patients are diagnosed with an incurable tumor [7]. The ability to reduce mortality through early identification may be aided by patient screening and prevention. Although more recent methods and screening of closely targeted populations (particularly people with a family history) are being studied, screening large populations of the overall population is not currently thought to be an effective way to catch the disease in its early stages [8,9]. Screening methods include blood tests for PC markers including DUPAN-2, CA19-9, SPAN-1,

CA-50, cell surface-associated mucins (MUC), and heat shock proteins [10,11]. Surgical resection of the tumor with adjuvant systemic chemotherapy is the only form of treatment that gives the possibility of curing local disease [12]. There is realistically no cure for patients with locally advanced or metastatic illness. In individuals with both resectable and nonresectable illness, improvements in chemotherapy and radiation therapy have led to a slight increase in survival. Adjuvant chemotherapy (gemcitabine plus capecitabine or modified FOLFIRINOX (folinic acid, 5-fluorouracil, irinotecan, and oxaliplatin)) after surgery is available standard treatment option for patient with early PC [13]. Understanding the cause of PC and laying the groundwork for establishing new cancer control measures may be achieved by analysis of the epidemiology of the disease. Smoking has been widely recognized as the primary factor contributing to the high mortality rates of PC, despite the fact that the cause is still largely unclear [14,15]. More efforts may be made by healthcare professionals and policy makers to reduce the risk factors that go along with this cancer. These efforts could include promoting lifestyle modifications, awareness campaigns, and the implementation of more stringent smoking-related regulations. Photodynamic therapy (PDT) is a light-based therapy, which has been clinically approved for the treatment of a variety of diseases such as early-stage cutaneous, superficial, and hollow organ cancers in different countries [16]. Originally, this unique method involves three main components including an organic photosensitizers (PSs) dye for the absorption of excitation light (light-absorbing molecule), molecular oxygen, and nonionizing light, which leads to localized tissue necrosis by producing intracellular reactive oxygen species (ROS) [17]. ROS are a group of potent oxidative reagents that greatly affect cellular bioactivity and promote apoptosis [18−20]. After the administration of a PS, it selectively accumulated in tumor tissues due to enhanced retention time. This process is followed by irradiation with a light of a suitable wavelength, leading to the selective ablation of the malignant cells [21]. The destruction of tumors by PDT takes place through all or some of the following mechanisms depending on the type of cancer and the PS: stimulating the host immune system against the tumor, inducing acute inflammatory response at the target tissue, recruiting leukocytes to the target area, activation of antitumor T lymphocytes, decrease in the tumor microvasculature, induction of apoptosis or necrosis by reactive singlet oxygen ($^1O_2$) [22]. The goal of this chapter is to explain the principle concept of PDT and different nanoparticles (NPs) used in PDT, providing a detailed update of PDT strategies for the treatment of PC and highlighting the impact of PDT in combination with other available therapy for cure of this malignancy.

16.2 Principles of photodynamic therapy

Since ancient times, light has been employed in the treatment of numerous illnesses [23]. The sun was employed by the ancient Egyptian, Indian, and Chinese cultures to heal a variety of skin conditions, including vitiligo, psoriasis, and skin cancer [24].

Herodotus, a renowned Greek physician who is credited with inventing heliotherapy, highlighted the value of full-body exposure to the sun for the recovery of health. Sunlight was utilized to treat a variety of diseases in France during the 18th and 19th centuries, including tuberculosis, rickets, scurvy, rheumatism, paralysis, edema, and muscle weakness [25]. The use of light in the treatment of diseases was recognized at the start of the 20th century, and Niels Finsen received the 1903 Nobel Prize in Physiology or Medicine in recognition of his research in the field. Finsen discovered that lupus vulgaris, a skin disorder caused by tuberculosis, could be treated with sunlight or light from a carbon arc lamp with a heat filter. This finding heralded the advent of contemporary phototherapy [26,27]. The term "phototherapy" refers to the use of light to cure diseases. But in photochemotherapy, a photosensitizing agent must be administered; the agent is then located in the tissues, where light activates it [28]. Over 3000 years ago, the Indians and the Egyptians employed psoralens (a substance from plants that is sensitive to light) derived from natural plants to treat a variety of skin diseases. At the Mayo Clinic, R. Lipson and S. Schwartz developed the idea of PDT in 1960 after learning that injecting a hematoporphyrin derivative had both cancer diagnostic and therapeutic benefits (HpD). The photochemical interaction of three harmless elements including PS, light, and molecular oxygen underlies PDT, which motivates the selective damage of the target tissue. A PS that selectively accumulates in tumor tissue (during a drug-light interval) is administered (topically or intravenously) as part of the PDT treatment. This is followed by exposure to the appropriate wavelength light, which is typically in the red spectral region (600 nm) of the electromagnetic spectrum [29]. The PS does not directly interact with biomolecules; instead, illumination causes the production of ROS, including singlet oxygen ($^1O_2$), superoxide radicals ($O_2^{\bullet-}$), hydroxyl radicals ($HO^\bullet$), and hydrogen peroxide (H_2O_2). The target tissue may become damaged or possibly die as a result of these cytotoxic photoproducts' metabolic cascade. In PDT process, following light absorption, the PS undergoes a brief transition from its ground state—the singlet state—to an electronically excited singlet state—the 1PS*—which lasts for only a few nanoseconds or less. The surplus energy can be lost by fluorescence or heat production as this excited state decays to the ground state (internal conversion). However, spin conversion of the electron in the higher energy orbital allows the singlet state to develop into a more stable and long-lived electronic excited state (triplet state, 3PS*). This excited state has two different types of reactions or it can emit light (phosphorescence) to decay to the ground state. The triplet state has a longer lifetime (up to tens of microseconds), giving molecular oxygen (O_2) enough time to directly receive the energy. The type I reaction can also happen when the excited state of the PS interacts directly with a substrate, such as a cell membrane or molecule, resulting in the removal of hydrogen atoms from the substrate or the transfer of electrons, producing free radicals and radical ions. The oxidative damage caused by these radicals' reactions with molecular oxygen results in ROS such $O_2^{\bullet-}$, $HO^{\bullet}$, and H_2O_2, which can cause biological lesions. In type II reaction, the fundamental state of the PS is produced as a result of this energy transfer step. Due to its high reactivity and ability to interact with a wide range of biological substrates, singlet oxygen can cause oxidative damage and eventually cell death [30,31] (Fig. 16.1).

16.3 Elements of photodynamic therapy

PDT works with three non-toxic elements that create the desired effects in the area of PS distribution within target tissues, allowing for selective destruction. These three elements are PS (a light-sensitive compound), oxygen (O_2), and appropriate light, which are adapted to the absorption spectrum of the PS being used [32].

16.3.1 Photosensitizers agents in photodynamic therapy

In PDT, PS agents are considered as the critical backbone, which are irradiated by appropriate light in a specific wavelength and generate active intermediates. These active products largely determine the therapeutic efficiency of the whole PDT system. The significant aspects that should be considered for selection of suitable PS in the PDT system include amphiphilicity, good photophysical features (such as high quantum yields of 3PS*formation, high $^1O_2$ generation, and a proper triplet lifetime), fast clearance, high

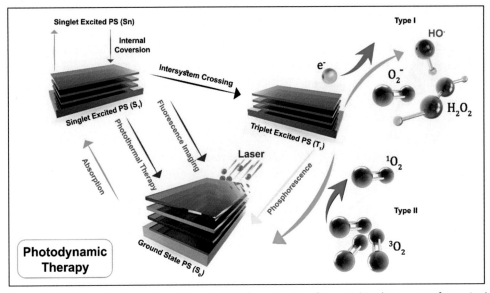

Figure 16.1 Schematic illustration of type I (ROS formation) and type II (singlet oxygen formation) in PDT. *ROS*, reactive oxygen species; *PDT*, photodynamic therapy.

degree of chemical purity, target ability, and light absorption property 600−80,000 nm, red to deep red region [32,33]. In addition, an ideal PS should be able to localize preferentially in tumors [34]. PSs are categorized into three major families, including (1) porphyrin and porphyrin derivative family, (2) chlorin family, and (3) dye family [21].

Verteporfin, m-tetrahydroxyphenylchlorin (mTHPC), chlorin e6 (Ce6), hemoporfin, porfimer sodium (Photofrin), aminolevulinic acid (ALA), and talaporfin, as well as pheophorbide a, are examples of FDA approved PSs [16].

16.3.2 Light (600−800 nm)

In PDT a variety of light sources, such as lasers, incandescent light, and light-emitting diodes (LEDs) were utilized. The light wavelength for tissue irradiation can be controlled using optical fibers and nonlaser light sources for example, standard lamps. LEDs have also been used as light sources in PDT. LEDs are more readily accessible in flexible arrays, less expensive, less dangerous, and thermally nondestructive. Light penetration into tumor tissue is exceedingly complicated because the light can be reflected, scattered, or absorbed. The type of tissue and the light's wavelength affect how far along these processes. Endogenous chromophores found in tissues, such as hemoglobin, myoglobin, and cytochromes, are primarily responsible for light absorption. By competing with PS in the absorption process, these endogenous chromophores can lessen the photodynamic process. Longer wavelengths of light, such as red light, enter into tissue more effectively because the amount of light that tissues absorb reduces as the wavelength increases [35]. The "tissue optical window" is the term used to describe the range between 600 and 1200 nm. Skin photosensitivity is increased by the shorter wavelengths (600 nm), which are more absorbed and less effective in penetrating tissue. However, longer wavelengths (> 850 nm) lack the energy to sufficiently excite oxygen in its singlet form and generate enough ROS. Therefore, between 600 and 850 nm tissue permeability, it is at its maximum. The "phototherapeutic window," which falls within this range, is mostly utilized in PDT [34,36]. Clinical effectiveness of PDT is greatly influenced by the light dose, light fluence, light fluence rate, light exposure time, and light delivery mode (single or fractionated). Light fluence, which is measured in J/cm^2, is the sum of exposed light energy over a sectional area of an irradiated point. Light fluence rate, which is measured in W/cm^2, is the incident energy per second over a segment of the irradiated location. According to several research papers, PDT benefits of low light fluence rates. The oxygen depletion in tissues, which results in a poor photo-degradation of the PS, is the main cause of the reduced efficacy of PDT for high light fluence rates. Additionally, it has been demonstrated that the light fluence rate affects the primary mechanism of cell death in the PDT. Importantly, the light source and the light dose should be optimized in PDT protocol. Once the treatment with PDT is inadequate or tumor cells are incubated in sublethal light doses, these cells have a tendency to live after the PDT [37] (Fig. 16.2).

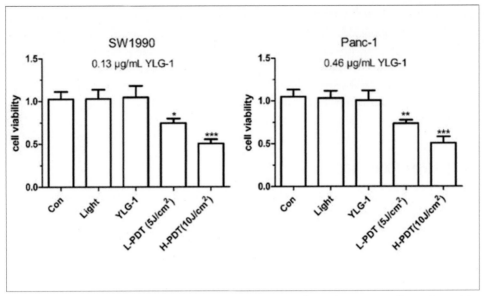

Figure 16.2 The effects of different doses of PDT (low 5 J/cm^2 and high 10 J/cm^2) on the viability of pancreatic tumor cells. First, two PC cell lines (SW1990 and Panc-1) were incubated with YLG-1 (a novel chlorine derivative PS) and then exposed to L-PDT and H-PDT. Cell viability decreased significantly in H-PDT treatment group. Reproduced with permission from reference [37]. *PDT*, photodynamic therapy; *PSs*, photosensitizers; *PC*, pancreatic cancer.

16.3.3 Oxygen

Apart from PS, the other key items affecting PDT efficiency are oxygen content in tumor tissues. Molecular oxygen is the third important part of PDT due to inducing the generation of ROS. The amount of oxygen in the tissues has a real impact on how well PDT works. Oxygen concentration depending on the density of the vasculature might fluctuate dramatically across various cancers and even between various parts of the same tumor. Lack of oxygen can be a limiting issue, particularly in deeper solid tumors, which are frequently distinguished by their anoxic microenvironment. As it was already noted, irradiating the tumor with a high light fluence rate has the potential to temporarily deplete the local oxygen supply. As a result, ROS production is interrupted and the efficacy of treatment is decreased. One of the major hurdles in the near future is the real–time assessment of tissue oxygen levels before and during PDT. Both the indirect and direct delivery of oxygen has been investigated as additional ways to boost oxygen availability in the tumor. Utilizing the catalase enzyme to convert the intracellular hydrogen peroxide into oxygen is one indirect method of raising the oxygen concentration in tumor cells [38]. In the PDT process, oxygen carriers such as perfluorocarbons, red blood cells, and hemoglobin are typically utilized to treat the hypoxia that is caused by tumors. This allows for the direct delivery of oxygen into tumors, which is the goal of the procedure [39–41].

16.4 Photodynamic therapy in pancreatic cancer

PDT is a minimally invasive technique that is clinically exploited in the treatment of multiple cancers, including PC [36]. In this modality, through a nonthermal cytotoxic effect, localized tissue necrosis was mediated by singlet oxygen [42]. PDT has various exceptional advantages over other conventional cancer therapies including low trauma, low side effects, less systemic toxicity, high selectivity (the PS is triggered once exposed to light), and reproducible treatment as well as high efficiency [43]. Depending on the PS, PDT protocol and tumor type, PDT induces several types of cell death, such as apoptosis, necroptosis, necrosis, and autophagy [44]. Three distinct mechanisms are involved in the destruction of tumors treated with PDT. In the first route, the generated ROS can destroy tumor cells by apoptosis and/or necrosis. PDT also can damage the tumor-related vasculature, leading to hemorrhage in tumor blood vessels, consequently, tumor death through lack of oxygen and nutrients occurred. Finally, PDT can stimulate an immune response against tumor cells and causes acute inflammation, consequently triggering the release of cytokines and stress response proteins [45—47]. For example, PSs, such as methylene (MB), have been shown to activate the necroptosis pathway, which is an inflammatory type of programmed cell death that is recognized by membrane permeabilization and cell swelling [48,49]. Considering the fact that most PDACs are resistant to chemotherapy and apoptosis pathways, inducing necroptosis pathways by PDT is a considerable alternative for activating the cell death pathways. One workaround addressing this context is reported by de Almeida et al. [48]. They utilized MB as PS with an absorption range at 655 nm to induce necroptosis pathway by activating different cell damage processes, including receptor-interacting protein kinase (RIP)-1 and RIP-3, mixed lineage kinase domain-like protein (MLKL) which, ultimately, results in plasma membrane pore formation [48,50].

16.5 Nanoparticles mediated photodynamic therapy for pancreatic cancer

During recent decades, there has been extreme focus on the application of NPs in the medicinal field [51—53]. In PDT therapy, during clinical modalities by conventional PSs, there are some limitations, such as inadequate PSs delivery and impaired $^1O_2$ yield, consequently low production of ROS, as well as low tissue penetration of light [54,55]. More importantly, there is no selectivity of PS to the tumor target so normal adjacent tissue also are damaged [56]. To overcome these difficulties and enhance the PDT efficacy, an increasing number of basic researchers have been reporting PDT treatments mediated by NPs [57,58]. Nanocarriers that can successfully incorporate the PSs, introduce oxygen to tumors, or enhance the penetration depth of irradiation to tissues are good candidates to boost the therapeutic outcomes of PDT [59].

Encapsulation of PSs with NPs enhances cellular uptake and biodistribution, avoids self-quenching, and increases solubility and stability of PSs in blood circulation, and increasing targeted delivery of PSs in tumors through the enhanced permeability and retention (EPR) effect result in significantly higher accumulation within pancreatic tumors and increase $^1O_2$ yield [60–62] (Fig. 16.3).

Different NPs, such as liposome and PLGA (poly (lactic acid-co-glycolic) acid) NPs [63], have been reported for various PS encapsulations for the treatment of PC [64]. AuNPs in combination with a PS were also reported for PDT. In this context, incorporation of AuNPs (5 nm) and verteporfin (VP, a commercially available PSs) in PLGA nanocomposites (PLGA@AuNPs-VP) for the treatment of PC were reported by Deng et al. The results revealed that the treatment of Panc-1 cells with PLGA @AuNPs-VP could decrease the cell viability after laser exposure (425 nm LED and 405 nm laser light) with an increase in the generation of $^1O_2$ in comparison to PLGA/VP NPs [63].

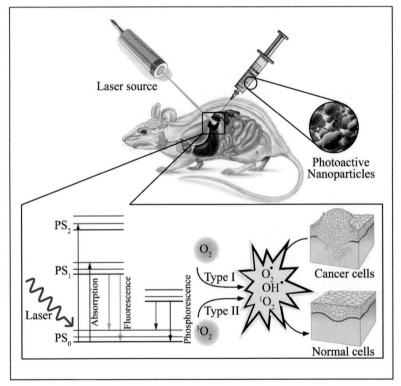

Figure 16.3 In PDT, as a light-based modality, reactive oxygen species produced in the pancreatic tumor via the energy transfer between a PS and molecularly dissolved triplet oxygen ($^3O_2$), leading to oxidative stress, prompt tumor death in vicinity of the PS. Incorporation of PS into NPs protects it from enzymatic degradation, overcoming graduation and enhancing the therapeutic efficacy. *PDT*, photodynamic therapy; *PSs*, photosensitizers; *PC*, pancreatic cancer.

16.6 Combination of photodynamic therapy with other therapies in pancreatic cancer treatment

The high complexity and heterogenicity of PC have pushed the studies to try combinatorial approaches and assess the parallel application of other therapeutic protocols with PDT to block this disease effectively. Combining PDT with other therapeutic strategy in the process of PDAC treatment has become innovative regimen in order to solve PDT's deficiencies such as recurrence and metastasis and limitations on superficial tumor types [17].

16.6.1 Combination of photodynamic therapy with radiation therapy

Single PDT faces the main challenge of the insufficient penetrating depth of visible light and PDT/RT suggested to overcome this limitation through the usage of near-infrared light or x-rays. Using an optimal combination of low-dose PDT and radiation therapy (RT) at 10 Gy, Bulin et al., demonstrated that PDT/RT combination can decrease the size of three different pancreatic spheroids (MIA PaCa-2, Capan2, and AsPC-1 cocultured with patient-derived PC-associated fibroblasts (pCAF)) and increase the necrosis response owing to the antiproliferation role of RT and the apoptosis and necrotic properties of PDT [65].

16.6.2 Combination of photodynamic therapy with immunotherapy

Immunotherapy as an artificial stimulation of the immune system is widely used for treatment of cancer with low side effects and notable therapeutic effects. However, the hypoxic TME, tumor heterogeneity, and immunosuppression made immunotherapy unsuccessful in several cancers including PC [66]. PDT triggered the direct destruction of cellular components, tumor vasculature, and also immunogenic cell death (ICD) [67]. In this cell death modality, the release of tumor-associated antigens, danger-associated molecular patterns, and different proinflammatory cytokines result in strong immune responses [68]. It was demonstrated that combining immunotherapy and PDT is a wealth of opportunities to eradicate PCs through various therapeutic mechanisms including the aid of checkpoint blockade [69]. In a study, Jang et al. isolated MIA-PaCa-2 cell-derived exosomes to use as a PS carrier (Ce6) and act as an immunostimulatory mediator. Ce6 was encapsulated into exosomes during exosomal reassembly (Ce6-R-Exo) to improve the photoacoustic signals and cause ROS generation in tumor cells effectively upon exposure to laser irradiation. Furthermore, Ce6-R-Exo increased the production of cytokines by CD8 T cells (Fig. 16.4). This combination approach (image-guided PDT and immunotherapy) exhibited promising results in tumor-bearing mice with minimal side effects [70].

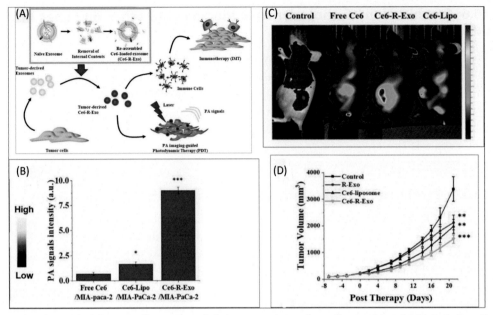

Figure 16.4 (A) Schematic illustration of Ce6 encapsulation by self-assembly of MIA-PaCa-2 cell-derived exosomes (Ce6-R-Exo). (B) Quantified intensities of photoacoustic signal in the MIA-PaCa-2 cells after being treated with free Ce6, Ce6-loaded liposomes (Ce6-Lipo), or Ce6-R-Exo. The photoacoustic signal from the Ce6-R-Exo group was higher than other groups. (C) In Ce6-R-Exo-treated group much stronger Ce6 fluorescence intensity was detected at the tumor site than in the free Ce6 group or Ce6-Lipo. (D) Tumor volume in the Ce6-R-Exo group (combination therapy group) significantly decreased in comparison to PDT treatment group (Ce6-liposome) and the immunotherapy treatment group (R-Exo). Reproduced with permission from reference [70]. *PDT*, photodynamic therapy.

16.6.3 Combination of photodynamic therapy with chemotherapy

In order to conquer hypoxic conditions within pancreatic tumors during PDT, Zhang and coworkers combined Fe^{3+} with porphyrins to make a porous coordination network (PCN) that further was loaded with paclitaxel with a high efficiency. The mesoporous PCN-Fe (III)-PTX NPs can participate in the Fenton reaction as an effective way to decompose H_2O_2 into O_2 with the capacity of ≈ 1 mg/L within 60 min. In PC cells, the generated O_2 was converted to $^1O_2$ under laser irradiation and pH change. After intravenous injection of PCN-Fe (III)-PTX to mice bearing PANC-1 tumor cells, complete inhibition of tumor growth within 16 days observed, thus providing an effective chemo-PDT (photodynamic therapy with chemotherapy) synergistic strategy [71]. To cite another example of chemo-PDT for PC treatment, Cho et al. [72] prepared a light-responsive NP system with conjugation of Ce6, caspase-3-specific cleavable peptide (KGDEVD), and monomethyl auristatin E (MMAE), a synthetic antineoplastic agent. Visible light irradiation induced the production of ROS, leading to the overexpression of caspase-3 by apoptosis in PCs. This phenomenon caused the MMAE released from nanostructure and promoted extensive apoptotic cell death in pancreatic tumor microenvironment [72]. In order to assess the effect of pancreatic tumor-stroma interactions on response to PDT, Karimnia et al. generated a heterotypic 3D model where primary pancreatic stellate cells and normal human fibroblast cell line were loaded in a Matrigel bead that was overlaid with a suspension of PDAC cells. In the next step, they exploited this 3d platform to test oxaliplatin, gemcitabine, and PDT treatment. The authors demonstrated that the PDAC cells were more resistant to chemotherapy due to the presence of stromal fibroblasts as expected, and more sensitive to PDT relative to cocultured fibroblasts. Importantly, by means of this heterotypic 3d platform, more physiological responses to drug treatments can be investigated, proposing that the PDT treatment can be exploited as a dominant tactic for stromal depletion [73]. Taken as a whole, by exploiting chemo-PDT, uniformly favorable outcomes, including a reduction in the dose of chemotherapeutic drugs as well as a decrease in the systematic toxicity, were achieved. PDT also has the potential to treat chemotherapy-resistant cancers. It was reported in PC that the overexpression of IAP family (inhibitors of apoptosis proteins) is important item to develop drug resistance by preventing caspase activities [74]. Therefore, block of IAP proteins can improve chemosensitivity of tumor cells. Zhu et al. reported a ROS-sensitive nanosystem for effective synergistic chemo-PDT using Ce6, gemcitabine (Gem), and a pro-apoptotic peptide that targets IAP family (Smac N7). At first, the pro-apoptotic peptide was conjugated to GEM by a vinyldithioether linker, which is sensitive to ROS. Then this peptide—drug conjugate (GVS) self-assembled with Ce6 (at the molar ratio of 1:1) to make Ce6-GVS NPs. In this system, ROS (generated by ce6 under 660-nm laser illumination) could trigger the cleavage of the vinyldithioether linker, and as a consequence, GEM and pro-apoptotic peptides released while the generated ROS can eradicate tumor cells at the same time [75].

16.6.4 Combination of photodynamic therapy with chemotherapy and immunotherapy

Progress in immunotherapy and immune checkpoint blockade for the treatment of different cancers is being made but it is too slow for PC due to molecular complexity involved in the progression of this lethal disease [76]. To address this issue, Ghosh et al. [69] applied a synergistic chemo-PDT-immunotherapy strategy to prepare porphyrin—phospholipid liposomes carrying irinotecan (IRI-PoP liposomes). Mice having KPC cell (PDAC) were treated with a combination of IRI-PoP liposomes (18 mg/kg) and laser (665 nm, 250 mW/cm^2) and anti-PD-1 + anti-CTLA4 mAbs (5 mg/kg, three times, at an interval of 3 days). Administration of antibodies along with IRI-PoP liposomes and laser therapy could induce considerable pancreatic tumor regression and postpone tumor regrowth [69]. This preliminary animal study provides a signal of the future potential role of chemo-photo-immunotherapy to fight against PC.

16.6.5 Combination of photodynamic therapy with sonodynamic therapy

Although PDT offers the opportunity to treat cancer with minimal side effects and high efficiency, its clinical application strongly is influenced by low tissue penetrative depth(≤ 1 cm). However, due to higher tissue penetration of ultrasound (≥ 10 cm) with no side effects in adjacent tissues, SPDT (photodynamic therapy with sonodynamic therapy) can overcome the tissue penetration limit of light [77]. In the SDT (sonodynamic therapy) approach, a sonosensitizing agent is induced by ultrasound and generates a large amount of ROS to eradicate tumor cells [78]. Insufficient oxygen supply in the hypoxic tumor microenvironment is another issue influencing the clinical application of PDT. In this way, Hu et al. [79] coincorporated a catalase and methylene blue (MB) into a nanoscale porous hierarchical zeolite with high enzyme activities of catalase (ZCM) to inhibit pancreatic tumors. Using real-time ultrasound imaging guidance, this nanostructure was inserted into the tumor area. In vitro results using singlet oxygen sensor green reagent exhibited that the $^1O_2$ generation was 3.7-fold higher for the ZCM nanocapsule treated group than the other groups including zeolite or zeolite-MB. The PDT tests were performed on ALB/c athymic nude mice having SW1990 pancreatic tumor cells. Under irradiation with laser at 635 nm (50 mW/cm^2, 10 min) pancreatic tumor cells are totally killed at 18 days [79].

16.6.6 Combination of photodynamic therapy with photothermal therapy

Photothermal therapy (PTT) has attracted great attention in cancer therapy because of its noninvasive properties and low side effects. In clinical practice, tissue oxygen–dependence is known as one of the serious drawbacks that should be considered for PDT, and interestingly PTT does not face this limitation. PTT has considerable merits in the treatment of solid tumors in hypoxic conditions. So, the combination therapy of PTT and PDT as an extraordinary therapeutic modality could mainly improve the ablation ability of tumors in clinic. In the related context, a combination therapy of PDT/PTT was reported by Li and coworkers [80] for treatment of PC. They synthesized a PS (namely DCTBT) through molecular engineering, with aggregation-induced emission properties, NIR-II absorption, and type I PDT and PTT function. Then this PS was incorporated into liposomes and further targeted by EGFR-targeting peptide. The results demonstrated that targeted DCTBT-loaded liposomes displayed tumor growth inhibition in a PANC-1 orthotopic model following synergistic treatment of type I PDT and PTT. This tactic displays great potential for overwhelming tumors in hypoxic conditions (Fig. 16.5) [80]. In another study, around this topic, a nanosystem (PSPP-Au980-D) consisting of perfluorocarbon-based bilayer-polymer (PFC-PS and PNIPAM) nanostructure introduced with outstanding oxygen loading capacity and PTT conversion capability in the NIR-II bio window. The PS silicon phthalocyanine

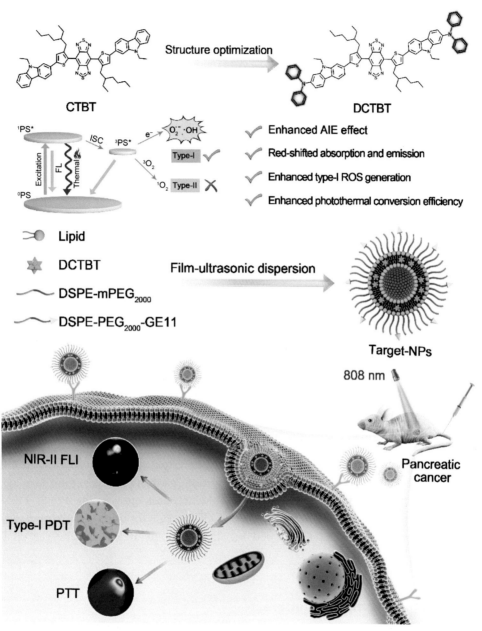

Figure 16.5 Schematic illustration of molecular design, and the application of NIR-II FLI-guided type-I PDT-PTT synergistic pancreatic cancer therapy. Reprinted with permission from referernce [80]. *PDT*, photodynamic therapy; *PTT*, Photothermal therapy.

(SiPc) was encapsulated into the interlayer and the outer layer was modified by AuNRs with extinction peak at 980 nm as the photothermal agent and doxorubicin (PFC/SiPc@PS@PNIPAMAu980-DOX). In this programmed cascade therapy, after irradiation, the PSPP–Au980-D with a 980 nm laser, oxygen, and doxorubicin was released from PFC, then a 680 nm laser was used to trigger PDT under high oxygen content. In this scenario, PDT and chemotherapy were collaborative with PTT to eradicate PC [81].

16.7 Summary and outlook

It is clear from the above studies that PDT, as a high-potential treatment method, is on the eve of clinical application for the treatment of PC. The first clinical study (phase I) in the world was designed by Bown et al. [82] on 16 patients with inoperable pancreatic adenocarcinoma. Three days before light delivery, mTHPC as a photosensitizing agent (0.15 mg/kg) was injected. No treatment-related mortality was observed and 44% were alive one year after PDT [82]. This group conducted another clinical study with verteporfin (liposomal benzoporphyrin derivative) instead of mTHPC [83]. Verteporfin exhibited reduced skin photosensitivity (24 h), rapid clearance by excretion in bile, and longer wavelength absorption peak (690 nm) as well as deeper tissue penetration compared with mTHPC [84]. In this phase I/II clinical study, 15 inoperable patients with locally advanced PCs received verteporfin (0.4 mg/kg). The result revealed that PDT in all patients could produce necrosis [83]. Other clinical studies also reported using PDT for the treatment of PC using porfimer sodium and Ce6 [85,86].

Despite this progress in these early phase studies, some problems should be addressed. More efficient and suitable PSs with high tumor selectivity, no considerable toxicity, and high ROS yield are essential for clinical application. On the other hand, the deep position and hypovascular structures of PC restrict the enough optical illumination and PS gathering in tumor tissues. In addition, gastrointestinal hemorrhage and duodenal obstruction are other issues that should be considered during PDT. These factors made a slow in the development of PDT for PC. In conclusion, along with other treatments, PDT is recommended for the treatment of PC, despite the challenges in the PDT field.

Declaration of competing interest

The authors declare that they have no competing interests.

References

[1] Mizrahi JD, Surana R, Valle JW, Shroff RT. Pancreatic cancer. Lancet 2020;395(10242):2008−20.

[2] McGuigan A, Kelly P, Turkington RC, Jones C, Coleman HG, McCain RS. Pancreatic cancer: a review of clinical diagnosis, epidemiology, treatment and outcomes. World J Gastroenterol 2018;24 (43):4846.

[3] Hidalgo M, Cascinu S, Kleeff J, Labianca R, Löhr J-M, Neoptolemos J, et al. Addressing the challenges of pancreatic cancer: future directions for improving outcomes. Pancreatology 2015;15 (1):8–18.

[4] Rawla P, Sunkara T, Gaduputi V. Epidemiology of pancreatic cancer: global trends, etiology and risk factors. World J Oncol 2019;10(1):10–27.

[5] De La Cruz MSD, Young AP, Ruffin MT. Diagnosis and management of pancreatic cancer. Am Fam Physician 2014;89(8):626–32.

[6] Siegel RL, Miller KD, Jemal A. Cancer statistics, 2018. CA: Cancer J Clin 2018;68(1):7–30.

[7] Raufi AG, May MS, Hadfield MJ, Seyhan AA, El-Deiry WS. Advances in liquid biopsy technology and implications for pancreatic cancer. Int J Mol Sci 2023;24(4):4238.

[8] Greenhalf W, Grocock C, Harcus M, Neoptolemos J. Screening of high-risk families for pancreatic cancer. Pancreatology 2009;9(3):215–22.

[9] Shin EJ, Canto MI. Pancreatic cancer screening. Gastroenterol Clin 2012;41(1):143–57.

[10] Hidalgo M. Pancreatic cancer. N Engl J Med 2010;362(17):1605–17.

[11] Cappelli G, Paladini S, d'Agata A. Tumor markers in the diagnosis of pancreatic cancer. Tumori 1999;85(1 Suppl 1):S19–21.

[12] Strobel O, Neoptolemos J, Jäger D, Büchler MW. Optimizing the outcomes of pancreatic cancer surgery. Nat Rev Clin Oncol 2019;16(1):11–26.

[13] Zeng S, Pöttler M, Lan B, Grützmann R, Pilarsky C, Yang H. Chemoresistance in pancreatic cancer. Int J Mol Sci 2019;20(18):4504.

[14] Ezzati M, Henley SJ, Lopez AD, Thun MJ. Role of smoking in global and regional cancer epidemiology: current patterns and data needs. Int J Cancer 2005;116(6):963–71.

[15] Weiss W, Benarde MA. The temporal relation between cigarette smoking and pancreatic cancer. Am J Public Health 1983;73(12):1403–4.

[16] Wang Y, Wang H, Zhou L, Lu J, Jiang B, Liu C, et al. Photodynamic therapy of pancreatic cancer: where have we come from and where are we going? Photodiagnosis Photodyn Ther 2020;31: 101876.

[17] Yazdian-Robati R, Bayat P, Oroojalian F, Zargari M, Ramezani M, Taghdisi SM, et al. Therapeutic applications of AS1411 aptamer, an update review. Int J Biol Macromol 2020;155: 1420–31.

[18] Bayat P, Farshchi M, Yousefian M, Mahmoudi M, Yazdian-Robati R. Flavonoids, the compounds with anti-inflammatory and immunomodulatory properties, as promising tools in multiple sclerosis (MS) therapy: a systematic review of preclinical evidence. Int Immunopharmacol 2021;95:107562.

[19] Tayarani-Najaran Z, Yazdian-Robati R, Amini E, Salek F, Arasteh F, Emami SA. The mechanism of neuroprotective effect of Viola odorata against serum/glucose deprivation-induced PC12 cell death. Avicenna J Phytomed 2019;9(6):491.

[20] Hassani FV, Abnous K, Mehri S, Jafarian A, Birner-Gruenberger R, Robati RY, et al. Proteomics and phosphoproteomics analysis of liver in male rats exposed to bisphenol A: mechanism of hepatotoxicity and biomarker discovery. Food Chem Toxicol 2018;112:26–38.

[21] Kwiatkowski S, Knap B, Przystupski D, Saczko J, Kędzierska E, Knap-Czop K, et al. Photodynamic therapy—mechanisms, photosensitizers and combinations. Biomed Pharmacother 2018;106:1098–107.

[22] Hou Y-j, Yang X-x, Liu R-q, Zhao D, Guo C-x, Zhu A-c, et al. Pathological mechanism of photodynamic therapy and photothermal therapy based on nanoparticles. Int J Nanomed 2020; 6827–38.

[23] Hamblin MR, Huang Y. Imaging in photodynamic therapy. CRC Press; 2017.

[24] Lee C-N, Hsu R, Chen H, Wong T-W. Daylight photodynamic therapy: an update. Molecules 2020;25(21):5195.

[25] Kelty CJ, Brown NJ, Reed MW, Ackroyd R. The use of 5-aminolaevulinic acid as a photosensitiser in photodynamic therapy and photodiagnosis. Photochem Photobiol Sci 2002;1(3):158–68.

[26] Dolmans DE, Fukumura D, Jain RK. Photodynamic therapy for cancer. Nat Rev Cancer 2003; 3(5):380−7.

[27] Li X, Lee S, Yoon J. Supramolecular photosensitizers rejuvenate photodynamic therapy. Chem Soc Rev 2018;47(4):1174−88.

[28] Rocha LGB. Development of a novel photosensitizer for photodynamic therapy of cancer. 2016, Universidade de Coimbra, Portugal.

[29] Ding H, Yu H, Dong Y, Tian R, Huang G, Boothman DA, et al. Photoactivation switch from type II to type I reactions by electron-rich micelles for improved photodynamic therapy of cancer cells under hypoxia. J Control Release 2011;156(3):276−80.

[30] Fitzgerald F. Photodynamic therapy (PDT). Nova Science Publishers; 2017. Incorporated.

[31] Yu Y, Wu S, Zhang L, Xu S, Dai C, Gan S, et al. Cationization to boost both type I and type II ROS generation for photodynamic therapy. Biomaterials 2022;280:121255.

[32] Kubrak TP, Kołodziej P, Sawicki J, Mazur A, Koziorowska K, Aebisher D. Some natural photosensitizers and their medicinal properties for use in photodynamic therapy. Molecules 2022;27(4):1192.

[33] Simões JC, Sarpaki S, Papadimitroulas P, Therrien B, Loudos G. Conjugated photosensitizers for imaging and PDT in cancer research. J Med Chem 2020;63(23):14119−50.

[34] Agostinis P, Berg K, Cengel KA, Foster TH, Girotti AW, Gollnick SO, et al. Photodynamic therapy of cancer: an update. CA: Cancer J Clin 2011;61(4):250−81.

[35] Liu J, Van Iersel MW. Photosynthetic physiology of blue, green, and red light: light intensity effects and underlying mechanisms. Front plant Sci 2021;12:619987.

[36] Correia JH, Rodrigues JA, Pimenta S, Dong T, Yang Z. Photodynamic therapy review: principles, photosensitizers, applications, and future directions. Pharmaceutics 2021;13(9):1332.

[37] Shen Y, Li M, Sun F, Zhang Y, Qu C, Zhou M, et al. Low-dose photodynamic therapy-induced increase in the metastatic potential of pancreatic tumor cells and its blockade by simvastatin. J Photochem Photobiol B Biol 2020;207:111889.

[38] Glorieux C, Dejeans N, Sid B, Beck R, Calderon PB, Verrax J. Catalase overexpression in mammary cancer cells leads to a less aggressive phenotype and an altered response to chemotherapy. Biochem Pharmacol 2011;82(10):1384−90.

[39] Cheng Y, Cheng H, Jiang C, Qiu X, Wang K, Huan W, et al. Perfluorocarbon nanoparticles enhance reactive oxygen levels and tumour growth inhibition in photodynamic therapy. Nat Commun 2015;6(1):8785.

[40] Luo Z, Zheng M, Zhao P, Chen Z, Siu F, Gong P, et al. Self-monitoring artificial red cells with sufficient oxygen supply for enhanced photodynamic therapy. Sci Rep 2016;6(1):23393.

[41] Cao H, Wang L, Yang Y, Li J, Qi Y, Li Y, et al. An assembled nanocomplex for improving both therapeutic efficiency and treatment depth in photodynamic therapy. Angew Chem 2018;130(26): 7885−9.

[42] Ayaru L, Bown SG, Pereira SP. Photodynamic therapy for pancreatic and biliary tract carcinoma. Int J Gastrointest Cancer 2005;35:1−13.

[43] Van Straten D, Mashayekhi V, De Bruijn HS, Oliveira S, Robinson DJ. Oncologic photodynamic therapy: basic principles, current clinical status and future directions. Cancers 2017;9(2):19.

[44] Miki Y, Akimoto J, Moritake K, Hironaka C, Fujiwara Y. Photodynamic therapy using talaporfin sodium induces concentration-dependent programmed necroptosis in human glioblastoma T98G cells. Lasers Med Sci 2015;30:1739−45.

[45] Lu Y, Sun W, Du J, Fan J, Peng X. Immuno-photodynamic therapy (IPDT): organic photosensitizers and their application in cancer ablation. JACS Au 2023;3:682−99.

[46] Kessel D. Critical PDT theory III: events at the molecular and cellular level. Int J Mol Sci 2022; 23(11):6195.

[47] Allison RR, Moghissi K. Photodynamic therapy (PDT): PDT mechanisms. Clin Endosc 2013;46 (1):24−9.

[48] de Almeida DR, Dos Santos AF, Wailemann RA, Terra LF, Gomes VM, Arini GS, et al. Necroptosis activation is associated with greater methylene blue-photodynamic therapy-induced cytotoxicity in human pancreatic ductal adenocarcinoma cells. Photochem Photobiol Sci 2022;1−16.

[49] De Silva P, Saad MA, Thomsen HC, Bano S, Ashraf S, Hasan T. Photodynamic therapy, priming and optical imaging: potential co-conspirators in treatment design and optimization—A Thomas Dougherty Award for Excellence in PDT paper. J Porphyr Phthalocyanines 2020;24(11n12):1320−60.

[50] Castano AP, Demidova TN, Hamblin MR. Mechanisms in photodynamic therapy: Part three—Photosensitizer pharmacokinetics, biodistribution, tumor localization and modes of tumor destruction. Photodiagnosis photodyn Ther 2005;2(2):91−106.

[51] Mirrezaei N, Yazdian-Robati R, Oroojalian F, Sahebkar A, Hashemi M. Recent developments in nano-drug delivery systems loaded by phytochemicals for wound healing. Mini Rev Med Chem 2020;20(18):1867−78.

[52] Mansouri A, Sathyapalan T, Kesharwani P, Sahebkar A. Aptamer-functionalized PLGA nanoparticles for targeted cancer therapy. Aptamers engineered nanocarriers for cancer therapy. Elsevier; 2023. p. 219−35.

[53] Wang S, Cheng K, Chen K, Xu C, Ma P, Dang G, et al. Nanoparticle-based medicines in clinical cancer therapy. Nano Today 2022;45:101512.

[54] Wan Y, Fu LH, Li C, Lin J, Huang P. Conquering the hypoxia limitation for photodynamic therapy. Adv Mater 2021;33(48):2103978.

[55] Ming L, Cheng K, Chen Y, Yang R, Chen D. Enhancement of tumor lethality of ROS in photodynamic therapy. Cancer Med 2021;10(1):257−68.

[56] Mathews MS, Angell-Petersen E, Sanchez R, Sun CH, Vo V, Hirschberg H, et al. The effects of ultra low fluence rate single and repetitive photodynamic therapy on glioma spheroids. Lasers Surg Med 2009;41(8):578−84.

[57] Liu J, Yin Y, Yang L, Lu B, Yang Z, Wang W, et al. Nucleus-targeted photosensitizer nanoparticles for photothermal and photodynamic therapy of breast carcinoma. Int J Nanomed 2021;16:1473.

[58] Moghassemi S, Dadashzadeh A, Azevedo RB, Feron O, Amorim CA. Photodynamic cancer therapy using liposomes as an advanced vesicular photosensitizer delivery system. J Control Release 2021;339:75−90.

[59] Zhao J, Duan L, Wang A, Fei J, Li J. Insight into the efficiency of oxygen introduced photodynamic therapy (PDT) and deep PDT against cancers with various assembled nanocarriers. Wiley Interdiscip Rev Nanomed Nanobiotechnol 2020;12(1):e1583.

[60] Day RA, Estabrook DA, Logan JK, Sletten EM. Fluorous photosensitizers enhance photodynamic therapy with perfluorocarbon nanoemulsions. Chem Commun 2017;53(97):13043−6.

[61] Charbgoo F, Taghdisi SM, Yazdian-Robati R, Abnous K, Ramezani M, Alibolandi M. Aptamer-incorporated nanoparticle systems for drug delivery. Nanobiotechnology in diagnosis, drug delivery, and treatment. Wiley; 2020. p. 95−112.

[62] You Y, Liang X, Yin T, Chen M, Qiu C, Gao C, et al. Porphyrin-grafted lipid microbubbles for the enhanced efficacy of photodynamic therapy in prostate cancer through ultrasound-controlled in situ accumulation. Theranostics 2018;8(6):1665.

[63] Deng W, Kautzka Z, Chen W, Goldys EM. PLGA nanocomposites loaded with verteporfin and gold nanoparticles for enhanced photodynamic therapy of cancer cells. RSC Adv 2016;6(113): 112393−402.

[64] Obaid G, Bano S, Thomsen H, Callaghan S, Shah N, Swain JW, et al. Remediating desmoplasia with EGFR-targeted photoactivable multi-inhibitor liposomes doubles overall survival in pancreatic cancer. Adv Sci 2022;9(24):2104594.

[65] Bulin A-L, Broekgaarden M, Simeone D, Hasan T. Low dose photodynamic therapy harmonizes with radiation therapy to induce beneficial effects on pancreatic heterocellular spheroids. Oncotarget 2019;10(27):2625.

[66] Zhou L, Zou M, Xu Y, Lin P, Lei C, Xia X. Nano drug delivery system for tumor immunotherapy: next-generation therapeutics. Front Oncol 2022;12:864301.

[67] Yang Y, Chen F, Xu N, Yao Q, Wang R, Xie X, et al. Red-light-triggered self-destructive mesoporous silica nanoparticles for cascade-amplifying chemo-photodynamic therapy favoring antitumor immune responses. Biomaterials 2022;281:121368.

[68] Krysko DV, Garg AD, Kaczmarek A, Krysko O, Agostinis P, Vandenabeele P. Immunogenic cell death and DAMPs in cancer therapy. Nat Rev Cancer 2012;12(12):860−75.

[69] Ghosh S, He X, Huang W-C, Lovell JF. Immune checkpoint blockade enhances chemophototherapy in a syngeneic pancreatic tumor model. APL Bioeng 2022;6(3):036105.

[70] Jang Y, Kim H, Yoon S, Lee H, Hwang J, Jung J, et al. Exosome-based photoacoustic imaging guided photodynamic and immunotherapy for the treatment of pancreatic cancer. J Control Release 2021;330:293–304.

[71] Zhang T, Jiang Z, Chen L, Pan C, Sun S, Liu C, et al. PCN-Fe (III)-PTX nanoparticles for MRI guided high efficiency chemo-photodynamic therapy in pancreatic cancer through alleviating tumor hypoxia. Nano Res 2020;13:273–81.

[72] Cho IK, Shim MK, Um W, Kim J-H, Kim K. Light-activated monomethyl auristatin E prodrug nanoparticles for combinational photo-chemotherapy of pancreatic cancer. Molecules 2022;27(8): 2529.

[73] Karimnia V, Rizvi I, Slack FJ, Celli JP. Photodestruction of stromal fibroblasts enhances tumor response to PDT in 3D pancreatic cancer coculture models. Photochem Photobiol 2021;97(2): 416–26.

[74] Lopes RB, Gangeswaran R, McNeish IA, Wang Y, Lemoine NR. Expression of the IAP protein family is dysregulated in pancreatic cancer cells and is important for resistance to chemotherapy. Int J Cancer 2007;120(11):2344–52.

[75] Zhu L, Lin S, Cui W, Xu Y, Wang L, Wang Z, et al. A nanomedicine enables synergistic chemo/ photodynamic therapy for pancreatic cancer treatment. Biomater Sci 2022;10(13):3624–36.

[76] Li X, Gulati M, Larson AC, Solheim JC, Jain M, Kumar S, et al. Immune checkpoint blockade in pancreatic cancer: trudging through the immune desert. Seminars in cancer biology. Elsevier; 2022.

[77] Xiao Z, Chen Q, Yang Y, Tu S, Wang B, Qiu Y, et al. State of the art advancements in sonodynamic therapy (SDT): Metal-Organic frameworks for SDT. Chem Eng J 2022;449:137889.

[78] Yang H, Liu R, Xu Y, Qian L, Dai Z. Photosensitizer nanoparticles boost photodynamic therapy for pancreatic cancer treatment. Nanomicro Lett 2021;13:1–16.

[79] Hu D, Chen Z, Sheng Z, Gao D, Yan F, Ma T, et al. A catalase-loaded hierarchical zeolite as an implantable nanocapsule for ultrasound-guided oxygen self-sufficient photodynamic therapy against pancreatic cancer. Nanoscale 2018;10(36):17283–92.

[80] Li D, Chen X, Wang D, Wu H, Wen H, Wang L, et al. Synchronously boosting type-I photodynamic and photothermal efficacies via molecular manipulation for pancreatic cancer theranostics in the NIR-II window. Biomaterials 2022;283:121476.

[81] Zhang S, Li Z, Wang Q, Liu Q, Yuan W, Feng W, et al. An NIR-II photothermally triggered "Oxygen Bomb" for hypoxic tumor programmed cascade therapy. Adv Mater 2022;34(29): 2201978.

[82] Bown S, Rogowska A, Whitelaw D, Lees W, Lovat L, Ripley P, et al. Photodynamic therapy for cancer of the pancreas. Gut 2002;50(4):549–57.

[83] Huggett MT, Jermyn M, Gillams A, Illing R, Mosse S, Novelli M, et al. Phase I/II study of verteporfin photodynamic therapy in locally advanced pancreatic cancer. Br J Cancer 2014;110(7): 1698–704.

[84] Wei C, Li X. The role of photoactivated and non-photoactivated verteporfin on tumor. Front Pharmacol 2020;11:557429.

[85] DeWitt JM, Sandrasegaran K, O'Neil B, House MG, Zyromski NJ, Sehdev A, et al. Phase 1 study of EUS-guided photodynamic therapy for locally advanced pancreatic cancer. Gastrointest Endosc 2019;89(2):390–8.

[86] Choi J-H, Oh D, Lee JH, Park J-H, Kim K-P, Lee SS, et al. Initial human experience of endoscopic ultrasound-guided photodynamic therapy with a novel photosensitizer and a flexible laserlight catheter. Endoscopy 2015;47(11):1035–8.

CHAPTER 17

Future prospect of nano-based drug delivery approaches against pancreatic cancer and expected pitfalls of the technology

K.R. Manu[1], Gurleen Kaur[1], Ananya Kar[1], Lopamudra Giri[1], Waleed H. Almalki[2], Neelima Gupta[3], Amirhossein Sahebkar[4], Prashant Kesharwani[5] and Rambabu Dandela[1]

[1]Department of Industrial and Engineering Chemistry, Institute of Chemical Technology, Indian Oil Odisha Campus, Samantapuri, Bhubaneswar, Odisha, India
[2]Department of Pharmacology and Toxicology, Faculty of Pharmacy, Umm Al-Qura University, Makkah, Saudi Arabia
[3]Dr. Harisingh Gour Vishwavidyalaya (A Central University), Sagar, Madhya Pradesh, India
[4]Applied Biomedical Research Center, Mashhad University of Medical Sciences, Mashhad, Iran
[5]Department of Pharmaceutics, School of Pharmaceutical Education and Research, Jamia Hamdard, New Delhi, India

17.1 Introduction

Pancreatic cancer is a devastating ailment that has a low survival rate and limited treatment options. Conventional therapy for pancreatic cancer includes surgery, chemotherapy, and radiation, but these treatments often have limited effectiveness and can cause serious side effects. In prevailing years, owing to its distinctive attributes, such as large surface area, size-tunable qualities, and surface chemistry, nanotechnology has become a viable method for cancer diagnosis, therapy, and management [1–7].

In the following chapter, we intend to provide a comprehensive outlook of pancreatic cancer treatment, focusing on the conventional therapy for pancreatic cancer, the prospects of nanotechnology in the treatment of pancreatic cancer, the various categories of nano-based systems delivering drugs, and the challenges associated with nano-based dosage transport systems for pancreatic cancer therapy.

Conventional therapy for pancreatic cancer includes surgery, chemotherapy, and radiation. Surgery is often the preferred treatment option for patients with localized pancreatic cancer, as it can potentially cure the disease. However, many patients are not eligible for surgery due to the advanced stage of their cancer. Chemotherapy and radiation are often used in combination with surgery or as the crucial treatment route for patients with advanced cancer. While these treatments can help shrink tumors and prolong survival, they often cause serious side effects and do not provide a cure for the disease [8–14].

Recent Advances in Nanocarriers for Pancreatic Cancer Therapy
DOI: https://doi.org/10.1016/B978-0-443-19142-8.00007-3

Nanotechnology has the potential to revolutionize pancreatic cancer treatment by improving drug delivery to tumor cells and reducing the after-effects of conventional therapy. Nanoparticles (NPs) are engineered to focus specific tumor cells and release drugs in a controlled manner, allowing for higher drug concentrations at the tumor site while minimizing toxicity to healthy tissues [15–21].

There are numerous forms of nano-based drug delivery systems that came to be studied for pancreatic cancer therapy. Hydrogel-based drug delivery systems are composed of hydrophilic polymers that can swell and retain water, allowing for sustained drug release [22]. Nanoemulsion-based drug delivery systems are oil-in-water emulsions that can improve drug solubility and stability [23]. Liposome-based drug delivery systems are spherical vesicles composed of phospholipids that can encapsulate drugs and improve their delivery to tumor cells [24]. Polymeric NP-based drug delivery systems are composed of biocompatible and biodegradable polymers that can be engineered to release drugs in a controlled manner [25]. Micelle-based drug delivery systems are composed of amphiphilic molecules that can self-assemble into micellar structures, allowing for improved drug solubility and stability [26].

Metallic NP-based drug delivery systems are composed of metallic particles that can be functionalized to target specific tumor cells [27]. Solid lipid NP (SLN)-based drug delivery systems are composed of lipids that can be engineered to encapsulate drugs and improve their delivery to tumor cells [28]. Quantum dot (QD)-based drug delivery systems are composed of semiconductor nanocrystals that can be engineered to fluoresce and target specific tumor cells [29]. Dendrimer-based drug delivery systems are composed of branched molecules that can be engineered to encapsulate drugs and target specific tumor cells [30]. Carbon nanotube–based dosage transport systems are composed of nanotubes made up of carbon that can be engineered to encapsulate drugs and target specific tumor cells.

While these nano-based drug delivery systems show promise in improving the effectiveness of pancreatic cancer treatment, they also present significant challenges. One of the main challenges is achieving targeted drug delivery to tumor cells while minimizing toxicity to healthy tissues. The size and surface properties of NPs can also affect their pharmacokinetics and toxicity. Additionally, there are regulatory challenges associated with the development and approval of nano-based drug transport techniques for clinical use [31].

We may say that the prospects of nanotechnology in pancreatic cancer treatment are promising, with various types of nano-based methods that have the ability to enhance dose delivery to tumor cells and lower the side effects occurred due to conventional therapy. However, these systems also present significant challenges that need to be addressed before they can be used clinically, and further research is needed to overcome these challenges and bring these innovative therapies to patients with pancreatic cancer.

17.2 Conventional therapy for pancreatic cancer

Conventional therapy for pancreatic cancer involves various treatment options that aim to slow down the growth of cancer cells, reduce symptoms, and improve the patient's quality of life. In this section, we aim to discuss the distinct types of conventional therapy for pancreatic cancer, their effectiveness, and their limitations. The different types of conventional therapies for pancreatic cancer are as follows.

17.2.1 Surgery

Surgical intervention is the elementary treatment option for pancreatic cancer. The aim of the surgery is to eliminate the tumor along with any affected tissues and lymph nodes. There are different surgical procedures depending on the dimensions and site of the tumor [32]. The most common surgical procedures are the Whipple procedure (pancreaticoduodenectomy) and distal pancreatectomy.

A procedure, known as the Whipple procedure, involves the extraction of the head of the pancreas, the duodenum (the first part of the small intestine), the gallbladder, and sometimes part of the stomach. The surgeon then reconstructs the digestive system by attaching the remaining part of the pancreas, the bile duct, and the remaining part of the stomach to the small intestine. This procedure is typically used for tumors that are situated in the head of the pancreas. Distal pancreatectomy involves the amputation of the body and the tail of the pancreas. This procedure is typically used for tumors that are localized in the body or the tail of the pancreas. The spleen may also be removed during this procedure. Surgery is the most effective treatment option for pancreatic cancer, particularly for tumors that are confined to the pancreas. However, surgery is not always possible, mainly if the tumor has expanded to other body parts.

17.2.2 Chemotherapy

Chemotherapy is a systemic therapy that focuses on the usage of drugs to damage the cancer cells. Chemotherapy drugs can be given orally or intravenously. Chemotherapy is usually administered before or after surgery to shrink the size of the tumor or destroy any remaining cells containing cancer.

The most universally used drug for chemotherapy is known as gemcitabine. Other chemotherapy drugs used for pancreatic cancer include FOLFIRINOX (a combination of fluorouracil, leucovorin, irinotecan, and oxaliplatin) and nab-paclitaxel (a protein-bound form of paclitaxel). Chemotherapy can have significant after-effects, which may include vomiting, fatigue, nausea, hair loss, and even a higher risk of infection. However, newer chemotherapy drugs and combinations have been developed that can be more effective and have fewer side effects [33].

17.2.3 Radiation therapy

In this type of therapy, high-energy radiation is used to eliminate cancer cells. It can be used alone or in combination with chemotherapy. Radiation therapy is often used to relieve symptoms such as pain and blockages in the digestive system. The most frequently used type of this therapy is called external beam radiation therapy for the treatment of pancreatic cancer. This involves directing a beam of radiation from outside of the body straight to the tumor. Brachytherapy is a radiation therapy type that comprises placing a small radioactive source inside the body close to the tumor. This concedes for a higher dose of radiation to be delivered directly to the tumor.

Radiation therapy can have significant side effects, including fatigue, nausea, vomiting, diarrhea, and skin irritation. However, newer radiation therapy techniques have been developed that can target the tumor more precisely and reduce side effects [34].

17.2.4 Targeted therapy

Targeted therapy is a type of remedy that focuses on specific molecules or otherwise pathways involved in the growth of cancer cells. It can be used alone or in combination with chemotherapy. Targeted therapy is based on the concept that cancer cells have specific characteristics that can be targeted by drugs, while healthy cells are relatively unaffected. This allows for more targeted treatment with fewer side effects.

One example of targeted therapy for pancreatic cancer is erlotinib, which affects the epidermal growth factor receptor (EGFR), a protein that is frequently overexpressed in the pancreatic cancer cells. Another example is bevacizumab, which targets vascular endothelial growth factor (VEGF), a protein that promotes the development of blood vessels that allocate essential nutrients to cancer cells. Targeted therapy can have significant side effects, including skin rash, diarrhea, nausea, and vomiting. However, because targeted therapy is more selective in its targeting of cancer cells, it generally has fewer side effects than traditional chemotherapy [35].

However, conventional therapy for pancreatic cancer has its limitations. Pancreatic cancer is often diagnosed at a radicle stage, making it challenging to cure. Even with aggressive treatment, the five-year survival rate for pancreatic cancer is less than 10%. Additionally, conventional therapy can have substantial side effects that can affect the patient's quality of life [36]. Future research should focus on developing new treatment options for pancreatic cancer that are more effective and have fewer side effects.

17.3 The prospects of nanotechnology in pancreatic cancer treatment

Nanotechnology is a rapidly growing field that involves the design, manufacture, and use of materials and devices on the nanoscale, typically ranging in size from 1 to 100 nm. This technology has shown great promise in the domain of cancer treatment, predominantly in the treatment of pancreatic cancer. Nanotechnology has emerged as a promising approach for cancer diagnosis, treatment, and management on account of its distinctive properties, including better and more surface area and size-tunable properties, along with surface chemistry [1].

Pancreatic cancer is one of the most deadly forms of cancer, with a survival rate of only 9% over a span of 5 years [37]. This cancer is often diagnosed in its advanced stages, making it difficult to treat using traditional methods such as surgery, chemotherapy, and radiation therapy. However, the unique properties of nanomaterials have allowed researchers to develop innovative approaches for the identification along with the curement of pancreatic cancer.

One of the most promising applications of nanotechnology in pancreatic cancer treatment is delivery of the drug. NPs can improve the pharmacokinetics and pharmacodynamics of drugs by increasing their bioavailability, stability, and retention time in the body. Moreover, NPs can selectively accumulate in tumor tissues due to the enriched permeability and retention effect, which allows for targeted drug delivery and reduced toxicity to normal tissues. Several studies have demonstrated the ability of nanotechnology-based systems for pancreatic cancer treatment, including gemcitabine-loaded liposomes, albumin-bound paclitaxel NPs, and curcumin-loaded dendrimers [38,39].

Development of NPs has been done for the usage in treatment of pancreatic cancer, including gold NPs, liposomes, dendrimers, micelles, metallic, carbon nanotubes (CNTs), polymeric, and QD-based NPs. These NPs can be functionalized with targeting moieties, such as antibodies or peptides, to specifically target cancer cells and minimize damage to normal cells. Additionally, NPs can be loaded with drugs or genes to enhance their efficacy and reduce systemic toxicity [40,41].

Another promising application of nanotechnology in pancreatic cancer treatment is the use of nanosensors for early detection of the disease. These sensors can detect specific biomarkers or changes in the microenvironment of the pancreas, which can indicate the presence of cancer cells. This early detection can lead to earlier treatment, better patient outcomes, and potentially even a cure for the disease [42]. Another potential application of nanotechnology in pancreatic cancer treatment is imaging. NPs can be used as contrast agents for imaging procedures, such as computed tomography (CT), along with positron emission tomography (PET) and also magnetic resonance imaging (MRI), to visualize the tumor and monitor treatment response. NPs can also be functionalized with fluorescent dyes or QDs to enable instantaneous imaging of tumor cells all through the surgery. These techniques can provide high-resolution images of the pancreas and surrounding tissues, allowing clinicians to better assess the extent of cancer and plan more effective treatment strategies [43].

Despite these promising developments, there are still several challenges that need to be overcome before nanotechnology can be extensively used in pancreatic cancer treatment. The biggest challenges are the development of safe and effective nanomaterials.

While many nanomaterials have shown great promise in the laboratory, their safety and efficacy in humans are still largely unknown. Another major challenge is the heterogeneity of pancreatic cancer, which makes it difficult to develop targeted therapies that can effectively treat all subtypes of the disease. There is also a need for improved methods for targeting and delivering nanoscale drug carriers to the pancreas [44,45].

Despite these challenges, the prospects for nanotechnology in pancreatic cancer treatment are very promising. With continued research and development, it is likely that nanotechnology will showcase an increasingly crucial role in the diagnosis and treatment of this deadly disease. By harnessing the unique properties of nanomaterials, researchers can develop innovative approaches to tackle one of the most challenging forms of cancer and ultimately improve patient outcomes and quality of life.

17.4 Applications of various types of nano-based drug delivery systems for pancreatic cancer therapy

The worst overall survival and death rates are associated with pancreatic cancer. Promising methods for the detection and treatment of pancreatic cancer include biological treatments that address the disease at the molecular level. One of the biggest challenges in treating pancreatic cancer is delivering drugs effectively. Pancreatic cancer has a very low overall survival rate due to the considerable resistance to chemotherapy and radiation treatment.

New developments in medication delivery technologies have enormous potential to enhance cancer treatment. Recent preclinical studies have demonstrated the effectiveness of using liposomes, NPs, and nanotubes of carbon to deliver anticancer medications as well as other agents such as small interfering RNA (siRNA), suicide genes, oncolytic viruses, small molecule inhibitors, and antibodies. Although employing ligand or antibody-directed delivery can increase the selectivity and sustainability of the medicine given, this poses a significant challenge. To combat this dreadful illness, innovative, focused, tumor-targeted medication delivery technologies are desperately needed. This study includes crucial details on prospective therapeutic targets for the treatment of pancreatic cancer and covers the state of the art in targeted medication delivery for the disease.

17.4.1 Hydrogel-based drug delivery systems

Hydrogels exist as three-dimensional systems of cross-linked polymers, which expand when exposed to water. Natural as well as synthetic polymers with their various physical elements and physio-chemical properties have been extensively used to prepare better and smarter hydrogels as a distribution center delivery procedure to treat a variety of diseases ever because the initial polymeric hydrogels were introduced by Wichterle and Lim in the late 1950s [46].

Hydrogels have become a benign and efficient depot-based delivery technology in cancer therapy due to their distinct physicochemical features. However, given the small quantity and homogeneity of hydrophobic pharmaceuticals loaded in hydrogel matrices, hydrogels have been restricted to conveying hydrophobic molecules rather than drugs that are weakly soluble in water as a dose delivery mechanism [47−51].

In quite recent investigations, hydrogels have been restricted to the networks made up of tiny micelles, with a mean size of a particle of about 200 nm, hence, increasing drug loading capacity. In composites, hydrogels enclose both the hydrophilic and the hydrophobic chemicals to regionally administer several medications in a specific dose because of their microsphere structure (hydrophobic core-hydrophilic shell) [52].

It is crucial to be able to provide the hydrophobic medications using systems that are hydrogel-based, especially for local chemotherapy [53], as many of the chemotherapeutic drug entrants have low aqueous solubility and have not been able to do the build-up to the necessary concentration range in injectable solutions to demonstrate techniques implemented in preclinical research and clinical trials [54]. Hydrogels can be sourced to improve the solubility in water of pharmaceuticals as well as produce longer drug release, improving the likelihood of intratumoral drug uptake over free medications.

Physical as well as chemical crosslinking techniques can be used to create injectable hydrogels on-site. Hydrogels that have been physically cross-linked have some advantages over those that have been chemically cross-linked because they do not need photo irradiation, liquid hydrocarbons, or crosslinking catalysts [55]. The generation and dissipation of heat during crosslinking, which can have an impact on the cells and medicines that have been integrated as well as the surrounding tissues, are also avoided by physical crosslinking techniques [56]. Moreover, for specific drug delivery applications, injection hydrogels can be focused to be biofunctionalized using different levels that have a resemblance to overly expressed and/or particular tumor cell indicators. With chemotherapeutic drugs, hydrogel formulations offer a potential way to prevent off-target effects [57].

17.4.2 Nanoemulsion-based drug delivery systems

The term "Nanoemulsion" refers to oil-in-water emulsions (represented as (o/w)) having standard droplet diameters between 50 and 1000 nm. Submicron emulsion and micro-emulsion are terminology used interchangeably when referring to droplet sizes that typically range from 100 to 500 nm. By changing the components of the emulsions, it is possible to switch between these three forms [58,59]. Depending on the type of oil used, oil/water nanoemulsions can preclude the hepatic first-pass metabolism, increase the emulsification of ineptly aqueous-soluble drugs by solubilizing all of them into the oil phase, increase the directional property of drug to the lymph, and

Table 17.1 Different types of surfactants used in making nanoemulsions.

Types	Examples
Nonionic surfactants	The Fatty alcohols and acid esters, along with glycerol esters
Anionic-surfactants	Containing carboxylate groups along with Soaps, sulfonates, and ions with a valency of two
Cationic-surfactants	Quaternary ammonium compounds and amines, e.g., cetyl trimethyl ammonium bromide

enable larger-scale production excluding the need for superior energy homogenization while the nanoemulsions protect compounds from intestinal degradation[60]. Due to the incredibly small droplet size category, which comparatively is substantially less than the span of the one to the 1000 m for ordinary emulsions, nanoemulsions have high kinetic stability [23]. They are particularly desirable systems for a variety of applications in the industry because of their increased kinetic stableness and low viscosity, along with optical transparency.

In addition to being compatible with one another and protecting the medicines from getting hydrolyzed and enzymatic degradation, nanoemulsions' ability to dissolve vast quantities of hydrophobics makes them suitable carriers for parenteral delivery [61]. Moreover, for this method of administration, the absence of sedimentation, creaming, or flocculation, as well as the substantial region of surface along with freely available energy, stipulate evident benefits over emulsions with prominent particle sizes. The highly wide interfacial region positively affects the transport and distribution of drugs as well as the ability to target them to certain areas [62]. To stabilize the system, three different types of surfactants are utilized in the creation of nanoemulsions, which are mentioned in Table 17.1.

The hydrophilic (water-attracted entity) head and a hydrophobic (water-repelling entity) tail make up each surfactant molecule's two components. Based on the polar segments found in the entity, surfactants are categorized [63]. In fact, nanoemulsions are erasing barriers to building more specialized and focused drug delivery. As a result, it is emerging as a top formulation choice and has begun a new phase in the area of drug administration.

17.4.3 Liposome- and niosome-based drug delivery systems

Drugs can be stored inside vesicular carriers of colloidal form such as the liposomes or the niosomes, and the makeup of these carriers can alter how quickly drugs are released. These lipid carriers can encapsulate both the hydrophilic pharmaceuticals and the hydrophobic medications.

Liposomes are tiny synthetic spherical vesicles that are between 30 nm and several micrometers in diameter. They include an aqueous core that may accommodate both

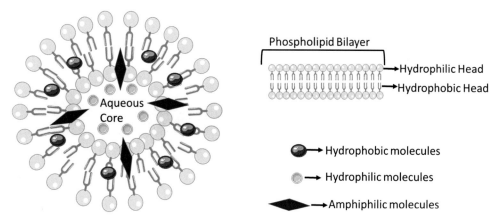

Figure 17.1 Liposome basic components representation.

hydrophobic and hydrophilic medicines and is encased with one or even more concentric lipid bilayers [64–69]. Because liposomes can be biodegraded and contain less toxicity than unrestricted pharmaceuticals, liposomes can be used to encase and enhance the intracellular administration of chemotherapeutic medications [70]. A general structure of liposomes can be represented in Fig. 17.1 [71].

The drug contained within a liposome is shielded from physiologically appearing processes such as enzymatic dilapidation, immunologic and chemical inactivation, and rapid clearance of plasma, which helps enhancing and prolonging the activity of the drug [72]. When paralleled to the free drug structure, the drug's negative side effects are reduced because of the liposome's reduced exposure to healthy tissue [71]. For liposomes to be safe, stable, and effective, the choice of the phospholipids, the head group, and the length of chain, in addition to the ratio of components, are essential factors [73].

Nonionic surfactant vesicles or niosomes are infinitesimal lamellar assemblies created when the cholesterol is combined with a nonionic surfactant of either the alkyl or di-alkyl polyglycerol ether class [74]. Due to intrinsic issues such as poor storage stability, quick leaking of aqueous-soluble pharmaceuticals in the vicinity of components of blood, and low encapsulation effectiveness, liposomes, however, do not demonstrate any notable advancements. Various applications of liposomes in pancreatic cancer can be described in Fig. 17.2 [75].

In comparison to liposomes, the niosomes are more active in an osmotic sense, have chemical stability, and have a prolonged storage time. The functional groups on their hydrophilic segments generate it simple to modify niosomes exteriors, and their nonionic nature results in high biological compatibility and low toxicity [76]. Niosomes are prepared by various methods such as dose delivery and gene therapy vectors, for example, thin-film hydration, ether injection, and micro fluidization [77].

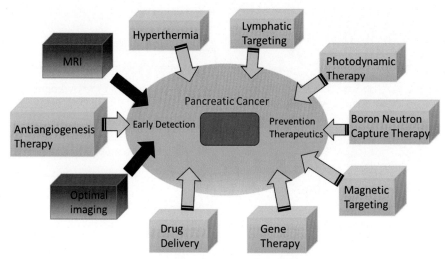

Figure 17.2 Various applications of liposomes in pancreatic cancer.

Recent years have seen an increase in interest in vesicular drug delivery methods including liposomes and niosomes. It is clear that niosomes are favored over liposomes as a means of medication delivery. Niosomes offer a simple, extended, focused, and efficient drug delivery technology with the capacity to load alike hydrophilic and lipophilic medicines [78]. Thus, more investigation and research are required in these areas in order to develop economically viable niosomal preparations.

17.4.4 Polymeric nanoparticle−based drug delivery systems

Polymeric NPs (PNPs) play a significant role in drug delivery because they meet the need for targeted distribution by encasing active ingredients and delivering them to the desired location. PNPs may be composed of synthetic or natural materials and may be biodegradable [79] or nonbiodegradable [80]. PNPs are heavily researched for drug delivery applications due to their decreased toxicity [81−86].

Several techniques have been used to create PNPs [87] depending on the applied objective and nature of medication, which is to be enclosed. These microparticles are widely employed to create nanomedicine by nanoencapsulating several beneficial bioactive chemicals and pharmaceuticals. PNPs that degrade naturally are highly favored because they have potential as a drug deliverance mechanism. These NPs have subcellular size and controlled release properties and are biocompatible with tissue as well as cells [88]. In addition, these nanomedicines can be biodegraded, avoid the reticuloendothelial type of system, are not toxic, nonthrombogenic, nonimmunogenic, noninflammatory, and do not stimulate neutrophils and are stable in blood. They are also applicable to varied molecules, including drugs, proteins, nucleic acids, and peptides [89].

Systems for delivering drugs through nanoparticulate emerge to be a workable and promising methodology for the biopharmaceutical sector. Compared to traditional drug delivery methods, they are better. Several strong medications that are otherwise challenging to administer orally can have their bioavailability, solubility, and permeability increased by them [90].

The frequency of medicine dosages will be decreased and patient compliance will rise with nanoparticulate drug delivery devices. Nanoparticulate systems for drug delivery will soon be able to make use of a wide range of biological pharmaceuticals, most of which have insignificant solubility in an aqueous environment, absorbency, and bioavailability [81]. By ensuring stability and maintaining their structure, NPs help reduce some of these medications' special issues. NPs also provide a controlled release and focused distribution, which makes for creative treatment [91].

17.4.5 Micelle-based drug delivery systems

Amphiphile micellar solutions are an efficient method of delivering medications to their targets. Water-insoluble medicines are easily soluble in the hydrophobic surroundings of the micelle core and loaded for distribution to the necessary sites [92−95].

Owing to their great solubilization ability, increased loading capacity, elevated bloodstream stability, certain therapeutic potential, and longevity, polymeric micelles have exceptional promise. The micelles in polymeric form are regarded as amphiphilic in aqueous systems, with the water-repellent component eliminated [96]. Polymeric micelles' special core-shell structure, whereby the hydrophobic portion creates a place for the encapsulating of these medicines, DNA, or protein through either chemical or physical amalgamating mechanisms, is a main factor why these micelles are used.

The adaptability of the shell or core structure of polymeric micelles is what distinguishes them from other colloidal delivery systems. The polymeric micellar structure's chemical adaptability enables the creation of specialized carriers that can be individually created in consideration of the pathophysiology of the illness, the location of the drug's engagement, and the suggested mode of administration [97].

Polymeric micelles have a variety of uses, but there are still several issues that need to be solved before they may be considered viable drug carriers. They include enhancing medication loading effectiveness even further, stabilizing blood-air injection, and facilitating transport through cell membranes [98]. Polymeric micelles are designed with the goal of creating formulations that, when administered systemically, could reach therapeutic medication levels. The effectiveness of polymeric micelles for drug loading is significantly influenced by the miscibility among pharmaceuticals and polymers [96]. The level of hydrophobic interface among both the drug and the micellar core determines how much of the medication is encapsulated. The findings from molecular empirical data and computer studies both point to a substantial role in polar contacts and hydrogen bonding among the medication entities [99].

In actual situations, it has been observed that the type and number of substituents on the hydrophobic block alter the loading effectiveness of specific medications in polymeric micelles [100]. Chemical conjugation, physical trapping through dialysis or emulsification, or both can be used to encapsulate the insoluble medicines in the micellar core [101].

Engineering the polymeric core of polymer form of micelles to improve the contact of the drug with the micelle core can control the release of drugs from the micelles. Two main processes—micelle dissociation followed by drug separation from monomers and drug-polymer link breaking inside of the micelle and diffusional outflow from the transport system are used to release the pharmaceuticals from the micellar core [102]. Polymeric micelles are among the best alternative carrier of drug-dose in comparison to other techniques [96].

17.4.6 Metallic nanoparticle−based drug delivery systems

Metal NPs can be coupled with antibodies, medicines, and other targeted ligands due to their ability to be synthesized in a variety of sizes, shapes, and surface modifications. This provides a broad spectrum of application possibilities. The form, size, surface area, existence or absence of certain functional groups at the surface, charge, and composition of metal NPs are important factors in determining how poisonous they are.

By leveraging the pathophysiology of the tumor cells, these metallic NPs enable efficient transport of anticancer medications into the tumors, changing the therapeutic results [103]. The capability of metallic NPs to dispense anticancer medicines precisely to the tumor location, avoiding off-target damage, makes them particularly effective for cancer therapy using targeting ligands [104]. The carrier system must not be eradicated from the body for an efficient targeted system for drug delivery in hopes of developing a superior pharmacokinetic property that will allow the anticancer agent to confer at the precise target spot [105].

Ligand-mediated targeting or alternating known as active-targeting is centered on specific molecular interfaces such as receptor–ligand-based associations and charge-based associations with substrate molecules [106]. It involves affinity-based detection and retention and aids uptake by the specified cells. The proteins, lipids, or surface molecules with high expression in tumor cells can all be considered target substrates [107]. For effective targeting of the tumor contained to the surface of the tumor cells, the surface is altered by chemically connecting the targeting ligands upon that interface of the metallic NPs [106].

Metallic NPs are crucial for the improvement of drug delivery in the remedy of cancer as well as for therapeutic, imaging, and diagnostic purposes. The development in developing metallic NPs is expanding at this time, which is causing more studies to be done on cancer, imaging, diagnosis, and therapies for anticancer treatment.

Target-specific NPs are being researched in order to reduce or eliminate the issues that are mostly experienced during the traditional therapy's medication delivery to the tumor location [108].

17.4.7 Solid lipid nanoparticle—based drug delivery systems

Solid lipid nanoparticles (SLNs) are a class of nanotechnology-based dosage transport system that has appealed considerable awareness in recent years. These particles are composed of a solid lipid core that is stabilized by surfactants, and they offer several advantages over traditional drug delivery systems. These advantages include the ability to encapsulate both hydrophilic and lipophilic drugs, high stability, biocompatibility, and controlled release of drugs. The usage of SLNs for the delivery of drugs has been investigated for various therapeutic applications, including cancer therapy. In particular, pancreatic cancer is a deadly illness that has inadequate options for treatment, and the usage of nanotechnology-based systems, including SLNs, has shown promise for improving the effectiveness of cancer treatment while diminishing the side effects [109].

SLNs-based drug delivery systems have been widely investigated for their potential applications in pancreatic cancer treatment. Several analyses have reported the development and evaluation of SLNs-based dosage transport for treatment. For example, SLNs loaded with the anticancer drug gemcitabine have been shown to enhance the anticancer activity of the drug both in vitro and in vivo[110,111].

An analysis reported the development of SLNs loaded with curcumin, a naturally occurring anticancer agent. The authors demonstrated that curcumin-loaded SLNs inhibited both the proliferation as well as migration of pancreatic cancer cells in vitro. Another study reported the development of SLNs loaded with docetaxel, a chemotherapy drug. The authors found that docetaxel-loaded SLNs enhanced the cytotoxicity of the drug against pancreatic cancer cells in vitro[112].

Apart from their usage as drug delivery systems, SLNs have also been utilized as imaging agents for pancreatic cancer. For example, SLNs loaded with fluorescent dyes can be used for optical imaging of pancreatic cancer cells [113].

Overall, SLNs-based drug delivery systems have a great future for pancreatic cancer therapy. Further research may be required to optimize the design and formulation of SLNs for specific drugs and to evaluate their safety and efficacy in clinical trials.

17.4.8 Quantum dot—based drug delivery systems

Quantum dots (QDs) are nanoscale semiconducting materials that have distinctive optical as well as electronic properties. These are strong candidates for several biomedical uses, such as medication delivery, because of these characteristics. QDs can be conjugated with therapeutic agents and selectively delivered to target sites, allowing for more precise drug delivery and reduced off-target effects. In recent years, QD-based drug delivery systems have received much attention for their potential applications in cancer therapy [114].

One such type of QD-based system for drug delivery for pancreatic cancer therapy involves the use of targeted NPs. These NPs are functionalized with ligands that can selectively bind to receptors overexpressed on pancreatic cancer cells, enabling targeted delivery of therapeutic agents. For example, QDs conjugated with gemcitabine, a common chemotherapy drug used in pancreatic cancer treatment, have been revealed to selectively aim at pancreatic cancer cells both in vitro as well as in vivo, leading to enhanced drug efficacy and reduced toxicity compared to free gemcitabine [115].

Another type of QD-based system for pancreatic cancer therapy involves the use of pH-responsive NPs. These NPs are designed to release therapeutic agents in response to the acidic environment of the tumor microenvironment. For example, QDs functionalized with pH-responsive PNPs have been shown to selectively release therapeutic agents in the acidic tumor microenvironment, leading to improved drug efficacy and reduced toxicity [116,117].

Furthermore, QDs have also been explored as imaging agents for pancreatic cancer diagnosis and treatment monitoring. QDs have unique optical properties that allow for high-resolution imaging of tumors in vivo. For example, QDs conjugated with antibodies specific to pancreatic cancer biomarkers have been used for the targeted imaging of pancreatic cancer cells both in vitro as well as in vivo [118,119].

In conclusion, QD-based drug delivery systems have a great ability for improving the usefulness and reducing the toxicity of pancreatic cancer therapy. Further research may be needed to optimize the design and efficacy of these systems for clinical translation.

17.4.9 Dendrimer-based drug delivery systems

Dendrimers are highly branched and nanoscale polymers with a defined structure, size, and surface chemistry, making them attractive as drug delivery vehicles. These molecules possess numerous surface functional groups, which can be modified to attach various therapeutic agents such as small molecules, peptides, and nucleic acids. The properties of dendrimers, such as high solubility, biocompatibility, low toxicity, and their ability to encapsulate and protect drug molecules, make them an ideal candidate for drug delivery systems [16,120−126].

Dendrimers have been investigated as a promising treatment for pancreatic cancer therapy due to their ability to overcome the limitations of conventional chemotherapy. Various dendrimer-based drug delivery systems, such as polyamidoamine (PAMAM), polyethyleneimine (PEI), and polypropylene imine (PPI) dendrimers, have been extensively studied for pancreatic cancer therapy [127−129].

PAMAM dendrimers have been used to compress or condense anticancer drugs such as gemcitabine and 5-fluorouracil (5-FU) to enhance their therapeutic efficiency. In vitro and in vivo experiments using pancreatic cancer cells revealed considerable tumor growth inhibition by the PAMAM dendrimer-gemcitabine complex. Similarly, PAMAM dendrimers loaded with 5-FU have shown enhanced antitumor activity and reduced toxicity compared to the free drug in preclinical studies. PEI dendrimers have also been investigated as a delivery system for pancreatic cancer therapy. PEI dendrimers loaded with siRNA targeting the KRAS oncogene have shown significant tumor growth inhibition and prolonged survival in pancreatic cancer mouse models. PPI dendrimers have been used to deliver chemotherapeutic drugs such as doxorubicin and paclitaxel. The PPI dendrimer-doxorubicin complex has shown improved therapeutic efficacy and lessened toxicity parallel to the unrestricted drug in preclinical studies. Similarly, PPI dendrimers loaded with paclitaxel have shown enhanced antitumor activity and reduced toxicity in pancreatic cancer cells [130].

Dendrimer-based transport systems have shown great potential for pancreatic cancer therapy due to their ability to overcome the limitations of conventional chemotherapy. The various dendrimer-based drug delivery systems such as PAMAM, PEI, and PPI dendrimers have shown enriched therapeutic efficacy and diminished toxicity compared to the free drug in preclinical studies. However, additional studies could be essential to fully evaluate the potential of dendrimer-based drug delivery systems for pancreatic cancer therapy.

17.4.10 Carbon nanotube—based drug delivery systems

CNTs are cylindrical structures composed of graphene sheets rolled into a tube-like shape. They are one of the most widely studied and versatile types of nanomaterials due to their distinctive mechanical, electrical, and thermal properties. CNTs can be single-walled or multiwalled, with different diameters and lengths, and can exhibit properties such as high strength, flexibility, and electrical conductivity. These properties make CNTs useful for a wide array of applications, comprising electronics, energy storage, and drug delivery. However, the likely toxicity of CNTs is a concern, and ongoing research is focused on understanding their environmental and health impacts [131].

They have gained significant awareness in the field of drug delivery. This is because of their small size and high surface area. CNTs have the potential to serve as effective drug carriers, allowing for specifically targeted and controlled drug delivery to specific cells or tissues. In recent years, research has focused on developing CNT-based transport systems for numerous diseases, also comprising cancer [132]. Several types of CNT-based drug delivery systems have been developed for pancreatic cancer therapy, including:

- Single-walled carbon nanotubes (SWCNTs): These are one-dimensional structures that have been shown to effectively deliver chemotherapeutic drugs to pancreatic cancer cells in vitro. SWCNTs can be functionalized by targeting moieties such as antibodies or peptides to improve their specificity and selectivity for cancer cells [133].

- Multiwalled carbon nanotubes (MWCNTs): These are cylindrical structures composed of several layers of graphene sheets. MWCNTs have been shown to have superior drug loading capacity compared to SWCNTs, making them ideal for delivering a higher concentration of therapeutic agents to cancer cells. Additionally, MWCNTs can be functionalized with targeting moieties and imaging agents for improved cancer cell detection and treatment monitoring [134].

- Carbon nanotube—based nanocomposites: These are hybrid structures that combine CNTs with other materials such as polymers or metals. These nanocomposites can be designed to have exceptional properties as improved biological compatibility and increased drug loading capacity. For example, the latest study testified the development of a CNT-polymer nanocomposite that improved the solubility and bioavailability of the chemotherapeutic drug gemcitabine, resulting in enhanced pancreatic cancer cell death in vitro [135].

- Carbon nanotube—based gene delivery systems: In addition to delivering chemotherapeutic drugs, CNTs can also be used as carriers for gene therapy. It has been demonstrated that CNTs effectively transfer siRNA and plasmid DNA to pancreatic cancer cells, inhibiting the growth of cancer cells and silencing their genes [136].

Overall, CNT-based transport systems have shown great potential for refining pancreatic cancer therapy. However, further studies are needed to optimize their design, improve their safety profile, and evaluate their efficacy in vivo. With continued research and development, CNT-based drug delivery systems may have the ability to revolutionize cancer treatment and improve patient outcomes.

17.5 Challenges of nano-based drug delivery system for pancreatic cancer therapy

Pancreatic cancer is a deadly and aggressive cancer that is difficult to treat due to its late diagnosis, rapid progression, and resistance to chemotherapy. Traditional chemotherapy has shown limited efficacy, and newer targeted therapies have not shown significant improvements in survival rates. Therefore, there is a critical need for innovative and effective therapies for pancreatic cancer. Nano-based drug delivery systems have developed as a favorable method for targeted drug delivery, enhanced bioavailability, and reduced toxicity. However, several challenges need to be addressed before their clinical translation [137].

One of the main challenges in the improvement of nano-based drug delivery systems for pancreatic cancer therapy is the complexity of the tumor microenvironment. The pancreatic tumor is characterized by a dense stromal matrix that creates significant barriers to drug delivery. The stroma consists of an extracellular matrix (ECM), fibroblasts, and immune cell components that form a physical and chemical barrier around the tumor cells. The dense stroma limits the penetration of chemotherapy drugs, antibodies, and NPs, thereby reducing their therapeutic efficacy. Moreover, the stroma creates a hypoxic and acidic environment that can affect drug stability and metabolism. Therefore, designing NPs that can penetrate the stromal barrier, reduce stromal content, and improve drug stability in the harsh tumor microenvironment is crucial for effective drug delivery [138].

Another challenge is the lack of specific biomarkers for pancreatic cancer. Targeted drug delivery relies on the identification of specific biomarkers present in the tumor cells. However, pancreatic cancer lacks specific biomarkers that can be used for targeted drug delivery. Therefore, developing new diagnostic and prognostic biomarkers for pancreatic cancer is crucial for the successful implementation of nano-based drug delivery systems. Recent advances in genomics and proteomics have enabled the identification of novel biomarkers that can be used for targeted drug delivery. For example, genetic mutations such as KRAS and TP53 are frequently observed in pancreatic cancer and can serve as potential targets for drug delivery [139].

Furthermore, there are concerns about the toxicity and biocompatibility of NPs. While NPs have shown promising results in preclinical studies, their toxicity and biocompatibility need to be thoroughly evaluated before clinical translation. The toxicity of NPs can be influenced by their size, shape, and surface charge. For instance, smaller NPs can penetrate deeper into tissues, but they can also induce greater toxicity than larger particles. Moreover, NPs can interact with various biological molecules, such as proteins and enzymes, which can affect their pharmacokinetics and biodistribution. Therefore, NPs must be carefully designed to minimize toxicity and maximize biocompatibility [140].

Another challenge is the potential for drug resistance. Pancreatic cancer cells can develop resistance to chemotherapy, which limits the effectiveness of treatment. The mechanisms of drug resistance in pancreatic cancer are complex and multifactorial. They can include alterations in drug metabolism, increased efflux of drugs, activation of pro-survival signaling pathways, and genetic mutations. Nano-based drug delivery systems can potentially overcome this challenge by delivering multiple drugs or combining chemotherapy with other therapies [141]. For instance, combining chemotherapy with immunotherapy can enhance the immune response against the tumor and overcome drug resistance. However, further research is needed to develop effective combination therapies that can disable drug resistance. Moreover, the heterogeneity of pancreatic cancer poses a significant challenge to drug delivery. Pancreatic cancer is characterized by significant intratumoral and intertumoral heterogeneity, which can affect drug efficacy and responsiveness. Intratumoral heterogeneity refers to the presence of different cell types within the tumor, such as cancer stem cells, immune cells, and fibroblasts, which can affect drug response. Intertumoral heterogeneity refers to the genetic and phenotypic differences between different tumors, which can affect drug sensitivity and resistance. Therefore, NPs that can target different cell types within the tumor and can overcome heterogeneity should be designed [142].

17.6 Conclusion and future perspective

Traditional treatments, such as surgery, radiotherapy, and chemotherapy, are still found to be sufficient, but due to particular adverse effects on healthy parts of the body, extra effort to improve cancer treatment methods is urgently needed. Nanocarrier-based methods have a significant implementation in biomedical uses, especially in chemotherapeutic drug distribution. Various changes are combined to surmount the constraints of traditional chemotherapy and decrease toxicity in various nanocarriers. Often these NPs exhibit preferred characteristics in regard to stability as well as toxicity in vitro, although in vivo toxicity and safety patterns may vary. As a result, comprehensive safety/toxicity experiments might also be conducted following in vivo applications. Novel treatments are indeed anticipated to attack both the tumor microenvironment and cancer cells, as well as impair cancerous cell communication systems in the stroma. Addressing signaling pathways that are prominent in both the stroma and the tumor sections could be beneficial. In conclusion, nano-based drug delivery systems hold great promise for pancreatic cancer therapy. However, several challenges need to be addressed before their clinical translation, including the complexity of the tumor microenvironment, the lack of specific biomarkers, toxicity and biocompatibility concerns, and drug resistance. Addressing these challenges will require collaboration among multidisciplinary teams of scientists, clinicians, and engineers to develop effective and safe nano-based drug delivery systems for pancreatic cancer therapy.

Acknowledgements

The authors acknowledge ICT-IOC, Bhubaneswar for providing necessary support. Rambabu Dandela thanks DST-SERB for Ramanujan fellowship (SB/S2/RJN-075/2016), Core research grant (CRG/2018/000782), and ICT-IOC startup grant.

References

[1] Manzur A, Oluwasanmi A, Moss D, Curtis A, Hoskins C. Nanotechnologies in pancreatic cancer therapy. Pharmaceutics 2017;9(4):39.
[2] Kesharwani P, Xie L, Mao G, Padhye S, Iyer AK. Hyaluronic acid-conjugated polyamidoamine dendrimers for targeted delivery of 3,4-difluorobenzylidene curcumin to CD44 overexpressing pancreatic cancer cells. Colloids Surf B Biointerfaces, 2015;136:413−23.
[3] Kesharwani P, Banerjee S, Padhye S, Sarkar FH, Iyer AK. Hyaluronic acid engineered nanomicelles loaded with 3,4-difluorobenzylidene curcumin for targeted killing of CD44 + stem-like pancreatic cancer cells. Biomacromolecules 2015;16(9):3042−53.

[4] Kesharwani P, Banerjee S, Padhye S, Sarkar FH, Iyer AK. Parenterally administrable nano-micelles of 3,4-difluorobenzylidene curcumin for treating pancreatic cancer. Colloids Surf B Biointerfaces 2015;132:138−45.

[5] Liu Z, Parveen N, Rehman U, Aziz A, Sheikh A, Abourehab MAS, et al. Unravelling the enigma of siRNA and aptamer mediated therapies against pancreatic cancer. Mol Cancer 2023; 22(1):1−22.

[6] Rehman U, Abourehab MAS, Alexander A, Kesharwani P. Polymeric micelles assisted combinatorial therapy: is it new hope for pancreatic cancer? Eur Polym J 2023;184:111784.

[7] Md S, Alhakamy NA, Aldawsari HM, Ahmad J, Alharbi WS, Asfour HZ. Resveratrol loaded self-nanoemulsifying drug delivery system (SNEDDS) for pancreatic cancer: formulation design, optimization and in vitro evaluation. J Drug Deliv Sci Technol 2021;64:102555.

[8] Ansari D, Gustafsson A, Andersson R. Update on the management of pancreatic cancer: surgery is not enough. World J Gastroenterol 2015;21(11):3157−65.

[9] Choudhury H, Gorain B, Pandey M, Kumbhar SA, Tekade RK, Iyer AK, et al. Recent advances in TPGS-based nanoparticles of docetaxel for improved chemotherapy. Int J Pharm 2017;529 (1−2):506−22.

[10] Choudhury H, Pandey M, Yin TH, Kaur T, Jia GW, Tan SQL, et al. Rising horizon in circumventing multidrug resistance in chemotherapy with nanotechnology. Mater Sci Eng C 2019; 101:596−613.

[11] Tekade RK, Tekade M, Kesharwani P, D'Emanuele A. RNAi-combined nano-chemotherapeutics to tackle resistant tumors. Drug Discov Today 2016;21:1761−74.

[12] Gorain B, Choudhury H, Nair AB, Dubey SK, Kesharwani P. Theranostic application of nanoemulsions in chemotherapy. Drug Discov Today 2020;25(7):1174−88.

[13] Pandey M, Choudhury H, Yeun OC, Yin HM, Lynn TW, Tine CLY, et al. Perspectives of nanoemulsion strategies in the improvement of oral, parenteral and transdermal chemotherapy. Curr Pharm Biotechnol 2018;19(4):276−92.

[14] Chadar R, Afzal O, Alqahtani SM, Kesharwani P. Carbon nanotubes as an emerging nanocarrier for the delivery of doxorubicin for improved chemotherapy. Colloids Surf B Biointerfaces 2021;208:112044.

[15] Yao Y, Zhou Y, Liu L, Xu Y, Chen Q, Wang Y, et al. Nanoparticle-based drug delivery in cancer therapy and its role in overcoming drug resistance. Front Mol Biosci 2020;7:193.

[16] Gorain B, Choudhury H, Pandey M, Nair AB, Iqbal Mohd Amin MC, Molugulu N, et al. Dendrimer-based nanocarriers in lung cancer therapy. Nanotechnology-based targeted drug delivery systems for lung cancer. Elsevier; 2019. p. 161−92.

[17] Gorain B, Choudhury H, Pandey M, Amin MCIM, Singh B, Gupta U, et al. Dendrimers as effective carriers for the treatment of brain tumor. Nanotechnology-based targeted drug delivery systems for brain tumors. Elsevier; 2018. p. 267−305.

[18] Singh AR, Desu PK, Nakkala RK, Kondi V, Devi S, Alam MS, et al. Nanotechnology-based approaches applied to nutraceuticals. Drug Deliv Transl Res 2021;12:485−99.

[19] Meher JG, Chaurasia M, Singh A, Chourasia MK. Carbon nanotubes (CNTs): a novel drug delivery tool in brain tumor treatment. Nanotechnology-based targeted drug delivery systems for lung cancer. Elsevier; 2018. p. 375−96.

[20] Kumari S, Choudhary PK, Shukla R, Sahebkar A, Kesharwani P. Recent advances in nanotechnology based combination drug therapy for skin cancer. J Biomater Sci Polym Ed 2022;33:1435−68.

[21] Rahiman N, Markina YV, Kesharwani P, Johnston TP, Sahebkar A. Curcumin-based nanotechnology approaches and therapeutics in restoration of autoimmune diseases. J Control Release 2022; 348:264−86.

[22] Li J, Mooney DJ. Designing hydrogels for controlled drug delivery. Nat Rev Mater 2016; 1(12):1−17.

[23] Jaiswal M, Dudhe R, Sharma PK. Nanoemulsion: an advanced mode of drug delivery system. 3 Biotech 2015;5(2):123−7.

[24] Olusanya TOB, Ahmad RRH, Ibegbu DM, Smith JR, Elkordy AA. Liposomal drug delivery systems and anticancer drugs. Molecules 2018;23(4):907.

[25] Begines B, Ortiz T, Pérez-Aranda M, Martínez G, Merinero M, Argüelles-Arias F, et al. Polymeric nanoparticles for drug delivery: recent developments and future prospects. Nanomaterials 2020; 10(7):1−41.

[26] Trivedi R, Kompella UB. Nanomicellar formulations for sustained drug delivery: strategies and underlying principles. Nanomedicine 2010;5(3):485−505.

[27] Chandrakala V, Aruna V, Angajala G. Review on metal nanoparticles as nanocarriers: current challenges and perspectives in drug delivery systems. Emergent Mater 2022;5(6):1593−615.

[28] Scioli Montoto S, Muraca G, Ruiz ME. Solid lipid nanoparticles for drug delivery: pharmacological and biopharmaceutical aspects. Front Mol Biosci 2020;7:587997.

[29] Devi S, Kumar M, Tiwari A, Tiwari V, Kaushik D, Verma R, et al. Quantum dots: an emerging approach for cancer therapy. Front Mater 2022;8(January):1−18.

[30] Wang J, Li B, Qiu L, Qiao X, Yang H. Dendrimer-based drug delivery systems: history, challenges, and latest developments. J Biol Eng 2022;16(1):1−12.

[31] Patra JK, Das G, Fraceto LF, Campos EVR, Rodriguez-Torres MDP, Acosta-Torres LS, et al. Nano based drug delivery systems: recent developments and future prospects. J Nanobiotechnol. 2018;16(1):71.

[32] Birk D, Beger HG. Lymph-node dissection in pancreatic cancer - What are the facts? Langenbeck Arch Surg 1999;384(2):158−66.

[33] Chun JW, Lee SH, Kim JS, Park N, Huh G, Cho IR, et al. Comparison between FOLFIRINOX and gemcitabine plus nab-paclitaxel including sequential treatment for metastatic pancreatic cancer: a propensity score matching approach. BMC Cancer 2021;21(1):1−11.

[34] Majeed H, Gupta V. Adverse effects of radiation therapy. StatPearls; 2022.

[35] Faller BA, Burtness B. Treatment of pancreatic cancer with epidermal growth factor receptor-targeted therapy. Biol Targets Ther 2009;3:419−28.

[36] McGuigan A, Kelly P, Turkington RC, Jones C, Coleman HG, McCain RS. Pancreatic cancer: a review of clinical diagnosis, epidemiology, treatment and outcomes. World J Gastroenterol 2018; 24(43):4846−61.

[37] Rawla P, Sunkara T, Gaduputi V. Epidemiology of pancreatic cancer: global trends, etiology and risk factors. World J Oncol 2019;10(1):10.

[38] Nanomedicine N, Ma M. Paclitaxel nano-delivery systems: a comprehensive review. J Nanomed Nanotechol 2013;4(2):164.

[39] Samanta K, Setua S, Kumari S, Jaggi M, Yallapu MM, Chauhan SC. Gemcitabine combination nano therapies for pancreatic cancer. Pharmaceutics 2019;11(11):1−25.

[40] Mody N, Tekade RK, Mehra NK, Chopdey P, Jain NK. Dendrimer, liposomes, carbon nanotubes and PLGA nanoparticles: one platform assessment of drug delivery potential. AAPS PharmSciTech 2014;15(2):388−99.

[41] Kenchegowda M, Rahamathulla M, Hani U, Begum MY, Guruswamy S, Osmani RAM, et al. Smart nanocarriers as an emerging platform for cancer therapy: a review. Molecules 2021;27(1):146.

[42] Wang J, He Z-W, Jiang J-X. Nanomaterials: applications in the diagnosis and treatment of pancreatic cancer. World J Gastrointest Pharmacol Ther 2020;11(1):1.

[43] Luo D, Wang X, Burda C, Basilion JP. Recent development of gold nanoparticles as contrast agents for cancer diagnosis. Cancers (Basel) 2021;13(8):1825.

[44] Leroux C, Konstantinidou G. Targeted therapies for pancreatic cancer: overview of current treatments and new opportunities for personalized oncology. Cancers (Basel) 2021;13(4):1−28.

[45] Su H, Wang Y, Gu Y, Bowman L, Zhao J, Ding M. Potential applications and human biosafety of nanomaterials used in nanomedicine. J Appl Toxicol 2018;38(1):3−24.

[46] Kopeček J. Hydrogels: from soft contact lenses and implants to self-assembled nanomaterials. J Polym Sci Part A Polym Chem 2009;47(22):5929−46.

[47] Sim~oes S, Figueiras A, Veiga F. Modular hydrogels for drug delivery. J Biomater Nanobiotechnol 2012;2012(2):185−99.

[48] Srivastava S, Mahor A, Singh G, Bansal K, Singh PP, Gupta R, et al. Formulation development, in vitro and in vivo evaluation of topical hydrogel formulation of econazole nitrate-loaded β-cyclodextrin nanosponges. J Pharm Sci 2021;110(11):3702−14.

[49] Gupta P, Sheikh A, Abourehab MAS, Kesharwani P. Amelioration of full-thickness wound using hesperidin loaded dendrimer-based hydrogel bandages. Biosensors 2022;12(7):462.

[50] Kesharwani P, Fatima M, Singh V, Sheikh A, Almalki WH, Gajbhiye V, et al. Itraconazole and difluorinated-curcumin containing chitosan nanoparticle loaded hydrogel for amelioration of onychomycosis. Biomimetics 2022;7(4):206.

[51] Alamdari SG, Alibakhshi A, de la Guardia M, Baradaran B, Mohammadzadeh R, Amini M, et al. Conductive and semiconductive nanocomposite-based hydrogels for cardiac tissue engineering. Adv Healthc Mater 2022;11(18):2200526.

[52] McKenzie M, Betts D, Suh A, Bui K, Kim LD, Cho H. Hydrogel-based drug delivery systems for poorly water-soluble drugs. Mol. 2015;20(11):20397–408.

[53] Cho H, Kwon GS. Thermosensitive poly-(d,l-lactide-co-glycolide)-block-poly(ethylene glycol)-block-poly-(d,l-lactide-co-glycolide) hydrogels for multi-drug delivery. J Drug Target 2014;22(7):669–77.

[54] Lipinski CA. Drug-like properties and the causes of poor solubility and poor permeability. J Pharmacol Toxicol Methods 2000;44(1):235–49.

[55] Nguyen MK, Lee DS. Injectable biodegradable hydrogels. Macromol Biosci 2010;10(6):563–79.

[56] Vashist A, Vashist A, Gupta YK, Ahmad S. Recent advances in hydrogel based drug delivery systems for the human body. J Mater Chem B 2013;2(2):147–66.

[57] Norouzi M, Nazari B, Miller DW. Injectable hydrogel-based drug delivery systems for local cancer therapy. Drug Discov Today 2016;21(11):1835–49.

[58] Bhatt P, Madhav S. A detailed review on nanoemulsion drug delivery system. IJPSR 2011;2(10):2482–9.

[59] Choudhury H, Zakaria NFB, Tilang PAB, Tzeyung AS, Pandey M, Chatterjee B, et al. Formulation development and evaluation of rotigotine mucoadhesive nanoemulsion for intranasal delivery. J Drug Deliv Sci Technol 2019;54:101301.

[60] Rajpoot P, Pathak K, Bali V. Therapeutic applications of nanoemulsion based drug delivery systems: a review of patents in last two decades. Recent Pat Drug Deliv Formul 2011;5(2):163–72.

[61] Lovelyn C, Attama AA. Current state of nanoemulsions in drug delivery. J Biomater Nanobiotechnol 2011;02(05):626–39.

[62] Anton N, Vandamme TF. The universality of low-energy nano-emulsification. Int J Pharm 2009;377(1–2):142–7.

[63] Sutradhar KB, Amin L. Nanoemulsions: increasing possibilities in drug delivery. Eur J Nanomed 2013;5(2):97–110.

[64] Kesharwani P, Md S, Alhakamy NA, Hosny KM, Haque A. QbD enabled azacitidine loaded liposomal nanoformulation and its in vitro evaluation. Polymers (Basel) 2021;13(2):250.

[65] Sheikh A, Alhakamy NA, Md S, Kesharwani P. Recent progress of rgd modified liposomes as multistage rocket against cancer. Front Pharmacol 2022;12:4024.

[66] Gorain B, Al-Dhubiab BE, Nair A, Kesharwani P, Pandey M, Choudhury H. Multivesicular liposome: a lipid-based drug delivery system for efficient drug delivery. Curr Pharm Des 2021;27:4404–15.

[67] Parveen N, Abourehab MAS, Shukla R, Thanikachalam PV, Jain GK, Kesharwani P. Immunoliposomes as an emerging nanocarrier for breast cancer therapy. Eur Polym J 2023;184:111781.

[68] Mohammadi G, Korani M, Nemati H, Nikpoor AR, Rashidi K, Varmira K, et al. Crocin-loaded nanoliposomes: preparation, characterization, and evaluation of anti-inflammatory effects in an experimental model of adjuvant-induced arthritis. J Drug Deliv Sci Technol 2022;74:103618.

[69] Hatamipour M, Hadizadeh F, Jaafari MR, Khashyarmanesh Z, Kesharwani P, McCloskey AP, et al. Formulation development and in vitro–in vivo anticancer potential of novel nanoliposomal fluorinated curcuminoids. Process Biochem 2022;122:250–7.

[70] Allahou L, Madani S, Seifalian A. Investigating the application of liposomes as drug delivery systems for the diagnosis and treatment of cancer. Int J Biomater 2021;2021:1–16.

[71] Guimarães D, Cavaco-Paulo A, Nogueira E. Design of liposomes as drug delivery system for therapeutic applications. Int J Pharm 2021;601(February):120571.

[72] Bozzuto G, Molinari A. Liposomes as nanomedical devices. Int J Nanomed 2015;10:975–99.

[73] Kapoor M, Lee SL, Tyner KM. Liposomal drug product development and quality: current us experience and perspective. AAPS J 2017;19(3):632–41.

[74] Alam G, Bali S, Kumar Verma N, Rai AK, Singh AP. Niosomes: an approach to current drug delivery - A review. Int J Adv Pharm 2017;06(02):6.

[75] Yang F, Jin C, Jiang Y, Li J, Di Y, Ni Q, et al. Liposome based delivery systems in pancreatic cancer treatment: from bench to bedside. Cancer Treat Rev 2011;37(8):633−42.

[76] Pardakhty A, Moazeni E. Nano-niosomes in drug, vaccine and gene delivery : a rapid overview. Nanomed J 2013;1(1):1−12.

[77] Baillie AJ, Florence AT, Hume LR, Muirhead GT, Rogerson A. The preparation and properties of niosomes—non-ionic surfactant vesicles. J Pharm Pharmacol 1985;37(12):863−8.

[78] Moghassemi S, Hadjizadeh A. Nano-niosomes as nanoscale drug delivery systems: an illustrated review. J Control Release 2014;185:22−36.

[79] Zhang Z, Ortiz O, Goyal R, Kohn J. Biodegradable polymers. Handbook of polymer applications in medicine and medical devices. William Andrew; 2014. p. 303−35.

[80] Steinbüchel A. Non-biodegradable biopolymers from renewable resources: perspectives and impacts. Curr Opin Biotechnol 2005;16(6):607−13.

[81] Kumari A, Yadav SK, Yadav SC. Biodegradable polymeric nanoparticles based drug delivery systems. Colloids Surf B Biointerfaces 2010;75(1):1−18.

[82] Amjad MW, Kesharwani P, Mohd Amin MCI, Iyer AK. Recent advances in the design, development, and targeting mechanisms of polymeric micelles for delivery of siRNA in cancer therapy. Prog Polym Sci 2017;64:154−81.

[83] Luong D, Kesharwani P, Alsaab HO, Sau S, Padhye S, Sarkar FH, et al. Folic acid conjugated polymeric micelles loaded with a curcumin difluorinated analog for targeting cervical and ovarian cancers. Colloids Surf B Biointerfaces 2017;157:490−502.

[84] Choudhury H, Gorain B, Pandey M, Khurana RK, Kesharwani P. Strategizing biodegradable polymeric nanoparticles to cross the biological barriers for cancer targeting. Int J Pharm 2019; 565:509−22.

[85] Singh V, Sahebkar A, Kesharwani P. Poly (propylene imine) dendrimer as an emerging polymeric nanocarrier for anticancer drug and gene delivery. Eur Polym J 2021;158:110683.

[86] Shukla R, Handa M, Lokesh SB, Ruwali M, Kohli K, Kesharwani P. Conclusion and future prospective of polymeric nanoparticles for cancer therapy. Polymeric nanoparticles as a promising tool for anti-cancer therapeutics. Elsevier; 2019. p. 389−408.

[87] Pinto Reis C, Neufeld RJ, Ribeiro AJ, Veiga F. Nanoencapsulation I. Methods for preparation of drug-loaded polymeric nanoparticles. Nanomed Nanotechnol. Biol Med 2006;2(1):8−21.

[88] Panyam J, Labhasetwar V. Biodegradable nanoparticles for drug and gene delivery to cells and tissue. Adv Drug Deliv Rev 2003;55(3):329−47.

[89] des Rieux A, Fievez V, Garinot M, Schneider YJ, Préat V. Nanoparticles as potential oral delivery systems of proteins and vaccines: a mechanistic approach. J Control Release 2006;116(1):1−27.

[90] Soppimath KS, Aminabhavi TM, Kulkarni AR, Rudzinski WE. Biodegradable polymeric nanoparticles as drug delivery devices. J Control Release 2001;70(1−2):1−20.

[91] Brannon-Peppas L, Blanchette JO. Nanoparticle and targeted systems for cancer therapy. Adv Drug Deliv Rev 2004;56(11):1649−59.

[92] Couvreur P, Puisieux F. Nano- and microparticles for the delivery of polypeptides and proteins. Adv Drug Deliv Rev 1993;10(2−3):141−62.

[93] Khurana RK, Beg S, Burrow AJ, Vashishta RK, Katare OP, Kaur S, et al. Enhancing biopharmaceutical performance of an anticancer drug by long chain PUFA based self-nanoemulsifying lipidic nanomicellar systems. Eur J Pharm Biopharm 2017;121:42−60.

[94] Kar A, Rout SR, Singh V, Greish K, Sahebkar A, Abourehab MAS, et al. Triblock polymeric micelles as an emerging nanocarrier for drug delivery. Polymeric micelles for drug delivery. Woodhead Publishing; 2022. p. 561−90.

[95] Kenguva G, Rout SR, Fatima M, Dubey SK, Alexander A, Abourehab MAS, et al. Solubility enhancement and drug release mechanism of polymeric micelles. Polymeric micelles for drug delivery. Woodhead Publishing; 2022. p. 41−64.

[96] Ahmad Z, Shah A, Siddiq M, Kraatz HB. Polymeric micelles as drug delivery vehicles. RSC Adv 2014;4(33):17028−38.

[97] Aliabadi HM, Lavasanifar A. Polymeric micelles for drug delivery. Expert Opin Drug Deliv 2006; 3(1):139–62.

[98] Kim S, Shi Y, Kim JY, Park K, Cheng J-X. Overcoming the barriers in micellar drug delivery: loading efficiency, in vivo stability, and micelle-cell interaction. Expert Opin Drug Deliv 2010;7(1):49–62.

[99] Patel SK, Lavasanifar A, Choi P. Roles of nonpolar and polar intermolecular interactions in the improvement of the drug loading capacity of PEO-b-PCL with increasing PCL content for two hydrophobic cucurbitacin drugs. Biomacromolecules 2009;10(9):2584–91.

[100] Shuai X, Ai H, Nasongkla N, Kim S, Gao J. Micellar carriers based on block copolymers of poly (ε-caprolactone) and poly(ethylene glycol) for doxorubicin delivery. J Control Release 2004; 98(3):415–26.

[101] Stock RS, Ray WH. Interpretation of photon correlation spectroscopy data: a comparison of analysis methods. J Polym Sci Part B Polym Phys 1985;23(7):1393–447.

[102] Lavasanifar A, Samuel J, Kwon GS. Poly(ethylene oxide)-block-poly(l-amino acid) micelles for drug delivery. Adv Drug Deliv Rev 2002;54(2):169–90.

[103] Ahmadi A, Arami S. Potential applications of nanoshells in biomedical sciences. J Drug Target 2014;22(3):175–90.

[104] Evans ER, Bugga P, Asthana V, Drezek R. Metallic nanoparticles for cancer immunotherapy. Mater Today 2018;21(6):673–85.

[105] Shittu KO, Bankole MT, Abdulkareem AS, Abubakre OK, Ubaka AU. Application of gold nanoparticles for improved drug efficiency. Adv Nat Sci Nanosci Nanotechnol 2017;8(3):035014.

[106] Pérez-Herrero E, Fernández-Medarde A. Advanced targeted therapies in cancer: drug nanocarriers, the future of chemotherapy. Eur J Pharm Biopharm 2015;93:52–79.

[107] Yoo J, Park C, Yi G, Lee D, Koo H. Active targeting strategies using biological ligands for nanoparticle drug delivery systems. Cancers (Basel) 2019;11(5):640.

[108] Neha Desai, Momin M, Khan T, Gharat S, Ningthoujam RS, Omri A. Metallic nanoparticles as drug delivery system for the treatment of cancer. Expert Opin Drug Deliv 2021;18(9):1261–90.

[109] Singh AP, Biswas A, Shukla A, Maiti P. Targeted therapy in chronic diseases using nanomaterial-based drug delivery vehicles. Signal Transduct Target Ther 2019;4:33.

[110] Alkhatib MH, Alshehri WS, Abdu FB. In vivo evaluation of the anticancer activity of the gemcitabine and doxorubicin combined in a nanoemulsion. J Pharm Bioallied Sci 2018;10(1):35.

[111] Affram KO, Smith T, Ofori E, Krishnan S, Underwood P, Trevino JG, et al. Cytotoxic effects of gemcitabine-loaded solid lipid nanoparticles in pancreatic cancer cells. J Drug Deliv Sci Technol 2020;55:101374.

[112] Nocito MC, De Luca A, Prestia F, Avena P, La Padula D, Zavaglia L, et al. Antitumoral activities of curcumin and recent advances to improve its oral bioavailability. Biomedicines 2021; 9(10):1476.

[113] Jiang S, Gnanasammandhan MK, Zhang Y. Optical imaging-guided cancer therapy with fluorescent nanoparticles. J R Soc Interface 2009;7(42):3–18.

[114] Shao L, Gao Y, Yan F. Semiconductor quantum dots for biomedicial applications. Sensors 2011; 11(12):11736–51.

[115] N'Guessan KF, Davis HW, Chu Z, Vallabhapurapu SD, Lewis CS, Franco RS, et al. Enhanced efficacy of combination of gemcitabine and phosphatidylserine-targeted nanovesicles against pancreatic cancer. Mol Ther 2020;28(8):1876–86.

[116] Chu S, Shi X, Tian Y, Gao F. pH-responsive polymer nanomaterials for tumor therapy. Front Oncol 2022;12(March):1–22.

[117] Wang X, Li C, Wang Y, Chen H, Zhang X, Luo C, et al. Smart drug delivery systems for precise cancer therapy. Acta Pharm Sin B 2022;12(11):4098–121.

[118] Liang Z, Khawar MB, Liang J, Sun H. Bio-conjugated quantum dots for cancer research: detection and imaging. Front Oncol 2021;11:4300.

[119] Fang M, Peng CW, Pang DW, Li Y. Quantum dots for cancer research: current status, remaining issues, and future perspectives. Cancer Biol Med 2012;9(3):151–63.

[120] Markowicz-Piasecka M, Mikiciuk-Olasik E. Dendrimers in drug delivery. Nanobiomaterials in drug delivery applications of nanobiomaterials. Woodhead Publishing; 2016. p. 39–74.

[121] Kesharwani P, Jain K, Jain NK. Dendrimer as nanocarrier for drug delivery. Prog Polym Sci 2014;39(2):268–307.

[122] Kesharwani P, Gajbhiye V, Jain NK. A review of nanocarriers for the delivery of small interfering RNA. Biomaterials 2012;33(29):7138–50.

[123] Kesharwani P, Banerjee S, Gupta U, Mohd Amin MCI, Padhye S, Sarkar FH, et al. PAMAM dendrimers as promising nanocarriers for RNAi therapeutics. Mater Today 2015;18(10):565–72.

[124] Sheikh A, Kesharwani P. An insight into aptamer engineered dendrimer for cancer therapy. Eur Polym J 2021;159:110746.

[125] Singh V, Kesharwani P. Dendrimer as a promising nanocarrier for the delivery of doxorubicin as an anticancer therapeutics. J Biomater Sci Polym Ed 2021;32(14):1882–909. Available from: https://doi.org/10.1080/09205063.2021.1938859.

[126] Fatima M, Sheikh A, Hasan N, Sahebkar A, Riadi Y, Kesharwani P. Folic acid conjugated poly (amidoamine) dendrimer as a smart nanocarriers for tracing, imaging, and treating cancers over-expressing folate receptors. Eur Polym J 2022;170:111156.

[127] Arora V, Abourehab MAS, Modi G, Kesharwani P. Dendrimers as prospective nanocarrier for targeted delivery against lung cancer. Eur Polym J 2022;180:111635.

[128] Kesharwani P, Chadar R, Shukla R, Jain GK, Aggarwal G, Abourehab MAS, et al. Recent advances in multifunctional dendrimer-based nanoprobes for breast cancer theranostics. J Biomater Sci Polym Ed 2022;33(18):2433–71. Available from: https://doi.org/10.1080/09205063.2022.2103627.

[129] Choudhury H, Pandey M, Mohgan R, Jong JSJ, David RN, Ngan WY, et al. Dendrimer-based delivery of macromolecules for the treatment of brain tumor. Biomater Adv 2022;141:213118.

[130] Reshadmanesh A, Rahbarizadeh F, Ahmadvand D, Jafari F, Sofla I. Recent advances in preclinical research using PAMAM dendrimers for cancer gene therapy. Int J Mol Sci 2021;22(6):2912.

[131] Aqel A, El-Nour KMMA, Ammar RAA, Al-Warthan A. Carbon nanotubes, science and technology part (I) structure, synthesis and characterisation. Arab J Chem 2012;5(1):1–23.

[132] Debnath SK, Srivastava R. Drug delivery with carbon-based nanomaterials as versatile nanocarriers: progress and prospects. Front Nanotechnol 2021;3(April):1–22.

[133] Sanginario A, Miccoli B, Demarchi D. Carbon nanotubes as an effective opportunity for cancer diagnosis and treatment. Biosensors 2017;7(1):9.

[134] Hwang Y, Park SH, Lee JW. Applications of functionalized carbon nanotubes for the therapy and diagnosis of cancer. Polymers 2017;9(1):13.

[135] Biswas MC, Lubna MM, Mohammed Z, Ul Iqbal MH, Hoque ME. Graphene and carbon nanotube-based hybrid nanocomposites: preparation to applications. Graphene and nanoparticles hybrid nanocomposites: composites science and technology. Singapore: Springer; 2021. p. 71–112.

[136] Zhang W, Zhang Z, Zhang Y. The application of carbon nanotubes in target drug delivery systems for cancer therapies. Nanoscale Res Lett 2011;6:1–22.

[137] Oberstein PE, Olive KP. Pancreatic cancer: why is it so hard to treat? Ther Adv Gastroenterol 2013;6(4):321–37.

[138] Greene MK, Johnston MC, Scott CJ. Nanomedicine in pancreatic cancer: current status and future opportunities for overcoming therapy resistance. Cancers 2021;13(24):6175.

[139] Sturm N, Ettrich TJ, Perkhofer L. The impact of biomarkers in pancreatic ductal adenocarcinoma on diagnosis, surveillance and therapy. Cancers 2022;14(1):217.

[140] Mitchell MJ, Billingsley MM, Haley RM, Wechsler ME, Peppas NA, Langer R. Engineering precision nanoparticles for drug delivery. Nat Rev Drug Discov 2020;20(2):101–24.

[141] Grasso C, Jansen G, Giovannetti E. Drug resistance in pancreatic cancer: impact of altered energy metabolism. Crit Rev Oncol Hematol 2017;114:139–52.

[142] Liu L, Kshirsagar PG, Gautam SK, Gulati M, Wafa EI, Christiansen JC, et al. Nanocarriers for pancreatic cancer imaging, treatments, and immunotherapies. Theranostics 2022;12(3):1030.

Index

Note: Page numbers followed by "*f*" and "*t*" refer to figures and tables, respectively.